Communicating
Your
Way to
SUCCESS

Dale Carnegie Success Series titles
published by Manjul Publishing House

◆*Living an Enriched Life*

◆*Become an Effective Leader*

◆*How to Jump-Start Your (Next) Career*

◆*10 Steps to a More Fulfilling Life*

◆*Overcoming Worry & Stress*

◆*How to Have Rewarding Relationships,*
Win Trust and Influence People

◆*Life Is Short Make It Great*

◆*Embrace Change for Success*

◆*Resolve Conflicts in Your Life*

Communicating Your Way to SUCCESS

DALE CARNEGIE

MANJUL

Manjul Publishing House

First published in India by

MANJUL

Manjul Publishing House

• 7/32, Ansari Road, Daryaganj, New Delhi 110 002 - India
Website: www.manjulindia.com

Registered Office:
• 10, Nishat Colony, Bhopal 462 003 - India

The Success Series:
Communicating Your Way to Success by *Dale Carnegie*

This edition first published in India in 2018
Second impression 2020

ISBN 978-93-87383-28-9

Cover Design by Trinankur Banerjee

This edition is authorised for sale in the Indian Subcontinent only.

Printed and bound in India by Thomson Press (India) Limited.

CONTENTS

PREFACE

....

COMMUNICATION IS A TWO-WAY STREET

There are four ways, and only four ways, in which we have contact with the world. We are evaluated and classified by these four contacts: what we do, how we look, what we say, and how we say it.

Dale Carnegie

These days, communication—what we say and how we say it—is a major factor of our success or failure. The great leaders of government, industry, and education are all skilled in their ability to communicate effectively with other people.

This skill is not necessarily inborn. Anybody who desires to can acquire it. All that is needed is will and determination.

Once we have improved our ability to communicate, we can more effectively present our ideas to our bosses, associates, customers, even our friends and family.

Imagine being able to communicate with more power and excitement. We can change a boring meeting into a dynamic, profitable one. We can inspire and motivate our associates to meet those deadlines and exceed our projected goals.

Much of day-to-day communication creates an opportunity for miscommunication and misunderstanding. Some of the language that is used might be easily understood within our own organization, but that jargon is often confusing for those outside our company or industry.

When we organize our thoughts and don't try to cover the entire range of a topic, we keep those listening to us on the same page because people like order and clarity. All professionals must be able to express their opinions clearly, concisely, and convincingly, especially in impromptu or unexpected situations. Those situations require courage, confidence, the ability to organize thoughts quickly, and the ability to express them in a coherent and persuasive way.

Communication is not a one-way street. It is not just the communicator giving a message to another party. To be effective it must be a two-way highway with feedback flowing from one party to the other on a continuous basis. The sender of the message must seek and receive feedback from the receiver. The communicator must be always assured that what is sent is understood and accepted by the receiver. To accomplish this, the sender must ask questions, observe what is observable and, if there are misunderstandings, correct them and assure that the corrections are understood. He or she must seek the acceptance of the communication by the receiver so that there exists a willingness to accomplish what is desired.

By following these fundamentals of good communication, not only will our messages get across more readily but also work will be accomplished with fewer errors and on time. Our people will be more efficient and happier, and we will be able to do our job as a manager with fewer problems and more satisfaction.

In this book, you will learn some strategies to improve both your oral and written communication—major steps toward becoming more successful in your job and in every aspect of your life.

You will learn how to perfect your oral communication skills from the day-to-day experience of talking one to one with another person—the art of conversation—to making public speeches to a large audience or presenting a report to members of a group or committee.

You will learn how to really listen to what the other person is saying so you fully understand the message. You will learn how your body language enhances or depreciates your message, and how to interpret the body language of your listeners.

You will also learn how to make your written communications—whether they are letters, memos, emails or text messages—clear, concise, complete and more appealing to the readers.

To get the most out of this book, read all of it first to absorb the overall concept of giving and getting ideas and information. Then reread each chapter and start applying the guidelines for achieving each of the areas covered. This will start you on the track to be a better communicator—a major step forward on the road to success.

Arthur R. Pell, Ph.D.
Editor

1

....

GETTING IDEAS ACROSS TO
OTHERS

Don M. was furious. "I explained in detail how to do that job. He told me he understood and now has messed it all up. It has to be done all over again."

How often has this happened to you? You give detailed instructions to a subordinate, explain a concept to an associate, describe a procedure to a customer—leave feeling that it is clearly understood and later find out it was not understood at all. Many problems could be avoided and much time saved if we could only be assured that what we communicate is received by the other party in the way we expected it to.

Is the Message Really Understood?

When Don gave his subordinate detailed instructions, what question do you think he asked when he completed his statement? You guessed right. He asked, "Did you understand?"

What do you think the subordinate answered? Again you're right. He surely said, "Yes, I do." Just because somebody says he or she understands does not mean he or she really does. Some people only think they understood what has been said and of course, they respond that they do understand. However, because their interpretation may be different from that of the person giving the information, there was no real understanding at all.

Other people understand only a part of what has been communicated yet assume they understand all of it. Still others do not understand it at all but are too embarrassed to tell their boss that they do not understand, so they say they do and try to figure it out for themselves. In these situations, no real communication has been accomplished and it is likely that errors will be made, misconceptions will develop; time will be wasted, tempers lost, and work will not be accomplished.

How do good communicators get their ideas across? Let's look at some of the responses to a survey made concerning office managers, factory supervisors, sales managers, and other administrative executives.

Betty M. office manager of a travel agency in New York City, reported that she never asks the employee if he or she understands the instructions. Instead, she asks the subordinate to tell her what he or she is going to do. "I give them a quiz," Betty told us. "If I give a clerk a project to complete, after I explain it, I ask her just what she is going to do. In case there is a different interpretation from what I had in mind, we can correct it on the spot before it becomes a problem. If the project is a complex one, I ask a variety of questions such as: 'What will you do if X happens?' and 'Suppose Y develops?'"

Among Betty's responsibility is teaching the clerical staff how to operate the computers used in making reservations and purchasing, and issuing airline tickets. She commented, "To be sure that I can depend on the clerk to operate that computer correctly, in addition to asking them questions, I have them show me on the computer just how they will handle a variety of problems. By having them actually work on the computer, I can see for myself how much they have learned and mastered."

Is the Message Accepted?

Understanding what is communicated is a basic criterion for good communication, but there is another factor which is equally important. What is communicated must not only be understood, the other party must accept it. The manager tells a clerk that an assignment must be completed by 3 o'clock in the afternoon. There is no doubt that the clerk knows exactly what the manager meant, but she says to herself, "no way." Do you think the job will be completed by 3? Not likely. Unless the person doing the job feels it is reasonable and attainable, he or she will not put forth the efforts to meet that time limit.

Louise R., who owns and manages a building maintenance service in Rock Hill, South Carolina, handles situations like this by soliciting the participation of her workers. Usually there is a team of men and woman involved in the project. She brings them together and first tells them what is required and the reason for the deadline. She then asks them when they think it can be done and what other suggestions they may have. Often they come up with solutions that are even better than what might have been determined solely by management.

From time to time, Louise learns from these meetings that overtime or extra help is needed and that her original estimate of time was overly optimistic. Because her people know she encourages their participation and listens to them, she gets more cooperation from them in tough situations when extra effort, energy and commitment are needed.

Plan What to Say

Whether we're addressing a group or having a one-to-one conversation, we should think out our message and how we plan to present it in advance. Sometimes we'll have to think on our feet with little or no time to prepare, but more often than not, when required to discuss something, we can prepare even on a short notice.

Know the Subject

On the job, we'll usually communicate with others about subjects we're thoroughly familiar with: the work we're doing, matters in our own area of expertize, or company-related problems. Still, we should review the facts to be sure that we have a hold on all the available information and are prepared to answer any questions.

From time to time, we may be asked to report on matters with which we are unfamiliar. Our company may want to purchase a new type of computer software, for example, and ask us to check it out.

> Learn as much as possible about the subject. Know ten times more than needed for the presentation.
> Prepare notes about the advantages and disadvantages of the proposed purchase, solution, and so on.

> Whether you are to make this report to one person (the boss, for example) or to a group of managers or technical specialists, be prepared to answer questions about any subject that might come up.

Know the Audience

Even the most skilled communicators fail to get their message across if the audience can't understand them. Half of good communication is understanding your audience. Choose words that your listeners can easily comprehend. If the people you are addressing come from a technical background, use technical terminology to communicate; the listeners would clearly and readily understand these special terms. But if you are to talk about a technical subject matter to an audience unfamiliar with it, drop the technical language. If your listeners can't understand your vocabulary, the message would be lost.

For example, Charles, an engineer whose work primarily involves dealing with other engineers is accustomed to using technical terms all the time. Now let's say he's called on to make a presentation to the company's finance department to arrange the funding for a new engineering project. It's Charles's responsibility, not the audience's, to ensure that the message gets across. If he can explain the technical matter in layperson's terms, he should do so. However, if it's necessary to use technical language, Charles must take the time to explain a term the first time he uses it, and at least once again if he feels that it needs reinforcement.

Those convinced against their will
are of the same opinion still.

Dale Carnegie

Speaking Clearly

We've all heard speakers who mumble, speak too fast or too slowly or have difficult-to-understand accents. If one does not articulate clearly, much of the message he or she is attempting to communicate would be lost to the listeners. Poor articulation is relatively easy to improve. Some ways to accomplish this will be discussed in Chapter 4.

Body Language

Some of the behaviors we exhibit without realizing it, can have an enormous impact on how we make an impression. Studies by social linguists regarding face-to-face communication determined that only seven percent of the message transferred from one person to the other was expressed in the words spoken. About 38 percent of the meanings were transmitted through vocal characteristics—tone of the voice, pauses, emphasis, etc.—and an astonishing 55 percent of the total message was communicated through visual signals we classify as "body language." Often we are not aware of how this affects the way we are perceived by others.

Posture

Good (or bad) posture can be seen even from a distance and registers instantly in the viewer's emotional brain. It is less subtle than other nonverbal gestures because it involves our entire body.

In research projects, participants assume that subjects with excellent posture were more popular, ambitious, confidant, friendly, and intelligent than those with a more relaxed stance.

Expect that improved posture will feel awkward and exaggerated at first. Work on standing straight, square-shouldered, and balanced lower body.

Of all facial expressions, the smile is the most influential. Smiling can actually cause others to be more receptive to our point of view. When we smile, the other person nearly always smiles back. More than just a mirroring, it reflects the sudden surge of warmth and well-being.

An insincere smile is more damaging than no smile. Don't try to smile warmly with just the jaw muscles. A believable smile uses the entire face and happens spontaneously when we process a positive thought about the exchange in which we are engaged.

When you smile at other people, you are telling them in a subtle way that you like them, at least to some degree. They will get that meaning and will like you better. Try the smiling habit. You have nothing to lose.

Dale Carnegie

Eye Contact

When we look at our listener, it implies confidence, honesty, and interest in that person. Lack of eye contact is usually interpreted as a sign of fear, dishonesty, hostility, or boredom.

Research shows that in job interviews, candidates give more complete and revealing answers when the interviewer maintains eye contact. In classes, student's comprehension and retention of materials are directly related to the instructor's eye contact. On the other hand, do not stare into the other person's eyes. Look at his or her entire face.

How to understand the body language of our listeners will be discussed in chapter 3.

Televise the Messages

We receive information from all five senses. Ideas and impressions develop from smelling, tasting and feeling, but most of the data that our mind processes come from hearing and seeing—audio and video. This has been significantly changed in this era of television. Television has merged audio and video so that those of us who have been brought up watching this medium from "Sesame Street" to today's news are accustomed to receiving information simultaneously through our eyes and ears. By applying this "simulcast" approach to our communication with other people, our messages will come across more effectively.

Don't Just Tell—Show!

In training her people to handle insurance claims, Joan found that when she drew a flow chart while describing the process, it was much more easily understood. As she taught each phase, she outlined them by drawing boxes around each step, as well as drew arrows showing the movement from step-to-step.

Steve learned, from failed experience, that telling his people how to do the job was not enough. Unless he took his trainees from place to place in the warehouse, they had difficulty in understanding what he was teaching. This was a very time consuming effort. He simplified the training by designing a model of the storerooms with which he could orient his people as he told them about the work they would be doing.

Many executives have flip charts or chalkboards in their offices so that they can use visual means to enhance their oral communications. By illustrating the subjects with charts, graphs, diagrams or sketches, what is being presented becomes far more effective. When there is a subject in which the listening is augmented by visual images, people tend to learn it faster and remember it longer.

One of the most popular professors at Syracuse University's School of Journalism was also a cartoonist. He drew cartoons and caricatures as he lectured. His colleagues scoffed at this and considered it very unprofessional. "He's just amusing his students—not teaching," they claimed. Yes, his students did find it amusing, but they absorbed a great deal more information than they would from just plain lecturing, and years later could still recall his teachings.

How to use visual aids effectively will be discussed in chapter 5.

Your purpose is to make your listeners see what you saw, hear what you heard, feel what you felt. Relevant detail, couched in concrete, colorful language, is the best way to recreate the incident as it happened and to picture it for the listeners.

Dale Carnegie

Creating Visual Images on the Telephone

The one media in which we still cannot use visual augmentation is the telephone. Yet, we can help our listeners "see" what we are saying by drawing word pictures. A word picture enables the listener to picture in the mind's eye what we are saying.

When we are asked for directions to our building, we say: "Take I-95 to Exit 23, that's Mulberry Street. Make a right off the ramp and drive to the fourth traffic light, that's 17th Avenue. Make a left on 17th Avenue and drive twelve blocks to Smith Road. Make a right on Smith Road and drive five blocks. We are number 2345 Smith Road."

That's clear. But now let's give these directions using word pictures: "Take I-95 to Exit 23, that's Mulberry Street. Make a right off the ramp and drive to the fourth traffic light. There's a Texaco station on your left and a McDonald's on the right. That's 17th Ave. Make a left on 17th Ave. Drive to the firehouse, that's Smith Road. Make a right and drive towards the yellow brick building on the left. That's our office, 2345 Smith Road."

Isn't that easier? The visitor does not have to count lights or blocks or look for street names. He or she can just seek out landmarks that have been visually presented.

Televise the Future

Successful sales people use word pictures. Audrey sells computers; in discussing the problems faced by one of her prospects, she learned that he was primarily concerned with the messy office that he supervised. "Papers and files are all over the place," he complained. "And I can never find the files that I need—they're always out, probably, in one of those piles."

After describing the technical aspects of her company's product, she said: "Let's look ahead to six months from now. You walk into the office. There are no piles of paper on desks and chairs. Your people are all working at their computers. You need a file; you sit down at a terminal and key in the file name. Instantly, the information desired appears on your screen. No waiting, No frustration."

Audrey has drawn a word picture of the future. The

manager does not require much imagination to visualize this and recognize the value of making the purchase.

Barriers to Clear Communication

No matter how good the preparation and presentation of our messages, often what is received is not exactly what has been sent. Barriers have cropped up, which impede the communication.

Some of these major barriers are psychological, not physical. We may have perfect articulation and choose our words wisely, but the static develops in intangible areas: assumptions, attitudes, and the emotional baggage each of us has.

Check Out Assumptions

We have a pretty good idea about what causes a particular problem and how to solve it. In discussing it with others, we assume that they know as much about it as we do, so what we say is based on the assumption that they have know-how even though they don't. As a result, we don't give them adequate information.

Be Aware of Our Attitude

Another barrier to communication is the attitudes of the sender and the receiver. A manager who is arrogant will convey his feelings in the way directions and informations are given. He or she may appear to be talking down to staff members. This causes resentment, which blocks communication. In order for the message to be received, it must not only be understood but also accepted by the receiver. When resentment develops, acceptance is unlikely.

An employee who is busy resenting the leader's attitude does not really "hear" what's being said. Good leaders avoid such indicators of arrogance as sarcasm and "pulling rank" when dealing with staff members.

Watch for Preconceptions

People tend to hear what they expect to hear. The message they receive is distorted by any information they have already heard about the subject. So if the new information is different from what's expected, they might reject it as being incorrect. Rather than actually hearing the new message, they may be hearing what their minds are telling them.

What does this mean? People must be trained to keep their minds open. When someone tells them something, they must make an extra effort to listen and to evaluate the new information objectively, instead of blocking it out because it differs from their preconceptions.

In communicating with others, try to learn their preconceptions. If they are people we work with regularly, we probably know how they view most of the matters we discuss. When presenting your views to them, take into consideration what they already believe. If their beliefs differ from yours, be prepared to make the effort to jump over those hurdles.

Prejudices and Biases—Ours and Theirs

Our biases for or against a person influence the way we receive their messages. We listen more attentively and are more likely to accept ideas from somebody we like and respect. Contrarily, we tend to blot out inputs from people we don't like, and reject their ideas.

Perception is reality in the mind of the perceiver. Unless our perception of a situation and of those with whom we are communicating are congruent, we would be working at cross-purposes.

Biases also affect the way subject matter is received. People turn a deaf ear to opposing viewpoints concerning matters about which they have strong feelings. Carol is a good example of such a person. As company controller, she is fixated on reducing costs. She won't even listen to any discussion that might increase costs no matter what the long-term benefits may be. To sell her on an original idea, we have to convince her how although there may be an immediate increase in costs, in the long run—it will be cost effective.

Many people are not even conscious of their own biases. Take the time to analyze why we have made certain decisions in the past. Have they been overly influenced by our biases? Follow these six steps:

1. Become aware of your biases.
2. Identify why you hold these biases.
3. Acknowledge shared characteristics.
4. Put your biases aside, and maintain an open mind.
5. Make an effort to consider other people's ideas objectively.
6. Don't allow a negative experience to revive your biases.

Be Aware of Our Emotional State

We've all had bad days. And on one of those bad days, one of our associates comes to us all excited about a new idea. How do we react? We probably think: "I have enough on my platter already, who needs this now?" Our mind is closed and the message doesn't come through. Not only must we be aware of our own emotional state when giving or receiving a message, we must also consider the emotional state of our subordinate.

An important project comes up and we go over to two of our staff members, Dan and Joan, to discuss it. Joan is enthusiastic about the job; Dan is skeptical. Why? Dan is annoyed because he is busy working on another project and he wants to concentrate on that. He feels we are inconsiderate to assign him another job.

Always test the temperature of the water before stepping into the tub. A brief conversation with Dan and Joan about their current activities would have brought out how much time Dan was spending on his current project. When presenting the new assignment, make the observation that what he is doing now is important, and you are happy with his progress. Show that the reason you chose him for the new assignment is because it will complement his current work.

Channels: The Distortion Between Sender and Receiver

In communication, a major source of interference and distortion is the path the message takes from sender to receiver. In many large organizations, communications must flow through set channels. The more extensive the channels, the more likely that distortion will occur. This can be illustrated in the popular party game where one person whispers an incident to his or her neighbor, who repeats it to the next person, and this continues around the room. By the time it is retold to the originator, the story is completely different.

It is not unusual for a piece of information passed orally "through channels" to be distorted at each station, so that what the receiver receives is not at all what the sender sent.

One way to alleviate this difficulty is to use written mode of communication. Writing is more difficult to distort, though interpretation of what is written may vary from station to station. Even so, writing has certain disadvantages: Many matters can't or shouldn't be communicated in writing. Writing is time consuming. For urgent matters and matters of transient interest, writing is not appropriate.

A more effective way is to shorten channels and allow for bypassing where feasible. The fewer stations along the way, the less chance for distortion. The main reason for using channels is to ensure that people who are responsible for a project are kept aware of everything that applies to it. This makes sense, but it is often overdone. If a matter involves policy decisions or major areas of activity, channels are important. But a great portion of the communication in companies concerns routine matters. Using channels for these may not only distort the message but could also slow down the work.

Be Open to Feedback

Perhaps the most challenging aspect of managing our external image is the difficulty in seeing ourselves as others see us. Research indicates that we are probably more critical of ourselves than others are of us. At the same time, we may be unaware of some of our own negative traits that need to be corrected.

These are some ways to gain an accurate view of our own external image:

➤ Viewing and listening to videotapes of ourself speaking at meetings.
➤ Rehearsing our talks in front of a mirror.

> Getting honest critiques from trusted associates.
> Carefully monitoring audience reactions.

It's a good idea to have a "coach" help identify and work with you to overcome communication problems. Help in this field is available in most communities by professional speech coaches or hands-on seminars like the Dale Carnegie's "High Impact Presentations" program.

Assigning Work

One of the most important communication functions of a manager or supervisor is assigning work to his or her staff. Often we hear the complaint: "I don't understand why my people can't follow orders. I give them clear instructions and still they get it all wrong."

How often have we made comments like that or heard other supervisors lament their people's inability to get things done right. Perhaps, the cause is not that our people are inept, but that we are not assigning work as effectively as it should be done.

Planning the Assignment

As pointed out at the beginning of this chapter, our message must be planned. Too often supervisors do not take the time to prepare assignments. They know what has to be done and assume that all that is necessary is to order a subordinate to do it, and it will be done.

Planning starts with having a clear concept of what must be accomplished. Even if we have done this type of work many times, it is important to think it through once again.

Think how the subordinate views this. If you had never seen this project before, what would you want to know? List the objectives you wish to attain, the information needed to attain it, the materials, tools, support sources and whatever else is needed to do the work.

A very important part of the planning is to determine who will be given the assignment. In selecting these people bear in mind the importance of the assignment. If it is one in which it is essential that the work be done immediately and with little supervision, choose people who have demonstrated competence in the past, in this type of work. However, if it is an area where there is adequate time for you to provide guidance, it may be advantageous to assign it to less skilled people, and use this project as a means of training and development of their skills.

Communicating the Assignment

Barbara was frustrated. She had given Carol a detailed description of what she wanted to be done and Carol had assured her she understood. Now, a week later, Carol turned in work that was all wrong. Her excuse: "I thought that's what you wanted."

Norman was upset. His boss had just given him a deadline that he felt was totally unrealistic. "He's out of line," Norman thought, "There's no way I can do this much work in such a short time. I'll do what I can, but I know I'm not going to make it."

As pointed out earlier in this chapter, the supervisor must assure himself or herself that the subordinate fully understands and accepts the instruction.

Get a Plan of Action

On assignments that will take any significant amount of time, ask the subordinate to prepare a plan of action before starting the job. This should—just what is to be done, when it is scheduled to be done, and what support may be needed.

Rita's assignment was to arrange travel plans for 20 salespeople from all over the country, to attend a meeting in Chicago. Before starting the assignment, she wrote a plan of action in which she covered every aspect of the assignment including notifying the salespeople, making airline and hotel reservations, and assuring that all the participants received their tickets within adequate time. The plan included timetables for starting and completing each phase and indication of what assistance she would need for the same. Going over this with her boss, she was able to iron out any misunderstandings or potential problems before starting.

Note that Rita put her plan of action into writing. By doing this, both she and her boss were able to check any time how the plan was proceeding and catch the problems-if any-early.

Follow-up

No matter how well any assignment is planned, it is incumbent upon a supervisor to follow-up from time to time to assure it is going according to the plan.

Alan believes that if he follows up too frequently, his people will feel that he doesn't trust them. "I want my people to be true participants. Once I agree to their plan of action, I must assume they will follow it. If I check them, I defeat what I am trying to project."

Alan has a point, but he still has the ultimate responsibility for the success of his department; the assignments are not properly completed, it would reflect on his ability. To assure that assignments are accomplished, follow-up is necessary. However, it can be achieved without causing the people to feel we don't trust them.

The key to Alan's philosophy of management is participation. Therefore, follow-up should be done in a participatory manner. Instead of Alan looking over his people's shoulders or surprising them with unexpected check-ups, the follow-ups should be built into the plan of action. When the subordinate develops the plan, checkpoints should be incorporated throughout the project. After certain phases of the project have been completed, the subordinate would meet Alan and go over what has been done. He or she should be encouraged to critique the work and perhaps suggest new or additional matters that might be incorporated in the assignment. Of course, Alan would make appropriate comments and suggestions as well. In this way the follow-up becomes part of the participative approach as well as acts as a stimulus to the subordinate to achieve even greater success in meeting the challenges of the assignment.

Cultivating Diplomacy and Tact

The way in which we communicate can elicit positive or negative emotions. If we communicate aggressively, without respect or sensitivity, defensive and angry emotions can prevent others from hearing the message we are trying to convey. Communicating with diplomacy and tact is an approach that combines strength and sensitivity and keep emotions at bay. When we communicate with diplomacy and tact, we adapt our style to the person we are speaking to in order to put them at ease.

Most people tend to follow an individual style of communication. Research on communication styles have commonly placed people into one of the four categories:

> *Friendly style:* These people are casual, amiable, relationship focused, helpful, and warm. They do not like to argue and they look for positive feedbacks.

> *Analytical style:* These people are formal, methodical, and systematic. They are impressed with data and details. They look carefully at evidences, and use them to find answers and solutions to the problems discussed.

> *Excitable style:* These men and women are demonstrative and expressive.
They are prone to use gestures in making their points. They are more concerned with the big picture than the details—their main concern is what's in it for them.

> *Pragmatic style:* These people are goal oriented and focused on the objectives to be achieved. Even if they have strong opinions and viewpoints, they are willing to consider other options when presented with them.

> *Diplomatic and tactful style:* These people establish rapport based on the style with which the other person communicates.

Earn the Trust of the People

To be a good communicator, we must gain the trust and respect of the people with whom we are relating. To earn this:

1. Take others' interests to heart; ask questions, learn what

motivates them, and help them to learn and grow.

2. Listen sincerely with ears, eyes, and heart and without prejudice and judgment.
3. Honor and find merit in differences of opinion, biases, and diversity.
4. Involve others in decisions, display an open and accepting attitude, and be receptive to new ideas.
5. Be willing to negotiate and compromise, and be a mediator between others who have different points of view.
6. Think before speaking. Consider the audience, relationship, and environment when choosing your words and actions.
7. Use inclusive language, and communicate with diplomacy, tact, and sensitivity.
8. Speak confidently, decisively, and with authority; and offer evidence when stating opinions.
9. Stand up for your beliefs and non-negotiable values.
10. Be a modest expert and be willing to defer to another's expertize.
11. Be reliable: keep confidences, fulfill promises, and keep commitments.
12. Refrain from mood swings. Act consistently, rationally, fairly, honestly, and ethically.
13. Be a stellar role model act professionally and always walk the talk.
14. Demonstrate trust in others reveal your own thoughts and feelings frankly and openly.
15. Be authentic—demonstrate congruency between your words and actions.
16. Be approachable and available as a resource.

17. Be realistic when communicating goals and outcomes.
18. Accept responsibility and admit mistakes, downfalls, and disadvantages.
19. Deal directly with others. Do not partake in gossip and never talk behind someone's back.
20. Share the glory—give others credit for accomplishments.

Sum and Substance

> Whether you are presenting your ideas to a group or to just one person, prepare what you're going to say before you say it.
> Speak clearly and distinctly so that you could be easily understood. Speak with enthusiasm so that your audience doesn't fall asleep.
> Be aware of your body language
> Be prepared to overcome barriers that distort your communication.
> Know and control your biases.
> In assigning work, plan what you would say, communicate it clearly to the assignees, get feedback on whether what you said was received; follow-up to assure that it is accomplished.
> Assure that what you have communicated is not only understood but also accepted by the other party.
> Be tactful and diplomatic in all of your dealings with others.

2

....

THE ART OF GOOD
CONVERSATION

The ability to engage in interesting conversations is one of the greatest personal assets a man or woman can have. It is a great aid to business and social success and also makes for greater enjoyment of the company of other people.

There is nothing that enables us to make so good an impression, especially upon those who do not know us thoroughly, than the ability to converse well. To be a good conversationalist, to be able to interest people, to rivet their attention, to draw them to us naturally, by the very superiority of our conversational ability, is to be the possessor of a very great accomplishment. It not only helps to make a good impression upon strangers, it also helps us to make and keep friends. It opens doors and softens hearts. It makes us interesting in all sorts of company. It helps us to get on in the world. It sends you clients, patients, or customers. It is the tool that would enable you to persuade people to accept your ideas, follow your leadership, and buy your products.

People who can talk well, who have the art of putting things in an attractive way, who can interest others immediately by their power of speech, have an advantage over those who may know more than they do about the subject, but who cannot express themselves with ease or eloquence.

Conversation is a tremendous power developer. However, talking without thinking, without an effort to express oneself with clarity and conciseness would work against you. Mere chattering, or gossiping is not impressive. It lies too deep for such superficial effort. Nothing else will indicate our fineness or coarseness of culture, our breeding or lack of it, as quickly as our conversation. It tells our whole life's story. What we say, and how we say it, will betray all our secrets, will give the world our true measure.

What Makes a Good Conversationalist?

Intellect, brainpower, expertize in a field can be helpful, but it is not the main reason through which a good conversationalist holds the attention of others.

We must make people feel our empathy, and that they have met a sincere person. Don't greet people with a stiff "How do you do?" or "Glad to meet you," without feeling any sentiment. Be accommodative and adapt to different dispositions. Look people you meet squarely in the eye and make them aware of your personality. Greet them with a smile and kind words, that would make them want to meet you again.

Be Cordial

To be an accepted conversationalist, we must cultivate cordiality. We must fling the door of our heart wide open, and not, as many do, just leave it slightly ajar to indicate to the ones we meet: "You may peep in a bit, but you cannot come in until I know whether you will be a desirable acquaintance." A great many people are stingy of their cordiality. They seem to reserve it for some special occasion or for intimate friends. They think it is too precious to give out to everybody.

Do not be afraid to open our heart; fling the door wide open. Get rid of all reservations; do not meet a person as though you were afraid of making a mistake and doing what you would be glad to recall.

A warm, glad handshake and cordial greeting will create a bond of good-will between you and the people you meet. They will say to themselves: "Well, there is a really interesting personality. I want to know more about this man or woman. They see something in me, evidently, which most people do not see."

Cultivate the habit of being cordial, of meeting people with a warm, sincere greeting, and an open heart; it will do wonders for you. You would find the stiffness, diffidence and indifference, the cold lack of interest in everybody, which now so troubles you disappearing. People will see that you really take an interest in them, that you really want to know and please them. The practice of cordiality will revolutionize your social power. You would develop attractive qualities that you never before dreamed of possessing.

It's Not Just What We Say, but How We Say It

Keep in mind that we express ourselves not only through the words we utter, but also by the tone of the voice, the expression of the face, our gestures, and our bearing.

When Charles W. Eliot was president of Harvard, he said: "I recognize but one mental acquisition as an essential part of the education of a lady or gentleman the accurate and refined use of the mother tongue."

There is no accomplishment, no attainment that we can use so constantly and effectively, which will help us make and keep friends, as fine as a conversation. There is no doubt that the gift of language was intended to be a much greater accomplishment than the majority of us have ever made of it.

Cultivate Conversational Skills

Most of us are bunglers in our conversations because we do not make an art of it. We do not take the trouble or pains to learn to talk well. We do not read enough or think enough. Most of us express ourselves in sloppy language because it is so much easier to do so than it is to think before we speak, to make an effort to express ourselves with elegance, ease, and power.

Poor conversationalists excuse themselves for not trying to improve by saying, "good talkers are born, not made." We might as well say that good lawyers, good physicians, or good merchants are born, not made. All the success that good doctors or merchants or scientists or teachers, indeed the elite of any career enjoy is a direct result of hard work. This is the price of all achievement that is of value.

Many people owe their advancement largely to their ability to converse well. The ability to interest people in conversation, and to hold them, is a great power. People who have a bungling expression, who know something, but can never put it in logical, interesting, or commanding language, are always placed at a great disadvantage.

It is a great treat to listen to people who have cultivated the art of conversation. Their language flows with such liquid, limpid beauty; their words are chosen with such exquisite delicacy; taste, and accuracy, there is such a refinement in their diction that they charm everyone who hears them speak.

We may think we are poor and have no opportunity in life. We may be situated so that others are dependent upon us, and we may not be able to go to school or college, or to study music or art, as we long to do. We may be tied down to a depressing environment or tortured with an unsatisfied, disappointed objectives. None of these should prevent us from becoming an interesting talker, because in every sentence that we utter, we can practice the best form of expression. Every book we read, every person with whom we converse, who uses good speech can help us.

Few people think excessively about how they are going to express themselves. They use the first words that come to them. They do not think of forming a sentence so that it will have beauty, brevity, transparency, and power. The words flow from their lips helter-skelter, with little thought, arrangement or order.

Good reading, however, will not only broaden the mind and introduce new ideas, but it will also increase one's vocabulary, which is a great aid to conversations. Many people have good thoughts and ideas, but they cannot express them because of the poverty of their vocabulary. Yet some people do not have the right words to clothe their ideas and make them attractive. They repeatedly talk around in circles, because when they want a particular word to convey their exact meaning, they cannot find it.

If we are determined to talk well, we must associate with educated, cultured people. If we seclude ourselves, though we may be a college graduates, we will be a poor conversationalist.

We all sympathize with people, especially the timid and shy, who have that awful feeling of repression and stifling of thought, when they make an effort to say something and cannot. Timid young people often suffer keenly in this area when attempting to express their thoughts at their schools or colleges. But even great orators have gone through similar experience when they first attempted to speak in public, and were often deeply humiliated by blunders and failures. There is no other way, however, to become a good conversationalist than by constantly trying to express oneself efficiently and elegantly.

If we find that our ideas fly from us when we attempt to express them, that we stammer and flounder about for words which we are unable to find, we may be sure that every honest effort we make, even if we fail in our attempt, will make it all the way easier for us to speak well the next time. It is remarkable, if we keep on trying, how quickly we can conquer our awkwardness and self-consciousness, and gain ease of manner and convenience of expression.

All good conversationalists have felt a power come to them from the listener that they never felt before, which often stimulates and inspires them to take up fresh endeavors. The mingling of thought with thought, the contact of mind with mind, develops new powers, as the mixing of two chemicals often produces a new third substance.

You can make more friends in two months by becoming interested in other people than you can in two years by trying to get other people interested in you.

Dale Carnegie

Be Truly Interested in Others

Many of us are not only poor conversationalists, but we are poor listeners as well. We are too impatient to listen. Instead of being attentive and eager to drink in the story or the information, we do not have enough respect for the talker to keep quiet. We look around impatiently, perhaps play out a pattern with our fingers on a chair or a table, hitch about as if we were bored and anxious to get away, and thereby, interrupt speakers before they reach a conclusion. In fact, we are such impatient people that we have no time for anything except pushing ahead, elbowing our way through the crowd to get the position or the money desired.

Impatience is a conspicuous characteristic of many of us. Everything bores us which does not bring more business, or more money, or which does not help to attain the positions for which we are striving.

Instead of enjoying our friendships, we inclined to look upon our friends as so rungs in a ladder, and to value them terms of the number of patients, clients, customers they send, or their ability to give a boost to our political position.

One cause for our conversational decline is a lack of empathy. We are too selfish, too engaged in our own welfare, and wrapped up in our own little world, and too intent upon our own self-promotion to be interested in others. No one can be a good conversationalist unless they are empathetic. We must be able to enter into another's life, to live it with the other person, in order to be a good listener or a good talker.

If we make ourselves empathetic we would be able to enter into the life of the people with whom we are conversing, and touch them along the lines of their interests. No matter how much we may know about a subject, if it does not happen to interest those with whom we are talking, our efforts would be largely lost.

It is sad sometimes, to see people standing around at the average reception or club gathering, dumb, almost helpless, and powerless to enter heartily into the conversation because they are too self-absorbed. They do not enter heartily into the lives of others, or abandon themselves to the occasion enough to become good talkers.

They are cold, reserved and distant because their minds are somewhere else, their affections on their own affairs. There are only two things that interest them: business and their own little world. If we talk about these things, they are interested at once; but they do not care about our affairs, how we get on, what our ambition is, or how they can help us. Their conversations will never reach a high standard while they live in such a feverish, selfish, and unempathetic state.

Be Tactful

Great conversationalists are always very tactful—interesting without offending. Some people have the peculiar quality of touching the best that is in us; others stir up the bad. Every time they come in contact they irritate us. Others are joyous and agreeable; they never inflame our sensitive spots. They radiate all that is spontaneous and sweet and beautiful.

Lincoln was a master of the art of making himself interesting to everybody he met. He put people at ease with his stories and jokes, and made them feel so completely at home in his presence that they opened up their mental treasures to him without reserve. Strangers were always glad to talk to him because he was so cordial and quaint, and always gave more than he got.

A sense of humor such as Lincoln's is of course a great addition to one's conversational power. Yet not everyone can be funny; and if we lack sense of humor, we only make ourselves ludicrous by attempting to be funny.

Good conversationalists, however, are not overly serious. They don't overwhelm us with miniscule details. Facts, statistics can be weary, so they supplement them with illustrations and anecdotes to make their points. Vivacity is absolutely necessary. Heavy conversations can be boring. But caution: if it is too light, although it may be amusing, it may not help achieve your objective.

Therefore, to be a good conversationalist we must be spontaneous, buoyant, natural, empathetic, and must show a spirit of good will. We must feel a spirit of helpfulness, and must enter heart and soul into things that interest others. We must get the attention of people and hold it by interesting them, and we can only interest them by a warm empathy—a real friendly empathetic attitude. If we are cold, distant, and unempathetic we cannot hold someone's attention.

Be open-minded and tolerant. People who violate a sense of taste, of justice, and of fairness, never interest others. They tightly lock all the approaches to their inner selves and the conversation is perfunctory, mechanical and without life or feeling.

To be a success anywhere, develop the power to express yourself in strong, effective, and interesting language. It is not necessary to give a stranger an inventory of your possessions in order to show that you have achieved something.

Our attitude, the spirit we radiate, our personality, will have everything to do with our conversational proficiency. The impression we make will be a tremendous factor in our success. Only then we would carry the conviction and give the impression of mastership, and that is half the battle won.

Learn and Remember Names

Remember, a person's name is, to that person, the sweetest and most important sound in any language.

Dale Carnegie

When meeting a new person, make a special effort to learn his or her name. Often names may be mumbled during an introduction, especially when more than one person is being introduced at the same time. If it is not clear, it is not impolite to ask for it be repeated. Using the name during the conversation helps set it firmly in our mind.

Follow these suggestions:

➤ Determine which part of the name to use. Americans usually use first names, unless the other person is significantly older or has higher authority, then use Mr./Ms. until he or she says, "First name, please." In other cultures, one always uses the formal 'Mr.', 'Mrs.' 'Ms.' or a title, 'Dr.', 'Professor', etc. unless invited to be less formal.

➤ Create a mind picture, linking the name with the person. Don't think in words—think in pictures. When we meet Julie, picture her bedecked with *jewelry*; Sandy reminds us of a beach, and George is visualized as standing at the edge of a *gorge*.

➤ Repeat the names immediately in your conversation, but don't overdo or it would look phony. Do it about once in three to four minutes of conversation, and when you leave.

➤ If the name is same as or similar to that of a relative, friend, or another person you know, picture the new person with that person.

➤ Most important, use it, use it, use it until it is firmly established in your mind.

Learn About the Other Person

When we meet a new person, it is important to get as much information about that person as possible. One way to obtain this is asking questions. However, this should not be an interrogation. Just a few well-chosen questions would get the ball rolling and the conversation would flow.

This is a delicate process, as we do not want to appear to be nosy. Ask only those questions which are appropriate for the situation in which you are involved. For example, some questions are appropriate when talking to a person on a business matter; others in social situations, etc.

In a social situation questions about the area in which one lives, hobbies or interests, family or mutual acquaintances are often good starters. Other good conversation openers are about schools or colleges they have attended, recent current events they participated in, or a comment made by the other person.

When meeting people in a business setting, good starters are questions about the industry and company the person represents, news items that affect that industry, questions about the nature of his or her job or career.

It's not necessary to have a list of questions we plan to ask. Once the conversation is underway, comments and responses would flow easily.

Conversational Styles

The manner in which we communicate with others, whether it is in a one-to-one conversation or when speaking to a group can influence how others perceive us. We may come across as passive, aggressive, or assertive.

Some of the traits manifested by passive people are:

- ➤ They are more concerned about others, often to their own personal detriment.
- ➤ They are often stressed internally, although it may not be obvious to others.
- ➤ They are likely to have low self-esteem.
- ➤ They are more concerned with being liked than being respected.

- They build others up even at their own expense.
- They take blame rather than blame others.
- They avoid confrontation.
- When action is needed, they ask for it indirectly in the form of a suggestion or as a wish.

The opposite of the passive style is the aggressive approach. Aggressive people manifest the following characteristics:

- They are overly self-centered.
- They are often internally stressed.
- They lack self-esteem, but will not admit it even to themselves.
- They are usually not liked or respected by others.
- They put others down by sarcasm or derogatory remarks.
- They try to control everything and everyone.
- When errors or failures occur, they blame others and never consider themselves responsible.
- They enjoy and seek confrontation with people with opposing views.
- If in a powerful position, they force others to follow.
- They are often verbally abusive to opponents.
- When action is needed, they present it in the form of a demand or command.

Effective communicators take a middle course. They are confident and assertive.

- They stand up for their own rights, but are also sensitive to others with whom they are speaking.
- If stressed, they deal with it and then move on.
- They have a strong, positive self-image.
- They are direct and honest.

- They earn the respect of others.
- They show their appreciation of others.
- They own up to their own errors and failures and expect others to own up to theirs.
- They do not seek confrontation. If others disagree, they will work to persuade them in a non-threatening, objective discussion.
- They are always willing to listen to others.
- When action is needed, they state what should be done, and work with others to accomplish it.

It is not easy to change our personality, but if we want to be better communicators, if we identify our style as passive or aggressive, we must make an effort to achieve the assertive, confident approach.

Our Telephone Personality

Every time we pick up the telephone—whether to make or receive a call—we leave an impression on the person at the other end of the line. Often, the only image that the person will have of us and our company will be derived from this conversation.

In face-to-face communication, there are many tools that help us to make good (or bad) impressions: our facial expressions, our gestures, and our use of props or visual aids. With the telephone, there is only one tool: our voice. Most people do not really hear themselves as others hear them. The best way to obtain a true concept of how we sound to others is to record several telephone calls and evaluate how they come across when we replay them. Most important, of course, is how we sound. Listen to those recordings and make the necessary changes needed to improve its quality.

Check the Attitude

One of the prime characteristics of effective dealing with others is to be friendly. Do we sound friendly on those recordings or do we sound annoyed? This call might have come at an inopportune time. We could be pressed by a demanding boss, a deadline that we were trying to meet, or a crisis in the department, but the caller does not know (or care about) this. We must discipline ourselves to put everything other than that phone call out of our minds.

If you are upset about something, before picking up the phone, take a deep breath, relax your muscles and clear your mind. Be calm, be attentive and the impression you wish to make—a genuine interest in what that person is saying—will be projected.

Telephone Tactics When Receiving a Call

Answer the phone promptly. In an official situation, the phone should not ring more than three times before it is answered. If you are on another call; either use your voicemail or put the current call on hold, pick up the new call and either request them to wait for a few minutes, or take the number and call back. If you plan to be away from our desk for more than a few minutes, arrange for somebody to take the calls or set the voicemail to answer after three rings.

Always state who you are immediately. Instead of saying "hello," say "Engineering Dept., Sam Johnson speaking." We cannot assume that the person who is calling knows who we are. If we do not know the caller, ask for his or her name. If it is an unusual name, ask how it is spelled. Write it down. When responding, use the caller's name. It demonstrates our sincere interest in that person and his or her problem. If we cannot provide the answers to the caller's questions within a very few minutes, it would be better to advise that we would call back rather than putting them on hold for a long time. If he or she prefers to hold the call or it takes longer than anticipated to respond, get back to them frequently so that they know that they haven't been abandoned.

One of the most irritating aspects of telephoning a company is to be told that you will be transferred to another person and then be disconnected. If it is necessary to transfer a call, always tell the person to whom they are going to be transferred to and give the caller that person's extension or phone number (if different from yours). It is also a good idea to obtain the caller's number, so that if disconnected, we can call them back to respond, not only to their direct questions, but also to implied objections.

When Martha called the Mail Order Department to complain about receiving damaged merchandise, she seemed upset when she was told to return it by United Parcel Service. The customer service representative recognized her concern and quickly told Martha that she did not have to make a trip to the UPS shipping center, but that they would arrange for UPS to pick up the package at her home.

By anticipating her concern, not only did the customer service representative make the customer feel better about the situation, but made a friend for the company.

Telephone Tactics When Making a Call

The beginning and end of a telephonic conversation are critical points. Begin the call with a welcoming attitude that shows you are glad to be talking to that person, and recognize that the call is important to them. If you are not known to that person, tell them who you are and why you are calling.

"Good morning Mrs. Samuels, as a mother who has children in our schools, I know you are concerned about the quality of education in this district. This is Blanche H., campaign manager for Diane McGrath, who is running for the school board presidency."

After making the presentation, listening and responding to questions, conclude in a positive way. "Thank you for your attention. I look forward to seeing you at the board meeting next Tuesday."

Plan all calls before picking up the phone. If you have to cover several items in a call, make a list of these items. Note the major points you wish to make for each of them. Follow your plan when talking and the call would be accomplished more effectively and in less time.

Listen to the other person. His or her responses may make it necessary to adjust your original plan. Ask questions and pay close attention to the responses. This is true for all communications, but particularly valuable with phone calls because we do not have the advantage of watching the non-verbal signals visible in face-to-face dealings. Learn to "read" the nuances of changes in inflection and voice tone. Think about the message you plan to send from the listener's point of view.

Small Talk

There is nothing really small about "small talk." This non-business style of conversation has the potential to build connections and become the foundation for ongoing relationships.

Becoming adept at small talks doesn't require an exhaustive knowledge of current events. It simply requires the ability to make the other person focus on his/her favorite topic, by asking questions that indicate interest. Even talking about the weather can be an ice-breaker. This is a sure-fire way to build rapport.

Be a Better Listener

Asking questions that will elicit appropriate information is the first step in getting to know people, but no matter how well chosen the questions we ask, unless we carefully listen to the responses, we would only understand a fraction of information that is provided. Honing our listening skills are important in all conversations.

Some techniques to help us become a better listener will be discussed in the following chapter.

Conversation Effectiveness Checklist

Review some recent conversations—whether it was in person or on the telephone. Did you:

> Smile? Even on the telephone, a smile is reflected in your voice and your attitude.
> If appropriate, use small talk to break the ice?
> Remember and use the person's name?

- Make a connection with the other person by observing his or her traits, values, or achievements?
- Establish common ground?
- Show respect for the other person's time?
- Show sensitivity to issues of diversity and avoid controversial subjects?
- Demonstrate a sincere desire to learn about the person by asking thoughtful questions?
- Fully listen and focus on what the person was saying?
- Ask how you can help?
- Talk in terms of the other person's interests?
- Tell them something of interest that they might not already know?
- Give sincere praise or a genuine compliment with evidence?

Sum and Substance

Dos for Good Conversation

- Do be prepared. A good conversationalist engages his or her listeners in a stimulating conversation. Hone your conversational skills by keeping up with trends and current events.
- Do learn the name of the other person and use it in the conversation.
- Do make eye contact. Looking directly at the other person is a indication that you are listening. Don't stare at the other person. Yes, look at their eyes, but move our eyes around so you could observe their entire face.
- Do speak clearly and audibly. If you are frequently asked to

speak up or to repeat yourself, you're probably not speaking clearly. Record and listen to your conversations.

> Do seek professional help from a voice coach to overcome poor speaking habits.

> Do use language and images familiar to the listener. You get more out of a conversation with someone who speaks and thinks like you do, than someone who uses a different vocabulary.

> Do speak the conversational style of the person with whom you're talking to.

> Do use different words and inflection when speaking to business associates than when conversing with the teenager down the street.

> Do stick to the topic. Conversation stealers are people who jump in on our story to change the focus to themselves or to something that they know more about.

> Do know when to speak and when to listen. Conversation should be a matter of give and take. Each person involved in a conversation needs to speak and each needs to listen. Participate but don't monopolize.

> Do express an interest in what's being said. Acknowledge statements with a nod, comment or question when appropriate.

> Do ask open-ended questions to promote communication—that is, questions that require more than a yes or no response.

Don'ts for Good Conversation

> Don't speak too fast or too slow. We've all been in conversations with people who talk so fast that we can't keep up, or so slowly that by the time they finish expressing their thought, we've forgotten the topic.

- Don't mumble or swallow your words.
- Don't talk too softly or too loud. Adjust your volume by the closeness or distance from your listener(s).
- Don't monopolize the conversation. Give the other person(s) a chance to talk.
- Don't brag or boast. A conversation should be an interchange of ideas and thoughts—not an ego-trip.
- Don't interrogate. Questions should be presented in a friendly and non-aggressive manner. Use open-end questions so the other person can express his or her ideas freely.
- Don't interrupt. Let the other person complete his or her comment before presenting yours.
- Don't talk over another person. Talking while the other person is still speaking is not only impolite, but your may miss the point he or she is making.
- Don't close your mind to what is being said. Open-mindedness is essential if you want to understand another's point of view.

3

....

LISTEN! REALLY LISTEN!

Do you really listen? Suppose one of your colleagues brings a problem to you and asks for help. You may begin by listening attentively, but before you know it, your mind wanders. Instead of listening to the problem, you're thinking about the pile of work on your desk, the telephone call you were planning to make when this colleague walked into your office, of the argument you had with your daughter when you drove her to school this morning. You hear your colleague's words, but you're not really listening.

This happens to all of us. Why? Our minds can process ideas considerably faster than we can talk. When someone is talking to us, our mind tends to race ahead and we complete the speaker's sentence in our mind—sometimes correctly, but often differently from what the speaker says. You hear what your mind dictates, but not what is eventually said.

This is human nature. But that is not an excuse for being a bad listener. Take the following test to determine how good a listener you are.

Evaluate Your Listening Skills

Answer 'yes' or 'no' to the following questions:

- Do you keep interrupting when somebody is trying to tell you something?
- Do you look at papers during the discussion?
- Do you come to the conclusion even before you hear the whole story?
- Does your body language signal lack of interest?
- Do you hear only what you want to hear and block out everything else?
- Do you show impatience with speakers?
- Do you spend more time talking than listening?
- Does your mind wander during the discussion?
- Do you think about your rebuttal or responses while the other person is still speaking?
- Do you ignore nonverbal signals from the speaker that might indicate that the speaker wants you to respond?

If you answered 'yes' to any of these questions, you should concentrate on improving your listening skills.

Becoming an Active Listener

An active listener not only pays close attention to what the other party is saying but also asks questions, makes comments, and reacts verbally and nonverbally to what is being said.

One way of improving your listening skill is to play an

active role. Instead of just sitting or standing with your ears open, follow these guidelines:

➤ Look at the speaker. Eye contact is one way of showing interest, but don't overdo it. Look at the whole person; don't just stare into his or her eyes.

➤ Show interest by your facial expressions. Smile or show concern when appropriate.

➤ Indicate that you are following the conversation by nods or gestures.

➤ Ask questions about what's being said. You can paraphrase "So the way I understand it is …" or ask specific questions about specific points. This technique not only enables you to clarify points that may be unclear but also keeps you alert by making you pay full attention.

➤ Don't interrupt. A pause should not be a signal for you to start talking. Wait.

➤ Be an empathetic listener. Listen with your heart as well as your head. Try to feel what other people are feeling when they speak. In other words, put yourself in the speaker's shoes.

Six Strategies to Become a Better Listener

You can become a better listener by keeping in check some of the main causes of ineffective listening, before they begin. All you have to do is make a few changes in your work environment and in your approach to listening:

1. Set your voice mail to pick up all phone calls right away. One of the most common distractions is probably the telephone. You want to give the speaker your full attention.

Answering the phone not only interrupts your discussion but also disrupts the flow of thoughts. Even after you've hung up, your mind may still be pondering over the call. If shutting off the phone isn't feasible, get away from the telephone. Go to an empty conference room. Even if there is a phone in the room, it probably won't ring as no one knows that you're there.

2. Hide the papers. If your desk is strewn with paper, your eyes will probably skim over them and before you realize you're reading a letter or a memo instead of listening. If you go to a conference room, take only the papers that are related to the discussion. If you must stay at your desk, put the papers in a drawer so that you won't be tempted to read them.

3. Don't get too comfortable. Robert L. tells of a particularly embarrassing situation: "Some years ago I was discussing a situation with another manager. As was my custom, I sat in my comfortable executive chair with my hands behind my head. Maybe I rocked a little, but fortunately, I caught myself before I dozed off. Ever since then, rather than taking a relaxing position when I engage in a discussion, I've made a point of sitting on the edge of my chair and leaning forward rather than backward when engaged in a discussion. This position not only brings me physically closer to the other person, but also enables me to be more attentive, and helps me to maintain eye contact. It also shows the other person that I'm truly interested in getting the full story he or she is relating and that I take seriously what is being said. And because I'm not quite so comfortable, there's less tendency to daydream."

4. Don't think about your rebuttal. It's tempting to pick up one or two points that the speaker is making and plan how you would respond to them. Do this and you'll probably miss much of the balance of what is being said, often, the really important matters. Concentrate on what is being said through the entire process.

5. Be an empathetic listener. Don't confuse empathy with sympathy. Empathy is putting yourself in the other person's shoes, so you know how he or she feels. Sympathy is feeling sorry for the situation a person faces. An empathetic listener will obtain a deeper understanding of what the speaker truly wants to convey.

6. Take notes. It's impossible to remember everything that is being said in a lengthy discussion. Even if you use shorthand, making lengthy notes keeps you from fully listening. Just jot down key words or phrases. Write down figures or important facts, just enough to help you remember. Immediately after a meeting, while the information is still fresh in your mind, write a detailed summary. Dictate it into a recorder, enter it into your computer, or write it in your notebook, whichever is best for you.

When dealing with people, remember you are not dealing with creatures of logic, but creatures of emotion.

Dale Carnegie

Seven Types of Listeners

Listeners often fall into one of the following categories:

The "Pre-occupieds"

These people come across as rushed and are constantly looking around or doing something else. Also known as multitaskers, these people cannot sit still and listen.

If you are a preoccupied listener, make a point to set aside what you are doing when someone is speaking to you.

If you are dealing with a preoccupied listener, you might want to ask: "Is this a good time?" or say: "I need your undivided attention for just a moment." Begin with a statement that would get their attention; be brief, and get to the bottom line quickly because their attention span is short.

The "Out-to-Lunchers"

These people are physically present, but mentally they are not. You can tell this by the blank look on their face. They are either daydreaming or thinking about everything and anything else but what you are saying.

If you are an out-to-luncher, act like a good listener. Be alert, maintain eye contact, lean forward, and show interest by asking questions.

If you are dealing with an out-to-luncher, check in with them every now and then to ask if they understood what you have said. As with the "pre-occupieds," begin with a statement that will catch their attention; be concise and to the point because their attention span is short.

The "Interrupters"

These people are ready to chime in at any given time. They are perched and ready for a break to complete your sentence for you. They are not listening to you but focused instead on what they want to say.

If you are an interrupter, make a point to apologize every

time you catch yourself interrupting. This would make you more conscious of it.

If you are dealing with an interrupter, when they come in, stop immediately and let them talk, or they would never listen to you. When they are done, you might say, "as I was saying before…" and then continue making your point.

The "Whatevers"

These people remain aloof and show little emotion while listening. They give off the impression that they are not at all interested in what you are talking about.

If you are a "whatever," concentrate on the full message, not just the verbal message. Make a point to listen with your eyes, ears, and heart.

If you are dealing with a "whatever," dramatize your ideas and ask questions to get their involvement.

The "Combatives"

These people are armed and ready for war. They enjoy disagreeing and blaming others.

If you are a "combative" listener, make an effort to put yourself in the speaker's shoes and understand, accept, and find merit in their point of view.

While dealing with this type of listener, when they disagree or resort to blaming: if the criticism is correct, thank them and take appropriate action; if it is not, rather than arguing, tell them you appreciate their suggestions and then go on with the balance of your message.

The "Analysts"

These people constantly take on the role of counselors or

therapists and are ready to provide you with answers even when you have not asked. They think they are great listeners and love to help. They are constantly in an-analyze-what-you-are-saying and fix-it mode.

If you are an "analyst," relax and understand that not everyone is looking for an answer, solution, or advice. Some people just like bouncing ideas off others to help them see the answers more clearly themselves.

If you are dealing with an analyzer, you might want to begin by saying: "I just need to run something by you, I'm not looking for any advice."

The "Engagers"

These are the consciously aware listeners. They listen with their eyes, ears, and hearts, and try to put themselves in the speaker's shoes. This is listening at the highest level. Their listening skills encourage you to continue talking and gives you the opportunity to discover your own solutions and let your ideas unfold.

> *You can close more business in two months by becoming interested in other people than you can in two years by trying to get people interested in you.*
>
> —*Dale Carnegie*

Watch the Body Language

All of us convey information with more than the words we use. What we say is often modified by the way we use our body, our facial expressions, our gestures, the way we sit or stand.

Wouldn't it be great if we could buy a dictionary of body

language so that we could look up what each gesture or expression mean? Then we could interpret what everybody is really saying.

Some people have tried to write such "dictionaries" that lists a variety of different "signals" and identify their meanings. For example, if the other person strokes his chin, "what could it mean?" "Ha! I know. He's pondering about the situation." Indeed, he may very well be thinking it over, but it might also mean that he didn't shave this morning and his chin itches.

The person across from you is sitting with her arms folded in front of her. Some "experts" interpret this to mean that she is holding herself in, blocking you out, rejecting you. Nonsense! Look at a roomful of people in a class, a lecture, or a theatrical performance. You will note that a good number of these people are sitting with arms crossed. Does that mean that they are rejecting the instructor or actors? Of course not, it's a comfortable way to sit, and if you are cold, it keeps you warm. On the other hand, if in the middle of a conversation, the other party should suddenly cross their arms, it might mean that at that point they are disagreeing with you.

There is No Universal Body Language

The fact that one cannot read body language indicates that there is no universal body language. Each of us has his or her own way of expressing ideas, feelings and nuances, nonverbally.

Why should this be? Body language is an acquired trait. We tend to imitate other people. It starts with our parents and is often closely tied in with our ethnic background. Two boys are born in Detroit, Michigan, but their parents immigrated to the United States from two different countries. One family came from a country where the usual way to express oneself was with gesticulation—you could not speak the language without using your hands. The other family came from a country where nobody gesticulated except when highly emotional. The two boys met for the first time in high school. The first boy was discussing a situation in his usual way—his hands moving wildly. The second boy thought: "My goodness, he's excited about this." When he responded in his usual quiet way, the first boy thought: "He's not even interested."

Cultural differences also affect the way one uses nonverbal communications.

Following the theft of money from a high school cafeteria in New York City, the principal interviewed all of the students who had access to the cash register. After the interviews he determined that the thief was a Latin-American girl and he suspended her. A social worker visited the principal about this and asked why he felt she was the thief. He responded: "All the other students looked me straight in the eye and said that they didn't do it. This girl wouldn't look me in the eye. She looked down at her toes throughout the interview. She's obviously guilty."

The social worker said: "Mr Principal, a well bred Latin-American girl is taught never to look straight into the eyes of an exalted personage as the principal, but to look demurely to the ground when talking to him." The cultural difference generated the body language and was misinterpreted by the principal.

A similar pattern may be determined by family habits. When anybody speaks to a member of Esther's family, they respond with frequent nods of their head. Most of us would interpret this to mean that they were agreeing with us. But as Esther pointed out when questioned about this—all it meant to them was that they have acknowledged what was being said.

Study Each Person's Use of Nonverbal Clues

If body language is an important aspect of communication, is there any way that we can learn to read it? There is no one hundred percent approach to reading body language. The only way to obtain a reasonably good interpretation of a person's nonverbal actions and reactions is to know the person with whom you are communicating. When you deal with the same people over and over again, by careful observation you can learn to read their body language. You note that when Claudia agrees with you, she tends to lean forward and when Paul agrees he tilts his head to the right. You observe that Esther nods no matter what you say, but when she is not sure of something, she has a puzzled look on her face even though she is nodding.

By making careful mental notes about each of the people with whom you communicate, you would be able to understand their nonverbal clues and interpret them properly. After a while, you may note that some gestures or expressions are more common among certain people you communicate with than others. From these you may make some generalizations when dealing with new people, but you must be careful not to put too much credence in those interpretations until you have had more experience with these people.

When the body language seems to contradict or skew the meaning of the words being spoken, or you are not sure what the signal being sent really means—ask a question. Get the person to communicate verbally what he or she really meant. By good questioning, you can overcome the doubts that the nonverbal actions induced and be able to deal with them.

The Feedback Loop

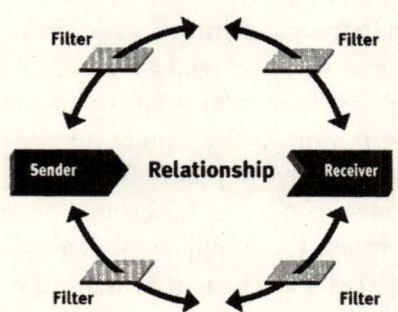

Good listeners recognize that communication is like a two-way radio. The sender sends a message to the receiver and the receiver responds. At that moment, the receiver has become the sender and the sender the receiver. In all of our communications, whether with friends and family, in social and community activities or on the job, we are constantly changing roles from sender to receiver and back again. Unless we recognize that we are always playing this dual role, our messages may degenerate into a one-person diatribe where no real communication would take place.

Just as in any radio interchange, static may develop between the sender's radio and receiver's radio causing distortion in the message. They filter the message so that what was received was not exactly the same message that was sent. This is more likely to occur when the message is long, or deals with complex matter. These distortions may emanate from the sender or from the receiver.

How Has the Message Been Received

In communication we alternate between being senders and receivers. We must be good listeners not only when we are the receiver, but also when we send a message, we must assure that the receiver has listened to what we have sent.

This is how it works: The sender sends a message to the receiver; the receiver responds. When this response is received, the sender, who has now become the receiver, filters this response through the mind's computer, which has been programmed to seek out clues as to how the message has been received. If what was sent was not what was received, a correction can be made in the next message.

> Myra: "Mike, I need to know what equipment is available, what material is in stock, time estimates and what people will be assigned to the project."
> Mike: "We have all the materials we need and we can get the job started on Monday."
> Myra: "Fine, but I still need the figures on each of the items I mentioned so I can write my report."

When Mike received Myra's message, his mindset was geared to getting the job started. Myra's objective was to obtain information for her report. The message was distorted by the perception each had of the purpose of the communication. This was corrected by Myra's next response. She picked up the clue and acted upon it.

Ask Questions

It is not always easy to pick up all the clues. To augment this—ask questions. After every four or five exchanges, ask a question to obtain reaction to what has been covered till that point.

"What problems do you anticipate may develop if we do it this way?"

"How much additional time will your people need to complete this phase?"

From the answers to your questions, you would be able to pick up additional clues and make necessary adjustments.

When the matters involved are complex, to be sure that the message has been received and understood, ask a few specific questions regarding the key points. This would help to quickly identify problem areas and provide immediate clarifications.

Observe Nonverbal Clues

Dr. Kim P., chief engineer of a technical facility, cautions: "My people are professionals and highly knowledgeable in their fields. They tend to rush ahead of me and anticipate what I would say. Often they are right, but there are times when they turn me off before I am finished, assuming they know what I am going to tell them. To overcome this I watch their nonverbal language carefully—their eyes, their facial expressions, their body language. If it appears to me that they are no longer listening, I stop talking for a few seconds and after a pause, ask a specific question on what I said. This brings them back on track."

Loren supervises several people who have limited knowledge of the English language. She depends on observing body language for feedback. She says: "If I see a blank expression on their face, I know I didn't get my message across. I repeat it in simpler words and demonstrate non-verbally what has to be done."

When You are the Receiver

When your boss is giving instructions and you are not sure just what is meant, create your own feedback loop—ask questions.

Don't wait till the end of the discussion, when he or she asks: "Do you have any questions?" All through the discussion, at appropriate moments, ask questions related to what has just been brought up.

It may be in the form of paraphrase: "So the way you want this to be done is..." restating in your own words how you have interpreted the instruction. If it is wrong, it can be clarified, and if it is right, immediate approval will reinforce it.

In some cases a specific question on a specific point will augment your interpretation and avert errors that could have been made. By the end of the discussion, not only would you have a clear picture of what has to be done, but your boss would know that you have followed the instructions.

Sum and Substance

To be an effective listener:

> Listen empathetically. Try to feel what the other person is feeling when he or she speaks.
> Remove all distractions. Turn off the telephone; remove all papers not pertinent to the conversation.
> Clarify any uncertainties after he or she has spoken. Make sure you understood what was said by rephrasing what you heard.

- Try to honestly see things through the other person's point of view.
- Don't jump to conclusions or make assumptions. Keep an open and accepting attitude.
- Show interest by your facial expressions. Smile or show concern when appropriate.
- Indicate that you are following the conversation by nods or gestures.
- Ask questions about what is being said. You can paraphrase, "So the way I understand it is…" or you can ask specific questions about specific points. This not only enables you to clarify points, but keeps you alert and paying full attention.
- Don't interrupt! A pause should not be interpreted as a time for you to start talking—wait.
- Observe the speaker's body language.
- Use the feedback loop. What is said may not be what was received. Search out filters and overcome them. To get back on track, restate your point or ask pertinent questions.

4

SPEAKING WITH CONFIDENCE
AND CONVICTION

When surveys were made concerning people's fears, speaking in public invariably appeared on the top of the list. Unlike some of the other fears, such as death, disease, or loss of job, overcoming the public speaking phobia is relatively easy.

Dale Carnegie expressed this most succinctly:

Is there any faintest shadow of a reason why you should not be able to think as well in a perpendicular position before an audience as you can sitting down? Is there any reason you should pay host to butterflies in your stomach and become a victim of the "trembles" when you get up and address an audience? Surely, you realize that this condition can be remedied, that training and practice will wear away your audience fright and give you self-confidence.

Preparation—The First Step for Successful Talks

In making a public speech, it is essential to be well prepared. How to do this in a business situation will be discussed in the next chapter. If, however, we are asked to talk to our child's class, a meeting of a community association, or any other group and have to choose a topic, the best route is to talk about something that we know and realize that we know. Don't spend ten minutes or ten hours preparing a talk; spend ten weeks or ten months—better still, spend ten years.

Talk about something that has aroused your interest; that you have a deep desire to communicate to your listeners.

Dale Carnegie tells the story of one of his class members, Gay K. Gay who had never made a speech in public before she enrolled in Mr. Carnegie's public speaking course.

She was terrified. She feared that public speaking might be an obscure art far beyond her abilities. Yet at the fourth session of the course, as she made an impromptu talk, she held the audience spellbound. She was asked to speak on, "The Biggest Regret of My Life." Gay then made a talk that was deeply moving. The listeners could hardly keep the tears back. Even Mr. Carnegie could hardly keep the tears from welling up in his own eyes. Her talk went like this:

"The biggest regret of my life is that I never knew a mother's love. My mother died when I was only a year old. I was brought up by a succession of aunts and other relatives who were so absorbed in their own children that they had no time for me. I never stayed with any of them very long. They were always sorry to see me come and glad to see me go. They never took any interest in me or gave me any affection. I knew

I wasn't wanted. Even as a little child I could feel it. I often cried myself to sleep because of loneliness. The deepest desire of my heart was to have someone ask to see my report card from school. But no one ever did. No one cared. All I craved as a little child was love—and no one ever gave it to me."

Had Gay spent ten years preparing that talk? No. She had spent twenty years. She had been preparing herself to make that talk when she cried herself to sleep as a little child. She had been preparing herself to make that talk when her heart ached because no one asked to see her report card from school. No wonder she couldn't talk about that subject. She could not have erased those early memories from her mind. Gay had rediscovered a storehouse of tragic memories and feelings hidden away deep down inside her. She didn't have to pump them up. She didn't have to work at making that talk. All she had to do was to let her pent-up feelings and memories rush up to the surface like oil from a well.

Speakers who talk about what life has taught them never fail to keep the attention of their listeners.

Dale Carnegie

Preparing a Talk When the Subject is Unfamiliar

Often, we could be asked to speak on a subject in which we have little or no experience. This generally occurs while making a business presentation. The purpose of most of these presentations is to get action of some kind—a commitment to purchase from a customer, the next step in the midst of a long project, a decision to change direction—all examples of common presentations.

In preparing this type of communication, begin with the end in mind—i.e., the action you want your listeners to take—and work back from that point. Then, when we would make the presentation, we seek an example or incident, which will capture attention and prepare the way for the desired action. By vividly reconstructing an incident we can make it the basis of influencing the conduct of others. It would be the evidence that convinces the audience to act. In communicating the example, we must recreate a segment of our experience in such a way that it tends to have the same effect on our listeners as it originally had on us. This would prepare us to clarify, intensify, and dramatize our points in a way that will make them interesting and compelling to listen to.

Following which we must obtain from research as much information as we can. A good presenter should know ten times as much about the subject than what would be necessary in the talk. Develop evidence to support your points. Effective use of evidence will be discussed in chapter 6.

Finally, prepare the conclusion. The way we end the presentation has been proven to be one of the best methods to motivate listeners to act. We will see that the end of the presentation yields positive results-especially, from the audience's point of view.

The Magic Formula for Dynamic Talks

We can avoid making rambling, incoherent, boring talks by using a simple, easy to apply three-step approach. This approach magically transforms our presentation into a vibrant, forceful speech.

The magic formula consists of three steps:

Incident: By citing an incident or an anecdote that illustrates the point that you plan to make is a sure-fire way to get and hold the attention of your listeners.

Action: Following an anecdote, point out what course of action you would want the audience to take.

Benefit: Conclude by showing how this action will benefit the audience.

If we wish to persuade others, we must be alert and alive ourselves. We must speak with sincerity and excitement. We must speak as to make our listeners feel that we believe in every word we say.

Incident

When delivering your report, always begin with the incident. Why? The incident captures the immediate attention of your listeners and makes the communication more conversational.

When using the Magic Formula, be sure that both your *action* and *benefit* steps are brief, clear, and specific. The incident must be based on an experience that taught you a lesson. Remember, your point must communicate what action you want your listeners to take. The more specific the *action* step, the better. To communicate clearly, identify one specific action and one specific benefit.

Action (Point)

The second step of the Magic Formula, the action, is what we want the audience to execute. It may be to buy our product, to write to the congressman, to stop smoking, or just to think more about the subject. Invest at least three times more time in preparing than you will in the delivery of your message.

Benefit

The third step of the Magic Formula, the benefit is what the listeners would receive by doing what is asked for in the action step.

For example, "By using this component, you will reduce the time spent and lower the cost in manufacturing your (name the product)."

"Quitting smoking will not only make you healthier and enable you to live longer, but will keep your families from the dangers of passive smoking."

Speak from the Listener's Point of View

Our ability to inspire others to embrace change is largely dependent on our ability to communicate from our listeners' point of view. Early in the presentation, we must build the trust of our listeners. Getting favorable attention and establishing the need to consider change must be accomplished quickly. The use of an incident is an effective way to do this. To be convinced, they must see the evidence that clearly—from their point of view—supports the need for change. The audience must not feel that they are being forced to change—they must see change as the logical option.

After establishing the need for change, we must illustrate both the advantages and disadvantages of each alternative. We should be are careful and ensure that the alternatives are considered from the point of view of our listeners and that they are designed and communicated in a credible and balanced fashion.

We must conclude with evidence to support that our belief is the best alternative and state what action should be taken and what would the benefits be for them. Thereby inspiring our listeners to embrace the specific change that will yield the desired results.

How to Prepare and Deliver Talks

Here are eight principles that will help immensely in preparing talks:

1. Make brief notes of the interesting things that you want to mention.
2. Don't write down the talks. If you do, we would be using written language instead of easy, conversational language; and when you would stand up to talk, you would probably find yourself trying to remember what you wrote down. That will keep you from speaking naturally and with spark.
3. Never, never, never memorize a talk word by word. If you memorize the talk, you are almost sure to forget it; and the audience would probably be glad, for nobody wants to listen to a canned speech. Even if you don't forget it, it would sound crammed. You would have a faraway look in your eyes and a faraway ring in your voice.
4. During a longer talk, if you are afraid that you would forget what you want to say, make some brief notes and glance at them occasionally.
5. Fill the talk with illustrations and examples. By far the easiest way to make a talk interesting is to fill it with examples.

6. Tell stories and anecdotes to illustrate the points. Tell how you or someone you know enforced that point. Give specific examples that you learned from research on the subject.
7. Become an authority on the subject. Develop that priceless asset known as *reserve power*. Know ten times more about the subject than what is required during the talk.
8. Rehearse the talk by conversing with friends—not necessarily a dress rehearsal, but try out the points of view that would be made during the conversation with others to get their reaction. This would enable you to discover how your jokes would be received, and which remark would elicit people's interest. This provides a reaction that is obviously not possible from just rehearsing a talk in front of a mirror.

Add Power to the Incident

To communicate effectively, we must use more than just our voice. We must also use animation or gestures. In other words—use the entire body. Natural, effective, and spontaneous gestures are extremely powerful for two reasons:

➤ Gestures stimulate and inspire the speaker. It wakes them up, loosens and relaxes them. By using gestures, we let ourselves go physically, mentally, and emotionally.

➤ Gestures also impact the listener. The emotional effect gestures have on a listener is both obvious and at times, even dramatic. Just think about some of the world's greatest communicators. In almost every case the use of natural, spontaneous gestures contributed to the effectiveness of the speaker and the impact of his or her message.

Be careful in how you use your body before an audience.

> Don't stand with legs and arms crossed.
> Don't place any barriers across your body such as a purse, papers, or a coffee cup.
> Don't stand with your feet spread apart.
> Don't cross arms in front of the body or at sides.
> Don't hold your head down with your eyes on the lectern (reading the script).
> Do hold your head straight, put your chin up, and chest out.
> Do hold your shoulders back.
> Do maintain eye contact with the group.
> Do smile appropriately.

> *Since most of us lose the spontaneity and naturalness of youth as we grow older, we tend to slip into a definite mold of physical and vocal communication. We find ourselves less ready to use gestures and animation ... In short, we lose the freshness and spontaneity of a true conversation.*
>
> *Dale Carnegie*

Five Steps for Better Articulation

For some people poor articulation reduces the effectiveness of their speech—and often many of us do not really know how we sound to other people. We do not hear ourselves as others hear us. As noted in the discussion of the telephone voice, only by listening to a careful recording of our speech that we can truly appreciate how we really sound. But, if we were to read into a recorder several paragraphs from a magazine, it would not be realistic. We must tape our voice without being aware it is being taped. A simple way to do this is to place a voice-activated tape recorder on your desk for a day. All our conversations that day—whether in person or on the telephone will be recorded. Listen to them and find out if you have any speech problems.

Improve Articulation

Danny is a supervisor. When he gives orders or instructions to his people, he mumbles. His words come across indistinctly and it is difficult to understand what he says. But his people are too embarrassed to tell him that he is mumbling, so they guess what he means—and often guess wrong. This results in errors, missed deadlines, and other problems.

Carrie is very bright. She thinks fast and speaks too fast because she's always trying to keep up with her thoughts. Unfortunately, her listeners cannot keep up with her and miss a good deal of what she says.

Darryl is just the opposite. He speaks very slowly. Although it is easy to understand what he is saying, his listeners often jump ahead of him, anticipating what they think he intends to say—often incorrectly.

Terry, Merry and Jerry interject extra sounds, words or phrases into their speech. Terry adds "er" to every word; Merry interjects, "Y'know" after every phrase and Jerry punctuates each sentence with "OK!" We call these and similar detracting sounds or expressions "word whiskers."

These are some of the most common problems in articulation. Most of the people who have these problems do not even realize they speak that way. By listening to tape recordings of their voices, they become aware that they are mumbling, speaking too fast or too slow or are adding sounds, words or phrases to their sentences.

All that is needed to correct these problems is awareness, and a careful listening to one's speech will do this. When people become aware that they mumble, they would make an effort to stop it. When a person knows that every fifth word uttered is "y'know," he or she will stop saying it.

Overcome Speech Defects

If a person has a serious speech defect like a stutter or a stammer, the chances are that he or she avoids situations that call for much oral communication. However, much has been learned in recent years to help such people. A well-known example is Anne Glenn, the wife of Senator John Glenn, who overcame a major stuttering problem and when her husband ran for office, made campaign speeches for him.

Ivan immigrated to the United States from Russia, and although he had learned English in his native land, his accent was very difficult for Americans to understand. A skilled engineer, he was stymied in his career growth because of this speech problem. At the suggestion of a career counselor, he sought the help of a speech therapist. In less than a year, Ivan's speech improved so much that he was promoted to a managerial position where he had to communicate with executives both within and outside of his company.

Speech therapy is available in universities and can be most helpful for people with speech defects of all sorts or difficult to understand foreign accents.

Tone is Critical

Claude speaks in a monotone. It is not difficult to understand what Claude is saying. His diction is very good. However, it is difficult to sustain one's attention because he has not learned to use inflection and modulation in his voice. People who speak in a monotone cannot hold the interest of their listeners. As in other speech problems, the speakers do not realize that they speak in a monotone. Listening to their own conversations would bring this to their attention and once aware, they could make efforts to overcome it.

Select Appropriate Tempo

The speed in which we speak also affects the message. If we wish to convey urgency or excitement, it is best to increase the tempo. If we speak slowly when we tell people that they should better work faster or they won't meet a deadline, we will not generate the sense of urgency that is required.

On the other hand, if we want something to sink in, we should say it more slowly. "We've had too many complaints about the quality of our work, if each of you would take one more minute to check your work, this could be overcome."

Control Voice Volume

Raising and lowering one's voice in a spoken message is the equivalent of adding italics to a printed page. Whether the voice ought to be raised or lowered, depends on the context of the message.

Careful: It is tempting to shout when one wants to emphasize a point. Shouting can be distracting or could even convey a negative message. Volume should be controlled so that we never speak too loudly or too softly. If we know we have a loud voice, it is especially important to control the volume. This is particularly important in public speeches where a microphone may be in use. Too high a volume can easily distort one's voice when amplified. Whether the voice is naturally soft or loud, careful attention to how it comes across and serious practice in projecting it can aid us in controlling the volume.

Whether we are speaking privately or publicly, if we follow these suggestions, we would easily be understood and would also make a more favorable impression on our listeners.

Twelve Ways to Make Our Listeners Like Us

In order to achieve an empathetic hearing of our messages, we must make our listeners like us. Here are twelve tested principles for winning listeners and influencing audiences.

1. *Consider yourself honored by being asked to address an audience—and say so!* Regardless of its size or type, it is nearly always a compliment to be asked to speak to a group. It is a matter of courtesy and good manners to acknowledge such a compliment. That is one way to make an audience like us.

2. *Appreciate your listeners sincerely.* Never speak before any group without finding out as much as you can about that group, beforehand. Then, spend a few seconds reminding the audience of some of its fine or unusual qualities that makes you proud to be chosen as its speaker.

3. *Whenever possible, mention the names of a few listeners.* A person's name is the sweetest sound in any language;

so, whenever possible, mention the names of a few people present in the audience. Note when political figures speak at a meeting, they almost always mention the names of local officials who are in the audience.

4. *Play yourselves down—not up.* Modesty usually inspires confidence and goodwill. For example, Abraham Lincoln was a master at this. One night during the Lincoln-Douglas debates, Lincoln was serenaded by a brass band; and as he stepped out into the dimly lit porch of the hotel to speak to the band, someone held up a lantern so that the crowd could see Lincoln's homely face. Lincoln began by saying: "My friends, the less you see of me the better you will like me." Lincoln knew the wisdom of the biblical advice: "He that humbles himself shall be exalted."

5. *Say "we"—not "you."* Never assume a condescending attitude towards the listeners. Bring all of them into the talk by using "we" instead of "you."

   The speaker says: "When *you* are worried, *you* ought to get so busy that *you* won't have time to think about *your* troubles." If he or she keeps repeating "you," the impression is that the speaker is lecturing and talking down to the audience.

   Instead say: "When we are worried, *we* ought to get so busy that *we* won't have time to think about *our* troubles." See the difference? When we use the word "you," we make ourselves offensive by seeming to take a superior attitude. A note of caution: The exclusive use of "we" tends to make a speaker sound equally condescending.

6. *Don't talk with a scowling face and an upbraiding voice.* Remember that the expression on your face and the tone of

your voice often speak louder than your words. Regardless of whether you are talking in private or public, you can't win friends with a scowling face and a scolding voice.

There is old Chinese proverb that we ought to cut out and paste inside our hats. It goes like this:

"A man without a smiling face must not open a shop."

Dale Carnegie

7. *Talk in terms of your listeners' interests.* All listeners are intensely and eternally interested in themselves and how to solve their problems. That is about all they are interested in. So, if you show them how to be happier, how to make more money, how to stop worrying and how to get what they want, they will listen to you gladly—regardless of what kind of voice we have, how we breathe, stand, look, gesture or what kind of grammar we use.

For example, when asked how did she manage to win friends so easily and become a more interesting conversationalist, a sales manager reported that she merely asked people, "How did you get into your line of work?" Then she centered her conversation on the response she received. She declared that this simple question had worked wonders for her, especially with strangers. Before addressing a group, find out what their main concerns are and allude to them in the talk.

8. *Have a good time while making the talk.* Unless we enjoy speaking, can we even hope that people would enjoy listening? No matter what our mental and emotional attitudes are, they are bound to be contagious. If we are

having a good time speaking, singing or skating, the people who are watching us or listening to us are also bound to have a good time. Emotional attitudes are as contagious as measles.

One may ask: "How can I have a rip-roaring good time making a talk?" The secret is simple: talk about something you have earned the right to talk about, something that puts sparkle in your eyes and feeling in your voice.

9. *Don't apologize.* We've all heard speakers begin by saying something like this: "I didn't know I was supposed to give this talk until two weeks ago, when the chairman told me I would have to fill in for the president." How about this opening remark? "Unaccustomed as I am to public speaking..." some speakers apologize before even starting. We should never accept an invitation to speak unless we are able to give it the necessary preparation. If we do the best we can do, no apologies are required. If we don't, no amount of apologizing will be acceptable. Apologies are usually an irritating waste of an audience's time.

However, if we are unavoidably late due to a grounded plane, a late train or some equally valid reason, we could explain the circumstances briefly and apologize courteously, and then get on with the talk before any more time is lost.

10. *Appeal to the nobler emotions of the audience.* To inspire an audience by stirring great emotions is not easy. We must first be deeply stirred ourselves. However, we are not often stirred that deeply. To align others to your way of thinking, show them how what you are proposing will in some way enable them to take part in repairing the world. Give them an example: When Susan Earl was soliciting

contributions to her favorite charity, "Heifer, International" she told how just by giving a small donation would enable a family in India to purchase a goat, which would provide milk for their children and a small income from selling the surplus.

Once this spark of noble emotion is lit and the flame plays over the speaker and the audience alike—the warm glow of this experience would be long remembered.

This is the age of dramatization. Merely stating a truth isn't enough. The truth has to be made vivid, interesting, and dramatic. You have to use showmanship. The movies do it. TV does it. And you will have to do it if you want attention.

Dale Carnegie

11. *Welcome the criticism—instead of resenting it.* Probably no other scientist who ever lived was criticized and denounced so outrageously as Charles Darwin, for his theory of evolution. Yet, he never uttered a harsh word against any of his critics. Instead, he thanked them saying that the primary purpose of his life was to uncover knowledge and discover truth, and when searching for truth, two minds were better than one. "If I am wrong," he said, "the sooner I am knocked on the head and annihilated, so much the better."

12. *Be sincere.* All the eloquence in the world would not make up for the lack of sincerity and integrity. To make the audience like you, you must inspire them with confidence in the honesty of your purpose. They may not agree with

your ideas, but they must respect your belief in those ideas if you are to be effective.

Welcome any criticism and respond with respect and humility. What we are speaks more loudly than what we say. Sincerity, integrity, modesty and unselfishness affect an audience deeply.

We prefer a clumsy speaker who radiates honesty and unselfishness to a polished orator who tries to impress us with their eloquence.

Introducing and Thanking a Speaker

If we chair a meeting or serve on a committee that has invited a speaker, we would probably be called to introduce the speaker. The introduction serves as a means of separating what has come before from what is about to be presented. It sets the stage for the audience to give its full attention to the person being introduced and the subject they will present.

The introduction also serves to identify the common ground between speaker and audience. It prepares the audience to accept the speaker because of his or her credentials and the relationship between what the speaker would offer and what the audience is interested in hearing. This is called the T-I-S method.

T—First, mention the *title* or *topic* of the presentation.

I—Identify why this topic is important or of *interest* to the audience.

S—Present the qualifications of the *speaker*. Make sure the qualifications mentioned establish the speaker's credibility to speak on the topic being presented; followed by the name of the speaker.

Preparing an Introduction

The TIS approach is not only an effective way to introduce a speaker, but could also be used if you are asked to address a group. Prepare a written introduction. Be sure it is printed or typed in large enough letters so that it can be read easily from the rostrum.

Present the introduction to the person who will be giving it well in advance of the presentation. Ask the person to read it over. Answer any questions that might arise. Encourage the person who would be introducing you to be brief, positive, and excited about the introduction.

Introducing Yourself

When we must introduce ourselves, the sequence of events changes. The first item would be our name and company or organization affiliation. Next would be the topic of the talk and its importance to the audience. In presenting your qualifications, indicate those aspects of your background that are relevant to the topic and the occasion.

Thanking a Presenter

As the chair of a meeting, we could find ourselves in a position to express our appreciation to the speakers for their presentations. Thank the speaker by acknowledging their contribution or the value of their message to the audience. The procedure should be succinct. You would be basically extending thanks on behalf of the entire group.

Guidelines for Thanking a Speaker Using the T I F Method

T—First, *thank* the presenter using their name.

I—Next, cite one specific area of *interest* from the presentation that made an impression on the audience.

F—Finally, make a *formal statement* thanking the speaker and again using their full name.

Sum and Substance

Keys to an Effective Talk:

> Learn as much as possible about the group being addressed.
> Know at least ten times more about the subject than required during the talk.
> Start with an incident that will illustrate the key point(s).
> Present evidence to substantiate the point(s).
> Pay attention to articulation, grammar, tone and tempo.
> Include animation and vocal variety.
> State clearly the action that the listeners ought to take.
> Point out the benefits of taking this action to them.
> Be prepared to respond to challenging questions.
> Maintain professional composure under pressure.
> Communicate clear, concise, positive messages.
> Sell strategic ideas to the organization.
> Communicate with competence and confidence.

5

MAKING GREAT PRESENTATIONS
TO GROUPS

The purpose of most business presentations is to get action of some kind. It may be a commitment to purchase from a customer, a decision to change a practice or procedure, acceptance of a plan or project, or similar actions. Even those presentations that seem to be simple "updates" call for some decision or action from someone.

To get the results we seek from our communication, our presentation must be well prepared. It must begin in a way that creates and holds the interest of our audience and end in a way that is clear and motivational.

Who is the Audience?

It is as difficult to satisfy the unknown expectations of an audience as it is to hit an unseen target. Even though it can

80

be done, it is a risky way to seek success. Part of the process of preparation is doing research to gather the following information about the audience:

Knowledge

Find out how much the audience knows about the subject. Ask yourself: "Is the audience better informed than I am?" Never face an audience unprepared, but also never fall into the trap of assuming that the listeners are ignorant and therefore, talking down to them.

Stanley L., an attorney, began his presentation to his supervisors at the City National Bank on the changes recently made in the labor law with a detailed statement of the new provisions. He noticed that his audience seemed bored and restless. At the first break, he spoke to some of the people and learned that they had recently attended a seminar on this. Had Stanley made the effort to learn what previous exposure the supervisors had in this area, he would not have had chosen to give so much time to the basics, but instead to the legal ramifications—aspects that they had not covered in their previous training.

Expertize

The skill level and sophistication of the audience is also important because that may determine our position on the issue. If the audience is made up of people with professional or technical backgrounds, the speaker can tailor the presentation to their level. If the participants in the meeting are mostly workers with specialized training, the speaker can prepare examples and techniques in line with their specialties.

Experience

This consideration is not only how much experience the audience has, but at what level and in what environment. Experience in a laboratory is significantly different from experience in the field or on the factory floor. They would relate better with examples and illustrations that fit in with their experiences.

Needs

In order to send the listeners home with a sense of satisfaction and a glad feeling for being present there, it is wise to address their needs. Theory is important when building evidence, but eventually you must show how the theory can be translated into action.

Wants

Similar to the needs of the audience is what the audience wants. Wants and needs are not always the same. If you only address their needs, it is difficult to satisfy an audience and move them to action.

Sally L. managed a boutique selling high priced handbags, costume jewelry, and accessories. She felt frustrated when the first speaker at the seminar she attended spoke only of the key requirements needed to operate a successful store. His suggestions were sound, but they did not excite her. However, the second speaker talked about the dreams she had about the perfect store. Sally was fully attentive and excited because they expressed not just what she needed, but the things she hopes for.

Goals

Determine the goals of the audience and keep them in mind as you plan your presentation. Before Allan L., a human resource consultant, prepared his talk on employee benefits to be presented to the H.R. staff of a client company, he discussed with the H.R. manager what short-term and long-term goals he had for the department. He was then able to gear his presentation to these goals, rather than talking in general terms.

What is the Purpose?

There are only a few purposes for a presentation. Following are the most accepted ones:

Convince

The purpose of many presentations is simply to get the audience to do something. The challenge is to persuade the audience to make a decision or to take an action.

Inform

Another logical purpose is to present information for the enlightenment of our audience. This format focuses on clarity and understanding.

Motivate

When an audience needs to change their opinion or take an unpopular action, the purpose of the presentation is to motivate. Motivation usually goes hand in hand with that of convincing.

Entertain

In one sense, every presentation should entertain. For the audience to be in a favorable frame of mind and open to being convinced, enlightened, or motivated, they need to be entertained. Entertainment is not necessarily based on humor, although that can be a big part of it. In the broadest sense, to entertain an audience is to make them glad they were there and glad we were the presenter.

What is the Message?

It hardly seems necessary to address the importance of having a message, but unfortunately sometimes presentations have no message or at least no easily discoverable message. They may be vague about the subject or there may be so many messages woven into the presentation that it is impossible to identify anything significant. Good speakers know what the message is and keep it in mind throughout the preparation, so that the presentation stays on track.

Be Creditable

As a representative of your organization speaking to a group,—be they customers, the Chamber of Commerce, a service club or a legislative committee—the impression you make determines how the audience will view your organization. Your clients or audience get an impression of your company through your ability to present the specified topics. Business audiences are reluctant to believe what is being said about a company or product unless they believe the person delivering the message.

Business people often make the mistake of overstating a company's ability by making claims, thus losing their (and their company's) credibility to perform or deliver. One must present accurate facts about one's organization. Facts should never be presented without presenting the benefits they could bring to the audience.

Opening a Presentation

The opening of a presentation differs from its content. Its distinct purpose is to elicit the audience's interest in the speaker and the message. Roger Ailes, in his book, *You are the Message*, states that we make an impression on our audience within seven seconds. Good or bad, an impression is made. In today's high-paced business world, those seven seconds are vital to gaining the trust of our audience and establishing professional credibility. If a bad first impression is made it is difficult—if not impossible—to correct it within the time of making a presentation.

With so much at stake, it is critical that our audience see us as real, believable, credible, professional, and trustworthy. Since understanding begins immediately upon opening a presentation, we must work on planning and delivering an impressive introduction. We should strive to be ourselves by being personal and natural, conveying trustworthiness and gaining the favorable interest of our audience. Start with something that will draw attention immediately. Here are some examples:

> "We all have the same amount of one very important asset—time."
> "Last year a million 'gadgets' were sold in the United States—and not a single person needed one."

Questions Based on Need or Interest

- "If there was a better way to market (name the product or service), you would be interested, wouldn't you?"
- "If I could tell you a way to avoid heart attacks, you surely would want to listen, wouldn't you?"

Mysterious Statement

- "When you fold your arms, which one is on top—the right or the left?" (This opening was used in a speech on habits and the difficulty of changing set habits.)
- "Your company's greatest asset will never show on a balance sheet!" (This was the opening to a speech regarding the value of the employees.)

Compliment

- "Your Chairman told me about your great support in improving community spirit and I congratulate you for it. What this shows about you is …" (The beginning of a speech given to a group of co-workers in the community after a luncheon.)
- "Sincere congratulations to the 121 percent sales increase which you achieved during the last budget year! What this shows about you is …" (Said by a sales manager at the beginning of a sales meeting.)

Note: When opening with a compliment, it is best to give a compliment that is based on something concrete or factual and not just an impression or hearsay, which could be misconstrued as insincere flattery.

Dramatic Incident

> "Last Thursday evening, as I approached my car, I observed a beautiful, sleek, red sports car race past me. All of a sudden I heard the tires screech. The brakes, firmly applied, slowed the car to a crawl as it made its way down the old gravel road with huge potholes. It then struck me that this situation was analogous to our own information system network. With some of the most contemporary softwares and equipments in the market, we are still attempting to transmit through an antiquated cabling system. It is only through a new fiber optic cabling network that we, like this beautiful sports car, will be able to capitalize upon our potential performance."

There are always three speeches for each one that you actually gave—the one you practiced, the one you gave, and the one you wish you gave.

Dale Carnegie

The Message

Once the opening has captured the attention of the audience, it is necessary to establish the theme or message of the presentation. As in a fine symphony where the composer reveals the theme and then proceeds to create variations on it, the presenter presents the message and then proceeds to develop it with facts, information, and evidence.

The opening is designed to get the attention of the audience. The message statement focuses attention on the subject. It can be a statement of intent, such as: "We are now going to examine the pros and cons of the new budget process." It can be a question such as: "What are the steps necessary to achieve a ten percent increase in market share next year?" Sometimes the message statement is presented as a proposal of logic such as: "If … is true, then … is also true, and … is the natural result."

Evidence Defeats Doubt

Using evidence is an essential part of an effective presentation. Questions that often arise in the minds of audience members— even if seldom asked—are: "Why should I listen to you?" "Why should I believe you?" "Who besides you says this?" When you need to convince others of your view, one of your primary tools should be the use of evidence. How to develop and use evidence will be discussed in chapter 6.

Closing a Presentation

The opening of a presentation should create a positive first impression. Whereas, the conclusion should solidify a positive lasting impression. Some examples

Summarize in a Few Words

- ➤ "In summary, the key points to remember are …"
- ➤ "Therefore, the action we need to take is …"

Appeal to the Nobler Motives

- ➤ "In the interest of the company."
- ➤ "For a better society."
- ➤ "To decrease famine."
- ➤ "Your contribution can save lives."

Throw Down a Challenge

> "It is up to you."
> "You are the only ones who can realize these goals."

Dramatize Your Ideas

> A slide showing the final project.
> A picture that indicates the team's progress.
> A token or lapel pin that is distributed to the audience.

Repeat the Most Important Point

> "… we will see our goals realized."
> "… your income will be increased by X%."

Use a Motivating Statement

> "No more financial worries."
> "Imagine your children happy, healthy, and safe."
> "You can have an extra hour with your family every day."

Use a Quotation

> Use direct quotes that are relevant.
> Be familiar with whom you are quoting.

Speak on a Personal Level

> "As Susan and Betsy have demonstrated, we can achieve this level of performance."
> "If we, as a team, follow Tom and John's example, we will realize our goals."

There is only one way… to get anybody to do anything. And that is by making the other person want to do it.

Dale Carnegie

The Questions and Answer Period

To effectively control a Q&A period, communicate clearly, in the beginning, how much time would be allotted to question and answer. This helps keep the questions and answers short and to the point.

The rule of thumb is to keep answers short. On certain occasions, it is advantageous to take the liberty of a longer answer, particularly if there was not enough time to develop that point in the presentation. However, short answers allows for more questions.

Be sure someone from the audience does not use the questioning privilege to make a speech. If that begins to happen, gracefully ask the person to ask a question. It is also important not to let any one person dominate the questioning period. It is our responsibility to remain in control.

If we do not know the answer to a specific question, say so. Honesty gains respect.

Opening the Question and Answer Period

Applause generally follows immediately after a presentation. Then it is simply a matter of saying: "I have ten minutes for questions and answers. Who has the first question?" This request says that we expect questions, and now is the time for the first one.

An expectant look on our face and a raised hand shows the audience what to do next. Look at the person asking the question, focus, and demonstrate good listening skills. Maintain a pleasant facial expression and welcome the question. Once you have heard and understood the question, turn to the rest of the audience, and paraphrase the question. By paraphrasing, you gain some time to gather your thoughts as well as make sure everyone else has heard the question. Probably what is most important is to remain in control and make it "your" question. Restatement of the question also gives you an opportunity to take the "sting" or the "barb" out of the question, if that was the intention of a hostile member of the audience.

What can you do when no one asks a question? Sometimes after a presenter asks for questions, the audience does not respond. Most often this simply means that our listeners are unsure of how "safe" it is to ask questions. Asking a question yourself would stimulate the audience. For instance, you could say: "A question that is often asked is …" and then answer the question. Then ask: "Who has the next question?" This usually sets the stage for further questions. Don't be overly afraid of a few seconds of silence. The audience wants to fill that silence as much as you do. If however, the audience still remains silent, ask another question and answer it. Twice is enough. Thank the audience for their attention, or repeat the closing of the formal presentation.

How To Close a Question and Answer Period

When you know your time is about to run out, ask: "Who has the final question?" This signals the audience that answering questions is about to come to an end. When you have answered the final question, gracefully thank the audience for its interest, or if appropriate, repeat the closing of the formal presentation.

Use of Visuals

Using visuals can enhance a presentation, but they also introduce potential barriers that must be crossed to attain an excellent presentation. For that reason the heart of the presentation must always remain the presenter, not the visuals.

The primary purpose of visual aids is to make the presentation more understandable to the audience. Your visuals should *support* your presentation, not *be* your presentation. Visuals also add color, drama, and pacing to the presentation. Choose the visuals based on the purpose, the size of the audience, the strategy and content of the message, the availability of resources to prepare them, and the thrust of the entire presentation.

Consider Visuals When:

➤ Presenting data to an audience that may be difficult to grasp: If statistical material is important, trying to compare data that can't be seen is difficult, if not impossible. It can also be boring.

➤ Listing several items or a series of items: If they have to be compared or if sequence is vital, seeing them is essential. It helps clarify steps and aids retention.

➤ Explaining a complicated process: This allows the audience to follow at their own speed. Since some people grasp relationships more rapidly than others, a visual accommodates both learning styles.

Retention is important. Only about 20% of what is heard is remembered. Only 30% of what is seen is remembered, but over 50% of what is heard *and* seen is remembered. Using visuals not only makes the presentation more interesting, but it is a significant factor in how much the listeners absorb and retain.

There are various types of visuals that we can use. Select and use the type that is appropriate for the audience, the points of the presentation, and for making the greatest impact. They range from high-tech computer generated presentations all the way down to simple flip charts on chalkboards or whiteboards.

With the development of high-powered, user-friendly presentation softwares and the advances and availability of projection equipment, computer-generated presentations are becoming the norm for delivery of professional presentations. PowerPoint, from Microsoft, is frequently used today because of its simplicity and its ability to facilitate more creative visual materials.

Computer presentations can be prepared in advance or can be created in front of the audience depending on the equipment, information, and expertize of the presenter. LCD panels and portable projectors allow computer-generated presentations to be transported and presented almost anywhere.

With so many presentations being made both in the business and educational arenas, and so much data generated by and stored on computers, it is only natural that computers play a role in creating visual aids.

Formats of Visual Aids

Whether the visual is prepared on a computer or it is in another form, there are various ways in which the information can be presented:

> *A bar or pie graph*: Charts and graphs can emphasize and simplify large amounts of information for the listeners.

Visuals cause listeners to focus and crystallize ideas rapidly, so, well-designed charts and graphs can accelerate decision-making, often providing the side benefit of shortening meetings—usually to the delight of all.

A bar chart is best used for comparing two items, such as total earnings between years. Bar charts can also be used to compare three or four elements, such as how a company stacks up against its three closest competitors.

To represent changes over time, a line graph works well. It's effective for detailing a company's month-to-month or year-to-year performance. It also allows viewers to quickly identify trends.

When we need to show the makeup of a complex element, such as the relative sizes of various parts of a whole, a pie chart is ideal. Pie charts quickly convey a subject's overall makeup by graphically representing the proportional relationships between the parts.

➤ *Video:* Professionally presented examples, illustrations, and demonstrations of the highest quality are possible through the use of video. The size and economy of equipments make video presentation practical for a variety of presentational opportunities. The recording, capturing, sending, viewing, editing, and printing of video images are easy, practical, and cost effective. Video can be used for the entire presentation, or certain points can be illustrated with 5-10 minute video segments in a presentation prepared primarily around another medium. Videos on a large variety of subjects can also be bought or rented. One can check what is available online or through a library.

➤ *35mm Slides:* While computer-based presentations have

made 35mm slides unnecessary, many people still consider them exciting, stimulating, and practical. It is an accepted way to show full-color, three-dimensional, still pictures. Like video, slides are most effective when limited to 10-15 minute segments of the presentation.

➤ *Overhead Transparencies:* When talking to small audiences or when computer technology is not available, a simple presentation tool is the overhead projector. The transparencies are easily produced in advance and speakers can write additional material on transparencies as part of the presentation.

➤ *Flip charts:* Flip charts provide spontaneous visual support to a presentation and often contain information provided by the audience; therefore, they have a great deal of credibility. They can be prepared prior to the meeting, or they can be created in front of the audience. This semi-permanent medium can provide continual reminders of points covered throughout a meeting or training process. Sheets from the flip chart can be posted around the room so participants can refer to them when desired.

➤ *White Boards:* White porcelain boards that can be written on quietly with bright colors and erased easily have replaced the old-fashioned chalkboard. The white board's usefulness is limited by the size of the group but is helpful for spontaneous participatory activities such as brainstorming.

Handouts

Additional information and summaries can be distributed at the presentation. They are often used to provide supporting data, worksheets, outlines, or questionnaires. They should be well designed and well printed because they carry the presenter's reputation. If the handouts are intended to replace note taking, they should be distributed at the beginning of the presentation, and the audience be informed of this fact. If they are to supplement what has been presented, they should be given at the end of the presentation.

Handouts can provide more depth to the presented information. The handouts can communicate information beyond bulleted topics presented on visuals.

Information that may be of interest to the members of the audience, but cannot be covered in the allotted presentation time, like references, resources, case studies and sidebars, can also be incorporated into handouts.

Sum and Substance

Here are some of Dale Carnegie's suggestions on making presentations from his book.

Public Speaking For Success:

> The opening of a talk is highly important. It should not be left to chance. It should be carefully worked out in advance.
> Show how the thing we want people to accept is similar to something they already believe.
> Use specific instances, cite concrete examples.
> Sprinkle the talk with phrases that create pictures using words that set images floating before one's eyes.
> The conclusion of a speech is its most strategic element. What is said last is what is likely to be remembered longest.
> Summarize, restate, and outline briefly the main points that have been covered.

- Be prepared to answer questions from the audience. Repeat or paraphrase the questions before answering them.
- Appeal for action. Make sure the audience knows what you want them to do.
- Get a good ending and a good beginning and get them close together. Always stop before your audience wants you to. The point of satiation is reached soon after the peak of popularity.

6

....

GETTING THE BEST OF AN
ARGUMENT

The word *argument* can be defined in several ways. One meaning is *disagreement* in which different views are expressed, often angrily. When it comes to this definition, Dale Carnegie was correct when he wrote: "The only way to get the best of an argument is to avoid it." An angry argument can only result in a no-win situation. Another definition of *argument*, however, is *debate and discussion* about an issue. When we consider *argument* in this context, we can with preparation and skill achieve a win-win result.

Selling an idea to another person—a boss, subordinate, customer or a co-worker—is in essence an argument to persuade that person to accept what is being presented. The objective is in some way to change how that person thinks or reacts on a specific matter.

When preparing to sell an idea—whether it is to the boss or to associates—follow the principles successful salespeople use to make sale. First get the attention of the listener. One effective way to do that is to ask a challenging question. Learn what problems the person(s) to whom we are making the presentation face and focus on that. For example, if customer service is of serious concern, ask: "If there was a way to keep abreast of your customers' satisfaction without increasing your customer service staff, would you want to know about it?"

This should get their attention and now you should be ready to present evidence to show how your idea would accomplish this.

The evidence must be pertinent to the subject and of course, meaningful to the listeners. Here are seven types of evidence that have been proven to be effective. They can be remembered by the acronym *DEFEATS*—the first letter of each method:

Demonstrations (show how something works)

Examples (personal experiences or experiences of others)

Facts (points that are specific, true, and can be proven)

Exhibits (a visual, chart, graph, picture, schematic drawing, or other tangible objects)

Analogies (relating a complex idea to something simpler and easier to understand)

Testimonials of experts (quoting a recognizable or credible source)

Statistics (numbers indicating increases, decreases, percentage changes, comparisons, trends, and summations)

Those convinced against their will are of the same opinion still.

Dale Carnegie

The Twelve Rules for Disagreeing Agreeably

In dealing with others there would certainly arise situations when we would disagree with one or more of the people with whom we are interacting. Expressing disagreement need not be antagonistic. Tact, tolerance, and understanding will enable us to disagree without being disagreeable.

Rule #1: Give others the benefit of the doubt.

Maybe the person who made that outrageous generalization isn't really insensitive. Maybe this person has had a painful experience that made him or her overreact. When instead of downsizing in order to make significant reductions in expenses, it was suggested that all emloyees take a cut in salary, Susan objected vociferously. She argued that highly productive workers should not have to make a sacrifice so less productive workers' jobs could be saved.   When pressed to determine why she was so adamant, we learned that in her previous job, she had accepted a similar solution to cost-cutting, but less than a year later, she and others were terminated anyway. Only by assuring that our company was financially sound enough to avoid this could persuade Susan to change her mind.

Rule #2: Listen.

After giving someone the benefit of the doubt, listen to learn and truly understand why this person holds this belief. We must let that person know that we have heard them and are genuinely trying to see things from their perspective.

Rule #3: Take Responsibility.

When disagreeing with someone, we must always take responsibility for our own feelings. Make a commitment to respond with statements using "I." When we begin our statements with "you" it sounds as if we are blaming and confronting them; this immediately makes the other person defensive and reduces the chance of our point of view being heard.

Rule #4: Use a cushion.

Connect or "cushion" a different opinion, starting with, "I hear what you're saying …" or "I appreciate your view on …." Again, begin with the word "I" and not "You" or it will sound confrontational.

For example: "I understand your concern about how this might slow down the process, but I have examined all the implications of the new approach …." Then restate how the suggested method will compensate for the initial slow-down.

Rule #5: Be Polite.

Remember that our objective is to align the other person's perspective to our own way of thinking. This can never be accomplished by being nasty or rude. Denigrating the other person by sarcasm or condescending humor will not accomplish this.

You can't win people by forcing ideas on them. Harold was an egotist who was so sure he was always right that he fought hard—no holds barred—to establish his points. He pounded the table, shouted, and antagonized his opponents by his arrogance. Such behavior not only makes everybody in the group uncomfortable, but most often results in lengthy and fruitless discussions. Even when his ideas were good, his demeanor defeated his purpose. If he had been polite and diplomatic, his excellent ideas would have been readily accepted.

Rule #6: Eliminate the word "but" or "however" from your vocabulary.

Acknowledging an individual's point of view followed by a "but" or "however" erases the acknowledgement.

Instead, use: "And…" or wait a moment silently and then, contribute your idea or opinion beginning with:

- "Let's also discuss …"
- "How about this angle …"
- "What would happen if …"
- "Have you ever thought about …"
- "Compare that idea with this idea …"
- "That's an interesting perspective."
- "I never thought about it that way."
- "I'm glad that we both agree on…."

Rule #7: State your point of view or opinion with relevant and factual evidence.

Keep emotions out of the equation by taking the time to reflect. Ask yourself: "What do I think?" "Why am I of that opinion?" "What evidence do I have to support my point?"

Rule #8: Let the other party save face.

Dale Carnegie taught us that to win friends and influence people we must always recognize and respect their individualities. When dealing with disagreements, we must never forget that. It is important to never make those who disagree with us feel inferior—even when their arguments are not valid.

Phil was one of those people who loved to point out people's errors. At meetings he would pounce on every error and gloat over his "superiority" to the person involved. Not only did that person lose face in front of his or her peers, but other members of the group also became upset. Such behavior destroys team spirit.

Rule #9: Be conscious of people's sensitivity.

Some people are very sensitive. Ashley is one of those people. She cannot accept criticism easily and becomes defensive when one of her ideas is turned down. We must be aware of this sensitivity so that we can correct or improve the situation with special care.

Instead of pointing out the areas with which we disagree, we should first compliment Ashley on all of the good points in her argument, then ask questions about the areas of disagreement. This will stimulate Ashley to rethink the situation and recognize how it can be improved.

By questioning rather that criticizing, we can get the best out of people without generating resentment. The employee rejects his or her own bad ideas and is encouraged to come up with better ones. This results in the honing of people's creative skills and obtaining more innovative ideas that would increase the effectiveness of a department.

Give consideration to other people's opinions. Let them sustain their feeling of importance.

Dale Carnegie

Rule #10: Give the other party a chance to solve the situation.

When Stephanie spoke to Harry about his frequent tardiness, she did not start with a diatribe on how lateness affects the work of the entire department and cannot be tolerated. Instead she asked: "What can you do to make it on time from now on?" By allowing Harry to come up with a solution to his own problem not only reaffirms the supervisor's faith in the employee, but also encourages employees to think about their problems and make their own decisions about them. People are more likely to follow solutions that they suggest with more commitment and enthusiasm than those superimposed on them.

There are times, particularly when the problem relates to job performance, when the supervisor must be very specific in calling attention to the employee's shortcomings. In such cases make the suggestions for improvement in positive terms. Don't say: "Your work is sloppy." It is far better to show specific examples of work that has not met standards and then ask what can be done to overcome the deficiencies. Reiterate your confidence in the employee and offer any assistance that can help.

Remember that the objective is to help the employee learn to be a better worker.

Rule #11: End on a positive note.

When Stephanie asked Harry what he can do to come in on time, he agreed to set his alarm clock at 6:15 instead of 6:30 from now on so he can avoid the occasional traffic delays that have caused his tardiness.

Stephanie agrees that this should help alleviate the problem. "Harry, I am confident that you will keep this commitment and from now on will be on time. Your contribution to our team is essential and this will assure that my confidence in you has not been misplaced."

Most importantly, give the other person support and assistance in helping them overcome whatever caused the problem. In this way, you would develop cooperative and productive relationships with people who would become valuable assets to the department.

Rule #12: Giving constructive feedback.

The effectiveness of communication can be enhanced when each party obtains honest feedback from the other. Nobody likes to be criticized, but a constructive critique, if done diplomatically, can be a significant contribution to a person's improvement.

Here are some suggestions on making feedback more acceptable:

> Get all the facts.
> Address the situation promptly and privately.
> Focus on the act or behavior, not the person.
> Give the person a genuine compliment first.
> First empathize, and then criticize. Reveal your own similar mistakes, and tell them what you did to correct them.

- Use your human relations skills. Do not order; instead ask questions and make suggestions.
- Show the benefits of changing the behavior.
- End on a friendly note and agree on how to move forward.

When you are on the receiving side of the feedback, keep in mind that the objective is to help us—not criticize us:

- Stay calm and hear the person out.
- Make sure you have a clear understanding of the problem.
- Be open to self-improvement and change.
- Trust that the person giving the feedback has good intentions.
- Do not react defensively.
- Don't offer excuses. If there are extenuating circumstances, specify them as facts not opinions.
- Thank the person for the feedback.
- Agree on how to move forward.

> *Praise people for what they do well, and then gradually help them with their shortcomings. This method will work well in an office, in a factory, in one's home, with spouse, children, parents, with almost anyone in the world.*
>
> *Dale Carnegie*

Problem Solving

Solving problems is an important part of most management jobs. Supervisors must deal with problems concerning operations, production, quality, personnel and sometimes marketing and financial areas. The most usual resource used to deal with these problems is the previous experience of the manager. If he or she has been involved in the type of work for any length of time, the chances are that similar problems have risen in the past. By applying what previously worked, there is a good possibility of resolving the problem.

Unfortunately, this does not always hold true. Sometimes a solution that had been successful in the past may not be effective this time. Although it appears to be the same problem, circumstances may be somewhat different. To avoid this, before tackling a problem, first make sure just what the problem really is.

Clarify the Problem

A major manufacturer of refrigerators had lost a significant share of its market to a competitor. In the past when market share had decreased, the reason for it was increased advertising on the part of the competitors involved, and it was overcome by increasing their own advertising. Using this past experience as a guide, they developed a good advertising campaign to overcome the current loss. To their surprise, the advertising did not help at all—in fact, the market share continued to decrease.

Further study showed that this time the competitor had not done any unusual advertising, but had increased the mark-up given to the retailers. This gave the retailer added incentive to push the competitor's product, even when the customer visited the store as a result of the new advertising. They had tackled the wrong problem. Study the problem—look for the real problem, it may not be what first appears to be.

Identify the Causes of the Problem

Often when we seek the cause of a problem, we see only the

tip of the iceberg. The problem is much deeper. We have an itchy rash, the dermatologist prescribes a salve, which we apply. The itching stops; the rash goes away. We think the problem is solved, but two weeks later it returns. What has happened? The doctor treated the symptom—the rash. True, the rash was a real problem, but it was not the real cause of the problem, which might have been an allergy or another medical situation. To find the real cause or causes of the problems in our jobs, we must look for the "critical factor(s)" from which the problem has arisen. This requires in-depth study and careful analysis.

Develop Several Possible Solutions

Typically, when faced with a problem, we may think of an immediate solution and rush it into effect. Just because a possible solution comes to mind immediately, does not mean that this is the best solution. It is far better to consider a variety of possible solutions before choosing the one to be tried.

Keep an open mind. Seek suggestions from the people who are closest to the problem—the people who work with the situation and will be involved in implementing the action that will be decided upon. Call on experts inside the company (or outside the company, if appropriate) to benefit from their experience and knowledge.

Be creative. People are more creative than they realize. By utilizing this often hidden power within us, innovative concepts can be uncovered that may solve our problems.

Determine the Best Solution

Once several alternatives have been developed, weigh all the factors and decide which is the best. To do this, it is necessary to review the problem and determine which of the solutions would be best suited to accomplish our goal.

List those items that are absolutely essential to the solution. These may include maximum cost, time limitations, use of personnel, and use of other resources. Then list those items that are not essential, but would make the chosen solution even better.

When the New Wave Hairdressers were seeking a new location, they listed the following as essential factors in making the decision:

1. The new location must be in an active shopping mall.
2. It should be no less than 4000 square feet.
3. The rent must be no more than $ "X" per month.
4. We can open for business no later than six months from now.

It would be nice if:

1. There was 4500 square feet for that rent.
2. The landlord would pay for redecorating costs.
3. There were no other hairdressers in the mall.
4. There were high fashion boutiques in the mall. These latter four are preferential factors.

New Wave would not even consider a location unless all of the essential factors are met. Then, by weighing the various preferential factors, they can determine which is the best deal for them.

Take Action

Once a decision is made, put it into effect. Each person involved in implementing the solution should be assigned his or her part, resources should be assembled and the action started. Managers should be on top of the situation. If there are some people on the staff who are not enthusiastic about the solution, "sell" it to them. Be available to help those involved to understand what has to be done, to demonstrate where appropriate, and help where needed.

Follow-Up

There are times when the type of problem requires a solution to which the company must commit itself for an extended periods (e.g., moving to a new location) of time. If the solution chosen does not work, there is little one can do to salvage it. Therefore, in such situations, the problem analysis must be performed with utmost skill. Fortunately, most problems faced by supervisors are not that permanent and can be reversed if they do not work.

When putting such a solution into effect, ask: "How long would it take to determine if this solution is working?" Then set a follow-up date accordingly. At that time, evaluate what has occurred so far and if it has not solved the problem, drop it and select one of the other alternatives. There is no reason to stick with a solution that is not effective when there are other alternatives available.

Customer Complaints

Until a perfect product, organization or company is invented, we would necessarily have to deal with negative issues from our customers. It is inevitable that problems will arise, and just as certain is the fact that some people who complain would be hard to please.

In addition to applying the principles discussed earlier in this chapter, we can effectively resolve complaints, build relationships, improve customer loyalty and retention by using the following eight-step process:

1. *Greet.* Always answer the phone or greet people in person as though you are happy to hear from them. Begin in a friendly way. This is easy to say, but can be difficult to do. We need to be able to "live in day-tight compartments" and separate any negative experiences from this customer contact. Even when the customer is a constant complainer, deal only with the current issue.

2. *Listen.* We often get the same kinds of complaints, so it becomes challenging to really listen to people. Give them an opportunity to vent some of their frustration. Be empathetic. Listen not only for facts, but also for feelings. Resist the temptation to start responding too quickly. Show that we are actively listening by brief interjections or repetition or by rephrasing the customer's comments.

3. *Ask Questions.* Ask questions to clarify the concern. It is important to recognize the need to resist responding until we understand exactly what issues the customer is concerned about.

Elementary questions capture the basic facts of the problem. This gives us an opportunity to take some of the emotion out of the complaint. For example: "When did this problem develop?"

Elaborative questions gather more details. This gives the customer a chance to expand on their feelings. These questions should be relatively short to encourage the customer to talk more. For example: "Tell me exactly what went wrong?"

Evaluative questions help us gain an understanding of the severity of the issue in the mind of the customer. For example: "What would you like us to do?" This is where we evaluate what steps we should take to satisfy the customer.

4. *Empathize.* Find a point of agreement with the person. This does not necessarily mean that you agree with the customer's complaint. This is where you show the customer that you heard and understood the concern and that you recognize its importance to them.

5. *Address the issue.* Now that the emotional issues have been addressed, you should do everything in your power to resolve the practical aspects of the complaint. You must take responsibility for the actions of your organization. If you need help to get back to the customer, do so quickly and thoroughly. This is your opportunity to turn a lemon into lemonade. People who have their problems successfully resolved tend to continue to do business with the same organization.

6. *Test questions.* Ask questions to test how well you have resolved the emotional and practical sides of the complaint. Give the customer another opportunity to talk.

7. *Offer additional help.* Ask what else you can do for this customer. This allows an opportunity to turn the conversation away from the complaint, which makes it easier to end on a positive note.

8. *Follow through.* Often complaints cannot be resolved completely during the first point of contact. Even if the complaint has been resolved, create a reason to contact the

customer again. For example, find a way to give added value. Also, look for ways to solve the root causes of problems within your organization.

Dealing with Negative Thinkers

In almost every organization, we will find people who are hostile about any new suggestions. Whenever we are for something, they're against it. They always have a reason that what we want to accomplish just can't be done.

The reasons for this negativity vary. It may stem from some real or perceived past mistreatment by the company. If that's the case, look into the matter. If the person has justifiable reasons for being negative, try to persuade them that the past is past and motivate them to look to the future. If misconceptions are involved, try to clear them up.

Negativity is often rooted in long-term personality factors that are beyond the ability of any manager to overcome. In that case, professional help is necessary.

Stop! Look! Listen!

A good rule in dealing with negative people is to acknowledge their arguments and persuade them to work with you to overcome their perceived problems, so that the project can move along. Make the person part of the solution rather than an additional problem.

Let's look at some of the problems negative people cause:

Resistance to change. Even people with a positive attitude are reluctant to change. It's comfortable to keep doing things the way they've always been done. Positive thinking people can be persuaded to change by presenting logical arguments. Negative people resist change just for the sake of resisting. No argument ever helps. They often do everything they can to sabotage a situation so that the new methods won't work and they can say, "I told you so."

Impact on group morale. Just as one rotten apple can spoil a whole barrel, one negative person can destroy the entire team's morale. Because the negativism that spreads from one person to another, it's tough to maintain team spirit under these circumstances.

When we present new ideas to negative people, get them to express their objections openly. Say something like this: "You have brought up some good points, and I appreciate them. As we move into this new program, let's carefully watch for those problems. However, we must give this new concept a try. Work with me on it, and together we'll iron out the kinks."

Negative Personalities

Anita exudes negativity. It's not what she says—it's how she acts. She takes any suggestion as a personal affront and takes on any new assignment with such reluctance and annoyance that she turns everyone off.

People such as Anita often don't realize how they come across to others. They probably act this way in their personal lives as well as on their jobs. They're the type of people who don't get along with their families, have few friends, and are forever the dissenters. A good start in dealing with such people is to have a heart-to-heart talk with them to let them know how their attitude affects your group's morale. Surprisingly, many negative thinking people have no idea that their behavior is disruptive to others.

Suggest that they enroll in a personal improvement program, such as the Dale Carnegie Course. Such programs have helped many people overcome negativity, resulting in not only improvement in their job performance, but their entire lives.

Work Towards a Win-Win Situation

If everybody isn't winning—nobody is truly winning. Creating "losers" ultimately results in lost customers, employee turnover, antagonistic work groups, and companies operating below potential.

By careful preparation and by keeping in mind the best techniques of dealing with people, we can present and sell our ideas to others and gain the great satisfaction of seeing our ideas carried out with enthusiasm by everyone involved.

Sum and Substance

There is no better summary of getting the best of an argument, whether it is with family members, social acquaintances, or on the job than Dale Carnegie's principles on persuading others to accept our ideas. They are:

1. Show respect for the other person's opinion. Never tell a person he or she is wrong.
2. If you are wrong, admit it quickly, emphatically.
3. Begin in a friendly way.
4. Get the other person to say, "yes" immediately.
5. Let the other person do a great deal of the talking.

6. Let the other person feel the idea is his or hers.
7. Try honestly to see things from the other person's point of view.
8. Be sympathetic with the other person's ideas and desires.
9. Appeal to the nobler motives.
10. Dramatize your ideas.
11. Throw down a challenge.

7

....

MAKING MEETINGS MORE MEANINGFUL

A frequently used and effective communication technique is meetings. It enables the communication to be delivered to a large group of people at the same time. But meetings can be a big waste of time if they're not organized properly.

In most businesses and organizations a good deal of work is assigned to committees. There's an old joke that says that a camel is a horse created by a committee. As long as there have been committees, they have had a reputation of not really being effective. Yet, often old aphorisms provide conflicting messages. Are committees made up of "too many cooks who spoil the broth," or do they benefit because "two heads are better than one?" Let's look at what can be done to make the committees on which *we* serve accomplish the mission for which they were created.

Establish Clear and Understandable Goals

When Leonard B. was appointed to chair a committee consisting of three other executives and himself to find a suitable location for a branch warehouse, he called a meeting to set specific goals and timetables. Rather than dictating these to his people, he conducted a participative planning session. Each of the members contributed ideas and together they came up with a workable plan. Because each of the committee members was involved in the planning, the goals were not only clear to each of them, but the entire group was committed to its accomplishment.

Every member of the committee should be given a specific assignment. The chairperson should learn the strengths and specific areas of expertize of each of the members and utilize these assets in making the assignments. Leonard had the advantage of knowing each of his team members as they had worked together for some time and was able to assign each of them meaningful assignments pertaining to areas where they could contribute most effectively.

However, if you chair a committee where some or all of the members are virtual strangers, learn as early as possible about each of them. When Carol was appointed to chair a PTA committee to study and make recommendations on the development of a program for more participation in classroom activities, she had only a casual acquaintance with most of the members. She made a point to meet each of them privately over the first few weeks to find out where they could do the most good. At the second meeting, she was not only able to make wise appointments, but as a result of these personal discussions, encouraged many of them to volunteer to take on significant aspects of the project.

Once the assignment is made, ask each of the committee members to develop a plan and a timetable for his or her assignment. These should be put in writing and submitted to the chairperson at the next meeting. To assure that the plan is being met, a follow-up system should be established.

Leonard's committee's goal was to find the location and arrange for the leasing of the facility within three months. So each of his members had to have the plans for his or her assignment ready two weeks from the first meeting. Follow-up discussions with each of the members were scheduled during the two week period after the second meeting and a third full committee meeting was scheduled at the beginning of the second month.

Carol's project was much longer. Her committee had a six-month deadline. Inasmuch as Carol's group consisted of nine people, she created three sub-committees for the three major aspects of the project and arranged to meet with each sub-committee once during the first and second month. Monthly meetings were scheduled for the entire committee to report and to share their ideas and accomplishments.

Resolving Disagreements

Whenever several people are involved in a project, there is likely to be some disagreements. It is the responsibility of the chairperson to resolve them. Carol faced this at her first meeting with a sub-committee. Two of the members agreed on a plan of action, but the third member firmly opposed it. Logically, a two to one vote might be used to choose the plan, but Carol recognized that it was necessary to win the full cooperation of the third member if the plan was to succeed.

She asked the dissenter to express her reasons for opposing the majority and listened carefully. She encouraged the others to think about these objections and together they were able to reach a consensus and develop a plan to which all of them could commit themselves. Some suggestions on how to deal with disagreements will be discussed later in this chapter.

Committee Reports

Once each of the members or sub-committees has completed the assigned work, the results are presented to the entire committee. These are discussed and final decisions or recommendations are made. Usually, a full report must be developed for submission to the person or persons to whom the committee is responsible. In most committees this is the end of the assignment. However, in some cases the committee may be responsible for implementing the action recommended.

Carol's committee had to submit a detailed report to the PTA Board. Inasmuch as each of her sub-committees had investigated a different aspect of the subject, she asked for written reports from each of them. After they had been discussed in the entire committee and decisions were made, the sub-committee revised their reports to reflect these decisions. Carol appointed one of the members to write the draft of the committee report. This was carefully reviewed and edited and copies sent to each of the committee members. At the final meeting of the committee, the report was approved.

Leonard's committee worked somewhat differently. Each of the members had been given a different aspect of the assignment. One member had studied traffic patterns; another cost factors and the third community desirability. Once this specialized information was obtained, several meetings were held to discuss the entire problem. From these a final recommendation and report was written. All the members contributed to the report and it was put into final shape by the chairperson. But this was not the end of the assignment. After the written report was submitted, Leonard had to meet his bosses to answer questions and defend some of the recommendations. Knowing that this was usual in these circumstances, the committee planned for the oral presentation and for questions or objections that might be raised. As a result Leonard was fully prepared to make a full presentation, answer questions, and rebut objections.

Successful committee work requires careful planning, assigning each of the aspects of the work to people who are competent, getting all of the members involved, and following up to assure that what is planned and assigned is carried out effectively. When you get each member to participate from the planning stage to the final report, the work of the group would go smoothly and the mission of the committee will be effectively accomplished.

Making Committees Work

We have often heard committee members complain: "What a waste of time. I could have accomplished so much more if I had spent this past hour at my desk!" In a recent survey, over 70 percent of the people interviewed felt they had wasted time in the meetings they had attended.

There is hope. Meetings can be made productive. Let's look at a few ways to conduct meetings more efficiently.

Limit Who Attends

Invite only appropriate participants. Some managers hold staff meetings on a regular basis—sometimes weekly or even daily. Quite often, many of the people who attend are not involved in the matters that are being discussed. By inviting only those who can contribute to the meeting or would be affected by what is being discussed, we can avoid wasting others' time and keep the meetings briefer.

When people who are usually invited to meetings are not invited, they may worry: "Why wasn't I asked? Is the boss giving me a hidden message? Am I on the way out?" Avoid this concern by explaining beforehand the new policy and why it is being instituted.

Plan an Agenda—and Stick To It

An agenda is the key to success or failure of a meeting. Plan the agenda carefully, covering all matters that are to be discussed. By determining in advance not only what subjects will be addressed, but the order in which they would be covered, the meeting will run more smoothly.

In establishing the sequence of topics at a meeting, put the most complex ones at the beginning of the program. People come to meetings with clear minds and are able to approach deeper matters more effectively early on. If the important issues are scheduled for later consideration, participants are less likely to be attentive, and might be distracted by what has been discussed earlier.

At least three days before the meeting, the agenda should be sent to all those people who are supposed to attend the meeting. This will allow them to study the topics of discussion and prepare their contribution.

Stick rigidly to the agenda. Topics not on the agenda should not be introduced unless it's an emergency. In that case, it to be placed on the agenda for the next meeting.

Get Everyone Into the Act

Attendees should be encouraged to study the agenda and be prepared to discuss each item. If specific data is needed to make a point, organize it into easy-to-follow visuals (for example, charts or hand-outs) and bring it to the meeting. Encourage discussion and create an atmosphere in which people can disagree without fear of ridicule or retaliation.

If pertinent, provide "takeaway" photocopies of diagrams, flow charts or other visuals that were projected. Distribute the copies to everyone at the meeting to ensure that they have a clear idea of the subjects discussed. These copies also serve as permanent reminders of the material; participants can refer to them later if necessary.

If there are heftier handouts or other dense reading materials, distribute them far enough in advance of the meeting to enable team members to study them. The focus of a meeting should be on expanding, demonstrating, and clarifying information—not to introduce brand new concepts, particularly complex technical material.

As the leader of the meeting, ask questions that stimulates discussion. Be open to questions and dissension. It's better to have people butt heads during the meeting than let them stew over their problems over a long period of time.

Don't Dominate the Meeting

Gus J. prided himself in running meetings. He boasted about how all his people contributed to the subjects discussed. His staff, however, had an entirely different perception of those meetings. "Gus tells us what he plans to do, then asks if we have any ideas. When one of us suggests something, he immediately rejects it, sometimes ridiculing the person who made the suggestion. So generally, we all agree. There is no real participation."

> *This is a hurried age we are living in. If you've got anything to say, say it quickly, get to the point and stop, and give the other person a chance to talk.*
>
> *Dale Carnegie*

Control Chatterboxes

Brad is one of those people who try to dominate a meeting. He always has something to say—usually not important, often a personal pet peeve which is always distracting.

Here are some tips on how leaders can attempt to keep Brad and others like him quiet:

> ➤ Take Brad aside before the meeting and tell him, "I know you like to contribute to our meetings and I appreciate it, but we have a limited amount of time and some of the other people want a chance to present their ideas. So let's give them a chance to talk, and you and I can discuss our issues after the meeting."

> ➤ If Brad still insists on dominating the meeting, wait until he pauses for a breath—which he inevitably must do—and

quickly say: "Thank you, Brad, now let's hear what Sue has to say."

> Announce that each speaker has only three minutes to make his or her point. Be flexible with others, but be strict with blabbermouths like Brad.

Close With a Bang

At the end of the meeting, after all the items on the agenda have been covered, the leader should summarize what has been accomplished. If team member received an assignment during the course of the meeting, have them indicate what did they understand with respect to the expectation and the course of action. This will give the leader and all the participants a feedback.

Take Notes

Take notes or assign a participant to take notes, so that there is no misunderstanding of what has been decided at a meeting. These need not be detailed transcripts of the entire discussion, but a summary of the decisions made on each issue. After the meeting, distribute copies of the notes not only to the attendees, but also to all the people who may be affected by what was determined. The notes would serve as a reminder to the participants of the meeting and as a communication to those who didn't attend.

Meetings in Volunteer Organizations

The same rules that apply to conducting business meetings should be applied in board meetings of volunteer organizations, such as religious groups, community associations, social clubs and similar societies. Sometimes these meetings are conducted in a more formal manner.

The usual structure of these meetings calls for starting with a reading of the notes from the previous meeting and, if necessary, making corrections on it. This may be followed by reports made by the chairs of various sub-committees, then a discussion of old business, followed by new business. An agenda covering the reports on "old business" is no problem, but there is little control over "new businesses."

Sandra was presiding over the board meeting of the Home Owners Association. It was 9 PM and they had just completed the old business section. As it was getting late, and Sandra had things to do at home, when she called for "new business," she crossed her fingers and hoped nothing would be brought up.

Sure enough, one board member had a pet project he was trying to promote, and the meeting went on for another hour.

To overcome this problem, suggest that the rules be changed. Instead of "new business," substitute, "suggestions for the next meeting." By doing this, although ideas may be introduced, no discussion can take place and the meeting will conclude much earlier. Control over the meeting is assured by sticking to the agenda. Other matters can be deferred until they can be incorporated into the agenda.

How to Disagree Without Being Disagreeable

Chairing a meeting does not always run smoothly. There are participants who disagree with you and are often adamant in their opinions. Here are some suggestions on how to deal with these people.

Accept the fact that the person disagreeing with you may

be right. You do not have all the answers. Ask questions to help understand where that person is coming from. Listen to fully understand and appreciate why this person holds that belief. Clarify any misunderstandings. He or she may not have fully understood your evidence. On the other hand, that person may have brought up some facts that you were not aware of and which may require you to reexamine your argument.

Often the reason for disagreement is emotional not factual. The person may be reacting negatively to your idea for some personal reason—perhaps a poor experience with a similar idea in the past of some facet of his or her personality. Arguing on the basis of evidence is futile. Try to determine the true reason for the disagreement and if possible, deal with it.

Do not become confrontational. Instead of saying: "You don't understand..." say: "The way I understand it ...." When we blame the other person for not agreeing with us, we put them on the defensive front and incur resentment that will work against ever convincing them to accept our ideas.

Reread the suggestions on how to disagree without being disagreeable in chapter 6.

Meeting Self-Evaluator

Next time we conduct a meeting, we can review our effectiveness with the following checklist.

Before the meeting:

1. Did we prepare an agenda for the meeting?
2. Did we distribute agenda to participants in advance of meeting?

3. Did we set starting and ending times for the meeting?
4. Did we prepare visuals and/or handouts?
5. Did we assign segments of the program to participants?
6. Did we appoint a participant to record the meeting by taking notes?
7. Did we arrange for all the equipment and supplies required:
   Chalk board and chalk
   Flip chart easel
   Flip chart pads and markers
   Computer & projector for powerpoint
   Overhead projector
   Slide projector
   Other

During the meeting:

1. Did we stick to the agenda?
2. Did we manage to obtain participation from all participants?
3. Did we keep blabbermouths and dominators under control?
4. Did we distribute assignments equitably?
5. Did we refrain from expressing our ideas until participants expressed theirs?
6. Did we encourage questions from participants?
7. Did we encourage other participants to answer questions asked by team members?
8. Did we summarize key points at the end of meeting?
9. Did we verify participants' understanding of their assignments before adjourning the meeting?
10. Did we end the meeting with a motivational statement or a call for action?

After the meeting:

1. Did we distribute notes from the meeting to the participants and others who may be affected?
2. Did we follow through on assignments made?
3. Did we gather feedback from participants about the meeting?

The more "yes" answers, the more effectively the meeting was conducted.

> *Successful people will profit from their mistakes and try again in a different way.*
>
> Dale Carnegie

Get the Most Out of Meetings

When we lead the meeting, we have control over how well it runs, but most of the times we are not the leader but a participant. By taking active steps before, during, and after the meeting, we can make every meeting that we attend a valuable learning experience.

When you are notified of the meeting, don't just enter it on your calendar and forget it until the scheduled time. It's worth taking the time to prepare for it.

Before the meeting:

› Study the agenda. Review the subjects that are listed. Even if you have enough knowledge about them, you should make sure that you are up to date on them. Review your files to find out know what's been done so far. If pertinent, read articles in technical or trade publications that cover the matters.

- If it is a new area or one with which you are not familiar with, carefully study the material provided. This is too important to just give it a cursory scan and expect to pick up the details at the meeting.
- Make notes on comments, ideas, or questions that you have about the subjects.

At the meeting:

- Participate: If you have comments, ideas, or questions, don't hold back. Caution: Don't just talk for the sake of talking. Make your points succinctly.
- Deal with disagreements. It's likely that some other participants may disagree with your view. Don't take it personally. In responding, stick to the facts. It's a discussion, not an argument.
- Work toward consensus. If the objective of the meeting is to solve a problem, contribute toward the solution. Listen to other views. They may be better than yours. Be ready to make compromises to attain satisfactory solutions.
- Don't dominate the meeting. Sometimes it's hard to hold back when you have ideas that you want to express. Give the others a chance to talk.
- Take notes on key decisions that were made, or on new information that you have learned.
- If assignments are to given to the participants, volunteer immediately for the assignment that most appeals to you. If you hold back, you may wind up with a job that is not as interesting and which you may not enjoy doing.

After the meeting:

Review your notes. Take action where required. If you were given an assignment, discuss it with the leader to assure you understood what is required and when it is expected.

Attending Meetings Outside

Many people attend meetings outside of the company. They may be seminars, trade association meetings or conventions, or conferences sponsored by organizations that have ideas or proposals that may be of interest to our company or us. These may be held within the company or outside the company's premises.

Here are some suggestions to help us make these meetings worth our time and attention.

Prepare for the meeting

Most conferences and conventions are announced months in advance. Prepare for this meeting in the same way as you would have for a company meeting. Usually an agenda accompanies the announcement. Study it carefully. Does any subject listed require special preparation? You may want to read up on unfamiliar subjects to help yourself comprehend and contribute to the discussion. You may want to re-examine your company's experience in that area so you could relate what is being discussed to your own organization's problems.

Meet new people

At the meeting, don't sit with your colleagues. You can speak to them any time. If attendees are seated at a table, make a point of sitting with different people at various stages of the meetings. Often at luncheon or dinner discussions, you pick up more ideas from your tablemates than from the speakers. Note the names and addresses of people you meet at these events. They may be a source of information or guidance in the future

When speakers from outside address a meeting, note their names and addresses. You may want to contact some of them for more information.

Keep an open mind

To get the most out of what a speaker says, keep your mind open to new suggestions. They may be different from what you honestly believe is best, but until you hear it all and think it through objectively, you wouldn't really know. Progress comes through change. This does not mean that all new ideas are good ones, but they should be heard out, evaluated and carefully and objectively considered.

Be tolerant

Sometimes you hear a speaker who immediately turned you off. You didn't like his or her appearance, clothes, voice, or regional accent so you either stopped listening or rejected what he or she said. Prejudice against a speaker keeps many attendees from really listening to what is being discussed or from accepting the ideas being presented.

Take notes

Note taking has two important functions: It helps organize what you hear while you are at the meeting, resulting in, systematic listening; it also becomes a source for future reference.

Keep an Ah Hah! page

Use this page in your notebook to list exciting ideas that you pick up at the meeting. These are items that you want to make sure you don't forget.

Ask questions

Don't hesitate to question a speaker when the opportunity arises. But don't waste time asking trivial questions. Avoid prefacing your question with lengthy comments. Be clear; be brief.

During a formal presentation, it is not appropriate to interrupt the speaker. If you have a question, jot it down on the last page of your notebook. This should act as a reminder to not to forget the questions that you want to ask when the opportune time comes.

Be an active participant

Contribute ideas. In most meetings there are people who willingly share ideas and information. Others just sit and listen. When asked why they did not participate fully, a commonly heard response is: "Why should I give my ideas to these people? Some of them are my competitors and I won't give away my trade secrets."

Nobody expects us to say anything that would damage our firm or its competitive position, but most discussions are not of this nature. They're designed to promote the exchange of ideas that are of value to most of the attendees. The experience of one organization helps the others. By contributing ideas, we provide richer experiences for others, which in turn results in a more fulfilling experience for ourselves.

After the meeting:

After the meeting, summarize what you learned. Review our notes while the meeting is still fresh in your mind. As soon as possible, write or dictate a report on the conference for the creation of a permanent file.

Report on what you have learned. Send a memo or brief report to your boss and your colleagues, who might find the information valuable. By sharing what you have learned, you add to the value of your firm and yourself, for attending the program.

Put it into practice

If nothing is done with what you learned at the meeting, it's has been a waste of time and money. Therefore, put what you have learned into practice.

Sum and Substance

> Every meeting should have a purpose, and the meeting's leader should make sure the purpose is accomplished.
> Several days before the meeting, prepare an agenda and distribute it to everybody who is expected at the meeting.
> Prepare materials and arrange for equipments intended to be used in advance and make sure the equipment required to show visuals is on hand. Make sure that there are enough copies of handouts for all participants.
> Establish a participative climate, facilitate participation by shy or reticent participants, and encourage all attendees to participate. Don't allow blabbermouths to dominate the meeting.

- By the time the meeting ends, participants should be clear about the subjects discussed. Give everyone a chance to ask questions and summarize what has been accomplished. Assure that if any participants received assignments during the meeting, they have understood what they are supposed to do and when to do it. End the meeting with a call for action or an inspirational message.
- We can get the most out of meetings or conferences we attend by following the suggestions made in the last section of this chapter.

8

PUT IT IN WRITING

"When I talk to somebody in person or on the telephone, I have no trouble making myself understood, but when I have to write a letter or a memo, I sound stilted and inadequate." This comment was not made by a high school dropout, but a graduate engineer with a master's degree in business administration. Many people who are articulate in oral communications freeze up when conveying their ideas on paper.

Part of the reason that this occurs is the mistaken notion that written words should sound more formal than the spoken message. This results in letters and memos that sound stiff and artificial.

Written words differ from spoken words because the meaning conveyed by oral communication is tempered by voice tone and body language. In addition, if the meaning is not clear, the speaker knows this immediately by the manner in which the message is received and the questions asked by the other party.

Some men and woman try to avoid a project that requires a written report. They feel inadequate and ill prepared to take on this assignment. There is no more reason to fear a written report than to give an oral report. It is a learnable skill and when mastered can enhance a person's career growth.

> *People who accept responsibility make themselves stand out from the others in the office, factory or in any walk of life, and they are the ones who get ahead. Welcome responsibility. Do this in little things and in big things and success will come to you.*
>
> *—Dale Carnegie*

In order to make sure that the written message comes across to the reader with the same impact as spoken words, the language of our letters and memos must be somewhat different from the language used in speaking. Yet, it need not be too different. The following suggestions will help you write in much the same way as you speak without sounding stilted.

Plan the Message Before Writing One Word

Think before writing. Deborah K. has received many compliments about her letters. She rightfully prides herself on this. Deborah outlines each letter carefully before dictating or writing it.

A study of Deborah's outlines indicate that she does not only list points to be covered, but puts them in order of importance so the letter immediately starts with what is of most interest to the correspondent. Rather than leading up to the critical information with background material, she states it immediately and follows it up with additional matters that are absolutely necessary to make the point.

For example, instead of the common beginning: "We are in receipt of your letter requesting information about our Model #1754, and so on," she writes: "Yes, our Model #1754 will solve your problem," and then provides evidence. Instead of ending: "Thank you for your inquiry," she concluded with: "We look forward to receiving your order." Statements such as these indicate a direct and dynamic response to the inquiry and precipitate immediate positive action.

TAB the Message

A good rule to follow is to carefully plan what we want to say before writing a single word. This simple process will help plan the letter or memo. It can be summarized in the acronym TAB, which provides clues to help us think clearly about what we want to write before writing it.

Think about the situation: Why am I writing this?
Action: What do I want to accomplish?
Benefit: How will this be of value to the reader?

Ask these questions and jot down the answers on a scratch pad. By "TAB-ing" our thoughts before we do the writing, we get a clear idea of what we want to convey. The list will help us organize all the information concerning the situation we're writing about—it will indicate what we want to accomplish, how to deal with it, and how those actions would benefit our readers.

Be Complete, Concise, and Clear

How can a letter be kept concise and still be complete and clear? Many writers include much extraneous material in a letter or memo. When Enrique returned from a business trip to Latin America, his report was ten pages long. It certainly was complete, but much of what he wrote was incidental information that had no bearing on his mission. He reported everything he saw and heard rather than concentrating on the objectives of his trip.

Ask these questions before writing a long letter or report: "What are the key matters to be discussed?"

"How can I present these matters in the most concise form and provide all the information as clearly as possible?"

After writing the first draft, reread each sentence and ask: "Is this sentence really needed?"

Avoid Jargon

The letter he was reading puzzled Gary. The writer kept referring to the advantages of dealing with an "OEM" and Gary had no idea what those letters meant. The writer incorrectly assumed that Gary knew they meant Original Equipment Manufacturer,' and by making this false assumption, failed to convey the message. Initials, acronyms and other jargon have a place when communicating with people in the fields where that jargon is used. One cannot assume that others will know these terms.

However, in writing a letter using the jargon of the field in which the recipient of the letter works, may result in an acceptance by the reader.

Use Short, Punchy Sentences

We may be impressed by our own excellent rhetoric, but the reader of our letter will find it much more understandable if we avoid complex, multi-phrase sentences. The simple declarative sentence is often the best. Instead of saying: "In light of the research in this field, it is our opinion that the program we are offering will facilitate the writing skills of the employees who undertake this training," say: "This program will teach your people to write better."

However, avoid structuring all sentences in the same manner. This will make the letter boring. Short and punchy—yes; simple and dull—no. Make the main points in capsule form like the headline of a newspaper story; supplement them with details where appropriate by using more varied word structure.

Get to the Point

Steer clear of complex sentence constructions or extravagant phraseology. Keep it as brief as possible, but make it punchy. One way of making points stand out is to write the item in the form of a bulletin:

- Headline the main point—use bold print.
- Break the body of the letter or memo into separate sections, one for each subsidiary point.
- Use an asterisk (*) or bullet (•) to highlight key points.
- Where appropriate, use graphs, charts, or other visual aids to augment the impact of your words.

Talk to the Reader

The message will be clearer and more easily accepted by the reader if it is written in the way we speak. Pretend the person who is going to read the letter or report is sitting in your office, or you are on the telephone with them. Be informal. Relax. Talk in the manner—the vocabulary, accents, idioms and expressions—which you usually use.

We wouldn't normally say: "Please be advised ..." or "We wish to inform you that because of the fire in our plant, there will be a ten day delay in shipping your order." Instead we would get right into the message: "Because of the fire in our plant, there will be a ten day delay in shipping your order." So why not write just that?

Use Direct Questions

A conversation is not one sided. One person speaks, and then the other responds, often with a question. "Yes, but how will this affect the quality?" By interjecting questions in the letter, we can draw the attention of the reader to specific points. After making a point, ask a pertinent question such as: "What additional applications can you find by installing this software?" This gives the reader a chance to reflect on your message in terms that are specific to his or her needs.

Write Like You Speak

When speaking we use *I*, *we* and *you* all the time. They're part of the normal give and take of our conversation. In writing we tend to be more formal. We use phrases like "It is assumed," "it is recommended," or sentences like: "An investigation will be made and upon its completion a report will be furnished to your organization." Why not clearly state: "We're investigating the matter and when we obtain the information we'll let you know."

Make the letter sound more personal. Use the addressee's name within the letter. If they are friends, we may use the first name, if business acquaintances, use the appropriate title (Mr., Mrs., Ms., Dr., etc.), and the last name, and instead of saying "the company will benefit by using this product," say "So you see, Beth, (or Ms. Smith), how using this product will benefit you."

Use Short, Snappy Sentences

The ordinary reader can take in only so many words before his or her eyes come to a brief rest at a period. If a sentence has too many words, chances are that the full meaning would be missed. Studies show that sentences of no more than 20 words are easiest to read and absorb. It is usually quite clear to see where one idea leaves off and another begins. Limit each sentence to one idea. Remember your objective is to get the idea across to the reader—not to create undying prose. It is also helpful to use short rather than long words.

Of course, technical language is appropriate while writing on technical matters to technically trained people. However, when writing to people who may not have the background in your area, avoid language and jargon that they are unlikely to possess.

Give Letters the Right Human Touch

Expressing our natural feelings personalizes the message. If it's good news, say you're glad; if it's bad news, say you're sorry. You should be as courteous, polite and interested as if the addressee is in front of you. Remember the person who is going to read the letter is a human being, they would be annoyed if the letter is cold and pleased if it is courteous and friendly.

Make Mail and Memos Memorable

Memos and letters are in a sense "visual," but when we read them, it becomes an audio input. We absorb the data by reading them to ourselves. The mind processes this in the same way that it deals with words that it hears. By augmenting memos and letters with visual aids, those documents become far more effective. Most people prefer to study a graph or chart than read a column of figures. By taking a little more time to convert information into graphic format, memos and reports could have much greater impact. For people who like to read figures, they can be included as back-up data. If drawings, photographs or other visual images can be used, the memo becomes a simulcast.

There are many computer programs available that can easily convert data into a variety of graphs and charts. And, if these charts are presented in color, the impact is enhanced. Where graphics are not applicable, use word pictures in the memos. Let's look at two memos about labor turnover:

"The turnover in the Shipping Department has caused a heavy workload for the shipping personnel, resulting in accidents, illness due to fatigue, and more resignations. This has led to orders not being shipped and customer complaints."

Now let's use some word pictures: "I walked into the shipping department this morning. Only six people were working instead of the full staff of ten. They were working under tremendous pressure trying to get the orders out. They had put in ten hours yesterday and I could see the fatigue in their faces and in the way they worked. One man was limping as a result of a minor accident. While I was there, three customers called complaining about not getting their orders when promised."

The first memo told the facts, but the second example allowed the reader of that memo to "see" the situation. By using visuals and word pictures where appropriate, communications— both oral and written—can become clearer and more dramatic.

Watch Grammar and Spelling

We can't always depend on a secretary to correct our grammar, sentence structure, and spelling errors. Today, many managers don't have secretaries or administrative assistants. They write their own correspondence. If you are weak in grammar or spelling, seek out a colleague to be your in-company "editor" for constructive review and suggestions. The "spell-check" feature in a word-processing program is a great help, as it catches most typos and misspellings, but you still must reread the document carefully. It can't catch all of them. Even if you are one of the lucky few who has an assistant, you should still check everything that goes out with your signature on it.

Ending the Letter

Before writing the final paragraph of a letter or memo, review what it is that you wish to accomplish. If the letter is a response to a request for information, did you provide the information requested? If the letter is intended to obtain action from the recipient, have you specified what action you demand?

Keep in mind that the final paragraph is your last chance to make your point. Just as a good salesperson always ends a sales call or sales letter by asking for the order, any good letter writer should ask at the end of the letter that the recipient take the action that the letter has addressed. A thank you is always appropriate, but by itself it is not enough. Instead of saying: "Thank you for your consideration," it is far better to end the letter with: "Thank you for signing and returning the enclosed maintenance agreement, which will assure you of worry-free use of your equipment for the next twelve months."

Letter writing can be improved by planning your letters and following the above suggestions to make each letter present your message in an easy-to-read, yet forceful style.

Dealing with Incoming Correspondence

As noted earlier in this book, communication is a two-way street. We not only send information, but also receive information. We learned how to be effective receivers of oral communication in previous chapters. How we receive written communications is also important.

Reading and responding to letters and memos can take an inordinate amount of time and energy.

Every morning, when Don M. emptied his in-basket, he would read each of the letters, memos, brochures and other items and carefully divide them into four neatly stacked piles. In the first pile, he placed letters and memos that required immediate response; in the second pile, those for which he needed additional information or could delegate to a subordinate; the third for materials on which he didn't have to take any action, just read them and file them away and the fourth was the junk mail that would be immediately discarded.

He scheduled a time for responding to his correspondences at a convenient time each day. At that time, he would reread each letter so he could respond appropriately. At another time during the day, he would reread the memos and letters in the second pile, obtain the required information or delegate it to somebody else. As he had already read the memos and letters in the third pile—those that did not require any action on his part, they were given to his secretary to be filed.

The time involved in reading and rereading each of those pieces of correspondence took an inordinate amount of Don's working day. We can deal with this much more effectively by following certain ideas:

Read a letter or memo once and take immediate action

When you read a letter the first time, make notes on a Post-It slip on the key points that would require a response. Then when you dictate or write your reply, it is not necessary to reread the entire letter. It may only save two or three minutes per letter, but if you respond to 30 letters a day, this saves 90 minutes that can be used on more productive matters.

Use the same approach with letters or memos for which you need additional information. During the first reading, note what information is needed, the source from which it can be obtained, to whom it should be delegated and any pertinent instructions.

Don't answer a memo with another memo

We receive a memo from the manager of another department asking for the current inventory of a list of items, specifying the items by name and stock number. Typically, we respond by writing a memo stating: "As per your request, here is the current inventory of the following items." Then we list each of the items by name and stock number and the quantity on hand.

It's more effective to just write the quantities next to the item name and number on the original memo. This saves considerable time and serves the purpose. In many cases copies are not even needed, but if there is a need, make a photocopy of the original memo with the noted data. A similar approach can be taken in replying to letters from outside the organization. If the inquiry made by the correspondent can be answered by a single sentence, just write the reply on the bottom of the letter received and send it back to the sender.

However, if it is company policy to answer correspondence in a more formal way, take the time to write a letter. Sometimes the image we present to our customers or the public is more important than time saved.

Delegate correspondence

Often the information requested in a letter or memo must be obtained from a subordinate. Instead of asking the subordinate to just obtain the information, give that person the full responsibility of writing the reply. This not only saves time, but gives the subordinate valuable experience in performing the entire task. In the beginning you would probably want to read and sign the final letter, but once the subordinate becomes more and more familiar with the areas covered, it may not be necessary for you to become involved at all.

Dump it

Many letters and memos are sent by other departments just to familiarize us to their contents and does not require any action. It is unlikely that we will ever need to see them again. Don't file them—just dump them! This may be a shocking thing to do in many companies, but there is no real need to save most of these memos. If in a remote situation a discarded file is needed, the person who wrote it and the person who received the original undoubtedly can provide us with a copy. Dumping letters and memos on which no action is required does not only save us time, but it saves considerable time for our clerical staff and keeps those file cabinets from becoming overstuffed.

The Email Explosion

As much attention to writing emails should be given as we do to the composition of standard letters and memos. Remember that email is a form of written communication. Many people think of it as a substitute for a phone call rather than a letter, so they dash off their messages with little or no consideration of style or even content. Unlike the phone call, email can be kept either electronically or as a printout, so it should be carefully planned and composed.

More and more inter and intra-office communications are now done via email. According to a poll conducted by Ernst & Young, 36 percent of respondents use email more than any other communication tool, including the telephone.

Today many managers, particularly the younger generation, use text messaging, sometimes called SMS (Short Message Service) with their mobile communication devices in addition to or instead of emails. The use of text messaging for business purposes has grown significantly during the first decade of the

21st century. Some practical uses of text messaging include the use of SMS for sending alerts (e.g. "The phone system is down"), for confirming delivery or other tasks, and for instant communication between a service provider and a client (e.g. stock broker and investor).

To use text messaging when sending more detailed information, follow the same suggestions presented here for sending effective emails.

Make Email Exciting, Expressive, and Engaging

Here are some tips to help write better emails and text messages:

> Think carefully about what needs to be written. If the message is more than just casual chitchat, plan it as carefully as a formal letter. If we're giving instructions, make sure the reader knows just exactly what action we're requesting. If we're answering an inquiry, make sure we've gathered all the information necessary to respond appropriately to the questions asked.

> Use a meaningful subject line. Our correspondent may receive dozens, even hundreds, of email messages each day. To ensure that our message will be read promptly, use a subject heading that will be meaningful to the addressee. For example, instead of "re your email of 6/25," use the subject line to refer to the information contained in the email (for instance, "Sales figures for June").

> Follow the suggestions given earlier in this chapter on writing letters and memos. Use the TAB approach. Use short, punchy sentences. Be clear, concise and complete. Keep to the point and be brief.

> If files are attached to the email, specify in the text which

files are attached, so the reader can check to make sure they all came through.

> Do not use abbreviations, jargon or short cuts unless you are sure the receiver understands them.

> Read the message carefully and spell-check it before clicking "Send now." If not satisfied, don't send it. Postpone the transmission. Review it, and then rewrite it. Make sure it's okay before it is sent.

If you believe in what you are doing, then let nothing hold you up in your work. Much of the best work in the world has been done against seeming impossibilities. The point is to get the work done.

Dale Carnegie

Email Clutter

Some people are so bogged down with email, they have no time to read it and still get other work done.

In many companies, employees spend an inordinate amount of time on the computer emailing jokes, personal messages, offerings ("I have six cute kittens looking for a home"), and information that is usually unimportant to most recipients. Some companies alleviate such clutter, or SPAM, in their regular email by setting up a special "classified ad" or bulletin board email address for these messages.

Another example of clutter is sending an email to an entire mailing list when only a few people on the list need the information. For example, some people, planning to take a day off, announce their plans to the "Everyone" list, thereby alerting 35 people, what only five or six people really need to know. Perhaps, they do so to puff up their own sense of self-importance, or more likely, they find it easier to send a message to everyone than to figure out who really needs to know and just click on those names. In replying to an email, don't click "reply all" unless *all* the recipients need to know the reply.

Email glut can result in the message being ignored or inadvertently deleted. Ask the receiver to acknowledge receipt of the email. If the matters involved are very important, follow up with a telephone call to ensure that the message was received and understood.

"Who's Reading my Emails?"

How private is our email? Not very. Sure, we may have a password and assume that it ensures privacy, but hackers have shown that they can easily break through even sophisticated systems. Assume anything we email can be intercepted. If confidentiality is required, email is not the medium to use.

Remember that any email sent via the company computer can be read by anybody in the company. Over the past few years there have been cases in which employees were fired because of emails they sent that violated company rules. The courts threw out their employees' claims of invasion of privacy.

More serious are the cases of people who have made comments or jokes in their email that were considered sexually or racially harassing. Printouts of such email have been entered as evidence in suits against employees' companies, even though company officials weren't aware of the messages. This has led to termination of the senders, as well as legal action against both the senders and the companies.

Email Versus Phone Calls or Visits

Many people tend to resort to email rather than make a phone call or a personal visit. Using email is often an easy way out. We don't have to leave our desks, and it's less time consuming than a telephone call. There's no time wasted in small talks or lengthy discussion about a project. All that's sent is the basic message. But often, that small talk and discussion on pros-and-cons is important. In addition, the phone call allows for instant feedback. It not only helps clarify the message, but it ensures that we and the other person both understand the matters involved in the same way.

Don't replace phone and personal contacts with email. Voice-to-voice or face-to-face contact with people with whom we deal with on a regular basis strengthens the personal relationship that is so important in building and maintaining rapport.

Summary of Email Dos and Don'ts

1. Do carefully plan emails and text messages.
2. Do read and re-read the message before clicking "send now."
3. Do inform recipients when the email doesn't require a reply. It will save both parties time and clutter.
4. Do use bullets instead of paragraphs. It makes it easier to read and grasp key points.
5. Do respond promptly to emails received, especially when immediate attention is required. Speed of communication is the chief advantage of this medium.
6. Don't send off-color jokes or stories on company email.

7. Do check whether an important email has been received by asking the respondent to acknowledge it and/or by following-up with a phone call.

8. Don't play games, or send or respond to chain letters or waste time on similar things on company time and on company computers.

9. Don't download pornographic material or items that are derogatory to any racial or ethnic groups on company computers. Remember that your emails can be read by anybody and may offend other people in the organization. It could lead to embarrassment and possibly charges of sexual or racial harassment.

10. Don't spread gossip or rumors through email. It's bad enough when gossip is repeated on the telephone or in person, but email exponentially expands the number of people receiving such information.

11. Don't use email to replace telephone or personal contacts. It is important to maintain voice-to-voice and face-to-face relationships with the people we regularly deal with.

12. Don't send a message to your entire list unless the message applies to everyone on it.

Writing Better Reports

Most managers have to write reports on their activities or on special projects assigned by their bosses. Not only are such reports often critical to the success of a project, but the writer is also judged by what and how he or she has composed the report.

Denise, the purchasing manager of a furniture company, was appalled as she read and reread the report submitted by

Gary, her new assistant. She had asked him to investigate which of several types of forklift trucks might best suit their needs. His report was totally unsatisfactory. Not only was it superficial and lacking in clear analysis, but it also omitted some of the key points necessary to make a logical decision.

The study would have to be repeated and this would seriously delay obtaining the equipment required. This was Gary's first significant assignment and Denise was very disappointed. Perhaps she had made a mistake in promoting him to this job.

Many people short-change themselves by submitting poorly developed, poorly thought-out and even more poorly written reports. Why? Perhaps they believe that if they present the basic data, it is adequate. A good report must be far more than just basic information. It should enable the reader to obtain enough knowledge of the subject covered so that he or she can make whatever decisions are needed. It should also be written in a clear and concise manner so the reader does not have to cut through a jungle of irrelevancies to get to the key areas of concern.

Get All the Facts

Careful planning must go into a report. When Gary was given the assignment to obtain information about the equipment, all he did was request some literature from the three leading manufacturers, abstracted a few facts, and summarized his findings in the report.

To be more effective what should Gary have done?

1. *Define the Problem:* What is the objective of the report? Much time, effort and money is wasted by not knowing

what is really wanted. Gary should have asked Denise to clearly define what she wanted to know. Unless the report writer is aware of how the report will be used, he or she may spend more time on secondary aspects of the situation instead of the really important areas.

2. *Get the Facts:* Once the objectives are clear, try to get all the information needed. Gary was right in obtaining the manufacturers' literature, but he did not go far enough. In addition, he should have discussed the situation with the people in his company who would be using the forklifts to learn what special problems they face and how the new equipment might help them. He should have interviewed sales representatives of local distributors of these trucks and talk to other users of this type of equipment to determine their opinions and perhaps to learn of other equipment that might be more appropriate for his needs.

3. *Analyze the Facts:* Once the information is accumulated, all the facts should be assembled, correlated and analyzed by listing and comparing the advantages and limitations of each type of truck, it would be easier to determine how they fit into the overall objectives desired. If there is a clear-cut advantage of purchasing one product, Gary should recommend it. However, it is better to present more than one alternative so that Denise can make her own decision.

In assembling and analyzing facts, it is helpful to systematically keep information together and in order. One good technique is to open a computer folder for the project and set up files within it for each major category of the study. Supplement this by making up a folder or envelope to place appropriate sales literature, reports of interviews, printouts of cost figures and the like. Pre-sorting the facts this way instead of throwing all the material together and sorting them later can save many hours of sorting and assembling.

Writing the Report

Once all the data is collected, assembled and evaluated, the report can be written. An effective business report must be easy to read. Its language and form should be familiar to the person or persons who would be reading it. An engineer writing a report for a non-technical management group should try to couch the report in as non-technical language as the subject permits.

The report writer has an advantage when it is known what management expects in terms of language, details of content, graphic material and the like. Gary should know whether Denise prefers terse, precise reports or a great deal of detail. Does she want graphs and charts or does she prefer statistical tables giving exact figures?

Know the reader. Gear the report to his or her interest and desires. The report is written for that specific individual, so tailor it to that person's preferences.

Dale Carnegie

Report Format

Although there is no ideal report style, the format suggested in the following paragraphs has proved to be effective:

Briefly State the Problem: "As you requested, here is the

information on the brands and models of forklift trucks for our warehouse."

Summary and Recommendations: Present the summary and recommendations at the beginning of the report. This will enable the executives to get the key information at once. They do not have to wade through realms of detail to find out what is recommended.

Detailed Back-up: This is the meat of the report. It presents all the details that support the summary and recommendations. Charts, graphs and statistical tables may make the report more understandable. Photographs, where appropriate, can be very helpful.

Watch the language: Keep it clear and to the point. There is no need to use an elaborate, pedantic style. Relate the language to the interests and background of the reader. Good usage and choice words are important. A report can be terribly dull if there is no variety in sentence structure, no color in vocabulary, too many clichés or too banal a style of writing.

How long should a report be? Long enough to tell the whole story—and not one word longer. Avoid repetition. A common fault in report writing is stating the same idea over and over again in different words.

Submitting the Report

Before submitting the report, we should proofread it carefully. Even a good report loses credibility when it has spelling errors, poor grammatical structure, and sloppy typing. Figures should be checked carefully. Reread it before forwarding. If possible, have another person who is knowledgeable of the subject, read it. Make whatever changes that are needed.

Attention to the finer points of obtaining and presenting information and ideas in writing reports will result in your being recognized as a person who can successfully accomplish an assigned job. It will enhance your image in the eyes of your bosses as a person who can communicate ideas and present information effectively.

Sum and Substance

> Plan the message before writing one word.
> Be Complete, Concise, and Clear.
> The message will be clearer and more easily accepted if you write just the way you speak.
> Use charts, graphs, photographs, etc. where appropriate, to clarify or expand the message.
> Watch the grammar and spelling. Your writing style reflects your competence.
> Give as much attention to writing emails and text messages as to writing a standard letter.
> In writing a report, get all the facts, analyze the situation and understand what the person(s) to whom the report will be submitted really wants and how he or she wants it to be presented.

Appendix A

....

ABOUT DALE CARNEGIE & ASSOCIATES, INC.

Founded in 1912, Dale Carnegie Training has evolved from one man's belief in the power of self-improvement to a performance-based training company with offices worldwide. It focuses on giving people in business the opportunity to sharpen their skills and improve their performance in order to build positive, steady, and profitable results.

Dale Carnegie's original body of knowledge has been constantly updated, expanded and refined through nearly a century's worth of real-life business experiences. The 160 Dale Carnegie Franchisees around the world use their training and consulting services with companies of all sizes, in all business segments to increase knowledge and performance. The result of this collective, global experience is an expanding reservoir of business acumen that our clients rely on to drive business results.

Headquartered in Hauppauge, New York, Dale Carnegie Training is represented in all 50 of the United States and over 75 countries. More than 2,700 instructors present Dale Carnegie Training programs in more than 25 languages. Dale Carnegie Training is dedicated to serving the business community worldwide. In fact, approximately 7 million people have completed Dale Carnegie Training.

Dale Carnegie Training emphasizes practical principles and processes by designing programs that offer people the knowledge, skills and practices they need to add value to their businesses. Connecting proven solutions with real-world challenges, Dale Carnegie Training is recognized internationally as the leader in bringing out the best in people.

Among the graduates of these programs are CEOs of major corporations, owners and managers of businesses of every size and every commercial and industrial activity, legislative and executive leaders of governments and countless individuals whose lives have been enriched by the experience.

In an ongoing global survey on customer satisfaction, 99 percent of Dale Carnegie Training graduates express satisfaction with the training they receive.

Appendix B

DALE CARNEGIE'S PRINCIPLES

Become a friendlier person

1. Don't criticize, condemn or complain.
2. Give honest, sincere appreciation.
3. Arouse in the other person an eager want.
4. Become genuinely interested in other people.
5. Smile.
6. Remember that a person's name is to that person the sweetest sound in any language.
7. Be a good listener. Encourage others to talk about themselves.
8. Talk in terms of the other person's interests.
9. Make the other person feel important—and do it sincerely.
10. To get the best of an argument—avoid it.
11. Show respect for the other person's opinion. Never tell a person he or she is wrong.
12. If you are wrong, admit it quickly, emphatically.

13. Begin in a friendly way.
14. Get the other person to say "yes" immediately.
15. Let the other person do a great deal of the talking.
16. Let the other person feel the idea is his or hers.
17. Try honestly to see things from the other person's point of view.
18. Be empathetic to the other person's ideas and desires.
19. Appeal to the nobler motives.
20. Dramatize your ideas.
21. Throw down a challenge.
22. Begin with praise and honest appreciation.
23. Call attention to people's mistakes indirectly.
24. Talk about your own mistakes before criticizing the other person.
25. Ask questions instead of giving direct orders.
26. Let the other person save face.
27. Praise the every slightest improvement. Be "hearty in your approbation and lavish in your praise."
28. Give the other person a fine reputation to live up to.
29. Use encouragement. Make the fault seem easy to correct.
30. Make the other person happy about doing the thing you suggest.

Fundamental Principles for Overcoming Worry

1. Live in "day—tight compartments."
2. How to face trouble:
   Ask yourself: "What is the worst that can possibly happen?"
3. Prepare to accept the worst.
4. Try to improve on the worst.
5. Remind yourself of the exorbitant price you can pay for worry in terms of your health.

Basic Techniques in Analyzing Worry

1. Get all the facts.
2. Weigh all the facts—then come to a decision.
3. Once a decision is reached, act!
4. Write out and answer the following questions:
   - What is the problem?
   - What are the causes of the problem?
   - What are the possible solutions?
   - What is the best possible solution?

Break the Worry Habit Before It Breaks You

1. Keep busy.
2. Don't fuss about trifles.
3. Use the law of averages to outlaw your worries.
4. Cooperate with the inevitable.
5. Decide just how much anxiety a thing may be worth and refuse to give it more.
6. Don't worry about the past.

Cultivate a Mental Attitude That Will Bring You Peace and Happiness

1. Fill your mind with thoughts of peace, courage, health and hope.
2. Never try to get even with your enemies.
3. Expect ingratitude.
4. Count your blessings—not your troubles.
5. Do not imitate others.
6. Try to profit from your losses.
7. Create happiness for others.

Life is SHORT, Make it GREAT!

Life is SHORT, Make it GREAT!

DALE CARNEGIE

MANJUL

Manjul Publishing House

First published in India by

Manjul Publishing House

• 7/32, Ansari Road, Daryaganj, New Delhi 110 002 - India
Website: www.manjulindia.com

Registered Office:
• 10, Nishat Colony, Bhopal 462 003 - India

The Success Series:
Life is Short, Make it Great!

This edition first published in India in 2018
Second impression 2020

ISBN 978-93-87383-48-7

Cover Design by Trinankur Banerjee

Printed and bound in India by Thomson Press (India) Limited.

CONTENTS

Preface

Wake up and live! You are not destined to be unhappy, consumed with fear and worry, suffer ill health, and feel rejected and inferior. You have within yourself the power to enrich your life—the power to overcome adversity and attain happiness, harmony, health and prosperity.

Whether you are at the brink of your adult life or well into it, it is never too late to evaluate what you have accomplished, what you wish you had accomplished, and what you can accomplish in the years ahead. Even if your life so far has not been as rewarding as you had hoped, no matter what your age, you can still make your future not just better, but truly great.

In this book you will learn from the principles set forth by Dale Carnegie, expanded by his successors, and applied by the millions of men and women who have followed these principles, how to program your approach to the variety of situations you meet in your life. You will learn how to diagnose your strengths and weaknesses and how to enhance those strengths and overcome the weaknesses.

Among the aspects of life enrichment that you will acquire from this book are:

✓ How to balance the key phases of your life: personal, family, job and career, social activities and others
✓ How to minimize stress and worry
✓ How to develop a health-oriented life style
✓ How to interact most effectively with others
✓ How to become a charismatic person
✓ How to deal with difficult people
✓ How to take control of your emotions

Plus many more ways of mastering and enjoying your life as outlined in the Table of Contents.

To make these principles work for you, you must first understand how you currently deal with life's vicissitudes. To help you identify these traits and pinpoint your special needs, you will find in this book self-administered inventories to measure what you do when faced with the many of these areas. Among these are how to:

✓ Assess the balances and imbalances in your life
✓ Measure how much stress you face and how you deal with it
✓ Analyze how you cope with the performance and progress in your job and career
✓ Test your "charisma quotient"
✓ Evaluate how well you really listen
✓ Measure your "emotional intelligence"
✓ Score your skills in dealing with the conflicts you face.

The advice and suggestions presented here will enrich your life. They are not theoretical. They are not sermons or philosophical discourses. They come from years and years of experience by people just like you who have applied them and have changed their lives from average, mediocre existences to satisfying, rewarding, meaningful, and often exciting lives.

To make this book more than just a book that you read then store in your bookcase, you have to develop a plan to convert what you read into action steps. As you read each chapter, take the self-assessment inventories, identify and then apply them to your life. Concentrate on those concepts that are specific to your needs and write a plan on how you will implement them. This is only the beginning. You must incorporate them into your life style. Review your plan periodically so you will avoid regression to old habits.

Now's the time to start.

Read.

Learn.

Apply.

Join the millions of others who through the teachings of Dale Carnegie as well as his successors have overcome their problems and worries, have transformed their life style and have made their lives truly great.

Arthur R Pell,
Editor

1

A GREAT LIFE STARTS WITH A
PERSONAL VISION

*The dictionary—which, unlike the computer, is an
essential leadership tool—contains multiple definitions of
the word mission. The most appropriate here is "purpose,
reason for being," vision, by contrast, is "a picture or
image of the future we seek to create," and...how we
intend to live as we pursue our mission.*

Peter M Senge

We hear, over and over again, about the power of a compelling personal vision. We hear it without fail from top motivational speakers, and it is hard to find a book on self-development or organizational development that does not testify to the importance of creating one. Yet over and over, in audiences attending Dale Carnegie events, fewer than ten percent will answer yes when asked if they have a concise written statement of their vision for the future.

Why? Let's face it, this is perhaps the most difficult question of all. *What do I want my life to mean? What is my purpose?* These are questions men and women have been grappling with for centuries. Nevertheless, the importance of committing the time, energy, and effort to finding and defining this all-important vision still remains.

So what will we get out of this effort? Why bother? What will this vision help us to accomplish? The answer is that lasting achievement and true excellence are high aspirations with high value attached to them. As such, they are not easy to acquire. In order to obtain these rare commodities, one must be willing to face an enormous amount of frustration, difficulty, and disappointment. In order to confront these adversities, one needs a compelling, magnetic future filled with desirable outcomes.

Vital Vision, Vital Life

An exciting, well-articulated vision can bring vitality and excitement into our daily activities. A vision helps us put meaning into our actions. Often, we feel as though what we are doing at any given moment has very little to do with whom we are and what we are becoming. A vision, used over time, helps us weed out the activities that hold us back.

Ultimately, such a vision captures our strengths, values, deepest beliefs, and the unique quality that makes us who we are. It is very personal. It touches us at the deepest level. It is moving!

This process turns our dreams and mission into reality. There are four major stepping-stones to this:

- Definition of purpose/mission/vision
- Specific, measurable goals along the way
- Habits that reinforce the goals and accomplish them
- Activities that establish and reinforce the habits

With a bit of daily effort, it is possible to slowly but surely move toward our ultimate purpose and weed out needless activities. This will lead us to find more fulfillment and satisfaction. Let's start with the first step.

What Do I Want Out of Life?

Many books and pages have recently been devoted to establishing distinctions between a purpose, a mission, and a vision. In practical terms, all three mingle to form the driving force of our lives. They can and should be combined into one concise statement. For our purposes, we will refer to this as the Personal Mission Statement.

What makes an effective Personal Mission Statement, and why bother going to the trouble of putting it on paper? The process of determining our direction will help us develop effective goals. Singular, clear, and specific goals help us make better decisions. Ultimately, our decisions pave the roads we walk in life. As we understand and commit ourselves to what we want most, it becomes clearer which decisions lead there and which do not. The process of putting this down on paper helps clarify it and forces us to truly answer the all-important question—what do I want out of life?

This is a critical step we must take if striving for higher degrees of excellence in our lives is important to us. A dynamic mission helps us make the changes necessary to accomplish it. It should extract a magnetic pull on us, which helps us eliminate those activities that lead us astray. Motivation flows from an exciting purpose in life. It gives us strength, fortitude, forbearance, and the will to withstand short-term sacrifice and adversity in pursuit of grander goals or achievements and, ultimately, excellence.

How Do We Put Our Vision Together?

There is no absolute formula for finding one's purpose, but research and interviews with successful individuals reveal the following steps:

1. Make a list of what you enjoy doing most.
2. Make a list of all your significant achievements and accomplishments.
3. Imagine a future twenty years from now. What would you like to be doing? Why?
4. What are you doing in this long-term future? Ask, "What would a typical day look like in this ideal future?" Schedule it out.
5. In what ways will you be different from the way you are now?
6. Make a list of at least twenty-five of your beliefs.
7. Make a list of your most important values.
8. Write out clearly what you want your three major accomplishments in life to be.
9. Write your epitaph. How do you want to be remembered?

Thinking about and making these lists will help us see our desired future in clearer detail. We will see patterns begin to emerge.

A Personal Mission Statement is often just that—personal. What other people think about it is not as important as what we think! We must understand that everyone's mission in life is as unique as our own.

A Personal Mission statement should:

- Be magnetic and exciting
- Appeal to the heart and mind
- Capture what is unique about us
- Create a view of a future that is better than today's reality
- Exhibit our deepest values and beliefs

These are five absolute criteria. Read the statement carefully. Is it exciting? Does it help you see where you are going? Will it help to pull you through the inevitable conflict, sacrifice, and make tough choices? Don't be surprised if it takes time to make it just right. You will know it when you get it. It will feel right as you ask your intuitive self for help.

Goals/Objectives and Priorities

Goals flow from our personal mission; they are the signposts on the way to excellence. They are destinations we reach and pass as we move toward our mission; the stairway of significant steps that build the future. They must be carefully thought out. As we clarify our personal mission, it is critical to break it down into various areas that we can focus on.

In setting goals, it is first critical to establish the type of person we need to become in order to navigate the road to our personal mission. What do we need to learn? What needs to change about us? Often, in setting goals, we concentrate too much on what we want, and neglect who we are becoming. Who we are establishes what we get in life. Pay particular attention to setting specific self-improvement goals that will allow you to accomplish your goals more quickly and effortlessly.

Goals need to be long-term and short-term. Start with the long-term goals first. Look at your Personal Mission Statement. Imagine yourself already there. What are the significant accomplishments you have made to get there? Consider all of the goal areas. What needs to be accomplished to get you to this exciting future? Answer these questions carefully, and you will have a solid set of long-term goals.

The Magic of Habits

"We forge the chains we wear in life," Charles Dickens wrote. The question is, are the chains we are forging confining us or creating a tie line to our dynamic future? Aristotle said, "First we make our habits, then our habits make us." It is absolutely critical for anyone serious about achieving excellence to pay very close attention to weeding out bad habits and building positive ones.

Habits are both our worst enemies and our best friends. They are impersonal, take discipline to establish, and yield predictable results. This holds true whether a habit is desirable or undesirable. Believe it or not, bad habits require as much effort to establish as good ones do. There is a price to be paid for bad habits as well as good ones. What we suggest is: make the habits you possess a conscious choice rather than an assumed reality.

Habits, first and foremost, must help us accomplish our goals. If, for instance, we set a major goal to improve our health and fitness, then we will need to build habits that reinforce this goal. Perhaps an eating habit will need to be established to include no less than two pieces of fresh fruit per day or an exercise routine requiring a twenty-minute walk per day. It might be necessary to stop an undesirable habit of eating candy bars. Once solid habits congruent with our goals have been established, we have effectively locked in success. It actually becomes more preferable to perform the new habits, because they become comfortable and reward us with the satisfaction that we are moving toward our exciting future, as opposed to away from it. Excellence occurs when we begin to take pride in these habits, perform them with skill, and enjoy the process!

Only Two Habits At a Time

Take a look at your long-term goals. What habits does the person you are trying to become possess? Make the longest possible list. Next, make a list of all the bad habits you now possess that will have to be dropped, as you become the person capable of actualizing your long-term goals. Ensure that the lists are thorough.

The next step is to prioritize them. Which new habits have to be established first, and which undesirable ones have to be eliminated? This is a critical step. Experience reveals it is best to take habits one or two at a time only. Trying to tackle them all at once, helter-skelter, inevitably leads to such radical change and shock that we are not capable of sustaining the effort.

Determine a way to track your progress daily to remove and establish habits. Perhaps a checklist in your journal will help, or an entry in your daily calendar as a reminder will do the trick.

Breaking it Down, Making it Real

The final step in this process is breaking it all down to the day-to-day level. What are the activities we need to engage in today that will lead us toward these habits, goals, and, ultimately, our purpose? These go into our daily to-do list.

First, look at your monthly objectives. Although this may seem tedious at first, it is critical to look at the monthly objectives every day before establishing the daily activities that need attention on your to-do list. Human beings have a tendency to do what is visible but unfortunately, what is readily visible is not always what is most important. What people tend to give attention to is usually not what will help them attain their long-term future. We need to make the important factors in life visible so we can focus on them.

Once again, avoid the tendency to create your daily to-do list from the papers on your desk or the requests you get from others. Create it from your monthly objectives, first. Fill in the rest of the time with the other tasks that are critical. Establish the habit of reviewing your monthly objectives daily, and you will be marching down the road of excellence.

2

A GREAT LIFE MEANS LIVING UP
TO OUR HIGHEST VALUES

If you are not in the process of becoming the person you want to be, you are automatically engaged in becoming the person you don't want to be.

Dale Carnegie

Character is determined by what we do subconsciously, habitually. It's said that building character is always about *adding qualities*, not subtracting them. Adding good qualities automatically takes care of the negative aspects.

Greg S. Baker, a pastor and author, tells the story of a young man who was always late for his college classes because he kept hitting the snooze button on his alarm clock. To cure himself, before he took a nap he'd set his alarm to go off in five minutes, and would make sure to leap up as soon as it went off. He did that a dozen times. The next morning he did not hit "snooze."

Reverend Baker tells a similar story about himself. He was always reclusive and introverted, which is not good for a pastor. So he trained himself to greet everybody before they could greet him. This wasn't always easy—think about having to out greet the very extroverted. Sometimes he had to shout down a hall in order to be the first to say hello, but he ultimately found himself being friendly to people and more outgoing without ever having to think about it again.

Old habits cannot be thrown out the upstairs window, they have to be coaxed down the stairs one at a time.

Mark Twain

A Code to Live By

Our values determine what is good and what is bad. Our ethics determine how we act regarding what is good and what is bad. Ethics involve a set of standards that tells us how we should behave. No person with strong character lives without a code of ethics.

Ethics is more than doing what we *must* do. It's doing what we *should* do. Because acting honorably sometimes means not doing what we *want* to do, ethics requires self-control. It's a commitment to do what is right, good, and honorable. We must ask ourselves if we are willing to pay the price for making an unethical choice. Are we willing to sacrifice our pride, integrity, reputation, and honor by making such a choice?

Because doing the right thing can cost us more in friendship, money, prestige, or pleasure than we may want to pay, practicing ethics also takes courage. The right thing to do isn't usually the easiest thing to do, but learning to say "no" when we feel like saying "yes" builds character. We learn what is good and ethical from the role models in our lives. Trusting relationships are the foundations of all ethical decisions.

The best defense against ethical lapses is to commit in advance to a set of ethical principles—our own personal code that defines our standards of right and wrong. It helps us resist temptation and becomes the basis for making ethically sound decisions.

There is no limit to an ethical code—it can be as simple as one sentence or contain many paragraphs of personal thought and intent.

> *From right understanding proceeds right thought; from right thought proceeds right speech; from right speech proceeds right action; from right action proceeds right livelihood; from right livelihood proceeds right effort; from right effort proceeds right awareness; from right awareness proceeds right concentration; from right concentration proceeds right wisdom; from right wisdom proceeds right liberation.*

Buddha's Path to Liberation

When it's up to us to set ethical standards, say in a family, we must set boundaries, but reasonable ones. The key words are *reasonable* and *clear*. Nobody likes vague rules or guidelines. Have a clear purpose to place behind the boundaries. Explain and reinforce the *why* behind the *what*. "Because I said so," didn't work when we were children and it doesn't work now either. Communicate boundaries in a positive manner and keep the focus on what to do, rather than what not to do. For example, "Keep confidences" is a positive suggestion, a much better one than "Don't gossip."

Give others an opportunity to contribute to the process of establishing appropriate boundaries. Children are actually entirely capable of coming up with stricter boundaries than parents. Whatever their origin, boundaries should be enforced consistently and fairly. Have the courage to stand behind them.

Ethics Self-Assessment

We all like to think the best of ourselves but sometimes it is necessary to take a hard look at what our day-to-day behavior is like. Are we living up to our own expectations for ourselves or are we making compromises? Understanding our behavior and knowing our limits can help us to change how we act.

Answer the following questions in the way in which you would most likely respond, not in the way in which you think you should respond.

1. You are employed full-time and are offered a project on the side that would provide additional income but would be a conflict of interest with your full-time job. You:
    a. Take the offer because you know no one will find out and no harm will be done.
    b. You really need the money so you take the job and do the best to keep the two jobs separate.
    c. Discuss the opportunity with your boss and mutually determine if this is okay to do.

2. You know your friend has had too much to drink and they are about to drive home. You:
   a. Let them leave since they only live a few miles away.
   b. Ask them if they are okay to drive and trust them when they say yes.
   c. Insist on hailing them a cab or having a designated driver take them home.
3. You have just won a substantial amount of money in a golf tournament. That evening you learn of a golf rule that would have cost you the tournament. No one witnessed the mistake. You:
   a. Keep it to yourself, as it was an honest mistake.
   b. Are too embarrassed to say anything and vowel never to do it again.
   c. Confess and give back the money.
4. You take your 12-year-old daughter to the movies and notice that there is a $4.00 difference between adult and child admission prices. Children are defined as 11 years old and under. You:
   a. Ask for one adult and one child ticket.
   b. Ask your daughter what she thinks you should do and then do whatever she suggests.
   c. Ask for two adult tickets.
5. Your friend is making copies of copyrighted videos to give to his friends. You:
   a. Don't say anything since everyone else is doing it and he's not making any money from it.
   b. Call the authorities, anonymously.
   c. Tell him this is wrong and suggest that he stop.

6. You have an expense account at work and have been turning in personal expenses and charging them as business. A colleague of yours has just been fired for this. You:
   a. Vow to stop.
   b. Don't say anything but figure out how much you have charged improperly and repay your debt before charging any legitimate business expenses again.
   c. Tell your supervisor what you have done, vow to stop, and repay everything.
7. You and your spouse are dining at a fancy restaurant. When the bill arrives, the expensive bottle of wine you had is missing from the bill. You:
   a. Pay the bill and leave a normal tip as you feel the meal and wine was overpriced to begin with.
   b. Pay the bill as it is but leave a larger tip than you planned.
   c. Tell the waiter about the error.

Dale Carnegie points out: If I don't trust you, I will not view you as credible, nor will I respect you. If I don't respect you, I will not see you as credible or trustworthy.

Clear-Eyed, Not Blindsided

Most of our day-to-day decisions don't necessarily involve right or wrong; rather they involve priorities, efficiency, planning, and managing resources. Then there are those decisions that involve right and wrong within our ethical boundaries. These situations are often time-pressured, emotional, and complicated. It becomes all too easy to be blindsided by temptation. We are often forced to make ethical choices reactively.

In the middle of an ethically sensitive situation is the worst time to try to determine our ethical standards. We have to review the information, anticipate consequences, consider others, and manage our emotions, then act. Ethical decisions happen quickly, but the consequences can last a lifetime. That's why careful consideration is important. A code of ethics can help. It determines direction in our lives.

Dale Carnegie suggests these considerations:

1. Think about the impact of the action on all the stakeholders! Stakeholders are those people affected by a decision. Before we do anything, determine who is likely to be helped or harmed, and avoid or reduce the harm. Good questions to ask ourselves are, "What if the roles were reversed? How would I feel if I were in the shoes of one of the stakeholders?"

2. Our Ethical Code is our ground rule for life. Weigh choices and options to determine if they meet your Ethical Code.

3. Our Ethical Code (trust, respect, responsibility, fairness, community service) outranks and overrides unethical motivations (money, power, popularity).

4. The long run outranks the short run. Ask, "what are the possible consequences of my actions in the short term and long term?"

5. Choose the option that will produce the most good. If we are still unsure about what to do, go with the choice that will produce the most good for the most people. To make tough decisions, eliminate choices that have nothing to do with ethical values. Then, pick the most ethical option left.

If you have clear values and standards, making decisions is easy.

Roy Disney

Watch for "Internal Text Messaging"

Just as we have text messages that alert us to new information, important communication, or even warn us of problems, our instincts also send us "internal text messages" in sticky situations. If we pay attention, they will alert us of potential problems or ethical dangers.

We can recognize these internal messages by various code names:

- TGR (The Golden Rule)—Treat others the way you want to be treated.
- POS (Parent Over Shoulder)— Would you want your Mom, Dad, Grandparent, or favorite relative to know what you were saying or doing?
- CIW (Child Is Watching)—Would you want your child to know what you are saying or doing?
- FPN (Front Page News)—How would your choice look on the front page of the local newspaper? Can you clearly and fully justify your thinking and your ethical choice?
- EOD (End of Day)—If, at the end of the day, a major portion of the population did it, would it be a good thing?
- WH5 (Who, What, When, Where, Why)—What is an ethical decision that you are facing or anticipate facing? What will you do?

The highest values are the ones that elevate the world around us. Dale Carnegie was clear on the value of gravitating always toward the kinder, gentler way.

> *I care not what others think of what I do, but I care very much about what I think of what I do. That is character.*
>
> Theodore Roosevelt

3

....

PERSONAL POWER:
FIND IT AND KEEP IT

Even a toad has four ounces of strength.

Chinese Proverb

We often lose perspective because we stop seeing the assets that we are bringing to a stressful situation. Such personal assets as experience, intelligence, diligence, common sense, and interpersonal skills are tremendously important for creating positive outcomes in such situations. If we're concentrating on the negatives, even when it comes to our assets, we might have fallen prey to the common "glass half full or the glass half empty" syndrome. If we check out the people we know who continually see the glass half empty, we see that they don't usually have overflowing glasses, do they?

An Inventory of Assets

The act of adding up our assets is also a valuable occasion for some straight-shooting inventory taking. Most of us are used to looking at the concept of taking inventory as a negative, an anxiety-producing procedure, but when using it as a tool in a stressful situation it's useful to turn it around, starting this inventory with what we own, what we bring to the table, and that almost always includes qualities and attributes that we overlook, to our detriment.

> *The interesting stuff is the information that's known to others but unknown to us. These blindside moments are rare and precious gifts. They hurt, perhaps (the truth often does), but they also instruct.*
>
> Marshall Goldsmith

One idea is to ask a very objective, dispassionate friend to help us list our valuable assets. This must be a person entirely free of people-pleasing tendencies. It should not be a family member or a partner of any kind, but obviously it must be a person who watches us closely, someone we let into our life. We will be amazed at the gifts—our gifts—that they have come up with and are offering back to us. Our next assignment will be to believe and act on this list.

Believe in Ourselves

A major aspect of the mental perspective is a healthy belief in ourselves. One way to begin is to remind ourselves of all the achievements we've enjoyed in our lives and the individual strengths we bring to any situation.

An ancillary reward is that if we believe in ourselves, others will believe in us too. In this way, we overcome self-doubt and move forward steadily.

I read and walked for miles at night along the beach, writing bad blank verse and searching endlessly for someone wonderful who would step out of the darkness and change my life. It never crossed my mind that that person could be me.

Anna Quindlen

All around us is a world trying its best to change us. Too often we cooperate with it instead of honoring our uniqueness, our distinction. It's not only our fingerprints that stand out among the billions of others; it's our particular personas that are ours alone.

Think of those who have changed our cultural, political, and even culinary landscapes over the last few decades. Most of them stood out because they had the courage to believe in their own styles of doing things, often their own eccentricities. It wasn't easy being green, perhaps, but at least they weren't beige.

Self-Belief, Not Self-Defeat

Your chances of success in any undertaking can always be measured by your belief in yourself.

Robert Collier

A healthy belief in ourselves is an essential ingredient in a great life. It sounds obvious, but if belief in oneself were more common, it would be a different world. There would be less people pleasing, which is just another term for lying.

We recognize self-belief when we see it in others. As a matter of fact, it's the quality in people we're most happy to have around us, whether we've arrived there ourselves or not.

People who exhibit a lack of belief in themselves aren't humble or right-sized. On the contrary, they're a burden to others, and tend to be anxious, maybe needy, and often angry. On the other hand, the truly self-realized can be relied upon in social, family, and work situations, and are trusted to be themselves. They are free enough in spirit to have fun, even when they're working; and being secured in themselves, they show up for others.

No Masks to Hide Behind

People who believe in themselves don't put on other masks for us to deal with either. They aren't playing chameleon, leaving us to guess whether they're people pleasing or not at any given moment, or whether what they say and how they act can be trusted.

Self-belief should not be confused with self-aggrandizement, boasting or lack of humility. As a matter of fact, it's been said that we only show a true sense of humility when we acknowledge our worth instead of always making others more important. Secure people aren't always fishing for compliments or fighting for respect, so they're easier to be around.

What earns you their respect in the end is whether you are you. And whether what you are embodies what they want to become.

James M. Kouzes, Leadership Scholar

Another Recommended Exercise

We'll learn a great deal about ourselves by projecting forward to our retirement party. What can a fantasy about an event in the far future reveal about our charisma and personal power now? Picture the party and fill in these blanks:

"I would want members of my family to say…"
"I would want members of my work team or staff to say…"
"I would want my superiors to say…"

Now decide what personal qualities we can enhance during the next six months in order to guarantee that these people, who have observed us closely, have reason to say the most gratifying things about us.

Dale Carnegie suggests six ways to build self-confidence and personal power:

Self-Acceptance

This comes from our ability to accept ourselves as human beings while focusing on our positive qualities, strengths, and unique traits that make us who we are. When we focus on these areas, both confidence and self-esteem are positively influenced. It is all too common for people to focus on their weaknesses instead of their strengths. We must help ourselves, and others by focusing on the positive.

Self-Respect

The key here is to focus on our past successes and achievements and to appreciate ourselves for the good we have done. When we spend time contemplating our successes, our perspective changes and self-respect and self-confidence develops. A valuable exercise is to create a "Success Inventory." This is a list of successes and accomplishments that we have had throughout our lives.

Self-Talk

When we add the two categories above together, we create a self-talk backed up by evidence. Self-talk is simply a way to remind us of those attributes and accomplishments of which we are most proud. This is a tool to take back control of the only thing we have ultimate control over—our thinking.

Take Risks

We can approach new experiences as opportunities to learn and grow. As we take risks, we expand our comfort zone. Doing so opens us up to new possibilities and can increase our sense of self-acceptance and self-respect.

Be Yourself

When we add all of the above, self-confidence and self-esteem increases, and we are more likely to be ourselves. Nothing zaps self-confidence more than envying others and trying to imitate those we envy. If we learn to accept and to be our unique selves, people will be drawn to us, and our feelings of self-worth will increase even more.

Create a Support System

No matter how self-confident we are, there will always be events and individuals that can zap our self-confidence. Think about the people in your life who make you feel good about yourself and who exude positive energy. When down, seek support from these people.

Dale Carnegie suggests writing down for ourselves: a brief pep talk, say about three things we're most proud of, and also writing about a risk we will take in the near future.

4

THE BEAUTY OF A BALANCED LIFE

*Happiness is not a matter of intensity, but of balance
and order and rhythm and harmony.*

Thomas Merton

Most of us aspire to live a balanced life. That is, we
prefer to spend the appropriate amount of time on
each area of our life, simply because we feel better
then. Yet we often feel that our lives have somehow fallen out
of balance. Sometimes it's due to a relatively temporary cause,
such as an accident or injury, a workplace change, or a move.
In other cases, feeling out of balance is more chronic. We feel
that way day after day, month after month, even year after year.
We should look at the important issue of balance and analyze
the current levels of energy and time that we are devoting to

each area. This allows us to set ourselves on a path that will result in a greater sense of balance.

Work, family, health, community, spirituality, our personal life, our social life, and finances are basically the main areas of our lives.

Which Way are We Tipping?

It's wise to periodically assess our current level of satisfaction with the degree of energy and time we are devoting to these various areas, and commit to actions that will bring our lives further into balance.

The time spent on our career too often goes beyond the normal workweek, especially with travel or commuting time, and bringing work home. The health arena comprises exercise, diet, psychological counseling, and other lifestyle choices.

Our communities are often where we can right the balance, giving back with something we enjoy, whether coaching or serving on a board or council. We can also rebalance by focusing on spirituality in our lives. This could include formal activities such as worship or study or a wide range of other pursuits such as yoga, meditation, tai chi, as well as regular retreats.

> *Be aware of wonder. Live a balanced life—learn some and think some and draw and paint and sing and dance and play and work every day.*
>
> Robert Fulghum

Our lives are often like an icy sidewalk. We stand at one end and have to walk to the other, and can slip and fall suddenly at any time. Depending on our degree of urgency, we may step out gingerly or make a break for it, hoping for the best. Either way, moving quickly or slowly, there's a possibility that we will slip and fall if we don't maintain our balance.

As we start to lose our balance, we find ourselves taking much more time than we had planned in one area of our lives, and not nearly enough time in others. This condition may evolve over time, or show itself quite suddenly, via an unexpected turn of events. Here are some common events that can throw off the sense of balance in our lives. They are, so to speak, our external icy spots:

Injury or illness, job change, employee turnover, the stress of major projects, a catastrophic event, such as fire, flood, or the death of a loved one. Others are travel, marriage or divorce, graduations or weddings, and relationship issues.

Then there are the internal icy spots, which are perhaps not as obviously things that can throw our lives out of balance. Dale Carnegie suggests that these are some internal icy spots:

Exhaustion, procrastination, self-pity, poor time management, criticizing, condemning, complaining, and lack of enthusiasm.

A Little Balance Test

Here are some questions. Answer them with a True or False.
- Work consumes more of my time than I would like.
- I rarely do something just for myself any more.
- My days are totally booked with activities.
- I don't use all my work-related vacation and personal days.
- I spend less and less time on outside interests and hobbies.

- I rarely go to movies, concerts, museums and so on.
- I often miss important family events.
- I bring work home with me often.
- I spend little time with friends any more.
- I feel tired most of the time.
- I am more irritable than usual.
- I complain more than usual.
- I do not enjoy my work as much as I used to.
- I do many things out of a sense of obligation to others.
- I have little sense of accomplishment, everyday.

If you answered "True" more than three times, your life may be drifting out of balance.

Dale Carnegie's "Balance Basics"

It's wise to revisit Dale Carnegie's classic list of basic principles that promote balance in our lives. The list is titled "Cultivate a Mental Attitude that Will Bring You Peace and Happiness," from his timeless best seller, *Stop Worrying and Start Living*.

1. Fill your mind with thoughts of peace, courage, health, and hope.
2. Never try to get even with your enemies.
3. Expect ingratitude.
4. Count your blessings, not your troubles.
5. Do not imitate others.
6. Try to profit from your losses.
7. Create happiness for others.

The best and safest thing is to keep a balance in your life.

Euripides (484 BCE - 406 BCE)

Rebalancing Tools

Think about the different elements in your life. They may fall into the categories of career, finances, health, family, social life, yourself, your community and your spiritual life. If any of these are taking over your life or being neglected consider what is in your control so you can reprioritize and find a balance that works for you.

Career: Go home from work on time, ask for cooperation in balancing your life, and negotiate a change with your current employer.

Finances (including savings, investments, reducing debt, purchases and bill-paying): Resist the temptation to buy the latest innovation, technological or otherwise; organize your finances, and set more money aside for future needs.

Health (including diet, exercise, sleep, drinking, smoking): Go to bed and get up at the same time each day, exercise three or four times per week and get proper nutrition.

Families: Often the first priority in our lives, though other areas often crowd out the family because "they'll always be there." Schedule family reading time, have family outings, and plan a traditional family meal each week at the same time.

Social Lives: Think of a group of people you would like to entertain, or an old friend you haven't seen in a while. See if you can arrange some time to get together at a dinner party, a movie or cultural event, lunch or coffee time.

You: Isn't there something you enjoy doing and haven't for a while? It might be golf, crafts or hobbies, listening to jazz or cooking Cajun. Doing something for yourself will bring in your life a much better sense of balance. Reward yourself every day with at least thirty minutes of free time and just slow down.

Community: It bears repeating: Giving back to our communities is a foolproof way to bring balance into our lives. It gives us a stronger sense of giving, gratitude, and selflessness. What is one gift that we could give back to the community? We don't have to commit a tremendous amount of time at first. We can start small and build on our sense of community purpose. It helps us to develop compassion, patience and tolerance for others, gives us meaning for our spare time, if there is any, and perhaps offers a chance to give back in an area where we've received much.

Spirituality: Sometimes we feel highly connected spiritually, and sometimes we lose that feeling. What is one commitment we could make to bring more balance into our spiritual life? Consider worship, meditation, prayer, group encounters, retreats, or study. There are many ways to revitalize your spiritual life. Try to maintain a positive mental attitude, expect the unexpected, and learn to laugh at life's experiences.

Next to love, balance is the most important thing.

John Wooden

Be Realistic

Balance isn't meant to command equal slices of the pie for each area of our lives. Balance also appears in our lives as realism, common sense. For instance, if we've just spent a term or more on a community board, that may be enough for community activism. If we've been slacking when it comes to work, we may need to imitate a workaholic till we catch up. And our sense of balance will change over time, too. Any number of internal and external factors can influence how satisfied we are at any given moment with the energy and time we are devoting to various aspects of our lives.

It's impossible to achieve perfect balance in each of these areas all of the time. To attempt that would be... well, unbalanced.

5

A GREAT LIFE MINIMIZES
STRESS AND WORRY

Worry is interest paid on trouble before it falls due.

William Inge

S tress is an all-too-familiar word these days. In some settings, it's almost worn as a badge of honor. "I've got so much on my plate, I'm all stressed out," we hear from those perhaps expecting others to be impressed at the amount of responsibility they're entrusted with. We sometimes think complaining about stress makes us sound important, while more than likely we sound like someone *wanting* to sound important. Stress isn't really very productive, after all. Why do athletes get massages before performing? So they'll remain all tense and stressed? No. Research has actually shown that muscles are *stronger* on the playing field when they are relaxed, not tense.

A Stress Checklist

There are ways to measure stress. Here's one. We'll rate ourselves from one to five when considering these statements:

1. I am usually even-tempered when it comes to stressful, worrisome situations.
2. Others view me as being able to keep stress in perspective.
3. I don't dwell on stressful situations.
4. I take time-out when I'm under stress.
5. I don't overreact to bad news.
6. I treat people the same whether I'm stressed or not.
7. I get involved in physical activities to let go of stress.
8. I have realistic expectations of others and myself.
9. I ask for help when I need it.
10. I get eight hours of sleep most nights.
11. I keep my sense of humor in stressful situations.
12. I have friends and colleagues whom I trust and can be honest with.
13. I periodically remind myself to slow down.
14. I practice relaxation techniques, such as deep breathing, yoga, or meditation.
15. I focus on my strengths, not my weaknesses.

This list contains many clues, not only about identifying stress and practicing stress free behaviors, but about some practices that dramatically—and often quickly—free us from this destructive twenty-first century disease.

Choose a Different Viewpoint

A situation is stressful when it automatically begins to occupy more and more of our thoughts. We become more irritable, less cooperative, and more distant from others under stress. The major question in determining whether or not we can easily de-stress is to answer the question: how much control do we *really* have over the issue? Very often we will wisely decide we have no power over it at all, and only then can let it go.

We've all had the experience of feeling very stressed out and worried about a situation on one day, then feeling calmer and more positive a day or two later. Assuming that the situation itself remains worrisome, the only thing that has changed is *our perspective*. The factors determining our stress perspective lie both within and without our control.

What the Unflappable Do

A Mayo Clinic study on stress found that resilient people:
- Use humor
- Use their experience as a means to learn to cope
- Maintain an optimistic/hopeful outlook
- Understand and accept change
- Establish goals and work toward them
- Engage in self-examination
- Maintain their sense of self-esteem

Dale Carnegie recommends keeping our energy and spirits high so as to prevent fatigue and the worry that often comes with it. He suggests resting before we are tired, learning to relax, even as we are working, putting enthusiasm into our work, and not worrying about insomnia. Good working habits that can prevent worry and stress are:
- Clearing the desk of all papers except those relating to the immediate problems at hand

- Doing things in the order of their importance
- Solving a problem as soon as we face it, if the facts are at hand that are necessary to make a decision
- Learning to organize, deputize, and supervise

Fatigue makes cowards of us all.

Vince Lombardi

Questioning Stress

Let's keep stress in perspective by evaluating how many of the currently stressful circumstances in life are actually out of our control and therefore not worth worrying about. Is it worthwhile to destroy our peace by trying to put an end to a civil war in Asia that even the United Nations cannot control? Or single-handedly trying to cut the national debt? Or, for that matter, trying to change a teenager hell-bent on acting out?

Dwelling on what we can't control anyway locks us into a perspective of hopelessness. It's far more productive to focus on the situations we can influence, at least to some degree. If we can't change a family member's personality or lifestyle, we can at least change our reactions.

Sources of Work Stress

There are so many kinds of work stress coming at us every day that most of us find it challenging just to keep up and cope appropriately. We try to stay on top of the workloads, responsibilities, and the expectations that others have of us. We manage this through our level of organization, discipline, and flexibility. We try to maintain good work habits and consistent performance but, at the same time, we feel the pressure of work-related stress, including:

- Deadlines
- Crises
- Demands from family, children, customers, vendors, or employees
- Reorganization/relocation
- Promotions, moving a household, or reassignments

We first make our habits, and then our habits make us.

John Dryden

Stress Reduction Through New Work Habits

"Work" doesn't always get done in an office. We work all day long at home, in our gardens, our garages, our childcare, our kitchens. And in all of these areas we often employ outmoded habits.

We can change them, and by doing so we can eliminate a great deal of stress, enhancing our chances for a great life. Anyone can fall into unproductive habits over a period of time. We drift into routines that are inefficient, become less and less organized, or experience deterioration in our work attitudes. Often, we slip into unproductive work habits without realizing it. Over time, we become comfortable with these work habits, and it turns out to be difficult to break the patterns we have established.

By identifying our inefficiencies and committing to new work habits, we can become more productive and less stressed at work. We have a greater sense of achievement as we gain more control over our management of time, our organizational skills, and our attitudes.

Work Habits Self-Assessment

Rate yourself on a 1–5 scale. One means that it is not very descriptive of you; five means that it is very descriptive of you.

1. I manage my time well. 1 2 3 4 5
2. I have a systematic, organized approach to completing work. 1 2 3 4 5
3. I work ahead of deadlines, not behind them. 1 2 3 4 5
4. I take a team-oriented approach to managing my work. 1 2 3 4 5
5. I have a neat, organized work area. 1 2 3 4 5
6. I work from a daily, weekly, and/or monthly plan. 1 2 3 4 5
7. I involve others in helping me manage my workload. 1 2 3 4 5
8. I maintain accurate and accessible work records. 1 2 3 4 5
9. I can easily locate files and work materials. 1 2 3 4 5
10. I organize my work area and materials before leaving work. 1 2 3 4 5
11. I keep my focus on work, even in distracting situations. 1 2 3 4 5
12. I approach problem-solving systematically. 1 2 3 4 5

13. I periodically remind myself to   1 2 3 4 5
    slow down.
14. I stay "in the moment" and don't   1 2 3 4 5
    worry about the past or future.
15. I don't let criticism bother me.   1 2 3 4 5

Inefficient Work Habits That Add to Our Stress

As challenging as it is to handle ongoing stressful situations, we often add to workplace tension through our own poor work habits. Sometimes we develop these habits over time, unintentionally. We may not even be aware of how our work habits have affected our performance and our attitude. Some bad habits that add to our workplace stress include:

- Disorganization
- Chronic lateness
- Procrastination
- Lack of follow-through
- Harboring resentments
- Resistance to change

We have three areas of opportunity when it comes to changing our work habits and reducing our stress. The first area of opportunity is our use of time. The second is our ability to organize our work. The third opportunity is in our attitude control. Examining our current work habits in each area gives us a basis for improving our skill in each category and replacing old habits with new, more productive habits.

The second half of a man's life is made up of nothing but the habits he has acquired during the first half.

Fyodor Dostoyevsky

Time Management to Reduce Stress

One critical habit to address in reducing workplace stress involves our productive, or non-productive, use of time. How do these positive work habits compare to our own?

Showing up early

Showing up early has no downside. It gives us extra time to gather our thoughts and get prepared, and consequently we are sure to make a better impression in every situation. All the way around, this work habit reduces stress.

Maintaining a daily planner

Whether it's software or plain paper, we need a daily planner to make sure to be on top of all the details of our days. Time spent in planning reduces time spent in execution, and thorough daily planning is a key stress-reduction tool.

Being present

How many times do we meet or converse with people, and our minds are really on something completely separate from the subject under discussion. We are physically present, but mentally in a totally different place. Believe it or not, this mindlessness, lack of presence, can add to our stress.

Avoiding procrastination

Everyone is motivated in different ways. We should seek to find what inspires and energizes us to tackle work issues, instead of putting them off. Commit to a regular schedule of work output and project completion.

Setting priorities

No one likes reaching the end of the day or week feeling as though we didn't accomplish our most critical tasks. It is less stressful to set and adhere to priorities than it is to feel we are getting further and further behind in our workload.

Protecting our private time

Some anxiety-provoking work habits, such as bringing work home or staying late at work, are more exhausting than we may realize. Sometimes violating our private time with work can't be avoided, but if it becomes a habit, we can start to feel we don't have a life outside of work.

Reducing Stress with Organization

A second critical area for reducing work stress is our ability to stay organized. Which of these productive work habits do we utilize in organizing our work?

Simplifying our approach

What could we start doing, stop doing, or do differently in order to simplify our approach to what needs to get done? Many of us make our commitments more complicated than they need to be, and would benefit from a simpler approach.

Dropping unnecessary activities

Make a list of each activities carried out every day for a week, from driving the car to sitting in meetings. Which of these activities are not necessary and could be dropped? Try dropping those activities for a week or a month, and track changes in productivity results.

Writing things down

Do you have one notebook or planner where you write down ideas as they strike you, commitments as you make them, or other important notes? We feel less stressed when we know that we have captured important information and can refer to them whenever required.

Creating and following agendas

One common area of workplace disorganization is in the conducting of meetings, whether one-on-one or with a larger group. Agendas, especially when sent ahead of time, make meetings more organized and productive, and help make participants more comfortable and confident.

Finishing one task before starting another

A major source of disorganization comes from excessive multi-tasking. If we stay focused on a particular task until its completion, we will get it done in far less time, and we will stay far more organized. More on multi-tasking later.

Attitude Control to Reduce Stress

Our third opportunity to create new stress less habits concern attitude control. When we get our attitudes toward the tasks at hand under control, every other aspect of our productivity improves. How many of these are among your work habits?

Connecting with others and using their names

It's easy to become so self-focused that we begin to tune others out. This can add to a feeling of isolation and stress.

It is better to reach out and greet others, learn their names, and maybe even win friends in the process.

Letting things go

There comes a time in the course of our day when we realize it would be better to relax and accept the idea that everything might not turn out perfectly every time. When we are experiencing too much stress in a situation, we might ask ourselves, "Is this time where I should just let go?"

Taking charge

Our attitudes improve when we take charge of situations to guarantee that something gets done. We can, at the very least, take charge of our own workload, relationships, and attitude. When we hesitate or procrastinate about taking charge, we actually undermine our energy and make our work more stressful than it has to be.

Staying calm

Whatever it takes—counting to ten, taking deep breaths, going for a walk, or a short meditation, we are advised to concentrate on staying calm, to avoid overreacting, lashing out, or acting impulsively, which only adds to our stress level.

Appreciating the uniqueness in others

As much as we sometimes feel we would, it's not true that we would prefer everyone to be like us. It would be boring. Differences in backgrounds, perspectives, and work styles make life more interesting and vibrant, not less. Work on appreciating the unique strengths in others.

6

BURNOUT HAS NO PLACE IN
A GREAT LIFE

Burnout occurs everywhere, it's not confined to the workplace, and there's a difference between a bad day or two and actual burnout.

Most of us have days when we feel overloaded, bored, or unappreciated; when juggling all our responsibilities isn't noticed, let alone rewarded; and when it takes a superhuman determination to drag ourselves into work.

But workplace burnout isn't the same as simply being extremely stressed at work. Burnout may be the result of unrelenting stress, but it isn't the same as having too much stress. When we're stressed, we care too much, but when we're burned out, we don't see any hope of improvement. We don't want to get to that point.

My candle burns at both ends. It will not last the night.

Edna St Vincent Millay

Stress Versus Burnout

Stress, by and large, involves *too much*: too many pressures that demand too much of us physically and psychologically. When we are stressed, we can still imagine, that if we can just get everything under control, we'll feel better. Burnout, on the other hand, is about *not enough*. Being burned out means feeling empty, devoid of motivation, and beyond caring. People experiencing burnout often don't see any hope of positive change in their situations. If excessive stress is like drowning in responsibilities, burnout is being all dried up.

Stress	Burnout
Characterized by over-engagement	Characterized by disengagement
Emotions are over-reactive	Emotions are blunted
Produces urgency and hyperactivity	Produces helplessness and hopelessness
Loss of energy	Loss of motivation, ideals, and hope
Can lead to anxiety disorders	Can lead to detachment and depression
Primary damage is physical	Primary damage is emotional
May kill us prematurely	May make life seem not worth living

Burnout Prevention Measures

The most effective way to head off job burnout is to quit doing what we're doing and do something else, whether that means changing duties at work or even changing careers. For most of us, this is an extreme measure and not an option that we can or even would choose. It makes more sense to become aware of our level of stress and overload moving toward burnout so that we can take some preventive measures.

Remember, these caveats may be even more relevant to those who work for themselves and feel that pushing yourself is really all for the best!

Some of these burnout prevention measures are:

Clarify job expectations. Update a description of your job duties and responsibilities. During the discussion preceding that, you may be able to point out that some of the things you're expected to do are not part of your job description, gaining a little leverage by showing that you've been working over and above the parameters of your job.

Request a change. If it's job burnout you're experiencing, and your workplace is large enough, you might be able to move to a different location, office, or department. Even a change of scenery can help gain a new perspective.

Ask for different responsibilities. If you've been doing the exact same work for a long time, you can either take it upon yourself or ask the powers-that-be to try something new: a different sales territory, a different project, a different role.

Take time off. Go on vacation, use up your sick days, and ask for a temporary leave-of-absence. Do something to remove yourself from the situation. Set aside "Me Time" outside of work. While being a dedicated employee is admirable, being an indentured servant to your business will wear you down over time. When work is your life, your life is work, and burnout becomes inevitable. Know when to walk away from work. Schedule regular time away from work *each week*, preferably dedicated to a personal passion or hobby that clears your mind of any fog. Fishing, knitting, gym workouts, reading, painting or doing yard work are just a few of the ways people center themselves outside of work. You can use the time away to recharge your batteries and gain perspective.

Take regular breaks. Mental health is becoming increasingly important in the workplace, and more and more employers are recognizing the need for their employees to take frequent breaks to keep their minds sharp. If you're an employer, by allowing your employees a fifteen-minute break in the morning, a 30- to 60-minute lunch break (it's recommended that the break is taken outside of the office) and an additional fifteen-minute break before the end of the day, you will find that your or your employees' batteries are constantly at a full charge.

Create (or suggest) a unique break room. Conventional break rooms tend to be pretty plain—coffee machine, water cooler, and the usual no-frills, pretty depressing stuff. Some companies have started to stray from this—transforming break rooms into brief escapes from work, going so far as to set up televisions, game tables, and video game systems in their break rooms. One hospital in Rochester New York has a Nintendo Wii in its break room. Creating an environment for employees to briefly escape to for a reasonable amount of time will go a long way to prevent job burnout. If you're an employee, try suggesting such an inviting break room for your company.

Balance life and work. Work cannot be the all-encompassing focus of our life—especially if you hope to maintain a happy private life. Whether you live independently, with a significant other, or a whole family—kids and all—you need to manage your time between work and home effectively. When it's time to punch out, *punch out*. Go home to your family. Go to the movies with your partner or friends. Give your personal life just as much time and attention as you do to your work life. Otherwise, you will start to see problems and frustrations develop at home that will affect your work life and cause you to feel burned out.

Maintain a healthy lifestyle. Proper diet, exercise, enough sleep and choosing water over carbonated cans full of nothing but chemicals can drastically affect your behavior, even at work. All it takes is setting aside from thirty or forty minutes just three days a week to exercise, and making a greater effort to manage your diet. Doing so will benefit you directly in innumerable ways, and a positive lifestyle will lead to a more positive work experience.

Finding "Margins"

In his landmark book on stress, *Margin: Restoring Emotional, Physical, Financial, and Time Reserves to Overloaded Lives,* Dr. Richard Swenson wrote, "Margin is the space between our load and our limits." He suggests that we look for ways to add margins to our lives to add reserve. His theory is that we can't continue to add stress in our lives without making room for it by taking something out.

Just as the white space and the margins in a book make the book easier to read, the white space and the margins in our lives make us more flexible and open during change and stress. Other moves suggested by Dale Carnegie are:

Tap the Power of "Block Days"

Scheduling "block days" is an effective way to create space to think and renew. Block days can be used to create focus on workdays, or to take time off from work. People approaching overload often feel they can't take block days for a variety of reasons.

Create Space By Being Intentional

When we find ourselves moving up the curve toward overload, it is time to get aggressive with our strategy to avoid it. The following ideas are a few of many that have worked for professionals to help avoid overload and burnout.

Learn to say "No." With the myriad choices we make in any given time, we can take on too many things that aren't meaningful to us. It is important to establish a perimeter around the personal spaces of our lives. Be wary of overworking. Many people find it difficult to say "no" in the workplace. This typically leads to the accumulation of more and more workload each time they agree to lend a hand here or there, or take on a side project or something similar. Being a team player is important in the business world, and helping your colleagues from time to time is a surefire way to further your career. But if you aren't careful, other employees will take advantage of your generous, helping nature and all you'll get in return is stress from being overworked.

Simplify your life in general. It's been said that we only use twenty percent of what we own, but we must maintain 100% of it.

Cultivate contentment. Dale Carnegie said, "Let's fill our minds with thoughts of peace, courage, health, and hope, for our life is what our thoughts make it."

Slow the pace, eliminate hurry. Fast is okay; faster is okay; too fast is not okay. When we stretch our timeframe to the limit, we speed, we sacrifice quality in our work, we stress ourselves and others around us.

Get interested in people. Nourish relationships and cultivate a network of caring friends. Studies have shown that having good friends is an important factor in living a long and healthy life.

7

....

A GREAT LIFE BEGINS WITH
A HEALTHY BODY

Let's Check Our Speed Limit and... Slow Down

This may be the most difficult element of all in our hectic, fast-paced lives. Slowing down gives us a safer life and—despite what society tells us—a more productive one. By slowing down we are less likely to make mistakes, and typically have more thorough and successful results. Most importantly, slowing down restores that healthy perspective we mentioned earlier, the key to preventing stress in the first place.

Stress management experts consider slowing down to be a most crucial stress-reliever, and offer some tips. Slowing down, in this day and age, doesn't come naturally. It is a learned skill. But the more stress comes our way, the more we must learn how to slow down.

Many of us don't think it's okay to slow down. We believe deep down that by slowing down we are somehow being unproductive. This idea creates much anxiety in itself. So we continue to push ourselves harder and harder thinking that if we just keep moving and sacrificing everything else, we are somehow doing the right thing. However, many end up sacrificing their physical health and even their mental health by working this way instead of pacing, pacing, pacing.

There is not enough time. So we must go slowly.

Ancient Chinese saying

Learning to slow down during stress requires taking time to make a few changes in our lives.

First, we must give ourselves permission to slow down. What we tell ourselves matters a great deal. A hurried attitude inside can create more stress and anxiety than it's worth. Allow your attitude to reflect acceptance and give yourself permission to slow down whenever possible.

We must say "No" to things not on our priority list. Not only is it okay to say no to people, we do not have to explain. No is a complete sentence. Explaining only leads to the need and expectation of more explaining.

By slowing down we're taking time to smell the roses. But in order to do so, we have to remember to breathe! Take time to be grateful for the roses and all the things and people waiting to be noticed each day.

Instead of climbing a mountain full speed without stopping and carrying extra baggage, we are now climbing the mountain with the intention of stopping, resting, and enjoying what we see, maybe even taking a short nap. We reach the summit because we learned to balance the stress in our lives and make ourselves the priority.

One of the best ways to get perspective on stress and worry is to get healthy and get moving! Yet, the more stressed we are, the more likely we are to ignore our body's basic needs.

Taking Breaks is Most Productive

Many of us get going on work or projects and keep going until the job is finished, without taking a break. But a break is what allows the mind to cool off, relax, and go somewhere else for a while. Stand up, walk around, and let the body loosen up as well. Many of us spend more time sitting than sleeping. The human body simply isn't built to sit all day at a desk or for vegging out on the couch. To avoid the health risks, we need not just thirty minutes of daily exercise, but to take every opportunity to *get up* during the day. Some people place important items—phones, copiers, printers, and coffee pots—a distance away from their desks. One recommendation is to use a small cup for water, making that long walk necessary in order to fill it up.

Get up, stretch, and look out a window to give your eyes a healthy long view.

Take Deep Breaths, Slow Your Breathing

Remember as a child being told to take deep breaths and count to ten if you were upset? Our grandmothers knew what they were talking about. It's very important to monitor the way we are breathing. Under stress, people often hold their breath or use shallow, rapid breaths. Shallow breathing is the sign of stressed body.

Deep breathing is a biofeedback technique that communicates to our physical selves that we are going to be okay. Start by breathing in and out to a slow count of three, then four, and then five. You will feel the stress unwind and calmness set in.

Dy'Ann Suares, who guides clients to higher levels of awareness, suggests: "Our bodies shift in and out of contracted states, moment to moment. Anyone desiring to reduce stress, improve mental clarity, decrease pain of any kind, including emotional and psychological pain, can begin a simple practice of taking three deep breaths before retiring and waking in the morning. This practice of conscious attention to the breath creates new momentum and can be very effective over time. Oxygenation of the body is also essential. Breathing out toxins helps the body renew itself naturally."

Suares also recommends taking a deep breath every time we want to integrate new levels of understanding. If we aren't in the habit of practicing this, we would be astonished at how regular, slow, deep and even breathing helps to center, ground, and hold us.

As we breathe deeply into our lungs, we are feeding valuable oxygen into our depleted system. The instant sense of relief can be quite remarkable.

If we are standing and breathing in deeply, we bring strength to our posture, which gives an added sense of positivity as we open our chest and therefore our heart to those around us.

Breathing Exercise for Five Minutes of Relaxation

Inhale

Inhale slowly and deeply, filling your chest with air, counting four seconds to yourself 'One *and* two *and* three *and* four'. The count is to give you a nice and easy, even pace. Try to breathe as fully as you can without discomfort. Imagine your chest slowly filling with air, from your diaphragm to your collar.

Hold breath

When you have inhaled fully, hold your breath for another four seconds, again counting to yourself 'One and two and three and four'. This should be just a comfortable pause. Do not do it until you are blue in the face.

Exhale

Exhale – but do not blow. Just let the air out through your mouth slowly, saying to yourself 'Easy... easy... easy... easy.' Let out as much air as you can, down to the lower part of the lungs. Feel yourself relaxing as you do. Feel your shoulders, chest and diaphragm loosen up. As you exhale, think of the tension flowing out of your body.

Sleep-Deprived Are Not Really Sober

Our average sleep time is 6.9 hours on weeknights, which means that, whether we like it or not, we are not thinking as clearly as we could be. A study by David Dinges, the head of the Sleep and Chronobiology Laboratory at the University of Pennsylvania hospital says that the magic number is eight hours of sleep per night. Test subjects who logged a solid eight hours of sleep per night had very few, if any, attention lapses and no cognitive declines over the course of Dinges' two-week study, but subjects who got just six hours of slumber "were as impaired as those who, in another study, had been sleep-deprived for twenty-four hours straight—the cognitive equivalent of being legally drunk," the *New York Times* reported.

There is a small portion of the population—Dinges estimates it at around only five percent or even less—who, for what researchers think may be genetic reasons, can maintain their performance with five or fewer hours of sleep, just as there is also a small percentage who require nine or ten hours.

Eat Healthy Meals

Food is the fuel that drives our health, balance, energy, and stamina. There's evidence that too much pressure is not just a mood killer. People who are under constant stress are more vulnerable to everything from cold to high blood pressure and heart disease. Although there are many ways to cope, one strategy is to eat stress-fighting foods. "Everyone knows food is fuel for the body, and when we're stressed, says Victoria Maizes, M.D., Executive Director of the Program in Integrative Medicine at the University of Arizona, "we need to focus on having better fuel."

In order to be at our physical and mental best in stressful situations, we need to eat healthy, replenishing meals. At each meal, ask, "What could I do to make this a more healthy meal?"

Food, Our Fuel

"A long-term diet low in nutrients can deplete your reserves of minerals and vitamins," says Narmin Virani, R.D., and L.D.N., a clinical dietician at the Benson-Henry Institute for Mind Body Medicine at Massachusetts General Hospital in Boston. "These nutrients go a long way in helping you pull through stressful situations. And without them, the going simply gets tougher." Food cannot fix the stress problem all by itself, but experts agree that good nutrition is a key to the problem. Foods fight stress in different ways. Comfort food, such as oatmeal, boosts our levels of serotonin, the brain chemical with the calming effect. Other foods reduce cortisol and adrenaline, the stress hormones that do damage over time.

We can begin with cutting back on the worst offenders in our diets, thereby breaking the cycle. There are "power food" to replace the offenders with, and these are nothing exotic, hard to find or unpleasant. Some may surprise us with their power, since we may eat them for their pure pleasure. Here are just a few de-stressors:

Complex Carbs

Complex carbohydrates are the feel-good chemicals, and are digested more slowly. They're in whole-grain breakfast cereals, some breads and pastas, and that old-fashioned bowl of warm oatmeal. They stabilize blood sugar levels.

Simple Carbs

We are usually warned against simple carbs, which include sodas and sweets, though it's agreed that they can relieve irritability for a short time. Since they are digested quickly, simple sugars lead to serotonin spikes.

Black Tea and Other Surprises

Research suggests that drinking a cup of black tea can help us recover from stressful events more quickly. One study compared people who drank four cups of tea daily for six weeks with people who drank a tea-like placebo. The real tea drinkers reported feeling calmer and had lower levels of cortisol after stressful situations. Coffee, on the other hand, can boost levels of cortisol.

Other Anti-Stress Secret Weapons

Pistachios can soften the impact stress hormones have on the body. Adrenaline raises blood pressure and gets your heart racing when you're under stress. Eating a handful of pistachios every day can lower blood pressure, so it won't spike as high when that adrenaline rush comes.

Oranges make the list for their wealth of vitamin C. Studies suggest this vitamin can reduce levels of stress hormones while strengthening the immune system. If you have a particularly stressful event coming up, you may want to consider supplements. In one study, blood pressure and cortisol levels returned to normal more quickly when people took 3,000 milligrams of vitamin C before a stressful task.

The magnesium in spinach helps regulate cortisol levels and tends to get depleted when we're under pressure. Too little magnesium may trigger headaches and fatigue, compounding the effects of stress. One cup of spinach goes a long way toward replenishing magnesium stores. Not a spinach eater? Try some cooked soybeans, or a filet of salmon, also high in magnesium.

To keep cortisol and adrenaline in check, make friends with fatty fish. Omega-3 fatty acids, found in fish like salmon and tuna, can prevent surges in stress hormones and protect against heart disease. For a steady supply, aim to eat three ounces of fatty fish at least twice a week.

One of the best ways to reduce high blood pressure is to get enough potassium—and half an avocado has more potassium than a medium-sized banana. In addition, guacamole offers a nutritious alternative when stress has you craving a high-fat treat.

Almonds are chock full of helpful vitamins. There's vitamin E to bolster the immune system, plus a range of B vitamins, which may make the body more resilient during bouts of stress. To get the benefits, snack on a quarter of a cup every day.

Crunchy raw vegetables can fight the effects of stress in a purely mechanical way. Munching celery or carrot sticks helps release a clenched jaw, and that can ward off tension headaches.

Carbs at bedtime can speed the release of serotonin and promote better sleep. Heavy meals before bed can trigger heartburn, so stick to something light like toast and jam.

Meditate: Go Straight to Your Center

The Mayo Clinic recommends meditation for stress relief, stating, "If stress has you anxious, tense and worried, consider trying meditation. Spending even a few minutes in meditation can restore your calm and inner peace. Anyone can practice meditation. It's simple and inexpensive, and it doesn't require any special equipment. And you can practice meditation wherever you are—whether you're out for a walk, riding the bus, waiting at the doctor's office or even in the middle of a difficult business meeting."

Meditation can become a lifelong method for maintaining perspective. Those who practice meditation regularly assert that it is a calming, centering way to regain their perspective. We are fortunate that meditation has entered the mainstream, and is no longer considered unproductive, self-concerned navel-gazing. Life is fluid and fast-paced these days, to get the most from it, we need to stay connected to our center, through solitude and silence. When we are alone in meditation, we can delineate between where we end and others begin.

When we say we'll "meditate" on something, we mean we'll focus on it until we see its essence, its meaning for us. Milton Erickson said that meditation counteracts the elements of modern existence that give us such stress. Meditation shows us how the events of our lives are as big or small as we let them be. It lets us focus on the moments of life as they actually exist, freeing us momentarily from neurosis, obsession, anxiety. Chogyam Trungpa, the renowned Tibetan monk, said this: "Meditation is simply the creation of a space in which we are able to expose and undo our neurotic games, or self-deceptions, our hidden fears and hopes. Becoming more clearly aware of emotions and life situations, the space in which they occur might open us to more panoramic awareness. A compassionate attitude, a warmth, develops at this point. It's an attitude of fundamental acceptance of oneself while still retaining critical intelligence."

A successful way of meditation is to simply count the breaths, in and out. Another is to silently say, "thinking" every time an intrusive thought pops up. There are as many different ways to meditate, as there are people. Meditation is the ultimate de-stressor.

Take Part in Yoga, Tai Chi, or Martial Arts

Sometimes referred to as "moving meditation," these forms of exercise have been used for centuries as ways to stay healthy, focused, and flexible. They are great methods for releasing physical energy in a positive, healthy way.

Practice Yoga

Yoga can be an effective method to reduce stress and anxiety.

Yoga's series of postures—some with names from nature—and controlled breathing exercises are a popular means of stress management and relaxation. Not that long ago yoga seemed foreign and exotic, as did meditation. Today, yoga classes teaches the art of breathing, and meditation are offered nearly everywhere—from trendy health clubs in big cities to community education classes in small towns to hospitals and clinics.

Yoga is considered a mind-body type of complementary and alternative medicine practice. Yoga brings together physical and mental disciplines to achieve peacefulness of body and mind, helping us relax and manage stress and anxiety. Traditional yoga philosophy requires that students adhere to this mission through behavior, diet and meditation. But if we're just looking for better stress management—whether because of life's daily hassles or a health problem—and not an entire lifestyle change or way of life, yoga can still help.

With its quiet, precise movements, yoga draws our focus away from our busy, chaotic day and toward calm, as we move our bodies through poses that require balance and concentration.

Yoga has many styles, forms and intensities. Hatha yoga, in particular, may be a good choice for stress management. Hatha is one of the most common styles of yoga, and some beginners find it easier to practice because of its slower pace and easier movements. But most people can benefit from any style of yoga—it's all about personal preferences.

Yoga poses, also called postures or asanas, are a series of movements designed to increase strength and flexibility. Poses range from lying on the floor while completely relaxed to difficult postures that may have us stretching our physical limits. Controlling our breathing is another important part of yoga. In yoga, breath signifies vital energy. Yoga teaches that controlling our breathing can help control our bodies and quiet our minds.

The Power of Gentle, Time-Honored Tai Chi

Another way to reduce stress is tai chi. The ancient art of tai chi uses gentle flowing movements to reduce the stress of today's busy lifestyles and improve health. Tai chi is sometimes described as "meditation in motion" because it promotes serenity through its gentle movements that connect the mind and body. Originally developed in ancient China for self-defense, tai chi evolved into a graceful form of exercise that's now used for stress reduction and to help with a variety of other health conditions.

Tai chi, also called tai chi chuan, is a noncompetitive, self-paced system of gentle physical exercise and stretching, a series of postures or movements performed in a slow, graceful manner. Each posture flows into the next without pause, ensuring that the body is in constant motion. Tai chi is appealing because it's inexpensive, requires no special equipment and can be done indoors or out, either alone or in a group.

8

HOW TO DEVELOP GREAT
PERSON-TO-PERSON SKILLS

*If out of reading this book you get just one thing—an
increased tendency to think always in terms of the other
people's point of view and see things from their angle—if
you get that one thing out of this book, it may easily
prove to be one of the building blocks of your career.*

Dale Carnegie
How to Win Friends and Influence People

Skillfully Leading Others from Compliance to Commitment

Are we born influential? Or do we develop influence?
Both, it seems. Some people are born into roles, or a
station in life that positions them to be influential.

Others work hard to develop themselves, and the ability to influence may become a bi-product, whether desired or undesired. Yet even those born into a position of status must work hard to develop a real ability to influence people in a positive way.

Influence fits hand-in-glove with leadership. As we develop an ability to influence, we often gravitate toward leadership role. Our motives for influencing others will eventually be known, and if they are less than worthy, our influence will be diminished.

Dale Carnegie is most well-known for his book, *How to Win Friends and Influence People*, which is filled with example after example of applications of thirty "win-win" human relations principles. If we were to boil all thirty of these principles that the author discovered down to one, it would most likely be *respect*. Most people would agree that we would rather have commitment than compliance from others.

Some of the key words connected with compliance are status, obligation, role, standing, position, station, and rank. Key words we think of when we think of commitment, however, are connection, corresponding, interest, relationship, association, and recipient.

We can all do the sort of research Dale Carnegie did by thinking of those people we consider influential and listing their notable qualities, values, or skills.

Become a Friendlier Person

Dale Carnegie's famous suggestions for becoming a friendlier person always bear repeating. There's a reason why they are among the most celebrated suggestions in the world—because they work, they are simple, and they improve our character as much as they improve our relationships. They are:

- Don't criticize, condemn or complain
- Give honest, sincere appreciation
- Arouse in the other person an eager want
- Become genuinely interested in other people
- Smile
- Remember that a person's name is to that person the sweetest sound in any language
- Encourage others to talk about themselves
- Talk in terms of the other person's interests
- Make others feel important, and do it sincerely

Using Stories to Influence Others

Stories impact our emotional side as well as our logic. They provide context as well as information. They connect on a psychological level that motivates and help listeners relate to us as people. They touch others on a multiple sensory level, and they intrigue all ages and cultures.

> *Nine-tenths of the serious controversies that arise in life result from misunderstandings, from one not knowing the facts which to the other seem important, or otherwise failing to appreciate the other's point of view.*
>
> Judge Louis D Brandeis

Practicing Everyday Leadership

To influence others' attitudes and behaviors, begin with praise and honest appreciation. Call attention to people's mistakes indirectly. Talk about your own mistakes before criticizing the other. Ask questions instead of giving direct orders. Let the other person save face.

Praise the slightest improvement and praise every improvement. Be hearty in your approbation and lavish in your praise. Give the other person a fine reputation to live up to. Use encouragement. If there is a fault, make it seem easy to correct. Make the other person happy about doing what you suggest.

We should concentrate on our strengths instead of always focusing on our weaknesses. By doing this we will rise to the expert level faster. Relying on others to complement our weaknesses is also recommended. Great leaders do recognize their weaknesses, but they also find people who excel where they fall short, and rely on them. Great leaders don't hide their weaknesses, they use them. They also avoid becoming set in their ways, so they often take the road less traveled.

Disagree Agreeably

"Think, cushion, and only then should you speak," Dale Carnegie advises. Think *about what you are thinking* and why you are thinking it, and what evidence you have. Evidence builds credibility and defeats doubt. Evidence is seen in demonstrations, examples, facts, exhibits, analogies, testimonials, and statistics.

The "cushion" Dale Carnegie mentions can consist of phrases such as "I hear you saying..." "I understand..." and "I appreciate your view...." He recommends avoiding words such as "but, however, and nevertheless," since they don't bridge, but divide. "Cushion" language avoids abruptness and potentially putting the other on the defense.

It's important to let others maintain their dignity, even during times of conflict, and to reassure people of their value. Create an environment where both sides can learn.

Common Ground, Always Available

Look for ways to build common ground between you and the person who has made an error by first establishing rapport. Rapport is a reservoir of good will and mutual trust accumulated over a long period of fair treatment. When you meet, begin by putting that person at ease and reducing their anxiety. Help him or her feel comfortable. Communicate in an empathetic manner and then conversationally bridge to the issue at hand.

It will soon come time to deal with the issue. During this step, you must focus on the problem and not the person. Eliminate personal pronouns to depersonalize the problem. It was the action that was wrong, not the person who did it. You want to give the other person a chance to explain what happened and then let that person know what you know about the problem.

You should listen to understand and to determine whether he or she is accepting responsibility or blaming and avoiding responsibility. The goal is to gather facts and information in order to be able to accurately identify the problem and why it happened. Reduce defensiveness by asking questions and not jumping to conclusions. The different perspectives will surface, and the root cause of the problem would be identified.

Options, Commitment, Accountability

The next steps are meant to remedy the problem, to reduce the chance of the mistake happening again, and to restore the person's performance. They also involve planning to devise a way to keep the problem from occurring again.

The step of exploring options together should be handled differently with the person who accepts responsibility, than with the one who blames and avoids taking responsibility. With the responsible person, effective questioning, listening, and coaching can be used to encourage him or her to suggest ways to correct the situation. Such a person can be involved in a problem analysis and decision-making process and will be more likely to be committed when they help provide the solution. For the "blaming" or "avoiding" one, expectations may first need to be reaffirmed and lessons given in the acceptance of responsibility to restore accountability.

Where the Erring Need Help

In establishing commitment, focus on the person. Obviously a person who has erred feels, to some degree, like a failure and is likely to be less inclined to approach the next opportunity with confidence. Therefore, he or she needs help to see the situation in a different context.

The person in question needs to be reassured of his or her value and importance and of the support and encouragement of others and should end up motivated to achieve optimal performance because he or she perceives a solid relationship is possible. Commitment to restoring a high performance level and your commitment to his or her success should be affirmed.

The "blaming" or "avoiding" person should leave the discussion with a sense of accountability and an understanding of what the other's expectations are.

Title

Our relationships are defined by the amount of trust they exhibit. Dale Carnegie called trust the result of competency plus compassion. Since our tendencies influence our relationships, it serves us to learn what our tendencies are and how they relate to others.

Each of the lettered rows below contains four words or phrases. From each row, circle one word or phrase that most closely describes you. Choose only one from each row.

A	a reporter	a futurist	a realist	a co-ordinator
B	people-oriented	detail-focused	values-focused	forward-thinking
C	a dreamer	a driver	a doer	a peace keeper
D	decisive	inspiring	reliable	considerate
E	meets deadlines	brings people together	keeps things on track	has sense of mission
F	dramatic	curious	relaxed	focused
G	knows how things should be done	knows what has to be done	knows where he or she wants to be	knows what questions to ask
H	reviews methods	anticipates problems	solves problems	resolves conflicts
I	gets results	assures results are appropriate	makes sure things are done right	focuses on outcomes
J	charismatic	prepared	easy-going	aware

Your Tendencies: Score Sheet

Instructions

Circle the words or phrases you circled on the previous page on this Score Sheet. Total the number of items circled in each column. Rank the columns from lowest (4) to highest (1).

	Visionary	Achiever	Facilitator	Analyzer
A	a futurist	a realist	a coordinator	a reporter
B	forward-thinking	values-focused	people-oriented	detail-focused
C	a dreamer	a driver	a peacekeeper	a doer
D	inspiring	reliable	considerate	decisive
E	has sense of mission	meets deadlines	brings people together	keeps things on track
F	dramatic	focused	relaxed	curious
G	knows where he or she wants to be	knows what has to be done	knows how things should be done	knows what questions to ask
H	anticipates problems	solves problems	resolves conflicts	reviews methods
I	focuses on outcomes	gets results	makes sure things are done right	assures results are appropriate
J	charismatic	prepared	easy-going	aware

	Visionary	Achiever	Facilitator	Analyzer

Total:____ Total:____ Total:____ Total:____
Rank:____ Rank:____ Rank:____ Rank:____

Different Tendencies, Different Roles

The four tendencies identified in the previous exercise translate into important roles. They can be described as follows:

Visionary

Focuses primarily on the big picture. He or she looks at long-term, desired outcomes and the general direction of the team and its processes. As such, the Visionary can provide a much-needed sense of mission, direction, and leadership that others cannot. *On the down side, the Visionary often ignores the details and fails to do what is necessary to get things done.*

Achiever

The people who can be most counted on to accomplish tasks. He or she is often a diligent worker with an outstanding level of technical expertise and will do the utmost to complete any assigned task. *However, in the desire to get things done, the Achiever often overlooks the contributions of others and may be seen as "difficult to work with."*

Facilitator

By far the best at working with people. In doing so, he or she tries to ensure that processes are established and upheld. When conflicts arise, the Facilitator can be counted upon to step in and make things right by getting all the parties to appropriately discuss their differences. *This can also be a disadvantage because, with this kind of attention to process, the facilitator often neglects to complete tasks on time.*

Analyzer

In a team setting, the Analyzer is the conscience of the team. He or she reviews the team's decisions and approaches and compares them to the common purpose to make sure the team stays on track. As such, the Analyzer can often provide the ethical and procedural compass that teams require. *However, in doing so, the Analyzer often remains in the reactive mode and is often not seen as a self-starter or as someone who can perform a task alone.*

The following grid presents brief descriptions of how people can work together. Select your tendency on the left and read across how you can best work with other roles.

	Visionary	Achiever	Facilitator	Analyzer
Visionary	Keep in mind that as Visionaries, you are both looking toward to tomorrow, but you have to work with others to get things done today.	Try to translate your vision of the future into things the Achiever can accomplish, and the tasks required.	Combine your inspiration with the Facilitator's skills to establish a process that combines your vision and the common purpose.	Empower the Analyzer to examine the tasks and processes to ensure that they are in keeping with the vision and common purpose.

Achiever	Seek out the Visionary's counsel to ensure that your tasks are making a difference in terms of the big picture.	Divide tasks clearly with other Achievers to ensure the best results.	Ask the facilitator for ways the process can support the tasks. Try to adapt some of his or her people skills to your own style.	Encourage the Analyzer to review your work to help you improve, and ensure that your efforts support the common purpose.
Facilitator	Remind the Visionary of the process required to get to the long-term results. Allow his or her vision to mold the processes you use.	Value the Achiever's contributions to accomplishing the common purpose and suggest processes to help him or her work with others on the team.	Work together to establish processes that consider the needs of all the members of your team.	Ask the Analyzer about the extent to which the team's processes are supporting the common purpose.

Analyzer	Help the Visionary to see that the longterm goals and the common purposes are interrelated.	Allow the Achiever to take the lead on time-sensitive tasks while supporting him or her with advice and guidance.	Once the Facilitator has established a process, work within that process to achieve the common purpose.	Work with other Analyzers to keep your comments positive and supportive and to encourage team unity.

9

....

CHARISMA: SUCCESS'S GREATEST INGREDIENT

Test Your Charisma Quotient

Charisma comes from a Greek word meaning "gift" or "favor." The dictionary defines charisma as "personal magnetism; the ability to inspire enthusiasm, interest, or affection in others by means of personal charm or influence." Whether in the office or not, we know when we're in the presence of charisma. But we don't always know when we possess it ourselves. Here's a way to find out.

Instructions: Give each statement a rank by checking the first answer that comes to mind. If you answer honestly, this will offer an instant picture of your tendencies in action: charismatic or not.

Seldom/Sometimes/Most of the time

1. At social and professional gatherings, people are drawn to me and seek out my company.   %   %   %

2. I express my emotions freely.   %   %   %

3. I am self-confident and completely myself and natural in social and professional settings.   %   %   %

4. I take a genuine and sincere interest in others and welcome diverse views.   %   %   %

5. I am energetic, enthusiastic, and passionate about my beliefs, values, work, and leisure.   %   %   %

6. I enjoy being around people, I am a warm and friendly person, and have an inviting personality.   %   %   %

7. I am adept at thinking on my feet and responding well under pressure.   %   %   %

8. I have an easy time convincing, persuading, and inspiring others to act or change.   %   %   %

9. I enjoy speaking in public.   %   %   %

10. People have the tendency to want to get to know me better.   %   %   %

Mistakes That Destroy Charisma

- Not being confident or authentic
- Poor human relations and communications skills
- Demonstrating poor listening skills; pretending to listen or listening just to respond
- Procrastinating or acting indecisively when decisions must be made
- Being defensive or not taking responsibility for mistakes
- Playing favorites or bullying
- Being controlling, arrogant, or uncompromising
- Having a negative attitude, being critical, and complaining often
- Dishonest or poor work ethics and questionable values
- Passing judgment or not receptive of others' ideas
- Inability to think quickly and perform well under pressure
- Lack of emotion, passion, and enthusiasm
- Flaunting knowledge, being conceited, or having a smug attitude
- Making false promises, contradicting yourself, or not holding confidences
- Not engaging or connecting with others on a personal and professional level
- Ordering or telling people what to do instead of asking
- An inability to influence, convince, and inspire others
- Not showing sincere gratitude, appreciation, and recognition
- Lack of focus, disorganization, things falling through cracks

- Asking close-ended questions or inappropriate ones
- Using negative body language or incongruent behavior
- Using unexciting words to communicate mundane stories

Small Talk is NOT Always That

The non-business style of communicating, conducted on a relatively surface level has the potential to build connections and become the foundation for an ongoing, more serious relationship. Becoming adept at small talk doesn't require an exhaustive knowledge of current events. It simply requires the ability to focus the other person on his or her favorite topic, and to ask questions that indicate your interest. This is a sure-fire way to build rapport.

Dale Carnegie suggests thinking of five different questions we could ask without appearing nosy or intrusive, to get us thinking in the right direction about this potentially important conversational opportunity that could appear at any given time. Smiling is helpful, and pleasantries that are genuine should be on the agenda, nothing forced. Observing the other's traits, values, or achievements creates an instant connection, perhaps even establishes common ground. Show respect for the other's time constraints, and avoid controversial subjects, being sensitive to issues of diversity. Ask thoughtful questions.

Be in the moment, focusing on what the other is saying. Be a resource; ask if you can help, if help is needed. Tell the other something of interest that he or she might not already know. Offer a genuine compliment, adding evidence, if possible, showing your sincerity and thoughtfulness.

The Three "C's" of Charisma

Communication, connection, and confidence are charisma's three C's.

Communication: What we say. Our questioning skills, our ability to listen and maintain eye contact. Speaking in terms of the other person. Using image-based words to paint vivid pictures.

Connection: How we say it. Our ability to engage and show emotion. Being authentic, genuine, and sincere. Focusing on others.

Confidence: How we look. How we act. How we sound. Having a positive attitude. Exuding enthusiasm and personal power.

Charismatic leaders generally exhibit such attributes as extraordinary emotional expressiveness, self-confidence, self-determination, and freedom from internal conflict.

—From the book *Charismatic Leadership: The Elusive Factor in Organizational Effectiveness* by Conger and Kanungo

The Charismatic Communicator Adapts

Nobody recommends being a chameleon, but to be seen as a charismatic communicator, Dale Carnegie suggests adapting our communication style to the person we are speaking to, in order to put him or her at ease. Persuasive and influential communicators will establish rapport, based on the communication style of the other. Spend time on the subject that is comfortable for the other. Use pacing and language suitable to the style of the other, and be conscious of the element of time, based on the style of the other.

What are these styles? Research on communication styles will commonly place people in one of four categories:

Friendly Style ("Why?"): Casual, amiable, relationship focused, helpful, warm, from the heart, likes positive feedback.

Analytical Style ("How?"): Formal, methodical, systematic, logical, data oriented, seeks answers, details and solutions, likes evidence.

Excitable Style ("Who?"): Demonstrative, expressive, uses gestures, paints the big picture, and likes to hear what's in it for them.

Dominating Style ("What?"): Efficient, focuses on goals and objectives, has strong viewpoints and opinions, decisive, likes to be presented with options.

How Our Image Can Help Others See Us As Charismatic

How we look. Consider your manner of dressing, your grooming, even your accessories. Facial expression and your habitual gestures.

How we act. Your demeanor, body language, attitude, and what you display of your character.

What we say. Your vocabulary, the facts you present, your knowledge, and the stories you tell.

How we say it. Your voice, tone, pitch, and speed or tempo.

Sixteen Tips For Increasing the Charisma Quotient

1. Create a good and memorable first impression. Be conscious of the ways in which you project yourself. Small gestures, such as shaking another person's hand, or remembering another person's name, create a memorable first impression.

2. Hold a positive attitude and project positive energy and body language. Maintain optimism about yourself, about others, and about life in general. Breathe "life," passion, and enthusiasm into every interaction.

3. Relax and speak conversationally. Speak with passion, energy, and enthusiasm, and use pauses to create emphasis.

4. Learn to think on your feet, ad-lib in impromptu situations, and be prepared to respond well under pressure.

5. Be knowledgeable and informed. Know what's going on in the world, and specifically in your area of expertise.

6. Captivate with your speech. Maintain congruency between what you say and how you say it. Be believable, genuine, and sincere. Be articulate and modulate your voice so others can hear you. Be a great storyteller and your image-based words to paint vivid pictures.

7. Engage others by being focused and attentive to them. Make them feel as though they are the most important person in the room.

8. Be respectful to others and yourself. Show respect to others even when you disagree with them. Always maintain self-respect. Be sensitive to diverse issues and speak with diplomacy and tact.

9. Build connections and trust with others. Mirror their body language and mannerisms to put them at ease.

10. Be human. Feel your emotions and tune into others' emotions. Allow emotions to come through in your actions and speech. Hear the emotions in other people's words and respond to them.

11. Never be intimidated by other charismatic people. Maintain drive and determination to reach your mission, vision, and goals.

12. Maintain humility and modesty. Focus on other people's success. Let your successes speak for itself. Give sincere compliments, recognition, and appreciation freely.
13. Treat every person you meet as important. Show warmth and acceptance for people you come in contact with.
14. Stand out from the ordinary. Be reasonably controversial, take risks, and propose out-of-the-box ideas.

And the fifteenth secret? Have fun and maintain a good sense of humor! When we enjoy our life, our work, and ourselves others will be drawn to our energy and exuberance.

10

MAKE THE FIRST IMPRESSION
A GREAT ONE

"You never get a second chance to make a first impression" is an honored old truism. Luckily, it's possible to become mindful enough to always be ready to present the best possible first impression, at any time.

Here are some Dale Carnegie observations about presenting a great first impression.

Eye Contact

Effective eye contact implies that a person is self-confident, honest, interested, in control, and comfortable with the interaction. Lack of eye contact is often interpreted to mean that the individual has something to hide, doesn't want to be in the situation, is intimidated, fearful, or ashamed. It can also imply avoidance, boredom, nervousness, or dishonesty.

Research show that in job interviews, candidates give longer and more revealing answers when the interviewer maintains consistent eye contact. In the classroom, students' comprehension and retention can be directly correlated to the teacher's level of eye contact.

There is one notable exception, however. When disclosing highly personal information, we usually avoid eye contact. Men, especially, disclose less personal information if eye contact is too intense.

Analysis of Effective Eye Contact in Business:

Intensity

The gaze is prolonged and focused, and accompanied by such signs of acceptance and friendliness as soft facial expressions, relaxed body language and vocalizations that indicate interest and attention. Prolonged, focused eye contact without the softening context can seem threatening or aggressive.

Location

Pupil-to-pupil eye contact is ideal when the objective is to convey specific info with an emphasis on accuracy. In other situations, it may be more comfortable to break the direct eye contact occasionally or soften overall by moving our focus slightly. For a gentler connection, try resting your gaze:

- just below one brow of the other person
- at the bridge of the nose
- near the inner corner of the eye

All of these *feel like* direct eye contact, but without the harshness.

Looking lower than the other's eyes is often interpreted as a sign of subservience or lacking in confidence, so break eye contact by moving focus upward or outward instead.

Duration

Forget any "rules" about how many seconds of eye contact you should maintain. How attentive can we be to the other person's communication if we are unconsciously ticking off some arbitrary time limit?

Maintaining eye contact 60–70 percent of the time is considered good—longer when communicating specific information for retention. An excellent guideline is to maintain eye contact, with only brief "rest" periods all the time, unless there is a specific reason to direct your gaze elsewhere.

In a group situation, maintain eye contact with someone all the time. Distribute eye contact carefully to include all participants. Including challenging people, or those you know disagree with your position, your eye contact conveys a high degree of self-confidence. It also conveys a level of comfort and acceptance toward the opinions of others.

We'll seem stronger if we usually wait for the other person to break eye contact. We should occasionally break it ourselves, however, to avoid appearing intimidating and to let the other person feel important.

We can even communicate confidence by the way in which we break eye contact. A jerky in-and-out motion appears nervous or furtive, while a slower, more controlled movement implies assurance.

Situational Variables

When we are standing/sitting opposite the other party, they expect more eye contact; when we are standing/sitting side-by-side, they expect less.

The closer we are, the more intense direct eye contact seems, and therefore the less of it is expected—in an elevator, for example.

Cultural Variables

Don't force eye contact if the other person is obviously avoiding it. Some cultures (and individuals) have different expectations about eye contact than the typical Americans. When we sense that might be the case, we should make the other person comfortable by minimizing eye contact, or we will seem pushy and intimidating.

Handshakes

Handshakes are believed to have originated on medieval battlefields as a forearm-to-forearm grip to check for concealed weapons, and a good handshake is equally disarming today in a psychological sense, creating a connection that makes the other person more open to accepting us and to communicating himself or herself honestly.

In one university study, researchers left a quarter in an airport phone booth. After someone else used the phone, the researcher approached, explained that he had accidentally left his quarter and asked if the individual had found it. Over half of the respondents lied. The researcher then added a handshake and greeting before inquiring about the quarter, and the number of dishonest responses decreased by 66%!

In today's business climate, the handshake is the only universally safe and acceptable form of touching others, and the bond it can create is very strong. Take every opportunity to accept or initiate handshakes with colleagues of both genders.

Variations On the Handshake Theme

Wrapping our other hand around the person's hand is appropriate when our intent is to indicate extra warmth, congratulations, and condolence. This type of handshake might be used when reconnecting with an old acquaintance or to subtly express personal concern within a business environment.

Other Forms of Touching

A secondary touch on the upper arm or shoulder elevates the level of intimacy in a handshake. If we have any doubt about which greeting is expected, we might offer our hand first. If the other party escalates the contact into a hug, the grasped hands keep the embrace from becoming too intimate.

If we want to discourage the possibility of a hug, we should initiate our handshake from a slightly greater distance; it is far more difficult to move into a hug with more space between two bodies. We can still create the impression of a warmer greeting by initiating the handshake more quickly and holding the grasp a bit longer than usual.

Departing Handshake

Since it is virtually the only physical contact expected in business, don't miss the opportunity to shake hands again at the conclusion of an interaction. If the exchange has been a positive one (or if you want to put a more positive spin on a slightly negative interaction), make the departing handshake a little bit more intimate than the first one, using a firmer grip, extended duration and/or positive facial expression to communicate warmth and acceptance to the other person.

Body Language

Smiling

Smiling causes people to respond more warmly to us and may even make them more agreeable to your point of view.

In the 1984 presidential election, a particular television commentator was observed to smile when he mentioned Reagan, but not to smile when he mentioned Mondale. A post-election survey found that his viewers voted for Reagan in far greater numbers than a control group of other individuals with the same demographic profile.

Throughout his presidency, Reagan's televised speeches were interspersed with warm, cordial smiles. After the fact, viewers of both parties were shown tapes of the speeches and their responses recorded. Each time the president smiled, the viewers smiled back at the video monitor.

What do we believe about people who smile? Studies show that most people interpret smiles to reflect confidence, competence, caring, and trustworthiness. It has been repeatedly documented that judges and juries of defendants who don't smile treat courtroom defendants who smile more leniently.

A good smile involves both cheek muscles and eye muscles— in effect, the whole face. Practice in front of a mirror to see and feel the difference. Of course the easiest way to generate a genuine, full-face smile is to maintain a positive attitude about the interaction in which you are involved.

Posture

Because it is seen instantly, posture causes an immediate and unconscious reaction in a viewer. Studies correlate positive beliefs about popularity, self-confidence, ambition, friendliness, and intelligence with great posture.

Posture is especially important for individuals who need to compensate for some other image disadvantage—those who are shorter, have weak voices, can't yet afford good clothes, or are overweight, or less attractive.

Maintaining good posture also makes us mentally sharper by allowing our lungs to function more effectively, thereby allowing more oxygen to reach your brain.

Standing Posture

If we stretch to maximum height by elongating our torso area, this simple correction may add an inch to our overall height and add immeasurably to our professional presence. Practice this technique until it becomes second nature.

Keeping shoulders squared, practice this by standing against a wall; press back until both shoulders touch the wall. Maintain this body alignment and move away from the wall. Although this may feel unnatural at first, it will become more comfortable with practice.

Note: It's good to stand with our arms relaxed at our sides and observe the position of our hands. If they naturally rest with the palms facing backward, rather than inward toward the body, you need to pay particular attention to developing a more squared-shoulder stance.

Keep a balanced appearance by centering your weight equally on both feet. Shifting the weight slightly toward the balls of the feet and leaning ever so slightly forward creates the subtle impression that we are very interested and attentive.

Seated Posture

Sit slightly forward and erect, not slouched in the chair, to appear energetic and actively engaged. Keep the body relatively balanced but not perfectly symmetrical. An exactly centered position looks awkward and self-conscious. Arrange arms in an asymmetrical position to communicate relaxed confidence.

Head Movements

We can use our head, literally, to enhance our professional presence, tilting our head slightly to make eye contact with someone who is much taller or shorter. Moving our eyes to look down appears snooty or demeaning; looking up seems submissive or imploring.

We're advised to keep our head erect rather than tilting it to the side. Any tilt can make us seem confused, not too bright, or even flirtatious. Avoid bobbing up and down in agreement; we can easily seem too anxious to please. Affirm agreement with a speaker with a slow, purposeful nod, vocalizing or raising an eyebrow instead.

Reading Others' Body Signals

Body language usually communicates a more honest message than words. Don't evaluate an isolated gesture or movement, but do watch for a pattern of clues that confirms or contradicts the spoken communication.

A collection of such "open" body signals as relaxed arms, open palms, soft facial expressions, eye contact, smiles, and leaning forward can usually be interpreted as an indication of an accepting response by the other person.

An array of such "closed" signals as crossed arms, clenched fists, a set jaw, or furrowed brow, lack of eye contact, frowning, and moving away usually sends a collective message of hostility, rejection, and avoidance.

11

MEETING NEW PEOPLE IS
ESSENTIAL FOR A GREAT LIFE

Meeting new people is easier if we can keep in mind just two questions to ask ourselves: "What do I want to know from this person?" and "What are the sample questions I might ask?"

The old joke about meeting someone in a club invariably involves the question, "Do you come here often?" Actually, if one could say it with a straight face, that's a perfectly good opener, but it certainly won't work for, say, a church supper or a party, though it could be effective in a gym setting.

Reinvent Party Talk

When meeting new people, remember that we all find it wonderfully satisfying when others ask what's going on with us in a sincere way. But we can show that interest without resorting to the same old conversational gambits that have been used for many generations as we initiate conversations. It's not that difficult to be creative, and it pays off. We make a better first impression, for instance, by asking the origin or meaning of a family name as a creative way to follow up an introduction. That may very well lead to mentioning of places and regions we've been to, or would like to visit.

Inquiring about names of the children in a family can often lead to discussions of how the names were chosen and what they mean. Questions about animals in the household are also useful for generating conversation. Animal names are often good for a chuckle and a good-natured mutual conversation, especially if both parties share a love for the same breed or species.

Not Only "What Do You Do?" but "How Do You Do It?"

Finding out the location of your new acquaintance's home can lead to a query about activities for families in the area, for instance, along with the standard questions about the age and style of the house, the amount of land, and so on. This line of conversation can easily lead to a colorful topic of benign and wholehearted interest on the part of many—gardening. Unlike a discussion of sports or religion, your preference for roses is not going to raise the hackles of your companion who adores irises.

It might be time to put the overworked "What do you do?" to rest, at least if we're going to leave it there. Expressing a genuine—not robotic—interest in people's jobs can be refreshing, especially if their own families have long ago lost interest in why they leave the house every morning. Chances are a new acquaintance's line of work does not resemble ours. What a goldmine of possibilities! "How has engineering changed in the last couple of years?" "Do you find that regularly looking up from the computer is as good for your eyesight as they say it is?" "As a waitress, have you seen changes in what your customers order lately?" "What advice would you give a newcomer to your field?"

"What's the last place you visited?" is likely to spark a lively conversation, whether you have been to that place or are eager to know why you should visit there. This conversation can expand onto many richly diverse paths, including food, music, vegetation, languages, and so on. Even finding out where your new acquaintance travels on business can produce good conversational results. "Do you know a restaurant in Rome where they speak English and children are welcome?" "Will they send me bulbs from Holland if I choose some when I'm there?" "Can you hire a private driver in China?" "Weren't you worried about your safety in Egypt?"

Tunes, Teams, and Trouble

If there's music playing while you are preparing to strike up a conversation, a comment on it might be in order. We can always find something good to say about music; it may be lively, even if our preference is for another kind. "I haven't heard this since I was riding around in my first Mustang," will undoubtedly lead to a run of charming nostalgia, and "I used to play this for my mother just to annoy her" will definitely get a laugh and maybe amusing follow-up. Music references are valuable because they can spin off onto interesting tangents, too. "If this were a little faster, we'd be able to Limbo, the way we did on our last cruise," for example, or, "My daughter tried to put this song on my iPod, but Dylan won that spot."

Sports conversations take on a life of their own, as do hobbies. Sometimes even spotting a key chain or a bumper sticker or a baseball cap worth commenting on can speed conversation along, but only if we can be sportsmanlike about a rival team.

And then there's the shark-infested subject of politics. There's traditionally been a bright yellow string of police tape around this one, and for good reason—unless we have a pretty good idea that the one we're talking to, votes the same way we do or is uncommonly open-minded. Broad social issues—*very* broad—might be safer territory, or non-incendiary comments about goings-on in distant parts of the world. But even these topics can lead to domestic disputes, however polite, and often depending on the amount of liquid indulgence involved.

We should be careful in these social situations, but not *too* hesitant, or we might miss a great chance at a successful "chance" meeting that could lead to anything, from a business contact to marriage.

And, don't forget, if the lull in the conversation ever grows large enough to walk an elephant through, it's always perfect respectable to resort to "My tomatoes are praying for rain!"

Reliable Phrases

It's handy to have some phrases at hand that are guaranteed to keep a fledgling conversation from flagging, especially if the situation is at all tense or anxiety provoking. Here are some transitional phrases that Dale Carnegie recommends: "In what way?" "Give me an example." "How so?" "Tell me more."

"Can you say that a different way?" "That word has so many different meanings. Can you tell me what it means to you?"

There are also "ladders" leading to common ground. Here are some:

Look at the other person. Ask questions. Don't interrupt. Don't change the subject. Express emotion with control. Respond appropriately.

How to "Break in" Politely

Some examples of phrases used in bridging, or gently introducing yourself, are:

"I just heard you mention something about…" "Did I hear you say you were from…" "I thought I heard you were recently in New York." "I find it interesting that you just spoke about…"

Moving On: Possible Ways to Exit a Conversation

It's often more difficult to leave a conversation gracefully than it is to enter it. Here are some helpers:

"It's been great talking to you. I've been trying to connect with the person over there for a while, so please excuse me."

"I've been wanting to go over there to ask that fellow a question. It's been nice talking to you."

"I need to take care of something. It was nice to meet you."

"Please excuse me. I'm meeting a colleague right about now. It was a pleasure meeting you."

Listening to *Really* Hear

What we say is proof of how well we listen.

Marshall Goldsmith

Be a good listener. Dale Carnegie says there are five levels of listening: pretending to listen, listening to respond, listening to learn, listening to understand, and empathetic listening.

Act as if there will be a quiz at the end of your conversation, Dale Carnegie suggests. Try rephrasing what you hear to make sure you got it right. Concentrate on the message, not the delivery. Turn off your minds as much as possible.

To find out how good a listener you really are, you can answer these questions with an "Always, Usually, Occasionally, or Rarely" score.

1. I find that people need to repeat information to me.
2. I experience incidents of miscommunication more than others do.
3. I tend to tune people out if their delivery is slow or the material dry.
4. I find myself finishing sentences for others.
5. I notice that people voice their frustrations with me regarding lack of follow-up or unmet expectations.
6. I steer others away from what they are saying with my comments.
7. I tend to multi-task when I am listening to other people.
8. I feel uncomfortable asking for clarification from the speaker.
9. When someone comes to me with a problem, I have the tendency to want to fix it or give advice.
10. I fake paying attention.
11. I form a response in my mind before the speaker finishes.
12. I need to take notes to remember what is being said.

13. I make assumptions based on the appearance of the speaker.
14. I am easily distracted when someone is speaking to me.
15. I tend to do most of the talking in conversations.
16. I ask questions that indicate I was not listening.
17. I display an open and accepting attitude toward the speaker.
18. I am in the loop on important communications at work.
19. When approached with a question, I offer complete attention.
20. I concentrate on what's being said, even if it is of little interest.
21. I listen to the other's point of view, even if I disagree.
22. I maintain eye contact with the speaker.
23. I try to understand the point of view of those who disagree with me.
24. I can briefly and accurately summarize what someone said.
25. I give the other a chance to explain fully before responding.
26. I observe the speaker for nonverbal cues.
27. I am open to criticism.
28. I give verbal or nonverbal encouragement to the speaker.
29. I check to make sure I have interpreted the message correctly.
30. I try to "be with" the person speaking by putting myself in his or her shoes.

Listening Skills Scoring

Score yourself in the following manner:

Questions 1–16

- 1 point —Always
- 2 points —Usually
- 3 points —Occasionally
- 4 points —Rarely

Questions 17–30

- 4 points —Always
- 3 points —Usually
- 2 points —Occasionally
- 1 point —Rarely

Results

- 104–120 You are a skilled listener. Obtain a second opinion to make sure you have an accurate perception of your listening skills.
- 95–104 Listening is a top priority for you.
- 85–94 You listen when it's convenient for you.
- 75–84 You are an occasional listener.
- Below 75 You are brutally honest and have great potential for improvement.

12

A GREAT LIFE COMMUNICATES
ACROSS GENERATIONS

The big danger when it comes to intergenerational communication is that each generation is sure it knows *exactly* what the other is like. For instance, we who are of a certain age are sure we know what it would be like to attend a board meeting at a company run by a very young person, right? We know that everybody would be on Twitter, nailed to their smart phones, texting their opinions, heads down, thumbs busy.

We know we wouldn't like it, that we would definitely prefer a meeting where the CEO at least formalizes the meeting by submitting a page with a few written mentions of "things going on in the company."

Well, surprise! Bringing that single piece of yellow legal paper into the boardroom is exactly the way Mark Zuckerberg,

CEO of Facebook, starts his board meetings, same as he did when Facebook was just beginning.

And Mark is twenty-six years old.

So much for that stereotype!

Looking for the Unexpected

Because of the aging of the population, it's not unusual for any gathering, or family, or office to comprise these four distinct generations, all existing within the same four walls, all expecting to get along together. Research tells us that it's the communication-taking place between two or more people that helps define their relationship.

Ours is a society where grandparents are even called upon to raise grandchildren, so it's doubly important for the communication to be clear. Communication is what enables family members to make their changing needs known and also the means by which each can learn how best to function as a cohesive unit. It doesn't only go one way, either. Children aren't the only ones who should be working toward understanding. Older generations would do well to acquaint themselves with the unique challenges of their grandchildren: drugs, violence, and sexual activity, to name just three.

Tom Boyle, director of the Learning Technology Research Institute in the UK, coined the term NQ, for Network Quotient, the ability to form connections with others. According to Boyle, NQ is more important than IQ when intergenerational communication is needed. Each generation living and working side by side has its own unique mindset, work style and ways of communicating. No kind of team, family or work-relation, is possible without bridging those gaps.

The following are considered to be the generational groups we deal with today, whether in families, in society, or at work:

Traditionalists or Veterans: Born between 1925 and 1944, Traditionalists are age 60 and older and number approximately 75 million in the work-force. In communicating with them we build trust through inclusive language, such as "we" or "us." Words are gospel. They should lean toward the formal and should be congruent with body language. They will not share their thoughts without trust, and do not like their time wasted. They prefer face-to-face or written communication.

Baby Boomers: Born between 1945 and 1964, Baby Boomers range in age from 71 to 40 and number approximately 80 million in the work force. To them we speak in an open and direct style with plenty of body language. We answer questions frankly and thoroughly and expect to be pressed for details. We don't use controlling, manipulative language, and we ask for or provide options to demonstrate flexible thinking. We use face-to-face or electronic communications.

Gen Xers: Born between 1965 and 1981, Gen Xers range in age from 50 to 35 and number approximately 46 million in the work force, comprising the smallest group of workers, according to the US Department of Labor. We learn their language and speak it. We're brief, concise in order to hold their attention, challenging them and asking for their input. We share information with them immediately and often, using an informal communication style, listening and showing respect for their opinions. We use email as the primary communication.

Millennials or Nexters or Gen Yers: Born between 1980 and 2000, Millennials range in age from 16 to 36 and number 76 million in the work force. We let words paint visual pictures to inspire, motivate and keep them focused. We use action verbs to challenge them, and are never condescending, showing respect through our language. We constantly seek their feedback, using humor, encouraging them to think outside the box and challenging them to explore new paths or options. We use email, texting, IM, and voicemail as primary communication tools.

Healthy Differences Promote Growth

The Dale Carnegie system offers insights to help us honor, appreciate, and identify with different generations. As we learn to connect and communicate more effectively with one another, differences can actually be viewed as healthy instead of disruptive, providing exciting opportunities to collaborate on innovative solutions.

Successful cross-generational relationships are most likely when each takes the following suggestions:

- Be interested in generational differences. Don't dismiss them offhand.
- Know your own generation. Characteristics different from yours may surprise you. Certainly becoming aware of them will open your eyes and change your attitudes.
- Know other generations and their characteristics, at least in general.
- Avoid holding grudges left over from clashes with other generations.
- Nurture positive feelings toward different generations. In other words, don't nurture the negative, and when

you notice positive feelings coming up, encourage them.

- Focus attention on your thoughts, feelings, and behavior, remaining mindful instead of unconscious, driven by knee-jerk reactions.
- Recognize how your perceptions affect all of your encounters. When you look at it this way, perception is everything.
- Be aware of the impact your behavior has on other generations.

It's Not a One-Shot Deal

Certain positive attitudes, principles, and concepts must be performed consistently to ensure success and effectiveness in dealing with people who are different from us. Very little gets integrated enough to become new behaviors in one shot.

Here are some valuable keys to understanding each other across the generations:

If you are a Veteran (1925-1944), and you are talking to other Veterans, you work together well in a structure where you each know your status. You should solicit ideas from each other to keep current, and use human relations skills to get along.

Talking to Boomers, you are warm and friendly. You ask questions and avoid telling them what to do. You should let them tell you how it's going, then ask permission to make suggestions about improvement.

Talking to Gen Xers, you recognize that independence is logical to them. You give them the end result needed, and hold them accountable. You should allow them freedom to complete it their way.

Talking to Millennials, you should realize that this is the generation actually most like your own, with a sense of civic duty, morality, and optimism. You can learn from their impressive technological skills and work together to get things done.

If you are a Boomer (1945-1964), and if you are talking to Veterans, you value their knowledge, wisdom, and experience. You should recognize that their need for structured hours and responsibilities demonstrates loyalty and commitment.

Talking to other Boomers; you work well as a team, respecting each other's opinions and needs, focusing on the needed results. You comfortably stand up for your beliefs.

Talking to Gen Xers, you capitalize on their ability to adapt quickly and independently. You should help them develop the people skills they need in order to grow.

Talking to Millennials, you should realize they work well as a team, just as you do. You should model the human relations skills you're good at as well as the value of being focused on others.

If you are a Gen Xer (1965-1981), and you are talking to Veterans, you should be patient with their learning curve when it comes to technology and offer them structure. You should show them support and give them an attitude of respect, especially if you must give them assignments.

Talking to Boomers, you should encourage them to read and learn more about technology, if that's your role in their lives. You should recognize that keeping long hours is often their way of contributing.

Talking to other Gen Xers, you can be direct and clear. You both value the need for freedom and independence. You can use your human relations skills to avoid misunderstandings.

Talking to Millennials, you should respect these younger workers' technological skills, using them to your advantage. You should capitalize on your common need to have fun and lead a balanced life.

If you are a Millennial (1980-2000), and if you are talking to Veterans, you realize that you are similar in attitude and outlook. You should respect their experience and learn the processes and procedures they have expertise in.

Talking to Boomers, you can learn from their sense of teamwork and capacity for collective decision-making. You can help them learn technology in an encouraging atmosphere.

Talking to Gen Xers, you should learn from their practicality and use their sense of self-reliance as a balancing factor and a compliment to the group dynamic.

Talking to other Millennials, you work together as a team and know how to pool resources to get things done. You'd do well to seek out mentors so you grow in new ways.

Breaking the Ice Gently

With each generation making an effort, it's less likely that differences in opinion will be automatically attributed to the age differences of the people involved. But communication skills don't happen overnight, and should be given time to develop. Experts recommend starting with a safe subject, using a conversational tool known as an ice breaker, building a dialogue from there till similarities are found and rapport is achieved. Deeper levels of involvement in each other's lives then will seem more natural.

When it comes to sharing the lives of others and trying to communicate across generation gaps, movie watching doesn't usually generate much thought-provoking discussion. But if the movie is chosen by a member of a generation seeking better understanding of another, it can be used as a forum for questions, answers, and interpretation. When a grandparent and grandchild watch Casablanca and Trainspotting together, for instance, there will undoubtedly be questions posed on both sides.

The Medium Says It All

Gaps in communication seem to be encouraged by the way media is developing over the years. Veterans, traditionalists, grew up listening to the radio, which encouraged them to use their imaginations. Families listened together and talked about what they were listening to.

Boomers grew up watching television, where verbal and non-verbal clues helped them interpret story lines.

Gen Xers grew up using the Internet, focusing exclusively on the written word and largely functioning in isolation, despite the illusion of virtual "communities," in some cases.

Millennials grew up with networks, with information accessible anytime, anywhere, and without any need for human interaction.

The result: four distinct communication styles, each one solidly sure it's perfectly understood by the other three. One element that each of them can agree on, however, is the need for giving and receiving sincere appreciation, praise, and recognition. Dale Carnegie's formula for success with this, whether we are praising accomplishments or character traits and strengths, suggests:

(1) Telling the recipient what you admire in him or her.

(2) Then following it up by explaining why you said that. What evidence do you have to support what you said? This gives your appreciation credibility and distinguishes it from flattery. "The reason I say that is...." Then perhaps ask a question to get them talking.

13

FIND GREAT SATISFACTION IN
HIRING OR BEING HIRED

*If you create an environment where the people truly
participate, you don't need control. They know what
needs to be done and they do it.*

Herb Kelleher
Co-founder, Southwest Airlines

If we were hiring, we'd do well to hire engaged employees
with these qualities. If we're employed, these are the
attributes we aim to have:

Engaged Employees:

- Have positive attitudes and spread positive energy
- Have high integrity

- Take pride in their work
- Demonstrate commitment and go the extra mile
- Are willing to accept responsibility
- Are self-confident and energetic
- Are self-starters, self-driven, self-disciplined, and show initiative
- Feel intellectually connected and personally satisfied
- Are creative, imaginative, and innovative
- Are team players and supportive of others
- Show interest and get involved
- Speak well about the organization

Dale Carnegie's Rules of Engagement at Work

Walk the talk. Be enthusiastic and fully engaged with your company, your job, and your employees. Get to know your staff and colleagues and take an interest in them as individuals. Learn what motivates them, what they want to achieve, and why this is important to them.

Earn trust, respect, and credibility by fulfilling promises, keeping confidences and commitments, and acting consistently, fairly, rationally, honestly, and ethically. Be authentic and approachable.

If you're hiring, *match the right person to the right job.* By learning your employees' strengths and work styles you can make the best use of their individual and unique talents and skills.

Play to strengths. Build on an individual's strengths rather than focusing on weaknesses. Without ignoring opportunities for performance improvement, focus more energy on what's being done right. Approach each employee as an individual having a distinctive and unique contribution. Demonstrate trust by delegating, empowering, and then letting go.

Instill a sense of purpose in your employees. Involve them in projects as fully as possible by communicating the big picture goal. Ensure they understand how the department contributes to the company's success, and how their individual roles impact the outcome. Everyone needs to know his or her efforts make a difference.

Set clear and realistic expectations and define expected outcomes. Maintain open lines of communication and "check in" with employees on a regular basis. Keep your staff consistently updated on the progress and status of projects. Ask for feedback from your staff on how projects are going and what you can do to make their job easier.

Ask, don't tell. Create buy-in from employees by collaborating with them on projects, department policies, ground rules, and so on. Encourage creativity, innovation, and decision-making input from staff. Implement their ideas to show that you value their opinion and trust their expertise.

Learn to listen empathically—with your eyes, ears, and heart. Listen without judgment in order to understand and connect with your employees.

Demonstrate strength and sensitivity. Communicate with diplomacy and tact, and learn to negotiate and compromise.

Equip, don't restrict. Discover what your employees need to learn in order to improve, grow, and succeed. Ensure that they have the time and resources they need to perform effectively and achieve their goals.

Foster an environment of respect, where outstanding work

is valued. Offer consistent and frequent feedback to employees, and recognize and reward efforts and accomplishments in ways that are meaningful to individuals.

Provide constant and sincere encouragement, and provide opportunities for growth and development. Provide mentoring, coaching, and training opportunities. Reward efforts, not just results.

Honor diversity. Promote healthy discussions, disagreements, and differences of opinion.

Promote and support rapport building among your staff to develop a compatible and cooperative team environment. Encourage employees to get to know each other better. Build communication opportunities in meetings, teambuilding activities, group lunches, and after-hour functions. Offer peer mentors, coaches, or someone they can connect with to help them stay engaged when challenges arise.

Encourage individuality in office space and environment. Allow employees to make their space their own with pictures, color, plants, inspirational items, trophies, etc.

"A," "B," and "C" Players

"A" Players

"A" players are ambitious, go-getters, have a desire to be promoted, and put their career first.

"A" players are charismatic, have high self-esteem, and will make waves when necessary.

"A" players tend to get caught up in the internal politics of an organization.

"A" players possess high-energy, are on the fast track and make the most demands of senior management.

"B" Players

"B" players are capable, steady performers who place great importance on the balance between work and life outside of work.

"B" players consistently produce good work and are dependable and reliable. They are self-sufficient.

"B" players ignore the gossip and politics and just get on with their work. They are a source of continuity.

"B" players are low maintenance, are seen as "grounders," and are often the go-to people because they have longevity with an organization and have been through all the changes and restructuring.

"C" Players

"C" players operate on cruise control, only working as hard as they have to.

"C" players do not strive to get better.

"C" players are not very proactive.

"C" players will do what is asked and nothing more.

Consider what types of tasks or jobs we might assign to each type from the chart. Which type are we? "A" Players provide challenges, "B" provides security, "C" provides structure.

Motivating Workforce Personalities

Tips for motivating the four common workplace personalities. Where do we fit in this list? Who would we prefer to work with?

A. Materialistic. These employees are often all work and no play. They typically live to work and are driven by job title, authority, and achievements. *Motivate them with bonuses, promotions, professional incentives, and so on.*

B. Sponge. These employees are usually driven by learning new things, challenges, new projects, brainstorming, innovating, and creating. *Motivate them with training opportunities and look for workshops, conferences, and seminars that they can attend.*

C. Connector. These people are typically driven by collaborating and socializing with others and working in teams. *Motivate these people with awards, photos, plaques, and public recognition for their roles in their teams.*

D. Work-Life Balancer. These people are typically driven by the freedom to pursue their personal hobbies as well as professional goals. They likely work to live, not live to work. *Motivate them with personal incentives such as time off, gift certificates to events or favorite restaurants, and so on.*

Think Money is the Only Workplace Motivator? Think Again

> *The number one reason people leave an organization isn't inadequate pay or benefits. It's the day-to-day relationship with their immediate superior.*

John Putzier, Business Writer

What makes employees tick? Some of the Dale Carnegie findings are surprising and enlightening. It seems that pay raises are not the only motivators, not by a long shot. Quality of life and a promising future are great motivators when it comes to job retention. Some of these findings might very well give us ideas about our own job advantages, ones we never thought of seeking out or requesting from our higher-ups.

- *A positive relationship with one's manager*

The Human Resource Development Organization reports that in a recent Gallup Poll of 400 companies, an employee's relationship with his or her direct boss is found to be more responsible for retention than pay or job perks. Fair and inspiring leadership, including coaching and mentoring, is what retains employees. Another Gallup Poll revealed that a key indicator of employee satisfaction and productivity is an employee's belief that the boss cares about the employee and can be trusted.

- *Recognition and appreciation*

Some people are driven more by other forms of incentives than by money. In a study by Employee Retention Headquarters, appreciation and involvement are cited more than money when it comes to what keeps employees happy. They need to be convinced, verbally and nonverbally, that management respects their position and that they are important to the success of their organization. They enjoy celebrating milestones and victories, publicly and privately, verbally and in writing, promptly and sincerely.

- *Stimulating and fulfilling work*

An American Society for Training and Development newsletter suggests that, for most workers today, stimulating and valuable work is more important than salary and advancement. It's hard to put a price tag on enthusiasm and excitement for a job. Managers who foster employee involvement, and include them early on in projects, obtain more creative ideas and create greater employee investment and pride in the outcome. Employees who actively participate in decision-making on a broad spectrum of issues help create an environment that they like and one in which they want to remain.

- *A clear career path and growth opportunities*

By providing opportunities for growth, both personally and professionally, employees are less likely to look elsewhere. Providing training opportunities with respect to new skill development and career development is an indication that a manager is willing to invest on behalf of the employee. This is the key to employee retention. Encouraging employees to join professional organizations by paying their membership fees and giving employees the time off and admission fees needed to attend lunches and conferences motivates employees. Companies who have a high retention rate hold a reputation for hiring from within. A jointly agreed upon career path (not necessarily "up" the hierarchy) will gain the commitment of employees and buy-in of organizational goals and direction.

- *Managers who respect a balanced life*

Organizations who walk the talk of the balanced life concept have higher retention than those who believe that the employee should eat, breathe, and sleep work. Acknowledging and respecting the importance of family and personal life prevents burnout and fosters loyalty. According to the Human Resource Development Organization, employers need to be aware of work-life quality issues. They must be willing to offer flexible schedules and be sensitive to dual career, childcare, and parent care challenges.

- *Competitive compensation and benefits*

Money is important, but it is less important than we might think. Employees expect to be paid fairly and competitively. They feel entitled to the standard benefits of health insurance and retirement plans. In a survey of food companies, 92% of respondents indicated that a $10,000 annual salary increase would not prompt them to change employers if they were receiving personal and professional development coaching.

> *A worker's desire to do a good job is priceless. It is one of the core components of a successful business. A company's steadfast willingness to value and appreciate will pay dividends by creating an upbeat workplace, better two-way communication, higher productivity, better customer service and loyalty, and ultimately a flourishing business.*

> Noelle Nelson,
> Author and Employee Recognition Expert

14

FOR A LIFE THAT'S GREAT,
DELEGATE!

*The single greatest cause for failure in managers is their
inability to delegate.*

J C Penney

Whether we're talking about scout troop leadership, a major corporate committee or organizing a church tag sale, delegating is the answer to burnout and a prescription for progress. Delegation not only helps us, but it develops and trains others. However, it is important to follow up and communicate clear performance standards when delegating.

Here are some questions to answer that will make it clear whether we need to delegate or not.

- Do you take work home?

- Do you still handle jobs you had before your last promotion?
- Are you interrupted for advice and information on a frequent basis?
- Do you work out details others could handle?
- Do you notice that you keep your hands on too many projects?
- Do you work longer hours than others?
- Do you spend time doing tasks for others that they could do themselves?
- Do you find you're "in" basket full when you return after a few days?
- Do you find yourself becoming involved in projects you thought you had given to someone else?

The Six "D's" of Productivity

Dale Carnegie training points out that there are six ways of dealing with work overload, and some are better than others. Dumping and dropping are the least recommended, doing and distributing carry an "average" rating, while delegating and deputizing are by far the most effective.

Don't Delegate Lightly

The decision to delegate should be made with these steps in mind:

Step #1: *Identify the right person or opportunity.*

What project or task could be delegated—not dumped—to someone on my team? Where is there an opportunity to build people? Identify who is ready for a growth step.

Step #2: *Meet with the right person for the job.*

Have a meeting with the one who is already prepared for the right opportunity. Go over the facts about the delegation.

Step #3: *Sell the need or opportunity. Be sure it's seen as win-win.*

In your meeting, sell the benefits of accepting the delegation. If there are no benefits to that person, then you are probably dumping and not delegating. Find a way to make the assignment win-win for both. Be attentive to their workload and be prepared to help *them* delegate some of their work to someone else, if possible.

Step #4: *Review and create an action plan with the person.*

After the delegation has been accepted, give the person time to think about the results and how he or she will achieve them. Work together on an action plan describing what is to be done, and how. Or guide the person to create such a plan.

Step #5: *Coach and train.*

Show your delegate how to do things that may be unfamiliar. Coach him or her through the process the first time, to insure things are done right. It may take a little more time the first time, but after you have begun to free yourself up from this job, task or project, you can begin to use your new found time more productively.

Step #6: *Turn it loose—let it go.*

Make sure the other person is empowered to do the job. When the time is right, turn the job loose, to the level you both are comfortable with, in order to achieve the results. Resist the urge to micro-manage, but, on the other hand, don't abdicate all control. Find a balance that works for you both and that empowers the other to get things done in his or her own style, but with a degree of measurability and accountability built in.

Step #7: *Reward! Celebrate Successes.*

Recognize big and small moves in the right direction, proportionally. Give praise informally in the form of pats on the back as well as formally in the appropriate manner.

You Haven't Successfully Delegated If:

You buy it back...

New accountability comes hand in hand with delegation, and along with that comes the temptation to buy the assignment back or to put it in limbo. It's the language we use that will give us clues as to whether or not the delegation is complete.

We are buying it back if we are saying,

"Let me think about . . ."

"I'll let you know when . . ."

"Leave it here, I'll . . ."

"I'll check with . . ."

"I'll make a draft of . . ."

"After I finish . . ."

With phrasing like this, the delegation is negated. The assignment remains with you, no matter what else has been said. There will be no progress until you rectify it.

Or you put it in limbo...

Phrases such as this point to that problem:

"Send me a memo and . . ."

"Why don't you check with . . ."

"Draft a proposal and . . ."

"See me later about . . ."

"Let me know if I can help . . ."

"We'll have to do something . . ."

You'll know the delegation deal is done if you're saying . . .

"I know you can do . . ."

"I'm counting on you to . . ."

"I gave it to you because . . ."

"What are you going to do . . ."

"What's your plan for . . ."

"I know you'll get it done . . ."

With phrases like these, it's clear that the accountability has been shifted. The delegation is complete, and progress is much more likely.

15

DEALING WITH DIFFICULT
PEOPLE CAN HAVE GREAT
RESULTS

Many of us seek to avoid difficult people because
confronting the person or situation can be exhausting
and emotionally draining. Yet avoiding these people
or situations can have a worse result. It can lead to unresolved
conflicts and miscommunications, which waste enormous
amounts of time and energy, can destroy our morale, and
impact our productivity and peace.

> *To be agreeable, all that is necessary is to take an*
> *interest in other persons and in other things, to recognize*
> *that other people as a rule are much like one self, and*
> *thankfully to admit that diversity is a glorious feature*
> *of life.*

> Frank Swinnerton

At the heart of the Dale Carnegie Training is the belief that in any situation or relationship, the only thing we can control is ourselves. It is important to recognize that our perceptions, biases, attitudes, behaviors, feelings, and communication style can either help or hinder the situation.

A List of Things Under Our Control

It might be a good idea to review the list of actions Dale Carnegie suggests we take as we seek to manage difficult people, gain cooperation, and reduce conflict. We can rank these from one to ten, with one being what we do best and ten being the action that has the most opportunity for improvement.

- Give others the benefit of the doubt
- Know our "hot" buttons
- Avoid getting defensive or taking things personally
- Listen to understand and tune in to body language
- Keep a positive attitude
- Try to see things from the other person's point of view
- Negotiate and compromise when appropriate
- Avoid making assumptions
- Learn to give and accept constructive feedback

What is your biggest opportunity for improvement here?

The most immutable barrier in nature is between one man's thoughts and another's.

William James

Dealing with Different Kinds of Difficult People

Unless they are family, we can often side step the most difficult people in our lives—except at work. Though they can't be avoided when they're in the next cubicle, they can be dealt with. Here are some types of difficult people and what to expect from them:

There are the *nay-sayers*. These people are habitually negative and have a pessimistic view of the world. Also known as grouches, they may come across as angry, arrogant, depressed, and frustrated. They might criticize others and complain often. The nay-sayers say: "That will never work," "You've got to be kidding," "Want to bet?"

The *immovables,* also known as bullies, are people who resist change, either outwardly by being combative, or in a passive-aggressive way. They might seem to agree to change, but sabotage the implementation of it. They say, "We tried that already," or, in a work situation, "Management doesn't know what it's like."

Nine-to-fivers work nine to five, nothing more, and nothing less. They are quick to tell you that something is not their job. They do the minimum to get by and get a paycheck. They say "That is not my job," "I don' have time to do that," and "It's time to go home."

Gossipers find joy in getting into everyone's business and creating diversions by spreading rumors. People who say one thing to our face and another thing behind our back fall into this category. Their pettiness may be a sign that they are lonely, and work is one of their only sources of interaction.

Violinists have a general "woe is me" attitude. They may stay late or do extra work, but then complain about the workload.

They are constantly whining about how busy they are and how other things take priority over what we need them to focus on. They might say, "I get all the hard jobs." "I was here until nine last night, trying to straighten this mess out." "I don't know when I'll get to this; I have three projects on my plate."

Blamers are quick to point the finger at anyone but himself or herself when mistakes have been made. These people always have an answer as to why they are not accountable for the error. They may also be experts at making excuses and procrastinating. They might say "I got those numbers from someone else." "I was told that this was not a high priority."

Twelve Tips for Negotiating and Compromising with Difficult People

Negotiating is the process of attempting to agree on a solution. Compromising, or settling on a mutually agreeable solution, is the result of successful negotiations. Compromise is all about being flexible. It means being able to generate alternate solutions when we've "hit the wall." Whether it involves a person we can't get along with, an idea we know will work but others are reluctant to adopt, a change in systems at work or home, or a turf war that needs ending, learning to negotiate and compromise is essential to our success.

Here are Dale Carnegie's suggestions:

1. *Have a positive attitude*. Our attitude is essential to the outcome. We have a much better chance of coming to mutual gains if we approach the negotiation as an opportunity to learn and achieve a win-win outcome.

2. *Meet on mutual ground*. Find a mutually agreeable and convenient physical space to meet that is comfortable to

everyone involved. Agree on when to meet and how much time is available to devote to the process. Whenever possible, deal with negotiations face-to-face and be careful about using the phone and e-mail, since the absence of facial expressions, vocal intonation, and other cues can result in a negotiation breakdown.

3. *Clearly define and agree on the issue.* Agree on a statement of the issue, using simple and factual terms. If the situation is multifaceted, search for ways to slice the large issue into smaller pieces and deal with one issue at a time.

4. *Do your homework.* Take time to plan. You must not only know what is at stake for ourselves, but you need to know the other side's concerns and motivations. Take into consideration any history or past situations that might affect the negotiations. Know the must-haves (nonnegotiable items) and nice-to-haves (negotiable items). Determine what would constitute the best resolution, a fair, reasonable, and a minimally acceptable deal.

5. *Take an honest inventory of yourself.* Determine your level of trust in the other person and the process. Be conscious of aspects of your personality that can help or hinder the process.

6. *Look for shared interests.* Get on the same side by finding and establishing similarities. Since conflict tends to magnify perceived differences and minimize similarities, look for common goals, objectives, or even gripes that can illustrate that you are in this together. Focus on the future, talk about what is to be done, and tackle the problem jointly.

7. *Deal with facts, not emotions.* Address problems, not personalities. Avoid any tendency to attack the other person or to pass judgment on his or her ideas and opinions. Avoid focusing on the past or blaming the other person. Maintain a

rational, goal-oriented frame of mind. This will depersonalize the conflict, separate the issues from the person involved, and avoid defensiveness.

8. *Be honest*. Don't play games. Be honest and clear about what is important to you. Equally important is to be clear and communicate why your goals, issues, and objectives mean so much to you.

9. *Present alternatives and provide evidences*. Create options and alternatives that demonstrate willingness to compromise. Consider conceding in areas that might have high value to the other person but are not that important to you. Frame options in terms of the other person's interests and provide evidence for your point of view.

10. *Be an expert communicator*. Nothing shows determination to find a mutually satisfactory resolution to conflict more than applying excellent communication skills. Ask questions, listen, rephrase what you have heard to check for understanding, and take a genuine interest in the other side's concerns. Reduce tension through humor, let the other "vent," and acknowledge their views. Focus less on your position and more on ways in which you can move toward a resolution or compromise.

11. *End on a good note*. Make a win-win proposal and check to make sure that everyone involved leaves the situation feeling they have "won." Shake hands, agree on the action steps, who is responsible for each step, how success will be measured, and how and when the decision will be evaluated. Be open to reaching an impasse for non-critical issues—agree to disagree.

12. *Enjoy the process*. Look at the benefits of learning from other people's point of view. People report that after overcoming

conflict and reaching an agreement, the relationship grew even stronger. Reflect and learn from each negotiation. Determine the criteria to evaluate the process and the solution.

Other Dale Carnegie suggestions for dealing with difficult people are:

Show genuine concern or interest. Respect people's privacy. Ask questions. Remember that people's perspectives are influenced by life experiences. Take some risks. Be honest and transparent. Listen without judgment. Recognize that you have your own "baggage" as well.

Things to avoid: prying, making assumptions, taking things personally, and "fixing their problem."

16

EVERY CONFLICT CAN HAVE A
GREAT RESOLUTION

When the elder John D. Rockefeller was setting up the Standard Oil Company, he said, "The ability to deal with people is as purchasable a commodity as sugar or coffee, and I will pay more for that ability than for any other under the sun."

The ability to deal with people is even more important today with the pressures of our fast-paced environments. Being able to handle conflict in a productive way is frequently mentioned as one of the most challenging skills for anyone to acquire. Day- to-day conflicts can undermine the best of plans and projects and the most well intentioned team of people or family.

A New Look At Conflict

Dale Carnegie points out that conflict, which we often

greet with trepidation at home, is actually a normal part of business activity. Few operations are perfect, and mistakes occur that need to be resolved. The result is what could be seen as conflict.

Conflicts actually provide good opportunities to demonstrate flexibility and charisma. There is an emotional side to conflicts, which needs to be addressed with an emphasis equal to that placed upon resolving the actual situation.

The positive side: as in nearly all relationships, when we work through issues and look at conflict as a growing experience, the relationship can grow even stronger.

Don't be afraid of opposition. Remember, a kite rises against, not with, the wind.

Hamilton Wright Mabie

Score Yourself on Your Conflict Reactions

Record your reaction to the following statements. Read each item carefully and place a number from the answer scale next to each statement.

1–Seldom
2–Sometimes
3–Most of the time

1. _____I can be swayed to someone else's point of view.
2. _____I shut down people who I disagree with.
3. _____I address the issue at hand diplomatically and do not attack the individual.
4. _____I think that others try to "bully" their way with me.

5. _____I express my thoughts and beliefs tactfully when they differ from those just expressed.

6. _____Rather than offer my opinion when I disagree with someone, I keep it to myself.

7. _____I listen to other people's point of view with an open mind.

8. _____I let my emotions get the best of me.

9. _____I raise my voice to make my point.

10. _____I tend to belittle other people when making my point.

11. _____I look for ways to negotiate and compromise with others.

12. _____I have been told I am too pushy.

13. _____I make sure I have my opinion heard in any controversy.

14. _____I think conflict in meetings is necessary.

15. _____I am the most vocal in meetings when trying to get my point across.

Scoring:

Add the total score from questions 1, 2, 4, 6, 8, 9, 10, 12, 13, 14, 15,_____

Subtract the sum of the score from questions 3, 5, 7, 11,_____

Total:

What Does Your Score Mean?

1–4: "Passive"—You may be such a pushover that you allow difficult people to walk all over you. You will benefit from learning to stand up for your ideas and opinions in a diplomatic and tactful way.

5–10: "Assertive"—You are professionally assertive when dealing with people, particularly difficult people. Continue to be open to listening to different points of view, and express your ideas and opinions appropriately.

11 and higher: "Aggressive"—You may be so combative that people might avoid interacting with you. You will benefit from learning to listen and express your opinions more effectively.

Ideas for Handling Interpersonal Conflicts

- Ask yourself, "How much do my personal biases and prejudices affect this relationship?"
- Write down three behaviors that you could change in order to reduce the conflict in this relationship. Commit to following through on these changes for at least three months.
- Ask the other person involved how you could defuse the existing conflict. Encourage feedback that might seem brutally honest.
- Put yourself in their position. How do you think they view your commitment to reducing conflict in your relationship? Why?
- Make a list of five strengths that you see in the other person. Then list five ways that improving this relationship would benefit you.

Ideas for Handling Conflicts About Direction

- Ask yourself, "Am I clear on the direction or vision?"
- Clarify the discrepancy so that it can be easily described in neutral words, and take action.

- Ask permission to address the discrepancy with the other person in a friendly, non-confrontational way, so that you can gain agreement.
- Use "I" and "we" messages rather than "you" messages.
- If there is a difference in values, always go with the higher value.
- Make authentic commitments.

17

KEEPING COOL IN THE MIDDLE
OF CONFLICT IS A GREAT FEAT

Strong emotions, such as anger and distrust, are both a cause and a result of a conflict. These emotions often conceal the issues in dispute. The emotions are real, though, and must be addressed for the conflict to be resolved comfortably for everyone involved.

There is a cycle that most conflicts follow. It starts with an event we interpret in such a way that it leads to conflict, and is followed by a series of emotional, physical, and attitudinal responses. It can be clear when others are caught up in this cycle, but typically is harder to see when we are.

The cycle begins with an event that launches the potential conflict. It could be a relatively insignificant encounter or something that turned into a big issue.

Any event can trigger conflict:
- Something that was said or overheard
- News or gossip
- An interaction with another person
- A work crisis

Interpretation

We apply our own interpretation to the event. Our experiences, insecurities, prejudices, and attitudes toward the event and the person are all factors that influence our interpretation, both consciously and subconsciously. Our interpretation of the event is critical to the subsequent responses we experience in the cycle:
- I think that person just insulted me.
- I don't think they meant anything by that.
- That news is totally wrong.
- I need to find out more about what I heard.
- That person was really rude to me.
- That person is having a bad day.

Emotional Response

Our interpretation of the event triggers an emotional response. Many times the other person is unaware of the emotion that has been triggered in us.

Depending on our interpretation, our emotional response could be:
- Anger, resentment, hurt
- Calm, centered, unperturbed
- Our emotional response could be anywhere in-between

Physical Response

Medical experts have long studied the connection between our emotions and our physical well being. It is widely accepted that emotional issues often trigger physical health issues. During periods of conflict, it is not unusual to experience:

- Sleeplessness
- Nervousness
- Irritability
- Headaches
- Stomach Aches

Attitudinal Response

When we go through conflict situations, our attitude inevitably changes toward those involved. If the relationship was friendly and warm prior to the conflict, our attitude might noticeably change to being more guarded and cool. At its worst, our attitude could become hostile toward the other person after the conflict situation has passed.

If the conflict is resolved to everyone's satisfaction, we might have a more respectful and open attitude toward the other person than we had before.

Effect

As we respond to the other with a changed attitude, it has a long-term effect on our relationship. The next time we find ourselves in a conflict situation involving this person, we are either in a better or worse position to resolve it successfully, depending on the attitudes that have prevailed between us since our last encounter.

The Risk of Anger

The interpretation of the conflict situation leads to the emotional response. One common emotional reaction in a conflict situation is anger. People are often under pressure to make important decisions in a short period of time. Under such circumstances, people may get angry and act in overly confrontational ways, which they later regret.

We run a serious risk if we allow ourselves to spontaneously give in to feelings of anger, without carefully processing them first.

Anger disrupts conflict situations by:

- Damaging trust
- Impairing judgment
- Leading us to diminish concern for the other person's preference
- Pushing us to neglecting our own goals

Processing Anger

Anger management experts say that anger is often the emotion that is expressed when the individual doesn't want to or doesn't know how to express true emotions. These emotions often obscure the issues in dispute. In other words, anger is often expressed to cover up feelings of:

- Hurt
- Humiliation
- Shame
- Distrust
- Disappointment
- Frustration
- Confusion
- Worry
- Fear
- Embarrassment

Anger, if not restrained, is frequently more hurtful to us than the injury that provokes it.

Seneca

Destructive Emotional Expressions

Blame

All of us have participated in a conflict situation where the people involved spent more time trying to pin blame than to solve the problem. Blaming others is clearly a way used by individuals and groups to defer blame from themselves. It rarely, if ever, leads to a solution of the issue at hand.

Attacking the other person

Like blaming, attacking is a defense mechanism used to deflect responsibility for the outcome of the conflict. If the conflict is entirely the other person's fault, then we don't have to be responsible for changing ourselves in order to resolve it. Attacking the other person tends to provoke defensive retaliation, destructive escalation, or withdrawal on the other person's part.

If we repress it

Trying to suppress these emotions seems like a useful strategy, until they eventually come out. Some people are generally socialized to conceal or repress their anger. Many of us have had the experience of a colleague or customer bursting out in a fit of unexpected anger. Our normal reaction in those situations is to think that the other person has something seriously wrong with them.

Keys to Healthy Emotional Expressions

- *Attempt to name the emotion accurately*

If angry emotions surface, stop and think about the real emotion that you are experiencing. Then, instead of calling it anger, call it what it is.

- *Be non-judgmental*

Healthy expressions address the issue or the frustration, but do not judge or condemn the other person.

- *Express in a direct, straightforward manner*

No games, no hiding, no manipulation. Healthy emotions are communicated honestly and directly. Consider using a metaphor to describe the emotion to help the other person understand.

- *Don't blame or attack the other*

There is no reason to make your anger an attack on the other person. Use "I" messages ("I feel this way about it...") to make sure you don't start attacking or blaming.

- *Convey the truth that others do not cause your feelings*

Other people's behavior can affect our feelings, but the other person doesn't cause our feelings. If you find yourself wanting to say, "You make me feel angry," stop and think about what is really making you feel angry or upset.

Dialogue: Talk Through the Issue

Stop and Cool Off

There's little point in trying to talk through the issue when both people are upset. Give it a little time. Let tempers cool down. Focus on something or someone else for a period of time. Come together when each party has achieved some sort of equilibrium.

Talk and Listen to Each Other

Don't hide from the other person or give the silent treatment. Keep talking. Express yourself honestly and openly. Use metaphors to describe your emotional and physical reactions. And, above all, listen to what the other party has to say without filtering or judging their message.

Find Out What You Both Need

These dialogues too often focus on complaints, rather than developing ongoing solutions. Determine what each party must have from the situation and strive for a solution where everyone's needs are met.

Brainstorm Solutions

Each party to the conflict has a vision of an ideal outcome for themselves. The challenge is to avoid forcing your solutions on the conflict situation, and instead allow solutions to emerge out of creative thinking on everyone's part.

Choose the Idea You Both Can Live with

In most conflicts, a compromise is more likely than the other party completely agreeing with our solution, or us completely agreeing with theirs. One of the ways to break out of a negative conflict cycle with the other person is to find solutions that you both feel are fair under the circumstances.

Create a plan and implement it

To make sure that the conflict does not re-emerge, make a new blueprint. Plan for ways of working together that will keep misunderstandings and emotional outbursts to a minimum. Most important, agree on it together and move on it at once, without hesitation.

Sample Conflict Dialogue

Setting Up the Dialogue

- "I'd like to get together and talk through the issue."
- "When would be a good time for you?"

Getting Started

- Greet the person and thank him or her for meeting with you.
- "What I thought we could do, if it is okay with you, is talk through the issue. Is that okay?"

Dialoguing

- "Why don't we both tell each other our interpretation of this event? Would you like to go first or should I?"
- Listen attentively to the other person. Don't explain, interrupt, or justify.
- "So what I hear you saying is . . . ." (Recap what you heard)

- "What do you feel you personally need from this situation?"
- Describe your interpretation in straightforward terms and use a metaphor to describe your emotional and physical response.
- "What would be important for me is . . ."
- "So, if we can find a way to get what we both need, we may be able to move past this conflict?"

Brainstorming Solutions

- "Let's talk about some possible solutions. What are some of the ideas you have been thinking about?"
- "Here are some of mine . . ."

Finding a Solution

- "It looks like we both agree on . . ."
- "Are there any other issues?"
- "How do you think we can work this out?"

Creating a Plan

- "What should be our plan for moving forward?"
- "How will we follow up with others?"
- "Is there anyone else who needs to know about our plan?"

Appreciation

- Thank the person for meeting.
- Tell what you admire about him or her in a sincere way.
- Back up your thought with specific evidence from this meeting.
- Make a commitment to move forward with the plan and shake hands.

18

CONTROLLED EMOTIONS
GREATLY SERVE US

Some of us are far better at getting a job done, and some are far easier to work with than others. The defining factor is Emotional Intelligence (EI). Emotional Intelligence means being aware of our own emotions, understanding them, and managing them (in ourselves and others) to bring about positive results. EQ (Emotional Intelligence Quotient) is the measurement of Emotional Intelligence.

Research shows that in business positive energy and emotional control results in high productivity, smart decisions, high retention rates, good morale, and strong teamwork; and the results would be the same in a family instead of an office. Studies have shown that raising the overall EQ in any group positively affects the bottom line. The good news is that, whereas our IQ is set in early adulthood, EQ can be developed over our lifespan.

Sometimes it's not that easy to understand the connection between what we think, how we feel, and how we behave. That's why it's very helpful to discover our current emotional fitness level, explore how our emotions and "hot buttons" that affect our performance, and apply tips for maintaining positive energy and controlling emotions in difficult situations.

Emotional Intelligence Competence

Daniel Goleman, author of *Emotional Intelligence* and *Working with Emotional Intelligence*, defines EI as: "The capacity for recognizing our own feelings and those of others, for motivating ourselves, and for managing emotions well in ourselves and in our relationships."

Mike Poskey, vice president of ZERORISK HR, Inc., a Dallas-based human resources risk management firm, identified five competencies that contribute to success in the workplace. The first two deal with how we manage relationships. The last three with how we manage ourselves.

1. Intuition and Empathy: Our awareness of others, feelings, needs, and challenges. This competency is important in the workplace because it:

- Helps us understand others' feelings and perspectives and sense what others need in order to grow, develop, and master their strengths
- Improves our customer service by allowing us to anticipate, recognize, and meet the needs of customers
- Improves our ability to be sensitive to others and to leverage a diverse workplace

2. Social Skills and Political Correctness: Our skill at gaining desirable responses in others. This competency is important in the workplace because it:

- Helps us communicate effectively; influence and persuade others by sending clear and convincing messages
- Improves our leadership skills, teamwork, and the ability to manage change, negotiate, resolve conflicts, gain consensus, and collaboration

3. *Self-awareness:* Knowing and understanding one's preferences, resources, and intuitions. This competency is important in the workplace because it:

- Improves our ability to recognize our own emotions and their effects and impact on those around us
- Helps us assess, understand, and accept our strengths and limitations
- Increases our self-confidence and self-esteem

4. *Self-Management:* Managing one's internal states, emotions, and resources. This competency is important in the workplace because it:

- Improves our self-control by managing negative emotions
- Increases our ability to gain trust and to be held accountable
- Improves our flexibility and comfort with change, new ideas, and new information

5. *Self-expectations and Motivation:* Emotional tendencies that guide or facilitate reaching goals. This competency is important in the workplace because it:

- Helps us conscientiously strive and commit to achieving our self-imposed standard of excellence
- Increases our ability to motivate ourselves and others and to be optimistic when faced with obstacles
- Improves our ability to take initiative by being a self-starter and self-driven

Used with permission from ZERORISK HR

More About the Emotional Intelligence Quotient

The four pillars of EQ are:

1. Self-awareness
2. Self-management
3. Social awareness
4. Relationship management

Interesting Research and Facts About EQ

- We can learn to be more emotionally aware and mature in managing emotions.
- Women and men score the same on self-awareness, but women score higher on relationship management.
- Within each profession, the best performers have the highest EQs.
- High EI and EQ are directly related to high productivity.
- Research indicates a connection between high EI and health. If you are in touch with your emotions and know how to deal with them properly, you are less prone to stress, which can cause illness. People who have mastered their emotions are much better off when something extreme happens in their lives.

I'm trying to never get mad at outside influences—the gallery, a bad bounce, or the weather. I'm pointing the finger at myself. If some problem or anxiety is bothering me, I try to bring it out, dissect it logically and deal with it. That's why I'm playing better. I'm more comfortable with myself. I'm more me.

Hale Irwin, Professional Golfer

Surprising Reasons Why Improving Emotional Intelligence in Business Pays Off

- The Hay Group states one study of forty-four Fortune 500 companies that found salespeople with high EQ produced *twice the revenue* of those with average or below average scores.
- In another study, technical programmers demonstrating the top ten percent of emotional intelligence competency were developing software *three times* faster than those with lower competency.
- One recent study conducted by a Dallas corporation found that the productivity difference between its low-scoring emotional intelligence employees and its high-scoring emotional intelligence employees was *twenty times*.
- Another study in the construction industry yielded results showing workers with low emotional intelligence had a higher likelihood of *getting injured* while on the job.

A fool gives full vent to his anger, but a wise man keeps himself under control.

Proverbs 29:11

Dale Carnegie's Tips for Controlling Emotions

- Identify the emotion and what caused you to feel that way.
- Communicate what you are feeling in a calm manner.
- Do not allow your emotions to fester.
- Keep a journal.
- Face trouble by asking, "What is the worst that can happen?" Accept the worst, and try to improve the situation.
- When an emotional situation arises, ask yourself:
  —What is the emotion?
  —What are the causes of the emotion?
  —What are the possible reactions?
  —What is the wisest reaction?
- Don't hold grudges or waste time trying to get even.
- Refrain from indulging in mood swings. Act consistently under a variety of circumstances in order to build trust.
- Eliminate stress by getting your house in order—do not let things pile up.
- Keep busy.
- Pick your battles—keep things in proper perspective and don't fuss about trifles.
- Cooperate with the inevitable—don't worry about the past, and instead, focus on the future.
- Count your blessings.
- Stay healthy by eating right, exercising, and getting enough sleep.
- Find moments of comic relief, and laugh often.
- Give to others.
- Socialize with positive people.
- Pamper—but don't indulge—yourself.

Six Steps to Maintaining One's Cool

- *Get cerebral.* Get a grasp on your thoughts and emotions and draft a note or email saying what's on your minds. Don't send it.
- *Ask for input.* Run the situation by someone impartial and ask for an honest point of view.
- *Get physical.* Get out of Dodge. Take a walk or partake of some physical activity.
- *Reflect.* Look at the situation from another point of view and think about how we may have contributed.
- *Sleep on it.* Review your notes or email in the morning, and decide if the situation is worth the energy or if it is something to let go.
- *Pick your battles.* Either let it go or confront the situation.

When dealing with people, remember you are not dealing with creatures of logic, but creatures of emotion.

Dale Carnegie

19

MULTI-TASKING CAN BE GREAT—
WHEN IT WORKS

With technology changing at lightning speed, increasing daily workloads, and demands coming from multiple sources, increased productivity is the order of the day. As a result, multi-tasking has become a necessity to succeed in business. In fact, for most of us, multi-tasking has become second nature. But are we doing it right?

In the evening, I'll have my PC running, and IM boxes pop up while I'm cooking dinner. It's an easy way for me to answer questions and field requests in between all of the other things that have to be done.

Anne Altman,
Managing Director, IBM

Four Myths About Multi-Tasking

We can actually do more than one thing at a time.

According to research by neurologists, when we are doing two things simultaneously, the brain processes things in a strict linear sequence. Hal Pashler, professor of psychology at the UCSD, conducted an experiment in which he tested the brain's ability to respond to two different sounds in quick succession. He found that the brain stalls fractionally before responding to the second stimulus. The second sound is heard, but it requires time, if only milliseconds, to organize a response. In addition, research has shown that the habit of students who try to learn or study while listening to music adversely affects learning.

Women are better at multitasking than men.

This myth began with a consideration of homemakers and gender. Since women were more often the homemakers, they were presumed to be better at multi-tasking or task switching. This assumption has been carried to the work environment, however. The truth is, the ability to toggle from task to task is not necessarily a skill that comes easily to women. The skill is not gender specific. Some do it frequently and naturally. Others do it when necessary.

Multi-tasking leads to burnout.

More likely the number of hours spent working, the pace with which we work, and leisure-work balance plays more of a role in burnout than multi-tasking or alternating between a variety of tasks.

People are born multi-taskers.

The ability to multi-task, or switch back and forth from various tasks and activities may come more naturally to some people than others. However, much has to do with the job we hold, the amount and kind of responsibilities delegated to us, the number of hours available to do the job, and the quality of work we are expected to deliver.

> *When you really study precisely what people's brains are doing at any moment, there's less concurrent processing than you might think. The brain is more of a time-share operation. When fractions of a second matter, we're better off not doing another task.*

Hal Pashler
Professor of Psychology at the University of
California at San Diego

Excessive Multi-Tasking	Effective Multi-Tasking	Excessive Compartmentalizing
Tends to "wing it" without a plan, goals, schedule, or priorities	Tends to plan ahead and stay disciplined to priorities, staying on task, and achieving goals	Tends to over plan and be too structured
Tends to bite off more than they can chew and have hands in everything	Tends to take on only what they know they can accomplish	Tends to underestimate the amount of work they can accomplish

Things may fall through the cracks, and the quality of work can suffer	Has a system in place to keep track of unfinished business and delivers high quality and timely work	Tends to be overly detail-oriented, meticulous, and a perfectionist
Enjoys being in control and has a difficult time asking for help, delegating, empowering, and letting go	Tends to ask for help, delegate, empower, and let go when necessary	Tends to think they are the only one who can do the task at hand
Tends to be too flexible and says "yes" to everything	Tends to exercise good judgment, make good decisions, and remain flexible when the need arises	Tends to be inflexible and avoids taking on additional tasks in order to guarantee meeting
Often appears disorganized and chaotic	Tends to be organized and make good use of time	Appears highly organized and dislikes unscheduled interruptions
Tends to have a short attention span, is preoccupied, and is unable to focus or concentrate	Tends to focus or concentrate on the task at hand	Tends to get in the zone and focus or concentrate to the disregard of others
May lose sight of the big picture	Remains calm and keeps the big picture at the forefront	Tends to neglect everything else but the big picture
Tends to focus on quantity versus quality of work	Tends to regard quantity and quality of work with equal importance	Tends to place more emphasis on quality of work than quantity

Fifteen Principles for Successful Multi-Tasking

1	**Different strokes for different folks**. There is no right way to multi-task. Play to your strengths and pick the tactic that is best for you. Some people need to block time and work without distractions; others thrive on interruptions and are more efficient when dealing with them in real time.
2	**Get organized and stay organized, both physically and mentally**. The more organized we feel, the better we are able to focus and concentrate on the task before us. Get rid of clutter and clear your desk of anything not pertinent to your goals for the day.
3	**Think ahead**. Plan each day, use a calendar or planner to create a schedule, and publicize your availability. Use timers or alarms to adhere to a schedule as much as possible. Include a daily variety of activities; prevent boredom and seeking interruptions and diversions.
4	**First prioritize goals, then compartmentalize**. Discriminate by using prime time for prime activities. Block time for urgent tasks and use after hours for less urgent activities. Alternate between time consuming and smaller projects to gain a sense of accomplishment. Break down large projects into stages by identifying good stopping points to task-switching. Remain vigilant and disciplined to your goals and priorities.

5	**Be honest with yourself**. Know your limits—when you can and can not task-switch. Give your undivided attention to critical tasks that require full concentration. Have a separate space designated to work on high priority projects, and step away from the phone and computer.
6	**Don't over commit.** Stay in control of your day and learn to say no, diplomatically and tactfully. Use call forwarding and disable the new mail alert on your computer when working on critical projects that demand your full concentration.
7	**Keep a positive attitude and remain flexible.** Expect the unexpected, stay calm, and exercise patience when things pop up. Rely on your past experiences to deal with the unexpected. If it cannot be put on your schedule to deal with later, take note of where you left off, resolve the situation, and return to what you were doing.
8	**Use breaks and interruptions to your benefit.** Step back, gain perspective, think creatively, and review and reward the progress you have made.
9	**Be creative to maximize efficiency.** Know when you personally can save time by bundling activities. Optimize your time and maximize productivity by making the most of free times and delays, and by pairing automatic or routine tasks.

10	**Don't waste your brain power.** Understand all the capabilities of the technology you use, and use them. Simplify your life and automate tasks as much as possible (i.e. phone speed dial, keyboard shortcuts, etc.). Keep frequently used resources at your fingertips. Invest in time-saving devices at the office and at home.
11	**Remember your human relations skills and make people your first priority.** Be courteous and show respect by giving individuals your undivided attention. The most important thing to know about technology is when to shut it off.
12	**Practice.** Switching tasks requires resetting our brain each time. If you practice, it can become more automatic and less stressful.
13	**Get over yourself.** Learn to ask for help, delegate, empower, and let go of tasks that don't have to be done by you. Keep the lines of communication open and be sure that colleagues and team members are in the loop so they are better able to lighten your load.
14	**Stay healthy.** Let your mind re-boot, slow down, and take a breather to be more efficient and accomplish more in less time. You can channel your energy more effectively when you eat well, stay hydrated, and take a break to stretch and exercise.

| 15 | **Review each day and analyze where the time was spent.** Note opportunities for improvement in productivity. Take 15 minutes at the end of the day to think about the next day and prepare your plan of attack. |

Pairing Tasks to Increase Efficiency

- Backup the computer when leaving house or office for lunch or an appointment
- Run virus scan program when leaving the office for the day
- Listen to a book on audio while driving
- Use a hands-free Dictaphone to record thoughts or dictate a letter while driving
- Read hands-free while walking on the treadmill or riding a stationary bicycle
- Watch the news or listen to music or a recorded book while exercising
- Catch up on a relationship by walking or running with a friend or family member
- Accomplish light chores (dusting, watering plants, etc.) while watching television
- Cook dinner in a slow cooker (crock pot) while at work
- Watch television or listen to music or a book on audio while cooking
- Wrap gifts or clip coupons while watching television

Take all the swift advantage of the hours.

William Shakespeare

20

....

FOCUS ON THE GREATNESS
YOU WANT

Get in the Zone: Ways to Concentrate and Focus

Think of the brain as a computer. Isn't it true that when we are working within multiple programs and have numerous windows open on our screen, our computer has the tendency to slow down or even lock up? According to research, the same thing happens in our brain. When we perform multiple tasks that require our undivided attention, our brain can get overloaded. To switch tasks successfully, the brain must marshal the resources required to perform the new task while shutting off, or inhibiting, the demands of the previous one. But how do we focus on that one job when we have so many other tasks waiting to be done? Use the FOCUS acronym to help concentrate solely on the task before us:

F	**Filters**. Remove all external filters such as noises and odors that may create a diversion. Stay in the moment by steering clear of distractions and interruptions. Use blinders and ear plugs if necessary.
O	**Organize** your space and pay attention to logistics—lighting, ventilation, comfortable chair, etc. The more organized we are, the less we worry about things falling through the cracks. The more comfortable we are, the better we are able to concentrate.
C	**Commit** to memory. Be vigilant about keeping good records, using a planner or calendar to create schedules, and backing up these records. Once you write something down, or record it electronically, you will never forget it. This will allow you to compartmentalize, let things go, immerse yourself, and focus purely on the task at hand.
U	**Understand** what needs to be done, break it into manageable size pieces, and set time limits or points at which to break. Keep reminders of your ultimate goal and what's in it for you. You must also reward yourself for the completed portion of the task.
S	**Scrutinize**. Act as if you are a proofreader and see the project or task as if for the very first time or the very last time. Challenge yourself to learn something new.

A Model for Organizing and Prioritizing

Our typical day spent as a responsible adult, in or out of an office, is concerned with activities that are either *past-focused, present-focused,* or *future-focused.* All three are intrinsic to ensuring productivity and success, and have no right or wrong value associated with them. It's not better or worse to spend time on a future-focused activity rather than a past-focused activity. They are both absolutely necessary.

The decision we have to make is based on where to direct our energy at any given moment. For example, compiling the figures on last month's household expenditures or business sales performance is past-focused, while budgeting for next quarter is future-focused. Both are finance and accounting-related, and the later two may well be interconnected, but they are looking in opposite directions.

Present-focused activities are those in our immediate range of vision and hearing. Telephone calls and face-to-face appointments fall into this category. Even with the same business function, there are past-present-future activities.

Let's focus on business. Here are a few:

Past focus	Present focus	Future focus
Analyzing turnover	Training	Succession planning
Managing expectations	Meeting expectations	Setting expectations

Why Does This Model Work?

Using Past-Present-Future as an organizing model is a simple means to determine what needs to be accomplished today, in all three categories. By carefully thinking through each of these timeframes—past, present, and future—we can be sure that we are organized and adequately prepared.

Once we have placed all of our activities and tasks into these categories, it is a matter of prioritizing them accordingly: What has to be accomplished first in each category?

Past focus:

What repairs do I need to make? What messages do I need to return?

What reports do I need to create or review? Who is waiting for follow-up contact from me?

Present focus:

What meetings are on my calendar today? What urgent matters have arisen today? What is my commuting or travel schedule today? What deadlines must I meet today?

Future focus:

What arrangements (travel, invitations, vacations, conferences, etc.) do I need to make? What projects or proposals do I need to prepare?

What deadlines are coming up?

Prioritizing

Some obstacles to handling competing priorities:

> Lack of focus and motivation
> Getting bogged down by minutiae
> Constant disruptions and interruptions
> Too much to do in too little time
> Too few resources to get the job done

- Poor planning and organizational skills
- Tendency toward procrastination
- Inability to establish priorities and keep on schedule
- Inability to delegate effectively
- Inability to make timely decisions
- Time-consuming and ineffective meetings

The Essentials of Prioritizing

1. *Record All Activities*: Write down all your multiple demands, competing priorities, tasks, and activities for the day or week.

2. *Determine Primary Goals*: List your primary goals for the day or the week.

3. *Consider the 80/20 Rule*: Determine which 20% of activities will yield 80% of the results, bringing you nearer to your goals.

4. *Evaluate Important versus Urgent*: Decide which of the activities are the most important versus the most urgent. At this stage, take into consideration how certain items affect others and the consequences for not accomplishing certain tasks (for example, someone might need something from us in order to do his or her job).

5. *Rank*: Use a ranking system to begin planning. For example:
   - "A" tasks have high priority and must be completed immediately.
   - "B" tasks are moderately important but can be done after the "A" tasks.
   - "C" tasks are of low-level importance and can be tackled in our spare time.

6. *Create a Schedule*: Indicate deadlines for each task and

estimate the time involved to complete the task. Create a schedule keeping in mind any tasks that may be linked together to increase productivity. For example, can we couple something of lesser priority with something of greater importance?

7. *Revisit Goals and Adjust*: Review your goal(s) and the rewards of doing the task on time, and make any necessary adjustments.

8. *Purge*: Get rid of items on your list that remain at the bottom and will realistically not get done.

21

ORGANIZE FOR A GREAT LIFE

Focus is what the magnifying glass uses to set the newspaper afire. It's the opposite of being all over the place, leaving mixed messages everywhere. Scattered efforts produce scattered, ungrounded results. Reining in our efforts is the only way to succeed at anything.

Focus produces organization. Or is it the other way around? Either way, only as we organize our schedules, our daily lives, and our work, with results in mind, can we take on the challenges that we all face today in staying on top of highly detailed responsibilities, constantly changing workplace and other situations, and ever-broadening scopes of control.

Organization Allows Focus

As we progress in life and acquire more authority, organizing and prioritizing daily, weekly, and monthly responsibilities become progressively more demanding. We are all challenged at home and at work by the need to keep track of obligations, follow up on projects, attend to details, determine current status and future planning.

Solid skills in organizing and prioritizing are highly admired traits, in or out of the office. By strengthening these skills, we strengthen our image within society, our families and our organizations.

Some of us resist being too neat and organized. We almost feel as if too much organization is contrary to our image. We can find things in our office, even if everything looks piled up and disorganized. We actually thrive on the energy and risk of seeming chaos. To us, taking time to develop organized work habits seems almost petty, compared with the urgency and importance of the workload. Chaos becomes a sort of badge of honor, and proof of our indispensability.

To those of us who pride ourselves on knowing there's "a place for everything" and "everything in its place," we can't understand how the other group can accomplish anything. Their chaos seems not only incomprehensible, but almost dangerous. We ponder the accomplishments other people might achieve if they'd at least clean off their desks. Yet, every time we ask one of those people for something, he or she seems to magically produce the item out of the piles on that desk.

These represent differences in style, personality, and self-direction. They don't represent the difference between good people and bad people. Yet, we are often quick to judge another person's style of personal organization.

There are four compelling reasons for becoming more organized.

We make a better impression on others.

Even if we tend toward chaos in our own organizational style, we secretly admire those who are consistently well organized and efficient. Organizational skill is a highly admired quality, and most of us aspire to be better at it than we currently are.

We feel less stressed.

While forming new organizational habits can itself be stressful, the eventual benefit is one of feeling less anxiety and more peace of mind. Taking chaos and turning it into organized priorities has a calming effect on us.

We move toward our goals of professionalism and promotability.

Most of us are motivated to be professional and respected in our business environment. In turn, this typically opens opportunities for career advancement. Our organizational skills have more and more value each time we accept additional responsibilities.

Organization on our part often makes it easier for others to work.

A systematic person is easy to dovetail with others to achieve joint goals. Organized persons inspire faith as well as set good models for achievers.

Make an Organizational Assessment

Rate how true the following statements are for you based on this scale:

    1 for "Always"

2 for "Sometimes"

3 for "Almost Never"

_____I am able to find needed items easily and quickly.

_____I maintain a daily priority list.

_____I'm thorough in my follow-up plans.

_____I schedule my activities ahead of time.

_____I can adequately absorb today's crisis into my priorities.

_____I arrive at meetings well prepared.

_____I review each day's priorities the night before.

_____My work area is generally orderly.

_____I meet deadlines without having to do everything at the last minute.

_____My colleagues, friends, and family view me as being well organized.

_____I am viewed as priority-driven.

_____I avoid multi-tasking as a rule.

_____I have balance when it comes to work, family, friends and social life.

_____I confirm meetings and appointments one-to-two hours in advance.

_____I arrive early for meetings.

The higher your point total, the more you need to commit yourself to organize and prioritize.

Dale Carnegie's Suggestions About Organizing Schedules

- Allow ourselves 25% extra time for each daily activity.

  For example, if you have a two-hour meeting at 10:00 AM,

block the calendar from 9:45–12:15. That way your schedule cannot be as easily disrupted by delays and interruptions.

- Every night, go over your schedule and priorities for the next day. This helps us to get off to a time-efficient start each morning, and helps us rest easier at night. This is a good time to use Past-Present-Future activity organization.

- Confirm meetings an hour or two before the scheduled time. If there is a change in the meeting time, you have ample time to make schedule adjustments and complete other priorities. It is also a courtesy to others involved in the meeting, and demonstrates your commitment to be organized.

- Schedule activities using Block Time. Block Time gives us uninterrupted periods of concentrated effort on our priorities. It requires both self-discipline and the cooperation of our colleagues. When working on a task in block time, eliminate all other distractions. If it is possible, turn off phones, e-mail, and the Internet.

Suggestions On Organizing Activities and Work Projects

- *Don't leave things where they don't belong.* Sometimes, in haste, we set something in the corner, on the wrong pile of work, or even in the wrong room. This results in inefficient use of our time as we search for things that aren't where they are supposed to be, and try to accomplish tasks amid growing clutter.

- *Take a few minutes every day to pick up and put clutter away.*

This saves us from having to devote large blocks of time to big clean-ups. Clutter belongs in either a designated area or the wastebasket.

- *First thing in the morning, work on your first priority.* Don't do anything else until this is done. This reduces the stress of carrying unfinished priorities around with us all day. Ask a family member or colleague to support you in this effort by avoiding interruptions.

- *Avoid multi-tasking if possible.* A variety of studies have shown that multi-tasking can be less efficient and makes tasks more complicated; this in turn, makes us more prone to stress and more likely to make mistakes.

- *Clear your desk of everything except your current priority.* Sometimes, in order to clear our minds and focus, we need to clear our field of vision and remove distractions. Even if it means simply moving something from the desk to the top of a file cabinet or table, we will at least have a clean desk to work from, and an uncluttered view.

Tips for Organizing Our Lives

- *Use a "capture tool."* A capture tool, such as a notebook or PDA, can be used for instantly recording ideas, data, or reminders. You don't have to rely on your memories to keep everything on track, and you have peace of mind knowing that critical information has been captured.

- *Pursue life balance.* We hear a lot about balancing work and home. We can take it further and spread our time out with community service, physical exercise, socializing, or pursuing hobbies. When we commit time to other areas of our life, it gives us breathing space from our day-to-day pressures.

- *Combine personal and business schedules into one planner.* That way we can see all of our obligations at a glance. We avoid the stress of accidentally double-booking time because we didn't have our business or personal calendars with us. It is also a good way to see the overall picture of our life organization, and observe the amount of balance we are achieving.

- *Arrive early at each event of the day.* There is almost no downside to arriving early at scheduled events. You can always use the extra time to return calls, complete a priority activity, or just take a breather for a few minutes. Imagine a life where you are always arriving at the last minute, or worse, arriving late.

Procrastination, the Sneaky Saboteur

It has been my observation that most people get ahead during the time that others waste.

Henry Ford

The interesting thing about procrastination is that it seems to be intended to make our lives more pleasant, but instead can add stress. When procrastination sabotages our success, because we actually seek out distractions unrelated to our job or wait to the last minute to complete a mammoth project, stress is inevitable.

On the other hand, it works to set time limits to doing

something unrelated to the task at hand. Taking a break can leave us feeling more motivated and focused. Doing something creative can help us get our juices flowing, find solutions to problems, and overcome roadblocks.

The causes and dynamics of putting off an important or unpleasant task vary from person to person and from task to task for the same person. For instance, someone might delay doing an expense report, but will fill out a performance review immediately.

Common Causes of Procrastination:

- Being overwhelmed by unrealistic goals
- Not having or buying into a vision
- Fear of failure or success
- Being too hard on yourself
- Being a perfectionist
- Unable to concentrate
- Lack of focus and discipline
- Lack of motivation
- Not feeling valued or appreciated

The Downward Spiral of Procrastination

First, we need to achieve some outcome.

Second, we delay and rationalize to invent advantages of a delayed start.

Third, we delay more and more, until finally the task has to be done, usually with haste.

Fourth, we repeat the process, knowing we can get away with it.

Tips to Overcome Procrastination

- Just do it. The obvious solution is to simply do the task as soon as practical, while we have enough time to do the job correctly.
- Avoid any reward for delay, or to pass the work on to someone else besides, or an escape from the task altogether.
- Remember that a prioritized to-do list, a daily schedule, and a simple record and reward procedure will do wonders.
- Recognize and change negative thoughts and attitudes about the task. Instead, think of the enjoyment and the relief when the task is completed.
- Break big jobs down into manageable tasks and get started. Try just a plan to tackle five minutes of the project and you might find you have worked longer than planned.
- Do the hardest things first.
- Give yourself a pep talk. Muster up motivation and enthusiasm about the job or task. Talk to the right people and get re-energized.

22

IT'S GREAT TO WIN FRIENDS
AND INFLUENCE PEOPLE

Dale Carnegie, famed author of *How to Win Friends and Influence People* was the master of that subject. He lists twelve ways to influence people:

1. Keep a positive attitude. Don't take resistance personally. Resistance or objections simply evidence a need for more information.
2. Be prepared and observant. Notice how the other side uses words to convey ideas and speak their language.
3. Be passionate and speak with sincere conviction.
4. Create a safety zone by asking questions, acknowledging concerns, and rephrasing the other's point of view.
5. Find something positive and build on it.
6. Explain what's in it for the other and talk in terms of

the other person's point of view. Paint a picture or make statements that are conceivable and believable.

7. Capture attention by making your point:
   - Interesting and clever
   - Valuable and clear
   - Important and vital
   - Useful, relevant, and applicable
8. Appeal to the nobler motives.
9. Dramatize your ideas.
10. Throw down a challenge.
11. Involve the reluctant person by collaborating with them. Or simply say:
   - "I need your help."
   - "What do you think?"
   - "Let's give it a try and see how it works."
12. Ask for support and shake hands on it.

Every single person you meet has a sign around his or her neck that says, "Make me feel important." If you can do that, you'll be a success not only in business, but in life too.

Mary Kay Ash
Founder, Mary Kay Cosmetics

Make Strength-Based Comments

Strength-based comments should be a part of every leader's repertoire, to be used frequently and genuinely.

Dale Carnegie uses the acronym PIER to display the elements of what he calls a Crowning Statement:

- *Praise*—be specific and genuine
- *Illustrate*—use an example
- *Elaborate*—suggest how this quality will help them
- *Reinforce*—top it off with a final positive statement

Example of a Crowning Statement:

"The person I'm about to present this certificate to is someone who lights up the room with her smile all day (P). During the break, she went out of her way to meet me (I). I believe this quality of her will continue to help her become a great leader (E). She was a great asset to the class today (R). Please help me welcome: Susan Jones."

We'll Win the World By Sharing the Glory

> *No one who achieves success does so without acknowledging the help of others. The wise and confident acknowledge this help with gratitude.*

> Alfred North Whitehead

Sharing the glory is not just a nice thing to do for people. It is a powerful motivator that reinforces and rewards the most important outcomes that people create, at work or in society or within the family. When we recognize people effectively, we reinforce the actions and behaviors that we most want to see repeated. Sharing the glory is simple, immediate, and powerful reinforcement.

Principles for Sharing the Glory

1. Look for the best in others.

Dale Carnegie said that any fool can criticize, and most

fools do! It takes an exceptional person to routinely see the strengths in others, instead of their weaknesses. When we try honestly to see the best in others, we begin to see people from a completely different point of view, and learn to value others more.

2. Write it down.

Telling someone about a strength that you see in him or her is a very positive gesture. Even better, why not put it in writing? Not only can the person read it over again, they can show the written compliment to others.

3. Pass it along.

Norman Vincent Peale wrote, "I've trained myself to listen for any word of approval or praise that one individual speaks about another—and to pass it on." Passing along a compliment is easy! Simply say, "I heard someone say something good about you, and I agree. I'd love you to hear it too..."

4. Catch them in the act.

Be there to witness and applaud achievements as they happen. "Sharing the Glory" means sharing the experience, not just throwing in "Way to go!" from a distance. When we personally observe others as they grow and achieve, they know that our recognition is sincere and genuine.

> *When you hear something pleasant related to you about another person, you are being given a choice. You can absorb it and let it stop right there—or you can deflect it to hit the real target.*
>
> Norman Vincent Peale

Ways to Share the Glory

- If you're in the workplace, make a special effort to introduce your support staff to clients and other associates involved in the project. If the recipient is not work-related, make a great effort to introduce him or her to people related to the project or effort, and give credit where credit is due.
- Write informal positive sticky notes about people's contributions to the overall project, placing them where they can be seen.
- Inform the team or helpful colleagues about the end result of projects or proposals.
- Include everyone who has lent a hand in wrap-up meetings and celebrations, however small their contributions.
- Publicly acknowledge the contributions of others when speaking publicly or to the press.
- Tell people specifically how they contributed. Sincerely let them know that they were indispensable to the end result, and in what way.

Appendix A

....

ABOUT DALE CARNEGIE

Dale Carnegie was a pioneer in what is now referred to as the human potential movement. His teachings and writings have helped people all over the world become self-confident, personable, and influential individuals.

In 1912, Carnegie offered his first course in public speaking at a YMCA in New York City. As in most public speaking courses given at that time, Carnegie started the class with a theoretical lecture, but quickly noticed that the class members looked bored and restless. Something had to be done.

Dale stopped his lecture and calmly pointed to a man in the back row and asked him to get up and give an impromptu talk about his background. When the student finished, he asked another student to speak about himself, and so on until everybody in the class had given a brief talk. With the encouragement of their classmates and guidance from Carnegie, each of them overcame their fright and gave satisfactory talks. "Without knowing what I was doing," Carnegie later reported, "I stumbled on the best method of conquering fear."

His course became so popular that he was asked to give it in other cities. As the years went by, he kept improving the content of the course. He learned that the students were most interested in increasing their self-confidence, improving their interpersonal relations, becoming successful in their careers and overcoming fear and worry. This resulted in the emphasis of the course being shifted from public speaking to dealing with these matters. The talks became the means to an end rather than the end itself.

In addition to what he learned from his students, Carnegie engaged in extensive research on the approach to life of successful men and women. He incorporated this into his classes. This led to the writing of his most famous book, *How To Win Friends and Influence People*.

This book became an instant best seller and since its publication in 1936 (and its revised edition in 1981), over 20 million copies have been sold. It has been translated into 36 languages. In 2002, *How to Win Friends and Influence People* was named the #1 Business Book of the 20th Century. In 2008, *Fortune Magazine* listed it as one of the seven books every leader should have in his or her bookcase. His book, *How To Stop Worrying and Start Living*, written in 1948 has also sold millions of copies and has been translated into 27 languages.

Dale Carnegie died on November 1, 1955. An obituary in a Washington newspaper summed up his contribution to society:

Dale Carnegie solved none of the profound mysteries of the universe. But, perhaps, more than anyone of his generation, he helped human beings learn how to get along together—which seems sometimes to be the greatest need of all.

About Dale Carnegie & Associates, Inc.: Founded in 1912, Dale Carnegie Training has evolved from one man's belief in the power of self-improvement to a performance-based training company with offices worldwide. It focuses on giving people in business the opportunity to sharpen their skills and improve their performance in order to build positive, steady, and profitable results.

Dale Carnegie's original body of knowledge has been constantly updated, expanded and refined through nearly a century's worth of real-life business experiences. The 160 Dale Carnegie Franchisees around the world use their training and consulting services with companies of all sizes in all business segments to increase knowledge and performance. The result of this collective, global experience is an expanding reservoir of business acumen that our clients rely on to drive business results.

Headquartered in Hauppauge, New York, Dale Carnegie Training is represented in all 50 of the United States and over 75 countries. More than 2,700 instructors present Dale Carnegie Training programs in more than 25 languages. Dale Carnegie Training is dedicated to serving the business community worldwide. In fact, approximately 7 million people have completed Dale Carnegie Training.

Dale Carnegie Training emphasizes practical principles

and processes by designing programs that offer people the knowledge, skills and practices they need to add value to the business. Connecting proven solutions with real-world challenges, Dale Carnegie Training is recognized internationally as the leader in bringing out the best in people.

Among the graduates of these programs are CEOs of major corporations, owners and managers of businesses of every size and every commercial and industrial activity, legislative and executive leaders of governments and countless individuals whose lives have been enriched by the experience.

In an ongoing global survey on customer satisfaction, 99 percent of Dale Carnegie Training graduates express satisfaction with the training they receive.

Appendix B

DALE CARNEGIE'S PRINCIPLES

Become a Friendlier Person

1. Don't criticize, condemn or complain.
2. Give honest, sincere appreciation.
3. Arouse in the other person an eager want.
4. Become genuinely interested in other people.
5. Smile.
6. Remember that a person's name is to that person the sweetest sound in any language.
7. Be a good listener. Encourage others to talk about themselves.
8. Talk in terms of the other person's interests.
9. Make the other person feel important—and do it sincerely.
10. To get the best of an argument—avoid it.

11. Show respect for the other person's opinion. Never tell a person he or she is wrong.

12. If you are wrong, admit it quickly, emphatically.

13. Begin in a friendly way.

14. Get the other person to say "yes" immediately.

15. Let the other person do a great deal of the talking.

16. Let the other person feel the idea is his or hers.

17. Try honestly to see things from the other person's point of view.

18. Be sympathetic with the other person's ideas and desires.

19. Appeal to the nobler motives.

20. Dramatize your ideas.

21. Throw down a challenge.

22. Begin with praise and honest appreciation.

23. Call attention to people's mistakes indirectly.

24. Talk about your own mistakes before criticizing the other person.

25. Ask questions instead of giving direct orders.

26. Let the other person save face.

27. Praise the slightest improvement and praise every improvement. Be "hearty in your approbation and lavish in your praise."

28. Give the other person a fine reputation to live up to.

29. Use encouragement. Make the fault seem easy to correct.

30. Make the other person happy about doing the thing you suggest.

Fundamental Principles for Overcoming Worry

1. Live in "day-tight compartments."
2. How to face trouble:
    a. Ask yourself, "What is the worst that can possibly happen?"
    b. Prepare to accept the worst.
    c. Try to improve on the worst.
3. Remind yourself of the exorbitant price you can pay for worry in terms of your health.

Basic Techniques in Analyzing Worry

1. Get all the facts.
2. Weigh all the facts—then come to a decision.
3. Once a decision is reached, act!
4. Write out and answer the following questions:
    a. What is the problem?
    b. What are the causes of the problem?
    c. What are the possible solutions?
    d. What is the best possible solution?

Break the Worry Habit Before It Breaks You

1. Keep busy.
2. Don't fuss about trifles.
3. Use the law of averages to outlaw your worries.
4. Cooperate with the inevitable.
5. Decide just how much anxiety a thing may be worth and refuse to give it more.

6. Don't worry about the past.

Cultivate a Mental Attitude That Will Bring You Peace and Happiness

1. Fill your mind with thoughts of peace, courage, health and hope.
2. Never try to get even with your enemies.
3. Expect ingratitude.
4. Count your blessings—not your troubles.
5. Do not imitate others.
6. Try to profit from your losses.
7. Create happiness for others.

10 STEPS to a MORE FULFILLING Life

Dale Carnegie Success Series titles
published by Manjul Publishing House

◆*Living an Enriched Life*

◆*Communicating Your Way to Success*

◆*How to Jump-Start Your (Next) Career*

◆*Become an Effective Leader*

◆*How to Have Rewarding Relationships,
Win Trust and Influence People*

◆*Overcoming Worry & Stress*

◆*Life Is Short Make It Great*

◆*Embrace Change for Success*

◆*Resolve Conflicts in Your Life*

10 STEPS to a MORE FULFILLING Life

DALE CARNEGIE

Manjul Publishing House

First published in India by

Manjul Publishing House

• 7/32, Ansari Road, Daryaganj, New Delhi 110 002 - India
Website: www.manjulindia.com

Registered Office:
• 10, Nishat Colony, Bhopal 462 003 - India

The Success Series:
10 Steps to a More Fulfilling Life by *Dale Carnegie*

This edition first published in India in 2018
Second impression 2020

ISBN 978-93-87383-32-6

Cover Design by Trinankur Banerjee

This edition is authorised for sale in the Indian Subcontinent only.

Printed and bound in India by Thomson Press (India) Limited.

CONTENTS

PREFACE

Some people enjoy a fulfilling and enriched life. They are magnetic; so sunny, so bright, cheerful, and attractive that they never have to force or even to request an entrance anywhere. The door is flung wide open, and they are invited to enter. Their very presence is soothing and pleasing. They know how to persuade, almost without uttering a word. They are popular in their social and community groups, and in their jobs and careers they move ahead rapidly.

It is hard to escape the charm in a gracious personality. It is difficult to snub the person who possesses it. There is something about that person that pulls you towards him or her and no matter how busy or how worried you may be, or how much you may dislike to be interrupted, somehow you want to interact with this person nonetheless.

Men and women are human magnets. Just as a steel magnet drawn through a pile of rubbish will pull out only the things that have an affinity for it, so we are constantly drawing to us and establishing relations with the things and the people that respond to our thoughts and ideals.

Our environment, our associates, and our general condition are the result of our mental attraction. These things have come to us on the physical plane because we have concentrated upon them, have related ourselves to them mentally; they are our affinities, and will remain with us as long as the affinity for them continues to exist in our minds.

Whether or not we will live a truly fulfilling life will depend in a great degree upon the quality of the impression we make upon others. It means everything, therefore, to develop a magnetic, forceful personality.

Wouldn't you like to be such an irresistible person? Well, you can. These traits are not necessarily inborn—anybody who truly desires to develop a warm, outgoing, welcoming personality can do so—if he or she masters the techniques that contribute to one.

This is not a very difficult thing to do. Everyone can cultivate the ability to please and the strength of character that will make him or her felt as a real force in the world.

Dale Carnegie and his successors have shown us the way in their courses and in their writings. In this book we have synthesized these principles into 10 steps that will guide readers to a more fulfilling life. These steps are listed in the table of contents preceding this preface.

To get the most out of this book, read all of it first to absorb the overall concepts. Then reread each chapter, and start applying the guidelines for achieving each of the areas covered. This will start you on the track that has brought success, happiness, and enrichment to the millions of men and women who have studied and implemented Dale Carnegie's teachings.

Arthur R. Pell, Ph.D.
Editor

Step 1

....

DEVELOP A GOOD SELF-IMAGE

While our interactions and relationships with others are critical to having a fulfilling life, our first priority must be having a good relationship with ourselves. If we lack a sense of our self-worth, we don't have a chance of projecting an image of ourselves as someone that others will want to know and trust. Creating a good self-image, and holding that image out to the world, are the first order of business in our success and happiness.

Believe in yourself! Have faith in your abilities! Without a humble but reasonable confidence in your own powers you cannot be successful or happy.

Dale Carnegie

1

We Must Love Ourselves

"Love your neighbor as you love yourself." This or similar injunctions have been proclaimed in the Old and New Testaments and in the writings and doctrines of most religions and philosophies throughout the ages.

However, most of the sermons and discussions of this tenet center on the first three words. They concentrate on how we treat others, assuming that the loving of ourselves is a given.

Unfortunately, this is not always the case. Too many people do not love themselves. They are unhappy about their appearance, their personality, their capabilities, and many, many other aspects of their lives.

In order to live a satisfying, rewarding life, we must first learn to truly love ourselves. This is the first step on the ladder to an enhanced life. Loving ourselves does not mean we must be totally egocentric. Loving ourselves is the foundation on which we will build our approach to the way we relate to all the people with whom we relate in our lives. Self-love leads to self-confidence, self-esteem, and being viewed positively by others. Self-love enables us to love others.

The ancient Hebrew philosopher, Hillel, stated this concept succinctly. "If I am not for myself, who is for me? And if I am only for myself, what am I?"

Wouldn't it be powerful if you fell in love with yourself so deeply that you would do just about anything if you knew it would make you happy? This is precisely how much life loves you and wants you to nurture yourself. The deeper you love yourself, the more the universe will affirm your worth. Then you can enjoy a lifelong love affair that brings you the richest fulfillment from inside out.

Alan Cohen,
American Business Executive

Building Self-Confidence

Loving ourselves helps in developing and maintaining self-confidence. Some elements of self-confidence include:

Self-Acceptance

Self-acceptance comes from our ability to accept ourselves as human beings while focusing on our positive sides—our strengths, positive qualities, and traits—that make us who we are. When our focus is on these areas, both confidence and selfesteem are positively influenced. It is all too common for people to focus on their weaknesses instead of their strengths. Doing this does more damage than good. We must help ourselves and others focus on our positive qualities.

Formulate and stamp indelibly on your mind a mental picture of yourself as succeeding. Hold this picture tenaciously. Never permit it to fade. Your mind will seek to develop the picture... . Do not build up obstacles in your imagination.

Norman Vincent Peale

Self-Respect

The key to developing self-respect is to focus on our past successes and achievements and to respect ourselves for the good we have done. It is far easier to dwell on failures. Others are only too eager to point them out to us. Our perspective changes and our confidence builds when we spend time contemplating our successes.

A valuable exercise to perform is to create a Success Inventory. This is a list of successes and accomplishments that we have had throughout our lives. At first it may be difficult to build a list, but with persistence we can keep adding to our list and building our confidence. Begin with a file folder, and start putting positive symbols and records of our successes in it today. These may include letters from teachers commending our schoolwork, memos from employers about contributions made in our jobs, emails from customers or clients thanking us for good service, letters of thanks from nonprofit organizations where we contributed time and effort, and similar papers. In addition, create a log in which we can enter our accomplishments and conduct of which we are particularly proud. When we feel blue or inadequate about a current situation, we can read this file and remind ourselves that we succeeded before and can do it again.

Positive Self-Talk

All of us engage in "self-talk"—the things that we repeat to ourselves about ourselves. When we add the above items together, we create positive self-talk backed up by evidence, an argument that would hold up under scrutiny. The stronger and more compelling the evidence, the more believable and powerful is the message. This positive self-talk is a tool to take back control of the only thing we really have ultimate control over—our thinking.

Risk Taking

We can also build our self-confidence by being willing to take risks. We can approach new experiences as opportunities to learn rather than occasions to win or lose. Doing so opens us up to new possibilities and can increase our sense of self-esteem. Not doing so inhibits personal growth and reinforces whatever belief we may have that a new possibility is an opportunity for failure.

Some people never take risks. They always play it safe. Most likely they will always be just average mediocre performers. They will never have any real successes. By not taking the chance that something they supported might not work out, they avoid the "agony of defeat," but never experience "the thrill of victory."

The turtle is a living fortress. Its impervious shell protects it from all harm. However, if the turtle wants to move, it must stick its head and neck out from the shell, exposing it to the dangers of the environment. Like the turtle, if we want to move ahead we cannot surround ourselves with perfect protection. We have to stick out our necks in order to progress.

Taking risks does not mean one must be a daredevil. Reasonable people take reasonable risks, but by definition, a risk may not succeed. Successful business executives take risks with every decision they make. However, they maximize their chance of success by careful research and analysis before making the decision. But when that decision finally has to be made, the manager must be willing to risk the possible loss of money, time, energy, and emotion. Without risk, there is no possibility of gain. By taking chances, even if the outcome is not what we would most like, we show both others and ourselves that we are confident in our abilities.

Expect the Best

There is no more uplifting habit than that of bearing a hopeful attitude, of believing that things are going to turn out well and not ill; that we are going to succeed and not fail; that no matter what may or may not happen, we are going to be happy.

In building our self-confidence, there is nothing else so helpful as the carrying of this optimistic, expectant attitude— the attitude that always looks for and expects the best, the highest, the happiest—and never allowing oneself to get into a pessimistic, discouraged mood.

We must believe with all our heart that we will do what we were made to do. We must never for an instant harbor a doubt of it, and entertain only "thought-friends"—ideals of the thing we are determined to achieve. We must reject all "thoughtenemies"— all discouraging moods, everything which would even suggest failure or unhappiness.

It does not matter what we are trying to do or to be, so long as we always assume an expectant, hopeful, optimistic attitude regarding it. This will put us on the road to grow in all our faculties, and how we improve generally.

Building Self-Esteem

Self-esteem may be defined as feeling good about oneself. People with high self-esteem believe that they are more likely to succeed than fail in most things they do. They know that other people respect them. This does not mean that one is unrealistically optimistic about everything one does. All of us have bad days and experience times when everything seems to go wrong. Persons with high self-esteem can accept untoward events and not let them overwhelm or deflate them.

In a study conducted by the Gallop Organization for *Newsweek*, 89 percent of the respondents said that self-esteem is important in motivating a person to work harder and to succeed. Sixty-three percent said that time and effort spent in developing self-esteem is worthwhile, while only 34 percent felt that time and effort could be better spent on work.

Many people have little self-esteem and a very low opinion of their own capabilities. They look upon themselves as failures and when they do succeed, they consider it a fluke. Why should this be?

Kevin was a bright and personable young man, but he didn't consider himself either bright or personable. He felt that he was dull and would never achieve anything in his life. Despite his high grades in school, he did not apply for top-level colleges because he felt he was not good enough to be accepted. His guidance counselor probed to discover why he had such low selfesteem. Kevin's father was a dynamic corporate executive who demanded perfection from his children and was never satisfied with less than perfect performance. When Kevin received a grade of 90, his father wanted to know why it was not 100. His father dominated the family dinner conversations and rejected any disagreements with his ideas by any of the children. Because he could never seem to please his father, over time, Kevin developed the feeling that he was an inadequate person.

Sarah had always been a self-confident child. She excelled in school and had demonstrated talents in art and music. However, when she completed college and entered the work world, she tried a series of unsatisfactory jobs—and was unhappy and unsuccessful in each of them. Her self-confidence eroded, and she began to feel that she would never succeed in life.

Steve had been a successful salesman for many years, but one spring he ran into a slump. Nothing he did seemed to work, and he didn't close any new deals. He began to feel that he was past his prime. "I've lost it," he thought. "I'll never make another sale."

Kevin had developed deep-seated psychological problems, and it is unlikely that he'd be able to repair his self-esteem without professional help. At the suggestion of his guidance counselor, he started a series of sessions with a psychotherapist, who helped him see that he was immensely capable, and helped him develop a healthy idea of his worth.

Most people with low self-esteem, however, do not need psychologists. They can help themselves. Sarah knew she had the ability to succeed. She realized that her failures were not due to lack of capability, but perhaps to wrong choices in the jobs she held. She thought, "I was good in school and in the work I did with my art and music. I have been a success, and I can be one again."

With that attitude, she rethought her career plans and began seeking jobs in areas closer to her real interests. This resulted in locating a job that used her talents and in which she was deeply valued by her supervisor and coworkers.

Steve's sales manager was concerned about Steve's slump—not just because of its effect on business, but because of its effect on Steve. He talked to Steve at length. "Steve," he said, "you haven't changed in any way—slumps can happen to anybody. You have what it takes. You are a good salesman. You can make it." With his boss's encouragement, Steve faced his next prospect with greater confidence and made the sale. This was the first step in rebuilding his flagging self-esteem.

Self-esteem is important—not only to success in our endeavors, but also to our total well-being. People with high selfesteem are happier and often healthier people than those without it. We must keep up our morale. Don't let failures get us down. We will suffer failures and disappointments in our lives, but by dwelling on our successes, on the good times, our self-esteem will remain high and help us overcome the temporary downturns.

So long as you are still worried about what others think of you, you are owned by them. Only when you require no approval from outside yourself can you own yourself.

Neale Donald Walsch,
American Author

Unless we have confidence in our abilities and faith in our determination to succeed, we will never even get started on the road that leads to the achievement of our goals. We must expect great things from ourselves. This faith brings out the best that is in us. As the old saying states:

> Life's battle does not always go
> To the stronger or the faster man;
> But soon or later, the man who wins
> Is the one who THINKS he can.

People who are not self-confident put a lot of weight on what others think in order to determine how they feel about themselves. They avoid taking risks due to fear of failure and generally do not expect to be successful. They often put themselves down, discount positive feedback, and subscribe to harmful assumptions that perpetuate self-defeating thought patterns and a negative attitude. Some self-defeating thought patterns include:

- *Extreme Thinking*: One failure may lead us to feel, "I am a total failure when my performance is not perfect."

- *Eminent Disaster*: Assuming that disaster lurks around every corner and comes to be expected. For example, a single negative detail, a bit of criticism, or a passing comment darkens all reality. "I blew that presentation and now I'll never get promoted."

- *Magnification of the Negative*: Good performance doesn't count nearly as much as poor performance. "I know I had the best sales record the last quarter, but that was just luck. Now I'm back to my real self. I'm just making quota this quarter."

- *Overemphasis on "should" statements*: "Should" statements are meant to push us toward the "perfect" outcomes, but must be followed by a realistic thought process that establishes what we need to do to get to where we "should be." Many times we just look at where we are and freeze with fear when we see we are not close to where we should be. Instead, this should be the time to stop, plan out our action steps, and begin to implement our plan.

There are times when any one of us may doubt our abilities and our accomplishments, and find our self-confidence plummeting. To make matters worse, we emphasize and dwell on what we think others think of us in order to determine how we feel about our ability and ourselves. This mind-set can lead us to avoid taking risks due to fear of failure. This kind of reinforcement can lead us to put ourselves down, discount positive feedback, and subscribe to harmful assumptions that perpetuate self-defeating thought patterns and a negative attitude.

Never forget that self-confidence is an integral part of selfesteem. Before we can gain the confidence in decisions we make, we must believe in ourselves. We must truly feel that we are someone of worth. If we do not have self-esteem, how can we be *confident* that our decisions are worthwhile?

No man is free, who is not master of himself.

Epictetus,
Greek Philosopher

We Are Who We—Not Others—Think We Are

Too often, we are more concerned about what others think of us than what we think about ourselves. William Becker, a midtwentieth- century clergyman and writer, admonished his readers, "Never mind what people think of you. They may overestimate or underestimate you! Until they discover your real worth, your success depends mainly upon what you think of yourself and whether you believe in yourself. You can succeed if nobody else believes it, but you will never succeed if you don't believe in yourself."

The more you like yourself, the less you are like anyone else, which makes you unique.

Walt Disney

The Self-Image That We Project

Our image is the way in which we express ourselves to the outside world. Some people have a strong, positive idea of who they are, and they send that idea out to others. There is something about their personalities that eludes the photographer, that the painter cannot reproduce, that the sculptor cannot chisel. This subtle something, which every one feels, but which no one can describe, which no biographer ever put down in a book, has a great deal to do with their success in life.

Certain personalities are greater than mere physical beauty and more powerful than learning. People who possess this magnetic power unconsciously impress every one with whom they come in contact. The moment people come into their presence they have a sense of enlargement. It broadens their horizons; they feel a new power stirring through them. Wouldn't it be great if people reacted to us in this way?

The First Impression We Send

Each time a new person meets us, that person takes just thirty seconds to form a whole laundry list of impressions, beliefs, or assumptions regarding who we are and what we are about. And those assumptions are far more significant than how much we paid for our clothes and whether or not our hair color is natural. Those impressions encompass everything from our education level to our financial situation, our career success, even things as subjective as our honesty and integrity. All those beliefs are formed, almost subconsciously, in the first thirty seconds.

The old adage: "You can't judge a book by its cover," makes good sense, but unfortunately, most of us do judge people by their "cover"—their appearance and demeanor. Indeed, some people make a decision about an individual in the first thirty seconds of contact.

If a negative or undesirable impression is made on that first contact, it may permeate all relations with that party for years to come. It takes a little thought and effort to establish the basis for making good impressions, but it is well worth the effort. Keep in mind that we'll project a much better image to others when our ideas about ourselves are positive and loving.

How can you have charisma? Be more concerned about making others feel good about themselves than you are making them feel good about you.

Dan Reiland,
America Clergyman

We Can Develop a Great Image

When Robert met Lisa, his new boss, he was impressed by her pleasant personality. Something about the way she projected herself made Robert feel confident in her, admire her, and feel comfortable with her. He thought, "This woman has charisma. I wish I could be like her."

We may think that people like Lisa were born that way. Some facets of our personalities are inborn—our physical appearance, basic intelligence, and some talents—but each of us has the capacity to make the most of our innate traits and to develop them to give us that type of personality that others will admire.

The important thing to remember is that a pleasant, welcoming image can be *developed*. It's not easy to grow into the charismatic person that we want to be, but it starts with a strong desire and commitment to develop an outgoing, cheerful, optimistic, and positive demeanor—an image that will win the approbation of the men and women with whom we interrelate. If we truly love ourselves and have a strong desire and commitment to do so, we can develop that magnetism.

Our Physical Appearance

When people meet us, the first factor to enter in their impression of us is how we look. Appearance plays a major part in how we are perceived. It can be an effective door opener . . . or a door closer. Every salesperson knows the frustration of not being able to get to a prospect because he can't get past the so-called "gatekeeper"—the receptionist, secretary, or subordinate who screens out unwanted callers. In a sense, a person's first impression of us is the most powerful gatekeeper of all. It often determines whether that person lets us in, figuratively as well as literally.

Some of the factors that may impress others either positively or negatively are beyond our control. We cannot change our basic physical appearance, but we can make the most of our assets and minimize what may be perceived to be defects. One does not have to have movie-star good looks to make a positive imprint.

The bulk of the cues to our external image are transmitted visually. Research reveals that visual impulses are transmitted directly to the emotional center of the brain, bypassing the normal routing systems and forming responses almost instantaneously.

Good grooming, appropriate dress, a pleasant smile, and proper manners are the first steps in making a good personal impression. We can maximize our chances for success by dressing in a way that communicates positive messages about our abilities and us. With the widespread adoption of business casual dress codes, there is no one right way to dress for business today. We must do some research to find what is appropriate in our industry, region, and culture.

Appearance and personality are only the first step in creating and maintaining the image others have of us. We must develop it by becoming genuinely interested in other people.

Dale Carnegie

Maintaining a Positive Attitude

Attitude is important in every area of the image we project, but nowhere is it more critical than in our attitude toward ourselves. Eleanor Roosevelt is often quoted as saying, "No one can make you feel inferior without your permission."

Most of us—even the most seemingly successful—carry around a mental suitcase full of negative messages about ourselves. They may have come from parents, teachers, bosses, colleagues, or even our own imaginations, but we have the capacity to recolor those messages and make positive beliefs our conscious choice.

A positive attitude toward others will go far to enhance the image we project. If we believe in our hearts that the world is full of friends, we will wear that belief like a well-fitting suit, and it will send a signal to those we meet that indeed, we are someone they want to be friends with. I we don't look at each day as a blessing to be enjoyed and savored, we will have an unhappy and most likely unproductive life.

Some people harbor for years a bitter hatred or a great jealousy toward others. Although they may not be aware of it, such a mental attitude does not allow the possessors to reach the highest levels of their abilities and destroys their happiness. And not only this; but they radiate their destructive atmosphere, thus prejudicing people against them, arousing antagonism, and constantly handicapping themselves all along the line.

We cannot do our best work while we harbor revengeful or even unfriendly thoughts toward others. Our faculties only give up their best when working in perfect harmony. There must be good will in the heart or we cannot do good work with heart or hand. A kindly attitude, a feeling of good will toward others will lead to a life of peace and equanimity. It will minimize discord in our lives and help us maintain harmonious relations with others.

We cannot carry secret hatreds and grudges, jealousies, and revengeful feelings without seriously impairing our own reputation. Many people wonder why they are not popular, why they are disliked generally, why they stand for so little in their community, when it is really because of their bitter, revengeful, discordant feelings, which kill personal magnetism.

On the other hand, if we maintain kindly, loving, helpful sympathetic thoughts, feel friendly toward everybody, and carry no bitterness, hatred, or jealousy in our hearts, we will create an attractive happy and sunny image.

The men and women who have succeeded best in life have always been cheerful and hopeful, who went about their business with a smile on their faces, and took the changes and chances of this mortal life, facing rough and smooth alike as it came.

We can often make our situation easier, get more salary, and win promotion, make more sales, be a more effective manager or professional by always being cheerful and bright, and at the same time have a pleasant, happy time themselves.

Do you like to associate with people who are grumpy, down in the dumps and unhappy, or do you like to associate with people who are happy and radiant? Their feelings and attitudes are just as contagious as the measles. So you ought to radiate what you want other people to have.

Dale Carnegie

Smile

Charismatic people know how and when to smile. A smile is a sign of friendliness. It is the human equivalent of a dog wagging its tail. Of course, we cannot nor should we smile all of the time. A smile is not something we put on mechanically as we put on a hat. A real smile is merely an outer expression of an inner condition. It is quite possible to be gracious and charming in a manner without actually smiling. There are situations in which a smile is totally inappropriate, and certainly nobody should smile constantly.

A smile must come from the heart. It pushes its way outward and shows in our eyes, our voice, and our actions. Act cheerful and we'll feel cheerful. We cannot fake a smile. A phony smile looks just that way—phony.

Dale Carnegie offers some suggestions on the art of smiling. He noted that first, we must have the right mental attitude toward the world and its people. Until we do, we will not be highly successful. But even smiling perfunctorily will help, for it will create happiness in others and that will act as a boomerang for us. To generate a pleasant feeling in another will make us feel more pleasant and pretty soon we will mean that smile.

Also, when we smile, we will be stifling any unpleasant or artificial feeling we may have been experiencing within ourselves. Try the smiling habit; it's a wonderfully simple way to feel good inside and to tell the world around us that we're someone nice to have around.

Let us make one point, that we meet each other with a smile, when it is difficult to smile.

Mother Teresa

Sending Out an Image of Enthusiasm

Charismatic people are enthusiastic about their lives, their work, their relationships, and their goals. The word "enthusiasm" comes from two Greek words meaning "the God within," and it comes from deep within ourselves. Enthusiasm cannot be faked. Pretending to be enthusiastic by artificial gestures, phony smiles, and exaggerated comments is easily detected. If we believe that what we are doing is worthwhile, meaningful, exciting, and achievable, it will show up in our demeanor and our actions.

People who are enthusiastic about themselves and their actions undertake their work with the assurance of success. Employees who go to their tasks with energy, determination, and enthusiasm, give confidence to their employer that the thing they undertake will not only be done, but that it will also be well done. The world has always made way for enthusiasm. It multiplies our power, raises whatever ability we have to its highest.

Enthusiasm is a great business getter. It is so contagious that, before we know it, we are infected with it, even though we try to brace ourselves against it. If our heart is in our work, our enthusiasm will often cause a would-be customer to forget that we are trying to make a sale.

There is something in assuming the part we wish to play and playing it with enthusiasm. If we are ambitious to do big things, we must be enthusiastic about ourselves and assume the part it demands.

Often the work we do may not be exciting or even interesting. It may be dull, boring, and fatiguing. We should look for something in it about which we can generate enthusiasm. This may be finding a way to do it better or faster or setting quantitative or qualitative goals that we must stretch to reach. If we cannot find ways to create such enthusiasm in our jobs, find another activity in the community, our family, our church, or a political or social group and devote ourselves to it.

There is something in the atmosphere of enthusiastic people, who believe they are going to win out, something in their very appearance that wins half the battle before a blow is struck.

Enthusiasm permeates the atmosphere and imparts to others the assurance that we can do the thing we attempt. As time goes on we are reinforced not only by the power of our own enthusiasm but also by that of all who know us. Our friends and acquaintances affirm and reaffirm our ability to succeed, and make each successive triumph easier of achievement than its predecessor. Our self-poise, confidence, and ability increase in direct ratio to the number of our achievements. The very intensity of our enthusiasm in doing the thing we attempt is definitely related to the degree of our achievement.

Enthusiasm is the dynamics of our personality, Without it, whatever abilities we may possess lie dormant; and it is safe to say that we all have more latent power than we ever learns to use. We may have knowledge, sound judgment, good reasoning facilities; but no one—not even ourselves—will know it until we discover how to put our hearts into thought and action. With an enthusiastic demeanor we project an image of confidence and competence.

When we are enthusiastic about something we are doing, the excitement, the joy, the inner feeling of satisfaction permeates the entire activity. It is not always easy to be excited about many of the things we have to do on a day-by-day basis, but is possible if we only make the effort.

Enthusiasm is the secret ingredient of success for the most successful people as well as the generator of happiness in the lives of those who possess it.

What goes on in the mind is what determines the outcome. When an individual really gets enthusiasm, you can see it in the flash of the eyes, in the alert and vibrant personality. You can see it in the verve of the whole being. Enthusiasm makes the difference in your attitude toward other people, and other people's attitude toward you. It makes the big difference between being just an "average Joe or Jane" and a charismatic person.

Norman Vincent Peale

Sum and Substance

- In order to live a satisfying, rewarding life, we must first learn to truly love ourselves. This is the first step on the ladder to an enhanced life. Self-love leads to self-confidence, self-esteem, and how others view us.

- Self-esteem is best defined as feeling good about oneself. People with high self-esteem believe that they are more likely to succeed than fail in most things they do.

- We will suffer failures and disappointments in our lives, but by dwelling on our successes instead of these failures, our selfesteem will remain high and help us overcome the temporary downturns.

- Too often, we are more concerned about what others think of us than what we think about ourselves. They may overestimate or underestimate us. Our success depends mainly upon what we think of ourselves. We can succeed if even if nobody else believes it, but we will never succeed if we don't believe in ourselves.

- A pleasant, welcoming image can be developed. Although some facets that make up our image are inborn—our physical appearance, basic intelligence, and some talents— each of us has the capacity to make the most of our innate traits and to develop them to give us that type of image that others will admire.

- Personality traits can be acquired. People are not all created equal. We must recognize that all do not have equal intelligence, equal physical strength, or equal levels of energy, but with effort we can become charismatic. We can choose and work to develop the personality traits we wish to acquire. The key is application.

- People who are enthusiastic about themselves and their actions undertake their work with the assurance of success. The world has always made way for enthusiasm. It multiplies our power, raises whatever ability we have to its highest.

Step 2

SET AND REACH ACHIEVABLE
GOALS

All successful people start with a goal. Establishing goals and working toward their achievement is an important step one must take on the long road to success. By knowing where we are going and how we plan to get there, we will be able to focus our time, energy, and emotions—and start on the right track toward reaching those goals.

A ship that has broken its rudder may keep everlastingly at it, may keep on a full head of steam and sail around endlessly, but it never arrives anywhere. It never reaches any port unless by accident, and if it does find a haven, its cargo may not be suited to the people, the climate, or the conditions. The ship must be directed to a definite port for which its cargo is adapted, and where there is a demand for it, and it must aim steadily for that port through sunshine and storm, through tempest and fog. So a person who would succeed must not drift about rudderless on the ocean of life, but must not only steer straight toward a destined port when the ocean is smooth, when the currents and winds serve, but also must keep the course in the very teeth of the wind and tempest, and even when enveloped in the fogs of disappointment and mists of opposition.

Start with a Dream

We start with a dream—a vision of the future. In the dream we are rich, happy, and maybe even famous. Most people do dream of such a future, but in most cases, that's all it will ever be—a dream.

Successful people have had those dreams too, but they turned those dreams into goals and in turn into reality. Their dreams were not vague hopes for success, but dreams of specific achievements that they aimed for. Edison dreamed of a world in which electric energy would light up the night. Beethoven dreamed of music that would make the spirit soar. Bill Gates dreamed of computer software that would enable everybody—not just big organizations—to utilize the power of computers. Great actors, artists, musicians, writers, accountants (yes, accountants!) dreamed—not just of fame, but of the way they would utilize their talents to achieve success.

Dreaming is not limited to geniuses. All successful people report that their success started with a hope, a dream, which led to a goal, which led to a plan of action and inevitably to accomplishing the goal.

Dreaming is not limited to the young. It is never too late to have a new dream that leads to new goals that lead to new successes. It is astonishing what people who have had their dreams late in life have accomplished. Benjamin Franklin was past fifty before he began the study of science and philosophy. Milton, in his blindness, was past the age of fifty when he sat down to complete his epic poem, *Paradise Lost*.

Dreaming is not limited to biases and prejudices of the times. For countless years, women have been restricted in what they can attempt to accomplish. Their career goals were limited to what were considered "female jobs." It took determination and courage to even think about other options. One example is Elaine Pagels, Princeton professor and best-selling author of books on Gnosticism and early Christianity. She said she was educated at a time when girls were taught not to even consider serious careers. She felt free to follow what she loved; only later discovering she could make a living out of it. Her dream had become her goal.

If you want to live a happy life, tie it to a goal, not to people or things.

Albert Einstein

In the nineteenth century, Frederick Douglass, born into slavery, did not let his race or condition of servitude stop him from learning to read and write and eventually to become a leader of his people. In the twenty-first century, Barack Obama broke the race barrier to become the first African American president of the United States.

Today, many of these barriers are gone in most career areas. For example, in most law, medical, and other professional schools in the United States, half or more of the students are women. As an employer, it is illegal to discriminate against someone because of his or her race, gender, or faith.

When it comes to realizing our dreams, even brains are second in importance to will. Only those people with an iron will and determination that nothing shall impede them are sure that with perseverance and grit, they will succeed. Dreams become goals and goals become achievements to those who strive long enough and hard enough.

Converting Dreams Into Goals

Unfortunately, too many dreamers remain just that—dreamers. The dreams remain dreams. When we convert dreams into goals, they are no longer fantasies, but objectives that we can set before us as a road map to success. We must bring to our dreams a purpose, a determination that we will do all that we can to make them come true.

A woman who had a dream and converted it into a successful goal is the clothes designer, Rachel Roy. Roy's love for fashion was inspired by the movies she saw as a child. The clothes the women on the screen wore seemed to give them an aura of confidence and success. Rachel dreamed that she could create the same aura for herself and other women, a sophisticated look that would create positive self-esteem.

She and her family went school shopping once a year. She was disturbed by the lack of interesting clothing choices in a local store and was convinced that if she had the opportunity she could create better styles. Her mother told her that this was the job of a buyer. Now she could put a name to her dream: buyer. At that moment, she said, her dream became her goal—to become a buyer in the fashion field.

Roy's first job was as stock clerk. She moved rapidly to assistant manager to personal shopper to stylist in various stores. She was soon designing fashions and was on the road to a senior position in her company.

When her husband, Damon Dash, wanted to start an independent clothing line, Roy had a decision to make—to stay with her own successful career, or to start over with Dash. She chose to begin anew, throwing herself into the job, working in every capacity, tracking everything she did to contribute, and involving herself in as many facets of the business as possible. She wanted to make herself irreplaceable. After about six years, Rachel was confident she could run a business herself and formed her own company. Her designs were acclaimed by the industry, and today she is considered one of the foremost designers in the fashion industry.

There is a significant distance between the wishers and the doers. Rachel Roy was more than a dreamer and a wisher. She turned her dream into a goal and worked hard to achieve that goal.

If We Believe, We Will Achieve

The very habit of expecting that the future is full of good things for us, that we are going to be prosperous and happy, that we are going to have a fine family, a beautiful home, a successful career, and are going to stand for something, is the best kind of capital on which to start our life.

What we try persistently to express what we intend to achieve, even though it may not seem likely or even possible. We always try to express the ideal, and we visualize it as vividly as possible and try with all our might to realize it. It is more likely we will achieve those things we would like to come true in our lives, whether they be robust health, a noble character, or a superb career. It is only when desire crystallizes into resolve that it is effective. It is the desire coupled with the vigorous determination to realize it that produces the creative power. It is the yearning, the longing and striving together that produce results.

If we wish to improve ourselves in any particular, we must visualize the quality as vividly and as tenaciously as possible and hold a superior ideal along the line of our ambition. We must keep this persistently in the mind until we feel its uplift and realization in our lives. We are born to win, to conquer and to lead triumphant lives. We should be a wonderful success in our chosen work, our relationship with people and in all other phases of our lives.

Prosperity begins in the mind and is an impossibility while the mental attitude is hostile to it. It is fatal to work for one thing and to expect something else, because everything must be created mentally first and is bound to follow its mental pattern. We cannot become prosperous if we really expect or half expect to remain poor. We tend to get what we expect, and to expect nothing is to get nothing.

When every step we take is on the road to failure, how can we hope to arrive at the success goal? It we are facing the wrong way, with a black, depressing, hopeless outlook, we may work as hard as we like, but our efforts will be in vain.

Thoughts are magnets that attract things like themselves. If our mind dwells upon poverty and disease, it will bring poverty and disease. There is no possibility of producing just the opposite of what we are holding in our minds, because our mental attitude is the pattern, which is built into our lives. Our accomplishments are achieved mentally first.

The terror of failure, the fear of financial loss and of possible humiliation keep multitudes of people from obtaining the very things they desire, by sapping their vitality and incapacitating them, through worry and anxiety, from the effective, creative work necessary to give them success.

The habit of looking at everything constructively, from the bright, hopeful side, the side of faith and assurance, instead of from the side of doubt and uncertainty; and the habit of believing the best is going to happen, that the right must triumph; the faith that truth is bound finally to conquer error, that harmony and health are the reality, and discord and disease the temporary absence of it—these are the attitudes of the optimist, which will ultimately reform the world.

Evaluating Ourselves For Success

We cannot depend on others to set us on the road to success. It depends entirely on ourselves. Before we can determine what goals can get us started on this journey, we must first evaluate ourselves. We must search deep inside of our mind and pull out from it what it is we really want out of life and what assets we have that will lead us to reaching that goal.

We must be realistic. We may want to establish a goal that appears to be desirable, but we may not have the abilities needed to achieve it. We may dream of being a movie star or an opera singer, but we don't have the talent needed. Our dream career may be in areas that are not feasible for us to attempt. On the other hand, we may have aptitudes and skills that we don't realize we have and that can lead to a satisfying and profitable career.

How can we find out? Look deeply inside ourselves. A careful introspection will bring this out. Most adults already know what they can and cannot do, what they like and do not like. It may not be obvious, but introspection enables us to reveal our best inclinations and abilities.

What we have to do is go systematically over our education, previous experience, hobbies, and interests. Look for those aspects of our lives in which we have been successful and in which we achieved satisfaction and joy. These are indicators of the areas in which we will succeed in the future. But this is only the beginning. Look beyond what we have accomplished and think of what we can accomplish.

Successful people learn at the very outset of their careers just what funds they can draw upon. We must take an inventory of all our possible assets and resources. Let's not just look at what we have accomplished thus far in our lives, but what we know we can accomplish. The great majority of young people start on their careers with little knowledge of their skills, and they usually discover them piece by piece over time.

Too many people never discover more than a small percentage of their ability and rarely rise above low-paid, lowlevel positions. They plod along in mediocrity, yet they have resources, if they could only detect them, that could lift them into superior positions. Somehow, they do not come into the right sort of ambition-arousing environment or do not come in contact with the necessary ideas or mentors to ignite the giant power of their hidden strengths.

Oneness of Purpose

Successful people strongly believe that one must be totally committed to one's goals. There is great power in a resolution that has no reservation in it—a strong, persistent, tenacious purpose which burns all bridges behind it, clears all obstacles from its path, and arrives at its goal, no matter how long it may take, no matter what the sacrifice or the cost.

To succeed we must concentrate all the faculties of our minds upon one unwavering aim, and have the tenacity of purpose that leads to defeat or victory. Every other inclination that tempts us must be suppressed.

We must plant the seeds in our minds that will enable us to accept and implement our goal. To nourish these seeds, we should write out a clear, concise statement of our objective and what we intend to do in order to achieve it. We should then read this statement aloud, twice daily, once just before retiring at night, and once after arising in the morning. As we read, we must see and feed and believe we are already achieving the goal.

Establishing Goals

Peter always knew he wanted to be an engineer. As a child his primary interests were mechanical. In school he excelled in math and science. His career goals were solid and he followed them through college and into the business world.

Most of us are not as fortunate as Peter. We only have vague concepts of careers as a child and adolescent, and often "fall into" our careers by fortuity. However, it is never too late to establish goals—not only in our job and career but also in all aspects of our life.

Jeanne floundered through several jobs after college. She had majored in marketing, but her first job in that field bored her to tears. She shifted to sales, but was unhappy and stressed. Her next job, as a paralegal in a law firm, really excited her and created an interest in becoming an attorney.

She set a new long-term goal—to become a criminal lawyer. She requested transfer within her firm to work for their senior attorney who handled criminal matters. She attended law school at night and will receive her law degree shortly. Now she has set a goal to work in the office of the public defender to gain experience before starting her own practice.

> *If you've been unsuccessful in something you've wanted very much to do, don't give up and accept defeat. Try something else. You have more than one string for your bow—if only you discover that string.*
>
> Dale Carnegie

Guidelines for Setting Goals

To make goals more than just pipe dreams, they should combine the following elements:

Clearly Articulated

Indicate in clear terms what we wish to accomplish. Be specific and firm in stating the goal. For example, saying "My goal is to be the best salesperson in my company"" sounds good, but it is better to be more specific: "My goal is to reach a sales volume of xx dollars for the next fiscal year; and ten percent more each year for the next three years." Now we know the target and our subconscious mind will help concentrate our efforts on reaching those figures.

Reasonable

Unless the goals set can be attained, goal setting is meaningless. To assure a goal's reasonableness, break the long-term goal into attainable sub-goals. For example: Long-term goal: exhibit my paintings in a prestigious art gallery within three years. Intermediate goals: To complete xx canvasses by December of next year; to mount a showing at a local art gallery by July of the following year; to be reviewed in an art journal by December of that year. Short-terms goals: To finish one painting each month; to bring my work to xx galleries each month for the owner's assessment.

Inspiring

If we set a goal that is too easily attained, it will not motivate us to do more than minimum work. We should set goals that will inspire us to keep moving ahead and to work that much harder to achieve them. Achievers recognize that once a goal is reached, they should immediately set another goal that will make them stretch and continue to improve and grow.

Action Based

Unless the actions that will be taken to implement the goals are noted, the goals are no more than dreams. In addition to its physical components, action has mental and emotional components as well. Mentally, we must be prepared to think about our goals every spare moment and what actions must be taken to realize them. Emotionally, we must not allow ourselves to be fearful or overwhelmed. We must simply remember our determination and take one step after another. If we meet with opposition along the way, we must not permit ourselves to give in to discouragement.

Measurable

It is not always possible to quantify goals. Some goals can be measured in financial or other numerical terms. We can set sales figures that we wish to attain by the month, quarter, or year—in terms of units of product or dollar value. We can set production goals by amount. Even intangible goals, which cannot be quantified, can be established in measurable terms. The major goal can be broken into segments and timetables set for the completion of each segment. In this way we can measure how close we are in reaching each of the segments and fine-tune our activities to assure that they will be accomplished in a timely manner.

Committed to Paper

One way to assure that goals will not be forgotten or lost in our hectic day-to-day lives is to write them down. Make a list of longterm goals; break them into intermediate and short-term goals. Write them in large letters and post them where we can see them every day—over our desk, on the refrigerator, on the mirror. Read them, memorize them, re-read them and ask each day: "What am I doing to accomplish these goals?"

Flexible

There are times when circumstances change, and the goal we set is no longer realistic or relevant to the business world. Economic conditions may not be favorable for starting a particular enterprise; technological innovations may have made the goal obsolete; we may have made errors in our research and the goal is not feasible. This does not necessarily mean the goal must be abandoned altogether. It may just require new thinking or more study. If faced with such a situation, review what has transpired and make necessary adjustments.

One often fails to meet a set goal. Don't become frustrated and give up. Review what has transpired, evaluate the situation and make necessary adjustments.

Jason had expected he would be promoted to store manager after serving two years as assistant manager. It didn't happen. Rather than quit in frustration, Jason reviewed the situation. His company had opened six to ten new stores each year for the past six years, and he had based his goal on the premise that his company would continue to open several new stores each year. But business had dropped off in the most recent year; only two new outlets were opened. But this year business had improved and he knew that additional openings were being considered. By adjusting his goals, he extended his timetable for another year and most likely will reach it.

Require Effort

Once we have reached a goal, set another that will make us stretch to continue to improve and grow. When Ben started his physical fitness program. he was told that if he swam thirty laps in half an hour, he would keep in good shape. It didn't take him long to achieve that goal. Most people of his age—the late fifties— would have been content to keep swimming at that pace, but Ben learned that in the twenty-five-yard pool that he used, thirty-six laps was equal to one-half mile. He immediately strove to reach that new goal.

Public Knowledge

In most weight-loss programs, participants are advised to let their families know how much weight they intend to lose and to keep their families advised of their progress. Why? When we share our goal with others, they will support us in helping reach it. When we are tempted to give up, they encourage us to continue.

Karen had dropped out of college when she married so she could work until her husband completed his education. Then she planned to return and get her degree. The birth of her children changed this plan. Now, ten years later, Karen has been able to resume her education. Managing a house, working an eight-hour day, and going to school at night is tough. From time to time, Karen feels it's not worth the effort. But because her husband, children, and friends know how important finishing school is to her, they help her with errands, cheer her on, and encourage her to keep going.

Review Our Progress

Not all goals can be quantified so that they can be easily measured, but when this is possible, set specific standards and timetables. When not quantifiable, develop a way of measuring how close we come to attaining our goals.

When Lee set his sales goals for the year, he expected to increase his annual volume by 8 percent. This meant he would have to open at least four new accounts or increase the sales of his current customers. He broke this down into monthly goals that could be easily measured against his actual sales. If business did not measure up to the monthly goal, he could take necessary steps immediately to get back on track.

As Human Resources Director of her organization, Kathy could not set quantifiable goals. Her objectives for the next twelve months included setting up a new training program for wordprocessor operators, studying and reporting to management on a new type of benefits package, and designing a performance review system for administrative and professional personnel. She broke each of these objectives into segments and set timetables for each segment. In this way she could measure how close she was to reaching each of the segments and fine-tune her activities to assure she would accomplish all of them by the end of the year.

Reach high, for stars lie hidden in you. Dream deep, for every dream precedes the goal.

Rabindranath Tagore,
Indian Nobel Prize Winning Author

The Planning Process

Let's look at an example of effective goal setting. Let's say we are a hardware distributor that has been selling its line primarily to building contractors. We would like to expand it to the consumer market—selling to hardware and building supply outlets and to the hardware departments of department stores and discount chains.

Here is an eight-point approach we may take.

Point 1: Desired Outcome

Our first point is the end result of the project. It is a picture of what we ultimately want. This should be clearly stated and agreed upon by all members of the management team.

Point 2: Our Present Circumstances

Examine the current situation. What are our strengths and weaknesses in marketing our products now?

Point 3: Set Goals

Now we are ready to define and set realistic goals to successfully carry out the scope of the project. Without such goals, we drift. Goals should be specific in terms of processes and resources. How much of our time and effort will be devoted to the new markets and how will this affect our current markets?

As noted earlier in this chapter, our goals should be readily measurable by objective data. What market share should we work to achieve in each of the four quarters of the first year of the process?

Goals should also be time specific. Determine the amount of time needed for each phase of the process including the planning, the start-up of each phase, and the implementation of the program.

Point 4: Action Steps

In order to achieve goals, priorities must be established and specific action steps taken. Our actions steps should set forth their requirements in terms of money, material, and equipment, so that we can establish a reasonable budget. Such action steps should include:

- Who will do the job? Can we accomplish our goal with our current sales and marketing staff? If so, what training will they need? Will we need to hire additional sales and marketing people? If so, what skills and experience should we seek?

- Methods to be used. What must we do differently to attain this new market?

- Who will be responsible for coordinating the entire effort?

Point 5: Cost

Another aspect to planning is determining the budget for, and cost of, each action step. Costs include personnel, equipment, material, and any other costs required to achieve the goal.

Point 6: Timetables

Deadlines should be set and communicated so there is a clear understanding and short-term, intermediate, and long-range targets can be met. When establishing timetables, be realistic. Put the schedule in writing to avoid misunderstandings.

Point 7: Implementation

An important, yet overlooked, part of implementing a plan

is making sure that all involved understand their role in achieving the goals. Commitment to agreed-upon results must be established.

Point 8: Follow-Up/Measurement

A critical part of the goal achievement process is to keep accurate records, analyze why deviations have occurred, and take action to correct any challenges. Concentrate on those factors critical to reaching the goal. Control points should be set at key intervals so deviations from the goals can be identified rapidly, adjusted, or reevaluated at the earliest stages of the process.

By establishing a well-conceived plan, we will be able to focus on our true objectives, measure our progress, and assure that what is most important to us in our job or other aspects of our life will be accomplished.

> *When defeat comes, accept it as a signal that your plans are not sound, rebuild those plans, and set sail once more toward your coveted goal.*
>
> Napoleon Hill, Author,
> *Think and Grow Rich*

Sum and Substance

- Successful people report that their success started with a hope, a dream, which led to a goal, which led to a plan of action and inevitably to accomplishing the goal.

- Before we can determine what goals can get us started on this journey, we must first evaluate ourselves. We must search deep inside of our minds and determine what it is we really want out of life and what assets we have that will lead us to reaching that goal.

- Developing goals that are reasonable and achievable is the first step to success.

- Follow these guidelines for setting goals:
  Goals should be clearly stated.
  Goals should be reasonably attainable.
  Goals should be inspiring.
  Goals should be action based.
  Goals should be measurable.
  Goals should be written down.
  Goals should be flexible.
  Goals should require effort.
  Goals should be shared with others who can support us.

- Goals should be reviewed periodically to measure our progress.

- A written, well-conceived action plan is important to our achieving our goals.

Step 3

....

TREAT OTHERS WELL

One of the most common reasons people do not get along well with others is that they assume that everybody shares their personal desires and psychology. We can't always know what drives someone else to act, or to respond to an event in a certain way. But we can have an understanding of the kind of treatment that most people appreciate and respond favorably to, and we can employ our understanding for good interpersonal relations. Here are some tips that will enable us to get along well with the people we encounter.

Recognition As An Individual

We would be wise to remember that in any group of people—at the workplace, at home, or on the softball field—each person is different from us and from the other people in the group.

Each person likes to feel that we recognize these differences and treat him or her as a special person, not as an interchangeable standard part. We must develop the practice of listening and observing the people with whom we relate and learn to appreciate the ways in which they are unique. Learn their strengths and limitations, their likes and dislikes, how they act and react and tailor the way we deal with each of them to their individualities. By paying attention to these differences, we learn that each has one or more special concerns about his or her relationships and activities. For example, let us assume we are supervisors or team leaders in our organization. We observe that Joe, one of our team members, is highly security-conscious and will take no risks for fear of failing and maybe jeopardizing his job. We note that Betty is very ambitious and wants to move up as fast as she can. Among our other associates, Sam and Lil need constant reassurance, while Karen is always trying new approaches. By keeping these individual differences in mind, we will be able to work most effectively with each of them and help them obtain what they want most from us.

Different Versus Preferential Treatment

Some managers are concerned that by "catering to the whims" of each worker, they would have to treat each person differently and that would not only be chaotic, but could lead to accusations of unfairness.

But because people are not all the same, we must make adaptations in our dealing with each of them to attain the same overall objective—getting the job done effectively. This does not mean that we accept lower standards or tolerate poor behavior from some of our staff members. By dealing with people in a way that inspires them to give their best, we are performing our managerial functions in the best possible manner. This will make a happier as well as a more productive work environment and will help each person—ourselves included—reach the desired goals.

Policies and procedures should be established, clearly communicated to the employees and administered in a consistent manner. Cindy and Sandy both have tardiness problems. The boss likes Cindy and is not too fond of Sandy. She enforces the disciplinary action for tardiness for Sandy, but lets Cindy get away with a light reprimand. Not only will Sandy be upset with this turn of events, but the other people in the department will consider this unfair. People who commit the same offenses should receive the same treatment.

People respond emotionally—not rationally—when their self-interest is in jeopardy. The desire for fair treatment is deep seated in the emotional makeup of all people. Favoritism is the greatest of demoralizers. It destroys the feeling of security in others who fear that their own efforts and worth are not being recognized.

Pride in Work

Regardless of whether we are in a supervisory or a more junior position, we most likely have pride in our job. We have earned the position we now hold and are proud of our accomplishments. Our bosses appreciate our work and consider us an important part of the company. If we can instill this sense of pride in everyone around us, it will lead to higher morale and commitment.

Appreciation and praise should be given whenever appropriate. Dale Carnegie encouraged us to be "hearty in our approbation and lavish in our praise," and this advice applies no matter what situation we are in. Everyone likes to hear that he or she is a valued part of the whole. Maybe our sister-in-law does a great job cleaning up the kitchen, or our babysitter's willingness to play with our children make them happy to have him show up. When people know that their work is appreciated, that behavior is encouraged and is more likely to be the norm.

The importance of having one's contribution be appreciated was reinforced by a report of the Society for Human Resource Management, based on a Gallup Poll of four hundred companies. It confirmed that an employee's relationship with his or her direct boss has a greater influence on retention than pay or job perks. Fair and inspiring leadership, including coaching and mentoring, retains employees. Another Gallup Poll revealed that a key indicator of employee satisfaction and productivity is an employee's belief that the boss cares about the employee and can be trusted.

Similarly, a study by Employee Retention Headquarters cited appreciation and involvement as more crucial than money to employee happiness. Staff members need to be convinced, verbally and nonverbally, that management respects their position and that they are important to the success of their organization. Treating others well means promptly and sincerely celebrating milestones and victories with them, whether publicly and privately.

Sense of Belonging

Many organizations boast of the esprit de corps that they generate. Team spirit is essential to successful group activity. People like to feel that they are a part of something bigger than themselves: a team, a social group, a military unit, or a company. People are happier, more cooperative and productive when they identify with their group—especially a successful and effective group. People brag about having served in the U.S. Marine Corps long after their service has been completed. People proudly tell others they are employed by IBM, Microsoft, Apple, General Motors, Sony, Toyota, or other prestigious companies.

How can we build this feeling of community in those around us? Good managers build team spirit by keeping objectives clearly in front of their staff members and giving all staff members the chance to participate in determining how they will meet these objectives. By getting people involved in decisions that affect their work, they feel that they are important to the department and this solidifies their commitment. If they are enthusiastic about the job, they will be motivated to do their best.

Treat people as if they were what they ought to be and you help them to become what they are capable of being.

Johann Wolfgang von Goethe

Billy never forgot his first boss. He recalls, "I thought up a great idea that could increase production in my department. All excited, I went to the boss to tell him about it. He never even listened. He said, 'You're paid to work, not to think. Go back to your desk.' I never suggested another idea while I was on that job."

People who work on the job have a great deal of insight into the operation and often come up with good suggestions. All of us are more creative than we think we are. We should make a practice to encourage everyone to make suggestions and take each one of them seriously. If an idea is not acceptable, explain why, but never ignore it—and never belittle it.

Team members and associates should feel free to discuss their personal progress with their manager. Some supervisors inadvertently erect a barrier between themselves and their staff members so that associates do not feel comfortable approaching them. We may not realize this, but if our employees rarely come to us with their problems, it does not mean that there are none. It is more likely that the employees do not feel free to discuss them with us.

The benefits of open communication are apparent in any situation. You may remember how the manufacturer Johnson & Johnson recalled about 31 million bottles of Tylenol at a huge expense to the company when it was revealed that some of the capsules had been tampered with. The candor and quick action of the company's executives was heralded in the media, and the company's stock rebounded relatively quickly. This event (over thirty years ago) generated tremendous good will toward the organization and set a new standard for businesses in responding to a crisis.

Opportunity to Thrive

No one wants to be bored. Treating others well involves ensuring that they thrive. In a work environment, several surveys have shown that to many workers stimulating and valuable work is more important than salary and advancement. It's hard to put a price tag on enthusiasm and excitement for a job. Managers who foster involvement of employees and include them early on in projects, obtain more creative ideas and create greater employee investment and pride in the outcome. Employees who actively participate in making decisions on a broad spectrum of issues help create an environment that they like and one in which they want to remain.

If provided with opportunities for growth both personally and professionally, employees are less likely to look elsewhere. Providing training opportunities with respect to new skill development and career enhancement is an indication that a manager is willing to invest on behalf of the employee. This is critical to employee retention. We can show our interest in staff members by encouraging them to join professional organizations (and by paying the membership fee) and giving employees the time off and admission fees needed to attend lunches and conferences. Companies who have a high retention rate hold a reputation for providing upward mobility for their staff members. A jointly agreed upon career path will gain the commitment of employees and ensure their acceptance of organizational goals and direction. In fact, 92 percent of respondents to one survey indicated that even a substantial annual salary increase would not prompt them to change employers if they were receiving personal and professional development coaching.

Recognize Others' Needs

We may not always anticipate others' specific needs, but we

can always be mindful that others have interests that don't involve us. If our roommate is studying, we don't enter the room and turn on the TV. In the workplace, organizations that demonstrate an awareness that employees need a balanced life have higher retention rates than those that believe that the employee should eat, breathe, and sleep work. Acknowledging and respecting the importance of family and personal life of employees prevents burnout and fosters loyalty. According to the Society for Human Resource Management, employers need to be aware of quality of work-life issues. They must be willing to offer flexible schedules and be sensitive to childcare constraints, parental care challenges, and even the balance between the employee's career and that of his or her partner.

It had long since come to my attention that people of accomplishment rarely sat back and let things happen to them. They went out and happened to things.

Leonardo da Vinci

Eight Ways to Treat Others Right in the Workplace

1. Let each person know how he or she is getting along.
2. Help staff members improve their performance and their contribution by coaching and guidance.
3. "Be hearty in our approbation and lavish in our praise."
4. Tell people in advance about changes that will affect them and, if possible, why the change is being made.
5. Make the best of each person's ability.
6. Look for ability that is not being used, help that person develop that ability and utilize it.

7. Never block a person's opportunity for advancement.
8. Give people freedom to control the way they do their jobs. Encourage them to suggest better methods and approaches.

Know and Overcome Our Biases

People often make decisions based on factors they may not even realize are biases.

After the Achilles Heel Company rejected Juan G. for a sales job, he was hired by a direct competitor and became the best salesperson on their staff. When Achilles' sales manager was asked why he had rejected Juan, he said: "I guess I wasn't sure how well he would fit in."

How many good people have we rejected—at the workplace or socially—because of our conscious or subconscious biases?

The word "bias" means "slant." For example, in hiring, we tend to lean toward those who fit our preconceived notions of what will or will not make for success in that job. Often these preconceptions are wrong—based on concepts that do not necessarily hold up when carefully examined. The word "prejudice" means "prejudgment." The decision is made on the basis of some superficial characteristic before a real evaluation of qualifications is conducted.

Sometimes we reject people because of a specific personal characteristic that annoys us. Remember that our perspective is ours alone, and is not necessarily shared by others. For example, the fact that Lisa reminds you of your ex-girlfriend is not an experience that others will have, and they will not be put off by her.

People Like Ourselves

Our biases are based on not only on how a person speaks, looks, or dresses, but also on other aspects of his or her background. People tend to feel more comfortable with people they consider like themselves. We tend to be biased in favor of people who have similar backgrounds, who attended the same school, or even live in the same community.

The president of a bank was of Christian descent. By strange coincidence, most of the people he personally hired or promoted had Christian backgrounds. Occasionally an unusually competent person from another background might be promoted to a management job—but never a Muslim. Why? He subconsciously distrusted Muslims after the September 11th attacks.

On the surface this action may appear to be sensible. After all, people who work together must be compatible. But not only was this illegal—discrimination based on religion—but allowing a person's religion to be a major hurdle in his or her career may eliminate high-potential people who could have been significant contributors to the company's success.

It's Not Bias—It's Fact

Jack was annoyed. "I am not biased," he explained when criticized for his choice of salespeople. "You have to be goodlooking to be successful in sales. People do judge a book by its cover. Buyers are more likely to spend time with an impressivelooking person. They turn the plain ones away."

However, when Jack was asked to compare his salespeople's results with those of other managers who did not put as much emphasis on looks when hiring, he realized that his "fact" was not true. The best salesperson in the company was Mark, a man Jack had refused to hire in his territory because he was overweight. "Customers would be turned off by a fatty," he explained. Jack's boss pointed out that Mark was a smart, engaging person who others enjoyed spending time with. Jack's subjective bias was not shared by other people, was unfair to Mark and others with weight issues, and got in the way of good decision making.

Uncovering Our Own Biases

Most people accept the fact that we should evaluate someone be based on his or her whole background. Because many biases are subconscious, however, many of us do not realize what our biases are. Biases are emotional, not logical. Only by careful selfanalysis can we become aware of them.

One way to do this is to review the job openings we have filled—either by hiring or promotion—over the past year. Look at the people we have chosen. Do they have any one special characteristic in common? Do they have the same type of appearance, speech, or ethnic background as one another?

Give special attention to the rejected applicants, particularly those who never proceeded beyond the first interview or consideration. Were they really unqualified? Did they have something about them that we could not define, but just didn't like? If so, it could have been good personnel intuition—or be honest—were our biases showing?

Understanding Our Attitude—A Self-Assessment

In order to better understand our attitudes regarding the

cultural differences between ourselves and of others, write, "agree" or "disagree" next to the following statements:

1. As a child, I was raised to celebrate specific holidays related to my country of origin or religious beliefs.
2. As an adult, I am proud of the culture in which I grew up and the clear rules of behavior I learned.
3. My religion requires me to observe specific traditions as an act of faith.
4. By choice, there are additional observances each year that are important to me based upon my interests, religion, gender, age, or other factors.
5. Most of my associates know little or nothing about my background and values.
6. I believe that religious and cultural observances should be a private matter.
7. I am familiar with the cultural backgrounds and religious beliefs of my friends and associates.
8. I respect and celebrate the cultural observances and traditions of others.
9. I openly share the significance of my own cultural celebrations.
10. I believe that only the official holidays of this country should be honored publically.
11. I find some of the customs, traditions, and/or observances of people from different cultures to be curious or offensive.
12. Our community would be more harmonious if all of us shared the same values.

Evaluation of Responses

If the response was "agree" to items 1–4:

This may indicate a strong connection to our own cultural and religious traditions and values. On the one hand, this connection may provide us with a strong sense of purpose, offer guidance for ethical behavior, and be a comfort in unfamiliar or stressful situations. On the other hand, our personal experiences and strong beliefs may make it harder for us to accept or tolerate views that differ from the ones we hold.

If the response was "agree" to items 5–6:

This may indicate that we are reserved about openly expressing our own values and believe that others should behave likewise. On a positive note, this approach may avoid conflict and confrontation when differences do exist. At the same time, a lack of awareness could actually cause problems based upon insensitive comments or behaviors to which others may take exception.

If the response was "agree" to items 7–9:

These answers may be interpreted as demonstrating openness to others and viewing differences as being interesting rather than irritating. A benefit of these attitudes is that they can lead to building rapport with colleagues. A downside may be that others could see us as less than strong in our own convictions.

If the response was "agree" to items 10–12:

By agreeing with these statements, we may be viewed as being a purist in terms of cultural values and mores. An advantage of holding these ideas may include fostering a homogeneous environment when willingly embraced by all. A possible disadvantage is that such attitudes can easily alienate members of the group who hold differences of opinions and practice other styles.

> *As we become ever more diverse, we must work harder to unite around our common values and our common humanity.*

William Jefferson Clinton

Making the Most of Diversity

Once we become aware of and take steps to overcome our biases, we should examine the entire concept of relating to people with diverse backgrounds. We should make it a major goal to achieve a successful relationship with people different from ourselves.

The first phase of making the most of diversity is to make a concerted effort to become aware of the cultural diversity that exists in our organization, church, community or other venues.

The second phase of making the most of diversity is for us to encourage people to talk about their cultural differences. Two things must be remembered concerning cultural diversity:

- People should remember it is difficult to address cultural differences without resorting to stereotypes. In the purest form, there is no such thing as a stereotypical person. No person is exactly like another person and no individual is a clone of another member of a group.
- As diversity grows, so does the complexity of communication and the necessity to make greater efforts in developing improved communication skills.

Awareness and discussion can cause a clearer picture of cultural diversity. Appreciation and understanding of cultural diversity is more than just tolerating differences among individuals or groups, but supporting and nurturing them. A variety of ideas, talents, skills, and knowledge is a desirable attribute of any organization.

Providing a supportive and nurturing environment and exposing group members to new issues, ideas, information, and cultures, enhances our opportunities for growth and success. It also creates opportunities for character development by teaching tolerance and respect for people and by encouraging concern for equity. A culturally diverse coalition that values and nurtures people from all backgrounds is worthy of active participation.

Making the most of diversity requires the commitment of all involved. Changing prevailing attitudes and assumptions is not easy. Often the best we can hope for is to change behaviors rather than deep-seated attitudes. Members of a diverse coalition must be committed to multiculturalism and to addressing issues related to cultural difference.

The Rise of Multiculturism

People in most countries today face the problems inherent in working with diverse groups. From the middle of the twentieth century, companies in Europe and Asia have "imported" workers from less developed countries to work in their workplaces. We have seen mass emigrations of Turks to Germany, Algerians to France, Indonesians and South Asians to Saudi Arabia, Koreans to Japan, and many others.

Early in our history, the American experience differed from that in other countries because the early immigrants relatively rapidly assimilated into the American lifestyle. This is not what has happened in recent times.

Under the traditional melting-pot theory, immigrants who settled in America would shed the ways of the old countries and blend happily into one people. This type of assimilation has been replaced by the multicultural concept. More recent immigrants tend to hang on to their native cultures and integrate them with the culture of their new environment without abandoning them.

Since the 1960s, the idea of a single monoculture has begun to deteriorate. It has given way to a more pluralistic society that continues to evolve through cultural integration and influence. These changes are commonly evident in fashion, dietary habits, entertainment, music, literature, and sports.

Such diversity enables all of us to capitalize on unique skills and areas of expertise. We can learn much by mutual understanding and appreciation of individual differences. Strengthening people's sense of positive cultural identity is an important aspect of establishing a successful relationship among all involved. Individuals may consciously or subconsciously interject ethnic values, attitudes, or behaviors into the dynamics of the larger group.

Understanding is the first step to acceptance.

J K Rowling

Managing Cultural Diversity

To make the most of cultural diversity, programs and protocols should include:

1. *Recruitment.* Try to include people in our organization that are representative of the community.

2. *Diversity Training.* Become aware of the cultural diversity of the group. Try to understand all its dimensions and seek the commitment of those involved to nurture cultural diversity. Address the myths, stereotypes, and cultural differences that interfere with the full contribution of members.

3. *Communications Within Coalitions.* Remove the major barriers that interfere with people from diverse cultures working together. The best method to do this is through understanding and practicing better communication:

- ✓ Learn to listen. Listen for what is really being said, not what we want to hear.
- ✓ Invite others to be a part of the discussion.
- ✓ Learn to communicate clearly and fairly.
- ✓ Do not judge people because of their accent or grammar.
- ✓ Test for understanding. Ask questions to be certain we are clear on what is being said.
- ✓ Adapt our communication style to fit the situation. Be explicit. Individuals from different cultures may react differently to certain language and tone. Know with whom we are communicating.
- ✓ Use language that fosters trust and alliance. Each person wants to succeed in this venture. Be calm and positive.
- ✓ When conflicts arise, the problem may result from style rather than content. Strive for understanding. Review, revise, and revisit our main objective to be certain the

content is clear. How we say something may be more important than what we say.

4. *A Focus on Similarities.* Men and women, whites and people of color, managers and workers are different from one another, but their similarities outweigh such differences. An appreciation and acceptance of both commonalities and differences are essential to effective relationships.

5. *Maintain the Commitment.* Continue to revisit the various activities that ensure the awareness, understanding, communication, and nurturing of a culturally diverse organization.

6. *Provide Strong Leadership.*

✓ In every area in which we participate, on or off the job, articulate pluralistic vision and values for that organization; show ways in which they are an integral part of that organization's mission and vision.

✓ Encourage and support discussion among people about the meaning of diversity and pluralism; show how to implement programs that can accomplish those goals.

✓ Demonstrate ethical commitment to fairness and to the elimination of discrimination in its relationships to other people, groups, and organizations.

✓ Understand the dimensions of diversity, use inclusive and valuing language, quote diverse sources, readily adapt to differences in communication styles of diverse people, display respect for human differences, and be aware of and comfortable about dealing with diversity issues.

✓ Value ongoing personal learning and change, solicit

views and opinions of diverse people, invite feedback about personal behavior and blind spots, and be open to belief modifications and actions based on feedback.

✓ Mentor and empower diverse individuals and encourage others to do so as well.

Quick Tips for Working with People of Different Cultures

➤ Most people appreciate a sincere effort to reach out, be greeted in their own language, and to have their beliefs acknowledged. Don't worry about making mistakes.

➤ It may take longer to build rapport and trust with people from different cultures. Be patient.

➤ Ask people involved to let us know at any time if we do something that is offensive in their culture.

➤ Thoroughly explain the procedures that we propose to conduct and the reason for doing them.

➤ Communicating with people who have limited proficiency in our language requires extra care. If the material is technical or complex, use a trained interpreter; for simpler matters, get help from another associate who has a good knowledge of both languages involved.

➤ As much as possible, use words (not gestures) to express our meaning. Gestures that are acceptable in our culture may be offensive or meaningless in other cultures.

➤ Explore how the person views the matter being discussed.

Sum and Substance

• Treating others well begins with a recognition that each person is an individual.

- We must do our best to meet the different needs of different people and still treat everyone fairly and equally.
- By instilling our staff members with pride in their work, we help to ensure a productive and happy group of employees.
- Our staff members will be more committed to the organization if we actively seek their ideas and innovations.
- In the workplace and elsewhere, it is paramount to remember that we are not the sole focus of others' lives.
- Make a point of accommodating the many needs that our staff members have the many demands on their time.
- Make a point of coaching and praising others at work.
- We may harbor biases toward those we see as different from ourselves. It is prudent to closely examine our behavior toward others to uncover our biases so that we can work toward alleviating them.
- As multiculturalism has become increasingly the norm around the world, we must take advantage of what those from other backgrounds have to offer. Within the workplace, we will want to implement inclusive practices to best welcome and integrate people of all nationalities and faiths.

Step 4

....

BECOME A GOOD
CONVERSATIONALIST

The ability to engage in interesting conversation is one of the greatest personal assets a man or woman can have. It is a great aid to business and social success and also makes for greater enjoyment of the company of others.

There is nothing that enables us to make so good an impression, especially upon those who do not know us thoroughly, than the ability to converse well. To be able to interest people, to rivet their attention, to draw them to us naturally, by the very superiority of our conversational ability, is to be the possessor of a very great accomplishment. It opens doors and softens hearts. It makes us welcome and engaging in all sorts of company. It helps us to get on in the world. It sends us clients, patients, customers, and friends. It is the tool that will enable us to persuade people to accept our ideas, follow our leadership, and buy our products.

People who can talk well, who have the art of putting things in an attractive way, who can interest others immediately by their power of speech, have a very great advantage over those who may know more than they do about the subject, but who cannot express himself or herself with ease or eloquence. In fact, research shows that noncognitive skills, those that go toward socialization, are much more important in terms of professional success than we traditionally think.

> *There are four ways, and only four ways, in which we have contact with the world. We are evaluated and classified by these four contacts: what we do, how we look, what we say, and how we say it.*
>
> Dale Carnegie

Conversation is a tremendous power developer. However, talking without thinking, without an effort to express oneself with clarity and conciseness will work against us. Mere chattering, or gossiping, is not impressive. Nothing will indicate our fineness or coarseness of culture, our breeding or lack of it, as quickly as our conversation. It tells our whole life's story. What we say, and how we say it, will betray all our secrets, will give the world our true measure.

What Makes A Good Conversationalist?

Intellect, brainpower, and expertise in a field can be helpful, but they are not the main reasons a good conversationalist holds the attention of others.

We must make people feel our empathy, feel that they have met a sincere person. Instead of greeting people with a stiff "How do you do?" or "Glad to meet you," without any feeling or sentiment in it, we should look people we meet squarely in the eye and make them feel our personality. Give them a smile and kind word that will make them glad to meet us.

Be Cordial

Cultivate cordiality; fling the door of our heart wide open. Don't just leave it slightly ajar, as much as to say to people we meet, "You may peep in a bit, but you cannot come in until I know whether you will be a desirable acquaintance." A great many people are stingy with their cordiality. They seem to reserve it for some special occasion or for intimate friends. They think it is too precious to give out to everybody.

This warm, glad handshake and cordial greeting will create a bond of good will between us and the people we meet. They will say to themselves, "Well, there is a really interesting personality. I want to know more about this man or woman. They see something in me, evidently, which most people do not see." This ability to engender a strong feeling of connectedness with others is a trait mastered by President Clinton. Those who meet him invariably say that they feel he is really looking right into their hearts when he speaks with them. Such a feeling creates an immediate warmth and intimacy.

It's Not Just What We Say, But How We Say It

Keep in mind that we express ourselves not only through the words we utter, but also by the tone of our voice, the expression on our face, our gestures, and our bearing.

Looking others in the eye and really listening to what they are saying is enormously impactful. If someone feels that we are not genuinely engaged in our conversation with them—if we look around the room, if our facial expression is not one of attention and compassion, or if, heaven forbid, we look at our device when someone is speaking—we send the signal that the other person is not important to us. That is a great way to lose someone's interest in getting to know us better or to do business with us in the future.

We will know when we have related well with someone. All good conversationalists have felt a power come to them from the listener that they never felt before, and which often stimulates and inspires to fresh endeavor. The mingling of thought with thought, the contact of mind with mind, develops new powers, as the mixing of two chemicals often produces a new third substance.

> *Conversation should be like juggling; up go the balls and plates, up and over, in and out, good solid objects that glitter in the footlights and fall with a bang if you miss them.*
>
> Evelyn Waugh,
> British Writer

Be Truly Interested In Others

Nervous impatience is a conspicuous characteristic of many of us. Everything bores us which does not bring more business, or more money, or which does not help to attain the positions for which we are striving.

Instead of enjoying our friends, we're inclined to look upon them as so many rungs in a ladder, and to value them in proportion as they send us patients, clients, customers, or show their ability to give us a boost for political position.

Develop Empathy

One cause for our conversational decline is a lack of empathy. We are too selfish, too busily engaged in our own welfare, and wrapped up in our own little world, too intent upon our own selfpromotion to be interested in others. No one can make a good conversationalist who is not empathetic. We must be able to enter into another's life, to live it with the other person, to be a good listener or a good speaker.

If we would make ourselves agreeable, we must touch others along the lines of their interest. No matter how much we may know about a subject, if it does not happen to interest those to whom we are talking, our efforts will be largely lost.

Too many people are cold, reserved, and distant, because their minds are somewhere else, concerned only about their own affairs. There are only two things that interest them; business and their own little world. If we talk to them about these things, they are interested at once; but they do not care about our affairs, how we get on, what our ambition is, or how they can help us. Their conversation will never reach a high standard while they live in such a feverish, selfish, and unsympathetic state.

The most fruitful and natural exercise for our minds is, in my opinion, conversation.

Michel de Montaigne,
French Essayist

Be Tactful

Great conversationalists have always been very tactful. They are interesting without offending. Some people have the peculiar quality of touching the best that is in us; they are joyous and agreeable. They never inflame our sensitive spots. They radiate all that is spontaneous and sweet and beautiful. Others stir up our less desirable qualities. Every time they come into our presence they irritate us.

Be open-minded and tolerant. People who violate a sense of taste, of justice, and of fairness, never interest or attract others. They lock tight all the approaches to their inner selves and the conversation is perfunctory, mechanical, and without life or feeling.

Put Others At Ease

Lincoln was master of the art of making himself interesting to everybody he met. He put people at ease with his stories and jokes, and made them feel so completely at home in his presence that they opened up their mental treasures to him without reserve. Strangers were always glad to talk with him because he was so cordial and quaint, and always gave more than he got.

A sense of humor such as Lincoln had is, of course, a great addition to one's conversational power. But not everyone can be funny; and, if we lack the sense of humor, we will embarrass ourselves by attempting to be funny.

Good conversationalists, however, are not overly serious. They don't overwhelm us with miniscule details. Facts, statistics can be weary so they supplement them with illustrations and anecdotes to make their points. Vivacity is absolutely necessary. Heavy conversation can be boring, but, on the other hand, if our conversation is too light, although it may be amusing, it may project to others that we are vapid and superficial.

Therefore, to be a good conversationalist we must be spontaneous, buoyant, natural, sympathetic, and must show a spirit of good will. We must feel a spirit of helpfulness, and must enter heart and soul into things that interest others. We must get the attention of people and hold it by interesting them, and we can only interest them by a warm sympathy—a real, friendly sympathy. If we are cold, distant, and unsympathetic, we will not attract others to us.

How we project our ideas, our attitude, the spirit we radiate, our personality, will have everything to do with our conversational proficiency. The impression we make will be a tremendous factor in our success.

Learn and Remember Names

When meeting a new person, make a special effort to learn his or her name. Often names may be mumbled in an introduction, especially when more than one person is being introduced at the same time. If it is not clear, it is not impolite to ask that it be repeated. Using the name during the conversation helps set it firmly in our mind.

Follow these suggestions:

- Determine which part of the name to use. Americans usually use first names, unless the other person is significantly older or has higher authority, then use Mr./Ms. until he or she says instructs you to do otherwise. In other cultures, one always uses the formal "Mr",

"Mrs", "Ms", or a title, "Dr", "Professor," etc. unless invited to be less formal.

- Create a mental picture linking the name with the person. Don't think in words—think in pictures. When we meet Julie, picture her bedecked with *jewelry*; "Sandy's" dappled hair reminds us of a beach, and "George" is visualized as standing at the edge of a gorge.

- If the name is the same as or similar to that of a relative, friend, or another person we know, picture the new person with that person.

- Repeat the name immediately in conversation, but don't overuse it. Numerous repetitions will appear deliberate. Use the other person's name about once in three to four minutes of conversation, and when we leave.

- Most importantly, repeat the name to ourselves until it is firmly established in our mind.

Remember, a person's name is, to that person, the sweetest and most important sound in any language.

Dale Carnegie

Learn About the Other Person

When we meet a new person, it is important to get as much information as possible about him or her. One way to do so is by asking questions. This should not be an interrogation. Just a few well-chosen questions will start the ball rolling and the conversation will flow.

This is a delicate process, as we do not want to appear to be nosy. Only ask those questions that are appropriate for the situation in which we are involved. For example, some questions are appropriate when talking to a person on a business matter; others in social situations, etc.

In a social situation, questions about the area in which one lives, hobbies or interests, family or mutual acquaintances often are good starters. Other good conversation openers are about schools or colleges attended, recent current events (but be wary of politics, we don't want to engage in a disagreement) or pick up on a comment made by the other person and ask about it. We can also tell someone that we like her shoes, top, or handbag (this approach can be a bit more challenging when speaking with a man), to start up a discussion.

When meeting people in a business setting, good starters are questions about the industry and company the person represents, news items that affect that industry, and questions about the nature of his or her job or career.

It's not necessary to have a list of questions we plan to ask. Once the conversation is underway, comments and responses will flow easily.

Listen! Really Listen!

Conversation is a two-way street. One way is what we say; the other is what the other party says. Too often we are so involved in what we are saying, or in thinking about what we want to say next, that we do not give adequate attention to what the other person is saying.

Suppose someone brings us a problem and asks for help. We may begin by listening attentively, but before we know it, our mind may wander. Instead of listening to the problem, we're thinking about the pile of work on our desk, the telephone call we planned to make when this person walked into our office, or of the argument we had with our daughter when we drove her to school this morning. We hear words, but we're not really listening.

This happens to all of us. Why? Our minds can process ideas considerably faster than we can talk. When someone is talking to us, our mind tends to race ahead and we complete the speaker's sentence in our mind— sometimes correctly, but often differently from what the speaker says. We hear what our mind dictates, but not what eventually is said.

This is human nature. But that is not an excuse for being a bad listener. Take the following test to determine our listening habits.

Evaluate Our Listening Skills

Answer "yes" or "no" to the following questions:

1. Do I keep interrupting when somebody is trying to tell me something?
2. Do I look at papers during the discussion?
3. Do I come to conclusion before I hear the whole story?
4. Does my body language signal lack of interest?
5. Do I hear only what I want to hear and block out everything else?
6. Do I show impatience with the speaker?
7. Do I spend more time talking than listening?
8. Does my mind wander during the discussion?
9. Do I think about my rebuttal or responses while the other person is speaking?

10. Do I ignore nonverbal signals from the speaker that will tell me the speaker wants me to respond?

If the answer was yes to any of these questions, our listening skills need improvement.

Becoming an Active Listener

An active listener not only pays close attention to what the other party says, but asks questions, makes comments, and reacts verbally and nonverbally to what is said.

One way of improving our listening skill is to take an active role as a listener. Instead of just sitting or standing with our ears open, follow these guidelines:

Look at the speaker. Eye contact is one way of showing interest, but don't overdo it. Look at the whole person; don't just stare into his or her eyes.

Show interest by our facial expressions. Smile or show concern when appropriate.

Indicate that we are following the conversation by nods or gestures.

Ask questions about what's being said. One way is to paraphrase: "So the way I understand it is..." or ask specific questions about specific points. This technique not only enables us to clarify points that may be unclear but also keeps us alert and paying full attention.

Don't interrupt. A pause should not be a signal for us to start talking. Wait.

Be an empathetic listener. Listen with our hearts as well as our heads. Try to feel what other people are feeling when they speak. In other words, put ourselves in the speaker's shoes.

Set voice mail to pick up all phone calls right away. One of the most common distractions during a conversation is a ringing phone. Answering the phone when conversing with somebody not only disrupts the flow of our thoughts, but also it is rude. It sends the message to the person with whom we're speaking that they are not as important as the person calling. If we know we are expecting an important call, inform the person with whom we are speaking that we must answer the phone and apologize for the interruption.

If shutting off the phone isn't feasible, get away from the telephone. Go to an empty conference room. Even if there is a phone in the room, it probably won't ring, as no one knows that we're there.

Hide the papers. If our desk is strewn with paper, we'll be tempted to skim over them and lose our focus on the discussion. If we go to a conference room, take only the papers that are related to the discussion. If we must stay at our desk, put the papers in a drawer and close our documents on our screen so that we won't be tempted to read them. And of course, we must not look at our mobile device during the conversation.

Don't get too comfortable. Robert L. tells of a particularly embarrassing situation: "Some years ago I was discussing an event with another manager. As was my custom, I sat in my comfortable executive chair with my hands behind my head. Maybe I rocked a little, but fortunately, I caught myself before I dozed off. Ever since then, rather than take a relaxing position when I engage in discussions, I've made a point of sitting on the edge of my chair and leaning forward rather than backward. This position not only brings me physically closer to the other person, but also enables me to be more attentive and helps me to maintain eye contact. It also shows the other person that I'm truly interested in getting the full story he or she is relating and that I take seriously what is being said. And because I'm not quite so comfortable, there's less of a tendency to daydream."

Don't think about our rebuttal. It's tempting to pick up one or two points that the speaker is making and plan how we will respond to them. Do this and we'll probably miss much of the balance of what is being said, often the really important matters. Concentrate on what is said through the entire process.

Take notes. It's impossible to remember everything that's said in a lengthy discussion. However, even if we use shorthand, making lengthy notes keeps us from fully listening. Just jot down key words or phrases. Write down figures or important facts, just enough to help us remember. Immediately after a meeting, while the information is still fresh in our mind, write a detailed summary.

> *When dealing with people, remember you are not dealing with creatures of logic, but creatures of emotion.*
>
> Dale Carnegie

Conversational Styles

The manner in which we communicate with others, whether it is in a one-to-one conversation or when speaking to a group, can influence how others receive us. We may come across as passive, aggressive, or assertive.

Some of the traits manifested by passive people are:

- They are more concerned about others, often to their own personal detriment.
- They are often stressed internally, although it may not be obvious to others.
- They are likely to have low self-esteem.
- They are more concerned with being liked than being respected.
- They build others up even at their own expense.
- They will take blame rather than blame others.
- They avoid confrontation.
- When action is needed, they will ask for it indirectly in the form of a suggestion or as a wish.

The opposite of the passive style is the aggressive approach. Aggressive people manifest these characteristics:

✓ They are overly self-centered.

✓ They are often internally stressed.

✓ They lack self-esteem, but will not admit it even to themselves.

✓ They are usually not liked or respected by others.

✓ They put others down by sarcasm or derogatory remarks.

✓ They try to control everything and everyone.

✓ When errors or failures occur, they place blame on others and will never consider themselves responsible.

✓ They enjoy and seek confrontation with people with opposing views.

✓ If in a position of authority, they insist that others follow.

✓ They are often verbally abusive to opponents.

✓ When action is needed, they present it in the form of a demand or command.

Effective communicators take a middle course. They are confident and assertive.

- They stand up for their own rights, but are sensitive to those of the person(s) with whom they are speaking.

- If stressed, they deal with it and then move on.

- They have a strong, positive self-image.

- They are direct and honest.

- They earn the respect of others.

- They show their appreciation of others.

- They own up to their own errors and failures and expect others to own up to theirs.

- They do not seek confrontation. If others disagree, they will work to persuade them to their point of view in a non-threatening, objective discussion.

- They are always willing to listen to others.

- When action is needed, they state what should be done, and work with others to accomplish it.

It is not easy to change our personality, but if we uncover that we have a passive or aggressive communication style, we'll want to be better communicators. We must make an effort to achieve the assertive-confident approach.

Telephone Conversations

Every time we pick up the telephone—whether to make or

receive a call—we are leaving an impression on the person at the other end of that line. Often, the only image that person will have of us and our company will derive from this conversation.

In face-to-face communication, there are many tools that help us to make good (or bad) impressions: our facial expressions, our gestures, and our use of props or visual aids. With the telephone, there is only one tool: our voice. Most people do not really hear themselves as others hear them. The best way to obtain a true concept of how we sound to others is to record several telephone calls and evaluate how they come across when we replay them. Most important, of course, is how we sound. As noted above, listen to those recordings and make whatever changes needed to improve its quality. Note that some people have developed the habit of speaking too loudly while on mobile phones. Ask your friends if you have that habit, and if so, be very mindful of the volume level of your voice when on a business call.

Our Attitude

One of the prime characteristics of effectively conversing with others is to be friendly. When we listen to recordings of ourselves on the phone, do we sound friendly on those recordings or do we sound abrupt or annoyed? The call may have come at an inopportune time—we may be pressed by a demanding boss, a deadline that we are trying to meet, or a crisis in the department, but our caller does not know (or care about) this. We must discipline ourselves to put everything other than that phone call out of our mind. That includes turning away from our computer screen during the call. If we're on Facebook while we're speaking, we think that we're cleverly "multitasking," but in fact, we're giving poor attention to two things.

If we are upset about anything, before picking up the phone, take a deep breath, relax our muscles and clear our mind. Be calm, be attentive and the impression we wish to make—a concerned interest in what that person is saying—will be projected.

Good Telephone Manners When Receiving a Call

Answer the phone promptly. In a business situation, the phone should not ring more than three times before it is answered. If we are on another call, either use our voicemail or put the current call on hold, pick up the new call and either ask the caller to wait for a few minutes, or take the number and call back. If we plan to be away from our desk for more than a few minutes, arrange for somebody to take the calls or set the voicemail to answer after three rings.

Always state who we are immediately. Instead of saying "hello," say "engineering department, Sam Johnson speaking." We cannot assume that the person calling knows who we are. If we do not know the caller, ask for his or her name. If it is an unusual name, ask how it is spelled. Write it down. When responding, use the caller's name. It demonstrates our sincere interest in that person and his or her problem. If we cannot provide the answer to the caller's questions within a very few minutes, it is better to advise that we will call back rather than have the caller hold for a long time. If he or she prefers to hold or it takes longer than anticipated to respond, get back frequently so the caller knows that he or she has not been abandoned.

One of the most irritating aspects of telephoning a company is to be told that we will be transferred to another person and then be disconnected. If it is necessary to transfer a call, always tell the person to whom they will be transferred and give the caller that person's extension or phone number (if different from ours). It is also a good idea to obtain the caller's number, so that if disconnected, we can call back.

Respond, not only to direct questions, but also to implied objections. When Madeline called the mail order department to complain about receiving damaged merchandise, she seemed upset when she was told to return it by United Parcel Service. The customer service representative recognized her concern and quickly told Madeline that she did not have to make a trip to the UPS shipping center, but that they would arrange for UPS to pick up the package at her home. By listening carefully to the caller and responding her concern, the customer service representative not only made the customer feel better about the situation, but he also made a friend for the company.

Good Telephone Manners When Making a Call

The beginning and end of a telephone conversation are critical points. Begin the call with a welcome attitude that shows we are glad to be talking to that person and recognize that we appreciate his or her willingness to speak with us. If we are not known to the person we are calling, introduce ourselves and state why we are calling.

"Good morning, Mrs Samuels, as a mother who has children in our schools, I know you are concerned about the quality of education in this district. This is Blanche H, campaign manager for Diane McGrath, who is running for the school board presidency."

After making the presentation, listening and responding to questions, conclude in a positive way. "Thank you for your attention. I look forward to seeing you at the board meeting next Tuesday."

Plan all calls before picking up the phone. If we have to cover several items in a call, make a list of these items. Note the major points we wish to make for each of them. Follow our plan when talking and the call will be accomplished more effectively and in less time than if we don't plan ahead.

It may seem like unnecessary advice to receive, but really listen to the other person. His or her responses may make it necessary to adjust our original plan. Ask questions and pay close attention to the responses. This is true of all communications, but particularly valuable when on the telephone because we do not have the advantage of watching the nonverbal signals given in face-to-face dealings. Learn to "read" the nuances of changes in inflection and voice tone. Think out the message we plan to send from the listener's point of view.

Small Talk

There is nothing really small about "small talk." This nonbusiness style of conversation has the potential to build connections and become the foundation for ongoing relationships.

Becoming adept at small talk doesn't require an exhaustive knowledge of current events. It simply requires the ability to focus the other person on his or her favorite topic—and ask questions that indicate interest. Even talking about the weather can be an icebreaker. A little small talk before a business discussion is a surefire way to build rapport.

Watch the Body Language

All of us convey information with more than the words we use. What we say is often modified by the way we use our body, our facial expressions, our gestures—the way we sit or stand all convey meaning.

Wouldn't it be great if we could buy a dictionary of body language so that we could look up what each gesture or expression means? Then we could interpret what everybody is really saying.

Some people have tried to write such "dictionaries." They list a variety of different "signals" and identify their meaning. For example, the other person strokes his chin. What can this mean? "Ha! I know. He's pondering the situation." Indeed, he may very well be thinking it over, but it might also mean that he didn't shave this morning and his chin itches.

The person across from us is sitting with his arms folded across his chest. Some "experts" interpret this to mean that he is holding himself in, blocking us out, rejecting us. Nonsense! Look at a roomful of people at a class, a lecture, or a theatrical performance. We will note that a good number of these people are sitting with arms crossed. Does that mean that they are rejecting the instructor or actors? Of course not. It's a comfortable way to sit, and if we are cold, it keeps us warm. On the other hand, if in the middle of a conversation, the other party should suddenly cross her arms, it might mean that at that point she is disagreeing with us.

There Is No Universal Body Language

While there is no simple, universal body language, this does not mean that one cannot read body language. Each of us has his or her own way of nonverbally expressing ideas, feelings, and responses.

Why should this be? Body language is an acquired trait. We tend to imitate other people. It starts with our parents and often is closely tied in with our ethnic background. Two boys are born in Detroit, Michigan, but their parents immigrated to the United States from two different countries. One family came from a country where the usual way to express oneself was with gesticulation. You could not speak the language without using your hands. The other family came from a country where nobody gesticulated except when highly emotional. The two boys met for the first time in high school. The first boy was discussing a situation in his usual way—his hands moving wildly. The second boy thought: "My goodness, he's excited about this." Then he responded in his usual quiet way and the first boy thought, "He's not even interested."

A similar pattern may be determined by family habits. When anybody speaks to a member of Chelsea's family, they respond with frequent nods of the head. Most of us would interpret this to mean that they were agreeing with us. But as Chelsea pointed out when questioned about this, all it meant to them was that they acknowledged that they heard what was being said.

Study Each Person's Use of Nonverbal Clues

If body language is an important aspect of communication, is there any way that we can learn to read it? There is no 100 hundred percent accurate approach to reading body language. The only way to obtain a reasonably good interpretation of a person's nonverbal actions and reactions is to know the person with whom we are communicating. When we deal with the same people over and over again, by careful observation we can learn to read their body language. We note that when Claudia agrees with us, she tends to lean forward and when Paul agrees he tilts his head to the right. We observe that Kat nods no matter what we say, but when she is not sure of something, she has a puzzled look on her face even though she is nodding.

By making careful mental notes about each of the people with whom we communicate, we will be able to understand his or her nonverbal clues and interpret them properly. After a while, we may note that some gestures or expressions are more common among the people we communicate with than others. From these we may make some generalizations when dealing with new people, but we must be careful not to put too much credence in those interpretations until we have had more experience with these individuals.

When the body language seems to contradict or skew the meaning of the words being spoken, or we are not sure what the signal being sent really means, ask a question. Get the person to communicate verbally what is really meant. By good questioning, we can overcome the doubts that the nonverbal actions induced and be able to deal with them.

Body language is a very powerful tool. We had body language before we had speech, and apparently, 80 percent of what you understand in a conversation is read through the body, not the words.

Deborah Bull,
British Dancer and Writer

Conversation Effectiveness Checklist

To assess the way we employ the advice in this chapter, review some recent conversations—whether they were in person or on the telephone. Did we:

➤ Smile? Even on the telephone, a smile is reflected in our voice and our attitude.
➤ If appropriate, use small talk to break the ice?
➤ Remember and use the person's name?

Make a connection with the other person by observing his or her traits, values, or achievements?

➤ Establish common ground?
➤ Show respect for the other person's time?
➤ Show sensitivity to issues of diversity and avoid controversial subjects?
➤ Demonstrate a sincere desire to learn about the person by asking thoughtful questions?
➤ Fully listen and focus on what the person was saying?
➤ Ask how we can help?
➤ Talk in terms of the other person's interests?
➤ Tell them something of interest that they might not already know?
➤ Give sincere praise or a genuine compliment, along with the evidence for our statement?

Sum and Substance

Dos for Good Conversation

- DO be prepared. A good conversationalist engages his or her listeners and stimulate conversation. Hone our conversational skills by keeping up with trends and current events.

- DO learn the name of the person with whom we are speaking and use it in the conversation.

- DO make eye contact. Looking directly at the other person is a indication that we are listening. But don't stare at the other person. Move our eyes around so we observe their entire face.

- DO speak clearly and audibly. If we are frequently asked to speak up or to repeat ourselves, we probably are not speaking clearly. Record and listen to our conversations so we learn whether we are easy to hear and understand when we speak.

- DO use language and images familiar to the listener. We get more out of a conversation with someone who speaks and thinks like we do, than someone who uses vocabulary differently.

- DO speak the language style of the person with whom we're talking. Use different words and inflection when speaking to business associates than when conversing with the teenager down the street.

- DO stick to the topic. Conversation stealers are people who jump in on our story to change the focus to themselves or to something that they know more about.

- DO know when to speak and when to listen. Conversation should be give and take. Each person involved in a conversation needs to speak and each needs to listen. Participate but don't monopolize.

- DO express an interest in what's being said. Acknowledge statements with a nod, comment, or question when appropriate.

- DO ask open-ended questions to promote communication— that is, questions that require more than a yes or no response.

Don'ts for Good Conversation

- DON'T speak too fast or too slow. We've all been in conversations with people who talk so fast that we can't keep up or so slowly that, by the time they finish expressing their thought, we've forgotten the topic.

- DON'T mumble or swallow our words.

- DON'T talk too softly or too loud. Judge our volume by the closeness or distance from our listener(s).

- DON'T monopolize the conversation. Give the other person(s) a chance to talk.

- DON'T brag or boast. A conversation should be an interchange of ideas and thoughts—not an ego-trip.

- DON'T interrogate. Questions should be presented in a friendly and nonaggressive manner. Use open-end questions so the other person can express his or her ideas freely.

- DON'T interrupt. Let the other person complete his or her comment before presenting ours.

- DON'T talk over another person. Talking while the other person is still speaking is not only impolite, but we may miss the point he or she is making.

- DON'T close our mind to what is being said. Openmindedness is essential if we want to understand another's point of view.

To Be an Effective Listener:

- Listen empathetically. Try to feel what the other person is feeling when he or she speaks.

- Remove all distractions. Turn off the telephone; remove all papers not pertinent to the conversation.

- Make sure we understood what was said by rephrasing what we heard. Clarify any uncertainties after the other person has spoken.

- Try honestly to see things from the other person's point of view.

- Don't jump to conclusions or make assumptions. Keep an open and accepting attitude.

- Show interest by our facial expressions. Smile or show concern when appropriate.

- Indicate that we are following the conversation by nods or gestures.

- Ask questions about what is being said. We can paraphrase, "So the way I understand it is…" or we can ask specific questions about specific points. This not only enables us to clarify points, but keeps us alert and paying full attention.

- Don't interrupt! A pause should not be interpreted as a time for us to start talking. Wait until we are certain that the other person has completed his statement.
- Observe the speaker's body language.

Step 5

SPEAK IN PUBLIC WITH
CONFIDENCE AND CONVICTION

S urveys show that speaking in public is on the top of
the list of people's fears. Fortunately, this is a fear that
is easily overcome.

Structuring the Informational Presentation

An innovative presentation will keep our audience intrigued,
but it's best to save the innovation for the subject matter. In
terms of how we make our presentation, following a traditional
structure helps to ensure our success.

Opening: Statement of Topic

Our opening statement in which we lay forth the topic should
be brief and clear. It should leave no question in the listeners'

minds as to the subject matter of the presentation. This is especially true when the presentation is part of a longer series of presentations, such as a staff meeting or full-day training session.

State Key Message: Desired End Result

Our key message statement should give the audience a clear picture of the main message of our presentation. It is simple, direct, and tells the audience where we are going with the information. It should answer this question in our audience's mind: "Why should I listen to this presentation?"

We should follow our key message statement with the central points we will make and the expected results, in straightforward language. In general, the fewer words, the better when stating our points. To emphasize the key message of our presentation to inform, we succinctly restate the key message or the desired end result of our presentation after giving the central points. This leaves our listeners with a message that they will remember long after the presentation.

Types of Evidence

Once we have told our audience what we want to convey, we must present evidence to support it. There are several forms of evidence we could use. As we think about ways in which to support our statements, we might think about the evidence that we've seen lawyers use in court, either in the movies or on TV. (Or, if we've sat through a trial or we're a lawyer, in real life.) Types of evidence include facts and statistics, as well as:

Analogies, in which we compare our topic with something that all audience members will understand.

Testimonials, which are statements by those who are familiar with the subject matter about some aspect of it.

Demonstrations, in which we show the audience how something happened or might have happened—remember Atticus Finch throwing the ball to Tom Robinson in *To Kill a Mockingbird*?

Examples, such as stories that show our subject matter in application, are an engaging way to make our topic come alive for our listeners.

Exhibits, which are visual aids that explain the information we're trying to convey in a form to which the audience can relate. Presentations are more interesting and engaging when we find ways to use visual aids to make our points. Turning data into a graph or chart makes our message more quickly and easily understood. Diagrams and photographs pull our listeners' attention to our presentation. Consider handouts as a way to make information accessible to our audience after a presentation.

Flip charts or chalkboards are simple visual means to enhance our presentations. By illustrating the subjects discussed, what is being presented becomes far more effective. People tend to learn faster and remember longer a subject in which the listening is augmented by visual images.

One of the most popular professors at Syracuse University School of Journalism was also a cartoonist. He drew cartoons and caricatures as he lectured. His colleagues scoffed at this practice and considered it very unprofessional. "He's just amusing his classes, not teaching," they claimed. Yes, his students did find it amusing, but they absorbed a great deal more information than they would from the lectures alone. Years later, his students could still recall his teachings.

There are many forms of visual aids. Among these are:

- Charts
- Graphs
- Photographs
- Diagrams
- Handouts
- Working models
- Videos

The format we use in showing our visuals depends on the type of visual and the size of the audience. For small groups, charts, graphs, diagrams, and the like can be posted on the walls of the room or displayed on an easel. Videos could be shown on a small TV screen or on as a PowerPoint on a laptop or desk computer. Chalkboards can be used where appropriate.

Visuals can also be used in one-to-one communication. In training her people to handle insurance claims, Joan found that the process was much more easily understood when she drew a flow chart as she described it. As she taught each phase, she outlined it by drawing boxes for each step and arrows showing the movement from step to step.

Steve, a warehouse manager, learned from difficult experience that telling his employees how to do the job was not enough. Unless he brought his trainees from place to place in the warehouse, they had difficulty in understanding what he was teaching. This was a very time consuming effort. He simplified the training by designing a model of the storerooms with which he could orient his staff members as he told them about the work they would be doing.

For larger audiences, charts, graphs, photos and related material can be shown as PowerPoint slides. Videos or slides can be projected on a large screen. Statistical tables and charts showing large sets of numbers are best presented as handouts. Our presentation will be more interesting and persuasive if we use a variety of types of evidence to support our message.

Closing

Restate the key message. Reiterate what we want the participants to do:

✓　Take a specific action
✓　Practice a new technique
✓　Prepare a plan to implement the points discussed
✓　Train others in the areas covered in the talk
✓　Other pertinent action

By summarizing our major points, we leave the audience with a final impression that is clear and memorable. If transitioning into a question and answer session, repeat the summary after the Q and A. Lastly, as we conclude, thank our audience members for their attention and commitment.

Structuring the Persuasive Presentation

Perhaps our talk is aimed at getting our audience members to do a particular thing, or we want them to leave the room with a particular belief. To do so, we can modify the above presentation outline slightly using the three components that follow in the body or our talk. These guides to presenting content help to guarantee that our presentation will be a vibrant, forceful speech.

1. *Incident*: Citing an incident or an anecdote that illustrates the point we plan to make is a surefire way to get and keep the attention of our listeners.

2. *Action*: Then point out what action we want the audience to take.

3. *Benefit*: Conclude by showing how this action will benefit the audience.

Incident

When delivering our presentation, we should almost always begin with an incident. The incident is based on an experience that taught us a lesson. It captures the immediate attention of our listeners and makes our communication more conversational.

Action

The second component of the magic formula, the action, is what we want the audience to do. It may be to buy our product, to write their congressman, to stop smoking, or just to think more about the subject. When using the magic formula, be sure that both our action and benefit steps are brief, clear, and specific. Remember, our point must communicate what action we want our listeners to take. The more specific the action step, the better. To communicate clearly, identify one specific action and one specific benefit.

Benefit

The third part of the magic formula is the benefit the listeners will receive by doing what is asked for in the action step.

For example, "By using this component, we will reduce the time spent and lower the cost in manufacturing (name the product)."

"Stopping smoking will not only make us healthier and enable us to live longer, but also will keep our families from the dangers of secondhand smoke."

Using the Formula to Advantage

Our ability to inspire others to take any action or to adopt a belief is largely dependent on our ability to communicate from our listeners' point of view. Early in the presentation, we must develop the trust of our listeners. Getting favorable attention and establishing the need to consider a new behavior or belief must be accomplished quickly. The use of an incident is an effective way to do this. To be persuaded to do a particular thing, they must see evidence that clearly, from their point of view, supports the stated need for action. The audience must not feel that they are being driven to a particular behavior or belief—they must see this behavior or belief as the logical option.

After establishing the need for the action, we illustrate both the advantages and disadvantages of each alternative. We are careful to ensure that alternatives are considered from the point of view of our listeners and that they are considered and communicated in a credible and balanced fashion.

We conclude with evidence to support what we believe is the best alternative and state what action to take or belief to hold and what the benefit is to them, thereby inspiring our listeners to embrace the specific conduct or understanding that will yield the desired results.

In preparing a persuasive presentation, we should with the end in mind—the action we want our listeners to take—and work back from that point. When we make the presentation, seek an example or incident, which will get attention and prepare the way for the desired action. By vividly reconstructing an incident we can make it the basis of influencing the conduct of others. It will be the evidence that convinces the audience to act. In communicating the example, we must recreate a segment of our experience in such a way that it tends to have the same effect on our listeners as it originally had on us. This will prepare us to clarify, intensify, and dramatize our points in a way that will make them interesting and compelling to our listeners.

Then we must obtain from research as much information as we can. A good presenter should know ten times as much about the subject than will be used in the talk. Develop evidence to support our points. Finally, prepare the close. The way we end the presentation has been proven to be one of the best ways to motivate listeners to act. We will see that ending with the benefit—from the audience's point of view—yields favorable results.

Speakers who talk about what life has taught them never fail to keep the attention of their listeners.

Dale Carnegie

How to Prepare and Deliver Talks

Here are seven principles that will help immensely in preparing talks:

1. If we are going to select our own topic, for example, if we are asked to talk to our child's class, a meeting of a community association, or any other group, the best route is to talk about something that we know and know that we know. Talk about something that has aroused our interest. Talk about something that we have a deep desire to communicate to our listeners. When we care about the subject matter, our enthusiasm will be conveyed to our audience.

2. If, in a longer talk, we are afraid we will forget what we want to say, we should make some brief notes and glance at them occasionally.

3. Don't write out the talks, because if we do, we will use written language instead of easy, conversational language; and when we stand up to talk, we will probably find ourselves trying to remember what we wrote. That will keep us from speaking naturally and with sparkle.

4. Never, never, never memorize a talk word for word. If we memorize the talk, we are almost sure to forget it; and the audience will probably be glad, for nobody wants to listen to a canned speech. Even if we don't forget it, it will sound memorized. We will have a faraway look in our eyes and a faraway ring in our voice.

5. Fill the talk with illustrations and examples, as noted above. By far the easiest way to make a talk interesting is to provide stories to illustrate our points. Tell how we or someone we know applied that point. Give specific examples that we learned from our research of the subject.

6. Become an authority on the subject. Develop that priceless asset known as reserve power. Know ten times more about the subject than will be used in the talk.

7. Rehearse the talk by conversing with friends. We need not necessarily give a dress rehearsal, but we should try out the points that will be made in conversation with others to get their reaction. This enables us to discover how our jokes will be received, and which remarks elicit people's interest. An "audience" of friends will provide us with reactions that are obviously not possible from just rehearsing a talk in front of a mirror.

Using Our Bodies When We Speak

To communicate effectively, we must use more than just our voice. We must also use physical animation or gestures—in other words, the entire body. Natural, forceful, spontaneous gestures are extremely powerful for two reasons: Gestures stimulate and inspire the speaker. Gestures wake us up, loosen and relax us. By using gestures, we let ourselves go physically, mentally, and emotionally. Gestures also impact the listeners. The emotional effect gestures have on listeners is both obvious and, at times, even dramatic. Just think about some of the world's great communicators. In almost every case the use of natural, spontaneous gestures contributes to the effectiveness of the speaker and the impact of his or her message.

Connecting with Our Audience

Professional presenters take their audience into consideration when planning a presentation. One of the major challenges of being a good speaker is making sure that we are not speaking above or below the level of knowledge and expertise in our audience. Many audiences will hold individuals with diverse levels of experience, which makes our task even more challenging.

Research Our Audience's Knowledge

When planning to give a presentation, we should do our best to learn as much as possible about our audience's familiarity with the subject. Don't assume that the audience is familiar with industry or company jargon, abbreviations, or slang. It takes little time to briefly define terms as we introduce them. If we commit to using actual words, rather than acronyms or abbreviations, we will ensure that everyone in our audience will understand our message.

And bear in mind that unless we are conducting a training session in which detailed directions may be necessary, most audiences don't need all the facts and figures, just those that are relevant to them. The challenge is finding a way to narrow subject matter to the specific presentation and give the audience enough information, and no more, within the allotted time frame.

Before we start taking notes for our talk, we should get answers to the following questions:

> How well-educated is this audience on the topic of my presentation?
> Am I talking, for example, to technicrats or end users, or both?
> Do I need to provide extensive background information to put my topic into perspective, or is this audience knowledgeable about the context of my message?
> What previous experience or education have the audience members had with the topic?

- ➤ Is this topic something they deal with every day or week, or is it new to them?
- ➤ If they are experienced with the topic, what kinds of issues or concerns have arisen in the past that they would like to see addressed?
- ➤ Do we have any reason to believe that our audience has a strong feeling about the topic of our presentation?
- ➤ If issues exist, what kinds of attitudes are reflected in this audience?
- ➤ What problems or criticisms have arisen with this audience concerning our topic?
- ➤ What personalities will be present that may carry personal bias for or against our key messages?
- ➤ Is this a group that needs all the detail we can provide, or are they just looking for a summary of the topic?
- ➤ How much will this group be impacted by our message? How much will we be asking them to change what they are already doing?
- ➤ Are there safety or policy issues in our message that require detailed information for the audience?

Twelve Ways to Make Our Listeners Like Us

In order to win a sympathetic hearing for our messages, we must make our listeners like us. Here are twelve tested principles for winning listeners and influencing audiences.

1. *Consider ourselves honored by being asked to address an audience—and say so!*

Regardless of the size or type of group we're asked to speak to, being asked to speak is always a compliment. It is a matter of courtesy and good manners to acknowledge such a compliment. That is one way to make an audience like us.

2. *Give our listeners sincere appreciation.*

Never speak before any group without finding out as much as we can about that group beforehand. Then spend a few seconds reminding the audience of some of its fine or unusual qualities that make us proud to be chosen as its speaker.

3. *Whenever possible, mention the names of some of the listeners.*

A person's name is the sweetest sound in any language; so, whenever possible, mention the names of some of the people in the audience. Note when political figures speak at a meeting, they almost always mention the names of local officials who are in the audience.

4. *Play ourselves down—not up!*

Modesty usually inspires confidence and good will. For example, Abraham Lincoln was a master at this. One night during the Lincoln-Douglas debates, Lincoln was serenaded by a brass band; and as he stepped out into the dimly lit porch of the hotel to speak to the band, someone held up a lantern so that the crowd could see Lincoln's homely face. Lincoln began by saying: "My friends, the less you see of me the better you will like me." Lincoln knew the wisdom of the biblical advice: "He that humbles himself shall be exalted."

5. *Say "we"—not "you."*

Never take an exclusive approach toward the listeners. Bring all of them into the talk by using "we" instead of "you." For example, should a speaker say "when you are worried, you ought to get so busy that you won't have time to think about your troubles," the impression is that the speaker is lecturing and talking down to the audience.

Instead say "when we are worried, we ought to get so busy that we won't have time to think about our troubles."

See the difference? When we use the word "you," we implicitly distance ourselves from the audience, and we may be perceived as taking a superior attitude.

6. *Don't talk with a scowling face and an upbraiding voice.*

Remember that the expression on our face and the tone of our voice often speak louder than our words. Regardless of whether we are talking in private or public, we can't win friends with a scowling face and a scolding voice.

7. *Talk in terms of our listeners' interests.*

All listeners are intensely and eternally interested in themselves and how to solve their problems. So, if we show them how to be happier, how to make more money, how to stop worrying and how to get what they want, then they will listen gladly.

For example, when asked how she about how she so easily won friends and became a more interesting conversationalist, a medical researcher reported that she merely asked people, "How did you get into your line of work?" Then she centered her conversation on the response she received. She declared that this simple question had worked wonders for her, especially with strangers. Before addressing a group, find out what their main concerns are and allude to them in the talk.

8. *Have a good time making the talk.*

Unless we enjoy speaking, how can we even hope that

anyone will enjoy listening? No matter what our mental and emotional attitudes are, they are bound to be contagious. If we are having a good time speaking, singing or skating, the people who are watching us or listening to us are also bound to have a good time. Emotional attitudes are as contagious as measles.

One may ask, "How can I have a rip-roaring good time making a talk?" The secret is simple: talk about something we have earned the right to talk about, something that puts a sparkle in our eyes and feeling in our voice.

9. *Don't apologize.*

We've all heard speakers begin by saying something like this: "I didn't know I was supposed to give this talk until two weeks ago when the chairman told me I would have to fill in for the president." How about this often-heard opening remark? "Unaccustomed as I am to public speaking..." Those speakers are apologizing before even starting.

We should never accept an invitation to speak unless we are able to give it the necessary preparation. If we do the best we can do, no apologies are required. If we don't, no amount of apologizing will be acceptable. Apologies are usually an irritating waste of an audience's time.

However, if we are unavoidably late due to a grounded plane, some equally valid reason, we might explain the circumstances briefly and apologize courteously, and then get on with the talk before any more time is lost.

10. *Appeal to the nobler emotions of the audience.*

To inspire an audience by stirring their loftier emotions is not easy. We must first be deeply stirred ourselves. To win others to our way of thinking, show them how what we are proposing will in some way enable them to take part in repairing the world. Give them an example. When Susan Earl was soliciting contributions to her favorite charity, Heifer International, she told those with whom she spoke how a small donation would enable the organization to donate a goat to a family in India, which would provide milk for the family's children and a small income from selling the surplus.

11. *Be sincere.*

All the eloquence in the world will not make up for lack of sincerity and integrity. To make audiences like us, we must inspire them with confidence in our honesty of purpose. They may not agree with our ideas, but they must respect our belief in those ideas if we are to be effective.

Welcome criticism and respond with respect and humility. What we are speaks more loudly than what we say. Sincerity, integrity, modesty, and unselfishness affect an audience deeply.

We much prefer a clumsy speaker who radiates honesty and unselfishness, to a polished orator who is trying to impress us with his eloquence.

12. *Organize our ideas carefully.*

Everyone has had the experience of listening to presenters who have not thought through and organized their material, so they jump from point to point randomly, leaving the audience confused and disengaged. Take the time to organize material so that it is logical and easy to follow. This will not only help our listeners understand our points, it will also help us remember the entirety of what we want to say.

Everything that can be thought at all can be thought clearly. Anything that can be said can be said clearly.

Ludwig Wittgenstein,
Twentieth-Century Philosopher

Assess Our Presentation Skill

To assess the way we currently deliver presentations, answer the following questions using "A" for always, "S" for sometimes, and "N" for never.

1. I carefully plan how to deliver my information._____

2. I use supporting visual aids to make my message easier to understand._____

3. I prepare handouts or a PowerPoint presentation to reinforce my message._____

4. I conduct question and answer sessions after delivering information._____

5. I follow up to make sure that listeners understood my message._____

6. I solicit feedback to see how well I communicated my message._____

7. I practice my presentations before delivering them.

_____

8. I use a structured approach to preparing my message.

_____

9. I research evidence to make my message more convincing.

_____

10. I use examples and illustrations to be more interesting.

_____

11. I narrow the content down to the most relevant information._____

12. I frequently summarize to keep my audience on track.
_____

13. I get feedback from my colleagues on my presentations.
_____

14. My audience stays engaged when I am presenting information._____

15. I am able to give a presentation with energy and enthusiasm._____

Our goal is to be able to train ourselves to respond with an "A" to all these questions.

Many talks fail to be clear because the speaker is intent on establishing a world record for ground covered in the allotted time.

Dale Carnegie

Think as wise men do, but speak as the common people do.

Aristotle

Soliciting Feedback

Business professionals look for ways to get feedback on the clarity and relevance of their presentations. Some of the ways that we can receive feedback include:

Conduct a Q and A Session

The questions that are asked by our audience tell us whether our message was clear. It's the most immediate way to get feedback from our listeners. If there are questions that indicate a lack of clarity, we can take the opportunity to restate our point, and perhaps offer additional evidence to support our message.

Follow Up with a Survey

Surveys may be distributed at the end of the presentation itself or as a follow-up. Email surveys allow time for the presentation to be processed by the participants before making an evaluation of our message, but we may not receive many responses.

Ask for a Detailed Evaluation

Before the presentation, ask specific people if they would be willing to give us feedback after our presentation. Tell them our goals for the presentation and the skills we are trying to improve. Ask for ways to make the message easier to understand and the ways in which we can enhance our performance in future presentations. In considering the responses, look for suggestions that we can express visually, such as with charts or graphs.

Test for Knowledge

"Testing" our audience to see whether we've successfully conveyed our message can be done in several ways. One is to question the group at the end of the presentation to see how well they remember our key information. Another way is to create a test that will assess the retention of our message with our listeners. Other ways include follow-up telephone calls or emails.

Sum and Substance

- When presenting information to an audience, we should:

  Open with a statement of our topic.

  State our key message and the result that we desire.

  Provide evidence for our message, using a variety of forms, such as exhibits and analogies.

  Close with a restatement of our main message and the desired action.

- When presenting a persuasive talk, we should:

  Use the three components of effective persuasion in the body of our presentation—cite an incident, state the desired action, state the benefit to the audience members.

- Good speech-giving principles include:

  Pick a topic that we are excited about.

  Make notes for use as we speak.

  Don't memorize our talk.

  Use examples and illustrations.

  Research our topic well so we are an authority on the subject matter.

  Rehearse our points by speaking with friends.

  Use gestures and movement judiciously to keep ourselves inspired and our audience engaged.

- Make a point of relating to our specific audience.

  Research our audience to learn its level of knowledge about our topic.

  Win our audience over by being sure to thank them for their attention, being modest and sincere, using inclusive language and pleasant expression, and by organizing thoughts so that we are easy to follow.

- Assess our ability to deliver presentations effectively so that we can improve our efforts.

- Solicit feedback from our audience for use in future talks through:

  Question and answer sessions. Post-talk surveys.
  Post-talk tests of our audience's understanding.
  Requesting specific feedback from a select number of listeners.

Step 6

MANAGE GOOD RELATIONSHIPS

As pointed out in Step 3, to have a harmonious environment wherever we are, we must get treat others with fairness and respect and become familiar with how they act and react in a given situation. Good relationships, of course, are a two-way street, and so we will want to ensure that others treat us with fairness and respect as well.

Be Respected by Others

Here are seven guidelines to help us earn and keep the respect of others. These guidelines were designed for use at the workplace, but they apply to any situation in which we are dealing with others.

1. Be trustworthy and keep confidences. Understand when it is and when it is not appropriate to share conversations and strategies.

2. Develop an "open door" policy. Give others our complete attention when they speak and encourage them to express their concerns and interests.

3. Always use good manners, good listening skills, and appropriate language, and display congruency between our words and actions.

4. Build positive relations with all staff members in our organization and with outside contacts such as customers and suppliers.

5. Be confident, energetic, and a self-starter. Anticipate challenges and options to overcome them. Today we hear people referred to as "high maintenance" or "low maintenance." We want others to see us in the latter category, as someone who takes charge appropriately and doesn't create problems without exceptional cause.

6. Run efficient and focused meetings and provide detailed information to all involved.

7. Be reliable, consistent, and accountable.

Here are seven destructive behaviors that hold us back. Again, this list was created to help us bring our best selves to work, but unflattering conduct will have a negative impact on those around us regardless of where we engage in it.

1. Failure to keep a confidence with colleagues, peers, and direct reports.

2. Clock-watching, taking excessive and inappropriate breaks, and leaving urgent tasks unfinished and messages unanswered.

3. Failure to offer our point of view to senior management before a decision has been made.

4. Persistence with our point of view after a decision has been made.
5. Inappropriate dress, language, and insensitivity to diversity issues.
6. Failure to participate in discussions with senior management and with staff.
7. Inability to immediately bounce back and regain composure after a frustrating or difficult time.

Dealing with Difficult People

Of course, we are bound to encounter others who require a little extra effort when it comes to managing good relationships. Some people are stubborn, unreasonable, or even belligerent. Let's look at some techniques to keep our interactions smooth and positive.

Sensitive People

We undoubtedly have people with whom we interface who are extremely sensitive. They can make our lives miserable or make them an ever-changing challenge. We can't ignore these folks; we have to deal with them, so here are some suggestions.

Overly sensitive often respond poorly to criticism, and whenever we make even the slightest criticism of their work, they pout and get defensive and accuse us of picking on them.

The best way to deal with very sensitive individuals is to be diplomatic. Begin by praising the parts of assignments that they have done well. Then make some suggestions about how they can do better in unsatisfactory areas.

Kathy's fear of being criticized has made her overly cautious in all areas of her work. Rather than risk a slight error, she checks, double-checks, and then rechecks everything she does. This process may minimize her exposure to criticism, but it's so time-consuming that it slows down her entire team. Worse, she stalls in making decisions, claiming that she needs more information. Even after she gets the information, she passes the buck to someone else.

To help people like Kathy, follow these guidelines to help them overcome their fears:

> Assure them that, because of their excellent knowledge in their field, their work is usually correct the first time and doesn't have to be checked repeatedly.

> Point out that occasional errors are normal and that they can be caught and corrected later without reflecting on the ability of the person who made the errors.

> If more information is needed before making a decision, guide them toward resources to help them obtain it. If we feel that they have adequate information, insist that they make prompt decisions.

> If they try to pass the buck to us, and ask us what to do, tell them that it's their decision and to make it quickly.

In most cases, overly sensitive people have the expertise and do make good decisions. They may need our reassurance to help convert their thinking into action.

Short-Fused People

We may come into contact with individuals who seem to get overly angry when something doesn't go their way. For example,

Terry is a good worker, but from time to time he loses his temper and hollers and screams at his coworkers and even at us. He calms down quickly, but his behavior affects the work of the entire team, and it takes a while to get back to normal performance. We've spoken to Terry about his temper several times, but it hasn't helped.

It isn't easy to work in an environment in which people holler and scream, particularly if we're the target. Because the victims of a tirade may be unable to work at full capacity for several hours afterward, this situation cannot be tolerated.

Here are some suggestions for dealing with someone who has temper tantrums:

➤ After the person calms down, have a heart-to-heart talk. Point out that we understand that it's not always easy for someone to control his or her temper but that such tantrums aren't acceptable in the workplace.

➤ If another outburst occurs, send the person out of the room until he or she can calm down. Let the person know that the next offense will lead to disciplinary action.

➤ When someone is throwing a tantrum, walk out of the room! Say we'll return after he or she calms down. Wait ten minutes, then try again. Assure the person that this isn't a personal attack but a means of correcting a situation.

Caution: It's not a good policy to leave an upset person alone in our office. If the event occurs in our personal space, insist that the other person leave the room.

➤ Stay calm. Follow the old adage, "Count to ten before opening our mouth."

Negating Negativity

Almost every organization has one or more negative people— people who find something wrong with everyone, every situation, and every idea. Whatever we are for, they're against it. They always have a reason that what we want to accomplish just can't be done. They can tear down our team with pessimism. Let's look at some of the problems negative people cause:

• *Resistance to change.* Even people with a positive attitude are reluctant to change. It's comfortable to keep doing things the way they've always done them. Positive-thinking people can be persuaded to change by being presented with logical arguments. Negative people resist change just for the sake of resisting. No argument ever helps. They often do everything they can to sabotage a situation so that the new methods won't work and they can say, "I told you so."

• *Impact on team morale.* Just as one rotten apple can spoil a whole barrel, one negative person can destroy the entire team's morale. Because the negativism spreads from one person to another, it's tough to maintain team spirit under these circumstances.

The reasons for a team member's negativity vary. It may stem from some real or perceived past mistreatment by our company. It's worth our effort to look into the matter and find out if that's the case. If the person has justifiable reasons for being negative, try to persuade him or her that the past is past and to look to the future. If misconceptions are involved, try to clear them up.

On the other hand, there are those for whom negativity is

simply part of their personality—a perspective that is beyond us to overcome, but that we must manage nonetheless.

Firstly, in dealing with negative people, acknowledge their arguments and persuade them to work with us to overcome their perceived problems so that the project can move along. Make the person part of the solution rather than an additional problem.

When presenting new ideas to negative people, get them to express their objections openly. Tell them, "You bring up some good points, and I appreciate them. As we move into this new program, let's carefully watch for those problems. We must give this new concept a try. Let's work together on it, and iron out the kinks."

Critical People

There are some people whose main joy in life is to point out the flaws and errors of others.

People who play this game are either trying to show their superiority, or compensate for their inferiority by making sure that we all see the imperfections of those around us. Because they usually have no original ideas or constructive suggestions, they get their kicks from catching other people's errors, particularly their boss's. They try to embarrass us and make us uncomfortable.

When we experience critical people pointing out an error, we need not give them any satisfaction. Make a joke about it ("What a blooper!"), or smile and say "Thanks for calling it to my attention before it caused real problems." If those who like to criticize see that we're not riled by their game, they'll stop and try to get their kicks elsewhere.

Dealing with Unhappy People

There's likely to be at least one unhappy person in any group. We all experience periods when things go wrong at home or on the job and it affects the way we do our work and how we interact with other people. As a supervisor at work, we should be alert to this likelihood and take the time to chat with the person. And of course, as a friend or coworker, there is no reason why we can't offer some comfort to someone having a difficult time. Giving a person the opportunity to talk about a problem often alleviates the tension. Even if the problem isn't solved, it clears the air and enables the person to better function.

Some people, however, will always be unhappy about something. At the workplace, they are often dissatisfied with work assignments. Even when we comply with their requests and accommodate their complaints, they're not satisfied. They seem to feel that they are never given enough respect and they're never taken into consideration. They display their unhappiness by being negative.

For example, If Jill's request for change in her vacation time is denied, she may get angry and let it show both overtly and subtly in her attitude.

We can never make everyone happy. Rebuilding the morale of people who believe that they've been treated unfairly takes tact and patience. As a manager at work, we can avoid some unfair situations by making sure—at the time a decision is made—to explain the reasons behind the decision. In the vacation example, we could explain that the company sets up the vacation schedule months in advance and that two other employees are taking their vacations at that time. Then make it clear that the group can't spare another member at that time. We may even suggest that the unhappy person try to find another staff member who will trade vacation time.

The Unreasonable Boss

But what can we do if the difficult person with whom we must interact is our boss? Some bosses seem to be more vocal with their criticism than others, and may feel that they simply must correct their staff with frequency.

When Jack was asked why he was always harping at his employees, he responded: "That's the boss's job." Jack had always worked for bosses who criticized, condemned, and complained, and he assumed that was the way to supervise others.

Arlene was a perfectionist and she couldn't tolerate people who did not meet her high standards. She lost patience with people who did not learn rapidly and accurately and would often express her displeasure loudly and sarcastically. Arlene told herself that she was no pushover, and she was not going to be afraid to speak her mind. She hadn't learned that she could do so in a way that was fruitful and supportive, and ultimately would get better results.

Most of us have no control over who will be our boss. We may have a great relationship with our supervisor, but when he or she leaves the job, the replacement has an entirely different management style that we find intolerable.

Since we can't expect to change our boss's behavior, the best way to work through this situation is to concentrate on what we can change—which is our responses to it. Try these tactics:

1. *Remember that unjust criticism is often a disguised compliment.* Sometimes people are so insecure in their own success that they criticize others as a way to make their own mistakes seem smaller. If someone is unjustly criticizing us, it won't take long for others to figure it out.

2. *Do the very best we can at our jobs.* We can't control the boss's attitude or what he or she says about us. But we can control how well we perform our job. People in management will notice our performance.

3. *Try honestly to see things from the other person's point of view.* Put ourselves in that person's place—with all its stresses and concerns—and we may find some clues to that behavior. It doesn't excuse what he or she does, of course, but our empathy might start to break down the barriers that frustrate us.

Life's challenges are not supposed to paralyze us; they're supposed to help us discover who we are.

Bernice Johnson Reagon,
American Composer and Singer

4. *Speak well of our supervisor.* It may feel counterintuitive, but it is actually helpful to say kind things about a difficult supervisor. Give our boss a fine reputation to live up to. Tell others how important he or she is the company. Accentuate even the smallest positive trait. Then, no matter what our supervisor does, treat him or her as though he or she is living up to that reputation. Even the nastiest person has a hard time being mean in the face of continuing kindness.

5. *Work on the relationship.* Let our supervisor know that we want to have a good relationship with him or her, then ask what we can do to make the working relationship smoother. If

it feels appropriate, we might want to apologize for whatever it is that seems to have gone awry in our interactions. Assure our boss that we want to make the company successful first and foremost.

6. *Ask for advice*. If our supervisor is feeling threatened by our expertise, give him or her a few chances to show his or her wisdom. Ask our boss to share opinions in areas where he or she really does know more than us.

7. *Correct errors immediately*. If we find that our supervisor is spreading untruths about us, inform him or her that we know what was said and that it isn't true. Don't be rude, just state that there must have been some miscommunication, and we want to set the record straight.

8. *Don't expect our supervisor to change overnight*. As mentioned earlier, we can't change other people; we can only change our reaction to their behavior. Manage each incident as it arises, and don't worry about what he or she might do tomorrow.

9. *Fill our mind with thoughts of peace, courage, health, and hope*. Go beyond the daily nuisances caused by our boss and look at life's nobler goals. Consciously choose to become a calm, content person who has the self-confidence to let others' criticisms roll off our backs.

10. *Count our blessings*. Remember to focus on the good in our lives. A loving family, for example, brings rewards that go well beyond any job.

The above suggestions are not limited to our bosses or even to our workplace. By applying them when we are faced with difficult people in social, community, or even family situations, they are just as effective.

Although the world is full of suffering, it is also full of the overcoming of it.

Helen Keller

When We Must Disagree

Disagreements are inevitable, but how we handle them can make a big difference in our relationships.

A good example is Patrick, the director of manufacturing of the Proper Paper Co., who was asked to make a preliminary recommendation to the company's senior management about investing in a new and unproven manufacturing process. The problem was that Patrick's boss, the vice president of operations, was totally behind the idea while Patrick had some serious reservations.

Patrick could defer to his boss and remain silent, of course, but he was certain that the result could be the end of the small paper mill. "I told you so" wouldn't mean much when sixty people were out of work. On the other hand, he could make a big fuss in front of the management team and point out exactly how wrongheaded his boss's assumptions were. That might work, but it also ran the risk of alienating top management and it would certainly destroy any chance of a good working relationship with his boss.

To help resolve this issue, Patrick called on his mentor, a retired executive from the first company Patrick had worked for after college. He suggested that Patrick take the middle ground by having a friendly disagreement. He suggested that Patrick prepare an informal presentation. It included:

1. *Acknowledge that there are several good points in his boss's plan.* Some aspects of the proposed process were very good. It definitely had promise; test runs at micromanufacturing sites had shaved time and money off the manufacture of coated papers without sacrificing quality. At the same time, the company definitely needed to look at new manufacturing processes if it was to remain competitive.

2. *Transition to his view.* Patrick couldn't negate his first comment by using words such as "but" or "however," because that would instantly establish that he was contradicting the ideas of his supervisor. Instead, after acknowledging that his boss's opinion was valid, he would take a slight pause then say, "I've thought of a few more factors that might influence our decision." This seemed a very neutral way to open up the conversation.

3. *Present the data.* At first, Patrick wanted to bring in reams and reams of reports to prove his case. He wanted to take out his anger at his boss by drowning the management team in paper. Instead, they boiled his argument down to just two main points: data suggested that the process became less efficient as it was expanded to bigger facilities and the process had yet to be tried at an operation of this company's size.

4. *End with a neutral statement.* Given the data, it made sense for Patrick to suggest that the company form a larger team to look at this option as well as others in greater detail. He could even appease his boss by saying it would be exciting if this new process, after further examination, proved to be the right opportunity for the company.

5. *Avoid anger.* Disagreements seldom proceed as planned. The mentor reminded Patrick that he could only provide the

information; he couldn't control the ultimate decision. If his boss argued, he could "agree to disagree," but he shouldn't get into a verbal battle. His job was to do what he felt was best for the organization, but not engage in an angry exchange.

It's not a surprise that top management agreed to Patrick's suggestion. His boss even agreed that it was the responsible thing to do. By thoughtfully presenting our ideas without undermining those of others, we can achieve the same results the next time we know we're going to disagree with someone.

Don't Criticize, Condemn, or Complain

If we want to have good relationships with others, we should consider how we like others to behave. We don't enjoy negative, critical people—why would we think that others do? We should make up our minds firmly at the very outset in life that we will not criticize or condemn others, or find fault with their mistakes and shortcomings. Faultfinding, indulging in sarcasm and irony, picking flaws in everything and everybody, looking for things to condemn instead of praise, are very dangerous habits. They are like deadly worms that gnaw at the heart of the rosebud or fruit, and will make our own lives gnarled, distorted, and bitter.

No life can be harmonious and happy after this blighting habit is once formed. Those who always look for something to condemn ruin their own character and destroy their normal integrity.

We all like sunshiny, bright, cheerful, hopeful people; nobody likes the grumbler, the faultfinder, the backbiter or the slanderer. The great American philosopher, Ralph Waldo Emerson wrote that "the world likes the man who sees longevity in his causes and good in the future, who believes the best and not the worst of people."

It is just as easy to go through life looking for the good and the beautiful, instead of the ugly; for the noble instead of the ignoble; for the bright and cheerful instead of the dark and gloomy; the hopeful instead of the despairing; to see the bright side instead of the dark side. To set our face always toward the sunlight is just as easy as to see always the shadows, and it makes all the difference in our character between content and discontent, between happiness and misery, and in our work lives, between prosperity and adversity, between success and failure.

Let us learn to look for the light, positively refuse to harbor shadows and blots, negative images, and the discordant. Let us hold to those things that give pleasure, that are helpful and inspiring, and we will change our whole way of looking at things, and we will transform our personality in a very short time.

Getting Others to Accept Our Ideas

While we don't want to act in a way that exerts undue influence on others, or that might be considered manipulative, there is nothing wrong with encouraging other people to accept our ideas. In fact, in the workplace, we are expected to make decisions and generate ideas that will move our organization forward. If we aren't even a little skilled at promoting our getting others to approve our efforts, we aren't very effective employees.

When Jennifer, human resources director of Sweet Sixteen Cosmetics Company, studied the time sheets, she saw that it was time to get creative in addressing some of the staff members' tardiness. The punishment of latecomers had not helped, and a plan to give awards to employees with perfect records had not led to significant improvement. A year earlier she had suggested initiating a flexible time schedule as an way to better accommodate the staff members, but her boss had turned it down cold. How could she reintroduce this idea now and change his mind?

Selling ideas is not much different from selling a product or service. By following the approaches of successful salespeople, we can persuade people to accept our concepts. The first step in any sales activity is to be properly prepared. No good salesperson would attempt to make a sale without careful preparation.

Clarify Our Ideas

Just as a salesperson must know his or her product thoroughly in order to be able to sell it, we must know as much as possible about the idea we want to sell. Before Jennifer even broaches the subject of flexible hours with her boss, she should know as much as possible about this concept. She should read the literature available about the subject, speak to executives at other companies that have adopted similar programs, and assess the attitudes of some of the employees who would be affected by it.

Evaluate the Benefit of Our Ideas

From our analysis of the subject, determine what this concept will do that no other concept is likely to do. In studying the experience of companies who use flexible time schedules,

Jennifer learned that tardiness was reduced significantly in all of the firms. She also learned that the productivity did not suffer, even though not all employees were available at the same time. It also made recruiting of new employees, particularly working parents, easier. Therefore, the outstanding feature of flexible hours is that it could combine these benefits. Jennifer summed it up this way: "It will reduce tardiness without loss of productivity and at the same time attract good people to the company."

Evaluate the Benefit to the "Buyer"

Every salesperson knows that the main concern of any buyer is:

"What's in it for me?" How will the company benefit by accepting our idea? Most companies are cost conscious, so we must be able to demonstrate how our idea is cost effective.

If we are selling the idea to a person with whom we work and know well, such as our immediate boss, we should know what his or her interests are. Prepare to tailor our presentation to these interests. If we can adapt what we offer to what the other person desires most, we have increased our likelihood of making the sale. We might all this the "buyer,s" Dominant Buying Motive (DBM). However, if the person to whom we are speaking is a virtual stranger, it is important to find out what is of real concern to that person. To learn his or her DBM, we must be prepared to ask questions to uncover the real interests. From other people who deal with this person, find out all we can about him or her. Try to meet with this executive before we make our presentation and ask good questions that might enlighten us. Direct questions such as:

"What do you wish to achieve in such and such an activity? What are your goals for this year?" or ask indirect questions such as: "What accomplishments in your past gave you most satisfaction? Why?" Listen carefully to the responses and we will pick up what it is that will really excite the buyer = his or her DBM.

Develop Evidence

Good salespeople always have evidence available to prove their points. In selling an idea at the workplace, perhaps the best evidence is the experience of other organizations that have successfully used similar concepts. Jennifer contacted several companies in her community that had been on a flexible time schedule for several years and was able to obtain considerable data on the benefits they derived from it. She also found out what problems they had and how they overcame them. By learning about the negatives as well as the positives, she was able to prepare for objections that her boss might present and develop the arguments to help rebut them.

Matching Our Plan with What Is Desired

Facts alone will rarely make a sale. The salesperson must be able to show how those facts translate into benefits to the buyer. In preparing to sell an idea, list each of the facts that make our idea worthwhile in one column and next to them in another column, identify the benefit they provide the buyer.

For Jennifer's flexible hour concept:

What Is Desired

Save $2,300 per month
Reduce turnover of staff
Increase productivity

What Is Offered

Reduce tardiness by 80%
Improve morale
Attract better workers

By showing how the idea we are selling will meet what the buyer wants, our presentation will come across in a positive and persuasive manner. Nobody wants to be "sold." Everybody wants to feel that he or she has purchased the thing that he or she wanted. By showing the person to whom we are presenting our idea how it fits into what he or she really wants, we are more likely to gain acceptance of the idea.

Now we are ready to make the presentation and sell our concept to the boss.

Making the Sale

Let's look at how Jennifer reintroduced her of flexible time to her boss, even though he had rejected that concept a year earlier. To do this, Jennifer carefully prepared her approach. She learned as much as she could about flexible time, investigated the experience of other companies that had successfully instituted the program, and identified its major advantage. She also analyzed what her boss wanted most for the company, his Dominant Buying Motive (DBM). She was now ready to make the presentation to the boss.

Salespeople often initiate a discussion with a prospect by commenting about the decor of the office or a picture on the wall or some other extraneous matter. When dealing with a person we work with, it is best to start with something we know will be of interest to that person. If he or she is "all business," then start right with the business at hand. "Doug, I know how concerned you have been about increasing productivity. One of the causes of this, as you know, is our difficulty in recruiting good clerical workers. If there were a way to attract more skilled people, you would want to know about it, wouldn't you?"

The only response Doug could make is "yes." Jennifer has presented the chief advantage of her concept and has gained immediate attention. She must now follow this up to determine Doug's specific interests.

Ask Questions and Listen to the Responses

Although Jennifer knows Doug's interests from her experience working with him, she should be prepared to ask specific questions about his objectives. If we are dealing with a person whom we do not know well, this part of the presentation may be the most important. It is essential to uncover what is most important to this executive, his or her DBM. We may learn that one person's major concern is cost effectiveness, while another is more interested in how a new product or practice will affect his or her image.

Many people are so anxious to "sell" their ideas that they do not really listen to what the "buyer" really wants. Some salespeople assume that because the price of their product is lower than those of the competitors, they can emphasize cost savings, so they do not listen to the prospect's concern about quality. Do not presuppose that the "buyer's" interests are the same as ours. Listen carefully to the answers to our questions and be prepared to pick up subtleties that can lead us to that person's real interests.

Presenting Evidence

In our preparation, we should have developed considerable evidence to back up the ideas we wish to sell. Once we know what the executive to whom we must sell the concept really wants, we can tailor the evidence to that person's desires. Jennifer knows that her boss, Doug, is a pragmatist. He will not accept vague theories, but is impressed by facts and figures. She also knows he measures all projects on cost effectiveness. To sell flexible hours to him, she must be ready to show him how it has worked in other companies, what it has cost, and how it paid off.

"Doug, I discussed this with Hilary Hendricks, the human resources manager of Fitrite Shoes. They instituted flexible hours three years ago. She pointed out that it reduced tardiness by 80 percent, saving them $2,300 per month. In addition, by attracting more people who prefer flexible hours, they have been able to recruit high caliber clerical workers and have reduced turnover significantly."

How should the evidence by presented? If we know the person to whom we are selling the concept—and in most cases, it is our own boss or other executives in our company—we should know how they like to receive information. Some people may be more easily reached with charts, graphs, and diagrams; others by cogent arguments or examples. By using the format that is most likely to impress our audience, we will have a greater chance of making the sale.

Handling Objections

Salespeople like objections. It helps them determine what the prospect really wants and enables them to face up to that and increase their chances of making the sale. Good salespeople anticipate what objections are likely to be presented and are prepared to counteract them. We should know the most likely objections that our boss may have to the concept we are selling and be prepared to deal with them.

Doug turned down the concept of flexible hours a year ago because he felt it would disrupt production. "If everybody comes in at different times, how can we get coordinated production? Suppose the supervisor needs critical information from a worker who has already left or hasn't arrived?" Jennifer was prepared to show how the companies she researched dealt with these problems and the results that ensued.

Closing the Sale

There are several approaches to closing a sale. Probably the most appropriate in selling an idea to an executive in our company is to ask him or her to help in evaluating our concept. Divide a paper into two columns. Head one: "Negatives" and the other "Positives." Immediately list the major objections that have been brought up in the "negative" column and write the countervailing argument in the "positive" column. Add to the "positive" column all the additional benefits that have been discussed. If we have done our homework, we should have many more positives than negatives. Then state: "Let's take a look at some of the reasons that may cause you to hesitate to accept this idea and weigh them against the reasons in favor of going ahead. In your opinion, which side weighs heavier?" The answer has to be the positive side.

Once we have obtained agreement that our concept is viable, ask, "Inasmuch as you agree that this is a good idea, I would like to discuss how this can be implemented." If the concept has to be sold by our boss to other executives before it can be adopted, suggest that we will by happy to assist him or her in preparing for that presentation.

By careful preparation and by following the approaches used by successful salespeople, we can present and sell our ideas to our boss and obtain that great satisfaction from being able to see our concepts accepted and carried out.

Sum and Substance

- To be respected by others, we must be polite, appropriate, and trustworthy.
- If we are obstinate and self-interested, we will not gain respect.
- Manage sensitive people by encouraging and reassuring them.
- Don't engage with someone having a temper tantrum. Stay calm and when the tantrum is over, let the person know that such behavior is not acceptable.
- Negative people should be acknowledged and allowed to express themselves. Make a point of letting them know that we hear them and will do our best to address their concerns.

- If people around us are critical, politely thank them for their input. They will lose interest in criticizing us.
- If our boss is difficult or critical of us, we must do our best to maintain a good relationship. It is up to us to simply do our best, and although it may feel counterintuitive, we should always speak well of our supervisor.
- Disagree politely. We can hold an opinion that is different from someone else's, and still show that person respect.
- If we want to influence people, we must earn their respect. Review the guidelines outlined at the start of this step.
- Selling ideas is not much different from selling a product or service. By following the approaches of successful salespeople, we can persuade people to accept our concepts.
- We should know as much as possible about the idea we want to sell.
- Evaluate the benefit of the idea that you are "selling" to the buyer. Be sure to convey the benefit in your sales pitch. Do not presuppose that the other person's interests are the same as ours. Ask good questions and listen carefully to the answers. Good salespeople always have evidence available to prove their points. In selling an idea, the best evidence is the experience of other organizations that have used similar concepts successfully.
- In our preparation we should have developed considerable evidence to back up the ideas we wish to sell. Once we know what the executive to whom we must sell the concept really wants, we can tailor the evidence to that person's desires.

Step 7

....

OVERCOME WORRY AND FEAR

Worry or fear of any kind is fatal to mental concentration and kills creative ability. Whether one is a scientist, artist, inventor or business tycoon, one cannot concentrate if filled with fear, worry, or anxiety.

When the whole mental organism is vibrating with disturbing emotions, efficiency is impossible. The things that enervate us and make us prematurely old, which rob us of joy, are not those that actually happen.

Success and happiness both depend on keeping ourselves in condition to get the most possible out of our energies. We should harbor in our minds that fear is the enemy of this very success and happiness. We must break the habit of anticipating catastrophes that will probably never come. Anxiety and fretting will not only rob us of peace of mind and strength and ability to do our work, but also of precious years of life.

Work kills no one, but fear has killed multitudes. It is not the doing things which injures us so much as the dreading to do them—not only performing them mentally over and over again, but anticipating something disagreeable in their performance.

How often have we awakened in the middle of the night in a cold sweat worrying over some problem we would have to face the next day or even far into the future? How frequently has our mind jumped to a problem that has us worried sick when in the midst of a joyous activity?

It is likely that every man or woman has had these pangs of worry hit him or her over and over again. Yet, if we look back weeks or months later at the matters about which we were so concerned, we often find that the problem that awakened us from a sound sleep or turned our joy into anxiety never developed or was much less of a concern than we had anticipated.

No problem was ever solved by worrying. If the energy we use worrying (and worry is a heavy energy consumer) was channeled into constructive approaches to solving our uneasiness instead of brooding over it, we would overcome our fears and trepidation and be healthier and happier people.

The happiest of people don't necessarily have the best of everything; they just make the most of everything that comes along their way. The brightest future will always be based on a forgotten past; we can't go forward in life until we let go of our past failures and heartaches.

Live in Day-Tight Compartments

In his book, *How to Stop Worrying and Start Living*, Dale

Carnegie cites the following comments by Dr William Osler, one of the great surgeons and philosophers of the early twentieth century, from an address he gave to a group of students at Yale University.

Dr Osler noted that on a large ocean liner, the captain has the power to seal off compartments of the ship if they may endanger the entire vessel. He then stated:

> Now each one of you is a much more marvelous organization than the great liner, and is bound on a longer voyage. What I urge is that you learn to control the machinery as to live with day-tight compartments as the most certain way to ensure safety on the voyage. Get on the bridge and see that at least the great bulkheads are in working other. Touch a button and hear, at every level of your life, the iron doors shutting out the past—the dead yesterdays. Touch another and shut off with a metal curtain, the future as tightly as the past. . . . The future is today…there is no tomorrow. Wasted energy, mental distress, nervous worries, dog the steps of one who is anxious about the future. . . . Shut close then the great fore and aft bulkheads, and prepare to cultivate the habit of a life of "day-tight" compartments.

Dr Osler did not mean to say we should not make any effort to prepare for tomorrow. But he did go on to say that the best possible way to prepare for tomorrow is to concentrate with all our intelligence, all our enthusiasm, on doing today's work superbly today. That is the best possible way to prepare for the future.

To help us shut the iron doors on the past and the future, Dale Carnegie suggests that we ask ourselves these questions and write down the answers:

- Do I tend to put off living in the present in order to worry about the future, or to yearn for some "magical rose garden over the horizon?"

- Do I sometimes embitter the present by regretting things that happened in the past—that are over and done with?

- Do I get up in the morning determined to "seize the day"—to get the utmost out of these twenty-four hours?

- Can I get more out of life by "living in day-tight compartments?

- When shall I start to do this? Next week? … Tomorrow? … Today?

The past is over; we cannot change it; the future is unknown, but today is a gift—that's why we call it the present.

Anonymous

Twelve Ways to Minimize Worries

It is easy to tell somebody to stop worrying, but to actually do it is another matter. Here are some ways that often help:

1. *Make a decision.*

When confronted with a worrisome problem, do not keep going over and over it ceaselessly in your mind. Face it once and for all and come to a decision.

Having made a decision, stick to it. It won't always be correct, but any positive action is usually better than no action at all.

2. *Decide where thought ends and worry begins.*

Remember, worrying is not the same as thinking. Clear thinking is constructive. Worry is destructive.

3. *If there is something we can do to solve a problem that is nagging us, do it.*

We should take every step possible to overcome it, so it no longer worries us. Several members of a Senior Citizens' Center in New York were worried about being mugged on their way to and from the center. The constant fear kept many of them in their lonely rooms and others came out to the center only with great anxiety. One of the men recognized that this worry was defeating all of them, and nobody was doing anything about it— except more worry. He shifted his thoughts from brooding to action. Result—an arrangement for several of the men and women to walk together through the "rough part of the neighborhood" at a specified time each day. Constructive thinking instead of destructive anxiety solved the problem.

4. *Mind our own business.*

Many of us create problems for ourselves by interfering too often in others' affairs. We do so because somehow we have convinced ourselves that our way is the best way and those who do not conform to our thinking must be criticized and steered to the right direction—our direction. If we mind our own business and give advice only when asked, we will have less to worry us.

5. *Hold no grudges.*

Although "brooding" might be distinct from "worrying,"

they are both wasteful, repetitive mental habits that we do not want to engage in. We may be tempted to brood over events that we believe were insulting or harmful. However, if we want to move on, it is essential that we cultivate the art of forgiving and forgetting. Life is too short to waste in such trifles. Forget, forgive, and march on.

6. *Believe in ourselves.*

We often worry that we are not recognized for our achievements. Our bosses or our associates rarely or never praise us. We must understand that there are many people who seldom praise anybody without selfish motive. They are quick to criticize us, but ignore our achievements. We put too much emphasis on how others view us. If we firmly believe in our own capabilities and strengths, we will worry less about other people's attitudes toward us.

We probably wouldn't worry about what people think of us if we only realized how seldom they do.

Olin Miller,
American Humorist

7. *Let go of jealousy.*

We all have experienced how jealousy can disturb our peace of mind. We may work harder than our colleagues in the office but they get promotions, and we do not. Our business is just breaking even, but our competitor is thriving. We envy our neighbor because he has a newer and more expensive car. Jealousy will not solve our problems, but will only lead to worry and insecurity. We must learn to accept what we have and work hard to improve it with a mind free of envy of others.

8. *Welcome change.*

Change is inevitable. No progress can be made without change. Yet too many of us fear change. It takes us out of our comfort zones. If changes are thrust upon us, instead of worrying that they will negatively affect us, focus on how they can make things better.

Jack couldn't sleep. He was worried sick. In a week his new boss would take over. A stranger. He had gotten along famously with his old boss, but when he retired, instead of appointing one of the old-timers to the supervisor's job, the company hired an outsider. "Maybe this new guy will be too tough; maybe he won't like me," he thought. For the next few days he was nervous on the job and had great difficulty sleeping. He noticed that his friend and coworker, Tony, didn't seem to be upset, so he asked him: "Tony, aren't you worried about the new boss?"

Tony shook his head. "Sure, I'm concerned. He could make big changes here. But I'm not worried. What is the worst thing that can happen? Well, the worst is he could fire me. But I've got valuable skills, and if he fires me, I know I'd just get another job.

There is no real reason he should fire me. I've done a good job and will continue to do so. If he makes changes, I can live with them—and if I can't, there are other jobs around for me. So why worry?"

Jack saw the logic in Tony's position and took his perspective to hear. He was able to work without worry and not lose more sleep. Sure, he would continue to be concerned, but rather than fantasize about all the things that could go wrong, he focused on his ability to go with the flow.

Keep in mind that change is not limited to what others foist upon us. We should always be studying how we do things and seek ways to do them more effectively. Suggesting changes entails risk. The change may fail, but self-confident people learn to accept risks and are resilient enough to not worry about occasional defeats and move on.

9. *Learn to accept the inevitable.*

After twenty-two years with her company, Elizabeth looked forward to retirement only eight years ahead. When the company announced it was going out of business, she couldn't believe it. All her plans were based on the security she had expected from her job.

Elizabeth cried herself to sleep each night. She had always prided herself on being self-sufficient, and now she would become dependent on her children. Within a few weeks, Elizabeth changed from a self-confident, cheerful person to a nervous wreck with migraine headaches and constant stomach disorder. Her doctor recognized that medication was not the therapy she needed. He suggested that she study Rheinhold Niebuhr's "Serenity Prayer"

> God grant me the serenity
> To accept the things I cannot change,
> The courage to change the things I can,
> And the wisdom to know the difference.

In time, Edith separated what could be changed (her attitude) from what could not (the company's closing.) With the support of her family and friends, she accepted the inevitable and began to work toward finding a new job and taking positive steps toward the new and exciting next phase of her life.

10. *Don't bite off more than we can chew.*

We often take on more responsibility than we are capable of carrying out. We want others to admire us so we take on more than we can handle. We must be aware of our limitations. When asked to take on a special assignment when we are overburdened, we should decline diplomatically.

11. *Keep our minds occupied.*

When our minds are not occupied with positive thoughts, we fill it with worries—often about matters that are trivial or even unlikely to happen. We must keep our minds occupied with positive, worthwhile matters. Reading inspirational books, listening to good music, meditating or concentrating on a worthwhile community project, an enjoyable hobby, or just about the joys and blessings of our lives will push out those worrisome thoughts.

12. *Don't procrastinate.*

In every job and in most aspects of our lives, we have to do things we don't enjoy doing. Many of us have the tendency to put off unpleasant tasks and work on those things we like. If we do the thing we like first, we will eventually have to do the one we dislike. This is self-defeating. If we get challenging activities out of the way, we can then look forward to the enjoyable ones.

13. *Learn from our mistakes.*

We all make mistakes. As noted above, we must take risks if we want to progress, and an integral part of any risk is possible failure. Successful people take risks with every decision they make. The risks can never be eliminated, but they can be minimized by careful analysis and planning. Without pain there is no gain.

When faced with failures, instead of worrying and brooding about them, we must study carefully the reasons for them and take steps to correct them, if possible. It is in our interest to seek alternative solutions and to analyze what caused the problems so that we won't make the same mistakes in the future.

When faced with a problem, first ask yourself: What is the worst that can happen? Then prepare to accept it. Then proceed to improve on the worst.

Dale Carnegie

Use the Law of Averages

Mike dropped out of college, and decided to hitchhike around the United States. His mother was frantic. She stayed up nights worrying about all the things that could happen to him. He would be killed, kidnapped, fall into a ditch, get arrested, take sick, fall into bad company, and so on. For weeks she didn't sleep, didn't eat, and couldn't enjoy any aspect of her life. All she did was worry.

She sought advice from an old friend, who reminded her that many thousands of youngsters had done the same thing. How many of them had any real misadventure?

Her friend suggested she do some research, and in fact, she learned that only a small percentage of these young people met with any harm. The law of averages was weighted heavily in favor of this boy returning with no trouble. Once my friend accepted this, her mind relaxed, she ceased worrying and her life returned to normal. Sure, she had squeamish thoughts from time to time, but they no longer dominated her life.

In due course, the boy returned home and to college. Had Mike's mother not put this in proper perspective, her health and personal equilibrium might have been destroyed.

You may not control all the events that happen to you, but you can decide not to be reduced by them.

Maya Angelou,
American Poet

Do Not Give In to Defeat

One important attribute of successful people is not that they always succeed, but that instead of worrying about their capabilities, they respond to failure or obstacles by bouncing back and redoubling their efforts. They are resilient, a quality of those with high emotional intelligence who are able to control stress and worry.

The power to hold on is characteristic of all people who have accomplished anything great; they may lack in some other particular, have many weaknesses or eccentricities, but they don't give up easily.

Success does not happen overnight. Steve Jobs and Steve Wozniak experienced failure after failure before they perfected their first successful Apple computer. Sure, they worried that they may never succeed, but they pushed worry aside and concentrated on overcoming the problems that they faced.

Never give up. There are chances and changes,

Helping the hopeful, a hundred to one;

And, through the chaos, High Wisdom arranges

Ever success, if you'll only hold on

Never give up; for the wisest is boldest,
Knowing that Providence mingles the cup,
And of all maxims, the best, as the oldest,
Is the stern watchword of "Never give up!"

Oliver Wendell Holmes,
American poet and philosopher

Rather than worry about not meeting success, we must continue our efforts with optimisim. The owner of a mine in Colorado drove a tunnel a mile long through the strata he thought contained gold, spent one hundred thousand dollars on it, and in a year and a half had failed to find the gold and gave up. Another company drove the tunnel just one yard farther and struck ore. So the gold of life may be to us only a yard away.

Benjamin Franklin exemplified this tenacity. When he started in the printing business in Philadelphia, he combined his office, workroom, and sleeping-facilities into one small room. He learned that another printer in the city had resolved to crush him. Franklin invited him to his room. Pointing to a piece of bread from which had been all the dinner he had eaten, he said: "Unless you can live cheaper than I can you cannot starve me out." Rather than worry about having his printing business ruined, Franklin simply resolved to do whatever it took to succeed.

If you can't sleep, then get up and do something instead
of lying there worrying. It's the worry that gets you, not
the lack of sleep.

Dale Carnegie

Conquering Fear

Even more serious than worrying is living in a state of fear. Worry is often an occasional facet of our lives, but fear dominates the lives of many of us.

When a publication interviewed twenty-five hundred persons, it found that they had over seven thousand different fears. The most frequently noted were fear of death, fear of loss of job, fear of public speaking, fear of poverty, fear of contagious diseases, fear of the development of some hidden hereditary taint, fear of declining health, fear of flying, and multitudes of superstitious fears.

Some people live in constant fear and do not know how to overcome the fears that terrify them. The dread of some impending evil is always present. Their happiness is poisoned with it so that they never take much pleasure or comfort in anything. It is ingrained into their very lives and prevents them from accomplishing worthwhile endeavors.

Sadly, some people are afraid of nearly everything. They are afraid to venture in business matters for fear of losing their money. They are inordinately concerned with what their neighbors think about them. Their whole lives are filled with fear, fear, fear.

When people are suffering from a sense of fear or foreboding, it affects everything they do in their jobs and in other aspects of their lives. Fear strangles originality, daring, boldness; it kills individuality, and weakens all the mental processes. Fear depresses normal mental action, and makes us incapable of acting wisely in an emergency, for no one can think clearly and act wisely when paralyzed by fear. When we become depressed and discouraged about our affairs, when we are filled with fear that we are going to fail, we attract the very thing we dread.

Program Ourselves to Defeat Fear

Fear is a mental habit that we have the capacity to easily destroy by simply changing the thought. Faith is its perfect antidote. While fear sees only the darkness and the shadows, faith sees the silver lining, the sun behind the cloud. Fear looks down, and expects the worst; faith looks up and anticipates the best. Fear is pessimistic; faith is optimistic. Fear always predicts failure; faith predicts success. There can be no fear of poverty or failure when the mind is dominated by faith. Doubt cannot exist in its presence. It is above all adversity.

Indeed, faith in ourselves and our abilities will go far to alleviate our fears. One of the worst forms of fear is the brooding over failure. It blights our ambition, deadens our purpose, and assures our defeat.

One way to overcome this is to write down everything that we think is going to turn out badly, and then put the list aside. When we retrieve it sometime in the future, we will realize what a small percentage of the doleful things ever came to pass.

We must make every effort to give up fearful thoughts just as we would quit any bad practice that causes us suffering. We must fill our minds with courage, hope and confidence. We must not wait until fear-thoughts become entrenched in our minds and our imaginations. When confronted with fears, take the antidote instantly, and the enemies will flee. There is no fear so great or entrenched so deeply in the mind that it cannot be neutralized or entirely eradicated by its opposite. The opposite suggestions will kill it. Remember Franklin D. Roosevelt's theme: "The only thing we have to fear is fear itself."

Fear is a bully and a coward, and all we have to do to conquer fear is to forget it is there. We can do it.

Dale Carnegie

In setting about the overcoming of fear, we must first understand what it is we fear. It is almost always something that has not yet happened; that is, it is non-existent. Trouble is an imaginary something that we think of, and which frightens us with its possibility.

In overcoming our various fears, follow each one out to its logical conclusion and convince ourselves that at the present moment the things we fear do not exist save in our imagination. Whether they ever come to pass in the future or not, our fear is a waste of time, energy, and actual bodily and mental strength.

Merely convincing ourselves that what we fear is imaginary will not suffice until we have trained our minds to throw off suggestions of fear, and to combat all thought that leads to it. This means constant watchfulness and alert mental effort. When the thoughts of foreboding, or worry, begin to suggest themselves, we must not indulge them, and let them grow big, but change those thoughts, and focus our minds in the opposite direction.

If the fear is of personal failure, instead of thinking how little and weak we are, how ill-prepared for the great task, and how sure we are to fail, we should think how strong and competent we are, how we have succeeded in similar tasks, and how we are going to utilize all our past experience and rise to the present occasion. We will then do the task triumphantly, and be ready for even more challenging ones. It is such an attitude as this, whether consciously assumed or not, that will carry us to yet higher places.

This same principle of crowding out the fear by a buoyant, hopeful, confident thought, can be applied to all the many kinds of fear that daily and hourly beset us. At first it will be hard to change the current of thought, to cease to dwell on somber and depressing things. An aid in the process is often advisable. A sudden change of work to something requiring concentration of mind will often act as a switch.

It is fear that keeps us perpetually struggling against terrific odds instead of overcoming them. This fear comes from the false belief of an inability to cope with the problem, such as the fear that one will not be able to provide for oneself, or for one's family. Convert that fear into faith and we will not fail.

Fear-thought, the archenemy of humankind, can be eliminated from the habit of thought—can be entirely eradicated—but only by facing it. As Emerson said, "Do the thing you are afraid to do and the death of fear is certain."

Sum and Substance

- When faced with a problem:
  - Ask, "What is the worst that can possibly happen?"
  - Prepare to accept the worst.
  - Try to improve on the worst.
  - Remember the exorbitant price we can pay for worry in terms of our health.

- To control worry, analyze what it is that is causing the worry:
  - Get all the facts.
  - Weigh all the facts—then come to a decision.
  - Once a decision is reached, act!
- Write out and answer the following questions:
  - What is the problem?
  - What are the causes of the problem?
  - What are the possible solutions?
  - What is the best possible solution?
- No problem was ever solved by worrying. If the energy we use was channeled into constructive approaches to solving our uneasiness instead of brooding over it, we would overcome our fears and trepidation and be healthier and happier people.
- We are best off focusing on the present, rather than brooding over the past or fear for the future. Live in daytight compartments that keep our minds on what is happening right now.
- Ways to Minimize Worries
  - Don't belabor decisions. Make the best decision we can, and stick to it.
  - Decide where constructive thought ends and worry begins.
  - If there is something we can do to solve a problem that is nagging us, do it.
  - Mind our own business. We make think that we have answers for others, but we needn't control how other people manage their issues.

- Hold no grudges.
- Believe in ourselves and our ability to cope with issues as they arise.
- Let go of feelings of jealously.
- Don't fear change, but see it as a welcome opportunity to grow.
- Learn to accept the things we cannot change.
- Don't bite off more than we can chew. We will have fewer worries if we don't take on responsibilities that are beyond our abilities.
- Keep our minds occupied. While engaged with something that interests us or requires our attention, we won't be worrying or following our fear.
- Do it now. If we are worried or fearful about an activity, go ahead and do it. Having the event behind us is much better than stewing over it.
- Learn from our mistakes. When we've made an error, analyze how we went wrong, so that we do not commit the same mistake again.

- Tenacity pays off. We must determine what we are going to do and then do it. Those who perpetually procrastinate or hesitate on which of two things to do first, will do neither.

- We have the capacity to easily destroy, neutralize fear by simply changing the thought.

- Faith is the perfect antidote to fear. Fear always predicts failure; faith predicts success.

- We must break the habit of anticipating catastrophes that will probably never come. Anxiety and fretting will not only rob us of peace of mind and strength and ability to do our work, but also of precious years of life.

- Worrying about our fears being realized increases the likelihood that they will be.

- Fear can be eliminated from the habit of thought only if we face it.

Step 8

....

BECOME A TRUE LEADER

One need not be born a leader; most people can be trained to be leaders, but there are characteristics that they must acquire to be truly great leaders. Over the years many studies have been made on what these characteristics are.

Although individual strengths and abilities may vary, research indicates that outstanding managers view the world in similar ways. The following represent the most commonly observed qualities of successful leaders:

1. *They hold strong values and high ethical standards.* We can learn much by following the philosophy of Sir John Templeton, the founder of the Templeton Fund, one of the world's most profitable mutual funds. He bases his business practices on the belief that the most successful people are often the most ethically motivated. Templeton says that such

people are likely to have the keenest understanding of morality in business, and can be trusted to give full measure and not cheat their customers.

2. *They lead by example, acting with integrity in both their professional and personal lives.* Effective leaders see the rules applying to everyone, particularly themselves. They set a high moral ground and they don't ask others to engage in behavior that they themselves would not engage in. They keep their word in their personal interactions as well as their business dealings, knowing that maintaining their integrity is not in any way conditional.

3. *They are knowledgeable about corporate and department goals and keep informed of changes.* The best leaders are not removed from their staff members or their business's challenges. They are available for advice and are willing to make hard decisions.

4. *They are proactive and self-motivated to achieve results.* Good leaders do not rest on their laurels, and they are never entirely satisfied with themselves. They keep up not only with the state of the art in their fields, but they improve their knowledge and understanding in a variety of areas. They read professional journals and magazines in their areas of interest. They take active roles in professional and trade associations not only to keep in touch with new developments but to share their ideas with colleagues from other organizations. They attend and participate in conventions and conferences and develop networks of people to whom they can turn to obtain knowledge or ideas over the years.

5. *They are strong communicators and exceptional listeners.* They listen to their staff members and recognize that those

they hire can contribute ideas and suggestions that may be even more valuable than their own. Good leaders establish cooperative, collaborative climates in which employees at every level know their participation in decisions are welcome.

6. *They are flexible under pressure and keep their emotions in check.* When faced with failure, their commitment keeps them from succumbing to defeat. They will not let failures or disappointments keep them from continuing to try and to encourage their followers to move forward.

> *The person who goes farthest is generally the one who is willing to do and dare. The sure-thing boat never gets far from shore.*
>
> Dale Carnegie

7. *They have positive attitudes.* Effective leaders know that the practice of positive thinking increases their ability tremendously, for two reasons. First, because it discovers latent ability, calling out hitherto unknown resources; and second, because it keeps the minds in harmony by killing fear, worry, and anxiety, and by destroying all the enemies of success and efficiency. As they are positive thinkers, their associates will most likely be positive thinkers.

8. *They nurture the cooperation and collaboration of their team.* Good leaders know that internal competition and strife are causes of low productivity. They encourage and reward cooperation among their staff members and the different departments of their business. They take the time to get to know what drives individual team members and enjoy motivating and helping them to succeed. Great leaders understand people—what causes them to act and react the way they do.

They recognize the importance of being a motivating factor for people—appealing to the drives and the feelings of others.

9. *Their minds are open to new ideas and they welcome suggestions.* Even after changes and improvements are made, they still look for even better ways to accomplish their goals.

10. *They recognize and maximize strengths in others.* Often people in positions of authority can compel subordinates to follow orders by dint of the power of their jobs. But such people are not true leaders. Yes, the orders will be followed but that is all that will happen. True leaders develop confidence and trust in their associates. (Note they think of them as associates—not subordinates.) This engenders a desire not only to follow the lead of the manager, but also to initiate, innovate, and implement ideas of their own that fit into the goals established.

11. *They hold themselves and others accountable for results.* They set standards, which are understood and accepted by their associates and work to meet those standards. They take immediate action to correct deviations. They recognize their own limitations and seek help when needed.

12. *They are efficient and manage their time effectively.* Strong leaders develop meaningful time schedules. They learn to prioritize and to minimize interruptions and distractions.

13. *They have vision.* Great leaders know what they want to accomplish and what steps they must take to achieve their goals. They look beyond meeting short-term objectives and keep the big picture clearly in their minds.

14. *They are not easily deterred.* When faced with failure they take the reins and fight to overcome the problem. A good example is Tom Monaghan, founder of Domino Pizzas. He

grew the company from a one-store pizza parlor to a chain of several thousand home-delivery outlets over a period of about thirty years. In 1989 he sold the company. After two and a half years, the company that had purchased the chain lost the momentum Monaghan had generated. In order to save the company, he bought back the company and returned to his former position as CEO. Under his guidance, the company expanded to over five thousand stores in the United States, and over three thousand in other countries.

The very essence of leadership is that you have to have vision. It's got to be a vision you articulate clearly and forcefully on every occasion. You can't blow an uncertain trumpet.

Theodore Hesburgh,
Former President, Notre Dame University

The Activities of a Successful Leader

One of the main reasons people are promoted into management and leadership positions is because they were effective at what they did in their job. When we get that promotion, our job is to get others to be able to do things as well as or better than we did them. A good worker has one skill set, and a good leader has an entirely different one. Thus, to serve well in a new supervisory position, we must hone a new group of abilities.

To be effective as a manager, we must balance people and process. Being too focused on the development of our staff members may put our productivity in jeopardy. If we're intent on fine-tuning everyone's skills and maximizing their aptitudes, we may be in a difficult situation if a key staff member leaves. Being too process focused means that great systems are in place; but the employees do not understand them fully nor do they want to. work within them. A people-focused manager would be likely to say, "Let's discuss the plan and why we do things." A processfocused manager might say, "here's the plan, and here,s how we do things." With the right balance, both commitment and productivity stay at their highest levels.

Balancing Motivation and Accountability

Some people believe that as soon as we try to hold people accountable for their work, they lose their internal motivation. This is not necessarily so. We can develop tools to hold people accountable for their goals, objectives, and commitments and stay motivated at the same time. With the right balance, we maintain good control over the results of our team and ourselves.

There is only one way . . . to get anybody to do anything.
And that is by making the other person want to do it.

Dale Carnegie

Communicating and Coaching for Results

Today, more than ever, a manager's job is to facilitate the growth of his or her staff members. When we can create an environment where people get results, develop new skills, and become successful, we are fulfilling our highest calling as a manager and leader of people. Communicating with strength and sensitivity, being a coach, and building people's abilities are a leader's highest priority.

One of the reasons people are promoted to manager is because they have demonstrated the skills and knowledge necessary to excel in their area of expertise. Now their success depends not on their personal achievement, but coaching others to succeed. Successfully transitioning from worker to manager demands a new frame of mind and set of skills. The following chart shows the differences between being a worker and being a successful leader:

Worker	Manager to Leader
Needs guidance and direction	Plans strategy, prioritizes, and channels action to support upper management
Conforms to structure	Provides structure and sets policy
Has short-term perspective	Has long-term perspective
Accepts and complies	Challenges, persuades, and influences
Demonstrates skills in particular areas	Finds opportunities to capitalize on individual strenghts
Wants to understand "What's in it for me"	Motivates, energizes, and gains commitment and buy-in
Avoids risks and conflict, and seeks continuity	Takes risks, continually re-evaluates, and embraces conflict and change
Uses analytical decision-making	Uses intuitive decision-making

Seeks to be heard and understood	Listens and seeks to understand
Identifies what is needed to excel on the job	Provides coaching, support, guidance, and resources to succeed
Seeks purpose	Provides purpose with enthusiasm, passion, and conviction
Craves trust, involvement, responsibility and ownership	Asks for input, then delegates, empowers, and holds people accountable
Needs reassurance and feedback	Provides consistent performance feedback
Thrives on appreciation and recognition	Consistently builds confidcence, shows appreciation, and shares the glory
Seeks a clear career path	Provides opportunity for growth

Don't Boss—Lead

Peter Drucker, one of the great management thinkers and writers, wrote: "Most of what we call management consists of making it difficult for people to get their work done."

What is it that managers do that instigated Drucker to write that? Many people in managerial or supervisory positions deal with their employees as if they were automatons—expecting them to follow procedures exactly and not use any of their own initiative, creativity, and brain power when working. They are so concerned with following rules, regulations, procedures, and routines that they overlook the potential that each human being working under their supervision may have.

Managers, who truly lead their people instead of directing their work, not only obtain better results for their organizations, but develop teams of people who are committed to working toward success in every aspect of their jobs and their lives.

Leaders Serve

The true leader serves his or her people—not the other way around. The typical geometric figure we associate with most organizations is the triangle. On the top is the boss who gives orders to middle management who gives orders to supervisors who in turn give orders to the workers. At the very bottom of the triangle are the customers who we hope will be satisfied by what we provide.

The purpose of each layer is to serve the layer above it. In the traditional approach, workers serve their supervisors, supervisors serve their managers and all eventually serve the big boss. The customer down at the bottom is virtually ignored. The triangle should be reversed. Top-level management should serve the middle level managers, who in turn serve their first line supervisors who are there to serve the workers—and all serve the customer.

Good leaders truly care about their staff members. They learn as much as they can about their strengths and limitations, their likes and their dislikes, how they act and react. They take the time to work with them, to give them the resources, the tools, and the know-how to do their job effectively. They do not get in their way by worrying more about whether every "i" is dotted and every "t" crossed.

When surveys are made on what people want from a boss, among the very top of the list is: someone who is there for me. This is a boss to whom a person can come with a question and not be afraid of being thought to be stupid, a boss on whom one can depend to provide information, training, and suggestions rather than make demands, and give orders and commands. This is a boss who helps develop the potential of people—not just use them merely as a means of getting a job done.

Empower Our Employees

Real leaders "empower" their people. This word empower has become a fad word in management today, but fad words often express concisely a currently accepted concept. It derives from a legal term meaning transferring certain legal rights from one person to another. In today's management parlance, however, it is used in a broader sense—to share some of the authority and control a manager has with the people who he or she manages. Instead of the manager making every decision as to how a job should be done, the people who will perform the job participate in doing this. When employees help decide the best way to achieve their goals, we not only obtain more varied information as to how a job can be done, but also the staff members have a great commitment to it success.

Managing Versus Leading

Managing emphasizes that people follow orders—often unquestioningly. "This is the way it's going to be done." Leading encourages creativity in people by soliciting their ideas both informally in day-to-day contact and formally in meetings, suggestion-programs, and similar activities. Managing is telling people what they will be accountable for. Leading empowers people—giving them the tools to make their own decisions within guidelines that are acceptable to all parties concerned.

Managing is more concerned with how the policies are followed, explaining rules and policies and enforcing them. Leading motivates people and teaches them how to achieve their (and the organization's) objectives. If it doesn't work out as expected, efforts are made to improve performance by more and better training. Helping people learn is the key tool in obtaining quality performance.

Managing concentrates efforts on *doing things right*; leading emphasizes *doing the right things*. There are times when it is necessary to manage—when for legal or similar reasons, it is essential that things be done according to the book. Of course, people in managerial positions must assure that things are done right. But this is not their main job. Enforcing rules may be necessary in such circumstances, but more important is to train and motivate people to be competent and desirous of doing their very best to meet the department and the company's objectives. To achieve this with one's staff members is the epitome of true leadership.

Good leaders are neither indecisive nor tyrannical. They are neither ignored nor feared by their associates. Capable supervisors have inner confidence plus the respect of their employees.

Let's look at a simple comparison between the way a boss manages and a leader leads:

The Boss	The Leader
Drives People	Guides People
Instills Fear	Inspires Enthusiasm
Says "Do"	Says "Let's Do"
Makes work drudgery	Makes Work Interesting
Relies upon authority	Relies upon cooperation
Says "I," "I," "I"	Says "We"

How Do We Become a Leader?

Some people are reluctant to take on leadership roles. To do so, they believe that they would have to have certain innate leadership traits such as charisma, or that intangible personality that would empower them to influence others.

It's true that some of the world's greatest leaders were born that way—they had that special charm that enraptured the public. But they are the exceptions. The majority of successful leaders are ordinary men and women who have worked hard to get where they are. Leading is easier if we have natural talents, but they're not essential. Each of us can certainly acquire the skills necessary to manage and lead people.

Leadership is an art that can be acquired. With a little effort anybody who desires to can learn to guide people in a way that commands their respect, confidence, and whole-hearted cooperation.

Acquiring the Art of Leadership

Many managers like to refer to themselves as "professionals," but is management really a profession? Professionals in other fields (such as physicians, lawyers, psychologists, and engineers) are required to complete advanced study and pass exams for certification. There are no such requirements to be a manager. Some managers may have special education such as degrees in business administration, but most are promoted from the ranks and have little or no training in management. Most managers learn primarily on the job.

More and more successful managers are making an effort to acquire skills through structured courses of study, but most managers still pick up their techniques by observing those of their bosses. The model they follow may be good. Too often, however, new managers are exposed to their bosses' outdated and invalid philosophies.

Leadership is an art that can be acquired. We can learn to guide people in a way that commands their respect, confidence, and whole-hearted cooperation.

To do so, let's look at some of the less-than useful ideas that prevail in our society about leading in business.

Myth 1: Management Equals Common Sense

When one manager was asked about his leadership training, he said, "When I was promoted to my first management job, I asked a long-time manager for some tips about how to deal with people who report to me. He told me, 'Just use common sense and you'll have no trouble.'"

What is "common sense," exactly? What appears to be sensible to one person may make be nonsense to another. Often the definition of common sense is culturally based. In Japan, for example, it's considered common sense to wait for a full consensus before making any decision; in the United

States, this technique is often derided as inefficient and a waste of time.

Cultural customs aren't the only cause for differing ideas about what constitutes common sense. Different people have different views about what is good and what is bad, what is efficient and what is wasteful, and what will work and what will not.

We tend to use our own experiences to develop our particular notions of common sense. The problem is, a person's individual experience provides only his or her own limited perspective. Leadership involves much more than the experience an individual may have. To be a real leader, we must look beyond common sense.

We wouldn't rely solely on common sense to help with financial or manufacturing problems. We would call on the best possible expertise in these areas for advice and information. Why then should we resort to a less pragmatic base in handling human-relations problems?

We can learn a lot about the art and science of management by reading industry-related books and periodicals in the field, attending courses and seminars, and actively participating in industry associations.

Myth 2: Managers Must Know Everything

Managers don't know everything. Nobody can. Accept that we don't have all the answers, but acquire the skills to get the answers. One effective way is to develop contacts with people in other companies who have faced similar situations. We can learn a great deal from them. Networking—making contacts with people in other companies to whom we can turn for suggestions, ideas, and problem-solving strategies—gives us access to these people when we need new information and ideas, and provides us with a valuable ongoing resource for assistance in solving problems.

> *One of the surest ways of influencing the opinion of others is to give consideration to their opinions and to let them sustain a feeling of importance.*
>
> Dale Carnegie

Myth 3: Managers Have to Be Tough

Management by fear is still a common practice. And it works—sometimes. People will work hard if they fear that they might lose their jobs, but what is the quality of the work they will do? The answer is "just good enough to keep from getting fired." That's why this technique isn't considered effective management. Successful management involves getting the willing cooperation of our associates.

(As an aside, we should note that a revolving door of staff members is not effective—just because we can fire people doesn't make it a good practice. It is hard on morale and requires us to find replacement workers, which is both a cost in time and money. Moreover, if our employees are union members, letting them go can be an onerous process.)

There are managers that act as slave masters. For years James Miller, management consultant and the author of *The Corporate Coach*, holds a contest for the Best and Worst Boss of the Year.

Employees did the nominating. Miller has reported that

he gets many more nominations for worst boss than for best boss. One of the chief reasons employees dislike their bosses, Miller found, is that these bosses are continually finding fault with subordinates, expressing sarcasm, gloating over failures, and frequently hollering and screaming at employees.

Why do people behave this way? Some people have always been screamed at—by parents, teachers, and former bosses—so they may assume that it's an effective communication tool.

Many of us raise our voices occasionally, especially when we're under stress. Sometimes it takes great self-discipline not to yell. Effective leaders, however, control this tendency. When we yell at people, we're admitting our failure to be real leaders. We cannot get the willing cooperation of our associates by screaming at them.

We can't keep good workers for long when we manage by fear. When jobs are scarce in our community or industry, workers might tolerate high-handed, arbitrary bosses. But when the job market opens up, the best people will leave for companies with more pleasant working environments. Employee turnover can be expensive and often devastating.

Myth 4: Praise Results in Complacency

Some managers fear that if they praise a team member's work, that person will become complacent and stop trying to improve (certainly, some people do react this way). The objective is to phrase our praise in a manner way that encourages the associate to keep continue the good work.

Other managers are concerned that if associates are praised for good work, they will expect pay raises or bonuses. And some folks might. But that's no reason to withhold praise when it's warranted. Employees should know how salary adjustments, bonuses, and other financial rewards are determined. If compensation is renegotiated at annual performance evaluations, team members should be assured that the good work for which they are praised will be considered in the evaluation.

Some managers consider praise irrelevant. One department head reported, "The people I supervise know that they're doing okay if I don't talk to them. If I have to speak to them, they know they are in trouble." Offering no feedback other than reprimands isn't effective, either. Remember, we want to use positive, not negative, reinforcement.

Of course, praise can be overdone. If people are repeatedly praised for every trivial accomplishment, the praise begins to feel superficial. Also, non-productive employees can think they're doing great if they are praised excessively.

Try the Platinum Rule

When we manage people, the biblical golden rule, "Do unto others as you would have others do unto you" is sound advice—but only to a point. People are not all alike; treating others as we want to be treated is not the same as treating them as they want to be treated.

For example, Linda prefers to be given broad objectives and likes to work out the details of her job on her own. But her assistant, Jason, is not comfortable receiving an assignment unless all the details are spelled out for him. If Linda delegates work to her assistant in the way she likes to have work assigned to her, she won't get the best results.

Sol needs continuous reinforcement. He's happy on the job only when his boss oversees his work and assures him that he's doing a good job. Tanya, however, gets upset if her boss checks her work too often. "Doesn't she trust me?" she complains. We can't do unto Tanya as we do unto Sol and get good results from each of them.

Each of us has our own style, our own approach, and our own eccentricities. To "do unto others" what as we would have them do unto us may be a less-than-effective way of managing people.

To be an effective manager, we must know each member of our team and tailor our method of management to each person's individuality. Rather than follow the golden rule, follow the platinum rule:

Do unto others, as they would have you do unto them.

Compromises must be made, of course. In some situations, work must be done in a manner that may not be ideal for some people. By knowing ahead of time what needs to be accomplished, we can anticipate problems and prepare our associates to accept their tasks.

Leaders Must Produce More than Optimum Performance

Production, performance, and profit are important aspects of our job as managers, but are these all we have to consider? Certainly, if a business is to survive, it must produce results. Equally important, however, is the development of its employees. If we ignore people's potential, our team's ability to attain results is limited. Instead, we reap short-term benefits at the expense of long-term success, and possibly even our business's survival.

When Eliot founded his computer components company, he was a pioneer in what was then a new and growing industry. Determined to be a leader in his field, he drove his employees to maintain high levels of productivity and kept his eye carefully trained on the profit picture, but he paid no attention to the development of his staff. His technical and administrative staff members were given little opportunity to contribute ideas or use their own initiative on their own projects. Over the years, Eliot's company saw reasonable profits, but it never grew to become an industry leader as he had hoped. Because he had stifled the potential and ambition of his employees, he lost many of his highly skilled staff members to other companies. And because he depended only on his own ideas, he missed out on all the innovative ideas his staff might have come up with.

Getting the Most From Our Employees

To get the most from each of our employees, we must understand them as human beings and work with them as individuals to help them make and meet commitments to perform even better than they have up to now.

As noted above, we must be aware others have their own personal, individual ways of being. We must deal with each of them according to his or her individuality, rather than expect them to respond to things the way that we would or try to get them all to do the same thing in the same way. Let's take the word "people," and by expanding on each letter obtain some hints on how we can achieve our goal of better relations with other people.

Personality

Each person has his or her own special personality. We must take the time to get to know how each of them acts and reacts, what turns them on—or off, and what really is of concern to them. A major error made by many people is to expect that others share their temperament and understanding. We are unwise to treat all people alike. Some people need much more attention than others, while some look upon our attention as prying or condescending. There are people who need constant reinforcement, while others only need an occasional pat on the back.

Exceptional Characteristics

Look for those traits that make each person stand out from others. Laurie is very creative. In her spare time she draws, sculpts, and writes poetry. How can that help in dealing with her? By appealing to her creativity, we can get Laurie to tackle difficult projects or contribute ideas and suggestions that may help solve job problems. Gary is a perfectionist. His work may be slow, but it is always accurate. By giving him assignments where quality is paramount, we will be using his skills most effectively.

Opportunity

Claudette's job was basically boring. But her boss recognized that she was eager to learn and would give her full efforts to her boring job if she could see how it could lead to more challenging work. By giving Claudette opportunity to learn about other jobs in the department, she was able to train and prepare for them, thus encouraging her to learn and grow.

Affording others with opportunity is not limited to the promotions. There are people who do not want the responsibility of senior positions, but seek chances to expand their knowledge or perform work that is of more interest to them. David considered himself a "people-person." He related well with other people, but in his job as an accountant he spends most of his time working by himself. By giving David the opportunity to train others in the department in various company procedures and to periodically conduct department meetings, his satisfaction with the job increased and his overall performance was enhanced.

Participation

People who work on a job have a lot more insight into how a job should be done that we may realize. When a new procedure has to be developed or a new project planned, have the people who will do the job participate in determining how it should be done. As the manager of the department, Kathy believed she knew exactly how the new project should be performed. After all, she had years of experience in this work. However, instead of designing the plan and then telling her people how it would be done, she brought them into the early stages of the planning procedure. Not only did they come up with some excellent ideas that Kathy had not considered, but because they were part of the planning process, they felt committed to work hard to assure it would succeed.

Leadership

Good leaders do not set goals for their staff members and tell them how to reach them. Good leaders work with their coworkers to encourage them to set their own goals and give them the tools they need to attain them.

► Fred was an intelligent man and a good worker, but Paul, his boss, felt he had much more capability than he was using. Fred was afraid to take the initiative on any project and continually came to Paul for instructions. To help Fred overcome this, Paul began giving Fred small projects and made him responsible for their completion. By gradually increasing the complexity of these assignments, Paul helped Fred develop the self-confidence he needed to really give outstanding performance.

Expectations

Let others know that our expectations are high. Do not be satisfied with mediocre work. Too many managers are delighted if their staff members meet minimum standards. This may be okay if business is flourishing, but when companies have to fight to stay alive, we need more than just meeting standards. Our people must be encouraged try to keep getting better and better. In fact, high expectations of others lets them know that they are considered competent and trustworthy. Asking others to be their best selves is a way to treat them with respect.

When their bosses, their families, and most importantly the people themselves see their performance improving, nothing can stop them from becoming real achievers.

By knowing those around us, using their individual

strengths, and treating them well, the group of which they are a part will flourish.

Sum and Substance

Effective leaders follow these principles:

✓ Team members respond better to participatory, rather than authoritarian, leadership.

✓ Associates should be given every opportunity to use their talents, skills, and brainpower.

✓ The good leader establishes a cooperative, collaborative climate in which all participants know their participation in decisions are welcome. Associates should be given every opportunity to use their talents, skills, and brainpower.

✓ Good leaders think of themselves as facilitators. Their job is to make it easy for their associates to accomplish their jobs.

✓ Effective leaders are ready to take the initiative, to act rather than react.

✓ The best leaders set high standards for themselves and then work hard to achieve their goals.

✓ They focus on getting things done and are not easily deterred.

✓ Leadership is an art that can be acquired. With a little effort anybody who desires to can learn to guide people in a way that commands their respect, confidence, and wholehearted cooperation.

✓ Don't boss—lead.

✓ Managers are often influenced by misconceptions and myths about management. Don't automatically follow in an old boss's footsteps.

✓ Be neither hard-boiled nor easy-going. The most effective supervisory style is somewhere between these two extremes. It is grounded on understanding human behavior and applying this knowledge in working with the people under our jurisdiction.

✓ Praise people for work well done. Unrecognized work is like an un-watered plant. Productivity will wither away.

✓ Follow the platinum rule: "Do unto others as *they* would have you do unto them."

✓ Make a point of getting to know the people we work with as individuals. By acknowledging each person's needs and strengths, we build good relationships and maximize the individual's contribution to the organization.

Step 9

....

HELP OTHERS TO SUCCEED

We are judged not only on the basis of our own performance, but also on how well the people we supervise perform. To be a successful leader, our primary goal is to develop and cultivate the skills and effectiveness of our team or subordinates.

Helping New People Get Started

How we orient and train new people joining our group will have a big impact on how well they adjust to the environment and their new tasks. Let's look at some examples.

Gloria felt unhappy and frustrated. This was her first day on the new job and nobody was paying much attention to her. She had spent most of the morning filling out papers in the Human Resources office and was then told to report to Carly Martin, her new boss. Carly had interviewed her before she was hired and, although she was all business at that meeting, she seemed to be a nice person. Now on her first day, Gloria wasn't so sure she made a good decision in taking the job. Carly had greeted her perfunctorily, assigned her a desk and gave her a job description to read. Two hours later, Carly still hadn't spoken to her.

The first day on the job can set the stage for success or failure, happiness or discontent, cooperation or rebellion. No matter how busy a supervisor may be, he or she must spend a significant amount of time with a new employee the day that person starts.

Develop Immediate Rapport

Plan for the arrival of the new person. Schedule our day so that we can spend at least two hours with that person immediately. If feasible, take him or her to lunch that first day. This is our chance to talk informally about the company and the department and to learn as much as we can about the new member of the team. Introduce him or her to each of the other members of the department and to persons in other departments with whom he or she will work. In making the introduction, always specify what kind of work that person does and tell him or her what the new employee will be doing. For example, we might say something like, "Marilyn, this is Gloria, our new market analyst. Gloria, Marilyn is in charge of our statistics section."

In introducing Gloria to more senior staff members, follow company protocol in whether first names or more formal address is used. Even if we call our boss Don, if Gloria is expected to refer to him as Mr Deane, introduce him as Mr Deane.

Orientation

Many companies have formal orientation programs for new people and this usually covers such things as company history, discussions of the products or services provided and descriptions of benefits, etc. In addition to this, a department head should discuss the mission of the department and how it fits into the overall picture.

It is important that a new person learn as quickly as possible who is who in the department and the company. Using an organization chart helps, but often the organization chart does not tell the entire story. On the chart, Don Deane, director of marketing, is our boss, However, Don is about to retire and Ken Maynard, the National Sales Manager, is being groomed to replace him. This is important for Gloria to know, but it doesn't show on the chart.

More difficult to convey to a new employee is the corporate culture. Each company has developed over the years a philosophy, a special approach to dealing with problems, a uniqueness that makes it the company that it has become. This "culture" is hard to put into words and often only can be absorbed by a new employee over time. However, there are certain aspects of the corporate culture in which the new employee should be steeped from the beginning.

One way to help an employee get started and learn the inner workings of the company is to assign one or, even better, two associates to each new person, who will be available to answer questions and guide him or her through the maze of company practices.

Clear and Meaningful Job Descriptions

A good start is to read the job description again. Does it truly describe the work that will be done? If the new employee were to use this, could he or she do what is expected in that job? In many companies a job description may be developed when the job was created and not changed for years. Most jobs are dynamic—they are always changing. Before starting the training of a new employee, reread the job description to determine if it is current, and if not, make necessary adjustments.

Once the new employee has studied the job description, the supervisor should discuss it with him or her. Ask that person to describe how the job is perceived. A detailed discussion of the nature of the work will clarify any misunderstandings that may have arisen from just reading the job description.

Train, Train, Train

No matter how much experience a person has in the field, it is still important that we give that person specific training in the methods and techniques we use. In previous jobs, he or she may have done things somewhat differently, may have had less stringent standards, or may have faced different problems. The more time spent in training a person in the beginning of that person's tenure with the department, the fewer problems will arise later on.

Who should do the training? In some organizations special trainers are utilized, but in most companies supervisors train their own employees. Because we are responsible for our team members' work, it is important that we take a significant role in the training. However, it is not always possible for the supervisor to give the time needed for complete training, so other employees may be used to assist. In choosing another person to help train new people, adhere to the following guidelines:

- The trainer should be thoroughly familiar with the job.
- Teach the trainer how to train. Don't assume that because a person knows the job, he or she can train others.
- Be sure that the trainer has a strong positive attitude toward the company and the job. If we use a disgruntled employee to do the training, that person will inject the trainee with the virus of discontent.
- Periodically arrange a feedback meeting with new employees to review what they have learned, where they need additional training, and to counsel them on how they can improve.

To get the employee started on the right foot and to assure that he or she will progress satisfactorily on the job, establish rapport immediately, orient carefully, train thoroughly, and give and get feedback regularly.

Communicating with Staff Members

Keith was puzzled. He had just spent ten minutes describing in detail to his team the process to follow on the new project. He considered himself a good communicator. This was borne out by the fact that most of his employees did fully understand, but somehow he couldn't get these instructions across to some of them. It wasn't so complex, why didn't they understand?

Like many people, Keith knew exactly what he wanted

done and assumed that just by projecting this to the other team members, they would know what to do. But the questions some of his employees asked showed they hadn't the vaguest idea of what was required.

People Absorb Information in Different Ways

Some people understand best by being told; others by being shown.

Tanya was a verbal person. She listened intently and usually fully comprehended the material. If not, she asked pertinent and thorough questions. Keith had no problem with Tanya. Gary learned by watching and doing. He compensated for his weakness in verbal skills by his mechanical comprehension. He could not maintain attention to long discussions and therefore missed key points, but if the project was diagrammed, illustrated, or presented by demonstration, he caught on immediately. So Keith showed Gary how to perform his part of the new process, and he had no difficulty in understanding it.

Consideration for Slow Learners

Everybody does not learn at the same pace. Some people take a lot longer to catch on to new concepts than others. This does not mean that they are stupid. Sally, one of the customer service representatives on Keith's team, was a slow learner. When she was assigned to the team, Keith had a great deal of difficulty in teaching her the work. He was about to give up on her, when her previous supervisor pointed out that, although she was a slow learner, once she mastered an area, she became one of the best workers in the group. He advised

Keith to be patient and his patience paid off as she became one of his most reliable and accurate team members.

Avoid Using Jargon

Every field, every trade, every profession has its private language—its jargon. This is fine when people in the field communicate with each other. However, more and more teams in business today come from a variety of disciplines. Some of the staff members may not be familiar with the jargon used by others.

Keith's background was in engineering, but his team consisted of customer service specialists, technical support people, and people from sales and marketing. From years of habit, Keith used technical terms and jargon quite often when discussing matters facing the group.

As these terms were not fully understood by nontechnically trained members, the communication was often less than successful. It took him some time to recognize this, and to teach those persons from nontechnical fields the necessary terminology and to avoid using jargon when it was not appropriate.

Get Continuing Feedback

Often we think that the people in the group understand what is desired, and then—after the work is well underway, we learn that they interpreted the instructions differently from what was meant.

To avoid heading in the wrong direction, get continuing feedback. At the time the instructions are given, ask questions about the key points as they are presented. Ask the listeners to tell us how they interpret our instructions. Where pertinent, ask just how they intend to follow the instructions. If it is something which can be demonstrated, have them show what they will do.

Correct any misunderstandings before the work starts. At various times during the course of the assignment, check with the persons involved to assure they are performing as expected. It is not necessary to keep looking over their shoulders, but set predetermined checkpoints at which we review progress with the associates and assure that what has been completed meets the standards we've set, so there are no unpleasant surprises at the end of the project.

As Keith's team consisted of both technical and nontechnical people, he often found that some of the marketing and customer service staff members lacked technical know-how that, although not essential to their work, would help them understand more clearly what they were doing.

He tried to give them a crash course in these technical aspects, but this was not sufficient. He found that he was spending an inordinate amount of his time answering questions on basic technical matters, and his own work suffered. To overcome this problem, he asked the technically savvy members of his team to help the nontechnical associates fully understand the terms used. This not only alleviated this burden on Keith, but gave the associates who needed this help an easier and more accessible means of obtaining it. In addition, empowering his staff members to resulted in a closer relationship among all of them, which led to an esprit de corps that contributed to the success of the group.

Lost Employees

Sometimes no matter what we do, there may be people in the group who just cannot seem to learn how to do their job. Before giving up and letting them go, try a different approach.

Jack had been a field representative in technical service for several years before being assigned to Keith's group. He was a hands-on mechanic, who found it difficult to learn the kind of work he was to do on the group's project. Keith told him, showed him, and worked with him. Nothing seemed to help. Keith realized that Jack seemed to be overwhelmed by the project. First, he explained to Jack how the project fit into the company's activities and what the goals for it were. He made sure that Jack had an understanding of the larger effort, so that he had some perspective on what he was trying to accomplish. He then broke Jack's work down into small tasks. By teaching Jack one task at a time, he overcame Jack's awe of the project and developed him into a valuable associate.

Be a Coach

Probably the most challenging part of the leader's job is molding the individual associates into a dynamic, interactive, highperformance unit. We have seen how athletic coaches shape up their teams and as leaders of our work teams, we can learn from them.

We do this by helping the members of the group develop their talents to optimum capacity. We keep them alert to the organization's goals and to the latest methods and techniques that will enable them to reach those goals. We help them learn what they don't know and to perfect what they do know.

A good example is Bob, an experienced salesman recently hired by the company. Because of his successful background, Bob did not expect his manager to give him much training. He assumed he would be oriented about the product line and sent into the field. But Bob's manager insisted on giving him the same extensive training as a less experienced sales trainee. Bob understood this. He had been a champion runner in high school but when he joined the university track team, the coach had given him as much attention and training as those team members who had never competed before.

Successful managers keep this in mind when bringing on a new employee. Even if he or she has had previous experience, it is necessary to understand the company's approaches to the job, which may differ from the employee's past experience. Most managers will not hesitate to do this with a person who has had no previous experience, but often neglect it with experienced personnel.

We have done lots of research over the past three years, and we have found that leaders who have the best coaching skills have better business results.

Tanya Clemens,
Vice President of Global Executive &
Organizational Development at IBM

Ten Tips on Coaching Associates

1. Meet with each associate on a regular basis to identify what that person can do to become more effective and what we can do to help.

2. Don't wait for a formal performance review to confront poor performance. Take action to correct it as soon as it is observed.

3. Keep a running record on each associate's progress. Include examples of successes and failures. Note areas where improvement is needed. Specify recommendations for that person's growth.

4. In training associates, keep in mind that people master tasks in small steps. Build the training by first giving the associate small tasks and work up to more complex tasks.

5. Encourage slow learners by praising their efforts and reinforcing the training to help them catch up.

6. Rather than working to achieve several goals at the same time, help associates build their skills by working on one goal at a time. Once on the way to meeting it, add another goal.

7. We should be a role model to associates by our own pursuit of learning and our application of new approaches to the work.

8. Pass on tips, information, and ideas that we acquire to team members. This may take the form of articles we read and clip, Internet resources we e-mail to them, or sharing new concepts verbally.

9. Assign associates responsibility for all or part of a project and give them the leeway to do it without our interference.

10. If our coaching session didn't result in improvement, ask these questions:
    - What was the purpose of the coaching session?
    - What did I do to achieve the purpose?
    - What action resulted from the session?

Have the team member answer the same questions, and compare the results.

Coaching the Team

As much work today is done in teams, it is not enough to train each member of the team to perform superbly. Equally important is merging the group members into a coordinated working unit.

For a new team, it starts with a thorough orientation on the objectives of the team—what is expected from each associate, and from the team as a whole. This can be done in group sessions or, when a new member is added, one-on-one.

Let's look at Erica, leader of an information technology team. When the team is assigned a new project, Erica spends the first day or more of the assignment discussing it with team members—both individually and as a group. She commented, "The more time I spend up front, the better the success rate." She draws on the experience that various team members have had with similar projects and together they plan the entire operation. As the project proceeds, she keeps tabs on each associate's progress and jumps in with assistance, added training, or whatever is needed to make him or her more effective on the job.

Give Pep Talks

Just as the coach of an athletic team gives pep talks to the team before the game and during breaks, team leaders find that pep talks stimulate production, and reinvigorate members when their enthusiasm wanes. A pep talk is more than yelling

"Go, team, go!" The effective team leader provides the team with understanding as to what they need to change to be more effective, and works with them to make those changes.

Pep talks help push the team forward for the short term— and often that's enough to pull it out of a rut. For more lasting effect, we must keep the team alert to its progress. It is important to praise every accomplishment, celebrate reaching interim goals, and give recognition to team members who do outstanding work.

Good leaders, like good coaches, also train people to give themselves pep talks. By showing associates that we have confidence in their ability and in helping them build up this selfconfidence, we are performing one of the most important functions of our job as manager/coach. Successful coaches work with people to keep up their spirits when they are depressed, to retrain them when they forget the fundamentals of the job, and to glory with them about their triumphs. They understand their personalities, and model motivational programs that will best take advantage of these factors. Effective coaches do not give up easily when some people do not meet expectations. They work with their employees and do their best to bring them up to the high standards set for the team.

Good leaders recognize superb performance as well as every improvement. When special achievements are accomplished, the leader praises the team and reiterates how the cooperative efforts of the team members contributed to the achievement. One manager makes a practice of having an impromptu pizza or ice cream party when a significant part of a project is successfully finished. Another manager hosts a barbecue at his home for all members and their significant others when a particularly complex project is completed.

> *Any fool can criticize, condemn, and complain, but it takes character and self-control to be understanding and forgiving.*
>
> Dale Carnegie

Create a Well-Motivated Team

Our coaching will be most effective if we know how to best motivate our particular staff members. If we don't have a good handle on this, we're bound to spend a great deal of our time just overcoming resistance to new work and new projects.

We often hear that people resist change. And in large measure, people resist change for which they for which they don't see the need, when the change is not appealing to them, or when they believe that they won't succeed in the changed environment. Whenever people are asked to change without their buy-in, we create resistance. The effective coach addresses his or her staff members' concerns about change, and creates an atmosphere where people are consistently motivated to attain high performance levels.

Provide Resources

The effective manager assures that all the resources needed for the training process are available. These include providing time, money, equipment, training aids, information, and upper level buy-in and support—and, most importantly, a personal commitment to succeed by all involved. We must ensure that the appropriate resources are in place and available. Nothing is as frustrating as being promised something and then not getting it. It can make everyone feel like they have been set up to fail.

A good coach will make his players see what they can become rather than what they are.

Ara Parseghian,
Football Coach, Notre Dame University

Be a Mentor—Develop Others to be Mentors

One of the best approaches to developing our staff members is to encourage experienced associates to mentor trainees. For example, a more experienced associate takes a younger employee under his or her wing and becomes that person's mentor. The person being mentored will get not only a head start for advancement, but also greater know-how about the work, the subtleties and nuances or contributing to the company, and the tricks of the trade.

It would be a major benefit to organizations if everybody had a mentor. As leaders, we should consider mentoring a job requirement not only for ourselves, but also for all experienced associates. By structuring a mentoring program, and assigning our best people the responsibility of mentoring a new associate, we take a giant step forward in making the newcomer productive and on the way to personal growth.

A structured mentoring program requires that people chosen to be mentors be willing to take on the job. Compelling someone to be a mentor is self-defeating. Not everybody is interested in or qualified to be a mentor. However, if in our judgment the person who declines the assignment is really qualified, but is shy or lacks the self-confidence, we should have a heart-to-heart talk about how by accepting the task, both the member and the team will benefit. Experienced people in the art of mentoring should train new mentors.

Both the mentor and the person who is mentored benefit from the process of mentoring. Obviously, those who are mentored learn much from the process, but equally importantly, the mentors gain by sharpening their skills in order to pass them on. It heightens the mentors' senses of responsibility as they guide their mentees through the maze of company policies and politics. It also makes them more effective in their interpersonal relationships.

A mentor is someone who sees more talent and ability within you than you see in yourself, and helps bring it out of you.

Bob Proctor,
Author, Speaker, and Success Coach

Ten Tips for New Mentors

When we are assigned to be a mentor, we should learn as much as we can about the art of mentoring. If we have had a successful experience with a mentor ourselves, we can use that as a model. If not, seek out another member who has been a successful mentor and learn from him or her.

Here are ten things to keep in mind:

    1. Know the work. Review the basics. Think back on the

problems we've faced and how we dealt with them. Be prepared to answer questions about every aspect of the job.

2. Know as much as we can about our company. One of the main functions of a mentor is to help the trainee overcome the hurdles of unfamiliar company policies and practices. More important, as a person who's been around the organization for some time, we know the inner workings of the organization—the true power structure—the company politics. That said, it is not wise to gossip or share opinions about a group or individual in our organization. We should only convey objective, factual information about how our organization works.

3. Get to know the trainee. To be an effective mentor, we must take the time to learn as much as we can about the person we are mentoring. Learn about his or her education, previous work experience, current job, and more. Learn his or her goals, ambitions, and outside interests. Observe personality traits. Get accustomed to his or her preferred ways of communicating— face-to-face, written memos, telephone, email, texting, and the like.

4. Learn to teach. If we have minimal experience in teaching, pick up pointers on teaching methods from the best trainers we know. Read articles and books on training techniques.

5. Be willing to learn. It is essential that we keep learning—not only the latest techniques in our own field, but developments in our industry, in the business community, and in the overall field of management.

6. Be patient. Some people learn more slowly than others. Taking a while to get accustomed to a new job does not mean that the individual is stupid. If the person we are mentoring does not catch on right away, be patient. Slow learners often develop into productive team members.

7. Be tactful. We are not drill sergeants training a rookie in how to survive in combat. Be kind. Be courteous. Be gentle but firm, and let the trainee know we expect the best.

8. Don't be afraid to take risks. Give the trainee assignments that will challenge his or her capabilities. Let the trainee know failures may occur, but that the best way to grow is to take on tough jobs. Failures should be looked upon as learning experiences.

9. Celebrate successes. Let the trainee know we are proud of the accomplishments and progress he or she makes. When something especially significant is achieved, let both the trainee and others know.

10. Encourage our trainee to become a mentor. The best reward we can get from being a mentor is that once the need for mentoring is done, our protégé carries on the process by becoming a mentor.

Mentoring is a brain to pick, an ear to listen, and a push in the right direction.

John Crosby
Business Executive

Correcting Errors

Even the most competent people will make errors in their work from time to time. It is the manager's responsibility to correct these errors. To maintain morale and to get the best from our staff members, we must do this without causing resentment or making the associate feel inadequate or inferior. Although we may become frustrated, upset, or even irate about the situation, this is not the time or place to lose our temper, rant and rave and bawl out the person who made the error. Address any situation as soon as it comes up. We should not wait until the situation reaches intolerable proportions, and then explode in a rage. So act early, while the situation and our responses are manageable.

The Nine R's in Correcting Errors

Here are some suggestions on how to diplomatically correct errors, teach the associate how to correct them, and avoid making future errors.

1. *Research*. Do the homework to make sure we have all the facts before discussing the issue with the associate. Our aim is not to build a case as much as gather information. We must keep an open mind and look behind the facts to better understand motivations.

2. *Rapport*. When we meet with the person who has made a mistake, it is best to begin by putting that person at ease and reducing the anxiety. One way to do this is to begin with honest appreciation that is supported by evidence. Instead of just giving a general compliment,

choose a behavior that we have observed. Maintain a policy of keeping our business relationships warm so the other person is open to our input.

Conduct the discussion in private. Don't say or do anything that may cause the person to feel embarrassed or lose face in front of others.

Adopt the attitude and actions we want the other person to exhibit. If we speak quietly and calmly, it is likely the other person will do so in return. If we view the fault as small and easy to correct, the other person may adopt the same attitude.

3. *Relate to the Situation.* Essential to success in correcting a problem is to focus on the problem and not the person. Eliminate personal pronouns and depersonalize the problem. It was the action that was wrong, not the person who did it. We want to give the other person a chance to explain what happened and then let that person know what we know about the problem. We should listen to understand and to determine whether he or she is accepting responsibility or blaming and avoiding responsibility. Our goal is to gather facts and information so we are able to accurately identify the problem and determine why it happened. By not being accusatory and not jumping to conclusions, different perspectives will surface, and the root cause of the problem should be identified.

Instead of attaching a negative label or trait to the individual, we should phrase our comments in non-accusatory terms. Here are some examples: instead of saying "There is not enough information about safety matters in the report," say, "This report is very comprehensive; it might be even more effective if the section on safety were more detailed..."

Instead of commenting: "Why were you so careless about these statistics?" We might say something like "The statistics need to be really accurate." If appropriate, supply an appropriate action step to help the individual alleviate the problem. "Joe Smith has the newest numbers you need. Can you get with him today?" or "Will you call Mary Ross at X-Tech to let her know the corrected shipping date?"

How the associate relates to the problem—their actions, attitude, and behavior in this discussion—will determine our next moves.

4. *Restore Performance.* The purpose of this step is to remedy the problem, to reduce the chance of the mistake happening again, and to restore the person's performance. It also involves devising a way to keep the problem from occurring again.

This step should be handled differently with the associate who accepts responsibility than with the one who blames and avoids taking responsibility. With the responsible employee, effective questioning, listening, and coaching can be used to encourage him or her to suggest ways to correct the situation. Involve the associate in the problem analysis and decisionmaking process.

For the blaming or avoiding employee, the manager

may first need to reaffirm performance expectations and coach him or her to accept responsibility and to restore accountability.

5. *Reassure.* This step is focused on the person. Obviously, a person who has made a mistake may feel, to some degree, like a failure and is likely to be less inclined to approach the next opportunity with confidence. Therefore, the manager needs to help the associate see the situation in a different context.

   The associate needs to be reassured of his or her value and importance to the organization and of the manger's support and encouragement. The associate should leave the meeting motivated to achieve optimal performance because he or she perceives a solid relationship with the organization.

   The blaming or avoiding person should leave with a sense of accountability and an understanding of what the company's expectations are. That person should also understand that we are interested in and committed to his or her success and growth.

6. *Retain.* If we handled the previous steps well, we have increased our chances of retaining the person and of enhancing his or her commitment. Forgiving errors also reinforces the morale of our whole team. This builds trust and increases the level of commitment and work ethic.

7. *Restate.* If performance is not improved or the associate does not seem to relate to the issue, our next move is to restate the facts, the seriousness, the policy, and

the proper remedy to the issue; this gives the person one more chance to do the right thing.

8. *Reprimand.* When people refuse to accept responsibility, we may have to formally remind them in some way prior to further action. Most organizations have established policies and procedures that must be followed before disciplinary action can be taken. This is particularly important in companies with contracts either with individual employees or with a labor union.

9. *Remove.* Sometimes we find that the employee is not a good fit for a particular task, project, or in some cases a major part of the department's activities. We may need to explore what his or her strengths, interests, and goals are and search for a better fit within the company for a better match. It is an injustice to employees and companies when we perpetuate a situation where individuals feel that they can never succeed.

The last resort after attempts to coach a poorly performing employee for desired performance have been unsuccessful is to remove him or her from this area of responsibility—to replace, reassign, or release them from the organization. Remember to comply with all the organization's policies when making this decision.

Sum and Substance

✓ The leader's job is to ensure that all members of the group or team know the organization's goals and the latest methods and techniques that will enable them to reach those goals.

They help them learn what they don't know and to perfect what they do know.

✓ To be a successful leader, our primary goal is to develop and cultivate the skills and effectiveness of our team or staff members.

✓ One way to help an employee get started and learn the inner workings of the company is to assign one or, even better, two associates to each new person, who will be available to answer questions and guide him or her through the maze of company practices.

✓ Before starting the training of a new employee, reread the job description to determine if it is current, and if not, make necessary adjustments.

✓ No matter how much experience a person has in the field, it is still important that we give that person specific training in the methods and techniques we use.

✓ At the time instructions are given, ask questions about the key points as they are presented. Ask the listeners to tell how they interpret our instructions. Where pertinent, ask just how they intend to follow the instructions.

✓ Just as a coach of an athletic team is constantly on the alert to identify areas where improvement can be made for each team member, so successful supervisors seek to work with each of their employees to hone their skills so they can become even more effective in their jobs.

✓ As much work today is done in teams, it is not enough to traineach member of the team to perform superbly. Equally important is merge the group members into a coordinated working unit.

✓ Just as the coach of an athletic team gives pep talks to the team before the game and during breaks, team leaders find that pep talks stimulate production, and reinvigorate members when their enthusiasm wanes.

✓ Good leaders recognize every improvement and good point. When special achievements are accomplished, the leader praises the team and reiterates how the cooperative efforts of the team members contributed to the achievement.

✓ One of the best approaches to developing our people is to mentor them. This gives the mentee both head start for advancement, and some helpful know-how about the work, the workings of the company, and the tricks of the trade.

✓ To avoid resentment and assure cooperation, when correcting an associate's mistakes, focus on the problem— not the person.

✓ In dealing with associates who have failed to meet performance standards, follow the "9 R" approach.

Step 10

....

LIVE A HARMONIOUS LIFE

All of us want to be happy and to live in a peaceful environment. But in our jobs, our home, or any aspect of our activities, conflicts may develop that disrupt the harmony of our lives.

Much has been written about creating and maintaining a happy family. In this book we will focus on maintaining harmony in the workplace. But keep in mind that most of the suggestions on handling conflict are also applicable in resolving conflicts in our families and our social and community groups.

As supervisors or team leaders, we must be alert to signs of conflict and take action to prevent it if possible, and to resolve it quickly if it occurs.

It is only natural that in any organization employing large numbers of people there will be misunderstandings, dissatisfactions, and just plain gripes. If no conflicts are called to management's attention, it does not necessarily mean that there are none. It may mean that there is no way for the employee to bring conflicts to the attention of management. The line of communication may be blocked somewhere along the way.

Problems that cannot be uncovered and adjusted or clarified fester in the minds of the aggrieved. At one time or another, perhaps at work or in our personal lives, we've undoubtedly found ourselves obsessing over what to do about a particular turn of events. The concern distracts us from what we want to attend to, and we have no peace. In the workplace, an employee's focus on an ongoing problem may manifest itself in poor work, purposeful slowing down on the job, absenteeism, and/or high turnover. It could lead to serious employee antagonism. It is important for employees to have a means of bringing complaints and conflicts to the attention of a person in the organization who has the authority to correct the problem.

Establishing Open Communications

Most people and organizations do a fairly good job of keeping the lines of communication open. To help resolve conflicts, we want to assure that a clear line of communication exists from the top management to every worker and equally importantly from every worker to top management. All company policies and procedures should be clearly imparted to all employees. This could be done in the form of an easy-to-read employee manual, and meetings of supervisors with their staff members to clarify and reinforce the manuals' contents. When specific violations occur, supervisors are encouraged to have a personal chat with offenders before disciplinary action is instituted.

Getting information from senior management to staff members rarely presents a problem; to get information from workers to the top managers is not that easy. The key person here is the supervisor or team leader, who will be most effective if he or she gains the confidence of his or her subordinates. Employees must feel that it is not only "safe," but also helpful to bring their complaints to their supervisor and that all complaints will be dealt with promptly and fairly.

Successful leaders see the opportunities in every difficulty rather than the difficulty in every opportunity.

Reed Markham,
American Educator

Keeping the Peace

If disagreements or hostility about an issue are kept hidden, they can have severe ramifications. The people involved will likely fail to cooperate on the area of disagreement, but also on other matters on which they may be working. All parties involved must make an effort to defuse the tension. Here are some guidelines:

1. Address the issue when tempers are cool. Little can be accomplished when participants are angry or emotionally distressed. If we feel the matter is too hot to handle at the moment, postpone dealing with it. If there is no urgency, we can schedule a meeting at a later date to discuss it. If it requires more rapid action, even a short break can serve to reduce the tension. Note, however, that we don't want to wait too long— tensions can become "embedded" in

people and the more they repeat the "negative story" to themselves, the more "true" it becomes in their minds.

2.   Before bringing the parties together, we may want to talk to each party separately to obtain his or her side of the story. Ask questions that elicit good information. Some good starting questions may be:

   •   Mara, tell me how you see this situation.
   •   When you discussed it with Corey, what did he propose?
   •   How did you react when he said that?
   •   Why did this upset you?
   •   Why do you think Corey cannot see your point of view?
   •   What can I do to help you?

   Then speak separately with Corey asking him similar questions.

3.   Choose a neutral setting. If the dispute is between leaders or members of different groups, bring all the parties involved into a conference room away from their usual work space. When the discussion is held in the workplace of one disputant, the other may feel ill at ease.

4.   If possible, treat the issue as a team problem. Let's say that two associates disagree about an issue. Solving this problem is more than a dispute between these associates; the problem affects the entire team.

5.   As the facilitator to the discussion, do not dominate it. Begin in a friendly way. For example, start with a comment such as, "As both of you know, completing this project on schedule is of utmost importance. Now we've run into a snag that we must overcome. Mara and Corey, this is

your project and you have differences on how to complete it. Let's discuss this and work together so we can reach agreement."

Peace is not the absence of conflict but the presence of creative alternatives for responding to conflict— alternatives to passive or aggressive responses, alternatives to violence.

Dorothy Thompson,
American Author

6. Neutralize the discussion. Avoid accusatory comments and making suggestions that one person or party is right or wrong. For example, instead of saying, "Mara, you haven't considered the cost factor," say, "let's look at the costs involved." Pointing out Mara's "failure" puts her on the defensive. This advice is equally true in situations outside the workplace. When our children are squabbling, it is best if we can refrain from immediately pointing out the failure or poor behavior of one of them.

7. Talk about the problem, not the person. Very often, opponents in conflicts find fault with one another and/or blame each other for the issue. We frequently hear things like, "She never pays attention to me," and "he is always telling me what to do." These types of statements reflect what's behind the problem, but don't address the issue at hand. In order to move the discussion along on a positive note, steer the discussion to the problem. For example, you might say something like, "Tell me how the workload is distributed," or "what aspects of the job are causing the most problems?"

8. Stop talking and listen. Remember the old saying. "There's a good reason we have two ears and only one mouth— to listen twice as much as we talk." Problems cannot be solved unless we learn all facets of them. Encourage the opponents to talk freely. Then listen and learn.

9. Act on what we hear. Our job is to resolve the conflict so the project can continue satisfactorily. If we succeed, we not only have solved a problem, but we'll also have made inroads in gaining the trust of our staff.

Moving Beyond Conflict Without Resentment

Managing our own emotional reactions is critical to keeping the lines of communication open. Dale Carnegie addressed the importance of this in his books, *How to Win Friends and Influence People* and *How to Stop Worrying and Start Living*. He identified many guidelines to help us move forward from conflict in a productive way and without harboring resentment, which are all listed in Appendix B. Let's look at how we can use some of these principles in conflict resolution.

See the Viewpoints of Others

It's best to try to ignore our own perspective when it comes to solving problems and to try honestly to see things from the other person's point of view.

The fund-raising committee meeting was at a standstill. Jody, who had chaired the last three fundraisers, was adamant that the traditional golf outing should be continued. "We've had a golfing event every May for years. The members look forward to it, and we always do very well financially."

Kat, the current chairperson, pointed out, "Jody, yes, golfing events have worked in the past, but the amount of money raised has declined each year. We must try something else. I think we should look into a silent auction. My favorite charity held one this last year. Lots of businesses, restaurants, and even resorts around the world were solicited to contribute. We made thousands and thousands of dollars."

Jody: "The golf outing not only brings in money, but gives our regular contributors a chance to treat guests to a great day out—and it gets newcomers interested in the organization too.

Kat: I understand your point of view. Giving our members a chance to participate is important, but we must face the facts. For years we've had the benefit of using the Springfield Country Club's course for free—but now that the club's closed, we'll have to find a new venue, and none of the other local courses are very appealing. With an auction, our most devoted members can solicit gifts from the many retailers and restaurants that they frequent. I'm sure we'd get some really valuable contributions that attendees would be happy to purchase."

After thinking about it, Jody agreed. "I guess you're right. Without the country club's course, we'll have a hard time attracting people to the event. The auction asks our members to participate in a different way, but I'm sure they'll be happy to reach out to those they know in the community on our behalf."

Don't Fuss About Trifles

Let go of little things that don't really matter. Decide just how much anxiety a thing may be worth and refuse to give it more. For the most part, it truly is all small stuff.

With an awareness that many disagreements don't really matter much in the long run, we should remember to pick our battles and address concerns that can have real impact on our goals and relationships. Sue and Stan were planning a weekend away by the beach. Sue felt that they must stay at the West Beck Inn, where they always stayed, but Stan felt that the inn had gotten too expensive over the past year. Rather than admit that she had a romantic attachment to staying at their usual haunt, Sue passive-aggressively starting speaking to him in one-word statements. After an hour of this, Stan said, "Sue, I can tell from your demeanor that something I've done or said is bothering you.

I'd love to know what it is." Sue thought, "How can you not know what it is?" but she remembered that as often as not, Stan actually didn't guess what was on her mind. She admitted to him that she interpreted his statement about the inn as an indication that he lacked fond feelings toward her. He said that he understood, and that he too was attached to the inn, but that he wanted to be able to enjoy their time away by not overspending. They agreed to look at less expensive options and ultimately found a little motel that they liked even better.

Cooperate with the Inevitable

If we can't change something that displeases us, we need to just learn to accept it. Sometimes a decision is made or a situation will continue regardless of our position toward it, and by griping or maintaining hostility toward it, we are merely "sawing sawdust." For example, Tim's dad was diagnosed with prediabetes. His doctor told him to lose some weight and to make a point of getting more exercise. Tim encouraged his dad to change his diet, and bought him a pair or walking shoes and a pedometer to use as an incentive to get out and walk more often. Tim's dad got angry at Tim for "trying to run his life," and refused to comply with the doctor's suggestions. Tim was very frustrated, but he learned to accept that the only person who could change his father's behavior was his father.

Whenever you're in conflict with someone, there is one factor that can make the difference between damaging your relationship and deepening it. That factor is attitude.

William James,
American Psychologist

Don't Seek Vengeance

In our society we tend to glamorize vengeance—in the movies and on TV, heroes are often people who seek revenge against those who have wronged them. In fact, however, seeking revenge is petty. If we've ever "succeeded" at it, we know that it doesn't provide any gratification, and just makes us feel bad in a different way. Anger, resentment, and hatred destroy our ability to enjoy our lives. Let's not let a situation or a person control our happiness.

Celebrate diversity, practice acceptance and may we all choose peaceful options to conflict.

Donzella Michele Malone,
Psychologist and Author

Personality Profile: Is It Me?

Too often we tend to blame others for causing conflict when the real cause may lie within ourselves.

To better understand ourselves and how we tend to act in situations of conflict, read each of the following items carefully and place a number from the following answer scale next to each statement:

1–Seldom   2–Sometimes   3–Most of the time

1. _____I can be swayed to adopt someone else's point of view.

2. _____I shut down people with whom I disagree.

3. _____When conflicts arise, I address the issue at hand diplomatically and do not attack the individual.

4. _____I think that others try to "bully" me.

5. _____I express my thoughts and beliefs tactfully when they differ from those of others.

6. _____Rather than offer my opinion when I disagree, I keep it to myself.

7. _____I listen to other people's points of view with an open mind.

8. _____When I disagree with someone, I tend to let my emotions get the best of me.

9. _____I raise my voice to make my point during an argument.

10. _____I tend to belittle other people when making my point.

11. _____I look for ways to negotiate and compromise with others.

12. _____I have been told I am too pushy.

13. _____I make sure I voice my opinion in any controversy.
14. _____I think conflict in meetings is necessary.
15. _____I am the most vocal in meetings when trying to get my point across.

Scoring:

Add the total score from questions 1, 2, 4, 6, 8, 9, 10, 12, 13, 14, and 15, then subtract the sum of the score from questions 3, 5, 7, 11. The resulting number is your final score. What does this number mean?

1–4: *Passive*—We tend to avoid conflicts. We might allow difficult people or people with different opinions have their way simply to dodge a disagreement, even if we are ill-served by the resulting situation.

5–10: *Assertive*—We are professionally assertive when dealing with difficult people or people with different opinions. This middle ground is a positive place to be on the scale: we share our ideas without being argumentative. We should continue to be open to listening to different points of view, and to express our ideas and opinions appropriately.

11 and higher: *Aggressive*—When we are not in agreement with others, we may be so combative that people avoid interacting with us altogether. We will benefit from learning to listen and express our opinions more effectively.

If you have learned how to disagree without being disagreeable, then you have discovered the secret of getting along—whether it be business, family relations, or life itself.

Bernard Meltzer,
Radio Commentator

Understanding Responses to Conflict

For most people, barriers to conflict resolution arise when their deep beliefs and/or convictions are challenged or threatened. To help "put out the fire" when disagreements arise, it's useful to understand the typical responses to conflict.

Conflict affects the people involved in a variety of ways. Indeed, most people are uncomfortable when faced with conflict.

One common response to a problem is to personalize it, or "make it about ourselves," and when we do so, emotions are invariably high. Rather than focusing on the problem, we shift the emphasis to our opponent, and the "attack" on ourselves.

For example, in a discussion on methods of introducing a new product, Beth, the organization's lead market strategist, made a proposal. Megan, a regional sales manager, disparaged her plan. "It's impractical," Megan said. "It's all theory. That approach will never work in the field." She let her antagonism toward staff people who have never been out in the field dictate her comments.

Beth should have responded by asking Megan for specific reasons why she thought the plan wouldn't work. But Beth felt that the statement was a personal affront. Instead, all she could think was, "That Megan is so short-sighted. She feels like she has all the answers, and she automatically opposes any ideas our marketing staff presents."

Those who can't separate problems and disagreements from personal affronts will make the conflict about themselves. They do not see the issue clearly. They tend to:

- Be sure about the matter involved beforehand, and will not even consider opposing views.

- Resent any opposition.
- Be reluctant to compromise on anything.
- Take no responsibility for causing conflict.
- Respond to conflict emotionally rather than intellectually. Unless these emotional reactions are put aside, this impasse will not only remain unresolved, but will probably occur over and over again. In this situation, the managers must recognize that their staff are not addressing the actual issue before them, and steer both parties back to a useful discussion.

Others may not personalize the disagreement, but feel isolated in their experience of it. In the belief that they are the only people feeling the tension or seeing the conflict, they retreat. This does nothing to change the situation.

Similarly, there are also those who assume that they are "out-matched" in any type of conflict. This frequently takes the form of the belief that the "opponent" has more clout. They believe that they will "lose" and do not pursue a resolution of the issue. By letting all staff members know that their opinions matter, and by providing concrete examples of how they can best share their concerns, the conflict can be addressed and resolved.

Note that extremely sensitive staff members may need extra coaching when it comes to sharing their problems with others. Managers and team leaders should make a point of frequently asking such individuals for their ideas and suggestions.

People who shy away from problems may be viewed as conflict avoiders. Generally, they:
- Prefer to pass issues on to another person in the group.

- Get upset when facing conflict cannot be avoided.
- Believe the leadership of the organization is responsible for dealing with conflict.

On the other hand, some individuals will not shy away from a conflict; they look forward to the battle and enjoy the adversarial process. Often such people sincerely believe that they are right, and are unwilling to accept any other solution. For example, Roger and Kyle, Roger's manager, strongly disagreed on how to deal with a problem. Roger felt that Kyle's suggested solution was inadequate and was absolutely certain that his idea for handling it was not the best way to resolve it. Nothing could make him change his mind. Kyle pointed out that the cost of Roger's idea was well above the approved budget and that although the lower cost alternative was not as foolproof as Roger's choice, it would serve the purpose for the short-run and enable them to keep the work flowing. He asked Roger to go along with his solution and promised to do his best to get approval for a higher budget so Roger's plan could be considered in the future.

By being clear that he had considered Roger's plan and that he respected Roger's idea, Kyle showed Roger that he was valued as a good contributor to the organization. Roger felt recognized, and although he did not get to see his plan unfold, he was nonetheless willing to support the alternative, less costly solution.

Those who seem to enjoy conflict (and who may even initiate it) could be characterized as combatants. They:
- Enjoy a good fight.
- Feel conflict is a mind-sharpener and generates creative solutions for problems.

- May set up conflicting situations.
- Are usually more satisfied with winning the argument than with obtaining a compromise.

Ideally, we want to view conflicts with an open mind and engage in them in a way that is constructive. We should aim to:

- See that as people view matters differently, conflict on some matters is unavoidable.
- Understand that many people do not bring conflict into the open, leading to resentment and lack of cooperation.
- Value conflict as a pathway to creating healthy discussion.
- Try to anticipate problems that may lead to conflict and take care of them before they explode.
- Use the conflict process as a means of developing more knowledge about the issues involved.
- Create win-win compromises to resolve problems.

Ethical Concerns

In some conflict situations, we may be unsure whether a person's request or demand is ethical or appropriate. For instance, a customer may request free merchandise, refunds, or expensive entertainment, which is not usual in our organization. In those cases, we may collaborate with members of senior management or an attorney as a way of making sure we are in alignment with our organization's values and business practices.

We build alignment through our shared values. Within communities, work teams, families, and other social systems, values serve as a framework that guide beliefs and behaviors.

Shared values give meaning to and influence events, communications, and interactions within groups, and they are the glue that holds people together so they may achieve common goals. Discovering the shared values of one's community, work team, committee, or family is mutually beneficial because values:

- Set ground rules or guiding principles for behaviors and actions.
- Shape the culture or environment in terms of language, rituals, practices, beliefs, and perspectives.
- Establish common ground from which to collaborate.

Collaboration

Sometimes the situation causing disharmony is complicated and difficult to resolve. Left on our own, we may have limited capacity for dealing with the many issues that might be involved in the dispute. On occasion, we're best off accessing the experience, expertise, creativity, and values of other professionals to bring the situation to a successful conclusion.

Collaborative solutions to conflicts enable everyone involved to feel that everything was done to resolve the situation professionally.

Collaboration may be defined as: the act of working together with one or more people in order to achieve something.

Collaborating with experts takes the pressure off us to have all the answers in a difficult situation, and brings diverse viewpoints to bear on a successful outcome.

Collaborating with others may also be an effective technique to solve personal conflicts. There are times when an outsider's objective viewpoint can make all the difference in helping us see viable solutions to what appear to be intractable problems.

We might want to bring in an expert or more experienced individual when:

Lack of Experience

Most of us feel uncomfortable in conflict situations where we have had little experience. If we are dealing with an unhappy customer, and we aren't familiar with his or her exact situation, we might want to collaborate with the sales or service departments to address the customer's concern.

Lack of a Skill Set or Knowledge

In some situations, we realize that our skills or our knowledge are not sufficient to professionally deal with the conflict. For example, we may need someone with more advanced computer skills, writing skills, or negotiation skills to help resolve the issue, or we may find ourselves in a situation where we need to collaborate with someone who has legal or accounting expertise. Collaborating with others provides an opportunity to learn from them and to further develop our own skills.

Lack of Objectivity

We all suffer from a lack of objectivity. We're used to seeing things from our own vantage point. This same concept applies to a group of workers. When people who have worked in the same company have had closely related training or have shared the same environment for a long time, they tend to think alike. When faced with problems, they tend to come to the same conclusions on solving them. Sometimes a different viewpoint is needed to bring a new and different approach to resolving the situation (indeed, many scientific breakthroughs are generated by people with little traditional knowledge of the field—such individuals are not limited by the conventional understanding of the topic). It can be very useful to look for partners with other points of view.

> *It's not the strongest species that survives, not the most intelligent, But rather the one that is most adaptable to change.*

Charles Darwin

Lack of Creativity and Innovation

In many conflict situations, the obvious choices for resolution are insufficient. In those cases, we look for collaboration with those who can help us think outside of our own perceptions.

At the close of World War II, the Ford Motor Company faced a major problem—returning to production of civilian cars after years of production of military combat vehicles. Henry Ford II, chairman of the company, recognized that to move ahead rapidly and effectively, he had to make major changes in management and to do this he had to go outside the company.

Ford had learned of a group of ten officers from the Army Air Force Statistical Control operation that had formed an organization to apply to business what had worked so well for them during the war. Ford hired the entire group of ten.

This group of "whiz kids" as they came to be known, helped the money-losing company reform its chaotic administration through modern planning, organization, and management control. The group worked collaboratively to revamp the company and make it highly profitable. One member of this group, Robert McNamara, became the first president of Ford outside the Ford family. This led to his appointment as Secretary of Defense by President Kennedy.

Lack of Personnel

Some conflicts require complicated, time-consuming solutions, and we recognize that moving through the problem is more than we can handle alone. Finding a good solution might involve having to contact a number of people or do research for fact verification. Look for the collaborative efforts of an expanded workforce when we are pushed past our available resources of time, skills, or knowledge.

Networking can be very helpful at times that we need to grow our staff. Successful people develop a personal network of other talented individuals from the beginning of their careers. It is easy to accomplish. When we meet new people—socially, at meetings of trade or professional associations, at community events—we should enter them in our networking file. Note in this file who the individual is, his or her expertise, where you met the person, and other pertinent information.

How Collaborative are We? A Self-Assessment Exercise

Collaboration and cooperation are not limited to the workplace. By adapting a collaborative approach to every phase of our activities, we will greatly enrich our lives.

The first step is to assess how collaborative we are. Check those statements that describe our attitude most of the time.

1. I listen more than I talk.

2. I ask people to tell me about their interests.

3. I try to imagine how I would feel if I were in the other person's situation.

4. When someone tells me about his or her experience, I reflect on my experiences.

5. I have a tendency to judge people's actions.

6. I try honestly to see things from the other person's point of view.

7. I form opinions based on how well people meet my expectations.

8. I'm generally sensitive to people's moods.

9. I prefer to work on my own.

10. I prefer to work with others.

11. I'm more interested in other people's actions than their feelings.

12. I get impatient when people talk to me about their feelings and opinions. I don't need a lot of detail; just what they need from me.

13. There's usually nothing I can do to solve someone else's problems.

14. I don't really have time to listen to everyone else's problems.

15. I want to know how the other person is feeling in a conflict situation.

16. I know how people on my team are going to react in most situations.

17. I prefer to work with people who share my interests and values.

18. I usually get great ideas from others.

If we checked statements 1, 2, 3, 4, 6, 8, 10, 15, 16, and 18, we are strong collaborators. If we checked statements 4, 7, 9, 11, 12, 13, 14, and17, we need to work on being more open-minded and patient in order to improve our collaborative skills.

A Process for Driving Collaboration

When implementing the procedure described below, we should keep in mind the shared values of the group with which we're working. Our colleagues will be more receptive to ideas that reflect their values. In addition, we should also try to be aware of how we performed on the assessment of our own collaborative nature. If there's an area that could use improvement, make a point of demonstrating that improvement in the problem-solving process.

1. *Clarify the goal.* The first step in driving collaboration is to clearly state the goal that we want to attain. Goals may vary from an immediate or short-term solution to a problem to a long-range objective.

2. *Assemble all the facts about the situation.* To come up with an impartial solution that includes input from everyone involved, we must to be able to identify and state the relevant facts about the conflict.

3. *Communicate the situation to all parties.* Every member

of our group needs to know all the information about the problem in order to best contribute to its solution. If we're aware of particular roles that we would like people to take in the collaboration process, convey that information to them.

4. *Request collaboration.* In the clearest language possible, we ask for collaboration and what we need from the other party.

Brainstorm with our collaboration partners to achieve the input we are looking for: creativity and innovation, additional resources, experience, etc.

5. *Consider possible options.* Most parties in the collaboration are going to expect that we have at least a few ideas beforehand on how the issue can be handled. Be open to hearing fresh ideas, and comments about your own solutions.

6. *Implement the action.* As early in the process as possible, we should put the solution to work.

7. *Follow-up.* Arrange a process for thorough follow-up on the solution's effectiveness. Set timetables for progress checks, and clearly set forth the ways that progress will be communicated.

8. *Evaluation.* After three months, or another period of time that makes sense in terms of the problem and the solution, check in one another to see how satisfied those affected by the solution are with the resolution.

The way to achieve success is first to have a definite, clear, practical ideal—a goal. Second, have the necessary means to achieve our ends: wisdom, money, material, methods. Third, adjust all your needs to that end.

Aristotle

Tips for Effective Collaboration

The steps outlined above will guide you through the process of collaborating to resolve problems in the workplace. Keep the following in mind as you proceed:

For collaboration to work well, the parties should not be assembled too early nor too late. A minor situation may not need to be addressed by a large group, and it might be best to first see whether it can be resolved without engaging a host of others. On the other hand, if we form a collaboration effort too late, we may be up against a deadline, or the issue may have escalated.

Remember too that resources of people, time, money, space, and support are all factors that play into successful collaboration. There is less investment in resources when we go it alone, but the return on investment is almost always greater in the long run when we use the ideas of many parties.

To maximize the talents and experience represented in the collaboration, all available plans, outlines, rough drafts, and goals should be shared. A defined plan is often the objective of the collaboration. Once the plan is in place, we may be able to manage obtaining the solution on our own.

Finally, we should note that collaboration rarely gets off the ground in cultures where management is highly controlling or where rigid boundaries exist between departments and work functions. Cooperative teams that value individual contributions are the most conducive to effective collaboration.

We do not act rightly because we have virtue or excellence,
but we rather have those because we have acted rightly.

Aristotle

Collaborating for Harmony in Our Personal Lives

In addition to applying good collaborative efforts on the job, here are other venues in which we can put them to work.

Community

There are numerous ways that we can be involved in our communities. Coaching a sports team, feeding the hungry, forming a neighborhood watch group, being a room parent, giving blood, and being involved in our political party are all ways of working with others to achieve a common goal. If we want to have a feeling that we are contributing to our community, and if we want to get to know others in our neighborhood, we should seek out some of these shared community commitments.

Social

Collaborative values can be expressed through our way of socializing. Playing in a sports league, joining a book club, attending concerts with friends, and other social activities enable us to enhance our collaborative skills. Today, a good deal of socializing revolves around health issues. Perhaps we workout at the gym and have friends there, or we follow a weight-loss plan with others. Moreover, each of us has personal interests, such as music, gardening, rock climbing, fishing, or collecting, and often we enjoy spending time with those who share our passion. Any activity where we're engaged with others can be an opportunity to collaborate or to fine-tune our collaborative abilities.

Education

Some of us are pursuing a degree; some of us have children who are pursuing theirs. Many of us are life-long learners. Education is a value that a lot of people share, and as a student or a parent (or as a teacher!) we can brainstorm and work with others to further the learning experience.

Spiritual

We don't have to attend the same place of worship to share the same spiritual values. Simple individual characteristics like humility, openness, caring, or empathy can all point to shared spiritual values, which provide the framework for collaborating toward the achievement of good in the world.

> *It's not hard to make decisions when you know what your values are.*
>
> Roy Disney

Our Personal Relationships

Of course, we need to collaborate all the time in our personal lives. In our society, being "headstrong" is often considered a strength, but in solving problems, it is much better to be openminded. When personal conflicts develop, the best solution will be a collaborative one in which everyone's interests are accounted for. When possible, be sure to enlist all parties in coming up with a consensus. Let's look more closely at a way in which we might resolve a conflict by using common interests as tools for the solution to a problem.

Sum and Substance

- Conflict that is not out in the open can be costly for an organization and for its staff members. We miss the chance to improve or make a change that can have a significant positive impact.
- Most people are uncomfortable when faced with conflict. It disrupts the routine, and makes them feel vulnerable.
- To resolve conflict take the pragmatic approach.
  - Anticipate problems that may lead to conflict and take care of them before they arise.
  - Use the conflict process as a means of developing more knowledge about the issues involved.
  - Aim for win-win compromise to resolve the problem.
- Guidelines when faced with conflict:
  - Address situation when tempers are cool.
  - Choose a neutral setting to discuss the issue.
  - Treat the issue as a team problem, if appropriate.
  - Do not dominate the discussion.
  - Ask questions that elicit good, factual information.
  - Take a neutralize position. Avoid accusatory comments.
  - Talk about the problem, not the people involved.
  - Stop talking and listen.
  - Act on what we hear.
- Some guidelines to help us move forward from conflict in a productive way and without harboring resentment are:
  - Try honestly to see things from the other person's point of view.
  - Don't fuss about trifles.
  - Accept things that we cannot change.

- ➤ Decide just how much anxiety a thing may be worth and refuse to give it more.
- ➤ Never seek vengeance. We are more satisfied if we turn the other cheek, rather than strike back at those we think have harmed us.

- We build alignment through our shared values. Shared values give meaning to our relationships and form the basis for finding resolutions to problems.
- By collaborating with others within and outside our organization, we can access the experience, expertise, creativity, and values of other professionals to bring problems to a successful conclusion.
- Our personal lives offer us countless opportunities to put collaborative skills to work. A great place to begin is to seek areas in which all parties have a common interest, and use that as a springboard for dealing with the problem.

Appendix A

ABOUT DALE CARNEGIE &
ASSOCIATES, INC.

Founded in 1912, Dale Carnegie Training has evolved from one man's belief in the power of self-improvement to a performance-based training company with offices worldwide. It focuses on giving people in business the opportunity to sharpen their skills and improve their performance in order to build positive, steady, and profitable results.

Dale Carnegie's original body of knowledge has been constantly updated, expanded, and refined through nearly a century" worth of real-life business experiences. The one hundred sixty Dale Carnegie Franchisees around the world use their training and consulting services with companies of all sizes in all business segments to increase knowledge and performance. The result of this collective, global experience is an expanding reservoir of business acumen that our clients rely on to drive business results.

Headquartered in Hauppauge, New York, Dale Carnegie Training is represented in all fifty of the United States and over seventy-five countries. More than two thousand seven hundred instructors present Dale Carnegie Training programs in more than twenty-five languages. Dale Carnegie Training is dedicated to serving the business community worldwide. In fact, approximately seven million people have completed Dale Carnegie Training.

Dale Carnegie Training emphasizes practical principles and processes by designing programs that offer people the knowledge, skills, and practices they need to add value to the business. Connecting proven solutions with real-world challenges, Dale Carnegie Training is recognized internationally as the leader in bringing out the best in people.

Among the graduates of these programs are CEOs of major corporations, owners and managers of businesses of every size and every commercial and industrial activity, legislative and executive leaders of governments, and countless individuals whose lives have been enriched by the experience.

In an ongoing global survey on customer satisfaction, 99 percent of Dale Carnegie Training graduates express satisfaction with the training they receive.

Appendix B

DALE CARNEGIE'S PRINCIPLES

Become a Friendlier Person

1. Don't criticize, condemn, or complain.
2. Give honest, sincere appreciation.
3. Arouse in the other person an eager want.
4. Become genuinely interested in other people.
5. Smile.
6. Remember that a person's name is to that person the sweetest sound in any language.
7. Be a good listener. Encourage others to talk about themselves.
8. Talk in terms of the other person's interests.
9. Make the other person feel important—and do it sincerely.
10. To get the best of an argument—avoid it.
11. Show respect for the other person's opinion. Never tell a person he or she is wrong.

12. If you are wrong, admit it quickly, emphatically.
13. Begin in a friendly way.
14. Get the other person saying "yes" immediately.
15. Let the other person do a great deal of the talking.
16. Let the other person feel the idea is his or hers.
17. Try honestly to see things from the other person's point of view.
18. Be sympathetic with the other person's ideas and desires.
19. Appeal to the nobler motives.
20. Dramatize your ideas.
21. Throw down a challenge.
22. Begin with praise and honest appreciation.
23. Call attention to people's mistakes indirectly.
24. Talk about your own mistakes before criticizing the other person.
25. Ask questions instead of giving direct orders.
26. Let the other person save face.
27. Praise the slightest improvement and praise every improvement. Be "hearty in your approbation and lavish in your praise."
28. Give the other person a fine reputation to live up to.
29. Use encouragement. Make the fault seem easy to correct.
30. Make the other person happy about doing the thing you suggest.

Fundamental Principles for Overcoming Worry

1. Live in "day-tight compartments."
2. How to face trouble:

- Ask yourself, "What is the worst that can possibly happen"
- Prepare to accept the worst.
- Try to improve on the worst.
- Remind yourself of the exorbitant price you can pay for worry in terms of your health.

Basic Techniques in Analyzing Worry

1. Get all the facts.
2. Weigh all the facts—then come to a decision.
3. Once a decision is reached, act!
4. Write out and answer the following questions:
   - What is the problem?
   - What are the causes of the problem?
   - What are the possible solutions?
   - What is the best possible solution?
5. Break the worry habit before it breaks you.
6. Keep busy.
7. Don't fuss about trifles.
8. Use the law of averages to outlaw your worries.
9. Cooperate with the inevitable.
10. Decide just how much anxiety a thing may be worth and refuse to give it more.
11. Don't worry about the past.
12. Cultivate a mental attitude that will bring you peace and happiness.
13. Fill your mind with thoughts of peace, courage, health, and hope.

14. Never try to get even with your enemies.
15. Expect ingratitude.
16. Count your blessings—not your troubles.
17. Do not imitate others.
18. Create happiness for others.
19. Try to profit from your losses.

Living
an
ENRICHED
LIFE

Dale Carnegie Success Series titles
published by Manjul Publishing House

◆*Become an Effective Leader*
◆*Communicating Your Way to Success*
◆*10 Steps to a More Fulfilling Life*
◆*How to Jump-Start Your (Next) Career*
◆*How to Have Rewarding Relationships,*
Win Trust and Influence People
◆*Overcoming Worry & Stress*
◆*Life Is Short Make It Great*
◆*Embrace Change for Success*
◆*Resolve Conflicts in Your Life*

Living an ENRICHED LIFE

Living

an

ENRICHED

LIFE

DALE CARNEGIE

MANJUL

Manjul Publishing House

First published in India by

Manjul Publishing House

• 7/32, Ansari Road, Daryaganj, New Delhi 110 002 - India
Website: www.manjulindia.com

Registered Office:
• 10, Nishat Colony, Bhopal 462 003 - India

The Success Series:
Living an Enriched Life by *Dale Carnegie*

This edition first published in India in 2018
Second impression 2020

ISBN 978-93-87383-30-2

Cover Design by Trinankur Banerjee

This edition is authorised for sale in the Indian Subcontinant only.

Printed and bound in India by Thomson Press (India) Limited.

CONTENTS

PREFACE

The longer I live, the more I realize the impact of attitude on life. Attitude to me is more important than facts. It is more important than the past, than education, than money, than circumstances, than failures, than appearance, giftedness or skill. It will make or break a company, a church, or a home. The remarkable thing is that we have a choice regarding the attitude we embrace for each day. We cannot change the inevitable. The only thing we can do is play on the one string we have, and that is ourselves. I am convinced that life is 10% what happens to me and 90% how I react to it. And so it is with you—we are in charge of our attitudes.

Dale Carnegie

Living an enriched life! Who would not want to get more out of the years they have on earth? We spend one-third of our lives asleep, at least one third working on our careers or taking care of our families and if we are lucky, the balance is created through recreational, cultural or religious pursuits or just through lolling around. Too many people live dull, drab lives, toiling in unsatisfying jobs, and using what free time they have in unrewarding pursuits.

In this book we will discuss some of the reasons we fall into these traps and provide some pointers to help overcome the problems and move forward to a better, more productive and more satisfying life.

Self-Confidence

The first matter to be discussed is Self-Confidence—the feeling we have about ourselves that we can accomplish anything we set out to do, is the essential element in living a full and meaningful life. The main reason many people never succeed in their jobs, their business ventures, and even in their personal lives is their lack of this key ingredient. Why do people lack self-confidence?

One common reason is that they have failed in some activity early in their lives and fear this will happen again. Another is that other people—their own parents, their teachers, their bosses—were never satisfied with their performance causing them to consider themselves failures.

Still others have tasted success only to have it followed by some sort of failure and have let that failure dominate their minds and doom them to a lack of self-confidence in anything they do. We will see how to overcome this and develop and maintain self-confidence along with a strong self-image.

Enthusiasm

A study of the lives of great men and women, whether they

are in government, business, science or the arts show that the one common trait all of them possess is enthusiasm about their work and their lives.

Enthusiasm is the secret ingredient of success as well as the generator of happiness in those people who possess it.

Enthusiasm makes the difference in one's attitude toward other people, toward one's job, and the world. It makes the big difference between a drab and an enriched life.

Setting and Achieving Goals

All successful people start with a goal. Establishing goals and working toward their achievement is the first step one must take on the long road to success. By knowing where we are going and how we plan to get there, we will be able to focus our time, energy and emotion, and start on the right track toward reaching those goals. We will study how to set goals that will inspire us to achieve high, how to assure that we do not deviate from those goals and how to overcome obstacles in reaching our goals.

Image

The image we project to people we meet is a major factor in the confidence they generate in us and whether or not they feel comfortable with us.

A pleasant, welcoming image can be *developed*. Some of the facets that make up our image are inborn—our physical appearance, basic intelligence and some talents—but each of us has the capacity to make the most of our innate traits and develop them to give us that type of image that others will admire.

It's not easy to grow into the person we want to be, but it starts with a strong desire and commitment to develop an outgoing, cheerful, optimistic and positive demeanor—an image that will win the approbation of the men and women with whom we interrelate.

We will learn how to make a good first impression, as well as how to maintain and improve that image.

Self-Motivation

Just wanting to accomplish our goals is not enough. We must constantly be cultivating the desire, the ambition, keeping those goals alive, being wholesome and healthy by active endeavor. This is the only way in which we can match our dreams with our realities. We will explore ways in which we can motivate ourselves to achieve our goals and learn techniques to move ourselves forward when we fall behind.

Be Positive

There is no uplifting habit better than that of bearing a hopeful attitude, of believing that things are going to turn out well and not ill; that we are going to succeed and not fail; that no matter what may or may not happen, we are going to be happy.

There is nothing else as helpful as the carrying on of this optimistic, expectant attitude—the attitude that always looks for and expects the best, the highest, the happiest—and never allowing oneself to get into a pessimistic, discouraging mood.

It is not always easy to remain positive, especially when matters do not go as we planned. We will learn how to overcome negativity and think affirmatively no matter what problems we face.

Be Courageous

Successful people have the courage to put their ideas into effect, the willingness to put their money, their efforts, their emotions into an enterprise in which they truly believe.

We must all take risks if we want to make progress in our jobs and in our lives. By careful analysis we can minimize the chances of failure, but we can never eliminate it. Without pain there is no gain. By always playing it safe, we may avoid that pain, but we will never feel the great joy and satisfaction that results from overcoming the obstacles and reaching our goals.

Bounce Back

Even when we have experience and know-how, we cannot always be successful. There will be times when we do fail, but we must not let the concept of failure overwhelm us. We learn from our mistakes and apply what we learn to overcome our failures.

Often disappointment or failure has a collateral consequence. It causes our morale to plummet and to destroy our self-confidence. Unless corrective action is taken immediately, this may deteriorate into self-pity, failure and unhappiness. We will explore how to deal with the psychological effects of defeats and restore our morale.

To get the most out of this book, first read all of it to absorb the overall concepts. Then reread each chapter and start applying the guidelines for achieving each of the areas covered. This will start you on the track to living an enriched life—a major step forward on the road to success.

—Arthur R. Pell, Ph.D.
Editor

1

....

BUILD UP SELF-CONFIDENCE

Believe in yourself! Have faith in your abilities! Without a humble but reasonable confidence in your own powers you cannot be successful or happy.

Dale Carnegie

When his company posted a position as a supervisor of a new department, Larry was tempted to apply, but after a moment he said to himself, "I'd like to move up, but I don't think I could handle it."

Susan made a suggestion to her boss for what she thought would improve productivity, but he pointed out several flaws in it. Susan's reaction: "I'm a failure. I just can't think things through. I'll never make another suggestion."

Claire was asked to chair a committee at her church. She told her husband: "I'd have to give talks to church members about this project. There's no way I could do that."

Eliot was the top salesman in his company for the first three months this year, but in the fourth month, he fell far behind. He said to himself: "I was lucky that first quarter, but the luck didn't hold and now I'm back where I belong—just barely meeting the quota. I knew it couldn't last."

What is the problem with these men and women? They all lack self-confidence. Each of them look upon themselves as basic failures, doomed to remain at the low end of the spectrum all of their lives.

There are times when any one of us may find ourselves doubting our abilities and our accomplishments and find our self-confidence plummeting. To make matters worse, we emphasize and dwell on what others think of us in order to determine how we feel about our abilities and ourselves. This mindset can lead us to avoid taking risks due to fear of failure.

Self-confidence is an integral part of self-esteem. Before we can gain the confidence in decisions we make, we must believe in ourselves. We must truly feel that we are someone of worth. If we do not have self-esteem, how can we be *confident* that our decisions are worthwhile?

Too often, we are more concerned about what others think of us than what we think about ourselves. William Becker, a mid-twentieth century clergyman and writer, admonished his readers: "Never mind what 'people' think of you. They may overestimate or underestimate you! Until they discover your real worth, your success depends mainly upon what you think of yourself and whether you believe in yourself. You can succeed if nobody else believes it, but you will never succeed if you don't believe in yourself."

The great Greek philosopher, Epicticus, said: "No man is free, who is not master of himself." Unless we have confidence in our abilities and faith and determination to succeed, we will never even get started on the road that leads to the achievement of our goals. We must expect great things from ourselves. This faith brings out the best that is in us. As the old saying states:

Life's battle does not always go
To the stronger or the faster man;
But soon or later, the man who wins
Is the one who THINKS he can.

We Are Who We (Not Others) Think We Are

People who are not self-confident put a lot of weight on what others think in order to determine how they feel about themselves. They avoid taking risks due to fear of failure and generally do not expect to be successful. They often put themselves down, discount positive feedback and subscribe to harmful assumptions that perpetuate self-defeating thought patterns and a negative attitude. Some self-defeating thought patterns include:

➤ Extreme Thinking: This is how Susan reacted to her boss's criticism of her suggestion. One failure led her to feel: "I am a total failure when my performance is not perfect."

➤ Imminent Disaster: Disaster lurks around every corner and becomes an expected outcome. For example, a single negative detail, a bit of criticism, or a passing comment darkens all reality. "I blew that presentation and now I'll never get promoted."

> Magnification of the Negative: Good performance doesn't count nearly as much as bad performance—That was Eliot's reaction.

"I know I had the best sales record the last quarter, but that was just luck. Now I'm back to my real self. I'm just making up to the quota this quarter."

> Overemphasis on "should" statements. "Should" statements are meant to push us toward the perfect scenario, but must be followed by a realistic thought process that establishes the "As is." Once these are established, we can plan on how to get from where we are to the "should be." Many times we just look at where we are and freeze with fear when we see we are not close to where we should be. This should, instead, be taken as a sign to stop, look and listen, so we could get on track.

> Being out of our comfort zones: From childhood on we develop an environment in which we are comfortable. In Sally's family, her father made all decisions. Children were told they were to be seen, but not heard. Today, as an adult, a wife, mother and employee, she is uncomfortable when asked to make decisions. Charlie spent many years as an administrative non-com in the US Army. He studied and followed the Army Regulations religiously. In his first civilian job after his retirement, he couldn't function efficiently because there were no equivalent written regulations in his company to guide him.

Sandra, the buyer of teen dresses for a local boutique was asked by her boss to narrate a fashion show, she was terrified. Speaking one to one to customers was routine and comfortable, but speaking to a group took her out of this comfort zone. Her boss suggested she take the Dale Carnegie Course to deal with this problem.

Dale Carnegie developed a method to help participants in his courses to overcome this discomfort by making each class member speak at least once in every class to an appreciative and encouraging audience. This has worked for thousands of participants in Dale Carnegie training programs, for over 90 years. It worked for Sandra, who now narrates fashion shows several times a year, and the compliments that she receives for her performance by her boss and her customers boosts her self-esteem.

Strategies for Developing Self-Confidence

The following strategies may help overcome self-defeating thought patterns:

Self-Acceptance

This comes from our ability to accept ourselves as human beings while focusing on our positive sides—our qualities, strengths, and traits—that make us who we are. When our focus is upon these areas of our self-image both confidence and self-esteem are positively influenced. It is all too common for people to focus upon their weaknesses instead of their strengths and therefore do more damage than good. We must help ourselves, and others to center on the positive pictures.

Focus on the Successes

The key here is to concentrate on our past success and achievements and to respect ourselves for the good we have done in the past. It is far easier to dwell on failures since others are only too eager to point them out to us. When we spend our time contemplating the many successes we have had in our lives, our perspective changes.

A valuable method of achieving this is to create an inventory of successes and accomplishments that we have had throughout our lives. At first it may be difficult to amass as complete a list as we would like but with persistence we can keep adding to our list and to our confidence.

Henrietta, a sales representative for a real estate firm in Orlando, Florida, received a letter from a client expressing her appreciation for helping her find her an "ideal home." Henrietta proudly showed it to everybody in the office. Her boss suggested that she set up a file in which she could place this letter and others she would get over time. He said, "This is your 'Success File.' These letters will cheer you up when things are not going great. They are evidence that you did it before and that you can do it again."

Henrietta followed his advice, but as every triumph she had was not substantiated with a letter, she added a "Success Log." In this log she listed her significant accomplishments— closing a tough sale, obtaining first sales rights for new homes from a major construction firm, making the most sales in the office for the month, etc.

All of us face slumps and down periods. Henrietta was no exception. When an "almost-sale" fell through, when faced with a dry spell, or when she just felt blue, she opened her "Success File," and reread those letters, reviewed the entries in her log. This restored her self-confidence and motivated her to get back to her real self.

Talk It Up

When we add the above two categories together and create a self-talk that is backed up by evidence, we will find that we have begin to believe the testimony. When a sports team is falling behind, the coach gives it a pep talk. We are our own coach, so we must give ourselves that pep talk. What do we say? We create an argument that would hold up to scrutiny due to the weight of the evidence. The stronger and more compelling the evidence is, the more believable and powerful the message. It is an internal discussion we must all have from time to time. This is a tool to take back control of the only thing over which we have ultimate control all the time—our thinking. In other words, we must psych ourselves to restore our self-confidence.

After Henrietta reviewed her success file, she created a self-talk based on the evidence in that file. She repeated it over and over again to herself and just as those coaches motivated their teams she motivated herself to renewed successes.

> *By talking to yourself every hour of the day, you can direct your thoughts towards those of courage and happiness, of power and peace. By talking to yourself about the things you have to be grateful for, you can fill your mind with thoughts that soar and sing.*
>
> *Dale Carnegie*

Know What You Want and How You'll Achieve It

1. Concentrate on the goal you want to attain. It is not sufficient merely to say: "I want a job with good potential." Be definite. "I want a job as a marketing researcher with opportunity to prove that I can move into management."
2. Create a definite plan for carrying out your desire, and begin at once—whether you are ready or not—to put this plan into action.
3. Write out a clear, concise statement of your objective and what you intend to do in order to achieve it.
4. Read this written statement aloud, twice daily, once just before retiring at night, and once after arising in the morning. As you read, you must see and feel and believe you are already achieving the goal.

Self-Confident People Take Risks

Approach new experiences as opportunities to learn rather than challenges to win or lose. Doing so opens one up to new possibilities and can increase your sense of self-acceptance. Not doing so turns every possibility into an opportunity for failure, and inhibits personal growth.

Some people never take risks. They always play it safe. Most likely they will always be just average, mediocre performers. They will never have any real success. By not taking the chance that something they supported might not work out, they avoid the "agony of defeat," but never experience "the thrill of victory."

The turtle is a living fortress. Its impervious shell protects it from all harm. However, if the turtle wants to move, it must stick its head and neck out from the shell, exposing itself to the dangers of the environment. Like the turtle, if we want to move ahead we cannot surround ourselves with perfect protection. We have to stick out our necks in order to progress.

Taking risks does not mean one must be a daredevil. Reasonable people take reasonable risks, but by definition, a risk may not succeed. Successful business executives take risks with every decision they make. However, they maximize their chance of success by careful research and analysis before making the decision. But when that decision finally has to be made, the manager must be willing to risk the possible loss of money, time, energy and emotion. Without risk, there is no possibility of gain.

It is the end of the ninth inning. The Red Sox lead the Yankees 2 to 1. The first two hitters strike out. Dave Winfield, the Yankee's ace hitter is at bat. The ball comes straight across the plate. Wham! a clean hit. Winfield races to first. He makes it easily. Should he try for a double?

In microseconds, Dave must decide if he should play it safe or take the risk of trying for that extra base which would put him in a scoring position. If he fails, the game is over, but by taking a chance he increases the possibility of turning defeat into victory. Winfield is a risk taker and if there's only a slightly better than even chance of success, he tried for the double. Champions have self-confidence. In life as well as in sports they will take chances. That is what makes them champions.

In his book *How to Stop Worrying and Start Living,* Dale Carnegie advises that when facing trouble: "Ask yourself: 'What is the worst that can possibly happen? then prepare to accept the worst; try to improve on the worst.'"

These principles can be applied in determining whether or not to take a chance on an innovative, radical or just different approach to a problem.

Gil Baker had not been able to obtain an appointment with Stan Green, the purchasing manager of a prospective customer. He had phoned, written letters and even "sat on his doorstep"—all to no avail. His colleagues advised him to forget Green and use his energies and time to develop other leads. But Gil was stubborn. There must be some way to get Green's attention. He learned that Green was to be a speaker at an industry workshop. "If I attend the workshop," thought Gil, "I can approach him after his talk, ask him some questions and then identify myself, so he'll at least know who I am."

His sales managers and co-workers discouraged this. "He'll be so mad that he never will speak to anybody from this company again."

Gil responded by applying Carnegie's principles. "What is the worst that could happen? He won't do business with us. That's not so bad because he isn't doing business with us now, so we have nothing to lose."

'Prepare to accept the worst: If I do not make an impression on him at the meeting, I'll give up working on that account."

"Try to improve on the worst: By carefully planning the questions I ask, I can demonstrate that I am truly knowledgeable about his business and this may overcome his reluctance to see me."

By taking a chance, Gil reached an "unreachable" prospect and opened a very profitable account for his company.

We must all take risks if we want to make progress in our jobs and in our lives. By careful analysis we can minimize the chances of failure, but we can never eliminate it. By always playing it safe, we may avoid that pain, but we will never feel the great joy and satisfaction that results from overcoming the obstacles and reaching our goals.

Aggressive versus Assertive

There is a difference between being a self-confident and assertive person and being an arbitrary and aggressive person. Most people appreciate boldness and confidence as long as it is not communicated with insensitivity. Many of the personal and corporate success stories that we know are the result of an individual or group of individuals assertively pressing on. Yet, there seems to be a lot of misconceptions about assertiveness versus aggressiveness or passivity. Assertive behavior has been defined as "... standing up for yourself in such a way that it does not violate the basic rights of another person."

The fundamental difference between assertiveness and aggressiveness is most often a self-esteem issue. Dale Carnegie's human relations principles teaches us to strike the balance. Instead of "walking over people" or "being walked on by people," it provides a way of "walking with people" to achieve a win-win result. Assertive communication is a human relations approach that combines strength and sensitivity.

The following chart (Figure 1) illustrates the difference between an assertive self-confident approach and an aggressive one:

Figure 1: Aggressive versus Assertive versus Passive

Aggressive	Assertive	Passive
Self-centered	Will stand up for their own rights while being sensitive to others	Concerned about others to the point of personal detriment
Often is stressed and stresses others	Deals with stressful situation and moves on.	Stressed internally though may not show
Often manifested as a result of poor self-esteem	Requires a strong self-image	Often manifested as a result of poor self-esteem
Direct to the point of inappropriateness	Direct, honest, appropriate communication	Indirect and often not to self
May not be liked or respected Puts down others	Often respected by others Builds others up	Often liked, but may not be respected Builds others up even at his own expense
Feels a need to control everything and everyone; holds others accountable but not themselves	Willing to take personal responsibility for their own actions	Holds themselves accountable, but not others
Confrontive—forces others to follow Restrictive	Tends to lead by example, does not seek nor avoid confrontations; Flexible with guidelines	Avoids confrontation—often overly apologetic; Strict guidelines for self, but not for others

Vocally abrasive	Open, yet sensitive, polite	Reserved, indirect, restrained
Extremely direct—forces thoughts, ideas on others	Direct but considerate	Avoids expressing feelings
Demands	Asks	Wishes

Help Others Achieve Self-Esteem

As parents, we can build self-confidence and self-esteem in our children. As managers, we can build self-confidence and self-esteem in our staffs. As teachers or coaches, we can build self-confidence and self-esteem in our students or teams. Teach them to believe in themselves. Give them the opportunity to express themselves.

Harvey Mackey, founder and CEO of Mackey Envelope Co., and author of many books on self-improvement, said in an interview in *Personal Excellence*:

> *Finally, it's important to give everyone a sense of being significant. In a bad environment, everyone feels like a victim. In a good one, people feel as if they have equal worth—perhaps not equal power, but equal worth. A production line worker may not be able to enforce his desires in the same way a senior executive can, but the production line worker has an equal chance to be heard, in the same way that the youngest child gets equal air time at the dinner table.*

What this all adds up to is one loud, clear message—you're special, and we care about you. For your child and your employee to succeed individually and the entire family or organization to thrive, each has to care about the other.

Sum and Substance

> Never allow yourself to think meanly, narrowly, poorly of yourself. Never regard yourself as weak, inefficient, diseased, but as perfect, complete, whole.
> Never even think of the possibility of going through life as a failure or a partial failure.
> Stoutly assert that there is a place for you in the world, and that you are going to fill it.
> Train yourself to expect great things of yourself. Never admit even by your manner that you think you are destined to do little things all your life. If you practice and persistently hold the positive, producing, opulent thought, this mental attitude will some day make a place for you, and create that which you desire.

2

....

BECOME TRULY ENTHUSIASTIC

Enthusiasm is the dynamic of your personality. Without it, whatever abilities you may possess lie dormant; and it is safe to say that nearly every man has more latent power than he ever learns to use. You may have knowledge, sound judgment, good reasoning facilities; but no one—not even yourself—will know it until you discover how to put your heart into thought and action.

Dale Carnegie

If there is one ingredient of success that surpasses all others, it is enthusiasm. Enthusiasm is an inner excitement that permeates the whole being. The word comes from two Greek roots: *en* meaning "in" and *theos* meaning "God."

Literally, the person with enthusiasm has God within. It is an inner glow—an ardent, spiritual quality deep inside a person.

An enthusiastic attitude is fundamental to self-fulfillment. It guides us towards positive thoughts and actions. It creates positive energy that improves our relationships with others, our willingness to be open to new ideas, and even our health. The reverse is also true. Dale Carnegie wrote that our fatigue is often caused not by work, but by worry, frustration and resentment.

Enthusiasm for life initiates within us the power to change our lives. Focus on the present to nourish that power. Enthusiasm for life facilitates our ability to release regrets about the past and worries concerning the future. We can't change the past, we can influence future outcomes with a positive, enthusiastic approach to the opportunities of the present.

When our thoughts are propelled by an enthusiasm for life, we find we have unlimited power to develop our own unique potential whether it be in business, sports, community life or family. In time, guilt, fear and worry are replaced by confidence and optimism.

Dale Carnegie wrote; "Remember, happiness doesn't depend on who you are or what you have; it depends solely on what you think. So start each day by thinking of all the things you have to be thankful for. Your future will depend very largely on the thoughts you think today. So think thoughts of hope and confidence and love and success."

Psychologists report that IQ tests have one important shortcoming. They fail to measure the "emotional drive"—the psychological term for enthusiasm. According to IQ tests, a person with a low score is usually rated as fit for only menial jobs, whereas a high score is considered practically a guarantee of success. This, we know is misleading. We have seen people with low IQ's suddenly "set on fire" by a new idea or a new line of work. It created within them the enthusiasm that leads them on to great success. We have also witnessed the opposite—very intelligent men and women who do not succeed in their lives.

When Mark Twain was asked the reason for his success, he replied: "I was born excited."

In his book, *The Excitement of Teaching,* William Lyon Phelps, a Yale University professor wrote: "With me, teaching is more than an art or an occupation—it is a passion. I love to teach, as a painter loves to paint, as a singer loves to sing, as a poet loves to write. Before I get out of bed in the morning, I think with ardent delight of my first group of students."

One of the chief reasons for success in life is the ability to maintain a daily interest in one's work, to have a chronic enthusiasm; to regard each day as important.'

Enthusiasm Leads to Action

Development of enthusiasm in individuals, groups, athletic teams, companies and total communities pays off in positive action—in success and happiness. This can be observed in athletic competitions. Norman Vincent Peale, one of Dale Carnegie's friends and colleagues tells the story of Vince Lombardi, one of the greatest football coaches of all time. When Lombardi was chosen to coach the Green Bay Packers (an American football team), he faced a defeated, dispirited team. He stood before them, looked over them silently for a long time and then in a quiet, but intense voice said: "Gentlemen, we are going to have a great football team. We are going to win games. Get that. You are going to learn to block. You are going to learn to run. You are going to learn to tackle. You are going to outplay the teams that come against you. Get that."

"And how is this to be done? You are to have confidence in me and enthusiasm for my system. The secret of the whole matter is what goes up on here (and he tapped his temple). Hereafter, I want you to think of only three things: your home, your religion, and the Green Bay Packers, in that order. Let enthusiasm take hold of you."

The men sat up straight in their chairs. "I walked out of that meeting," wrote the quarterback, "feeling ten feet tall."

That year the Packers won seven games—with virtually the same players that had lost ten games the year before. The next year they won the division title, and the third year, the world championship. Why? Because, added to hard work and skill and love of the sport, enthusiasm made the difference.

Dale Carnegie often quoted Frederick Williamson, one-time president of the New York Central Railroad:

"The longer I live, the more certain I am that that enthusiasm is the little-recognized secret of success. The difference in actual skill, ability, and intelligence between those who succeed and those who fail is usually not very great. But if two men are about equally matched, the man who is enthusiastic will often outstrip one who has first-rate ability, but no enthusiasm."

When Sir Edward Victor Appleton, who had been awarded the Nobel Prize in physics, was made Chancellor of the University of Edinburgh, *TIME* magazine sent him a cable asking him if he had any recipe for success. "Yes," he replied, "enthusiasm. I rate that even ahead of professional skill."

Thomas A. Edison said: "When a man dies, if he can pass enthusiasm along to his children, he has left them an estate of incalculable value." Experience proves that to be true. It is more than wealth, for enthusiasm will produce not only wealth but also a great zest for living.

Enthusiasm Comes From Within

Enthusiasm is not skin-deep. It must emanate from within a person. It rarely can be feigned for a sustained period of time. One way of generating a continued surge of enthusiasm is to set a goal and work toward it, and when it is accomplished set another goal and work toward it. The excitement and challenge it provides cannot help but keep one enthusiastic.

When feeling blue, some people sing to themselves to overcome their sadness. By acting happy they restore their happiness. The same principle applies to enthusiasm. If we stimulate animation and excitement for our work or other facets of our lives, we will usually find that we've stimulated ourselves right into the middle of the kind of emotional drive we are seeking.

How can you make yourself become enthusiastic? By telling yourself what you like about what you are doing and pass on quickly from the part you don't like to the part you do like. Then act enthusiastic; tell someone about it; let them know why it interests you.

Dale Carnegie

Find Something to Become Enthusiastic About

Do not confuse enthusiasm with noise, shouting or yelling. Dale Carnegie defines enthusiasm as an ardent spiritual quality deep inside—a suppressed excitement. He says: "If your heart is on fire with a desire to help others, you will be excited. Your excitement will radiate through your eyes, your face, your soul and your whole personality. You will be inspired and your inspiration will inspire others." To be truly excited about something, we must feel that passion deep inside ourselves. However, we are often required to do things about which we do not have that deep commitment. One way that helps develop enthusiasm is to find something in the assignment about which we can become excited. By focusing on this, real enthusiasm will be generated.

Carol had her first job as a junior associate after graduating from law school. She dreaded the time-consuming and dull work of researching cases in the law library, but unless this was done, the case her firm was trying could not be properly prepared. What would be the benefit to her from doing this necessary, but boring job? Carol realized that this was a test of her capability as a new lawyer in the firm. By concentrating on how finding details important to the case would reflect on her career, she became enthusiastic about seeking out these details and became truly enthusiastic about the assignment.

Become an Expert in the Subject

Learn as much as possible about the subject. Learning leads to knowledge and often engenders excitement about the matters learned.

When Andy was hired to be the assistant to the Town Supervisor, he expected to be involved in working on solving many of the political problems faced in the township. However, his boss assigned him to very routine work, such as checking on whether forms were filled out properly, assuring that documents were properly processed and handling similar detail work.

After a few months, he complained to the Town Supervisor, "The work you give me could be done by a high school drop-out. I'm a college grad and can be much more valuable to the office if you would give me higher level work." The Supervisor responded: "Andy, I hired you because I know you can be a great help to me in important matters, but understanding the basics of what we do here will give you the foundation needed to take on additional responsibilities. Rather than looking at these assignments as boring clerical details, study what they represent, why the details are needed and how they relate to the smooth operation of our office."

Andy took his advice. Instead of just checking for accuracy, he studied the material, asked questions about it and learned as much as he could about the process that ensued in resolving each issue. It was not long before he started looking forward to each day and to what new things he would learn.

The way to acquire enthusiasm is to believe in what you are doing and in yourself and to want to get something definite accomplished. Enthusiasm will follow as night follows the day.

Dale Carnegie

Try a Different Approach

Alfred M. represents a company that leases cranes to contractors in South Africa. He reported on how he applied the concept of enthusiasm to opening one of the toughest accounts in his industry.

The customer, whom he called "Mr. Smith," was always rude and usually in a violent temper. After two calls in which Smith refused to listen to his presentation, Alfred was about to give up, but he resolved not to lose his enthusiasm and to try once again.

Through the open door from the waiting room to Smith's office, Alfred could see him ranting and raving at another salesman. He almost physically pushed him out of the office and shouted: "Next!"

In Alfred's words: I walked into his office. He shouted, "You again—I told you 'no' already. Why are you bothering me?" Before he could say anything else, I smiled and without the tremor most salesmen had in their voice when addressing him, I said in my most enthusiastic manner. "I want all of your crane hire business."

He stood there behind his desk for about fifteen seconds, speechless. He looked at me in an odd way and said: "You sit there and wait for me," and left the room. When he returned a half hour later, he looked at me quizzically and snarled, "Why are you still here?" I told him that I had such a good deal for him that I wouldn't think of leaving until I could explain it to him. The result was an order amounting to 75,000 rands per month for a year's contract, with good possibilities for more business.

Self-Talk

In the previous chapter we discussed how giving oneself a pep talk is an effective way to gain self-confidence. It also works as a tool to engender enthusiasm for what we are doing.

Lisa's goal was to become a medical secretary. She completed the course required and set out to find a job. After several rejections due to her lack of experience, she became discouraged. When she went to her next interview, she paused before entering the building. "What's the use? I'll run into the same thing again." Instead of giving up, Lisa gave herself a pep talk. "I want this job and I have the technical know-how. I was the topper of my class in the school. I am a diligent and conscientious worker. I can do this job and will be a real asset to the doctor. She repeated this over and over again in her head as she waited for the doctor to see her. Her enthusiasm manifested itself in the answers to his questions and she was offered the job.

Some months later the doctor told her that when he saw from her application that she had no work experience, he had decided to give her just a courtesy interview and reject her. But he was so impressed by her enthusiasm, it convinced him to hire her. She carried that enthusiasm into the work itself and became a very successful medical secretary.

Enthusiasm is not merely an outward expression. It works from within. Enthusiasm is born of a genuine liking for what you are doing.

Dale Carnegie

Enthusiasm Can Overcome Adversity

Andrew Grove is a man whose triumph over adversity was fueled by his great enthusiasm. A native of Hungary, he had first been persecuted by the Nazis during World War II, and later by the Russians when they invaded Hungary in 1956.

He fled to America when he was 20 years old with only a few dollars in his pocket, and only a little knowledge of English. Despite many hardships he never lost his enthusiasm for obtaining knowledge and making a success of his life. By working any job he could find, he put himself through New York's City College, earning a Bachelor of Science degree in Chemical Engineering. He received his masters and Ph.D. from the University of California at Berkeley.

Andrew Grove has played perhaps the pivotal role in the development and popularization of the 20th Century's most remarkable innovation—the personal computer. The technologies pioneered by Grove and his associates, first at Fairchild Semiconductor and then at Intel, which he co-founded in 1968, made the entire personal computing revolution possible. The world has barely begun to scratch the surface of the technological and economic benefits that such revolution can bring.

He was no stranger to problems and setbacks, but he always managed to retain his enthusiasm and maintain his focus on what is important and what he does best: developing even faster, more affordable and more powerful technology.

Thanks to Andrew Grove's genius and vision, millions of people now have instant and inexpensive access to the kinds of information and entertainment about which even the elites of previous generations could only dream. In 1997, Andrew Grove was chosen by TIME magazine as their person of the year. A few years ago Grove learned that he had prostate cancer. He determined to fight it with the same energy and enthusiasm that he used to build Intel. As of now he is winning the battle.

Grove has shown us that opportunity for success and wealth is not restricted by adversity, persecution or poverty. By vision, enthusiasm and hard work, one can make the vision a reality and great things can be accomplished. Set backs—whether they are business problems or serious diseases—can be overcome if we have the enthusiasm to deal with them.

Dale Carnegie was so impressed by the following poem by the 19th century American philosopher, Samuel Ullman, that he had a plaque quoting it hung over his desk:

You are as young as your faith,
As old as your doubts;
As young as your self-confidence
As old as your fears;
As young as your hope,
As old as your despair.
Years may wrinkle the skin,
But to give up enthusiasm
Wrinkles the soul.

Attitude

A prerequisite for becoming an enthusiastic and self-motivated person is believing that things are going to turn out well and not ill; that we are going to succeed and not fail; that no matter what may or may not happen, we are going to be happy.

There is nothing else so helpful as the carrying of this optimistic, expectant attitude—the attitude that always looks for and expects the best, the highest, the happiest—and never allowing oneself to get into a pessimistic, discouraged mood.

We must believe that we will do what we were made to do. Never for an instant must we harbor a doubt of it. It does not matter what we are trying to do or to be, we should always assume an expectant, hopeful, optimistic attitude regarding it. It will enable us to grow in all our faculties.

Successful people treat themselves properly by encouraging themselves and by making their minds positive, to will be immune from all negative, discouraging thoughts.

The only world we will ever know anything about, the only world that is true for us at this moment, is the one we create mentally—the world we are conscious of. The environment we fashion out of our thoughts, our beliefs, our ideals, our philosophy is the only one we will ever live in. Another inspiration, new ideas will come tomorrow. Today we should carry out the inspiration of the day.

No human being has succeeded in trying to be somebody else, even if that person was a success. Success cannot be copied—cannot be successfully imitated. It is an original force—an individual creation.

Enthusiasm comes from within or from nowhere. We must be ourselves. We must listen to the voice within. There is room for improvement in every profession, in every trade, and in every business. The world wants people who can do things in new and better ways. Don't think that because your plan or idea has no precedent, or because you are young and inexperienced, that you will not get a hearing. People who have anything new and valuable to give to the world will be heard and will be followed. People who dare to think their own thoughts and originate their own methods, who are not afraid to be themselves, and are not a copy of someone else, gets recognition quickly. Nothing else will attract the attention of an employer or the rest of the world so quickly as originality and unique ways of doing things, especially if they are effective.

Control Your Thoughts

Considering that our mind governs everything in our world, its force has been singularly neglected and misunderstood.

Even when tribute is paid to its power, it is treated as something unalterable, a tool that could be used if one was born with the genius to do so. Of recent years, the control of thought, and its use to modify character already formed, to change even external surroundings, or at least their effect on one's self, and to bring about health, happiness, and success, is increasingly being studied and understood.

A strong man hypnotized into a belief that he cannot rise from his chair is actually powerless to do so until the spell is removed. A frail woman, nerved by necessity to save a life, can carry a person heavier than herself from during by fire or flood. In both cases the mental attitude, not the physical ability, determines the result; yet both acts are only work of muscles.

When a task to be done consists largely or wholly of mental acts, as most achievements, how much greater must be the determining power of the thought. The conquerors of the world, whether on battlefields, in trade or in moral struggles, have won by the attitude of mind with which they went to their work.

There is no certainty in the presence of doubt. Until we erase "fate" and "can't" and "doubt" from our vocabulary, we cannot rise. We cannot get strong while we harbor convictions of weakness, or be happy while we dwell on miseries or misfortunes

There's no way we can become well and strong by always thinking and talking about our bad health, saying that we never expect to be robust or well. Neither can we expect our executive faculties to be strong and vigorous while we perpetually doubt our ability to do what we undertake. Nothing so weakens the mind and renders it totally unfit for effective thinking as the constant acknowledgment of weakness, or doubt of one's ability to accomplish a task.

There can be no more important study, no higher duty owed to ourselves than that of thought-control and of self-control, which results in self-development. Perhaps because thought in itself is intangible, and most of us really have so little control over it, there is an impression that direction of mind action is a difficult and abstruse affair, something that requires hard study, leisure, and book knowledge to accomplish it. Nothing is further from the truth. All of us have within ourselves all that is required to remake our intellectual nature, our character, and resultantly, change our lives for the better.

Channel Enthusiasm Into Action

Self-confidence enables us to be enthusiastic about our activities and to accomplish results by eliminating fear, doubt, and uncertainty. The mind cannot act with vigor in the presence of doubt. There must be certainty, or there would be no efficiency.

We must concentrate on our goal, see before us the prize as though it were already won, while being intensely conscious of moving nearer to its achievement. This will generate the enthusiasm that helps us on our way. One by one obstacles vanish, and what once seemed too hard for human strength to accomplish appear plain and even simple. The greatest need of all is to keep the goal in sight and not let interest flag or inward vision waver.

Enthusiasm alone will not accomplish results. Outward work must follow inward contemplation. Wishes alone will not absolve us from the need of making effort, but it is a means for revealing to us what efforts we need to make and how to make them.

Ten Techniques Proven to Engender Enthusiasm:

1. Adopt a definite major purpose—that aspect of our job or our life in which we want to become more enthusiastic. Write out a clear statement of that purpose and our plan for attaining it.

   When Harry was elected chairman of the fund raising drive for his community center, his goal was to generate as much enthusiasm as he had about the project in other members of the committee and in turn the entire membership of the organization. He carefully thought out his plan of action, published it in the organization bulletin and had copies emailed to the entire committee. Now everybody involved was made aware of his plan and how he or she could help achieve it. But more importantly, he made large-print copies of it, and posted them on his bathroom mirror, on the refrigerator in his kitchen and on the wall next to his desk to keep himself notified and refreshed on his plan and to maintain his enthusiasm for it.

2. Attack the plan with a burning desire to make it work. Never let your enthusiasm for it fade. Think about it every day and every night. Let it become the dominating thought in your minds.

3. Don't procrastinate. Set to work immediately in carrying out your plan. Harry met with his committee and together they drew up an action program indicating who would do what, timetables, and expected results.

4. Set up procedures for follow-up. Too often the best-laid plans are nothing more than words because nobody checks progress. When what is planned does not happen, the enthusiasm of the start-up begins to fade. Harry set checkpoints so that each member could measure his or her own activities.

5. Setbacks and snags are most likely to occur. There are people who lose their enthusiasm if things don't go well. This is when your enthusiasm will act as an adrenaline shot and give others the energy to fight and correct it. It may be necessary to change direction—but not necessarily. Evaluate what went wrong. It may just require minor adjustments, but if serious problems developed, re-examine what occurred. However, if you find that you are significantly off track, it may be necessary to rethink the plan and rewrite it. By maintaining you enthusiasm, you could approach the problem not as an unpleasant chore, but as an exciting opportunity.

6. You are not alone. Just like an athletic team has its cheerleaders, you need a "cheer squad" to applaud you when you succeed and to boost you up when you are behind. However, unlike the college cheer leader, you should select men and women who are not only positive thinkers, but have knowledge and experience that can help you in your endeavors.

   Harry had a mentor, who had guided him in his career and never failed to encourage him when things were not going well. With the help of his mentor, he assembled a group of people who had previous experience in fund raising to guide over the rough spots.

7. Beware of pessimists. The world is filled with naysayers— men and women who always predict failure. They doom every effort and when setbacks do occur, instead of helping they say: "I told you so." Keep these people off your committee or team. If you are compelled to work with such people, you should surround yourself with optimists who can counteract their negativity.

8. Make a habit of being enthusiastic. Habits require reinforcement. Never let a day pass without devoting some time to furthering the plan.

9. Never give up on the idea that you will achieve your goal, no matter how far away that moment seems. When enthusiasm is waning, an "internal pep talk" will reinforce it.

10. Be positive at all times. Enthusiasm thrives on hope, confidence, selflessness, assurance and tolerance. Maintain that positive attitude and your project assuredly will move forward.

Ralph Waldo Emerson, who is considered the greatest of American philosophers, saw the value of enthusiasm. In one of his essays he wrote: "Every great and commanding moment in the annals of the world is the triumph of some enthusiasm."

Sum and Substance

> Enthusiasm is the little-recognized secret of success.

> Set a goal and work toward it, and when it is accomplished set another goal and work toward it. The excitement and challenge it provides cannot help but keep one enthusiastic.

> Study the subject. Learning leads to knowledge that leads to enthusiasm about the matters learned.

> By far the men and women who are most enthusiastic are those who are self-motivated. We are our own best motivators. If we believe in ourselves and in our inevitable success, we create within ourselves a never-ending source of enthusiasm.

> Always assume an expectant, hopeful, optimistic attitude. It will generate enthusiasm for whatever we are engaged in.

> Faith in ourselves enables us to be enthusiastic about our activities and to accomplish results by eliminating fear, doubt, and uncertainty. The mind cannot act with vigor in the presence of doubt. There must be certainty, or there would be no efficiency.

> Never give up on the idea that we will achieve our goal, no matter how far away that moment seems. An "internal pep-talk" will help when enthusiasm begins to wane.

3

SET AND REACH ACHIEVABLE
GOALS

All successful people start with a goal. Establishing goals and working toward their achievement is the first step one must take on the long road to success. By knowing where we are going and how we plan to get there, we will be able to focus our time, energy and emotion—and start on the right track toward reaching those goals.

A ship, which has broken its rudder, may keep everlastingly at it, may keep on a full head of steam, sailing around all the time, but never arrives anywhere. It never reaches any port unless by accident; and if it does find a haven, its cargo may not be suited to the people, the climate or the conditions. The ship must be directed to a definite port, for which its cargo is adapted, and where there is a demand for it, and it must aim steadily for that port through sunshine and storm, through tempest and fog.

So a person who wants to succeed must not drift about rudderless on the ocean of life, but must not only steer straight toward a destined port when the ocean is smooth, when the currents and winds serve, but also must keep the course in the very teeth of the wind and tempest, and even when enveloped in the fogs of disappointment and mists of opposition.

It Starts with a Dream

We start with a dream—a vision of the future. In the dream we are rich, famous and happy. Most people do dream of such a future, but in most cases, that's all it will ever be—a dream.

Successful people have had those dreams too, but they turned those dreams into goals and in turn into reality. But their dreams were not vague hopes for success, but dreams of specific achievements that they aimed for. Edison dreamed of a world in which electric energy would light up the night. Gates dreamed of a computer system that would enable everybody—not just big organizations—to utilize the power of computers. Beethoven dreamed of music that would make the spirit soar. Great actors, artists, musicians, writers dreamed, not just of fame but of the way they would utilize their talents to achieve success.

Dreaming is not limited to such geniuses. All successful people report that their success started with a hope, a dream. Men and women who have been queried about their achievements reported over and over again that it all started with a dream, which led to a goal, which led to a plan of action and inevitably to accomplishing the goal.

Dreaming is not limited to the young. It is never too late to have a new dream that leads to new goals that in turn leads to new successes. It is astonishing what people who have had their dreams late in life have accomplished. Benjamin Franklin was past fifty before he began the study of science and philosophy. Milton, in his blindness, was past the age of fifty when he sat down to complete his epic poem—*Paradise Lost*.

Dreaming is not limited to biases and prejudices of the times. For countless years, women have been restricted in what they can attempt to accomplish. Their career goals were limited to what were considered "female jobs." It took determination and courage to even think about other careers. One example is Elaine Pagels, Princeton professor and best-selling author of books on Gnosticism and early Christianity. She said she was educated at a time when girls were taught to not even consider serious careers. She felt free to follow what she loved; only later discovering she could make a living out of it. Her dream had become her goal.

Are you doing the work you like best? If not, do something about it. You will never achieve real success unless you like what you are doing. Many people have had to try several things before they knew what they wanted to do.

Dale Carnegie

Today the barriers are gone in most career areas. For example, in most law, medical and other professional schools in the United States, half or more of the students are women.

In the nineteenth century, Frederick Douglas, born into slavery, did not let his race or condition of servitude stop him from learning to read and write and eventually to become a leader of his people. In the twenty-first century, Barack Obama broke the race barrier to become president of the United States.

Even brains are second in importance to will. Vacillators are always pushed aside in the race of life. Only those with an iron will and determination that nothing shall impede them, are sure that with perseverance and grit, they will succeed. Dreams become goals and goals become achievements to those who strive long enough and hard enough.

Most of the things which make life worth living, which have emancipated us from drudgery and lifted us above commonness and ugliness—the great amenities of life—we owe to our dreamers.

Converting Dreams Into Goals

Unfortunately, too many dreamers remain just that—dreamers. The dreams remain dreams. When we convert dreams into goals, they are no longer fantasies, but objectives that we can set before us as a road map to success. We must bring to our dreams a purpose, a determination that we will do all that we can to make that dream come true.

A woman who had a dream and converted it into a successful goal is the clothes designer, Rachel Roy. Rachel's love for fashion was inspired by the movies she saw as a child. The clothes the women on the screen wore seemed to give them an aura of confidence and success. Rachel dreamed that she could create the same aura for herself and other women—a sophisticated look that would create positive self-esteem.

She and her family went school shopping once a year. She was disturbed by the lack of interesting clothing choices in a local store and was convinced that if she had the opportunity she could create better styles. Her mother told her that this was the job of a buyer. Now she could put a name to her dream: buyer. At that moment, she said, her dream became her goal—to become a buyer in the fashion field.

Her first job was as stock clerk. She moved rapidly to assistant manager, to personal shopper, to stylist in various stores. She was soon designing fashions and was on the road to a senior position in her company.

When her husband, Damon Dash, wanted to start an independent clothing line, Rachel had a decision to make—to leave her own successful career and start over with Damon. She chose to start over, throwing herself into the job, working in every capacity, tracking everything she did to contribute, and involving herself in as many facets of the business as possible. She wanted to make herself irreplaceable. After about six years, Rachel was confident she could run a business herself and formed her own company. Her designs were acclaimed by the industry and today she is considered one of the foremost designers in the fashion industry.

There is an infinite distance between the wishers and the doers. Rachel Roy was more than a dreamer and a wisher. She turned her dream into a goal and worked hard to achieve that goal.

The very habit of expecting that the future is full of good things for you, that you are going to be prosperous and happy, that you are going to have a fine family, a beautiful home, a successful career, and are going to stand for something, is the best kind of capital on which to start your life.

What we try persistently is what we tend to achieve, even though it may not seem likely or even possible. If we always try to express the ideal, and we visualize it as vividly as possible and try with all our might to realize it, it is more likely we will achieve those things we would like to come true in our lives, whether it be robust health, a noble character, or a superb career. It is only when desire crystallizes into resolve that it is effective. It is the desire coupled with the vigorous determination to realize it that produces the creative power. It is the yearning, the longing, and striving together that produce results.

If we wish to improve ourselves in any particular area, we must visualize the quality as vividly and as tenaciously as possible, and hold a superior ideal along the line of our ambition. We must keep this persistently in the mind until we feel its uplift and realization in our lives. We are born to win, to conquer and to lead a triumphant lives. We should be a success in our chosen work, our relationship with people, and in all other phases of our lives.

Believe, and Achieve

Prosperity begins in the mind and is impossible while the mental attitude is hostile to it. It is fatal to work for one thing and to expect something else, because everything must be created mentally first and is bound to follow its mental pattern.

We cannot become prosperous if we really expect or half expect to remain poor. We tend to get what we expect, and to expect nothing is to get nothing.

When every step we take is on the road to failure, how can we hope to arrive at success? It is about facing the wrong way toward the black, depressing, hopeless outlook, even though we may be working in the opposite direction that kills the results of our effort.

Thoughts are magnets that attract things like themselves.

If your mind dwells upon poverty and disease, it will bring poverty and disease. There is no possibility of producing just the opposite of what we are holding in our minds, because our mental attitude is the pattern, which is built into our lives. Our accomplishments are achieved mentally first.

The terror of failure, the fear of financial loss and of possible humiliation keep multitudes of people from obtaining the very things they desire.

The habit of looking at everything constructively, from the bright, hopeful side, the side of faith and assurance, instead of from the side of doubt and uncertainty; and the habit of believing the best is going to happen, that the right must triumph; the faith that truth is bound finally to conquer error; that harmony and health are the reality and discord and disease the temporary absence of it—this is the attitude of an optimist, which will ultimately reform the world.

Setting the Stage for Success

We cannot depend on others to set us on the road to success. It depends entirely on ourselves.

Before we can determine what goals can get us started on this journey, we must first evaluate ourselves. We must search deep inside of our minds and pull out from it what it is we really want out of life and what assets we have that will lead us to reach that goal.

We must be realistic. We may want to establish a goal that appears to be desirable, but we may not have the abilities needed to achieve it. We may dream of being a movie star or an opera singer, but don't have the talent needed. Our dream career may be in areas that are not feasible for us to attempt.

On the other hand, we may have aptitudes and skills that we don't realize we have and which can lead to a satisfying and profitable career.

How can we find out? By looking deep inside ourselves. A careful introspection will bring this out. Most adults already know what they can and cannot do, what they like and do not like. It may not be obvious, but introspection enables us to go beyond the obvious and think deeply about ourselves.

A good example of this is Shonda Rhimes, creator and executive producer of the television shows "Grey's Anatomy" and "Private Practice." Even as a child she knew that she would become a creative writer. She made up stories and spoke them into a tape recorder before she knew how to write. Her mother encouraged her by transcribing them, hence making them real.

What we have to do is go systematically over our education, previous experience, hobbies and interests. Look for those aspects of our lives in which we have been successful and in which we have achieved satisfaction and joy. These are indicators of the areas in which we will succeed in the future. But this is only the beginning. Look beyond what we *have* accomplished and think what we *can* accomplish.

Successful people learn at the very outset of their careers just what funds they can draw upon. We must take an inventory of all our possible assets and resources. Let's not just look at what we have accomplished so far in our lives, but what we know we can accomplish. The great majority of young people start on their careers with little knowledge of their mental capacities and they usually discover them piece by piece over time.

Too many people never discover more than a small

percent of their ability and rarely rise above low paid, low-level positions. They plod along in mediocrity; yet they have resources, if they could only detect them, it could lift them into superior positions.

Somehow they never come in touch with just the right kind of ambition-arousing material, ambition-arousing environment or the necessary material to ignite the giant power of their hidden strengths.

Oneness of Purpose

Successful people strongly believe that one must be totally committed to one's goals. There is great power in a resolution that has no reservation in it—a strong, persistent, tenacious purpose which burns all bridges behind it, clears all obstacles from its path, and arrives at its goal, no matter how long it may take, no matter what the sacrifice or the cost.

To succeed we must concentrate all the faculties of our minds upon one unwavering aim, and have the tenacity of purpose, which leads to defeat or victory. Every other inclination that tempts us must be suppressed.

Developing goals that are reasonable and achievable is the first step to success—whether it is in our career or any other aspect of our lives. We must plant the seeds in our minds that will enable us to accept and implement these goals.

Establishing Goals

Peter M. always knew he wanted to be an engineer. As a child his primary interests were mechanical. In school he excelled in math and science. His career goals were solid and he followed them through college and into the world of work.

Most of us are not that fortunate. We only have vague concepts of careers as a child and often "fall into" our careers by fortuity. However, it is never too late to establish goals—not only in our job and career but also in other aspects of our life.

Elvira S. floundered through several jobs after college. She had majored in marketing, but her first job in that field bored her to tears. She shifted to sales, but was unhappy and unsuccessful. Her next job, a paralegal in a law firm, really excited her and created in her an interest in becoming an attorney.

She set a new long-term goal—to become a criminal lawyer. She requested transfer within her firm to work for their senior attorney who handled criminal matters. She attended law school at night and received her law degree shortly. Further, she set a goal to work in the office of the District Attorney to gain experience before starting her own practice.

If you've been unsuccessful in something you've wanted very much to do, don't give up and accept defeat. Try something else. You have more than one string for your bow—if only you discover that string.

Dale Carnegie

Guidelines For Setting Goals

To make goals more than just pipe dreams, they should combine the following elements:

> *Goals should be clearly stated*: Indicate in clear terms what you wish to accomplish. Be specific and firm in stating the goal. For example, saying "My goal is to be the best salesperson in my company" sounds good, but it is better to

be more specific: "My goal is to reach a sales volume of so many dollars for the next fiscal year; and ten percent more each year for the next three years." Now you know the target and your subconscious mind will help concentrate your efforts on reaching those figures.

> *Reasonable*: Unless the goals set can be attained, setting goal is meaningless. To assure reasonableness, break the long-term goal into attainable sub-goals. For example, Long-term goal: exhibit my paintings in a prestigious art gallery in next three years. Intermediate goals: To complete X canvasses by December of next year; to mount a showing at a local art gallery by July of the following year; to be reviewed in an art journal by December of that year.

> *Goals should be inspiring:* If we set a goal that is too easily attained, it will not motivate us to do more than minimum work. We should set goals that will inspire us to keep moving ahead and to work much harder to achieve them. Achievers recognize that once a goal is reached, they should immediately set another goal that will make them stretch themselves to continue to improve and grow.

> *Goals should be action based:* Unless the actions that will be taken to implement the goals are noted, the goals are no more than dreams. Action requires activity—mental, physical, and emotional. Mentally, we must be prepared to think about our goals every spare moment and what actions must be taken to realize them.

> *Goals should be measurable:* It is not always possible to quantify goals. Some goals can be measured in financial or other numerical terms. We can set sales figures that we wish to attain by the month, quarter, or year—in terms of units

of product or dollar value. We can set production goals by amount. Even intangible goals, which cannot be quantified, can be established in measurable terms. The major goal can be broken into segments and timetables set for the completion of each segment. In this way we can measure how close we are in reaching each of the segments and fine-tune our activities to assure that they will be accomplished in a timely manner.

> *Goals should be written down:* One way to assure that goals will not be forgotten or lost in our hectic day-to-day lives is to write them down. Make a list of long-term goals; break them into intermediate and short-term goals. Write them in large letters and post them where you can see them every day—over your desk, on the refrigerator, on the mirror. Read them, memorize them, re-read them and ask each day: "What am I doing to accomplish these goals?"

> *Goals should be flexible:* There are times when circumstances change and the goal we set is no longer pertinent. Economic conditions may not be favorable for starting that new enterprise; technological innovations may have made the goal obsolete; we may have made errors in our research and the goal is not feasible. This does not necessarily mean the goal must be abandoned. It may just require new thinking or more study. If faced with such a situation, review what has transpired and make necessary adjustments.

One often fails to meet a set goal. Don't become frustrated and give up. Review what has transpired, evaluate the situation and make necessary adjustments.

Hugh had expected that he would be promoted to store manager after serving two years as assistant manager. It didn't happen. Rather than quitting in frustration, Hugh reviewed the situation. His company had opened six to ten new stores each year for the past six years and he had based his goal on the premise that his company would continue to open several new stores each year. Last year business had not been good and they had only opened two new outlets. But this year business had improved and he knew that additional openings were being considered. By adjusting his goals, he extended his timetable for another year and will most likely reach it.

> *Goals should be stretched:* Once you have reached a goal, set another that will make you stretch in order to continue to improve and grow. When Ben started his physical fitness program he was told that if he swam thirty laps in half an hour, he would keep in good shape. It didn't take him long to achieve that goal. Most people of his age—the late fifties— would have been content to keep swimming at that pace, but Ben learned that in the 25-yards pool that he used, 36 laps was equal to one-half mile. He immediately strove to reach that new goal.

> *Let others know our goals:* In most weight-loss programs, participants are advised to let their families know how much weight they intend to lose and keep them reminded of their progress. Why? When we share our goal with others, they will support us in helping reach it. When we are tempted to give up, they encourage us to continue.

Karen had dropped out of college when she got married, so she could work until her husband completed his education. Then she planned to return and get her degree. The birth of her children changed this plan. Now, ten years, later, Karen managed to resume her education. Managing a house, working an eight-hour day and going to school at night is tough. From time to time, Karen feels it's not worth the effort. But because her husband, children and friends know how important that goal is to her, they cheer her on and encourage her to keep going.

> *Review progress:* All goals cannot be quantified so that they can be easily measured, but when this is possible, set specific standards and timetables. When not quantifiable, develop a way of measuring how close you have come to attain your goals.

When Lee set his sales goals for the year, he expected to increase his annual volume by eight percent. This meant he would have to open at least four new accounts or increase the sales of his current customers. He broke this down into monthly goals that could be easily measured against his actual sales. If business did not measure up to the monthly goal, he could take necessary steps immediately to get back on track.

As Human Resources Director of her organization, Kathy could not set quantifiable goals. Her objectives for the next twelve months included setting up a new training program for word processor operators, studying and reporting to management on a new type of benefits package, and designing a performance review system for administrative and professional personnel.

She broke each of these objectives into segments and set timetables for each segment. In this way she measured how close she was to reaching each of the segments and fine-tune her activities to assure she would accomplish all of them by the end of the year.

We all have possibilities we don't know about. We can do things we don't even dream we can do.

Dale Carnegie

The Planning Process

A systematic approach to establish goals for a specific project should follow the following steps:

Step 1. Should-Be

This is the scope of the project. It is a picture of what you ultimately want, and who and how it would be beneficial. This should be clearly stated and agreed upon among senior managers, your team and yourself. If you have not done a good job of defining scope, planning the project will be almost impossible.

Step 2. As-Is

Examine the current situation. Where are you today? What factors help or hinder your efforts to carry out the project scope?

Step 3. Goals

Now you are ready to define and set realistic goals to successfully carry out the scope of the project. Without such goals, one tends to drift. Goals can be immediate, intermediate, or long-term. Achieving day-to-day goals (immediate goals) contribute to the achievement of intermediate and long-term goals. Review what constitutes a SMART goal:

- S = Specific in terms of processes and resources
- M = Measurable by objective data
- A = Attainable in that they can be achieved
- R = Relevant to your vision
- T = Time specific with a deadline

Step 4. Action Steps

In order to achieve goals, priorities must be established and specific action steps must be developed. In order for goals to be met, action steps should include:

- Requirements of the job
- Who will do the job
- Methods to be used
- How the different parts tie together and fit into the big picture
- How you want the results communicated (report, PowerPoint, etc.)

Step 5. Cost

Another aspect to planning is determining the budget for, and cost of, each action step. Costs include that of personnel, equipment, material and any other costs required to achieve the goal.

Step 6. Timetables

Deadlines should be set and communicated so there is a clear understanding of immediate, intermediate, and long-term targets to be met. When establishing timetables, be realistic. Work backward to determine when each phase should be completed. Put the schedule in writing to avoid misunderstandings.

Step 7. Implementation

An important yet overlooked part of implementing a plan is making sure that everybody involved understand their role in achieving the goals. Commitment to agreed-upon results must be established. Monitoring the implementation may result in modifying the scope of the plan and re-evaluation goals.

Step 8. Follow-Up/Measurement

A critical part of the planning process is to keep accurate records, analyze why deviations have occurred, and take action to correct any challenges. Concentrate on those factors critical to reaching the goal.

By establishing a well-thought out goal standard, you would be able to focus on your true objectives, measure your progress and assure that what is most important to you in your job or other aspects of your life be accomplished.

Sum and Substance

➤ All successful people report that their success started with a hope, a dream, which led to a goal, which led to a plan of action and inevitably, to accomplishing the goal.

➤ Before you can determine what goals can get you started on the journey, you must first evaluate yourself. You must search deep inside your mind and determine what it is that you really want out of your life and what assets you have that will help you in reaching that goal.

- Developing goals that are reasonable and achievable is the first step to success.
- Follow these guidelines for setting goals:

  Goals should be clearly stated.

  Goals should be reasonably attainable.

  Goals should be inspiring.

  Goals should be action based.

  Goals should be measurable.

  Goals should be written down.

  Goals should be flexible.

  Goals should be stretched.

  Goals should be shared with others who can support you.

  Goals should be reviewed periodically to measure progress.

4

....

HOW OTHERS SEE US

The old adage: "You can't judge a book by its cover," makes good sense but unfortunately, most of us do judge people by their "cover"—their appearance and demeanor at the first meeting. Indeed, some people make a decision about an individual in the first thirty seconds of contact.

First impressions are hard to overcome. If a negative or undesirable impression is made on that first contact, it may permeate all relations with that party for years to come. It takes a little thought and effort to establish the basis for making good impressions, but it is well worth the effort.

Create an Image of Success

When we meet successful people, we are often impressed by their pleasant personality. The image that we receive makes us confide in them, admire them, and feel comfortable with them. Sometimes we meet unpleasant people and are repelled by the image they project.

Our image—sometimes called our personality—is the way in which we express ourselves to the outside world. We are not only gregarious animals, liking to be in the sight of other people, but we have an innate propensity to get ourselves noticed, and noticed favorably. Much of this image comes from a fine, cultivated manner. Tact is a very important element, next only to fine manner—perhaps the most important. One must know exactly what to do, and be able to do just the right thing at the proper time. Good judgment and common sense are indispensable to those who are trying to develop a positive image.

One of the greatest investments one can make is that of attaining a gracious manner, cordiality of bearing, generosity of feeling—the delightful art of pleasing. It is infinitely better than money or capital, for all doors fly open to sunny, pleasing personalities. They are more than welcome; they are sought out for everywhere.

Personality Traits Can Be Acquired

Assuming that all people have equal rights and opportunities, we must recognize that all do not have equal intelligence, equal physical strength, equal levels of energy; yet whatever their status, they may rise by self-education and self-development. Those eager for knowledge, ambitious to excel, will naturally forge ahead. Consequently, we can choose and work to develop the personality traits we wish to acquire. Application is the great thing.

The important thing to remember is that a pleasant, welcoming image can be *developed*. Although some facets that make up our image are inborn—our physical appearance, basic intelligence and some talents—each of us has the capacity to make the most of our innate traits and to develop them to give us a type of image that others will admire.

It's not easy to grow into the person we want to be, but it starts with a strong desire and commitment to develop an outgoing, cheerful, optimistic, and positive demeanor—an image that will win the approbation of the men and women with whom we interrelate.

Maintain a Cheerful Disposition

Unless we have a mental attitude that is free of bitterness and guile and we look at each day as a blessing to be enjoyed and savored, we will have an unhappy and most likely unproductive life.

Some people harbor for years a bitter hatred or a great jealousy toward others. Although they may not be aware of it, such a mental attitude does not allow the possessors to reach the highest levels of their abilities, and destroy their happiness.

Moreover, they radiate their destructive energy thus prejudicing people against them, arousing their antagonism, and constantly handicapping themselves all along the line.

The mind must be kept free from bitterness, jealousy, hatred, envy, and uncharitable thoughts; free from everything which inhibits it, or there must be a penalty paid in terms of impaired efficiency, inferior work as well as loss of peace of mind.

We cannot do our best work while we harbor revengeful

or even unfriendly thoughts toward others. Our faculties only give up their best when working in perfect harmony. There must be good will in the heart or we will be incapable of doing good work. Hatred, revenge, and jealousy are poisons, fatal to all that is noblest in us, as arsenic is fatal to physical life.

A kindly attitude, a feeling of good will toward others is our best protection against bitter hatred or injurious thoughts of any kind. It will lead to a life of peace and equanimity. It will minimize discord in our lives and help us maintain harmonious relations with others.

We cannot carry secret hatreds and grudges, jealousies, and revengeful feelings without seriously impairing our own reputation. Many people wonder why they are not popular, why they are disliked generally, why they stand for so little in their community, when it is really because of their bitter, revengeful, discordant feelings, which kill personal magnetism.

On the other hand, if we maintain kind, loving, helpful sympathetic thoughts, feel friendly toward everybody, and carry no bitterness, hatred, or jealousy in our hearts, we will create an attractive, helpful, and sunny image.

Flaming enthusiasm, backed up by horse sense and persistence, is the quality that most frequently makes for success.

Dale Carnegie

People who can smile when things go wrong have a tremendous advantage over those whose courage collapses just as soon as they are in a hard place. People who can smile when everything seems to go against them will always project the image that they are made of winning material.

First Things First

When people meet us, the first factor that makes an impression on them is how we look. Appearance plays a major part in how we are perceived. Some of the factors that may impress others either positively or negatively are beyond our control. We cannot change our basic physical appearance, but we can make the most of our assets and minimize what may be perceived to be defects. One does not have to have movie-star good looks to make a positive impression.

The Critical Ten Seconds

Each time a new person meets us, that person takes just ten seconds to form a whole laundry list of impressions, beliefs or assumptions regarding who we are and what we are about.

And those assumptions are far more significant than how much we paid for our clothes and whether or not that's our natural hair color. Those impressions encompass everything from our education level to our financial situation, our career success, even things as subjective as our honesty and integrity. All those beliefs are formed, almost subconsciously, in the first ten seconds.

External Image

Our external image is what others observe first. It can be an effective door opener or a door closer. Every salesperson knows the frustration of not being able to get to a prospect because he can't get past the so-called "gatekeeper"—the receptionist, secretary, or subordinate who screens out unwanted callers. In a sense, a person's first impression of us is the most powerful gatekeeper of all. It often determines whether that person would let us in, figuratively as well as literally.

The bulk of the cues to our external image are transmitted visually. The newest brain research reveals that visual impulses are transmitted directly to the emotional center of the brain, bypassing the normal routing systems and forming responses almost instantaneously.

Good grooming, appropriate dress, a pleasant smile, and proper manners are the first steps in making a good personal impression. We can maximize our chances of success by dressing in a way that communicates a positive message about us and our abilities.

With the widespread adoption of business casual dress codes, there is no one right way to dress for business today. We must do some research to find what is appropriate in our industry, region, and culture.

The day before Phyllis was scheduled to be interviewed by the ABC Ad Agency, she went to the lobby of their building and observed how the women who worked there dressed. She noted that unlike the bank where she had formerly been employed, most women wore blouses and skirts or slacks— not dresses. So when she went for her interview, she dressed accordingly. Had she worn one of the outfits she had worn in the bank, she would not have presented an image of somebody who would fit into that environment. On the other hand, had she applied to another bank, dressing in casual attire would have made a poor impression.

Be Interested in Others

Remember that the person you are talking to is a hundred times more interested in himself and his wants and his problems than he is in you and your problems.

Dale Carnegie

Appearance and personality are only the first step in creating and maintaining the image others have of us. We must develop it by becoming, as Dale Carnegie said, "genuinely interested in other people."

If we make a point of showing sincere interest in somebody from the moment of initial contact, it will work more than anything else to develop instant rapport. We must make the effort to note that person's name and use it when addressing him or her.

In a business situation, listen intently to the problem or situation that the person has come to discuss and ask questions that show you are genuinely concerned. In social situations, show sincere interest when responding to the other person's comments and questions.

Alfred Adler, the famous Viennese psychologist said in his book *What Life Should Mean to You,* "It is the individual who is not interested in his fellow men who has the greatest difficulties in life and provides the greatest injury to others. It is from among such individuals that all human failures spring."

One of the characteristics that made Theodore Roosevelt one of the best-liked people of his time was the sincere interest he showed in every person he met. He would ask them about their families and listen to their ideas—no matter how humble their backgrounds. He took the time to get to know each of the members of the household staff of the White House and even years after he left office, when he visited the White House, he greeted each by name and commented about an interest that they had expressed or something they had done for him when he was the president. How could anybody keep from liking him?

If you want to make friends, greet people with animation and enthusiasm. When somebody calls you on the telephone, say "hello" in a tone that lets him or her know how pleased you are to receive the call. Showing a genuine interest in others not only wins friends, but also helps develop customers' loyalty to your company.

It was often said about Daniel Webster, the great orator and statesman that he gained the trust of every person he met. When asked why people had such an immediate reaction to him, they commented that unlike most politicians, he listened to what they had to say about themselves rather than talk about himself.

Be empathetic. Empathetic people put themselves in the shoes of the people with whom they interact. They not only hear what other's have to say, but feel what they feel when they say it.

First Impression on the Telephone

Often the first contact we have with somebody is on the telephone. The future relationships one would have with that person can be established by the impression one makes in this phone call. Jennifer was upset. The washing machine she had purchased only last month had broken down. She called the store and asked for the manager. After six rings, the call was answered: "Jones' Appliances, Please wait." She waited and waited and waited for what appeared to be an eternity. Just as Jennifer was about to hang up and dial again, the operator finally came back on the line:

"Jones' Appliances, can I help you?"

"May I please speak to the manager?"

"What for?"

"I bought a washer last month and it broke down."

"You don't want the manager, I'll connect you with service."

After another long wait, the service representative finally responded. Half way through Jennifer's complaint, he interrupted: "Sorry, we can't help you. You have to go to the manufacturer. You'll find the address on your warranty," and without waiting for a response hung up.

Do you think Jennifer will ever buy anything from that store again?

To make a good impression on callers, answer the telephone promptly. If you know that the person will have to wait for any length of time, let that person know approximately how long and suggest that you would be happy to call them back. In case the individual elects to wait, have somebody advise them that you are still looking into the problem, so they have the option of either continuing to wait or request that the call be returned.

When speaking with the caller, always let them talk until the complaint or message is fully explained. Do not interrupt. If you cannot help, give as much information as you can to enable the person to obtain the help needed.

Our Workplace Creates First Impressions

Gary's eyes scanned the room. It was certainly a busy office. People were scurrying back and forth; the desks he could see were piled with papers. Phones rang, and nobody answered. The one word that popped into Gary's head was "chaos." He began to have reservations about doing business with this organization. When he finally met with the company's representative, this first impression had predetermined his decision.

The company Gary visited might have been highly competent to handle Gary's business, but by not paying enough attention to the little things that add up to the impression made on visitors, everything that followed was almost automatically rejected.

When visitors enter the place of business, whether they are customers, bankers, potential employees, or government regulators, the impression made by the first sight influences the manner in which they perceive the company.

Obviously, a machine shop cannot be as spotless as a doctor's office, but it should at least be as neat as other machine shops.

It's a good idea for people to check their facility periodically to assure that it is clean and orderly; that tools and equipments are properly stored when not used; that desks are not overflowing with papers; and in general, that there is a business like atmosphere.

Correspondence Creates First Impressions

When Warren attended a time management seminar, he was told that the time spent on writing business letters could be shortened significantly if the writer would just jot down the response on the bottom of the letter received and mail it back to the person who sent it. Warren put this idea into practice immediately. It certainly did save time, but in doing this, the image of his company suffered.

In following up a sales lead that he had answered in this matter, he learned that the prospect decided not to do business with Warren's company because their response to his inquiry was "unprofessional."

Our correspondence represents us to the public. Our letterhead should be designed to represent the image we wish to present. Spelling and typographical errors can be interpreted as indicators of a careless or inefficient operation. Intelligent readers readily detect poor choice of words or incorrect grammar. Reread correspondence before mailing. Make sure all letters are error-free.

Nonverbal Communication

Some of the routine behaviors we exhibit on autopilot can be strengthened to help us communicate positive messages about ourselves to those with whom we interact. These superficial behaviors have an enormous impact on the impressions we make.

Sociolinguist Albert Mehrabian, in his exhaustive study of face-to-face communication, determined that only 7 percent of the message transferred from one person to the other was housed in spoken words. About 38 percent of the meanings were transmitted through vocal characteristics—tone of voice, pauses, emphasis, etc. And an astonishing 55 percent of the total message was communicated through visual signals we classify as "body language."

The famous presidential debates between the young John F. Kennedy and the much more experienced Richard Nixon are a classic example. Radio listeners who only received the verbal portion of the message felt that Nixon excelled, but millions of viewers who saw the additional nonverbal component on television had exactly the opposite impression. Nixon's facial expressions, his sweating and hand movements made a negative impression on the viewer.

Posture

Good (or bad) posture is seen even from a distance, and registers instantly in the viewer's brain. It is less subtle than other nonverbal cues because it involves the entire body.

In research projects, participants assumed that subjects with excellent posture were more popular, ambitious, confidant, friendly, and intelligent than others with a more relaxed stance.

Improving our posture may feel awkward and exaggerated at first. By observing the impact of an upright torso, squared shoulders, and balanced lower body in other people, we can see how impressive they look, and learn how to look equally impressive.

Using Our Head

The position of our head and the movements of our features play a significant role in nonverbal communication. We should keep a level head to make the maximum impression.

Of all facial expressions, the smile is the most influential. Smiling can actually cause others to be more receptive to our point of view. When we smile, the other person nearly always smiles back. More than just a mirroring, it reflects the sudden surge of warmth and well-being that our smile generates.

However, an insincere smile is more damaging than no smile. A believable smile uses the entire face and happens spontaneously when we process a positive thought about the interchange we are a part of.

Eye Contact

Effective eye contact implies confidence, honesty, and interest in the other person. Lack of eye contact is usually interpreted as a sign of fear, dishonesty, hostility, or boredom.

Research shows that in job interviews candidates give more complete and revealing answers when the interviewer maintains eye contact. In classes, student comprehension and retention of the materials are directly related to the instructor's eye contact.

Handshakes

In America and Europe, the handshake is a significant part of the introduction when meeting new people. An effective handshake communicates an unconscious but important message to others about our self-esteem, energy, and enthusiasm. A handshake also creates a personal connection that makes the other party more open and honest.

Feedback

Perhaps the most challenging aspect of managing our external image is the difficulty of seeing ourselves as others see us. Research indicates that we are probably more critical of ourselves than others are of us. And at the same time, we may be totally unaware of negative behaviors that need to be corrected.

Some ways to get an accurate view of our own external image include:

> Seeing and listening to ourselves on videotape
> Studying our mirror image as we speak
> Asking trusted colleagues for honest input
> Monitoring others' reactions to us—especially those whom we want to influence

Building an Impressive Image

When we describe someone with an effective executive image, we nearly always describe an individual with high credibility. Others can count on such a person's words and their ability to make positive things happen.

When we choose a new behavior and then follow through on that commitment, we build credibility with our most important audience—ourselves. We prove to ourselves that we have the personal power to overcome our reluctance and make things happen.

Our attitudes are intimately intertwined with our actions. It is virtually impossible to maintain a change in one without a change in the other. There is no "quick-fix" to shortcut, but each instance of taking positive action adds another link to the chain that holds up our executive image.

To help track your successes, think of one important professional goal—something that really matters to you— perhaps something you have been putting off or feeling reluctant to tackle.

Then take one step, however small, that will move you toward that goal. Analyze what has been done so far and what it accomplished. If you feel confident that it has been achieved, select another step, and so on until you reach the image you want.

Of course some of the shortcomings we see in ourselves need to be corrected, rather than accepted. By identifying and filtering out misconceptions that we may have about our weak points releases energy to work constructively on strengthening those weak areas.

Benjamin Franklin, in his autobiography, describes his fruitless attempts over the years to rid himself of numerous negative behaviors. However, he found great success when he decided to focus on a single behavior until he had eliminated it from his life; then he moved on to tackle another behavior.

Instead of worrying about what people say of you, why not spend time trying to accomplish something they will admire.

Dale Carnegie

Internal Image

Trying to create a positive image with others without first building a firm foundation of self-awareness and self-confidence is the equivalent of using Band-Aids when we need antibiotics. It is an attempt to treat surface symptoms rather than creating overall good health.

Interpersonal effectiveness rests on sharing ourselves with others, and it is simply too threatening for most of us to share openly until we have a high level of comfort with our own identity. We cannot give others the acceptance they desperately need unless we first give that same acceptance to ourselves.

You may have been advised to adhere to the concept of "fake it till you make it?" That can be an excellent strategy in the short term. When you face a new situation and feel the almost inevitable butterflies despite your inner belief in your resources—take a deep breath and dive in. And just like a dip in a swimming pool, your ability and energy will pull you to the top.

However, unless your self-confidence is solidly in place, you can't fool all the people all the time. So why bother trying? Instead, you should invest your time and energy in re-establishing a strong sense of personal value and ability.

Assurance can be nurtured in a variety of ways. One important tool for revitalizing our sense of self-confidence is a review of past accomplishments. One way of doing this is to keep a success file as discussed in Chapter 1 of this book. Reviewing your past successes is a sure way of reinforcing your self-image.

Maintaining a positive attitude is important in every area of executive image, but nowhere is it more critical than in our attitude toward ourselves. Most of us—even the most seemingly successful—carry around a mental suitcase full of negative messages about ourselves. They may have come from parents, teachers, bosses, colleagues, or even our own imagination, but we have the capacity to recolor those messages and make positive beliefs our conscious choice. How to overcome negativism and maintain a more positive self-image will be discussed in Chapter 6.

We can control the image we present to others by creating within ourselves the internal image that will radiate from us to the outside world. The time and effort we devote to developing a positive, warm, welcoming image will result in our acceptance by others and strengthen the relationships we develop in our business and social lives.

Sum and Substance

> A person's first impression of us is the most powerful gatekeeper of all. It often determines whether that person will let us in, figuratively as well as literally.

> Maintaining a positive attitude is important in every area of executive image, but nowhere is it more critical than in our attitude toward ourselves.

> One of the greatest investments one can make is that of attaining a gracious manner, cordiality of bearing, generosity of feeling—the delightful art of pleasing.

> To make a good impression on telephone callers, answer the telephone promptly. While speaking with the caller, always let them talk until the complaint or message is fully explained. Do not interrupt. If you cannot help, give as much information as you can to enable the person to obtain the help needed.

> We should take a look at our facility with the eyes of a stranger. Ensure that the place of business reflects an image of professionalism.

> Our correspondence represents us to the public. Spelling and typographical errors can be interpreted as indicators of a careless or inefficient operation. Reread correspondence before mailing. Make sure all letters are error-free.

> Try to see yourself as others see you. Make an effort to identify and correct negative behaviors.

> Unless you have a mental attitude that is free of negativity

and look at each day as a blessing to be enjoyed and savored, you will have an unhappy and most likely unproductive life.

> You can improve our external image if you follow Dale Carnegie's principles of dealing with others:

1. Don't criticize, condemn, or complain.
2. Give honest, sincere appreciation.
3. Arouse in the other person an eager want.
4. Become genuinely interested in other people.
5. Smile.
6. Remember that a person's name is to that person the sweetest sound in any language.
7. Be a good listener. Encourage others to talk about themselves.
8. Talk in terms of the other person's interests.
9. Make the other person feel important—and do it sincerely.

5

WE ARE OUR OWN BEST
MOTIVATOR

There is no better uplifting habit than that of bearing a hopeful attitude, of believing that things are going to turn out well and not ill; that we are going to succeed and not fail; that no matter what may or may not happen, we are going to be happy. But unfortunately, there are times when we may dim our chances for success at the very outset by expecting that we are going to fail, thinking that the chances are against us. In other words, if our mental attitude is not favorable to the success that we are after, it could sometimes even attract failure. Success is achieved mentally first. If the mental attitude is one of doubt, the results will correspond. This is the time when we must motivate ourselves to overcome these doubts and move on to success.

When we begin to doubt ourselves, when we feel things are not going right, we must give ourselves a pep talk. We must say—and say it out loud—that we are going to succeed. There is a force in spoken word that is not stirred by going over the same mentally. When we hear them they make a more lasting impression upon the mind. We know we are more powerfully impressed and inspired by listening to a great lecture or sermon than if we read the same thing in print. We remember the spoken word even when we forget the cold print that is carried to the brain. It makes a deeper impression on the inner self.

> *By talking to yourself every hour of the day, you can direct yourself to think thoughts of courage and happiness, thoughts of power and peace. By talking to yourself about the things you have to be grateful for, you can fill your mind with thoughts that soar and sing.*
>
> *Dale Carnegie*

We must visualize ourselves as achieving our goals. Follow the lead of successful people—think only of success. It is our responsibility to keep ourselves motivated.

What Do We Mean By Motivation

Let's look carefully at this word. Another word beginning with the first three letters M-O-T that's related to motivation is MOTION. Motivation involves putting one into motion—getting one to get up and *do* something. Another word that begins with the letters M-O-T is MOTOR. The great automobile pioneer, R.E. Olds remarked that he likens a person to an automobile. He reminds us that the propelling power in a car is its motor—its internal combustion engine. Each of us has a motor inside of us—an engine that is combusting internally to keep us in motion.

Just as the engine in the car requires fuel to make it go, we also require fuel to make us go. Just as all auto engines do not use the same kind of fuel—some cars use gasoline, some electric batteries, some steam—the same fuel does not motivate all people. Some people's motivation is fueled by a desire to make money; some to gain fame; some to create great art or music; some to perfect an invention; some to gain happiness and satisfaction.

Who will provide the fuel to motivate us? It may come from an employer who compliments us for exceptional production. It may come from awards given by universities, foundations or governments. It may come from the profits of a company we created or manage. It may come from a variety of outside sources. But by far the men and women who are highly motivated to succeed provide their own fuel. The best motivator is within our own minds. If we believe in ourselves and in our inevitable success, we create within ourselves a never-ending source of fuel to put and keep us in motion.

We must concentrate our efforts in order to marshal the forces within us to continually fuel us to be self-motivated. It starts with our attitude. We must stimulate our mind and our body to put out the extra effort needed to succeed. We must have faith in ourselves and in our goals to provide the foundation to sustain our motivation. This will be the foundation on which we will conquer obstacles and disappointments.

We Can Make It Happen

The reason why so many people fail to realize their ideals is because they are not willing to do their part to make it real. Remember that the longing, the desire to do a certain thing, is merely sowing the seed of our ambition. If we stop at this we will get about as much harvest as the farmer would get if he put his seed in the ground without preparing the soil, without fertilizing it, and keeping the weeds down.

We must back up that which our heart longs to realize with an honest purpose to do our best, and a dead-in-earnest effort to make our vision real.

The mere holding of desire to do so, no matter how persistently or strongly we hold it, will not help us to realize our dreams. We must not only sow the seed of desire and longing, but we must also do all the nourishing, cultivating, caring for, or we will only reap a harvest of weeds. We see men and women everywhere reaping a weedy harvest from the sowing of mere longings. These people can scarcely get enough out of their harvest to keep them alive, simply because they took no care of their seed after the planting.

The constant nursing, cultivating the desire, the ambition, keeping our heart's longings and soul's yearnings alive, wholesome and healthy by actively working to achieve them, is the only way in which we can match our dreams with our realities.

The framework of our life structure is invisible. It is on the mental plane. We are laying the foundation for our future, fixing its limits by the expectations we are visualizing. We cannot do anything bigger than we plan to do. The mental plans always come first. Our future building will merely be carrying out in detail what we are visualizing today. The future is simply an extension of the present. Our thought habit, our prevailing mental attitude determines our place in life. We are locating ourselves, settling what we are to be. It will be broad, ever growing, ever expanding, or it will become narrower, more restricted and stolid, according to our mental plan, and according to the vision we maintain.

Successful people, without knowing it, encourage themselves by making their minds positive, so that they could be immune from all negative, discouraging thoughts. Holding the thought of success, the prosperity ideal, constantly dwelling upon one's successful future, expecting it, working for it—these are, whether we know it or not, success, or prosperity treatments.

Stay Focused

Dave Thomas, born and raised in poverty, never lost faith in himself. He created the Wendy's Restaurant chain and built it into one of the most successful fast-food chains in the United States.

When he was asked about what he believed was important to his success, he responded:

"Stay focused on meeting your goals. Don't be distracted by trying to accomplish too many things at the same time. Without a doubt, motivation is a key to success. You must keep in mind what motivates you and prove to yourself that this motivation is honest and worthwhile. If too many different things motivate you, you'll become tangled up in a maze of all kinds of conflicts. It is imperative to stay focused. Figure out what your motivations are going to be in the next step.

Keep dreaming, but don't daydream: if you do it for praise, you are likely to short-change yourself in the end. Look at success firsthand so that you know how it works and what it costs to achieve it."

However, we must be careful not to let praise make us complacent or worse. Some people let praise go to their heads and are so overly impressed with themselves that they feel they've already made it and stop pushing ahead.

The opposite is also true. When we are criticized or our ideas are rejected, we give up too easily. Sure, we will not always be right, but if we are convinced we are on the right track, we must keep trying to accomplish our goals.

Don't let other people's opinion about you or your dream influence your self-motivation. If they are negative, don't let them discourage you; if they are flattering, don't become complacent.

Inside ourselves, we have to have a clear understanding of where we want to go and confidence in our ability to get there.

Don't fuss about trifles. Don't permit little things—the mere termites of life—to ruin your happiness.

Dale Carnegie

Listen—Challenge—Assess

We should challenge the praise as well as the criticism. Of course, we have to listen to what our boss says about us, but it's also helpful to know what co-workers and subordinates say about us. Equally important is to listen to what our spouse, our father or our mother or our biggest customer or contributor may say about us.

Successful people balance what they hear about themselves from others. We're all human. The boss may pat us on the back because we really deserve it. Then again, the boss may be patting us on the back because he is about to give us an arduous assignment.

It isn't wise or even necessary to look for a sniper behind every tree. Successful people are not cynics. We can't go marching around the world like a hard-core skeptic saying: "Just give me the facts, ma'am."

Not every compliment is phony; not every criticism is a trumped-up charge. That's why we need our own sense of direction and confidence about where we're headed.

We must stay attuned to the truth that there are millions of yardsticks to measure life. Picking the right one at the right time could be one of the biggest clues to self-motivation that can ever be learned. Keep motivated until the goal is reached.

Enjoy Your Work

We spend most of our lives at work. It's certainly easier to sustain a high level of commitment if we enjoy our work. So, we should do everything we can to enjoy ourselves at work. Just remember while we are having fun—it is a place to work! The fun part should support the work part, not detract from it.

Intel's founder and long-time CEO, Andrew Grove strongly believes that self-motivation comes from the satisfaction we get from our accomplishments. Each triumph generates the confidence to seek greater triumphs; each accomplishment leads to more accomplishments. Let's listen to what he has to say about self-motivation:

He lists six pointers that have helped him maintain his self-motivation:

1. *Celebrate achievements*: Try to provide as many interim milestones as you can, and supplant the long-term drive toward reaching a major result with a series of shorter steps. Then, use the occasions when one of these is achieved as an event to celebrate in some small way. However, you shouldn't let any celebration become a distraction to others who work. Poke gentle fun at each other, including the boss. Keep internal competition light.

2. *Rotate jobs*: Even if you stay with one organization, make every effort to rotate jobs occasionally. Even in the best organizations, any job can become tedious after a while. It is harder to create and sustain energy and drive if you have the same job forever. Rotating jobs and working in different assignments is an excellent way to keep your work interesting and to enrich our skills.

3. *Enjoy the people you work with*: Our co-workers are usually very important to us. Our activities at work are almost always connected with theirs. To do our work well, we are dependent on them, and they on us. The people we work with are a major factor in determining whether or not our work is pleasant, congenial, and maybe even fun. Often, our feelings toward the people we work with determine if we like going to work each morning. Problems with co-workers can significantly affect our work and the work of our entire group. Sorting out such problems is important for the benefit of our productivity, as well as for our emotional well-being.

4. *Enjoy the work*: It is impossible to like all of it. Sometimes you will chafe under its unrelenting nature, other times you will be bored, but overall you must enjoy it. Try to see how what you do makes a difference, and approach the work with a bit of zest, maybe even playfulness. Doing so induces a bit of levity when it's most needed and leads to camaraderie.

5. *Be dedicated to the work:* Be dedicated to the end result, the output, not how to get to it or whose idea it is or whether you look good or not. Respect the work of those who respect their work. Nobody is unimportant; it takes many people to make an organization function.

6. *Be straight with everyone:* This isn't an easy principle to stick to. There are various reasons or excuses to compromise a little here or there. We may reason that people are not ready to hear the truth or the bad news, that the time isn't right, or whatever. Giving in to those tempting rationalizations usually leads to conduct that can be ethically wrong and will backfire every time. When stumped, stop and think the way through to meaningful answers.

Believe in what you are doing and in yourself, and want to get something accomplished.

                                             Dale Carnegie

Enrich Your Jobs

Behavioral scientists generally agree that although we are motivated by such external factors as recognition, appreciation, challenge and, of course, fair treatment, the most effective motivator of all is the work itself. If we find our jobs boring and unchallenging, no matter how good these external motivators may be, we will have a tough time motivating ourselves. On the other hand, if we enjoy our work so much that we can't wait to come in every morning and hate to leave each evening, there is little else we need do to keep ourselves motivated.

Unfortunately, a great percentage of jobs in industry today are merely routine, and it is difficult if not impossible, to generate excitement about them. One way to overcome this is to find a way to enrich the job.

Competing Against Ourselves

Denise, a computer operator, works at her home, entering data provided by her employer into computer programs, developing spreadsheets and related assignments.

Once she mastered the techniques, she was able to perform them accurately and meet deadlines readily. After doing this for several months, it became so routine that Denise was easily bored and instead of looking forward to her assignments, she dreaded them and would find excuses to postpone starting her workday.

When her boss rejected her request for more varied work, she tried to find some way to overcome her apathy: "I'm a competitor," she told herself, "if I were in a contest to finish my work faster than my rivals, I would be excited about it. But as I have no rivals, I have to compete against myself."

When she received her next assignment, she timed each phase of it, checked it and corrected errors, and recorded it.

She continued this until she established a norm that factored in variations in the assignments and then competed against this norm on each assignment. The challenge of this competition re-motivated her and she's now thinking of other challenges to build into the job to reinforce her self-motivation.

We Can't Always Do It Alone

When Jennifer was hired as a claims processing clerk at the Liability Insurance Company, she found her job boring and stifling. The claims processing operation was an "assembly line." Each clerk checked a section of the claims form, passed it to the next clerk, who checked the next section, and so on. If an error or question on interpretation was discovered, it was put aside for handling by a specialist. From an operational viewpoint, this was highly efficient. However, it made the work dull and unchallenging. Jennifer spoke to her supervisor about it and suggested that the job would not only be more interesting but more efficient if it could be enlarged. Her supervisor agreed and together they devised a new system. The "assembly line" was replaced by a system in which each clerk checked the entire form, corrected errors and sought interpretations. This required added training and did slow the work down in the beginning, but it paid off not only for Jennifer, but also for the entire department by developing a highly motivated team of workers who were really interested in their jobs. Turnover, absenteeism, and dissatisfaction were significantly reduced, and once the system was fully established, speed and accuracy were increased.

Never Let Discouragement Dominate

One of the most successful men in American industrial history was Charles M. Schwab. Ever since he was a poor boy starting in life he gave himself success treatments.

He never let the determination to be successful and prosperous fade from his mind. If he had allowed himself to yield to the many discouragements he faced, he would never have become a great industrialist. He always triumphed over these negative, destructive, discouraging thoughts, by insisting on holding to the ideal of prosperity and success.

Your ideas, your visions, your resolutions come to you fresh every day. Act now. Another inspiration, new ideas may come tomorrow, but today you should carry out the inspiration of the day.

A vision flashes across the artist's mind with lightning-like rapidity. She keeps turning it over and over in her mind. It takes possession of her very soul, but she is not in her studio, or it is not convenient to put her vision upon canvas, and the picture gradually fades from her mind.

A strong, vigorous conception flashes into the brain of the writer, and he has an almost irresistible impulse to seize his pen and transfer the beautiful images and the fascinating conception to paper; but it is not convenient at the moment, and, while it seems almost impossible to wait, he postpones the writing. The images and the conception keep haunting him, but he still postpones. Finally, the visions grow dimmer and dimmer, and at last fade away and are lost forever.

It is the execution of a plan that creates success. Almost

anybody can resolve to do a great thing; it is only the strong determined character that puts the resolve into execution.

Of course, there are times when the idea or impulse comes at a time when it is not possible to execute it. We are on a long plane flight; we are in the midst of another major project; the idea comes to us in the middle of the night.

Great ideas need not die. Benjamin Franklin always had a pad and pencil handy—in his pocket, at his bedside, on his desk—in which he jotted down ideas as they came to him. He made a point to review these the moment he had time and to take action as soon as he could. Today we can speak or type our ideas into our PDA's or Blackberry's no matter where we may be.

Success Comes From Within

No human being has ever succeeded in trying to be somebody else, even if that person was a success. Success cannot be copied; it cannot be successfully imitated. It is an original force—an individual creation.

If we try to be somebody else and to express somebody else instead of ourselves, we are likely to fail. Power comes from within or from nowhere. We must be ourselves. We must listen to the voice within. There is room for improvement in every profession, in every trade, and in every business. The world wants people who can do things in new and better ways. Don't think, because a plan or idea has no precedent, or because you are young and inexperienced, that you will not get a hearing. If you have anything new and valuable to give to the world, it will be heard and considered. If you dare to think your own thoughts and originate your own methods, if you are not afraid to be yourself, and are not a copy of someone else, you will be recognized. Nothing else will attract the attention of an employer or the rest of the world as quickly as originality and unique ways of doing things, especially if they are effective.

Control Your Thoughts

Considering that mind governs everything in our world, we must channel it to be self-motivated. In recent years, the control of thought, and its use to modify character, to change even external surroundings, or at least their effect on one's self, and to bring about health, happiness, and success, have been more and more studied and understood.

When a task to be done consists largely or wholly of mental acts—as do most ways to gain success—how much greater must be the determining power of the thought. The conquerors of the world, whether on battlefields, in trade or in moral struggles, have won by the attitude of mind in which they motivated themselves to do the work they had to do.

Once we realize the inherent capacity for great things, convinced that we are intended to succeed, and that we can control our minds, we can revolutionize our lives and abolish most of our ills and troubles.

You can't get anywhere in this world without wanting to do something.

Dale Carnegie

We cannot expect ourselves to become well and strong by always thinking and talking about our bad health, or assuming that we will never be robust. Neither can we expect our executive faculties to be strong and vigorous if we perpetually doubt our ability to do what we undertake. Nothing so weakens the mind and renders it totally unfit for effective thinking as the constant acknowledgment of weakness, or doubting of our ability to accomplish our goals.

There can be no more important study, no higher duty owed to ourselves, than the understanding of thought-control and of self-motivation, which results in self-development. Perhaps because thought in itself is intangible, and most of us really have so little control over it, there is an impression that directing our minds is a difficult and mysterious affair, something that requires hard study, leisure, and book knowledge to accomplish. Nothing is further from the truth. Whatever the level of our education, the level of our culture, or however busy we may be, all of us have within ourselves all that is required and all the time needed to remake our intellectual nature, our character, and our life.

Every person will have a different task, different problems to solve, and different results to aim at, but the process is practically the same, and the transformation is no more impossible for one than for another.

Let us concentrate on our goal—see it in our minds as though it were already won, while we are all the while intensely conscious of moving nearer to its achievement. One by one obstacles will vanish, and what seemed once too hard for human strength to accomplish appears now plain and even simple. The greatest need of all is to keep the goal in sight and not let interest flag or inward vision waver from the very place in which we most desire to be engaged, in the very work we would love best to accomplish.

There is No Substitute For Work

Thinking about success is not enough. Outward work must follow inward contemplation. True meditation does not absolve us from the need of making effort, but it is a means for revealing to us what efforts we need to make and how to make them. Hold the thought and get to work. Start by holding the right thought, that is, the right mental attitude toward your goals, and then hustle for all you are worth to make your dream come true.

As a matter of fact, nothing happens until the mind moves it. Nothing starts in this world until thought precedes the action. Thought moves everything that is. It is the prime mover of the things we perceive through the senses.

It is the constant thinking about our business, the planning of ways and means to extend it, the schemes for its improvement and betterment that really enlarge it. Our thoughts, our planning, our enthusiasm, our dreaming of success—all these are vital forces that increases the power of our mental magnet to attract the thing we long for.

No matter what the nature of our work or our business, the habit of holding in mind the prosperous ideal, the happiness ideal, the good luck ideal, sets the mind in the direction of these ideals and helps wonderfully in our efforts to always face the light under all circumstances. This mental attitude builds up our confidence in ourselves. When we think more of ourselves, we will be self-motivated and see greater possibilities ahead.

Commitment

One of the most effective ways to motivate ourselves is to be firmly committed to what we desire to accomplish. When things go wrong, when obstacles seem unconquerable, when discouragement raises its face, our commitment will motivate us to keep up the fight.

Champions never say: "It can't be done." They try to find a way to overcome the obstacles. Even champions don't always win, but they never lose without first trying to win because they are committed to win.

Thinking

The basic component of self-motivation is thinking. Before commencing the project, it is essential that it be thought out. A superb performer thinks out how the job will be performed before its beginning.

In a complex operation, as much time must often be given to the planning as to the work itself. Before making a sales call, the successful sales representative thinks carefully about all of the possible problems that may develop and how they can be handled. Executives think about every ramification any of their decisions may cause before making that decision. This is also true of top performers in the theater, cinema, television or in sports. Norman Strauss, an industrial painting contractor in New York City, was faced with a major problem. His bid for the job of painting Madison Square Garden, New York's largest indoor sports arena was due by the end of the week.

The major problem was painting the ceiling, which was 110 feet above the first floor. The usual way of reaching the ceiling was constructing a pipe platform on which the painters would stand when they sprayed the ceiling. The cost of building the platform would be the same for all bidders. The only way to significantly reduce the bid would be to find some way to paint the ceiling without building the pipe platform. Everybody knew this couldn't be done, so why bother?

But Norman Strauss did not give up easily. He was committed to achieve success and ceaselessly devoted himself to solve the problem. On the way home that evening, Norman noticed an electric company repainting a high street light. To reach this light, they were using a "cherry picker," a truck with an elevator on its roof that could be raised to various heights. "Why not use cherry pickers to reach the ceiling at the Garden," Norman thought. The next day investigation brought out that it was feasible and economical. Strauss was able to submit a significantly lower bid than his competitors and obtained the job.

Self-Motivation Must Be Ongoing

Everyone who wants to keep growing, increase his ability, and multiply his talent, must strive to outdo his past records. They must be ready to take advantage of every legitimate opportunity, for personal improvement, for advancement in their business or profession.

Whatever anyone's business is, there is only one way to insure progress and that is by constantly endeavoring to better one's previous records. Spasmodic effort, no matter how vigorous, won't do it. It is the daily progress that counts most in the final averaging.

That we did a fine piece of work, a superb thing yesterday is no reason why we should rest on our laurels today. It should rather spur us to go ahead of it tomorrow.

We must never allow ourselves or anyone else to shake our confidence in ourselves, or to destroy our self-reliance, for this is the very foundation of all great achievement. When that is gone, our whole structure falls; as long as we have it, there is hope for us. Confidence unbounded, unshaken faith in ourselves, which even amounts to boldness at times, is absolutely necessary in all great undertakings.

Sum and Substance

> Follow the lead of successful people—think success-thoughts.

> The best motivator is within our own minds. If we believe in ourselves and in our inevitable success, we create within ourselves a never-ending self-motivating mechanism.

> Don't let other people's opinions about you or your dream influence your self-motivation. If they are negative, don't let it discourage you; if they are flattering, don't become complacent.

> If you enjoy your work so much that you can't wait to come in every morning and hate to leave each evening, there is little else that you need to do to keep yourself motivated.

> If you dare to think your own thought and originate your own methods, if you are not afraid to be yourself, and are not a copy of someone else, you will be quickly recognized.

> All of us have within ourselves all the time and capacity needed to remake our intellectual nature, our character, and our lives.
> Be firmly committed to what you desire to accomplish. When things go wrong, when obstacles seem unconquerable; when discouragement raises its face, your commitment will motivate you to keep up the fight.

6

....

ACCENTUATE THE POSITIVE

Maintaining a positive attitude is important in every area of the image we project, but nowhere is it more critical than in our attitude toward ourselves. Eleanor Roosevelt is often quoted as saying: "No one can make you feel inferior without your permission."

Most of us—even the most seemingly successful—carry around a mental suitcase full of negative messages about ourselves. Sometimes we do get positive pictures of ourselves from others. As suggested in Chapter 1—hold on to them! Start a file folder or notebook to collect acknowledgment, thank-you notes, stellar reviews, good evaluations, and other tangible evidence of your abilities.

Maintain a Hopeful Attitude

There is nothing else so helpful as the carrying of an optimistic, expectant attitude—the attitude that always looks for and expects the best, the highest, the happiest—and never allowing oneself to get into a pessimistic, discouraged mood.

We must believe with all our heart that we will do what we were made to do. Never for an instant harbor a doubt of it. We must entertain only "thought-friends"—ideals of the thing we are determined to achieve. We must reject all "thought-enemies"—all discouraging moods, everything which would even suggest failure or unhappiness.

It does not matter what we are trying to do or who we are trying to be, so long as we always assume an expectant, hopeful, optimistic attitude regarding it. This will put us on the road to grow all our faculties, and improve.

> *It isn't what you have, or who you are, or where you are, or what you are doing that makes you happy or unhappy. It is what you think about.*
>
> *Dale Carnegie*

Great Achievers Are Positive Thinkers

That one quality of persistently holding the faith in themselves, and never allowing anything to weaken their belief, has been the underlying principle of all great achievers. The great majority of men and women who have given civilization a great uplift started poor, and for many dark years saw no hope of accomplishing their ambition, but they kept on working and believing that somehow a way would be opened. Think of what this attitude of hopefulness and faith has done for the world's great inventors! How most of them plodded on through many years of dry, dreary drudgery before the light came. And the light probably would have never come but for their faith, hope, and persistent endeavor.

There is no other habit which brings so much value to our lives than always expecting the best ought to happen to us, and that of taking for granted that we ought to succeed in whatever task we undertake.

Many people foil their chances of success at the very outset by expecting that they are going to fail—thinking that the chances are against them. In other words, their mental attitude is not favorable to success, which they are after. It sometimes even attracts failure. Success is achieved mentally first. If the mental attitude is one of doubt, the results will correspond. There must be persistent faith and continuous confidence, in order to win.

A wavering, doubting mind brings wavering, doubting results.

Strive for the Rewards of Success

Many people are motivated by tangible rewards. They strongly desire to own a beautiful home, drive a luxury car, dine in expensive restaurants, stay at posh resorts—just be rich.

J. P. Morgan was one of the richest men of his generation. When asked why he continued to be motivated by money when he already had every luxury money can buy, he responded: "Money is the scorecard by which I measure my success. I don't need the money for its own sake, but by continuing to work to increase my wealth, I am proving to myself that I continue to be an achiever."

When Teddy L., one of the top ten sales representatives for his company was asked what motivated him to get out day after day and make call after call, he responded that he came from a poor family, lived in a cold-water flat in a tenement house all of his childhood. "I always dreamed," he said, "that one day I would own a house, a home like those the rich people in my town lived in. When I started selling, I was a mediocre salesman. I made just enough sales to meet my quotas and make a fair income to afford a comfortable apartment. Then one day I drove through the part of town where the rich people lived. I recalled my dream of having a house like theirs. I resolved then and there to make enough money to buy such a home."

"That day I went to a real estate office and obtained photographs of some of the houses in that neighborhood that were for sale. I tacked one of them on the table next to my bed; pasted another on my bathroom mirror; clipped another on the visor in my car. Every night before I went to bed, I looked at the picture; every morning when I shaved, I looked at the picture; every day as I drove to see my customers, I looked at the picture. I resolved that one day I would buy a house like the ones in those photos."

"I could visualize myself and my family living in that house. I could see us dining in the large dining room; relaxing in the parlor; each of my children playing in his own room; my wife cooking in a modern kitchen; all of us enjoying the tree-shaded lawn. These thoughts motivated me to press harder at each sales call; to make one more call each day; to learn and apply more effective sales approaches."

"Over the next few months my sales increased. Within a year my income had doubled and a year later, I was able to buy my dream house."

Rewards do not have to be tangible. Some people seek rewards in the satisfaction of accomplishing their dreams. John Burroughs was a successful man, but he was not a rich man. He lived in modest circumstances. Money was not important to him. He was probably the greatest naturalist of his time. He devoted his life to studying and writing about nature.

He received his reward from the great satisfaction of being among the wonders of nature. He said: "I live to broaden and enjoy my own life, believing that in doing so, I am doing what is best for everyone. If I ran after birds only to write about them, I should never have written anything that anyone else would have cared to read. I must write from sympathy and love—that is for enjoyment—or not at all. The work is pleasure and hence, the result gives pleasure."

By keeping in the front of our minds the reward we seek whether it is tangible—a new car, a fine home, money for our retirement, or intangible—satisfaction of accomplishing our dream, we will be motivated to work hard to achieve that goal and reap that reward.

Don't Look For Trouble

Some people always look at the dark side of every situation. Considering how unprofitable such efforts are, it is surprising how many people make a business of looking for trouble, or cultivating and coaxing it. No one ever looked for trouble yet found plenty of it. This is because one can make trouble out of anything if the mind is set that way. It is said that during the development of the West, in the days of rough frontier life, the men who always went armed with pistols, revolvers, and bowie-knives always got into difficulties, while the men who never carried arms, but trusted their own good sense, self-control, tact and humor, rarely got into trouble. The incident that meant a shooting affray to the armed men was merely a joke to the more sensible unarmed men. It is just so with the seekers of ordinary trouble. By constantly holding discouraged, dejected, melancholy, gloomy thoughts, they make themselves receptive to all that depresses and destroys. What to a cheerful person would be a trifling incident, to be laughed at and dismissed from the mind, becomes in the mind of the croaker, a thing of dread, an occasion for gloom and foreboding.

Imagination wrongly used, is one of our worst foes. There are people who live in perpetual unhappiness and discomfort because they imagine they are being abused, slighted, neglected, and talked about. They think of themselves as a target of all sorts of evils, being the object of envy, jealously, and all kinds of ill will. Most such ideas are delusions and have no reality whatsoever. This is the most unfortunate state of mind to get into. It kills happiness, it demoralizes usefulness, it throws the mind out of harmony, and life itself becomes unsatisfactory.

People who think such thoughts make themselves perpetually wretched by surrounding themselves with an atmosphere reeking with pessimism. It is as if they are always wearing dark glasses, which makes everything around them seem draped in mourning; they see nothing but black. There is nothing cheerful or bright in their world.

These people have talked poverty, failure, hard luck, fate, and hard times so long that their entire being is imbued with pessimism.

The cheerful qualities of the mind have atrophied from neglect and disuse, while their pessimistic tendencies have been so overdeveloped that their minds cannot regain a normal, healthy, cheerful balance.

These people carry a gloomy, disagreeable, uncomfortable influence with them wherever they go. Nobody likes to converse with them, because they are always telling their stories of hard luck and misfortune. With them, times are always hard, money scarce, and society "going to the bad." After a while they become pessimistic cranks with morbid minds, and people avoid them.

The most injurious and unpleasant way of looking for trouble is faultfinding, or continual criticism of other persons. Some people are never generous, never magnanimous toward others. They are stingy of their praise, rarely recognize merit in others, and are critical of their every act.

If you believe in what you are doing, then let nothing hold you up in your work. Much of the best work of the world has been done against seeming impossibilities.

Dale Carnegie

Don't Criticize, Condemn or Complain

We should make up our minds firmly at the very outset in life that we will not criticize or condemn others, or find fault with their mistakes and shortcomings. Faultfinding, indulging in sarcasm and irony, picking flaws in everything and everybody, looking for things to condemn instead of praise is a very dangerous habit to possess. It is like a deadly worm that gnaws at the heart of the rosebud or fruit, and will make life gnarled, distorted, and bitter.

No life can be harmonious and happy after this blighting habit is once formed. Those who always look for something to condemn ruin their own character and destroy their normal integrity.

We all like sunshiny, bright, cheerful, hopeful people; nobody likes the grumbler, the faultfinder, the backbiter or the slanderer. The great American philosopher, Ralph Waldo Emerson wrote: "the world likes the man who sees longevity in his causes and good in the future, who believes the best and not the worst of people."

Idle gossipers, serpent tongues, people who give vent to their tempers get only momentary satisfaction, and even afterward they are tormented by their own ugly natures and then wonder why people enjoy their lives and they do not enjoy theirs.

It is just as easy to go through life looking for the good and the beautiful, instead of the ugly; for the noble instead of the ignoble; for the bright and cheerful instead of the dark and gloomy; the hopeful instead of the despairing; to see the bright side instead of the dark side. To set our face always toward the sunlight is just as easy as to always see the shadows, and it makes all the difference in our character between content and discontent, between happiness and misery, between prosperity and adversity, between success and failure.

Let us learn to look for the light, positively refuse to harbor shadows and blot, negative images. Let us hold to those things that give pleasure, that are helpful and inspiring, in order to change our whole way of looking at things, and transform our personality in a very short time.

Optimism Leads to Achievement

Helen Keller, the blind and deaf woman who had every reason to bemoan her fate and be pessimistic said: "Optimism is the faith that leads to achievement, nothing can be done without hope."

The people who have succeeded in life have always been cheerful and hopeful people, who went about their business with a smile on their faces, and took the changes and chances of this mortal life as mature adults, facing rough and smooth phases of life alike.

Optimistic people have a creative power that pessimistic people never possess. There is nothing which will so completely sweeten life and take out its drudgery, nothing that will so effectively ease the jolts on the road, as a sunny, hopeful, optimistic disposition. With the same mental ability, the optimistic thinker has infinitely more power than the despondent, gloomy pessimist. Optimism is a perpetual lubricator of the mind; it is the oil of gladness that drives out friction, worries, anxieties, and disagreeable experiences. The life machinery of an optimist does not wear out as rapidly as people whose moods and temper scour, throwing the entire machinery out of harmony.

Change Negativism Into Positivism

Negativism never accomplish anything. There is no life in a negative person; nothing but deterioration, destruction, and death. Negativism is a great enemy of those who seek success. People who are always talking down to everyone, who are always complaining of hard times and bad business, poor health and poverty, attract all the destructive, negative influences about them, and neutralize all of their endeavors.

The creative principles cannot live in a negative, destructive atmosphere, and no single achievement can take place there. Therefore, negative people are always on the downgrade, always turning out failures. They lose the power of affirmation, and drift, unable to get ahead.

Negativism will paralyze ambition; poison our life; rob us of power. They will kill our self-confidence until we become victims of the situation instead of masters of it. The power to do is largely a question of self-faith and self-confidence. No matter what we undertake, we can never do it until we think we can. We will never master it until we first feel the mastery and do the deed in our minds. It must be thought out or it can never be wrought out. It must be a mentally accomplished before it can be a materially accomplished.

Many people scatter thoughts of fear, doubt, and failure, wherever they go; these take root in minds that might otherwise be free from them and therefore happy, confident, and successful.

Be sure that when you hold an evil or discordant thought toward another, something is wrong in your mind. You should call: "Halt! About face!" Look toward the sunlight; determine that if you cannot do any good in the world, you will not scatter seeds of poison and hatred.

If you hold kindly, charitable, magnanimous, loving thoughts toward everybody, you will not depress or hinder them, but will scatter sunshine and gladness instead of sadness and shadow; project help and encouragement instead of discouragement.

There are people who are always radiating thoughts of success, good health, joy, scattering sunshine wherever they go. These are the helpers of the world, the lighteners of burdens, and the people who ease the jolts of life and soothe the wounded and give solace to the discouraged.

You can be like them by learning to radiate joy, not stingy, or meanly, but generously. You must learn to emit gladness without reserve, to express it in the home, on the street, in the car, in the store, everywhere.

The best way to keep out darkness is to keep the life filled with light; to keep out negative thoughts, keep it filled with harmony; to shut out error, keep the mind filled with truth; to shut out ugliness, contemplate beauty and loveliness; to get rid of all that is sour and unwholesome, and contemplate all that is sweet and wholesome. Opposite thoughts cannot occupy the mind at the same time.

We should form the habit of erasing from the mind all disagreeable, unhealthy, death-dealing thoughts. We should start out every morning with a clean slate, blotting out from our mental gallery all discordant pictures, replacing them with the harmonious, uplifting, life-giving ones.

When Frank A., a successful Chicago marketing executive, was asked by a television interviewer how he "kept his cool" under the day to day pressures of his job, he responded that he never allowed himself to go to his office in the morning until he has put his mind into perfect harmony with the world.

If he had the slightest feeling of envy or jealousy, if he felt selfish or unfair, without the right attitude toward his partner or any of his employees, he simply did not go to work until his instrument was in tune, until his mind was clear of any form of discord. He said he discovered that if he starts out in the morning with a right attitude of mind toward everybody, he would infinitely get more out of his day than otherwise; that whenever he allowed himself to go to work in the past with negative thoughts dominating his mind, he did not obtain nearly as good results and he made those about him unhappy, to say nothing of the increased wear and tear upon himself.

Substitute Harmony For Discord

No matter whether we feel positive or not, we must affirm that we *do* feel positive, that we *will* feel positive, and that we are in a position to do our best to act positively. Say it deliberately, affirm it vigorously, and it will come true.

As the Bible says: "As a man thinketh in his heart, so is he." Many people who do only mediocre things really have a great deal of ability, but are so sensitive to friction that they cannot do effective work. If they only had someone to steer them, to plan for them, to keep discord away from them and help them to create harmony, they could do remarkable things. As most of us do not have such a "guardian angel," we must acquire this for ourselves. No one can exercise it for us, and we cannot accomplish anything very great in this world unless we are able to avoid succumbing to the thousand and one things that distract us. Unfortunately, there are times when we are disagreeable and irritable. This is not our real nature. The cause of our irritability and lack of harmony is because we are tired or stressed. We must learn to recognize when this may happen and make every effort to overcome it.

We often see people who have become absolutely unbearable, after a year of hard work, completely revolutionized when they return from a holiday or a vacation. They do not seem like the same people that they were before they went away. The trifles that would throw them into a fit of passion before their vacation do not affect them at all now.

As a squeaking axle indicates the want of a lubricant, friction or discord anywhere in the physical economy is a warning that something is wrong. A dispute at the breakfast table, or any little wrangling in the morning may destroy the peace of the household for the entire day. A moment's hot temper may destroy a very dear friendship for life.

In pursuing our daily activities, we force ourselves to work when we are tired and out of tune; when our spontaneity is gone, and our vital standards are low. We force ourselves by all sorts of stimulants and will power. We strain the delicate mechanism or our minds and bodies until they are often prematurely injured, overstrained, ruined for their finest work.

We ought to school ourselves in a way that no matter what happens we would not lose our presence of mind, and balance. We should always keep our equilibrium so as to be able, no matter what happens, to do the levelheaded thing, the wise thing, the right thing.

Remember happiness doesn't depend upon who you are or what you have; it depends solely on what you think.

Dale Carnegie

Self-Defeating Thought Patterns

Many times we find ourselves doubting our abilities and our accomplishments due to our lack of self-confidence and negative surroundings. To make matters worse, we emphasize and dwell on what others think in order to determine how we feel about our ability and ourselves. This mindset can lead us to avoid taking risks due to fear of failure. This kind of reinforcement can lead us to put ourselves down, discount positive feedback and subscribe to harmful assumptions that perpetuate self-defeating thought patterns and a negative attitude. Some self-defeating thought patterns include:

Extreme thinking

When things become all or nothing and there is no middle ground. We tend to think: "I am a total failure when my performance is not perfect."

Imminent disaster

Disaster lurks around in every corner and comes to be expected. For example, a single negative detail, piece of criticism, or passing comment darkens all reality. Our concern: "I blew the small presentation and now I'll never get promoted."

Magnification of the negative

Good things don't count nearly as much as bad ones. This leads us to feel: "I know I had the best sales record the last three months, but coming in third this month makes me feel terrible about myself."

Overemphasis on "should" statements

"Should" statements are meant to push us toward the perfect scenario. In order to achieve what should be, we must first assess the *as is* situation. Once this is established, we can plan on how to get from where we are now to the "should be." Just because we are not as yet close to the "should be" we should not be detered from moving forward and working toward it.

Boxing in

Boxing ourselves is a non-rational thought process in which we blame ourselves. It is easy to let initial defeats determine our long-term mindset. Don't fall into the trap of thinking: "I am a failure and I'll never be anything else."

Difficulty accepting compliments

When receiving a compliment, we should accept it and not mitigate it with comments like: "You like this presentation? It was nothing. I have done better." Say: "Thank you." In this way you indicate to the compliment giver that you appreciate his or her comments, but more importantly, you reinforce your own self-confidence and self-image.

Strategies for Developing Confidence

These self-defeating thoughts can turn us from optimists to pessimists, from positive to negative thinkers, from success oriented to defeat doomed. The following strategies may help us overcome self-defeating thought patterns:

Self-acceptance

Self-acceptance comes from our ability to accept ourselves as human beings while focusing on our positive sides—our qualities, strengths, and traits—that make us who we are. When our focus is upon these areas of our self-image both confidence and self-esteem are positively influenced. It is all too common for people to focus upon their weaknesses instead of their strengths and therefore do more damage than good. We must help ourselves, and others to focus on the positive pictures.

Self-respect

The key here is to focus on our past success and achievements and to respect ourselves for the good we have done in the past. It is far easier to dwell on failures since others are only too eager to point them out to us. When we spend our time contemplating the many successes we all have in our lives, our perspective changes, followed by our confidence.

Thought Control

There can be no better study, no higher duty owed to ourselves than that of thought-control, which results in self-development. Perhaps because thought in itself is intangible, and most of us really have so little control over it, there is an impression that direction of mind's action is a difficult and complex affair, something that requires hard study, leisure, and book knowledge to accomplish. Nothing is further from the truth. We have within ourselves all that is required, and all the time needed, to remake our intellectual nature, our character, and practically our entire life.

Concentrate on the goal

We must concentrate on our committed goal, to see before the mental eye the prize as though it were already won. Then, one by one obstacles will vanish, and what once seemed too hard for us to accomplish would now appear plain and even simple. The greatest need of all is to keep the goal in sight and not let interest flag or inward vision waver.

Sum and Substance

> There is no better uplifting habit than that of bearing a hopeful attitude, of believing that things are going to turn out well and not ill; that we are going to succeed and not fail; that no matter what may or may not happen, we are going to be happy.

> Whatever comes to us in life we create first in our minds. As the building is a reality in all its details in the architect's mind before a stone or brick is laid, so we create everything mentally that later becomes a reality with our achievement.

> By mental visualization of the ideal as vividly and sharply as possible will make our dream come true. By imagining something we truly want with the whole mind, and heart, and soul, by imagining it as if it were already true, will move it to its fruition.

> We need to tell our subconscious exactly what we want. When we know what our true desire really is, our subconscious mind will propel us unerringly towards it. We must believe

that what we want can happen. We must believe that it will happen.

> All great achievers have had the quality of holding the persistently faith in themselves, and never allowing anything to weaken the belief that somehow they will accomplish what they undertook.

> Success is achieved mentally first. If the mental attitude is one of doubt, the results will correspond. There must be persistent faith and continuous confidence in order to win. A wavering, doubting mind brings wavering, doubting results.

> There is no other habit which would bring as much value to our lives as that of always expecting the best of taking it for granted that we are going to win in whatever we undertake.

> The reason why so many people fail to realize their ideals is that they are not willing to do their part to make it real. The longing, the desire to do a certain thing, is merely sowing the seed of our ambition. We must back up that which our heart longs to realize with an honest purpose to do our best and an earnest effort to make our vision real.

> Power comes from within or from nowhere. Listen to the voice within. There is room for improvement in every profession, in every trade, and in every business. The world wants people who can do things in new and better ways. Because our plan or idea has no precedent, or because we are young and inexperienced, we fear that we will not get a hearing. If we have anything new and valuable to give to the world, we will be heard and followed.

> Until we erase "fate" and "can't" and "doubt" from our vocabulary, we cannot rise. We cannot get strong while we

harbor convictions of our weakness or be happy while we dwell on our miseries or misfortunes.

> Be firmly committed to what you desire to accomplish. When things go wrong, when obstacles seem unconquerable, when discouragement raises its face, our commitment will motivate us to keep up the fight.

7

....

BE COURAGEOUS

The determination to succeed and the willpower to exert the energy and time, to sacrifice immediate pleasures, to fight opposition, to overcome obstacles and challenges in the pursuit of our goals, is an essential ingredient on the road to success.

Successful people have the courage to put their ideas into effect, the willingness to put their money, their efforts, their emotions into an enterprise in which they truly believe.

While these achievers display astonishing boldness, they are not reckless gamblers. They prepare their moves with a ferocious intensity, and then fly into action.

We must take risks if we want to be better than average people. We cannot always "play it safe." Security is mostly a superstition. It does not exist in nature, nor do people in general experience it. Striving to avoid all danger can end up being no safer in the long run than outright exposure. Life is either a daring adventure, or nothing.

The great US Supreme Court Justice, Oliver Wendell Holmes puts it this way: "Security is an illusion, and repose is not the destiny of man."

Whether it be in the world of business, sports, or politics, the men and women who have achieved great success have manifested their courage by defying the odds, by jumping into dangerous waters, by making creative decisions; they have risked losing all because they never doubted that they would succeed.

The most dangerous situation in the world is that of people who have given up, who do not try to help themselves, who make no efforts to rise. No power in the world can do all the lifting. God Himself will not help those who will not help themselves. The determination to succeed is the ladder of our ascent. We must make sure that there are no weak rungs in our ladder.

We must develop the strength of our resolution. Unless our convictions are on the surface, we stand for nothing. Nobody will have confidence in us. Unless conviction takes hold of one's very being, there will be very little achievement in life.

Approach new experiences as opportunities to learn rather than occasions to win or lose. Doing so opens us up to new possibilities and can increase our sense of self-acceptance. Not doing so turns every possibility into an opportunity for failure, and inhibits personal growth.

Take a chance! All life is a chance. The man who goes furthest is generally the one who is willing to do and dare. The "sure thing" boat never gets far from shore.

Dale Carnegie

Become Involved

When Alex was a boy in Chicago, he and his friends were ardent Cubs fans. They were elated when their team won and unhappy when they lost. Alex felt the losses more than his friends. When the Cubs lost, he would be deeply depressed. After a particularly bad season, Alex thought: "It isn't worth it. I'm never going to get so involved with a team that I can feel this bad." From that time on he refused to commit himself to the Cubs or any team in any sport.

Alex carried this concept into all aspects of his life. His philosophy was: "If I don't become too involved, I can never be hurt." In his school and in his jobs, he always took the middle course. Indeed, Alex never did get hurt, but neither did he ever have any real joys. By not taking the chance that someone or something he supported might not work out, he avoided the "agony of defeat," but never experienced "the thrill of victory."

Be Committed

Dr. Robert Jarvik worked for years to develop an artificial heart. It had never been done and he was told by colleagues and other "experts" that it never could be done. Jarvik was not only willing to take the chance that all of his work would be for naught, but he was committed to keep trying until he did succeed.

Inventors and innovators have always faced ridicule. We have read how Fulton's steamboat was dubbed "Fulton's FOLLY" and how the first automobiles were greeted with the scornful accusation—"Get a horse." Edison had tried and failed hundreds of times before succeeding in inventing the light bulb. Inventors must commit themselves and be willing to suffer the taunts of others and bear the many doubts and disappointments of defeat after defeat before reaching their goals.

Don't Fear Dissent

Liz was upset. All of the people in the group seemed to agree that the idea under discussion would solve their problem. If she expressed her disagreement, the others might consider her stupid, or worse, a rebel. The safe course was to remain silent, but Liz was sure that the group had overlooked an important aspect of the problem. Liz took the risk of being rejected, but by saying what she believed, she enabled the group to look at the problem from a different angle and come to a more effective conclusion.

Taking risks does not mean one must be a daredevil. Reasonable people take reasonable risks, but by definition, a risk may not succeed. Successful business executives take risks with every decision they make. However, they maximize their chance of success by careful research and analysis before making the decision. But when that decision finally has to be made, the manager must be willing to risk the possible loss of money, time, energy and emotion. Without risk, there is no possibility of gain.

Prepare to Accept the Worst

In chapter 1, we learned that Dale Carnegie in his book *How to Stop Worrying and Start Living*, advised that when facing trouble: "Ask yourself: What is the worst that can possibly happen?" "Prepare to accept the worst; then try to improve on it."

We should use these principles when we have to make a decision on whether or not to take a chance on an innovative, radical or just different approach to a problem.

We must all take risks if we want to make progress in our jobs and in our lives. By careful analysis we can minimize the chances of failure, but we can never eliminate it. Without pain there is no gain. By always playing it safe, we may avoid that pain, but we will never feel the great joy and satisfaction that results from overcoming the obstacles and reaching our goals.

Most of us have far more courage than we ever dreamed we possessed.

Dale Carnegie

Have Faith

We cannot hope to succeed if we are timid, lack faith in ourselves, and do not have the courage of our convictions. We cannot always seek for certainty before we venture. Self-distrust is the cause of most of our failures. In the assurance of strength there is strength, and they are the weakest, who have no faith in themselves or their powers.

The failure, which overtakes so many merchants, is due, not so much to their lack of business talent, as to their lack of business nerve. We see many people who are endowed with brilliant capacities, but are cursed with indecision. They are prone to follow the instincts of a weak nature against the utilization of clear intelligence. The world is overcrowded with people who remain stationary, filling minor positions, and drawing meager salaries, simply because they have never thought it worth while to achieve mastery in the pursuits they have chosen to follow.

There are some people whose failure to succeed in life is a problem to others, as well as to themselves. They are industrious, prudent, and economical; yet after a long life of striving, old age finds them still poor. They complain of ill luck, they say fate is against them, but the real truth is that their projects miscarry because they mistake mere activity for energy. Confounding two things essentially different, they suppose that if they are always busy they must necessarily be advancing their fortunes, forgetting that misdirected labor is a waste of activity.

Courage Converts Dreams to Reality

One reason why many people do not achieve their goals is that they seem to look upon their dream, their ambition as a sort of fanciful mental picture, something that has no definite basis in reality. These people never take their life mission very seriously, and consequently never grow to their full stature.

They do not seem to realize that to make those dreams come true, they were meant to play definite and distinct individual parts in its accomplishment. Yet that is just what we are here to do. We were not thrown off as independent, unrelated units of the universe. People who have faith in themselves feel that their abilities can make their dreams a reality.

Abraham Lincoln was a very modest, unassuming man. When the first rumblings of the Civil War reverberated through the North and a presidential election was at hand, he put himself forward as leader of the nation. When the politicians were looking round for a suitable man for that great position,

Lincoln asked them why they did not nominate him. He said he felt within his breast the power to carry the nation through the threatened crises, and that he believed he would be elected. Coming from a less modest man this assurance would look like a boast, but Lincoln's motives were pure, and his faith, based upon a marvellous dedication for the work to be done, carried him to success.

The history makers have always had strong convictions with regard to their life work. They have believed in their vision, and the part they were to play. They have believed that their ambition foreshadowed a prophecy that it was the substance of things expected, and not a mere figment of the imagination.

In other words, people who have won out in the world have been profound believers in their destiny. The faith of such people impress us with a conviction of their power. We all feel that there is something about people who believe in their destiny that commands our respect, and homage. The world itself makes way for those who believe they were born to play a grand part in the human drama.

Lech Walesa—Liberator of Poland

One of the best examples of courage in recent times is Lech Walesa. Shakespeare said that some people are born great, some achieve greatness and others have greatness thrust upon them. Lech Walesa fits the latter. He seems to have come out of nowhere to lead his people in their fight against Communist oppression at a time when there was no Polish leader who would stand up to the tyrannical government.

As an electrician at the Lenin Shipyards in Gdansk, he was among the first to express discontent with the Communist government of Poland that was so dominated by the Soviet Union that Poland had become nothing more than a puppet state. As a religious Roman Catholic, he was bitter about the suppression of the church by the Communists.

Walesa was not alone, of course. Most of the workers at the shipyard had been disillusioned by the so-called "workers' paradise" that the Communists had proclaimed. Meanwhile, the unrest at the shipyard was growing stronger. The union members formed what at first was a secret group, which they named "Solidarity"—a word that had traditionally been the watchword of the union movement signifying the solidarity of workers against capitalists. Now this name took on a new meaning—a solid front of workers against the communists. Walesa stood out as leader of this group.

Why did he take on this awesome responsibility, even though knew that this could lead to arrest, imprisonment and perhaps torture by the police or even his death. He knew that he was putting his family in jeopardy?

Years later, when asked if he was afraid, he admitted that he was very much afraid, but he knew that somebody had to take the lead. He remembered the words of the one man he admired most, Pope John Paul II. "Learn to Conquer Fear," the pope had admonished. Walesa heeded the pope's powerful words.

Imprisonment and release

With such a mission in mind, Walesa stepped forward into history. His courageous stand at the Gdansk shipyards thrust him into the public eye all over the world. But it also resulted in a series of persecutions that tested Walesa's courage. He was arrested in 1981 and under martial law was interned in a hunting lodge in a remote part of the country for eleven months.

When he was finally released, a crowd estimated at 1,500 assembled outside his apartment building greeted him. Walesa's emotional and long-awaited homecoming demonstrated that he was still a leader of considerable charisma and, whether the Communist authorities liked it or not, an enormous political force in Poland.

He promised them: "In my future conduct I will be courageous but also prudent, and there is nothing negotiable in this regard. I will talk and act, not on my knees, but with prudence."

Over the next few years, both he and his wife, Danuta, were harassed by the police, brought in for interrogation —sometimes for several days—but he no longer feared them. Because he met with other leaders of Solidarity, he was threatened with another period of detention.

However in the end, the Polish government was reluctant to press the matter much further. After his release, Walesa told journalists that he had been ordered by his interrogators not to meet with Solidarity leaders again but, said the defiant Walesa: "I'll do it again. I will have another meeting."

The Nobel Peace Prize

Walesa was awarded the Nobel Peace prize in 1983. The news of his courage in the face of his defiance of the powerful Communist government drew cheers and praise around the world. Ronald Reagan hailed it as "a triumph of moral force over brute force." John Paul II, whose first return to his homeland in 1979 helped launch the Solidarity movement, sent Walesa a congratulatory telegram in which he applauded the award's "special eloquence." In the official citation, the five members of Norway's Nobel Peace Prize committee praised Walesa's fight for "the workers' right to establish their own organizations," adding that "a campaign for human rights is a campaign for peace."

Lech Walesa's courage was a major contributor to the demise of the Communist government in Poland once the protection from the Soviet Union no longer existed to support it. In 1990, Walesa, the brave electrician from Gdansk was elected president of Poland.

What Walesa's accomplishment teach us:

> No matter how humble our background, if we have courage and the commitment to pursue our goals, nothing can stop us.

> Like Walesa, we may have "greatness thrust upon us." Our challenge is not to fight oppression, but to achieve success. Our opportunity may be starting a business of our own or developing an uncharted sales territory. We may fear the consequences, but if we have confidence in ourselves, we will overcome obstacles and succeed.

Take the High Road

Barry and Leon were among the people laid off when a business in Milwaukee downsized. Leon looked upon this as a great disappointment and misfortune. He showed it in the depressed expression that marked his features. He looked as though he had lost his best friend and his last dollar. His shoulders drooped, his feet dragged, and his clothing was soiled and creased. He complained that he believed he had been born under an unlucky star; that he had been employed by that firm for several years, and had been faithful, loyal and hard working, yet, he had been discharged. He could see no use in trying again, because, he argued, if he had not been able to win out in the work in which he was experienced he did not see how he could be successful in anything else. He felt convinced he was a failure. This thought dominated his thinking and he came to believe that failure was his destiny. It was easy to see that this young man was suffering greatly from that demoralizing disease of discouragement.

On the other hand, Barry took an entirely different view of his layoff. He got up each morning with the attitude that this was a new opportunity for him. He continued to dress as neatly as if he were going to work. There was no sign of defeat in his face. His attitude was that of a winner. There was a look of determination, almost of defiance, in his eye. He appeared so cheerful and happy that friends thought he must have secured a good position. He informed them, however, that he was still hunting for a job; but declared that he had not the slightest doubt he would soon find one, and a better one than he had lost. He said—not boastfully but with an air of quiet conviction—that he would show the company who had discharged him that they did not know what they were giving up; that he had no intention of remaining a perpetual clerk or a perpetual anything else; that he intended to climb to the top; to be an employer himself, and he wanted the firm who had once been his employer to watch his progress.

Barry went on to get into business himself and became a

bigger success than his former employer ever was. Time would undoubtedly show him at the head of a larger business, and would prove that he has greater executive ability, more push, greater initiative, more originality, and resourcefulness than his former company had realized.

Now the difference between these two young employees marks the difference between a winner and a loser. The winner is a person who gets up after he has been knocked down, with more determination than before; a person who is stung into greater activity by some serious setback. A temporary failure does not mean much to such a person—it is only an episode in his life.

If you want to develop courage, do the thing you fear to do and keep doing it until you get a record of successful experiences behind you. This is the quickest and surest way ever yet discovered to conquer fear.

Dale Carnegie

Richard Branson—Courage in Business

Richard Branson, the entrepreneur who revolutionized the music industry when he established Virgin Records always sought new challenges. In 1984, he sold his company and decided to engage in an entirely new venture. He started Virgin Atlantic Airways. Why an airline? In the music business Branson traveled constantly and was appalled by the poor service that most airlines provided. Creating an airline that was truly customer conscious was a challenge that appealed to him. Like many entrepreneurs, he drew upon his direct personal experience as a customer in creating a new venture.

His boldness is exemplified by the act that he knew next to nothing about airlines. But, by this time he did know a lot about being an entrepreneur.

To develop an appeal before to the public, he took advantage of being a small company unhindered by bureaucratic red tape. He offered inexpensive flights between Newark Airport near New York City to Gatwick airport near London. Just as he had built Virgin Records by offering discounted prices, he now offered discounted airfares—appealing to the young consumers eager to save cash.

His strategy was simple: Develop an airline that he would like to fly on. Many people have ideas about such products or services, but only a true entrepreneur has the boldness to act on his ideas. Branson was such a man. Many observers thought he did not stand a chance competing against well-heeled British Airways. This did not deter Branson, and he plowed ahead.

It took several years of major losses before Virgin Atlantic began to make money. Despite advice by bankers and friends to give up before he lost all of his money, Branson pushed on. When asked by a newspaper reporter how one can become a multi-millionaire, Branson quipped, "A multi-millionaire is a billionaire who invested in an airline."

Today Virgin Atlantic flies to cities all over the world and is highly profitable. It is now the second largest British long haul international airline and operates a fleet of Boeing 747 and Airbus A340 aircraft to New York, Miami, Boston, Los Angeles, Orlando, San Francisco, Hong Kong, Athens, and Tokyo.

Branson's courage has extended into his personal life.

His participation in record setting boat and balloon races exemplify this courage.

What Branson's story can teach us:

> It isn't necessary to invent or create a new product or service to become a success. Branson studied the market and sought businesses that were already mature, but in his judgment, he sought to provide a better, more efficient or less expensive approach.

> Success involves risk. Branson took risks in all his ventures. Most notably in competing with the well-established British Airways. Branson found a niche that BA had neglected and Virgin Atlantic filled it by offering lower cost and better services.

> Branson had the courage of his convictions. He believed that his ventures would succeed and he didn't give up—even suffering years of losses—until success was his.

> If we contemplate going into a new venture or are currently engaged in our own business, we should keep Branson's experience in mind. If we truly believe in the product or service we are providing, we should have the courage to enter competitive markets. Branson didn't gamble. He was willing to take prudent risks based on the evaluation of a situation. He knew the odds and only took a risk when he felt things were in his favor.

Use It or Lose It

One reason why so many employees never reach the heights is because they cease trying to climb. They have never properly cultivated their ambition, never furnished the fuel that would keep it burning, growing brighter and larger. The decay of ambition in youth, its early deterioration is a sign of early decay in the individual. With the decline of ambition, determination and courage decline.

On the other hand, young people who keep the fires of their ambition burning brightly, who guard their ideal, cannot help turning out well. Those who let it sag, peter out in a short time, never amount to anything. Many a youth who felt confident that they would head up a corporation did nothing to feed their ambition, and today they are nobodies, of little value to themselves or the world.

No matter how conspicuous or well defined our talent, unless we exercise it continuously it will deteriorate. Nature's law, "Use or lose," is operative everywhere. There is no getting away from or ignoring it. Whether it is ambition, talent, or a seed planted in the ground, the law is inevitable. That which is not used, taken care of, or cultivated will slide backward.

Think of Achievement

By setting our minds toward achievement, everything about us would indicates success. We must express this in our manner, our dress, our bearing, and our conversation. Everything we do should speak of achievement and success.

It's a wonderful advantage in starting out every morning with the mind set toward success and achievement, by permeating it with thoughts of prosperity and harmony, whether by repetition of set formulas as some advise, or by concentrating our minds on what we are determined to accomplish. It will then be so much harder for discord to get into the day's work. If we are inclined to doubt our ability to do any particular thing, we must train ourselves to keep the thought that we have the courage to move forward firmly and persistently. It is the assumption of power, of self-trust, of confidence in ourselves, in our integrity, and our courage that cannot be shaken, that will enable us to become strong, and to do, with vigor and ease, the thing we undertake.

We will find that the perpetual holding of these ideals will change our whole outlook upon life. We will approach our problems from a new standpoint, and life will take on a fresh meaning. This perpetual affirmation will put us in harmony with our surroundings; it will make us content and happy. It will help us to build up individuality and personal willpower. It will make our brains clearer, our thoughts more effective. Keeping the mental machinery clean makes for vigorous thinking and decisive action.

Strengthen Courage and Defeat Fears

If we are deficient in any quality, we can strengthen it by constant affirmation. If we lack courage anywhere in our nature (and most people do), we can strengthen courage by constantly affirming that we are absolutely fearless, that we are courageous, that nothing can harm us. Reason that fear is simply the sense of danger, and when we have perfect confidence in ourselves, there will be no cause for fear.

Every time you feel a sense of fear come over you say: "I am absolutely fearless; there is nothing to fear; fear is not a reality; it is not the truth of being. It is only the absence of courage, based upon ignorance of the great cause." Emerson knew the virtue of this philosophy when he said: "Nerve us with incessant affirmation. Don't bark against the bad, but chant the beauties of the good."

Determine not to harbor anything in the mind that you do not wish to become real in your lives. Shun poisoned thoughts, ideas that depress and makes you unhappy as instinctively as you avoid physical danger of any kind. You must replace discordant or unhappy thoughts, or thoughts of weakness and misery with cheerful, hopeful, optimistic thoughts. Form the habit of suggesting to yourself some agreeable or pleasant subject, to dwell upon or think about, or take up some word or idea that will suggest pleasure, happiness, and harmony. You will be surprised to see how quickly you can change the whole course of your thoughts. When your thoughts are changed, your feelings will change. It will increase your courage and confidence, and this is half the battle won.

The Self-Talk

As noted in the first chapter of this book, when our fears or discouragement begin to enter our minds, by giving ourselves a pep talk we can strengthen our resolution. The self-talk is simply a way to create an argument that would hold up to scrutiny due to the weight of the evidence. The stronger and more compelling the evidence is, the more believable and powerful the message. It is an internal discussion we all must have from time to time. This is a tool to take back control of the only thing we should have ultimate control over all the time—our thinking.

> *Inaction breeds doubt and fear. Action breeds confidence and courage. If you want to conquer fear, do not sit home and think about it. Go out and get busy.*
>
> *Dale Carnegie*

Make a Decision and Do It

Chief among the causes that bring total failure or a disappointing result that or only a partial success is vacillation.

Many entrepreneurs have made their fortunes by promptly deciding at some nice juncture to take a considerable risk. Yet many failures are caused by poorly thought out changes and needless vacillation. Determined people, who know what they want to do and do it, always push; vacillators, however strong in other respect, fall behind in the race of life.

If you are vacillators, if you have acquired a habit of hesitating, or of weighting and considering and reconsidering, never quite knowing what you want, you will never be leaders.

This is not the stuff which leaders are made, for whatever else leaders may lack, they know their own minds. They know what they want, and make straight for it. They may make mistakes, they may fall down now and then, but they always get up promptly and push on.

People who decide quickly can afford to make mistakes; for no matter how many they make, they will get on faster than those who are timid, vacillating, and so afraid of taking a wrong course that they dare not start out to do anything. Those who wait for certainties, who stand on the brink of the stream waiting for somebody to push them in, never reach the other shore.

A great many people seem to have a mortal dread of deciding things. They do not dare to take the responsibility, because they do not know what it may lead to. They are afraid that if they should decide upon one thing today, something better may come up tomorrow and cause them to regret their first decision. These habitual wavers so completely lose their self-confidence that they do not dare to trust themselves to decide anything of importance. Many of them ruin naturally fine minds by nursing the fatal habit of indecision.

There are no two words in the English language that stand out in bolder relief to so great an extent as the words *I will*. There is strength, depth and solidity, decision, confidence and power, determination, courage, vigor and individuality, in the round, ringing tone which characterizes its delivery. It talks to us of triumph over difficulties, of victory in the face of discouragement, of a will to promise and strength to perform, of lofty and daring enterprises, of unfettered aspirations, and of the thousand and one solid impulses by which we master impediments in the way of progress.

Sum and Substance

> When faith in ourselves and in our mission is the dominant note in our lives, nothing can daunt us, no power can keep us from success. Whatever other weaknesses, defects or deficiencies we have, our faith will be a powerful conviction of our ability to perform the things we have undertaken.

> No matter how conspicuous or well defined our talents, unless we exercise them continuously they will deteriorate. Nature's law: "Use or lose," is operative everywhere. There is no getting away from or ignoring it.

> If we recognize the potency of affirmation, of the habit of holding in the mind persistently and affirming that we are what we wish to be and that we can do what we want to do, it would revolutionize our whole lives, it would exempt us

from most of our ills and troubles, and carry us to heights of which we scarcely dream.

> We cannot ever accomplish anything in this world until we affirm in one way or another that we can do what we undertake.

> The worst of all foes to success is sheer, downright laziness.

> Vacillation in making decisions will bring failure or a disappointing result or only a partial success in our endeavors.

> Opposing circumstances create strength. Opposition gives us greater power of resistance. Overcoming one barrier gives us greater ability to overcome the next.

> All doubts and fears, all pessimism and negative thinking poison the very source of life. They sap energy, enthusiasm, ambition, hope, and faith—everything that makes life strong, vital, and creative. Entertain only the mental friends of your ambition, those that will help realize your ideal, that will help to make your dreams come true, to match your vision with reality.

> Humankind was created to do things. Nothing else can take the place of achievement in this life. Real happiness without achievement of some worthy aim is unthinkable.

> The way to learn how to run is to run, the way to learn how to swim is to swim. The way to learn how to develop courage is by the actual exercise of courage in the business of life. By following the examples of great leaders like Lech Walesa, and Richard Branson, we can learn to exercise courage in our endeavors.

8

....

DEFEATING DEFEAT

We are often afraid of trying new ideas, new ventures, or unusual approaches to solving problems because we are afraid of failure. Fear of failure is a human trait. Nobody wants to suffer the pains of defeat, but no endeavor can succeed unless it is attempted and with every attempt there is the risk that it will not work.

Learn From Your Failures

All of us have failed in many of the things we have tried throughout our lives, but we learn from our mistakes and use what we have learned to overcome them. The first time we try something new, it is likely that we will not succeed. When little Tricia tried to put together her first jigsaw puzzle, she cried in frustration. The parts simply would not fit together.

But with patience and some guidance from her mother, she began to identify patterns and in a short while her failures turned into successes. The first time Johnny faced a pitcher in a baseball game, he just couldn't hit the ball. He struck out over and over again, until he got the knack needed to change misses to hits.

Keep Trying

Even when we have experience and know-how, we cannot always be successful. There will be times when we do fail, but we must not let the concept of failure overwhelm us.

R. H. Macy had to close his first seven stores, but instead of giving up as a "failure," he kept trying and became one of Americas leading retailers. Babe Ruth struck out over 1300 times in his career, but that is forgotten because of his 714 home runs.

Seek the Cause

Thomas Edison never gave up, but perseverance alone is not enough. Each time one of his experiments failed, he studied what caused the failure and kept seeking solutions. It is said that he failed almost 1000 times before developing the filament that made the light bulb work.

It is not just the great geniuses and sports champions who have faced and overcome failures and disappointments. All of us, in our jobs and in our personal lives must expect defeats from time to time and be prepared to defeat them.

Justine was upset. She had been sure that the changes she had recommended would speed up the payroll processing procedure, but to her shock, her changes had slowed it down.

Her boss's criticisms made her feel even more stupid about what she had done. But, rather than give up, she probed to find out what it was that caused the idea to fail. She realized that the concept itself was valid, so the cause had to be in the way it was implemented. By changing the manner in which the clerks were trained in the new procedure, she turned failure into success.

Minimize Risk

All new ideas are risky. If it has not been proven successful in the past, there is a good chance that it may not succeed now. When Paul developed a unique marketing plan for the introduction of a new product his company had developed, he recognized that there were many imponderables that might defeat his objective.

To identify what roadblocks might be encountered, he chose to market the product in three cities before developing the final plans for national distribution. From each test, he was able to learn probable problem areas and work to overcome them. By the time the national marketing campaign started, most of the bugs had been detected and corrected and the chances of success greatly increased.

Seek Alternative Solutions

If the new program Peter developed did not work, and work fast, the company would be in serious difficulties. Peter knew that this idea was good, but it was new and had never been tried. If it failed, there would be no time to evaluate the reasons and make adjustments. It just had to work immediately.

To protect himself and his company in the event of possible problems with the new program, Peter developed an alternative solution, less innovative and unlikely to be as effective as the basic plan, but serve as an interim solution. If the basic plan did not succeed, the problem would at least be under control. Further study could then be made to determine why the plan had not worked and additional steps be taken to enable it to succeed.

Psych Yourself To Succeed

When any plan or concept fails, the persons involved with it are likely to be depressed and some may easily give up. We must expect that failures occur and from time to time we may face defeat.

Andrea was devastated. She was so sure that her suggestions would have solved the situation, but despite all of her efforts, it just didn't do the job. "I'm a failure," she thought. "I'm just not up to this kind of challenge."

If this attitude persisted, not only would Andrea remain unhappy, but it would prevent her from thinking clearly about additional ways to tackle the problem.

We must accept that all of us fail from time to time and that it is not anything to be ashamed of. A self-talk will help remind us that failures are part of trying new things and unless we continue to innovate, we will be become stagnant.

We must remember all of the successes we have had—often after previous failures—and keep telling ourselves that we've done it before and can do it again. Failure is a temporary situation. We have overcome it in the past and we can and will overcome it and succeed again.

Support Staff When They Fail

Managers and supervisors have an added responsibility. They must be willing to deal with failures of their staffs. Of course, there will be times when a subordinate disappoints us by an unsuccessful endeavor. It is tempting to reprimand that person or worse, fire them. Hasty action may cause the loss or demoralization of a potentially good staff member.

A middle manager at IBM made a major misjudgment that cost the company over $100,000. When he was called into the office of Thomas Watson, the man who built IBM into the giant it now is, he expected to be fired. "It was my fault," he told the chairman, "I guess you want my resignation."

"Nonsense," said Watson, "I just invested over $100,000 in your training. Now learn from it and get back to work."

Managers must recognize that if their people are to grow, they must be given opportunities to fail. Otherwise they will fear to take any new, creative, or different approaches.

Getting Performance Back on Track

This does not mean we should ignore failures, errors or poor performance just to maintain the morale of staff members. It is the manager's responsibility to train them to be successful.

In Dale Carnegie Training, participants are taught a six-step approach to getting staff members to speed up their performance.

Step 1 Build common ground

First we should look for ways to build common ground between the person with whom we are working and us. Establish rapport. Rapport is a reservoir of good will and mutual trust accumulated over a long period of fair treatment. When we meet, begin by putting that person at ease and reducing their anxiety. Help him or her feel comfortable. Communicate in an empathetic manner and then conversationally get to the issue at hand.

Step 2 Cushion

Cushion language to avoid abruptness and the potential of placing the individual on defense. Look for a comfortable way to bridge from the conversational rapport building to the issue that needs to be addressed.

Instead of just saying: "that's wrong," cushion your comment by saying something like, "I see that you are on the way to solving this, may I suggest..." then state how improvement can be achieved.

Step 3 Focus on the problem—not the person

During this step, we must focus on the problem and not the person. Eliminate personal pronouns and depersonalize the problem. It was the action that was wrong, not the person who did it. We want to give the other person a chance to explain what happened and then let that person know what we know about the problem. We should listen to understand and to determine whether he or she is accepting responsibility or blaming it on others and avoiding responsibility. The goal is to gather facts and information to be able to accurately identify the problem and its cause. Reduce defensiveness by asking questions and not jumping to conclusions. The different perspectives will surface, and the root cause of the problem should be identified.

Step 4 Explore options together

The purpose of this step is to remedy the problem, to reduce the chance of the mistake happening again, and to restore the person's performance. It also involves planning to devise a way to keep the problem from occurring again. Encourage feedback. This step should be handled differently with the employee who accepts responsibility than with the one who blames and avoids taking responsibility. With the responsible employee, effective questioning, listening, and coaching can be used to encourage him or her to suggest ways to correct the situation. The employee can be involved in a problem analysis and decision-making process and more likely to be committed when they help provide the solution. For the "blaming" or "avoiding" employee, the manager may first need to reaffirm performance expectations and to coach for acceptance of responsibility to restore accountability. Check for understanding and seek to gain consensus.

Step 5 Establish commitment

This step is focused on the person. Obviously a person who has erred feels, to some degree, like a failure and is likely to be less inclined to approach the next opportunity with confidence. Therefore, the manager needs to help the employee see the situation in a different context.

The staff member needs to be reassured of his or her value and importance to the organization and of the manger's support and encouragement. The employee should leave the meeting motivated to achieve optimal performance because he or she perceives a solid relationship with the organization.

The member's commitment to restoring a high performance level and the organization's commitment to the associate's success should be affirmed.

Step 6 Hold accountable

The staff member should leave the meeting with a sense of accountability and an understanding of what the company's expectations are.

Sometimes we find that the employee is not a good fit with a particular task, project, or department. We may need to explore what the employee's strengths, interests, and goals are and search for a better fit within the company for a better match. It is an injustice to employees and companies when we perpetuate a situation where individuals feel that they can never succeed. The last resort after attempts to coach them for desired performance is to remove them from this area of responsibility.

Perseverance and Innovation

All endeavors we undertake cannot succeed. Interspersed with the joy of success is the bitterness of failure. By dealing with failures constructively, we can often turn those failures into successes.

When Lee Iacocca was fired from the Ford Motor Company he was at the lowest point in his career. How he turned this defeat into success in his new job as CEO of Chrysler is well known. In his autobiography, he reported that, immediately upon starting his new job, he was faced with the probability of an even more devastating defeat. Chrysler was on the verge of bankruptcy. A lesser person might have quit right then, rather than moving from one failure to another. But by innovative thinking and perseverance, Iacocca confronted this crisis and defeated it.

Change Direction

Don was more than an ordinary musician. His dream was to be a famous concert violinist. After graduating from the prestigious Juilliard School of Music, he entered several of the major competitions, but never finished in the top group of winners. After all those years of study, he realized that, although he was a competent violinist, he did not have what it takes to reach the top. He could have settled for less and become a member of a symphony orchestra—a job that would give him steady employment and still use his talents. However, Don had the desire to be at the top in his field—not just one of many musicians.

He carefully studied his options and noted a real dearth of knowledgeable musicians in the production end of the recording business. He was hired by a major record company as an Assistant Producer to work in the production of classical records. His talents and knowledge of his field soon led to his promotion—eventually to the head of this department.

Several years later, Don faced another crisis. The Classical Record Department, never a significant moneymaker, was cut back in a cost-saving reorganization. Don was laid off. Again, Don had to change direction. He set himself up as a consulting producer and offered his services to his former employer and other record companies. With his history of achievement in classical record production, he soon became one of the leading independent producers in his field.

On two occasions, Don rather than mourning his failures, turned defeat into success by analyzing his strengths and changing his direction to best use his talents.

Change Goals

When Christine received her last rejection letter from the medical schools to which she had applied, she was distraught. All her life she had planned to be a doctor. In college all of her courses were geared to a medical career. She was a bright student and had expected no problem in being accepted by a medical school. However, her grades in the science courses were lower than was desirable for medical training.

After two days of brooding, Christine realized she had to make some decision as to what to do now. She examined many choices in the medical field including applying to medical schools in foreign countries, getting a job in a medical-related field or repeating the science courses and raising her grades so she could apply again to those schools that had rejected her. None of these options appealed to her. Serious introspection, followed by discussions with friends, parents and advisors, made her realize that her low marks in science courses were not due to lack of capability, but because she had no deep interest in them. Over the years her real interests had changed, but this had not been reflected in her career aspirations.

By rethinking her goals and with the aid of vocational guidance counseling, Christine recognized that she had many talents and opportunities open in several fields. Changing her goals at this point in her life probably saved her from pursuing a career in which she might have been unhappy.

Returning to Past Successes

After many years as one of the top financial analysts in his firm, Joel was promoted to Division Controller. It didn't take Joel long to realize he was over his head in his new job. His strength was working with figures and now much of his work was dealing with people. He supervised a staff of 40 accountants, computer operators and clerks. He spent much of his time at meetings with other managers, personnel from banks and other financial institutions and his own top management. By the end of the first year, he had been talked to and counseled by his boss several times on the lack of performance in his department.

He was on the verge of resigning and looking for another job, when the Corporate Controller visited his division from the home office. "Joel," he said, "you were one of the best financial analysts we had in this company. Your analyses were brilliant. However, in your current job you are not successful. If you are willing to go back to your old job, I think you will be happier and certainly more valuable to the company."

To go backwards is usually looked upon as a defeat. It means admitting we could not succeed in the higher-level position and it is often a blow to one's ego. Yet, history is full of people who were promoted to jobs above their level of competence. People have different strengths and weaknesses. We should be able to accept that we cannot be all things to all people. By returning to his former position, Joel once again can be valuable to his company—and to himself.

Charles Kettering, the creator of the automobile self-starter and many other inventions, sold his company to General

Motors, where he was appointed vice-president in charge of several operations. Kettering was a terrible administrator and the departments he managed did not meet the standards set by the company. Kettering was finally relieved of his managerial duties and left to concentrate on inventions.

Both he and General Motors benefited because he could now work exclusively in the areas where he was at his best.

Failures and defeats should not lead to depression and mourning. Analyze the reason for the defeat and determine how you can change it into a successful endeavor.

Develop success from failures. Discouragement and failure are two of the surest stepping stones to success.

Dale Carnegie

Overcoming Disappointment on the Job

When Victor joined his company, he set as his goal to be the branch manager within five years. Four years later he isn't even close to reaching his goal. He feels unhappy, letdown and demotivated. His thoughts vary from dreaming of a sudden change in his fortunes to bemoaning his ill luck.

Why hasn't Victor met his goal? Perhaps it is due to circumstances being beyond his control such as a recession or a tough competitive situation. Or perhaps Victor has not demonstrated his best capabilities in the assignments given to him. If the former, Victor may have to set new goals or seek a new job where circumstances are more favorable.

Promotions Must Be Earned

However, the reason for one's failure to move up in the company may not be due to outside factors. It may be that Victor had not earned the expected promotion. Just putting in one's time is not enough. Victor should reevaluate his work, discuss with his supervisor how he can improve, and take additional training to prepare himself for advancement of his position.

Meredith was very upset. Her boss had retired and she expected that she would be promoted to her job. After all, she was the most senior person in the department and her work was always good. Not only did she not get the promotion, but the company brought in an outsider who knew nothing about the department—"It just wasn't fair."

Well, why didn't Meredith get her boss's job? When a company chooses a person for a leadership position, it is certainly going to consider a person's work record, reliability and competence, but it also must seek people with the characteristics that show that they have more than just technical competence. They must have those special ingredients that make them stand out. They must be people who have shown they are willing to stretch to do more than just the routine job.

Stretch

Jack, the executive vice-president, was meeting with Leo, a middle level manager who was about to retire. After they completed their discussion of the transition of Leo's work to his successor, Leo said: "Jack, there's something that has been on my mind a long time. It has bothered and frustrated me for years, but were I not retiring, I wouldn't have dared ask you. You and I started in this company at approximately the same time. You're the executive vice-president and I have never risen above the middle level of management. Where did I go wrong? I have done excellent work. My bosses have always given me excellent reviews. I've always done everything I have been asked to do and did it well. What did you do that I failed to do that put you so far ahead of where I am?"

"Leo, you just answered your own question. You always did everything you were asked to do, but that was all you did. I got where I am because I reached out to do more than what I had to do in my regular work. I volunteered to take on assignments nobody else wanted. I initiated ideas and sold these ideas to top management. Sure I took risks, because some of them may not have worked and cost the company money—and some of them did fail, but overall I made myself invaluable to the company. When I felt I had done all I could in the department where I was assigned, I asked for transfer to another department where I could learn more about the company and contribute in added ways. Doing one's job well is important, and is the basis for all else, but it is doing more than what one has to do that brings one to the attention of the top managers who decide who moves up."

Too many people are like Leo and Meredith and perhaps, Victor. They do good work and expect that is enough. It is important, but as Jack said, one has to stretch to really get ahead.

Understanding Why

If you are being by-passed while others are being promoted, think carefully what you can do to earn the right to be considered for the next opportunity. Answer these ten questions:

1. How can I make my current work more valuable to the company?
2. What can I do for this company that I am not doing?
3. In what ways can I improve how things are done in my department?
4. What new and different aspects of the work could I learn so I can be more valuable to this organization?
5. What steps might I take to let my bosses know I am willing to accept more responsibility?
6. What can I learn about what other departments are doing that might fit into my goals?
7. If I have gone as far as I can in my current job, are there other jobs within the organization I can do?
8. Are there assignments other people are reluctant to do that I might volunteer to perform?
9. How can I improve my accomplishments as a manager by getting my people to be better performers?
10. Am I willing to make the commitment and undergo the sacrifices and take necessary risks to earn the right to move up the management ladder?

Be the Master of Your Own Fate

Don't blame your frustrations on the system—unless it truly is the system. If an honest evaluation of why you are not reaching your goals shows that you can do something to overcome what is holding you back, identify what it is you are not currently doing and correct it. By taking overt steps to become an outstanding employee, not just a good worker, you will put yourself on the road to success.

> *We can all endure disaster and tragedy, and triumph over them—if we have to. We may not think we can, but we have surprisingly strong inner resources that will see us through if we will only make use of them. We are stronger than we think.*

> *Dale Carnegie*

Bouncing Back

It is not uncommon for a major disappointment, whether in business or in other aspects of one's life, to cause one's morale to plummet and to engender a grave blow to one's self-confidence. Unless corrective action is taken immediately, this may deteriorate into self-pity, failure, and unhappiness.

"I don't think I'll ever recover from the loss of this account." Clyde thought. He was deeply depressed. For several years his largest customer, the Lincoln Manufacturing Company, had accounted for 30 percent of his income. He had just learned that the company was going to close its plant in Toledo and consolidate its operations with their Houston facility.

For the next few weeks Clyde moped about bemoaning his loss. His sales manager gave him pep talks, encouraged him to try develop new accounts, gave him additional leads—but nothing seemed to help.

He called on the prospects, but his presentations were mediocre, his doubts about his abilities seeped through to the customer and he didn't make the sale.

These failures added to the original loss made the situation even worse. Clyde went into a state of deep gloom and seriously considered getting out of selling and seeking a less demanding career.

Set Realistic and Attainable Goals

Clyde had fought hard to become a successful salesman. It would be wrong to let all those good years go down the drain. With the help of his sales manager, he worked his way through the "mourning" stages that follows a serious loss. He finally accepted the fact that the loss of the customer had nothing to do with his competency. He still had the same capability and drive that had enabled him to sell to Lincoln and all his other customers over the years. He had to start afresh with renewed confidence and enthusiasm. The only way to obtain this confidence was by successful selling. He set new goals for himself and discussed them with his manager.

"Art, I'm going to replace that business in six months."

"Fine, Clyde, what is your plan of action?"

"I'll work, really work long and hard and I'll make it."

"I'm glad you feel this way, but let's study the market and set realistic goals. If you set too high a goal in too short a time, you are likely not to make it. It is more important for you to set lower goals that you are sure to reach and then work up from there."

Art was right. The best way to bounce back is to experience new successes. If the initial goals are too high, this is less likely to occur. By setting realistic and attainable goals, each time we reach a goal, we are adding credibility to the image we have of ourselves.

We are giving ourselves proof of our capability and this builds a solid foundation for our next step. Success breeds success and by following Art's advice, Clyde was not only able to replace his lost business but also increase his total sales over the next several months.

Focus on Past Achievements

Marybeth's marriage had been a disaster. Her ex-husband's constant berating had turned a vibrant, self-assured woman into a frightened, despondent defeatist. She had married just after her college graduation and although she wanted to teach, her husband persuaded her to take a clerical job in a bank. She felt she could do better, but he kept telling her she was not capable of any position of responsibility. He found fault with everything she did and inflated his ego by debasing her. After three years of this, she divorced him and tried to build her life anew.

She reviewed her past and realized that she was happiest and most successful when she was in college. She enrolled in the continuing education division of a local college. Her class participation, research reports, and excellent grades reinforced her image of herself as an achiever. This gave her the courage to apply for matriculation in a Master's degree program, where she did so well that she was asked to join the faculty when she attains her degree.

By focusing on past achievements and seeking opportunity to repeat them, Marybeth pulled herself out of her dejection and bounced back to a happy and satisfying life.

Convert "Worry" to "Concern"

Carlos couldn't sleep. He was worried sick. In a week his new boss would take over—a stranger. He had gotten along famously with his old boss, but when he retired, instead of appointing one of the old-timers to the supervisor's job, they hired an outsider. "Maybe this new guy would be too tough; maybe he won't like me."

For the next few days he was nervous on the job and had great difficulty sleeping. He noticed that his friend and co-worker, Tony, didn't seem to be upset, so he asked him: "Tony, aren't you worried about the new boss?"

Tony shook his head. "Sure, I'm concerned. He could make changes here. But I'm not worried. What is the worst thing that can happen? Well the worst is he could fire me.

If he fires me, I have acquired good skills here so I'd just get another job. However, there is no real reason he should fire me. I've done a good job and will continue to do so. If he makes changes, I can live with them—and if I can't, there are other jobs around. So why worry?"

Carlos took this to heart and was able to work without worry and not lose more sleep. Sure, he would be concerned, but by keeping these precepts on controlling worry, he was able to handle this situation with assurance.

Beating the Blues

All of us have within ourselves the capability of bouncing back and beating those blues that get us down when things go wrong. We can work to correct the tangible problems, but we also have to make overt efforts to overcome the psychological depression that may sap our strengths and energy.

When the *blues* hit, we must not let it dim our hope. The bright *orange* sun is still there. It is only hidden temporarily behind the *ebony* clouds. The path to those *silver* linings may be barred by *green* envy of others, distorted by *purple* rage or impeded by *yellow* lights that may make us overcautious. To get back into the *pink,* we must visualize our goals with *crystal* clarity and fan those *red* flames of our zeal to overcome our problems to a *white* heat of strength and determination that will enable us to leap over the *black* pits that block us from our goals and change the color of our lives from dark *gray* to glittering *gold.*

Sum and Substance

> All endeavors we undertake cannot succeed. Interspersed with the joy of success is the bitterness of failure. By dealing with failures constructively, we can often turn those failures into successes.

> We must expect that failures occur from time to time and condition ourselves not to let it depress us.

> If we are managers, it is our responsibility to encourage our staffs when they fail and train them to be successful.

> To succeed, good performance is not enough. To really get ahead, we must perform over and above what is expected of us, innovate and have the courage to take risks that may not work out.

> To cultivate a mental attitude that will bring peace and happiness, Dale Carnegie advices that we should:
> 1. Fill our minds with thoughts of peace, courage, health and hope.
> 2. Never try to get even with our enemies.
> 3. Expect ingratitude.
> 4. Count our blessings—not our troubles.
> 5. Do not imitate others.
> 6. Try to profit from our losses.
> 7. Create happiness for others.

Appendix A

....

ABOUT DALE CARNEGIE & ASSOCIATES, INC.

Founded in 1912, Dale Carnegie Training has evolved from one man's belief in the power of self-improvement to a performance-based training company with offices worldwide. It focuses on giving people in business the opportunity to sharpen their skills and improve their performance in order to build positive, steady, and profitable results.

Dale Carnegie's original body of knowledge has been constantly updated, expanded and refined through nearly a century's worth of real-life business experiences. The 160 Dale Carnegie Franchisees around the world use their training and consulting services with companies of all sizes in all business segments to increase knowledge and performance. The result of this collective, global experience is an expanding reservoir of business acumen that our clients rely on to drive business results.

Headquartered in Hauppauge, New York, Dale Carnegie Training is represented in all 50 of the United States and over 75 countries. More than 2,700 instructors present Dale Carnegie Training programs in more than 25 languages. Dale Carnegie Training is dedicated to serving the business community worldwide. In fact, approximately 7 million people have completed Dale Carnegie Training.

Dale Carnegie Training emphasizes practical principles and processes by designing programs that offer people the knowledge, skills and practices they need to add value to their businesses. Connecting proven solutions with real-world challenges, Dale Carnegie Training is recognized internationally as the leader in bringing out the best in people.

Among the graduates of these programs are CEOs of major corporations, owners and managers of businesses of every size and every commercial and industrial activity, legislative and executive leaders of governments and countless individuals whose lives have been enriched by the experience.

In an ongoing global survey on customer satisfaction, 99 percent of Dale Carnegie Training graduates express satisfaction with the training they receive.

Appendix B

....

DALE CARNEGIE'S PRINCIPLES

Become a friendlier person

1. Don't criticize, condemn or complain.
2. Give honest, sincere appreciation.
3. Arouse in the other person an eager want.
4. Become genuinely interested in other people.
5. Smile.
6. Remember that a person's name is to that person the sweetest sound in any language.
7. Be a good listener. Encourage others to talk about themselves.
8. Talk in terms of the other person's interests.
9. Make the other person feel important—and do it sincerely.
10. To get the best of an argument—avoid it.
11. Show respect for the other person's opinion. Never tell a person he or she is wrong.

12. If you are wrong, admit it quickly, emphatically.
13. Begin in a friendly way.
14. Get the other person to say "yes" immediately.
15. Let the other person do a great deal of the talking.
16. Let the other person feel the idea is his or hers.
17. Try honestly to see things from the other person's point of view.
18. Be sympathetic with the other person's ideas and desires.
19. Appeal to the nobler motives.
20. Dramatize your ideas.
21. Throw down a challenge.
22. Begin with praise and honest appreciation.
23. Call attention to people's mistakes indirectly.
24. Talk about your own mistakes before criticizing the other person.
25. Ask questions instead of giving direct orders.
26. Let the other person save face.
27. Praise the slightest improvement. Be "hearty in your approbation and lavish in your praise."
28. Give the other person a fine reputation to live up to.
29. Use encouragement. Make the fault seem easy to correct.
30. Make the other person happy about doing the thing you suggest.

Fundamental Principles for Overcoming Worry

1. Live in "day-tight compartments."
2. How to face trouble:
   Ask yourself: "What is the worst that can possibly happen?"
3. Prepare to accept the worst.
4. Try to improve on the worst.

5. Remind yourself of the exorbitant price you can pay for worry in terms of your health.

Basic Techniques in Analyzing Worry

1. Get all the facts.
2. Weigh all the facts—then come to a decision.
3. Once a decision is reached—act!
4. Write out and answer the following questions:
   - What is the problem?
   - What are the causes of the problem?
   - What are the possible solutions?
   - What is the best possible solution?
5. Break the habit of worrying before it breaks you.
6. Keep busy.
7. Don't fuss about trifles.
8. Use the law of averages to outlaw your worries.
9. Cooperate with the inevitable.
10. Decide just how much anxiety a thing may be worth and refuse to give it more.
11. Don't worry about the past.
12. Cultivate a mental attitude that will bring you peace and happiness.
13. Fill your mind with thoughts of peace, courage, health and hope.
14. Never try to get even with your enemies.
15. Expect ingratitude.
16. Count your blessings—not your troubles.
17. Do not imitate others.
18. Try to profit from your losses.
19. Create happiness for others.

Become
an
EFFECTIVE
Leader

Become an EFFECTIVE Leader

DALE CARNEGIE

MANJUL

Manjul Publishing House

First published in India by

MANJUL

Manjul Publishing House

• 7/32, Ansari Road, Daryaganj, New Delhi 110 002 - India
Website: www.manjulindia.com

Registered Office:
• 10, Nishat Colony, Bhopal 462 003 - India

The Success Series:
Become an Effective Leader by *Dale Carnegie*

This edition first published in India in 2018
Second impression 2020

Copyright © Dale Carnegie & Associates
Rights licensed exclusively by JMW Group Inc.
jmwgroup@jmwgroup.net

ISBN 978-93-87383-31-9

Cover Design by Trinankur Banerjee

This edition is authorised for sale in the Indian Subcontinant only.

Printed and bound in India by Thomson Press (India) Limited.

CONTENTS

PREFACE

Are successful managers more concerned with meeting established goals or leading the people they supervise? Effective managers know that in order to reach those goals, they must be true leaders, who guide, motivate, coach, and care for their associates. Balancing the skills between leadership and management should be the focus of all who aspire to succeed in their jobs.

It is important to examine the balance between what we are doing versus what we are leading others to do. How can we identify and leverage our leadership style to be the best we can be in order to get the best results for ourselves and our organization?

The way we see others and the assumptions we make about people and the world around us shape our reality and the environment in which we work. In this book we examine the lessons we have learned about leadership and the beliefs we form as a result of those experiences.

The Changing Role of the Manager/Leader

The world is rapidly changing and requires those in leadership and management positions to assume constantly changing roles and responsibilities. Whether we are in Europe, Africa, the Americas, or the Pacific Rim, competition constantly demands that we find better, more efficient, more productive, and more profitable ways to produce products and deliver services.

These demands are not limited to our competition— The expectations of our people, our internal and external customers, our suppliers, distributors, and business partners are increasing. In order for us to remain competitive in today's rapidly changing world, we lead and manage our organizations through the 21st century.

Create and Share a Vision

We must be creative and create a shared vision, and communicate effectively with our associates. We must encourage our people to step outside the box created by job descriptions and a minimalistic approach to the work world so that our companies will grow and prosper in today's world. It is critical that we hire and cultivate people who are capable of helping us move our organizations to the next level. We cannot do this ourselves nor can our people help us move to the next level, unless we first identify our goals and establish and communicate a clear vision to our associates. Once a shared vision is created and disseminated throughout the organization, the resultant empowered behavior catapults us to the next level. People cease viewing their role as task-oriented and instead become results-oriented. Clearly seeing outcomes inspires one and one's associates to take risks and responsibility. Leadership begins finding its own level in the organization. Clearly focused outcomes allow people to become more self-managed and to handle resources without senior level assistance.

Empowered behavior is driven by a shared vision, but neither is possible unless the vision is clearly communicated throughout the organization. Effective communication is the foundational skill of building effective teams, creating a unified sense of purpose, and moving our organization to the next level.

Balancing People and Process

When asked to identify the most significant personal characteristic needed by management, most senior executives say, "the ability to work with people." Leaders recognize the importance of production, distribution, engineering, sales, research and development, and they have management systems in place to organize, direct, and control activities in each area. However, when it is time to carry out executive decisions, they are carried out by people. The largest single operating expense in any budget is people. Planning, whether functional or strategic, is carried out and built around people. The most valuable asset an organization has is its people. In fact, most executives spend approximately three-fourths of every working day dealing with people. This means that we create the management system by which our organization functions and continually demonstrate leadership that allows those systems to achieve their objectives.

One of the main reasons people are promoted into management and leadership positions is because they were effective at what they did in their job. Now, as a manager, the job is to get others to be able to do things as well as or better than we did them. These require a totally different skill set. Our success requires making the transition from doing to leading in order to leverage our skills and our time.

To be effective as a manager we must balance people and process. Being too people focused mean that if a key person leaves, everything stops. Being too process focused means that great systems are in place; however no one understands them or wants to work within them. Process focus says: "Here's the plan and here's how we do things." People focus says: "Let's discuss the plan and why we do things." With the right balance, both productivity and commitment stay at their highest levels.

Balancing Motivation and Accountability

Without motivation nothing gets done but as soon as we try to hold people accountable they get demotivated, right? Not necessarily! There are tools to hold people accountable for their goals, objectives, and commitments, and stay motivated at the same time. With this balance, we have more control over results for ourselves and our team.

Today, more than ever, a manager's job is to build people. When we can create an environment where people get results, develop new skills, and become successful, we are fulfilling our highest calling as a manager and leader of people. Communicating with strength and sensitivity, being a coach, and building people are a leader's highest priority.

Handling Conflict and Negativity

No matter what we do there will always be the challenges with negative people and performance management. Our results, and the results of our team, depend on how those situations are handled. Fairness, consistency, and strength are required in the right places, at the right times and in the right way. Without this, morale can grind to a halt for everyone, effecting productivity, customer loyalty, and employee loyalty—all mandatory in today's highly competitive work force.

In this book we will tackle these and other problems leaders face and provide approaches that will enable us and our associates to improve productivity and at the same time develop skills, attitudes, and capabilities that will help all of us grow in our jobs.

To get the most out of this book, read all of it first to absorb the overall concept of dealing with our roles as leaders. Then reread each chapter and start applying the guidelines for achieving each of the areas covered.

Arthur R. Pell, Ph.D.

Editor

1

....

DON'T BOSS—LEAD

Peter Drucker, one of the greatest management thinkers, wrote: "Most of what we call management consists of making it difficult for people to get their work done."

What is it that managers do that instigated Drucker to write that? Many people in managerial or supervisory positions deal with their people as if they were automatons—expecting them to follow procedures exactly and not use any of their own initiative, creativity, and brain power when working. They are so concerned with following rules, regulations, procedures, and routines that they overlook the potential that each human being working under their supervision may have.

Managers, who truly lead their people instead of directing their work, not only obtain better results for their organizations, but develop teams of people who are committed to working toward success in every aspect of their jobs and their lives.

Do you know the most important trait a leader can have? It is not executive ability; it is not a great mentality; it is not kindliness, nor courage, not a sense of humor, though each of those is of tremendous importance. It is the ability to make friends, which boiled down, means the ability to see the best in others.

Dale Carnegie

Leaders Serve

The true leader serves his or her people, not the other way around. The typical geometric figure we associate with most organizations is the triangle. On the top is the boss who gives orders to middle management who gives orders to supervisors who in turn give orders to the workers. At the very bottom of the triangle are the customers who we hope will be satisfied by what we provide.

The purpose of each layer is to serve the layer above it. In the traditional approach, workers serve their supervisors, supervisors, their managers, and all eventually serve the big boss. The customer, down at the bottom is virtually ignored. The triangle should be reversed. Top level management should serve the middle level managers, who in turn serve their first line supervisors, who are there to serve the workers—and all serve the customer.

Leaders Serve their Staffs

J. Willard Marriott, the hotel entrepreneur, sums it up succinctly: "My job is to motivate my people, teach them, help them and care about them." Note that last item—care about them. Good leaders truly care about their people. They learn as much as they can about their strengths and limitations, their likes and their dislikes, how they act and react. They take the time to work with them, to give them the resources, the tools, the know-how to do their job effectively. They do not get in their way by worrying more about whether every "i" is dotted and every "t" crossed.

When surveys are made on what people want from a boss, almost the very top item is a *boss who is there for me*. This is a boss to whom a person can come with a question and not be afraid of being thought to be stupid; a boss on whom one can depend to provide information, training, and suggestions rather than make demands, and give orders and commands. This is a boss who helps develop the potential of people—not just use them merely as a means of getting a job done.

Empower Our People

Real leaders "empower" their people. This word *empower* has become a fad word in management today, but fad words often express concisely a currently accepted concept. It derives from a legal term meaning transferring certain legal rights from one person to another. In today's management parlance, however, it is used in a broader sense—to share some of the authority and control a manager has with the people who he or she manages. Instead of the manager making every decision as to how a job should be done, the people who perform the job participate in doing this. When people have some say in these determinations, not only will we obtain more varied information as to how a job can be done, but because they did participate, the workers become committed to its success.

Managing versus Leading

Managing emphasizes that people follow orders—often unquestioningly. "This is the way it's going to be done." Leading encourages creativity in people by soliciting their ideas both informally in day to day contact and formally in meetings, suggestion programs and similar activities. Managing is telling people what they will be accountable for. Leading empowers people—giving them the tools to make their own decisions within guidelines that are acceptable to all parties concerned.

Managing is more concerned with how the policies are followed, explaining rules and policies, and enforcing them. Leading motivates people and teaches them how to get the job done. If it doesn't work out as expected, efforts are made to improve performance by better training. Helping people learn is the key tool in obtaining quality performance.

Managing concentrates efforts on *doing things right;* leading emphasize *doing the right things.* There are times when it is necessary to manage—when for legal or similar reasons, it is essential that things be done according to the book. Of course, people in managerial positions must assure that things are done right, but this is not their main job. Enforcing rules may be necessary in such circumstances, but more important is to train and motivate people to be competent and desirous of doing their very best to meet the department and the company's objectives. To achieve this with one's people is the epitome of true leadership.

Good Boss—Bad Boss

Harry was the kind of boss that liked to be popular. He thought he was a good boss because everybody in his department liked him. He did not want to upset this popularity so he hesitated to enforce minor infractions of rules or correct minor errors in work. When a reprimand was called for, he would stall it for so long that the reason for it was often forgotten. However, praise was so common that it lost significance.

Teresa was tough. She believed that one had to crack the whip to get the work done. She was abrupt, dogmatic and her favorite expression was: "I am the boss. You get paid to work so you'd better work or else." She rarely praised her people and often bawled them out in front of the whole department.

Both Harry and Teresa had serious problems because neither of these extremes could really work. Let's look at what happened in each of these areas.

The Easy-Going Boss

When a manager does not control the department, the work will be affected. Production schedules will not be met, quality suffers, people take advantage of this leniency and absenteeism, tardiness, and general attitudes deteriorate. Harry's people feel leaderless and walk all over him.

Why will a manager become so lenient and easy-going to the point where the department suffers? Often it can be traced to a feeling of insecurity in one's own ability. Insecure persons demand approval from others to bolster one's own ego. Such people want to be popular, to be "one of the gang." They believe that leniency with subordinates will engender employee approval.

When Harry's boss discovers that the department is falling behind, Harry will be held accountable. Now, Harry gets nervous as it is clear that he has to reverse this rapidly. A natural reaction is to do an abrupt about-face. He begins to get tough and demanding. He jumps on his people, often hollering, and screaming. He begins to reprimand people for every minor violation and punish people for matters he had ignored only a week earlier. This causes resentment and uncertainty among his people. The work may pick up for a while, but as the nature of Harry's personality is quite the opposite of these actions, once things straighten out, he reverts to his old self.

Frequent changes in management style are more demoralizing than sticking to one style—good or bad. Our people cannot anticipate how we will behave. This uncertainty leads to poor morale and heavy turnover.

The cause of Harry's easy-going attitude stems from his own sense of insecurity. He has to build up his self-confidence—One way of accomplishing this is to become expert in the work one does. When a person is thoroughly knowledgeable about the work, there is a feeling of security in it that leads to self-confidence in all matters pertaining to the work. He should also study more about human relations and apply what he has learned to his job.

The Hard-Boiled Supervisor

Teresa has a similar problem. Although her style is quite different from Harry's, the results are much the same. She causes resentment among her people—consciously or subconsciously, they refuse to cooperate. Lower production, higher turnover, more absenteeism, numerous grievances, and generally poor morale are the usual evidences of such a lack of cooperation.

The cause of the tough approach as of the lenient one is insecurity. However, the "desire to please" attitude is replaced by a gruff manner and authoritarian veneer. It is more difficult for hard-boiled leaders to change, probably because they have a stubborn feeling that their way is the only way. Stubbornness is an integral part of their behavior pattern.

Again the solution requires a good knowledge of human relations. The supervisor must learn to praise more frequently, and how to administer effective reprimands without causing resentment and rancor. Teresa must learn to tone down her manner and speech to avoid arguments and to work more amiably with her co-workers and staff.

The Best Supervisor

The most effective supervisory style is somewhere between these two extremes. It is grounded on understanding human behavior and applying this knowledge in working with the people under his or her jurisdiction. He or she praises people for good work, but does not throw praise around lightly. Harry overdid praise to the point that none of his people felt that their remarkably good work was really appreciated. Teresa never praised her people so they felt that there was no point in doing remarkably good work.

Reprimanding, where called for, should be done in private and in a calm manner. Never raise one's voice and always give the employee the opportunity to tell his or her own side of the story. Listen attentively and do not interrupt. Give constructive criticism and be as specific as possible.

Do not reprimand in a bad mood or in anger. Do not get maneuvered into an argument. Avoid sarcasm and nagging.

Keep to the issues. Remember the purpose of a reprimand is to right a wrong. A good manager would not want to compound the wrong by creating resentment. Always emphasize the *what* rather than the *who*. Suggestions on how to give effective reprimands will be discussed in chapter 9.

Good leaders are neither wishy-washy hail-fellow-well-met characters nor tyrants. They are neither ignored nor feared by their subordinates. Capable supervisors have inner confidence plus the respect of their people.

Let's look at a simple comparison between the way a boss manages and a leader leads:

The Boss as The Leader

Instills Fear
Says 'Do'
Makes work drudgery
Relies upon authority
Says 'I,' 'I,' 'I'

Myths and Misconceptions

Myths and misconceptions that have governed people's thinking for years or for lifetimes are tough to overcome. As a manager, however, we must shatter them if we want to be able to move ahead.

Some people are reluctant to take on leadership roles. To do so, they believe that they would have to have certain innate leadership traits such as charisma, or that intangible personality that would empower them to influence others.

It's true that some of the world's greatest leaders were born that way—they had that special charm that enraptured the public. But they are the exceptions. The majority of successful leaders are ordinary men and women who have worked hard to get where they are. Management of people is easier if we have natural talents, but they're not essential. Each of us can certainly acquire the skills necessary to manage and lead people.

Leadership is an art that can be acquired. With a little effort anybody who desires to can learn to guide people in a way that commands their respect, confidence, and whole-hearted cooperation.

Many managers like to refer to themselves as "professionals," but is management really a profession? Professionals in other fields (such as physicians, lawyers, psychologists, and engineers) are required to complete advanced study and pass exams for certification. There are no such requirements to be a manager. Some managers may have special education such as degrees in business administration, but most are promoted from the ranks and have little or no training in management. Most managers learn primarily on the job.

More and more successful managers are making an effort to acquire skills through structured courses of study, but most managers still pick up their techniques by observing their bosses. The model they follow may be good. Too often, however, new managers are exposed to their bosses' outdated and invalid philosophies.

Some of these ideas noted below may have been valid in the past but are no longer effective; others were never true. Let's look at some of the many myths and misconceptions about management.

Management is No More than Common Sense

A manager was asked about his training when he started in management, he said, "When I was promoted to my first management job, I asked a long-time manager for some tips about how to deal with people who report to me. He told me, 'Just use common sense and you'll have no trouble.'"

What is "common sense," exactly? What appears to be sensible to one person may be nonsense to another. Often the definition of "common sense" is culturally based. In Japan, for example, it's considered "common sense" to wait for a full consensus before making any decision; in the United States, this technique is often derided as inefficient and a waste of time.

Cultural customs aren't the only cause for differing ideas about what constitutes common sense. Different people have different views about what is good and what is bad, what is efficient and what is wasteful, and what will work and what will not.

We tend to use our own experiences to develop our particular brands of common sense. The problem is, a person's individual experience provides only limited perspective. Although what we think of as common sense has been developed from our own experiences; an individual's experience is never enough to provide anything other than limited perspectives. Leadership involves much more than the experience an individual may have. To be a real leader, we must look beyond common sense.

We wouldn't rely solely on common sense to help with financial or manufacturing problems. We would call on the best possible expertise in these areas for advice and information.

Why then should we resort to a less pragmatic base in handling human-relations problems?

We can learn a lot about the art and science of management by reading industry-related books and periodicals in the field, attending courses and seminars, and actively participating in industry associations.

Managers Know Everything

Managers don't know everything. Nobody does. Accept that we don't have all the answers, but know that we need the skills to get the answers. One effective way is to develop contacts with people in other companies who have faced similar situations. We can learn a great deal from them. Networking—making contacts with people in other companies to whom we can turn for suggestions, ideas, and problem-solving strategies—gives us access to these people when we need new information and ideas, and provides us with a valuable ongoing resource for assistance in solving problems.

> *Don't you have much more fate in ideas that you discover yourself than ideas that are handed down to you? If so, isn't it bad judgment to ram your ideas down the throats of other people? Wouldn't it be wise to make suggestions and let the other person think out the conclusion for themselves?*
>
> *Dale Carnegie*

It's My Way or the Highway!

Management using fear is still a common practice. And it

works, sometimes. People will work if they fear that they might lose their jobs, but how much work will they do? The answer is "Just enough to keep from getting fired." That's why this technique isn't considered effective management. Successful management involves getting the willing cooperation of our associates.

Moreover, it's not that easy to fire people. Considering the implications of the civil-rights laws and labor unions—and in many cases the difficulty and costs associated with hiring competent replacements—firing people may cause more problems than keeping employees with whom we are not satisfied.

We can't keep good workers for long when we manage by fear. When jobs are scarce in our community or industry, workers might tolerate high-handed, arbitrary bosses, but when the job market opens up, the best people will leave for companies with more pleasant working environments. Employee turnover can be expensive and often devastating.

Praising Is Coddling Employees

Some managers fear that if they praise a team member's work, that person will become complacent and stop trying to improve (certainly, some people do react this way). The objective key is to phrase our praise in a manner that encourages the associate to keep up the good work.

Other managers are concerned that if associates are praised for good work, they will expect pay raises or bonuses. And some folks might. But that's no reason to withhold praise when it's warranted. Employees should know how salary adjustments, bonuses, and other financial rewards are determined. If compensation is renegotiated at annual performance evaluations, team members should be assured that the good work for which they are praised will be considered in the evaluation.

Some managers consider praise irrelevant. One department head reported, "The people I supervise know that they're doing okay if I don't talk to them. If I have to speak to them, they know they are in trouble." Offering no feedback other than reprimands, isn't effective either. Remember, we want to use positive, not negative, reinforcement.

Of course, praise can be overdone. If people are repeatedly praised for every trivial accomplishment, the value of praise is diminished to the point of being becoming superficial. Also, nonproductive employees can think they're doing great if they are praised excessively. Techniques on effective use of praise will be discussed in chapter 3.

Let's praise the slightest improvement that inspires the other person to keep on improving.

Dale Carnegie

Using the Whip Excessively

Sure, some managers still act as slave masters. Every year James Miller, management consultant and the author of 'The Corporate Coach,' holds a contest for the Best and Worst Boss of the Year. Employees do the nominating. Miller reports that he gets many more nominations for worst boss than for best boss. One of the chief reasons employees dislike their bosses, Miller found, is that these bosses are continually finding fault with subordinates, expressing sarcasm, gloating over failures, and frequently hollering and screaming at employees.

Why do people behave this way? Some people have always been screamed at—by parents, teachers, and former bosses—so they may assume that it's an effective communication tool.

We all raise our voices occasionally, especially when we're under stress. Sometimes it takes great self-discipline not to yell. Effective leaders, however, control this tendency. An occasional lapse is okay, but when yelling becomes our normal manner of communication, we're admitting our failure to be real leaders. We cannot get the willing cooperation of our associates by screaming at them.

Try the Platinum Rule

When we manage people, the Biblical golden rule, "Do unto others as you would have others do unto you" is sound advice, but only to a point. People are not all alike; treating others as we want to be treated is not the same as treating them as they want to be treated.

For example, Linda prefers to be given broad objectives and likes to work out the details of her job on her own. But her assistant, Jason, is not comfortable receiving an assignment unless all the details are spelled out for him. If Linda delegates work to her assistant in the way she likes to have work assigned to her, she won't get the best results.

Sol needs continuous reinforcement. He's happy on the job only when his boss oversees his work and assures Sol that he's doing a good job. Tanya, however, gets upset if her boss checks her work too often. "Doesn't she trust me?" she complains. We can't do unto Tanya as we do unto Sol and get good results from each of them.

Each of us has our own style, our own approach, and

our own eccentricities. To "do unto others" as we would have them do unto us may be the poorest way of managing people.

To be an effective manager, we must know each member of our team and tailor our method of management to each person's individuality. Rather than follow the golden rule, follow the platinum rule: *Do unto others as they would have you do unto them.*

Compromises must be made, of course. In some situations, work must be done in a manner that may not be ideal for some people. By knowing ahead of time what needs to be accomplished, we can anticipate problems and prepare our associates to accept their tasks.

Leaders Must Produce More than Optimum Performance

Production, performance, and profit are important aspects of our job as managers, but are these all we have to consider? Certainly, if a business is to survive, it must produce results. Equally important, however, is the development of its employees. If we ignore people's potential, our team's ability to attain results is limited. Instead, we reap short-term benefits at the expense of long-term success and even survival.

When Eliot founded his computer-components company, he was a pioneer in what was then a new and growing industry. Determined to be a leader in his field, he drove his employees to maintain high levels of productivity, and kept his eye carefully trained on the profit picture. But he paid no attention to the development of his staff. His technical and administrative staff members were given little opportunity to contribute ideas or use their own initiative on their own projects. Over the years, Eliot's company saw reasonable profits, but it never grew to become an industry-leader as he had hoped. Because he had stifled the potential and ambition of his employees, he lost many of his technical staff members to other companies. And because he depended only on his own ideas, he missed out on all the innovative ideas his staff might have come up with.

Sum and Substance

> - Leadership is an art that can be acquired. With a little effort anybody who desires to can learn to guide people in a way that commands their respect, confidence, and whole-hearted cooperation.
> - Don't boss—lead.
> - Managers are often influenced by misconceptions and myths about management. Don't automatically follow in an old boss's footsteps.
> - Be neither hard-boiled nor easy-going. The most effective supervisory style is somewhere between these two extremes. It is grounded on understanding human behaviour and applying this knowledge in working with the people under his or her jurisdiction.
> - Praise people for work done well. Unrecognized work is like an un-watered plant. Productivity will wither away.
> - Follow the platinum rule: "Do Unto Others as they would have you do unto them."
> - We must always be there for our people.

2

CHARACTERISTICS OF
SUCCESSFUL LEADERS

One need not be born a leader; most people can be trained to be leaders, but there are characteristics that they must acquire to be truly great leaders. Over the years many studies have been made on what these characteristics are.

Although individual strengths and abilities may vary, research indicates that outstanding managers view the world in similar ways. The following represent the most commonly observed qualities of successful leaders:

1. *They hold strong values and high ethical standards.* We can learn a lot by following the philosophy of Sir John Templeton, the founder of the Templeton Fund, one of the world's most profitable mutual funds. He bases his business practices on the belief that the most successful people are often the most ethically motivated.

He says that such people are likely to have the keenest understanding of the importance of morality in business, and can be trusted to give full measure and not cheat their customers.

Hard work combined with honesty and perseverance is the crux of the Templeton philosophy. "Individuals who have learned to invest themselves in their work are successful. They have earned what they have. More than simply knowing the value of money, they know their own value."

2. *They lead by example, acting with integrity in both their professional and personal lives.* Whether it is carrying out their own ideas or those of others, they work to assure that what has been planned is achieved. Nothing is more powerful in reinforcing leadership skills than success and achievements. Working hard to accomplish the goals set by the leader and his or her associates will enhance the probability of success and motivate the leader and the group to move ahead.

3. *They are knowledgeable about corporate and department goals and stay informed of changes.* The best leaders set high standards for themselves and then work hard to achieve their goals. Like everyone, we will make mistakes; and when we do, we must view these mistakes as learning experiences and try to turn them into successes. As it has been said: "If you've never made errors, you've never made decisions."

4. *They are proactive and self-motivated to achieve results.* They are never entirely satisfied with themselves. They keep up not only with the state of the art in their fields, but they improve their knowledge and understanding in a variety of areas. They read professional journals and magazines in their

areas of interest. They read extensively. They take active roles in professional and trade associations not only to keep in touch with new developments, but to share their ideas with colleagues from other organizations. They attend and participate in conventions and conferences and develop networks of people to whom they can turn to obtain knowledge or ideas over the years.

5. *They are strong communicators and exceptional listeners.* They listen to their people and recognize that the men and women, who although not in leadership positions themselves can contribute ideas and suggestions that may be even more valuable than his or her own. The good leader establishes cooperative, collaborative climates in which all participants know their participation in decisions are welcome.

6. *They are flexible under pressure and keep their emotions in check.* When faced with failure, their commitment keeps them from succumbing to defeat. In Chapter 1, we discussed how to regain self-confidence after suffering from defeat. Good leaders follow these advice. They will not let failures or disappointments keep them from continuing to try and to encourage their followers to move forward.

7. *They have positive attitudes.* The practice of positive thinking increases our ability tremendously, for two reasons. First, because it discovers ability which was locked up before, calls out hitherto unknown resources; and second, it keeps our minds in harmony by killing fear, worry, anxiety, destroying all the enemies of our success and efficiency. It puts our minds in a condition to succeed. It sharpens our faculties, makes them keener, because it gives a new outlook upon life;

and turns us about so that we face towards our goal, towards certainty, towards assurance, instead of towards doubt, fear and uncertainty. We must accentuate the positive in our thoughts and actions. If we are positive thinkers, our associates will most likely be positive thinkers.

8. *They nurture the cooperation and collaboration of their team.* Good leaders aren't complacent. They're constantly on the lookout for making innovations that will improve the way work is done, assure continuing customer satisfaction, and increase the profitability of the organization.

9. *Their minds are open to new ideas and they welcome suggestions.* Even after changes and improvements are made, they still look for even better ways to accomplish their goals. They take the time to get to know what drives individual team members and enjoy motivating and helping them to succeed. Great leaders understand people—what causes them to act and react the way they do.

10. *They recognize the importance of being a motivating factor for people—appealing to the drives and the feelings of others.* They take a genuine interest in the people with whom they interact. As Dale Carnegie succinctly pointed out: "You can make more friends in two months by becoming genuinely interested in others than you can in two years by trying to get others interested in you."

11. *They recognize and maximize strengths in others.* Often people in positions of authority can compel subordinates to follow orders by dint of the power of their jobs. But such people are not true leaders. Yes, the orders will be followed but

that is all that will happen. True leaders develop confidence and trust in their associates (Note they think of them as associates—not subordinates). This engenders a desire not only to follow the lead of the manager, but also to initiate, innovate, and implement ideas of their own that fit into the established goals.

12. *They hold themselves and others accountable for results.* They set standards, which are understood and accepted by their associates, and work to meet those standards. They take immediate action to correct deviations. They recognize their own limitations and seek help when needed.

13. *They are efficient and manage their time effectively.* They develop meaningful time schedules, learn to prioritize, and to minimize interruptions and distractions.

14. *They are creative and innovative.* They are not afraid to try new ideas. Good leaders aren't complacent. They're constantly on the alert for making innovations that will improve the way work is done, assure continuing customer satisfaction and increase the profitability of the organization. Their minds are open to new ideas and they welcome suggestions. Even after changes and improvements are made, they still look for even better ways to accomplish their goals.

15. *They have vision.* Great leaders know what they want to accomplish and what steps they must take to achieve their goals. They look beyond meeting short-term objectives and keep the big picture clearly in their minds. Theodore Hesburgh, former president, Notre Dame University, expressed this succinctly: "The very essence of leadership is that you have to have vision.

It's got to be a vision you articulate clearly and forcefully on every occasion. You can't blow an uncertain trumpet."

16. *They Focus on Getting Things Done.* We've all come across people in management positions who appear to have great attributes of leadership, but somehow never quite succeed. Somewhere along the line they have missed the boat.

Here is an example: When the ABC Distributing Co. hired Brian as a regional sales manager, they were extremely enthusiastic about him. He had come to them highly recommended. During the selection process, he had impressed the Marketing Manager with his thorough knowledge of their markets, his innovative ideas on how to increase business and his charming personality. During the first several months on the job, he developed a creative and comprehensive marketing program for his region. He spent weeks fine-tuning, writing materials, and creating graphics for it. This led to his making several impressive presentations to management and to the sales force. And that's where it ended. He was never able to actually go out and make the program work. When the Marketing Manager checked back with his previous employer, he learned that Brian had been a staff marketer—brilliant in that type of work—but he had never had line responsibility. He lacked that key ingredient of leadership—getting things done.

17. *They are not easily deterred.* When faced with failure they take the reins and fight to overcome the problem. A good example is Tom Monaghan, founder of Domino's Pizza. He grew this company from a one-store pizza parlor to a chain of several thousand home-delivery outlets over a period of about 30 years. In 1989, he sold the company. After two and

a half years, the company that had purchased the chain lost the momentum Monaghan had generated. In order to save the company, he bought back the company and returned to his former position as CEO. He revitalized the company and expanded it to over 5000 stores in the United States, and over 3000 in other countries.

Transitioning from Doing to Leading

One of the main reasons people are promoted into management and leadership positions is because they were effective at what they did in their jobs. When you get that promotion, your job is to get others to be able to do things as well as or better than you did them. These require a totally different skill set. The success requires making the transition from doing to leading in order to leverage our skills and our time.

Balancing People and Process

To be effective as a manager one must balance people and process. Being too people focused may result in situations where if a key person leaves, everything stops. Being too process focused means that great systems are in place, however no one understands them or wants to work within them. Process focus says: "Here's the plan and here's how we do things." People focus says: "Let's discuss the plan and why we do things." With the right balance, both productivity and commitment stay at their highest levels.

Balancing Motivation and Accountability

Without motivation nothing gets done but some people believe that as soon as we try to hold people accountable they get demotivated. This is not necessarily so. We can develop tools to hold people accountable for their goals, objectives, and commitments and stay motivated at the same time. With this balance, we have more control over the results for ourselves and our team.

> *If you do not like people generally, there is one simple way of cultivating the characteristic—just look for the good traits, you'll be sure to find some.*

> *Dale Carnegie*

Communicating and Coaching for Results

Today, more than ever, a manager's job is to build people. When we can create an environment where people get results, develop new skills, and become successful, we are fulfilling our highest calling as a manager and a leader of people. Communicating with strength and sensitivity, being a coach, and building people are a leader's highest priority.

One of the reasons people are often promoted to manager is because they have demonstrated the skills and knowledge necessary to excel in their area of expertise. Now, success depends not on personal achievement, but coaching others to succeed. Successfully transitioning from worker to manager demands a new frame of mind and set of skills.

Setting Goals and Planning to Achieve Them

The first step we must take in applying our leadership skills is to set goals. Like a good navigator, the effective leader determines what goals should be set and how and when to reach those goals.

Some people prefer the term "objectives". Goals and objectives are interchangeable terms that describe the purpose, or long-term results, toward which an organization's or individual's endeavors are directed.

There are people who like to set out on a journey without a map. They want to ride the currents, and hope that they'll find adventure and fortune—and sometimes they do—but leaders and managers in companies and other organizations can't afford to take those risks because they have responsibilities to their teams. They must know where they want to go, what they want to accomplish, what kinds of problems they may encounter along the way, and how to overcome those problems.

Unless we know exactly what we want to achieve, there's no way to measure how close we are to achieving it. Specific goals give us a standard against which to measure our progress.

The goals we set for accomplishing our team's mission must be in line with what the larger goals our organization sets for us. If we don't coordinate the objectives of what we plan to achieve for our job, department, or team with the objectives of the organization, we will be wasting our time and energy.

Goals are the foundation of motivational programs. In striving to reach our goals, we become motivated. In knowing the goals of our team members and helping them reach those goals, we help to motivate them.

In most organizations, overall big-picture goals are established by top management and filtered down to departments or teams, who use them as guides in establishing their own goals.

The Goal Setting Process

The process of setting goals takes time, energy, and effort. Goals aren't something we scribble on a napkin during our coffee break. We must plan what we truly want to accomplish, establish timetables, determine who will be responsible for which aspect of the job, and then anticipate and plan a resolution for any obstacles that may threaten to thwart the achievement of our goals.

Goals must be spelled out. They must be fully understood by all those who have to meet them. The managers—whether in the top echelon or in any other level of the management hierarchy—must not only be aware of the company's goals, but must be fully committed to them.

Benefits of Establishing Goals

> Establishing goals helps motivate the individuals who are performing the tasks. If people know why something is required they are more likely to learn to do it well and so accomplish the purpose than if they are just told to do it. People take pride in doing a good job. Unless they know the objectives of the job they are doing, they cannot really know whether they are doing satisfactory work or not.

For example, Neil, an engineering student, was in a cooperative education program in which he worked three months in industry and attended classes for three months. His job was in a research laboratory of a large plastics company, where he was assigned a routine testing job. The work was repetitive and dull; Neil soon lost interest in it, and his performance fell. The laboratory manager, seeing the effect on the work, took Neil aside and carefully explained the importance of testing, the use of the results and exactly how the work contributed to meeting the company's goal of producing a superb product. Once Neil understood the nature of the efforts he was making, his performance improved and he was soon producing top level results.

> Establishing goals provides consistence in planning. When several persons are engaged in making the plans for an organization, a thorough understanding of the goals will make it easier to develop plans that are in line with the overall objectives. Each person involved in the planning process keeps an eye on the major goals and fits his or her aspect of the planning into the whole picture.

> Establishing goals provides a sound basis for coordination and control. On the basis of these goals, performance standards can be set and these in turn become guideposts against which actual performance can be measured.

Build in Flexibility

Sometimes we just can't reach a goal. Circumstances may change. What once seemed to be viable may no longer be. Instead of becoming frustrated, we should be flexible.

Changing Goals with Changing Circumstances

All of us set goals based on certain circumstances we anticipate during the life of a project. Circumstances do change however, and original goals may have to be adjusted. To anticipate that end, many companies use a goal-setting program that involves three levels:

- Alternative 1: A main, or standard goal: What we plan to accomplish if everything goes well.
- Alternative 2: A slightly lower goal: If circumstances change and it becomes obvious that our main goal cannot be achieved, rather than starting from scratch in redefining our goal, we can shift to this alternative.
- Alternative 3: A higher-level goal: If we're making greater progress than we had originally thought we could, rather than being complacent about being ahead of target, shift to this alternative and accomplish even more.

Take, for example, PCX, a company in the metropolitan Philadelphia area that services and repairs computers. Its sales goal for one year was to open ten new accounts. To prevent loss of customers when a national competitor opened a service outlet in the same community, all the company's energies were redirected toward saving its current accounts. The goal of attracting new clients then had to be reduced.

On the other hand, if PCX was having a good year, its goals could have been accelerated. If PCX had gained eight new clients in the first half of the year, it could have automatically raised its goal to a higher level.

Getting the Team to Buy into the Goal-Setting Process

At a recent goal-setting seminar, one participant complained: "I have trouble getting people to buy in to the big picture concept. They're so absorbed in their individual jobs that they can't see beyond their own problems."

Here's how we can overcome this type of situation:

- Bring everyone in the department or on our project team into the early stages of the planning process.
- Discuss the major points of the overall plan.
- Ask each person to describe how he or she will fit in to the big-picture plan.

- Give each person a chance to comment on each stage of the project. Breaking a long-term goal into bite-size pieces that people can relate to can help them to see how their part in a project fits together with the other parts. They can also then see how to set overall team or project goals for the long-run.

- Become thoroughly familiar with each of the team member's goals. If their goals aren't in line with those of the company, department, or project group, demonstrate to them how applying their skills to meeting the team's goals enhances the opportunity to fulfill their own expectations.

The Planning Process

The entire team should be involved in developing the team's plans for each project or assignment. As supervisor or team leader, we should coordinate and lead the process. Assign particular aspects of the planning to the associates who are the most knowledgeable about them, coordinate the process, and make decisions that have a significant effect on the entire project.

Planning must be tied in with the organization's goals. Unless one adheres to these goals, planning will be haphazard. Once the goals are clearly defined, the planners must diagnose the problems that the plan is to cover. To do this certain steps should be followed:

> *Clarify the problem.* Make sure that each of the planners understand the problem in the same way. For example, if the objective of an overall plan is to increase sales, and one participant diagnoses the situation as problem in better sales techniques, while another sees it as a problem in pricing, no solution can be reached. To assure that the situation is clearly understood by all planners, ask these questions:

> *What must be done?* Is it to correct inefficiency? To prepare for contingencies? To change a method? Or some specific matter?

> *Why must it be done?* If it is not done, what will happen? Is the action essential to solve present problems or to prepare for the future? How will this action affect company goals?

> *When should it be done?* Is there an emergency? If not, what time-table should be established to accomplish it?

> *Where will it take place?* Are facilities available for the plan and its implementation?

> *Who will be assigned to develop the plan?* Will it be assigned to a special planning group or to the staff members who are engaged in the current operation and will be responsible for implementing it?

> *How will it be done?* In what manner will the plan be made and later implemented?

SOPs: The Company Bible

One frequently used type of planning is the establishment of Standard Operating Procedures (SOPs), sometimes called Standard Practices (SPs), that details the organization's plans and policies. Although progressive organizations usually restrict their SOPs to such matters as personnel policies, safety measures, and related matters. Many companies, however, either incorporate specific job methods and procedures into their "Bibles" or publish them in accompanying "instruction manuals." Providing policies and procedures for routine activities eliminates the need to plan anew for them every time they occur. Because SOPs set standards that everyone must follow, all employees working with the manuals can refer to them at any time, which ensures consistency in dealing with particular situations.

If we have to develop SOPs, keep them simple. SOPs too often become complicated because of manager's desires to cover every possible contingency. It can't be done. Managers will frequently have to make decisions based on many unforeseeable factors. SOPs should cover the common issues in detail, but leave room for managers (or non-managerial people, where appropriate) to make spontaneous decisions when circumstances warrant them.

SOPs should also be flexible. Don't make SOPs so rigid that they can't be changed when circumstances change. Plans may become obsolete because of new technologies, competition, government regulations, or the development of more efficient methods. Build into SOPs a policy for periodic review and adjustment.

Also keep in mind that not all plans are SOPs. Plans may be developed for special purposes, sometimes to be used only once, and sometimes for projects that last several months or even years.

Standard Operating Procedures are just one phase of planning. As mentioned, it's best if SOPs should cover only broad policy matters so that specific plans can be designed for new projects as they're created.

A Guide to Successful SOPs:

> Clearly state what actions are expected from each participant.
> Specify where deviations may be allowed and when they are not permitted.
> Test the SOP before making it final.

Obstacles to Enforcing Accountability

No matter how well our plans are designed, there are likely to be challenges from associates or other managers. Our results, and the results of our team, depend on how those situations are handled. Fairness, consistency, and strength are required in the right places, at the right time, and in the right way. Without this, morale can grind to a low for everyone, effecting productivity, customer loyalty, and employee loyalty—all mandatory in today's highly competitive work force. Here are some suggestions to deal with this:

> Make sure that all goals and objectives are clear and communicated to everybody involved and that they not only understand but accept them.
> Performance objectives should be clearly indicated. How this can be done will be discussed in chapter 5.
> Goals and standards should not be revised unless serious problems change the scope of the project.
> Assure that all stake holders buy into, and feel a sense of ownership of the goals and standards. Milestones and methods of measuring, monitoring, and communicating achievements are determined.
> Encourage associates to ask the right questions to uncover barriers to achieving results.

- Set and adhere to time schedules.
- Provide coaching and feedback techniques.
- Be aware of lack of motivation and burnout of those involved in the project and take action to overcome it.
- Establish relevant reward system for achievement of goals.

Principles for Holding Ourselves and Others Accountable

We, as leaders of our teams are primarily accountable for its success or failure. To assure success we have the obligation to see that our associates recognize that they too are accountable. Here are some guidelines to help in this:

- Make immediate, intermediate, and long-term goals.
- Align performance objectives with corporate strategy.
- Be aware of changes in the scope of the project and revise goals, procedures, and deadlines, if plans or projects change.
- Gain agreement and buy-in on established goals and standards.
- Consistently broadcast established goals, objectives, checkpoints, and milestones to all involved.
- Ask the right questions, confront challenges head-on, and seek input to eliminate barriers to reaching goals.
- Prioritize activities, stay focused, and manage time according to performance goals.
- Set up a mentor system and learn ways to effectively coach and give constructive feedback.
- Maintain enthusiasm, commitment, and motivation by giving sincere and consistent recognition.
- Develop a relevant reward system for the achievement of goals.

Sum and Substance

Effective leaders follow these principles:

> Team members respond better to participatory, rather than authoritarian leadership.
> Associates should be given every opportunity to use their talents, skills, and brainpower.
> The good leader establishes a cooperative, collaborative climate in which all participants know their participation in decisions are welcome.
> Good leaders think of themselves as facilitators. Their job is to make it easy for their associates to accomplish their jobs.
> Effective leaders are ready to take the initiative, to act rather than react.
> The best leaders set high standards for themselves and then work hard to achieve their goals.
> They focus on getting things done and are not easily deterred.

3

....

MOTIVATING OUR STAFFS

As our people report to work have we ever asked ourselves, "Are they happy to be here? Would they rather be working for somebody else? Is it just the salary we pay them or the benefits our company provides that motivate them to come to work?" These are important, but most companies today pay satisfactory salaries and offer comparable benefits packages. It has to be more than that. Psychologists tell us that there are five basic motivating factors in a person's relationship to his or her job.

Recognition as an Individual

Each of our people is different from us and from the other people in the group. Each person likes to feel that we recognize these differences and treat him or her as a special person not as an interchangeable standard part. Supervisors must listen and observe the people they supervise and learn to differentiate among them. Learn their strengths and limitations, their likes and dislikes, how they act and react and tailor the way we deal with each of their individualities.

By paying attention to these differences we learn that each has one or more special concerns about his or her job. We find that Joe is highly security conscious and will take no risks for fear of failing and maybe jeopardizing his job. We note that Betty is very ambitious and wants to move up as fast as she can. Among our other people, Sam and Lil need constant reassurance while Karen is always trying new approaches. By keeping these individual differences in mind, we will be able to work most effectively with each of them and help them obtain what they want most from us as their managers.

Pride in Work

Most people who have reached supervisory or management positions take pride in their jobs. They usually have earned the promotion and have significant accomplishments in their work. These men and women are considered an important part of the company. If we can instill this sense of pride in *all* our people, it will lead to higher morale and commitment.

To accomplish this each new employee should be given a thorough orientation on what the department does and how it relates to overall company activities. He or she should also be told how the specific job performed helps the department and the company accomplishes its mission.

Appreciation and praise should be given whenever appropriate. Dale Carnegie encouraged us to be "hearty in our approbation and lavish in our praise." When people know that their work is appreciated, a sense of pride develops, and is maintained.

Sense of Belonging

Many organizations boast of the *esprit de corps* that they generate. Team spirit is essential to successful group activity. People like to feel that they are a part of something bigger than themselves: a team, a social group, a military unit or a company. These feelings flow directly from pride in one's job, but that is only the beginning. People are happier, more cooperative, and productive when they identify with their group—especially a successful and effective group. People brag about having served in the U.S. Marine Corps long after their service has been completed. People proudly tell others they are employed by IBM, AT&T, Sony, Toyota or other prestigious companies.

How can we build this feeling of belonging in our people? Good managers build team spirit by keeping objectives clearly in front of their people and getting their people to participate in determining how they will meet these objectives. By getting people involved in decisions which affect their work, they feel that they are important to the department and this solidifies their commitment. If they are enthusiastic about the job, they will be motivated to do their best.

Flaming enthusiasm, backed up by horse sense and persistence, is the quality that most frequently makes for success.

Dale Carnegie

Fair Treatment

Policies and procedures should be established, clearly communicated to the employees, and administered in a consistent manner. Cindy and Sandy both have tardiness problems. The boss likes Cindy and is not too fond of Sandy. She enforces the disciplinary action for tardiness for Sandy, but lets Cindy get away with a light reprimand. Not only will Sandy be upset, but the other people in the department will consider this unfair. People who commit the same offenses should receive the same treatment.

People respond emotionally—not rationally—when their self-interest is in jeopardy. The desire for fair treatment is deep seated in the emotional makeup of all people. Favoritism is the greatest of demoralizers. It destroys the feeling of security in others who fear that their own efforts and worth are not being recognized.

Chance to Express Ideas

Billy never forgot his first boss. "I thought up a great idea that could increase production in my department. All excited, I went to the boss to tell him about it. He never even listened. He said, 'You're paid to work not to think. Go back to your machine.' I never suggested another idea while I was on that job."

People who work on the job have a great deal of insight into the operation and often come up with good suggestions. All of us are more creative than we think we are. We should make a practice to encourage our people to make suggestions and take each one of them seriously. If it is not acceptable, explain why, but never ignore it.

Employees should feel free to discuss their personal progress with their manager. Some supervisors inadvertently erect a barrier between themselves and their people so that associates do not feel comfortable to approach them. We may not realize this, but if our people rarely come to us with their problems, it does not mean that there are none. It is more likely that employees do not feel free to discuss them with us.

What Makes Employees Tick

Let's take another look at some of the factors that employees seek in their jobs:

Recognition and appreciation

As noted above, recognition is a key factor. This was reinforced by a report of The Society for Human Resource Management, based on a Gallup Poll of 400 companies. It confirmed that an employee's relationship with his or her direct boss is more responsible for retention than pay or job perks. Fair and inspiring leadership, including coaching and mentoring, retains employees. Another Gallup Poll revealed that a key indicator of employee satisfaction and productivity is an employee's belief that the boss cares about the employee and can be trusted.

Some people are driven more by other forms of incentives than by money. In a study by Employee Retention Headquarters, appreciation and involvement are cited more than money as what keeps employees happy. They need to be convinced, verbally and nonverbally, that management respects their position and that they are important to the success of their organization. They enjoy celebrating milestones and victories, publicly and privately, verbally and in writing, promptly and sincerely.

Stimulating and fulfilling work

In October 2003, ASTD (*American Society for Training & Development*) newsletter reported that for most workers today, stimulating and valuable work is more important than salary and advancement. It's hard to put a price tag on enthusiasm and excitement for a job. Managers, who foster involvement of employees and include them early on in projects, obtain more creative ideas and create greater employee investment and pride in the outcome. Employees who actively participate in making decisions on a broad spectrum of issues help create an environment that they like and one in which they want to remain.

A clear career path and growth opportunities

By providing opportunities for growth, both personally and professionally, employees are less likely to look elsewhere.

Providing training opportunities with respect to new skill development and career development is an indication that a manager is willing to invest on behalf of the employee. This is critical for employee retention. Encouraging employees to join professional organizations by paying the membership fee and giving employees the time off and admission fees needed to attend lunches and conferences motivates employees. Companies who have a high retention rate hold a reputation for hiring from within. A jointly agreed upon career path will gain the commitment of employees and ensure their acceptance of organizational goals and direction.

Managers who respect a balanced life

Organizations that walk the talk of a balanced life have higher retention than those who believe that the employee should eat, breathe, and sleep work. Acknowledging and respecting the importance of family and personal life of employees prevents burnout and fosters loyalty. According to the Society for Human Resource Management, employers need to be aware of quality of work–life issues. They must be willing to offer flexible schedules and be sensitive to dual careers, childcare, and parent care challenges.

Competitive compensation and benefits

Money is important, but it is less important than we might think. Employees expect to be paid fairly and competitively. They feel entitled to the standard benefits of health insurance and retirement plans. In a survey 92 percent of respondents indicated that a $10,000 annual salary increase would not prompt them to change employers if they were receiving personal and professional development coaching.

Motivating for Peak Performance

Our first job as a manager or leader is to develop the skills and abilities of each of our associates so that they can perform at top capacity. The best way to begin is to learn about each person as an individual.

We may think that all we really have to know about our associates is how well they do their work. Wrong! Knowing the members of our team requires more than just knowing their job skill—that's an important part, but it's only a part of their total make-up. Learn what's important to our associates—their ambitions and goals, their families, their special concerns—in other words, what makes them tick.

Method of Operation

Each of us has our own special way in which we do our work and the way we live our lives. This is our "MO" (Method of Operation). Study the way each of our staff members operates, and we'll discover his or her MO. For example, we might notice that one person always ponders on a subject before commenting on it, and another might reread everything she's worked on several times before starting new work. Being aware of these work styles helps us understand people and enable us to work with them more effectively.

By observing and listening, we can learn a great deal about our colleagues. Listen when they speak to us: listen to what they say, and listen to what they don't say. Listen when they speak to others. Eavesdropping may not be polite, but we can learn a great deal. Observe how our associates do their work and how they act and react. It doesn't take long to identify their likes and dislikes, their quirks and eccentricities. By listening, we can learn about the things that are important to each of them and the "hot buttons" that can turn them on or off.

To get the most from each of our employees, we must understand them as human beings and work with them as individuals to help them make and meet commitments to perform even better than they have up to now.

As noted above, we must recognize that all human beings are not the same and we must deal with each of them according to his or her individuality rather than trying to get them all to do the same thing in the same way. Let's take the word "PEOPLE" and by expanding on each letter obtain some hints on how we can achieve our goal of better performance through our people.

Personality

Each person has his or her own special personality. A manager must take the time to get to know how each of them acts and reacts, what turns them on or off, what really is of concern to them. A major error made by many supervisors is to attempt to treat all people alike. Some people need much more attention than others, while some look upon your attention as prying or condescending. There are people who need constant reinforcement, while others only need an occasional pat on the back.

Exceptional Characteristics

Look for those traits that make each person stand out from the others. Laurie is very creative. In her spare time she draws, sculpts and writes poetry. How can that help on the job? By appealing to her creativity, we can get Laurie to tackle difficult projects or contribute ideas and suggestions that may help solve job problems. Gary is a perfectionist. His work may be slow, but it is always right. By giving him assignments where quality is paramount, we will be utilizing him most effectively.

Opportunity

Claudette's job was basically boring. But her boss recognized that she was anxious to learn and would give her full efforts to her boring job if she could see how it could lead to more challenging work. By giving Claudette opportunity to learn about other jobs in the department, she was able to train and prepare for them; thus encouraging her to learn and grow.

Opportunity is not limited to possible advancement on the job. There are people who do not want the responsibility of supervisory or management jobs, but seek opportunities to expand their knowledge or perform work that is of more interest to them. David considered himself a "people-person." He relates well to other people, but in his job as an accountant he spends most of his time working by himself. By giving David the opportunity to train others in the department in various company procedures and to periodically conduct department meetings, his enthusiasm for the job increased and his overall performance was enhanced.

Participation

People who work on a job have a lot more insight into how a job should be done than we may realize. When a new procedure has to be developed or a new project planned, have the people who will do the job participate in determining how it should be done. As the manager of the department, Kathy believed she knew exactly how the new project should be planned. After all she had years of experience in this work. However, instead of designing the plan and then telling her people how it would be done, she brought them into the early stages of the planning procedure. Not only did they come up with some excellent ideas that Kathy had not considered, but because they were participants in the planning, they felt committed to work hard to assure it would succeed.

Leadership

Good leaders do not set goals for their people and tell them how to reach them. Good leaders work with their people to encourage them to set their own goals and give them the tools they need to reach them.

Fred was an intelligent man and a good worker, but Paul, his boss, felt he had much more capability than he was using. Fred was afraid to take the initiative on any project and continually came to Paul for instructions. To help Fred overcome this, Paul began giving Fred small projects and made him responsible for their completion. By gradually increasing the complexity of these assignments, Paul helped Fred develop the self-confidence he needed to really give an outstanding performance.

Expectations

Let people know that we expect high performance. Do not be satisfied with mediocre work. Too many managers are delighted if their people meet minimum standards. This may be OK if business is flourishing, but when companies have to fight to stay alive, we need more than just meeting standards. Our people must be encouraged to try to keep getting better and better.

Rewards for achieving goals often help. Mary Kay Ash, the founder of the Mary Kay cosmetics company, attributes the great success of her company to her practice of having her people keep setting higher and higher expectations for themselves—and then by rewarding them with some form of recognition when those goals are met.

When people are expected by their bosses, by their families and most important by themselves to keep improving their performance, nothing can stop them from becoming real achievers.

By knowing our people and working with them, and utilizing their individual strengths will result in the collective efficacy of our department and higher performance for the organization.

Money as a Motivator

Here's a mini-lesson in logic:

A: The more money we earn, the happier we are.
B: The more work we produce, the more money we earn. Therefore:
C: People will stretch to produce more, earn more and thereby will become happier.

But is it true? Sometimes, but not always. Assume A and B are both true, it should logically follow that C is true. Right? Sometimes it is, but often it is not.

Let's look into why money is not always the motivator that it logically appears to be.

Motivators versus Satisfiers

A team of behavioral scientists led by Frederick Herzberg studied what people want from their jobs and classified the results into two categories:

1. *Satisfiers* (also called maintenance factors): Factors people require from a job to justify minimum effort. These factors include working conditions, money, and benefits. After employees are satisfied, however, just giving them more of the same factors will not motivate them to work harder. Many of what most people consider motivators are really just satisfiers.
2. *Motivators*: Factors that stimulate people to put out more

energy, effort, and enthusiasm in their job. They make them really move.

To see how this concept works on the job, suppose that we work in a less-than-adequate facility, in which lighting is poor, ventilation is inadequate, and space is tight. Productivity, of course, is low.

In a few months, our company moves to new quarters, with excellent lighting and air-conditioning and lots of space, and productivity shoots up.

The company CEO is elated. He says to the board of directors, "I've found the solution to high productivity: If we give people better working conditions, they'll produce more, so I'm going to make the working conditions even better." He hires an interior designer, has new carpet installed, hangs paintings on the walls, and places plants around the office. The employees are delighted. It's a pleasure to work in these surroundings—but productivity doesn't increase at all.

Why not? People seek a level of satisfaction in their job—in this case, reasonably good working conditions. When the working environment was made acceptable, employees were satisfied, and it showed up in their productivity. After the conditions met their level of satisfaction, however, added enhancements didn't motivate them.

So What Does This Have to Do with Money?

Money, like working conditions, is a satisfier. We might assume that offering more money generates higher productivity. And we're probably right—for most people, but not for everyone. Incentive programs, in which people are given an opportunity to earn more money by producing more, are part of many company compensation plans. They work for some people, but not for others.

The sales department is a good example. Because salespeople usually work on a commission, or incentive basis, they're in the enviable position of rarely having to ask for a raise. If salespeople want to earn more money, all they have to do is work harder or smarter and make as much money as they want. Therefore, all salespeople are very rich. Right? Wrong!

How come this logic doesn't work? Sales managers have complained about this problem from the beginning of time. They say: "We have an excellent incentive program, and the money is there for our sales staff. All they have to do is reach out—and they don't. Why not?"

We have to delve deep into the human psyche for an answer. We all set personal salary levels, consciously or subconsciously, at which we are satisfied. Until we reach that point, money does motivate us, but after that no more. This level varies significantly from person to person.

Some people set this point very high, and money is a major motivator to them; others are content at lower levels. It doesn't mean that they don't want their annual raise or bonus, but if obtaining the extra money requires special effort or inconvenience, we can forget it.

For example, suppose that Derek is in our production group and that his salary is 60 percent of ours. His wife works, but we know by the nature of her job that it doesn't pay much. Derek drives a twelve-year-old car and buys his clothes at thrift shops. The only vacations his family has ever taken are occasional camping trips. We feel sorry for him. But now we can help Derek. We need several workers for a special project to be done over the next six Saturdays at double-time pay. When we ask Derek whether he wants the assignment, he says "No," and we can't understand why. It seems to us that he should be eager to make more money, but he has already reached his level of satisfaction. To him, having the Saturday off to be with his family is more important than the opportunity to earn more money.

This example doesn't mean that money doesn't motivate at all. The opportunity to earn money motivates everyone up to the point that they are satisfied. Some people, like Derek, are content at lower levels. As long as they can meet their basic needs, other things are more important to them than money. To other people, this point is very high, and they extend themselves to keep making more money.

By learning as much as we can about our associates, we learn about their interests, goals, and lifestyles and the level of income at which they're satisfied. To offer the opportunity to make more money as an incentive to people who don't care about it is futile. We have to find some other ways to motivate them.

Benefits: Motivators or Satisfiers?

Benefits are important in most companies. These companies provide some form of health insurance, life insurance, pensions, and other benefits to their employees. In fact, the benefits package is one of the factors that potential employees seek when they evaluate a job offer—but it isn't a motivator. Have we ever known anyone who worked harder because the company introduced a dental-insurance program?

Benefits are satisfiers. Good benefits attract people to work for a company, and they also keep people from quitting.

Keeping employees happy is not enough. The challenge is to develop high performance standards that challenge employees and motivate them to stretch to meet these standards. Some of these motivators are:

Recognition

Human beings crave recognition. People like to know that others know who they are, what they want, and what they believe. Recognition begins when we learn and use people's names. Of course we know the names of the men and women in our work group, but often we will be coordinating work with other groups, with internal and external suppliers, subcontractors, and customers. Everyone has a name; learn the names of those people. Use them. It's the first step to recognize each person's individuality.

Remember that a person's name is to that person the sweetest sound in any language.

Dale Carnegie

Recognition is not limited to using a name. In Warren's exit interview after quitting his job with the Building Maintenance Company, he was asked what he liked most and least about the company. Warren responded that although the salary and benefits were good, he never felt that he was part of the organization. "I always felt that I was looked at as nothing more than a cog in the machine," he said. "During the nine months I worked in the department, I made several suggestions, offered to take on extra projects, and tried to apply creative approaches to some of the work assigned to me. My boss didn't recognize all that I could have contributed."

Show We Care

Just as we have a life outside the company, so do our associates. A job is an important part of our lives, but there are many aspects of life that may be of greater importance: health, family, and outside interests, for example. Show sincere interest in the associate as a total person.

Virginia, the head teller of a savings and loan association in Wichita, Kansas, makes a point of welcoming back associates who have been on vacation or out for several days because of illness. She asks them about their vacation or the state of their health and brings them up-to-date on company news. She makes them feel that she missed them, and it comes across sincerely because she really did miss them.

Jacob, a grandfather, realizes that children are the center of most families. He takes a genuine interest in the activities of his coworkers' children and has even accompanied associates to school events in which their children participate. Some people may consider this situation paternalistic or intrusive, but Jake's true concern comes across as positive interest and has helped meld his team members into a working family.

Praise

Twice I did good and that I heard never. Once I did bad and that I heard ever.

Dale Carnegie

There are supervisors who never praise their people. They rationalize that people are supposed to do good work and need not be praised for doing what is expected of them. One crusty supervisor boasted: "I never praise people. They know they're doing OK if I leave them alone. If I have to talk to them, they're in trouble."

Human beings crave praise. We all want to know that other people recognize our accomplishments and achievements. This is especially important when the praise is from our supervisor or other people whom we respect.

Praise Must Be Sincere

Carol was about to leave the room to attend a meeting. She paused when she reached the door, turned around and said: "Gang, I want to let we know you're doing a great job," smiled and left the room. At the meeting she told her colleagues how she boosted the morale of her department by her parting remark. Back in her department, her people looked upon it quite differently. One of the men loudly commented to the others: "She's just given us her monthly positive reinforcement."

What Carol assumed to be a morale builder was perceived by her people to be insincere. Praise must be sincere and we can't fake sincerity.

One way to make praise truly sincere is to incorporate the reason for the praise into the praise itself. Instead of saying: "Good job, Joe," it is far more effective to say "Joe, the way you handled that customer complaint is a fine example of the professionalism we like to see in this department."

Combining Criticism With Praise

When an employee has to be criticized, many supervisors sandwich the criticism between praise. This is supposed to make the criticism more palatable. Often this does reduce the resentment which often accompanies censure. However, if the only praise given is always accompanied by some form of negative comments, the praise becomes meaningless. When the supervisor begins the praise, the employee is thinking: "OK, when does he throw it at me?"

Typically, the conversation goes: "Sam, you are one of our fastest workers and I appreciate that, *but* you make too many errors...." The minute Sam hears that word "but," his mind blocks out the praise. He knows the next words will be criticism.

Barry overcomes this by substituting "and" for "but:" "Sam, you are one of our fastest workers. I appreciate that, *and* you could become even more effective if you improved the quality of the work. Let's see what we can do together to help you in that."

The word "and" does not have the negative connotation of "but." The employee still retains the glow of the praise and is open to suggestions for improvement.

Fear of Praising

Some managers comment, "If I praise workers who are doing well more often than others, won't this be considered favoritism?"

Not necessarily. When recognition is clearly deserved, and extended to everybody who deserves it, this is not favoritism. Those who are not praised should realize that they have not earned it.

Another concern: "When a person's performance improves significantly, is it better to give them extra praise than somebody who has done good work all along?"

Excessive praise can arouse resentment in those who have always been performing in a desirable way. Also excessive recognition can convey the idea that we expect exceptional achievement to become routine. We must tailor the way we praise to the needs of the specific associate.

When that person reaches the standard that is expected, praise him or her for the accomplishment and point out that this is what the other good workers are doing and we appreciate it. Do this in front of co-workers, so all know that this praise is based on reaching this level and is not for exceptional work. Naturally, persons who still do better should receive special recognition.

Managers ask: "Should people be praised for performing average work consistently?" Everybody needs praise, but to give special recognition for routine performance is self-defeating. It gives the person no incentive to improve. Occasionally, the supervisor might compliment them on some special achievement or comment on their good attendance record. This should not be done on a regular basis or it loses its value. Praise should never be given on a schedule. "Today is the 14th, it's my day to praise Kathy," but given at a time when the circumstances warrant it.

Communicating Praise

Be immediate: The best time to praise is at the time the praiseworthy event occurs. When Alice presented her report to her boss, he immediately complimented her on completing it before the deadline. After he read it, he again praised her for its content.

Be specific: As mentioned earlier, incorporate what we are praising the person for with the praise itself.

Describe its value to the organization: "By beating that deadline, it enabled us to complete that project and solve our customer's problem to his satisfaction."

Encourage them to keep up the good work: "We have made great progress on this job and I know we will continue to use our excellent skills in helping us achieve our goals."

Five Tips for Effective Praise

As important as praise is in motivating people, it doesn't always work. Some supervisors praise every minor activity, diminishing the value of praise for real accomplishments. Others deliver praise in such a way that it seems phony. To make praise more meaningful, follow these suggestions:

1. Don't overdo it. Praise is sweet. Candy is sweet too, but the more we eat, the less sweet each piece becomes—and we may get a stomachache. Too much praise reduces the benefit that's derived from each bit of praise; if it's overdone, it loses its value altogether.

2. Be sincere. We can't fake sincerity. We must truly believe that what we're praising our associate for is actually commendable. If we don't believe it ourselves, neither will our associate.

3. Be specific about the reason for the praise. Rather than say, "Great job!" it's much better to say, "The report you

wrote on the XYZ matter enabled me to understand more clearly the complexities of the issue."

4. Ask for our associates' advice. Nothing is more flattering than to be asked for advice about how to handle a situation. Caution: This approach can backfire if we don't take the advice. If we have to reject an advice, ask the person questions about their suggestion until they see its limitations and rethink it.

5. Publicize praise. Just as a reprimand should always be given in private, praising should be done (whenever possible) in public. Sometimes the matter for which praise is given is a private issue, but it's more often appropriate to let the entire team in on the praise. If other team members are aware of the praise we give a colleague, it spurs them to work for similar recognition. In some cases, praise for significant accomplishments can be more widely publicized, such as when it's given at meetings or company events.

Give Them Something to Keep

Telling people that we appreciate what they've done is a great idea, but writing it is even more effective. The aura of oral praise fades away; a letter or even a brief note endures. We don't have to spend much money. It doesn't take much time.

Write Thank-You Cards

At the A&G Merchandising Company in Wilmington, Delaware, team leaders are given packets of "thank-you" cards on which the words *Thank You* are printed in beautiful script on the front flap, and the inside of the card is left blank. Whenever someone does something worthy of special recognition, that person's manager writes a note on one of the cards detailing the special accomplishment and congratulating the employee for achieving it. The recipients cherish the cards and show them to friends and family.

Plaques and Certificates

No matter what type of award we give to employees—large or small (cash, merchandise, tickets to a show or sports event, or a trip to a resort, for example)—it's worth spending a few more dollars to include a certificate or plaque. Employees love to hang these mementos in their cubicles or offices, over their workbenches, or in their homes. The cash gets spent, the merchandise wears out, the trip becomes a long-past memory, but a certificate or plaque is a permanent reminder of the recognition.

Motivating Marginal Workers

Who are our marginal workers? These are the people who meet our minimum performance standards, but rarely exceed them. They are not bad enough to be fired, but do not really carry their own weight. Motivating such people is a major challenge to leaders. What are some of the reasons we have marginal workers in our organizations?

Poor Selection

Debbie, a data entry clerk, is a marginal worker. Because data entry clerks were in short supply. Her boss Barbara, hired Debbie even though she did not quite meet the job requirements. Although she was still below the expected performance standard when she completed her probationary period, Barbara decided to keep her. "At least somebody is operating that computer," she rationalized, "and I'll keep working with her and make her productive."

Six months later, despite additional training and coaching, Debbie is still just barely meeting production standards. She does not have the innate capability to be truly productive.

Poor selection is one of the major reasons for marginal production. By establishing realistic job specifications and not compromising when hiring people—even when desperate to fill the job—the chances of selecting people who will succeed on the job will be enhanced.

However, no matter how good our selection procedures may be, errors may be made and the person hired may not make the grade. That is why probationary periods are so important. During this period, the supervisor should make sure the new worker knows what he or she is expected to do and the standards that must be met. Every effort should be made to help this person meet these standards through training, coaching, and special attention.

Be patient. Sometimes the reason for marginal production is not incapability but a lack of understanding or what is to be done. In designing a training program for new people, set specific standards and time tables. Make sure that the trainee is aware of them. If standards are not met at the specified time, we should work with the trainee to overcome the problems that may have caused this.

Every effort should be made to salvage the trainee, but if it fails, do not keep a person who barely meets minimum standards. Once probation is completed, it is much more difficult to terminate a marginal worker.

Good Workers Whose Performance Declines

Phil has been with the company for six years. His production has always been well above the minimum standard and his supervisor, Lil, looked upon him as one of her best people. A few months ago Phil's production began to decline. He seemed to have lost interest in the job.

Why does this happen to people like Phil? Sometimes it's due to personal problems. One's personal life and job life cannot be separated. If there are serious problems at home, it will affect our work.

Sometimes it's due to a real or perceived grievance. Some people keep their grievances deep inside themselves and it festers unless it is brought out and addressed.

In her discussion with Phil, Lil learned that Phil had set certain goals for himself which were not being met on the job. Although his work was praised and his reviews excellent, he had not reached the position he had hoped to reach at this stage of his career.

The supervisor should know the goals of his or her people and do what can be done to help them reach them. Let the worker know what he or she must do to attain the goals—including maintaining a high performance level, taking additional training on the job or through outside study, and pointing out how long it might take to achieve this. If it is not possible for the worker to meet his or her goals on this job, the supervisor and worker together should determine how the goals might be modified so that they could be met on this job.

Boredom

For years Ann was one of the best performers in her department. But now Ann was bored. She had been doing the same job for so long that she no longer enjoyed doing it. She found every excuse to take time off. When she was on the job, she gossiped with her co-workers, extended her breaks, and put out as little production as she could get away with.

One way a supervisor can help formerly productive workers return to productivity is to enrich the job by combining functions that were performed by several people into one job so that each worker does more diverse work. Another is to restructure the manner in which the work is done. This is achieved most effectively when the worker participates in the restructuring. People who work on a job can often come up with ideas to make the work more interesting and effective. Another approach to relieve boredom is to assign the worker special projects. Change of pace is a good antidote to boredom.

Coasters

Michael has been with the company for 22 years and in his present position for eight years. He's happy in his work, but also recognizes that due to the nature of his work and the organizational structure of the company, it is unlikely he will ever be promoted. His work is good; he knows he will never be fired unless he does something drastic, so consciously or subconsciously he decided that there is no point knocking himself out on the job. He'll just coast along until retirement.

Most companies have their share of such "coasters." They are good workers and can contribute to productivity, but they feel they've done their part. How can we remotivate such people?

Associated Products uses "coasters" for new product testing. When they are ready to introduce a new line, they test market it in key cities. Instead of using a test marketing company, they assign this to some of their "old-timers." By being involved in a new and important role shows them they are respected and it gives them an opportunity to do something new and different. This stimulation carries over when they return to their regular work.

Other companies have used these long-term workers as trainers and mentors of new people. Giving them this type of responsibility makes them more dedicated to the job and the company, and can convert them from marginal workers to productive members of the company team.

"My people couldn't care less about their jobs. If I don't keep pushing them, nothing will be accomplished," sighed Al.

"I don't have that problem at all," Carl responded. "My gang is always willing to put forth whatever effort is needed to get the job done."

What is the reason for these diametrically opposite attitudes of the workers that each of these managers supervise? Why is Carl's group so much more highly motivated than Al's? It could be the management style of the supervisor or it could be the work itself.

Behavioral scientists generally agree that although employee motivation is enhanced by such factors as recognition, appreciation, challenge and, of course, fair treatment, the most effective motivator of all is the work itself. If Al's people find their jobs boring and unchallenging, no matter how good a supervisor Al may be, he will have a tough time motivating them. On the other hand, if Carl's people enjoy their work so much that they can't wait to come in every morning and hate to leave each evening, there is little else Carl needs to do to keep them motivated.

Enrich the Job

Unfortunately, a great percentage of jobs in industry today are merely routine, and it is difficult, if not impossible, to generate excitement about them. One way to overcome this is to enrich the job.

When Jennifer was hired to head the claims processing department of the Liability Insurance Company, she inherited a department with low morale, manifested with high turnover, absenteeism, and disgruntled employees. The claims processing operation was an "assembly line." Each clerk checked a section of the claims form, passed it to the next clerk, who checked the next section, and so on. If an error or question of interpretation was discovered, it was put aside for handling by a specialist. From an operational viewpoint, this was highly efficient. However, it made the work dull and unchallenging. Jennifer reorganized the system. She enriched the job by eliminating the "assembly line." Each clerk checked the entire form, corrected errors and sought interpretations. This required added training and did slow the work down in the beginning, but it paid off in developing a highly motivated team of workers who were really interested in their jobs. Turnover, absenteeism and dissatisfaction were significantly reduced, and once the system was fully established, speed and accuracy were increased.

Get the Staff Involved

Engendering an attitude that the job to be done is mutual effort of management and labor, not "superiors" ordering "inferiors" to perform a task—will make the work more interesting and the people engaged in that work more highly motivated to accomplish the job.

When productivity expected is quantifiable, many companies establish production quotas for their workers. This is particularly true in sales and many manufacturing and office positions. Denise heads the Word Processing Section of her company. She has established specific quotas for most of her mass-mailing projects and can measure how well her people are doing by how close they come to meeting the quotas. Denise noted that even her best workers rarely would produce more than the quota. When she tried to increase the number of letters expected, she was faced with resentment and even overt opposition.

When a new project was being planned, instead of superimposing a quota for the project, Denise asked the people who would work on it to study the project. Managers and the workers together should establish quotas or goals that are attainable and acceptable by both. When a person has participated in establishing quotas, that person will feel committed to meet that quota and will willingly work to assure that it is met.

In his book, *How to Win Friends and Influence People*, Dale Carnegie anticipated what the behavioral scientists later promulgated. He wrote: "No one likes to feel that he or she is being sold something or told to do a thing. We much prefer to feel we are buying of our own accord or acting on our own ideas. We like to be consulted about our wishes, our wants, and our thoughts."

The One Best Motivator

Behavioral scientists generally agree that although employee motivation is enhanced by such factors as recognition, appreciation, challenge and, of course, fair treatment, the most effective motivator of all is the work itself. Work can become repetitious, boring, and unchallenging. Some ways to overcome this is redesign jobs to provide diversity, challenge and commitment.

Bring associates into the planning stages of new jobs. Get their input as to production or sales quotas, methods and performance standards. When people feel they "own" the job, they are more likely to put in all their efforts to achieve the goal.

Sum and Substance

Eight ways to give people what they want from their jobs

1. Let each person know how he or she is getting along.
2. Help them improve by coaching and guidance.
3. Be hearty in our approbation and lavish in our praise.
4. Tell people in advance about changes that will affect them and, if possible, why the change is being made.
5. Make the best of each person's ability.
6. Look for ability that is not being used, help that person develop that ability and utilize it.
7. Never block a person's opportunity for advancement.
8. Give people more freedom to control the way they do their jobs. Encourage them to suggest better methods and approaches.

4

....

STAFFING OUR ORGANIZATION

Most managers feel that filling a vacancy in their department is an annoying distraction from their real function. The time, energy and emotional drain that the hiring process involves takes them away from their regular duties, adds extra hours to their day, and worst of all, they fear that they will make the wrong choice and would have to go through the whole process over again in a few months.

In most large companies and in many smaller firms, the human resources department handles recruiting and selecting new employees. However, even when this is done, line supervisors and team leaders have to participate in the process. Almost always, they'll interview prospects. After all, they are the people to whom the person hired will report and they will be responsible for the new employee's success or failure.

In some companies there may not be an H.R. department or, if there is one, it is situated at the home office, so managers at branch facilities are required to do the hiring themselves.

Unfortunately, although these managers are usually skilled in performing work in their own specialty, they don't have the training and experience required for successful hiring. As a result countless errors have occurred—at the minimum, wasted time and effort, and at the worst hiring people who were doomed to fail.

As a supervisor or manager we cannot take this aspect of our job lightly. The men and women we hire will contribute to our success or cause us from meeting our objectives.

Develop Realistic Job Specifications

We can be more effective in selecting the people with whom we will have to work and upon whom we must depend to get the job done by starting the search with a realistic job specification.

Analyze the job carefully and determine just what background the new employee should bring to the job. We should ask ourselves as we list each requirement: "Is this really needed to perform the job?"

Jeff was seeking to fill a job for a customer service representative. One of the specs he established for this job was the requirement of a college degree. Is this realistic? Certainly there are advantages in hiring a college graduate for this job, but does this job really require skills that are acquired in college? Could a person with less formal education do the job just as well?

When Jeff was asked why he wanted a college grad for this job, he responded: "Why not? There are lots of college grads looking for jobs, I might as well take advantage of this and get the best I can." Does this make sense? Requiring more education (or any other qualification) than is really needed has more disadvantages than advantages. Sure, we may get smarter or more creative people, but because these people will not be challenged by the job, they will probably not be as highly productive as persons with less education. People who become bored with the job are the people who become gripers, have high absentee problems, and leave after brief tenures. More important, we may eliminate the best possible candidate for the job by putting the emphasis on the wrong aspect of background.

When Lynn obtained approval to add another accounting clerk to her staff, she told the H.R. department she needed somebody with at least ten years' experience in bookkeeping or accounting. Is this realistic? When asked why ten years? Lynn responded: "The more experience the applicant has, the more he or she will know—therefore will become productive for us more rapidly." Is there always a direct correlation between years of experience and expertize? Not necessarily. We all know people who have ten years on the job, but only have the equivalent of one year's experience. We also know others who acquire great skill in a very brief period of time.

Recognizing that years alone do not really measure expertize, Lynn rethought her specs. Instead of asking for ten years' experience, she set up a list of factors that the new employee should bring to the job and how strong he or she should be in each of them. By asking the applicants specific questions on each of these factors, she would be able to determine at an interview how much the applicant knew and what he or she had actually done in each area that is important to the job.

Does this mean that years of experience don't count for anything? No. Often the only way a person can gain the skills needed for a job is by actually working in a similar capacity. However, by emphasizing what they have accomplished rather than how long they have done it, we will make a better hiring decision.

Another requirement often found in job specifications is that the experience should have been in "our industry." True, often skills and job knowledge can only be acquired in companies that do similar work, but there are many jobs where the background in other industries is just as valuable and may be even better because the new employee is not tradition-bound and brings creative and innovative concepts to the job.

By limiting the population from which we can choose our new employee to only those in one industry, we may not only eliminate good people, but the job may remain unfilled for a long period of time. The H.R. manager of Associated Health Aids was frustrated. It was six months since the admin assistant to the Marketing Vice-President had left and the position was still vacant. The problem: The VP insisted that his assistant have experience in the health aids field. No applicants with that kind of experience had turned up. When asked why this background was needed, the VP told her that the admin had to know the language of the trade. How long would it take somebody who was not familiar with it to learn that "language?" Probably two to three months. Yet the company had already kept the job open for six months, when in a maximum of 90 days, the lack of this one "critical" requirement could have been overcome.

To avoid falling into the common traps in setting job specification, analyze the jobs carefully. Ask: "What must the applicant have that I either cannot do or do not want to spend time to train them to do?" These should be the essential specifications for that job.

If there are a large number of applicants for a position, we should also determine what preferential factors would be helpful. These factors can be used to help choose from among the applicants who have all of the essential factors. But even in establishing preferential factors, be sure they are realistic and do not eliminate good people. For example, a preferential requirement for a graduate degree when such educational background is not really important for the job may not be wise.

A vital part of every job specification is the indication of the intangible factors—often more significant in hiring the right person than some tangible requirements. Sure, we would all like to hire people with high intelligence, creativity, integrity, loyalty, positive attitudes, enthusiasm and the like. However, when listing the intangibles needed for a job, be sure they are put in proper perspective as it relates to that job. If the job calls for communication skills, specify which communication skills are needed: one-to-one oral communication? ability to talk to groups? telephone communication? writing letters and memos? creating advertising copy or brochures? power-point or other computer based communication techniques?

If the job calls for "attention to detail," specify what type of detail work. If the job calls for working under pressure, indicate what types of pressure: meeting daily deadlines? occasional deadlines? unpleasant working conditions? a tough boss? Analysis and description of the intangibles needed is just as important as analysis and description of education, experience and skills required.

By establishing realistic job specifications and screening our applicants to ascertain that they meet these specifications, we will staff our department with qualified people to form the team we need to meet our goals and objectives.

Screening Candidates

Once the job specifications are established, we must now begin our search for candidates. The people currently working in the organization often know other people who may qualify for the open positions.

Promoting or transferring a current employee to a new position is commendable and should be encouraged. Internal candidates are known factors. The company has seen them in action. They know their strengths and weaknesses, their personality quirks, their work habits, their attendance and punctuality patterns and all the little things that months or years of observation uncover. It also is good for employee morale and motivation. The problem, however, is that it limits the position only to current employees. In this highly competitive world, a company should attempt to find the very best candidate for open positions—and that person may not be currently on the payroll.

There was a time when companies boasted that when the Chairman retired, they hired a junior clerk. Everybody moved up a notch. It is likely that in a large organization there are many highly competent people who are available for filling the new openings and of course, they should be given serious consideration. However, a search for outside candidates may bring to the company skills and expertize that is now lacking and new ideas that often elude people in-bred within the organization.

Charlie used a variety of sources when a vacancy developed in his department and received over thirty résumés. They all looked good. Which ones should he see for the interview? When screening résumés, look for the following:

➤ *Does applicant meet the basic specifications?*

Don't waste time calling candidates who fail to meet the key requirements for the job.

➤ *Look for omissions.*

Many résumés omit dates of employment. This may be done to hide periods of unemployment or to leave an impression of having more or better experience than really achieved. One way to overcome this is to have all applicants complete a company application form. This can be mailed to them and returned before we determine who is to be interviewed. If there is a rush to fill the job, telephone or email the applicants in whom we are interested to obtain missing information.

➤ *Look for inconsistencies.*

An applicant may claim heavy background in one area, yet the companies for whom he or she worked are not involved in that area. For example, Jack's résumé played up his background in marketing consumer packaged goods, but, of his ten year's experience, only two years—several years ago—were with consumer oriented companies.

➤ *Look for progress.*

For the amount of years in the work force, has the candidate made appropriate progress in terms of advancement and earnings? Compare the backgrounds of the candidates as they relate to the job specifications and then as they relate to each other and select the best for the next stop—the job interview.

When talking with another person, listen attentively. Don't assume a bored attitude or allow an "I knew it" expression to flicker across your features.

Dale Carnegie

Getting the Most from an Interview

Here are some suggestions on conducting a meaningful interview. After making the applicant feel at ease by a friendly greeting and a few comments on non-controversial aspects of the applicant's background, begin the structured interview with some *open-ended questions*:

"Tell me about your experience with the XYZ Company."

"What background do you have in sales analysis?"

"Describe your most recent project."

On the basis of the responses received, focus on key aspects of the candidate's background in that area and *ask specific questions* based on details of what was done and accomplished.

Mae commented in response to an open-ended question on her most recent project that she had made a market study of the potential of a new product. Specific questions to elaborate and verify what she really did might include:

"How did you obtain the needed data?"

"What problems did you face in getting cooperation from the people involved?"

"How did you solve them?"

"What was the result?"

"Describe the steps you took in your analysis."

"What was the most difficult aspect of the project?"

By asking about specific facets of the project rather than

just accepting her statements, we will obtain a clear view of actual experience rather than the usual generalizations that are so often elicited in a job interview, and it will help identify the real accomplishments of the candidate.

Evaluate Personal Characteristics

We hire not only a person's job skills, but also the personal characteristics that the individual brings to the job. A person with good looks, charm, a gift of gab and a pleasant way makes such a good impression on us that we may be overly influenced by this veneer. To determine the true personality of the applicant, we must look beneath the surface.

By using "situational questions," true personality traits can often be uncovered. A situational question is one in which the candidate is asked to respond on how he/she handled delicate problems in the past or how hypothetical situations might be handled. For example, "A customer calls and is irate. The delivery promised has not arrived and the entire production schedule for this customer is in jeopardy. How did (or would) you handle this?" From the response, we can determine the candidate's integrity (would he/she lie about the delivery?), tact (was the candidate diplomatic?), and attitude (was he/she loyal to the company?).

As the interview is usually the primary tool used in making the hiring decision, it is important that it gives the interviewer the information and impressions needed to make this judgment. Here are ten traps that many interviewers fall into that prevent them from really learning as much as they should know about the people they are considering for employment.

1. *Not structuring the interview*: When Bill returned from an interview with the Chief Accountant of the Goody Gumdrop Candy Co., he was convinced that the interviewer had obtained little or nothing from the interview. Bill reported that the Chief Accountant had jumped from one subject to another—talking for a moment about education, then shifting to some phases of work experience, then back to schooling, over to attitudes, then to job objectives and finally, more questions on work background. Too many interviews are little more than informal chats. In order to make the interview more effective, the interviewer should follow a set pattern that will enable the interviewer to cover all the salient points systematically. It doesn't make any difference whether we start with education, the first job, the last job or objectives, so long as a structure is established and followed to cover all information. However, we must be flexible within the structure, so we don't fail to probe areas of interest just because they may not fit into our interviewing plan.

2. *Interviewing for the wrong job:* Some interviewers do not pay adequate attention to the job specifications. Barbara applied for a job analyst's position. The interviewer asked all kinds of questions on every aspect of H.R. administration except job analysis. Before an interview, study the specifications. Be familiar with the details and implications. Frame questions that will bring out those aspects of the applicant's background that indicates knowledge (or lack of it) of those specifications.

3. *Letting the applicant dominate the interview:* A savvy applicant can so dominate the situation that he or she

only tells us what is most favorable and manages to deemphasize negative facets. The good interviewer must maintain control. When we have an applicant who doesn't let us get one word in, who twists our questions to fit his or her desires, who keeps adding information which is not relevant, but is designed to boost his or her background, *cut it off*. We may say, "That's most interesting, however, would you mind giving me specific details on... (then indicate the specific area)." The best way to counteract an applicant's attempt at domination is to insist that he or she answer our questions to our satisfaction.

4. *Playing God*: One of the major complaints applicants have about interviewers is that they condescend to them. They act so superior that they feel uncomfortable. Because the interviewer has the power to hire or at least to refer the applicant on for further consideration, there is a tendency to "play God" and smugly savor this power. A little humility will pay off in better rapport, and a more effective interview will win friends for us and for our company.

Don't assume an air of importance. Never allow the other person to feel he is inferior to you in any sense.

Dale Carnegie

5. *Signaling the right response*: Some interviewers are so anxious to fill a job, they help the applicant respond correctly to their questions. They signal the expected answer "This job calls for ability to handle people. You do have this ability—don't you?" Nobody ever says, "No."

6. *Stifling the applicant*: When Henry was interviewed, he never had a chance to tell about his qualifications. The

interviewer first told him about the company, then he told him about the job, then about his own work. When he finally did ask a question, he interrupted Henry before he could finish his answer. An interview is a two-way conversation. If only one party dominates it—applicant or interviewer—it will not accomplish its purpose.

Susan stifled her applicant in another way. She wrote down everything the applicant said. It's OK to take occasional notes, but a word-by-word transcription will stifle the interviewee and keep the interviewer from listening fully to what is being said.

7. *Playing the District Attorney*: Martin loved interviewing people. His great joy was to "catch them" in some inconsistency. He would repeat questions in several forms to ascertain that the answers were the same. If he found an "error," he would pounce on the victim. He bragged about all the "phonies" he exposed, but more often than not the inconsistencies were inconsequential and he not only lost good potential employees, but left a poor impression on those applicants he interviewed.

8. *Playing Psychologist:* Just because we took Basic Psychology in college does not qualify us to be a psychologist. Some interviewers assume far more psychological knowledge than they have. They look for hidden meanings in everything the applicant says. They ascribe Freudian motives to work experience, family relations, attitudes and even casual comments made by applicants. The fact that they are not really qualified to make these judgments does not bother them one bit. They are so absorbed in their "psychological evaluations," they fail to determine if the applicant can or cannot do the job.

9. *"Falling in love" with the applicant*: Sometimes an interviewer is so impressed with one aspect of an applicant's presentation that it dominates the evaluation. It may be a person's appearance or charisma, or it might be the possession of a specific skill that is needed by the company. Although that trait may be impressive, there may be other important facts of the applicant's background that negate it. A good interviewer will recognize that this charm or skill is an asset, but it should be put in proper perspective. A well structured interview which allows for a careful evaluation of each factor needed for success in the job, will help overcome this.

10. *Failure to probe for details*: George was asked a series of questions on whether he had experience in several areas of work in his field. He answered each affirmatively, but to his surprise, the interviewer accepted his answer without probing to determine how much depth he had in each area. George could have easily misrepresented his background by outright false information or by exaggerating his knowledge. Good interviewing requires thorough exploration of the candidate's knowledge. Study the job specifications and frame questions based on what is expected in order to meet those specifications.

By careful planning of an interview and being cognizant of the pitfalls and avoiding them, we can make our interviews more meaningful and our hiring decisions more effective.

Don't interrupt the other person when talking. Let that person talk himself out. If you interrupt him you are implying that what he is saying isn't worth listening to.

Dale Carnegie

Verify

Wherever possible, contact the former employers of applicants in whom we have interest to verify that what they have told us is correct. To get meaningful information, try to speak to the applicant's direct supervisor rather than to the Human Resources department. The supervisor has had day-to-day observation of the candidate, where in most companies the only information H.R. has is what's in the files.

More and more companies are reluctant to give information about former employees to others, but it is worth the effort to try. One way to overcome resistance to giving information is to emphasize that we would like to *verify* information rather than ask for information. Before making a call, prepare a series of questions drawn from the applicant's application, résumé and notes from the interview. Be sure to choose significant aspects of the background to use so we can obtain maximum information in a limited amount of time.

Selecting the Best People

We have read a hundred résumés, interviewed dozens of applicants, and have narrowed it down to three or four people, all of whom have excellent experience and background for the job we are seeking to fill. Which one should we hire? This dilemma is faced by managers each time a job opening occurs. We must make this important decision based on the personal characteristics that make one person stand out from all the others. People with "hire appeal" are more likely to impress us than those who lack this intangible trait.

Experience has shown that unless these characteristics are superficial or contrived, they are indicative of success on a job. They are the human factors that enable people to work well with us, their co-workers, and others within or outside the organization with whom they will interrelate.

Appearance

In most contacts with people our immediate reaction is to their appearance. A person whose physical characteristics, dress, and presence are pleasant, neat and attractive, starts off on the right foot in most interpersonal relationships. This does not mean that we should judge the book solely by its cover, or that we should give preference to handsome men and beautiful women. Neatness, a pleasant countenance and good taste in dress and grooming are important. But be careful not to put overemphasis on appearance.

Barbara is an extremely attractive young woman. Over the past five years, she has had four jobs as a sales representative and has failed in all four. The sales managers were so impressed by Barbara's good looks, they assumed she would make an immediate favorable impression on prospects and become a successful salesperson. However, Barbara had little else to offer. She had been so accustomed to getting by on her appearance that she had never had to work very hard.

Do not interpret this to mean that appearance is not a factor to be considered. Many attractive people also have the skill, drive and capability to do a good job. Because many of us tend to put more emphasis than we should on appearance, we should look more deeply into all the aspects of a particularly attractive person's background before making a decision.

We Favor People Like Ourselves

Tom's associates were all alumni of his university. Even though Beth, a native of Iowa, worked in Chicago, three of her staff members were also from Iowa. When Tom and Beth were questioned on why they selected these people, their responses included comments on job qualifications, personality traits and intelligence, but neither manager considered the similarity of backgrounds as being a factor.

One tends to subconsciously favor people whose backgrounds are close to one's own. There is a comfortable feeling when dealing with people who have shared a similar environment or experience. This could be an asset in the sense that working relationships can be developed more rapidly and more easily. However, it may lead to choosing a less qualified candidate. Another limitation when all the people in a work group have analogous backgrounds is the inclination for them to think much alike and therefore, have less exposure to new ideas.

Self-Confidence

When Frank was interviewed he exuded self-confidence. He was not afraid to talk about his failures and unlike people who try to impress interviewers by bragging about their accomplishments, Frank was matter-of-fact about his successes. He projected an image of being totally secure in his feelings about his capabilities. It is likely that Frank will manifest this self-confidence on the job, enabling him to adapt readily to the new situation.

Fluency of Expression

Laura was able to discuss her background easily and fluently. She did not hesitate or grasp for words. When the interviewer probed for details, she was ready with statistics, examples, and specific applications. Not only does this indicate her expertise, but her ability to communicate—an essential ingredient in many jobs.

However, there are some glib people who can talk a great job, but have only cursory experience or knowledge of it. They learn and use the jargon of the field. To determine if an applicant is a talker but not a doer, ask in-depth questions and also probe for specific examples of their work. Glib phonies cannot come up with meaningful answers.

Alertness

Diane sparkled at the interview. She reacted to questions and comments with her facial expressions and gestures. We could see that she was on her toes. Alert, sparkling applicants are usually dynamic and exciting people who give all to their jobs.

Maturity

Maturity cannot be measured by the chronological age of a person. Young people can be very mature and older people may still manifest child-like emotions. Truly mature applicants are not hostile or defensive. They do not interpret questions as barbs by a "prosecutor out to catch them." They do not show self-pity, have excuses for all of their past failures or inadequacies. They can discuss their weaknesses as readily as their strengths.

Sense of Humor

Evan was a sourpuss. At no time during the interview did he smile or relax. Even when we tried to lighten up the interview with a humorous comment, he barely reacted. This may be due to nervousness, but more likely Evan is one of those very serious people who never look at the lighter side of things. They are difficult to supervise and impossible to work within a team. It is easier and much more fun to work with a person who has a sense of humor.

On the other hand, applicants who are too frivolous, who tell inappropriate jokes, laugh raucously or act inconsistently with the situation may be immature.

Intelligence

Although some aspects of intelligence may be measured by tests, we can pick up a great deal about the type of intelligence a person has at an interview. If the job calls for rapid reaction to situations as they develop, (e.g. sales) a person who responds to questions rapidly and sensibly has the kind of intelligence needed for the job. However, if the person is applying for a job where it is important to ponder over a question before coming up with an answer (e.g. research engineer), a slow, but well-thought-out response may be indicative of the type of intelligence required.

Watch for the "Halo Effect"

Rob is a computer wizard. Give him any type of problem that can be solved by a computer and he will develop a program to solve it. His bosses were so impressed with this capability that they promoted Rob to a position which required making decisions that could not be solved by computer. They assumed that because he was so good in one area, he must be good in all areas.

The opposite is the "pitchfork effect." The person involved has one negative characteristic that so dominates our evaluation of that person that we do not see his or her good points.

To avoid the prejudice of halo or pitchfork effects or other narrow approaches of evaluation, we should look at the whole person instead of at disparate traits.

Look for Success Records

"What is past is prologue." In selecting people for a new job, whether it be a promotion from within or hiring from the outside, the most significant factor is their past record. Successful people tend to continue to be successful. People with mediocre records tend to repeat their mediocrity. By evaluating what that person has accomplished in previous jobs or assignments, we can get a graphic picture of what they may do in the new situation. To determine and evaluate success patterns, ask applicants what they consider to be their major contributions in their previous jobs.

When Lee applied for a sales job, he had no specific experience, but his record of success in his previous administrative job showed that he could face and solve complex problems in a variety of areas. The Sales Manager recognized that this was a major asset in selling and selected Lee rather than some of the more experienced salespeople who were competing for the job. Within a few months, Lee proved that his pattern of success carried over into this new position and was on his way to becoming one of the best salespeople on the staff.

The way a person perceives the job also tells much about the candidate. Betty was the office manager of her company. Her major achievement was to keep the work flowing, putting out fires, and assuring that each assignment was completed on time accurately. That is good—if we want a "maintenance" type individual, one who can maintain operations as they are. However, if we need innovation or creativity, it would be better to seek someone who has introduced new systems which improved productivity or had reorganized a department to make it more efficient.

The accomplishments of which the applicant is proud of, also give more insight into his or her thinking about the nature of the work. In answer to the question of achievement, Gary, a candidate for a human resources executive position, proudly described how he created a bowling league and softball tournament for his company. His competitor for the position, Eileen, explained how she introduced a suggestion program which resulted in several cost-saving innovations. On the basis of these responses, which one is the better candidate?

Warmth

This very important intangible asset is a major ingredient of "hire appeal." It is difficult to describe but we know when it is there. The warm person is empathetic and shows real concern about the matters discussed. This person will talk freely about interpersonal relations. He or she is comfortable at the interview and makes us feel comfortable. An individual with this type of personality is at ease in any environment and will most likely fit into the department rapidly and naturally. They are likeable people and easy to live and work with.

Sensitivity to Feedback

The applicant who understands what we are projecting not only in our questions and in our comments, but with our body language will probably do the same on the job. This is an asset which is invaluable in the workplace. People like these are easy to train. They readily accept and implement instruction and criticism and work well with their peers.

Naturalness

A person who is natural and relaxed is probably a well integrated person. However, do not automatically negate a nervous applicant. To reach such a person and determine what latent characteristics may exist beneath his or her uneasiness calls for skill, patience, and determination. Their nervousness may be masking their real selves.

Giving Information to the Applicant

An important part of the interview is giving the applicant information about the company and the job. All the work and expense undertaken to get good employees is lost if the applicants we want don't accept our offer. By giving them a positive picture of the job at the interview, we are more likely to have a higher rate of acceptances.

When and what to tell about the job

Some interviewers start the interview by describing the job duties. Some give the applicant a copy of the job description in advance of the interview. This is a serious error. If an applicant knows too much about a job too soon, he or she is likely to tailor the answers to all of the questions to fit the job.

For example, we tell a prospect that the job calls for selling to department store chains. Even if the applicant has only limited experience in this area, when we ask, "What types of markets did you call on?" guess which one will be emphasized.

The best way to give information about duties and responsibilities is to feed it to the applicant throughout the interview—*after* we have ascertained the background of the applicant in that phase of the work. For example:

Interviewer: What types of markets did you call on?

Applicant: Drug store chains, discount stores, department stores, and mail order houses.

Follow this by asking specific questions about the applicant's experience in each of these markets. If the department store background is satisfactory, the interviewer might then say: "I'm glad you have such a fine background in dealing with department store chains as they represent about 40 percent of our customer list. If you should be hired, you'd be working closely with those chains."

If the background in this area was weak, the interviewer might say: "As a great deal of our business is with department store chains, if you should be hired, we would have to give you added training in this area."

Most interviewers give the applicant an opportunity to ask questions about the job and the company at some point (usually at the end) of the interview. The questions asked can give some insight into the applicant's personality and help us in our evaluation.

Are the questions primarily of a personal nature? (Such as vacations, time off, raises, and similar queries), or are they about the job? People who are only concerned about personal aspects are less likely to be as highly motivated as job-oriented applicants. Their questions can also be clues to their real interest in the job. If we feel from these questions that a promising candidate might not be too enthusiastic about the job, it gives us another chance to sell the prospect on the advantages of joining our company.

We are always 'selling' when we interview. It's important that we present our company and the job in a positive and enthusiastic manner. This doesn't mean that we should exaggerate or mislead the applicant. Tell the applicant any negative factors about the job at the interview, but show how the positive aspects outweigh them. For example, "This job does require you to work overtime for the first few months to acquire our complex technical training, but once you have mastered our system, it will enhance your expertize in this field."

Whether we are considering a current employee for promotion or we are hiring from the outside, it is imperative that every step be taken to assure the right decision is made. Be alert to the dangers of personal likes and dislikes, overemphasis on appearance and the halo or pitchfork effects. Look for a pattern of success in the past, a positive attitude toward the job, the type of intelligence patterns related to the job, and a warm, natural, mature personality.

Sum and Substance

> Before evaluating résumés, set up a list of key requirements. Unless the applicant meets these specifications, there's no point arranging for an interview.
> Don't take a résumé at face value. Read between the lines. Look for hidden negative factors.

- Have all applicants complete a company application. The résumé should be used as a supplement not a substitute for the application.
- Before conducting an interview, review the job specifications as well as the applicant's résumé and application form.
- A good interview should be structured, but flexible enough so that follow-up questions can be asked.
- Put the applicant at ease by asking non-threatening questions at the beginning of the interview.
- Check the references of prospective employees by speaking to his or her direct supervisor, not the H.R. department.
- When comparing candidates consider the whole person, not just work experience. Avoid the halo or pitchfork effects.

5

....

ENHANCING PERFORMANCE

Phil accepted the congratulations graciously. He had won the club championship for the third consecutive year. A reporter from the local paper asked: "Phil, you're our undisputed golf champ. What advice can you give the rest of us on how we can improve our performance?" Without hesitation, Phil responded: "It begins with the way you tee up."

Preparation

All performance whether it be on the golf course or on the job starts with preparation. Before the first ball is hit or the job assignment is undertaken, it is what is done to prepare for it that will make the difference between adequate and superb performance. In golf, teeing up is not just putting the ball on the tee, but all that has been done before the game to master it.

Technical Competence

The first step is to acquire as much knowledge about the subject as possible. Competency in one's job just as in any sport, starts with learning the basics and then the more complex aspects of the procedure. Becoming technically proficient in the field of one's endeavor is essential for top performance.

Darlene was intrigued by the new technologies in medical diagnosis and treatment. As a nurses' aid at Mercy Hospital, she observed but did not operate this new equipment. At every opportunity, Darlene went down to the department where this equipment was being used. She spoke to the technicians and was given literature she could study. She was particularly interested in the use of the ultrasound machine, which is used to identify many internal problems. She then enrolled in a training program, and became certified as a Registered Diagnostic Medical Sonographer and was transferred to full-time work in this capacity. Most people obtaining this certification would be satisfied to get such a job, but Darlene wanted to be more than just a good worker; she aimed to be the best possible technician. She continued her studies, and volunteered to work on special projects with the physicians using the equipment. In a relatively short time, Darlene was the most technically knowledgeable sonographer in the hospital and was on her way to a successful career in this field.

Training

Training does not stop when one has acquired technical competence. Even the best athletes will continue to train no matter how successful they are. They know that the need for training never ends.

Sam is a successful salesperson who does not believe he will ever complete his training. "There is so much I have to learn," he complains. Every year, Sam takes at least one training course in salesmanship or product knowledge. He reserves time every week to read books and listen to training tapes. This has resulted in Sam's continuing improved performance in servicing his customers and increasing his sales.

Teach Others

Another way to perfect our own skills is to teach others. Not only does this enable us to systematically review what we have been doing and reinforce it for ourselves, but one often learns from the trainee. Questions asked and suggestions made by the trainee can lead to more knowledge about one's own field.

Ann is the supervisor of word processing for a political action committee. With election time nearing, she hired two additional operators and had to train them. In order to assure that these trainees would be taught rapidly and efficiently, Ann set up a training plan. The process of developing this plan forced Ann to rethink many of the techniques that she had been using herself. She recalled some short cuts and special approaches that she had not used in years and came up with some new ideas. Once the training began, the interaction between Ann and the trainees stimulated her to improve her own performance and increase her personal productivity.

Trying

Champions never say. "It can't be done." They try to find a way to overcome the obstacles. Even champions don't always win, but they never lose without first trying to win.

Norman Strauss, an industrial painting contractor in New York City, was confronted with a major problem. His bid for the job of painting Madison Square Garden, New York's largest indoor sports arena was due by the end of the week. The major problem was painting the ceiling, which was 110 feet above the ground floor. The usual way of reaching the ceiling was constructing a pipe platform on which the painters would stand when they sprayed the ceiling. The cost of building the platform was the same for all bidders. The only way to significantly reduce the bid would be to find some way to paint the ceiling without constructing the pipe platform. Everybody knew this couldn't be done, so why bother?

But Norman Strauss did not give up easily. He believed that to achieve success one must never cease trying to solve a problem. On the way home that evening, Norman noticed an electric company repainting a high street light. To reach this light, they were using a "cherry picker," a truck with an elevator on its roof that could be raised to various heights. "Why not use cherry pickers to reach the ceiling at the Garden," Norman thought. Investigation the next day brought out that it was feasible and economical. Strauss was able to submit a significantly lower bid than his competitors and obtained the job.

Think

The final step in preparing for enhanced performance is thinking. Before commencing the game or the job, it is essential that it be thought out. A good golfer thinks out how he or she will play the hole before making that first drive. A superb performer thinks out how the job will be performed before beginning the project.

In a complex operation, as much time must be given to the planning as to the work itself. Before making a sales call, the successful sales representative thinks carefully about all of the possible problems that may develop and how they can be handled. Executives think about every ramification any of their decisions may cause before making that decision. This is also true for top performers in the theater, cinema, television, and in sports.

We can become superb performers by careful preparation for all of our endeavors, becoming technically proficient, and never ceasing training, teaching others, and keep trying—especially when things get tough.

The Performance Process

Performance standards are usually based on the experience of satisfactory workers who have done that type of work over a length of time. Whether the standards cover quantity or quality of the work or other aspects of the work, they should meet these criteria:

Specific: Every person doing a job should know exactly what he or she is expected to do.

Measurable: The company should have a touchstone against which performance can be measured. Measuring performance is easy when a standard is quantifiable; it is more difficult (but not impossible) when it isn't quantifiable. When a numerical measurement isn't feasible, some of the criteria may include timely completion of assignment, introduction of new concepts, or contribution to team activities.

Realistic: Unless standards are attainable, people consider them unfair and resist working towards them.

The Performance Results Description (PRD)

Enhancing performance—our own and that of our associates must be accomplished in a systematic manner. It starts with a look at our own position and the results that we are responsible for at the end of the day, month, and year. It continues both up and down in the organization to ensure there is alignment from the very top to the bottom.

The first step is to determine exactly what we wish to accomplish on this job and how it will be measured. To do this we must design a Performance Results Description (PRD). Unlike the prototypical job description that focuses upon what activities or tasks that should be done, the Performance Results Description is a picture of what the job looks like when it is being done well.

It is a results-oriented view that allows managers and employees to plot a path from the organization's vision, mission, and values to the individual's measurable job objectives. The Performance Results Description not only helps them discover and delineate individual job functions—which we refer to as Key Result Areas (KRA's)—but it correctly measures successful completion of those areas through clearly defined performance standards. This document is an alignment tool that establishes clear-cut individual accountability throughout the team, department, and organization.

As this is done, everyone in the organization is focused on accomplishing the vision, mission, values, and job objectives on a daily basis. This tool helps delineate and measure goals, provide clear-cut responsibilities, and establish accountability. People use technology to monitor a car's speed and performance with the speedometer and gasoline gauge. Leaders help define performance by identifying Key Result Areas and relevant performance standards in the workplace. This system frees people to measure and monitor their own performance while minimizing the need for traditional systems of measurement and discipline.

This view starts at the top with the organization vision, mission, and values, then moves to individual results that are always in alignment with the team, his or her manager and the mission of the organization.

When we maximize the performance process, we create an environment through our leadership where people are free to achieve the results the organization needs to stay competitive and exceed customer expectations; while at the same time assuring employee's personal and professional growth.

Major Components of the PRD

In developing the PRD for a job, we must determine:

> What is the purpose of this job? In other words, why does this job exist?
> What are we committed to in this job and why?
> What are the Key Result Areas—the areas in which specific results must be accomplished that, when achieved, fulfill the job function?
> Are these goals in alignment with the position goal, the vision, and mission of the organization?

Performance Standards Should Be Specific

To assure that these Key Result Areas are determined satisfactorily the performance standards should be specific, measurable, attainable, results-oriented, and time-phased. Among the things to be specified are:

> Deadlines
> Costs
> Duties
> Activities required to accomplish the Key Result Area
> Skills, Knowledge, and Abilities
> What is needed to accomplish this Key Result Area?

Performance Standards Should Be Measurable

Performance standards are tangible, measurable conditions that must exist before the job can be done well. These standards are focused on results, not activities. They should be outcome oriented.

Although we may create our own standards, once written, they are negotiable to the point of agreement with the next level of management. During the performance it can be shown that each standard was, or was not, accomplished. This makes it objective instead of subjective and removes fear from the performance review process.

Here are some "Acid-Test" questions used to determine the strength of a performance standard:

> Is it within our control or domain?
> Are we measuring results or just quantifying activities?
> Where are we expecting perfection?
> Is there any chance of misunderstanding the terms or

language? For example, words such as: "good", "many", "effective", "well done", "successful", "best", etc., are not measurable nor easily agreed on.

Any fool can criticize, condemn, and complain but it takes character and self-control to be understanding and forgiving.

Dale Carnegie

Below is a sample list of performance standards. Of course each job requires individual analysis. These are presented as an example to illustrate the process.

➤ A minimum of 30% of business increase in 2010–2011 fiscal year has been from new customers.

➤ All staff have completed their mandatory yearly recertification within one month of the anniversary of their date of employment, as required in certifying agency standards.

➤ All staff members have attended one training meeting per week in the past six months.

➤ Customer complaints about late deliveries have been reduced by 20% during 2010–2011 fiscal year.

➤ The restructuring of the employee orientation meeting to make it more enjoyable for the staff has been completed by June 15, 2010.

➤ The sales team has increased the level of repeat business from current customers in the pharmaceutical field by 17% between April 1 and September 30, 2010.

➤ The amount of break-ins and vandalism in our branch office has been reduced by 50% during 2010-2011 fiscal year, resulting in 10% lower insurance premiums.

- All graphic designing deadlines have been met every time with each client.

Formal Performance Appraisals

Usually before in most organizations, a formal evaluation of performance is conducted annually. Many leaders add an informal appraisal semi-annually or quarterly as a means of helping associates be aware of their progress.

Importance of Formal Appraisals

- They provide a framework for discussing the person's overall work record. The leader can use this meeting to recognize an employee's past successes and provide suggestions for even greater contributions.
- They enable leaders to measure all members of the group against the same criteria.
- They provide helpful data for determining what type of additional training associates need.
- In many companies, they're the primary factor in determining salary increases and bonuses.
- Their formality causes them to be taken more seriously than informal comments about performance.
- They can be used as a vehicle for goal setting, career planning, and personal growth.

Downside of Performance Appraisals

- They can be stressful for both leaders and staff members.
- It make some leaders so uncomfortable making associates unhappy that they overrate their performance.

> Many formal systems are inadequate, cumbersome, or poorly designed, which creates more problems than solutions.
> In some appraisals, good workers are underrated because their supervisors are afraid that these workers might become competitors.

Choosing the Best System

There are many formal appraisal systems that can be used. Let's look at the most frequently used programs:

Trait-based Systems

The most common evaluation system is the 'trait' format, in which a series of traits are listed and each is measured against a scale from unsatisfactory to excellent. Here is a typical example:

Traits:

> Quantity of work
> Quality of work
> Job knowledge
> Dependability
> Ability to take instruction
> Initiative
> Creativity
> Cooperation

Ratings:

Excellent 5-points; Good 4-points; Average 3-points; Needs Improvement 2-points; Unsatisfactory 1-point—this system seems on the surface to be simple to administer and easy to understand, but it's loaded with problems:

- *A central tendency:* Rather than carefully evaluating each trait, it's much easier to rate a trait as average or close to average (the central rating).
- *The "Halo Effect":* As discussed earlier in this book, some managers are so impressed by one trait that they rate all traits highly. Its opposite is the "pitchfork effect."
- *Personal biases:* Managers are human, and humans have personal biases for and against other people. These biases can influence any type of rating, but the trait system is particularly vulnerable.
- *Latest behavior:* It's easy to remember what employees have done during the past few months, but managers tend to forget what they did in the first part of a rating period.

As the trait-based appraisal is measured in numerical terms, it is tempting to use the scores to compare associates. Some companies encourage the use of the bell curve in making these ratings. The Bell Curve concept is based on the assumption that in a large population most people will fall in the average (middle) category, a smaller number in each of the poorer than average and better than average categories, and a still smaller number in the highest and lowest categories.

The trouble with the use of the bell curve in employee evaluations is that small groups are unlikely to have this type of distribution—and it may work unfairly against top and bottom level workers.

For example, suppose that Carla is a genius who works in a department in which everyone is a genius. However, Carla is the lowest-level genius in the group. In a bell curve for that group, she would be rated as "unsatisfactory." In any other group, she probably would be rated "excellent."

Or suppose that Harold's work is barely satisfactory but that his entire group is performing below average. Compared to the others if we use a bell curve, we have to rate him "excellent."

Every manager and group leader should be carefully informed about the meaning of each category and the definition of each trait.

Understanding *quantity* and *quality* is relatively easy. But what is *dependability*? How are *initiative, creativity*, and other intangibles measured? By developing training programs that include discussions, role-plays, and case-studies, standards can be established that everyone understands and uses.

Establish criteria for ratings. It's easy to identify superior and unsatisfactory employees, but it's tougher to differentiate among people in the middle three categories.

Keep a running log of each employee's performance throughout the year. It isn't necessary to record average performance, but we should note anything special that each person has accomplished or failed to accomplish. Some notes on the positive side may say, for example, "Exceeded quota by 20 percent," "Completed project two days before deadline," or "Made a suggestion that cut by a third the time required for a job."

Notes on the negative side may say, "Had to redo report because of major errors" or "Was reprimanded for extending lunch hour three days this month."

Make an effort to be aware of personal biases and to overcome them.

Gather information. Have specific examples of exceptional and unsatisfactory performance and behavior to back up the evaluation.

Results-based Evaluations

Rather than rating people on the basis of an opinion about their various traits, a more effective appraisal system focuses on the attainment of specific results. Results-based ratings can be used in any situation in which results are measurable. This system is obviously easier to use when quantifiable factors are involved (such as sales volume or production units), but it is also useful in intangible areas such as attaining specific goals in management development, reaching personal goals, and making collaborative efforts.

In a results-based evaluation system, the people who do the evaluation don't have to rely on their judgment of abstract traits, but instead can focus on what was expected from their employees and how close they came to meeting these expectations. The expectations are agreed upon at the beginning of a period and measured at the end of that period. During that time, new goals are developed to be measured at the end of the same period.

Here's how this system works:

> For every job, the manager and the people doing the job agree on the KRAs (Key Results Areas) for that job. Employees must accomplish results in these areas to meet those goals.

> The leader and the people assigned to the job establish the results that are expected from each person in each of the KRAs.

> During a formal review, the results that the associate attained in each of the KRAs are measured against what was expected.

> A numerical scale is used in some organizations to rate employees on how close they came to reaching their goals. In others, no grades are given. Instead, a narrative report is compiled to summarize what has been accomplished and to comment on its significance.

Some companies request that associates submit monthly progress reports compiled in the same format as the annual review. This technique enables both the associate and the leader to monitor progress. By studying the monthly reports, the annual review is more easily compiled and discussed.

When dealing with people, remember you are not dealing with creatures of logic, but creatures of emotion.

Dale Carnegie

The 360° Assessment

Multilevel assessments have become an increasingly popular approach, used to identify how a manager is viewed by his or her bosses, peers, subordinates, and even outsiders (for example vendors and customers). Usually referred to as 360° assessment, such reviews have been adopted by companies like General Electric, ExxonMobil, and other Fortune 500 corporations.

People do not see themselves as others see them. We perceive our actions as rational, our ideas as solid, and our decisions as meaningful. Traditionally, performance is evaluated only by one's own manager. This does give us insight into how our work is perceived by that person, but he or she is not the only person with whom we interact.

Even more complex is the evaluation of senior managers,

who frequently are not evaluated at all. When these executives are assessed by peers and subordinates, they may learn things about their management style that they were not aware of. Many are shocked to find out how people perceive them and, as a result, take steps to change their management styles.

Despite the advantages of multilevel assessments, there are also potential drawbacks. Feedback can hurt. Evaluators may not always be nice or positive. Some people see their role as assessor, as an opportunity to criticize other's behavior on the job.

Another flaw concerns conflicting opinions. Who decides who is right? Or what if an appraisal is biased? If the evaluator does not like the person being evaluated, the responses might be skewed negatively; if the assessee is a friend, the evaluation might be skewed positively. Often, people rating their bosses or other senior executives fear it is dangerous to be completely truthful.

In order to ensure that the 360° assessment has a better chance of producing a change, it is recommended that:

> The appraisal is anonymous and confidential.
> To have sufficient knowledge of the person being rated; the appraisers should have worked with the appraisee for at least six months.
> Appraisers should give written comments as well as numerical ratings. This enables their evaluations to be more specific and meaningful.
> To avoid "survey fatigue," don't use 360° assessments on too many employees at one time.

Employee Evaluation Interviews

Whether a point or results-based system is used, the results must be communicated to the associate. When supervisors are asked what aspect of their job they like least, firing employees is usually first, but right behind it is the evaluation interview. Supervisors do not mind telling good things to their people, but are uncomfortable in discussing shortcomings. Of course, employees feel the same way. They'd dread the evaluation interview and often are nervous, tense or defensive. To make this interview meaningful and productive, both parties should approach the meeting with the positive feeling that this is a constructive exercise.

Preparing for the Interview

Effective appraisal interviews must be carefully planned. Before sitting down with the associate, the leader should study the appraisal itself. It is helpful to make a list of the major areas to be covered. Note all the positive aspects of the performance—not just the areas where improvement is needed. Study previous appraisals. Note all of the improvements that have been made since the last appraisal. Prepare pertinent questions about past actions, steps to be taken for improvement, and future goals.

We should recall all we can about the employee's behavior patterns. Does he or she have any special problems or idiosyncrasies? If this person is known to be belligerent, negative, emotional or in any other factor that may make the interview difficult, be prepared to deal with it.

The meeting should be scheduled a few days in advance. Suggest that the employee review his or her own performance before the meeting. Many companies give the employee a blank evaluation form and ask them to rate themselves. This gives them the chance to give a serious and systematic look at their own performance and prepare them to discuss it at the meeting.

Discuss the Performance

Once rapport has been established with the interviewee, we should point out the areas of the job in which the person has excelled and those in which the standards were met. By giving specific examples, the employee will know that we really are aware of his or her positive qualities. Encourage the employee to comment.

Listen attentively, and then discuss those aspects of performance or behavior which did not meet the standards. Be specific. It is far more effective to give a few examples of where the employee has fallen below expectations than to just say, "Your work is not up to our standard." Performance standards should be clearly spelled out and understood by employees. It should be no surprise to them to be told that they are not meeting those standards. By showing them work with excessive errors, or reminding them of missed deadlines, would be accepted in a more positive way.

In every instance our concentration should be on the work, not on the person. Never say: "You were no good;" say: "The work did not meet the standards."

If the problems are not related to performance, but behavior, give illustrations of this as well—"Over the past several months I have spoken to you about being late. You are a good worker, your opportunities in this company would be much greater if you could only get here on time everyday."

Get Employee's Suggestion for Improvement

Once the situation has been presented, instead of making recommendations for improvement, ask the employee for his or her suggestions. Some employees will resist this. They will present excuses, alibis, and rationales for past actions rather than look forward to future improvement. Listen to them empathetically and encourage them to get it all out of their system. Once this is done, they will be more amenable to face the real situation and come up with viable ideas.

Ask, "In what way can I help you improve your performance?" Accept their recommendations where possible and work out a plan of action on how this can be accomplished. It is often helpful to suggest added training on the job or through outside sources.

We know our people and if in our judgment this employee is unlikely to come up with constructive suggestions, we should be be prepared to propose a few of our own.

Set Goals

If goals had been set at the previous annual review, reevaluate them. If they were met, congratulate the employee and learn just what was done to accomplish this. If they were not met, find out why, and determine what can be done to meet them over the given period of time.

The appraisal interview is not just a review of the past, but a plan for the future. Ask: "What would you like to accomplish over the next twelve months?" Elicit production goals, behavioral changes, and plans for advancement. This could also include personal goals such as obtaining additional education, participation in professional or trade association activities or other off the job endeavors that will enhance his or her career. As the manager, we should be supportive, but not make any promises or give false hope for advancement or career growth that may be beyond what we can offer.

Have the employee write down each goal then next to it indicate what he or she plans to do to achieve the goal. Give one copy to the employee and keep one copy with the employee appraisal form. Next year, use this as a part of the appraisal interview.

Most of the important things in the world have been accomplished by people who have kept on trying when there seemed to be no hope at all.

Dale Carnegie

Summarize

At the end of the meeting, we should ask the appraisee to summarize what has been discussed. Make sure that he or she fully understands the advantages and disadvantages of performance and behavior, the plans and goals for the next period, and any other pertinent matters. Keep a written record of these points.

Unless the employee is doing a poor job and this evaluation is a "last chance" before termination, end the meeting on a positive note—"Overall, you have made good progress this year. I am confident that you will continue to do a good job."

The employee evaluation process, if properly managed, can be a highly stimulating experience for both the employee and the supervisor. The interview should not be a confrontation, but a meaningful two-way interchange that leads to commitment of the employee to reach out for improvement and set and implement goals for the coming year that will lead to a more productive and satisfying work experience.

Performance Appraisals Dos and Don'ts

✓ Do develop a reservoir of goodwill. Be trustworthy.
✓ Do let the appraisee review all the data before the meeting.
✓ Do start with the positive.
✓ Do be a coach.
✓ Do put the spotlight on success.
✓ Do use accurate data for our assessment.
✓ Do coach, and correct. Depersonalize the mistakes.
✓ Do let the other person save face.
✓ Do praise the slightest improvement. Be hearty in our approbation and lavish in our praise.
✓ Do expect improvement.
✓ Do develop a mutual plan of improvement.
✓ Do revise the PRD, and set new performance standards where appropriate.
✓ Do end the appraisal with reassurance and a big reputation to live up to.

Try to adhere to these **don'ts:**

✓ Don't betray confidences.
✓ Don't save up any unpleasant surprises.
✓ Don't nag or whine.
✓ Don't be an adversary.
✓ Don't focus exclusively on failure.
✓ Don't criticize, condemn, or complain.
✓ Don't launch a personal attack.

✓ Don't humiliate the other person.

✓ Don't expect miracles.

✓ Don't ignore him or her until the next appraisal and expect much improvement.

✓ Don't end the appraisal on a negative note.

Sum and Substance

> For every job, set performance standards that are clearly understood and accepted by those who will perform the job.

> When people know what is expected of them, they can monitor their own performance on an ongoing basis.

> If the trait method is used to evaluate staff members, be careful to avoid the dangers of central tendency, the halo and pitchfork effects, personal biases, or an emphasis only on the most recent behavior.

> Results-oriented evaluations measure actual performance against predetermined expectations.

> Don't fear the performance review. It can be a beneficial and worthwhile experience. We can make it even more valuable by going into the review prepared to handle it in a constructive manner.

6

....

BE A COACH

Probably the most challenging part of the leader's job is molding the individual team members into a dynamic, interactive, high-performance unit. We have seen how athletic coaches shape up their teams and as leaders of our work teams, we can learn from them.

We do this by helping the members of the team develop their talents to optimum capacity. We keep our team alert to the organization's goals and to the latest methods and techniques that will enable them to reach those goals. We help them learn what they don't know and to perfect what they do know.

A good example is Bob, an experienced salesman recently hired by a company. Because of his successful background, Bob did not expect his manager to give him much training. He assumed he would be oriented about the product line and sent into the field. But Bob's manager insisted on giving him the same extensive training as a less experienced sales trainee. Bob understood this. He had been a champion runner in high school but his coach at the university had given him as much attention and training as those team members who had never competed before. Successful managers keep this in mind when bringing on a new employee. Even if he or she has had previous experience, it is necessary to work on the company's approaches to the job, which may differ from the employee's past experience. Most managers will not hesitate to do this with a person who has had no previous experience, but often neglect it with experienced personnel.

Helping Team Members Take Charge of Their Jobs

Our work group or team is made up of individuals. Each person in the group contributes to the success of the team's mission. To do that, each member must be skilled in the work he or she performs and motivated to do it superbly.

Here are some suggestions that have worked for many leaders:

> The leader encourages associates to master their jobs. When workers know their work well and perform it in a professional manner, they are on the track toward mastery of their work life. The coach not only trains new members of the group in the basics of their jobs, but works with all the members to keep them on the cutting edge of the latest technology, methods, and innovations. In addition, the leader encourages members to take the initiative in adding to their knowledge, to read, to take courses, to attend seminars, to learn from others—not just about specific aspects of the functions currently performed, but to broaden their knowledge of their profession or skill area. This gives

associates a feeling of comfort and confidence when faced with new challenges that arise.

> Training never ceases. Techniques of training can be learned by observing the athletic coach. The professional trainer, whether he or she is a coach or a manager, will start training with a thorough orientation on what must he acquired during the training. This can be done in group sessions (if more than one person is being trained) or by individual discussions. Training aids such as manuals, films, or tapes are helpful during this time.

Elena, the manager of data processing for a housewares distributor has an enviable record of success in getting new people started rapidly. When a new employee joins her department, Elena works with that person almost exclusively for the first few days. She says, "The more time I spend up front, the better the success rate." During this initial training, Elena gives her people thorough preview of the basics of the computers used in her department—no matter how much experience the new employee has already had. She says this gets them started correctly and helps eliminate any bad habit carried over from previous jobs.

> Training does not end when the new employee is allowed to work independently. No matter how long a person is on the staff, continual training and retraining should be a part of the manager's job. Successful leaders do not concentrate the training effort only on those people who are not performing satisfactorily, but make a practice of working with all of their people on a regular basis. Just as a coach of an athletic team is constantly on the alert to identify areas where improvements

can be made for each team member, successful supervisors seek to work with each of their people to hone their skills, so they can become even more effective in their jobs.

> Managers should have periodic individual training conferences with each of their people alongwith group meetings for all their staff. The manager should always be on the alert for any variations in the performance of each subordinate and give them suggestions and coaching to improve.

Aim for excellence. In most teams there are members whom we know can perform better. They do satisfactory, even good work, but we see in them a potential that is not being reached.

An example: Cathy, team leader of a market development team, felt that one of her associates, Christine, was one of those persons. She set up a meeting with Christine and told her: "Your work is good, I have no complaints about it, but I know that you could and should do better. Had you been less bright, I would've been satisfied with what you've been doing; but I see in you the capacity to be one of the very best people in this company. By being satisfied with mediocre performance, you're not aiming high enough. Let's together develop a plan to help you achieve what you are capable of achieving."

They jointly set goals and plan to reach them. Standards were established so they could measure how close Christine was getting to those goals. They met periodically to evaluate her progress. Within a few months, Christine was doing significantly more effective work and was on her way to an exciting and satisfying career.

> Get the members to participate. As discussed earlier in

this book, it has been shown that when people participate in decisions that affect them, they're more likely to work to achieve them. When a new project is assigned, instead of telling the assignees how to do it, we should work together with them in setting the procedures. Giving them some control over the way it will be done is another way of helping them take charge of their jobs.

> Encourage creativity. Most people feel they have some control over their jobs when their suggestions and ideas are taken seriously. Nobody expects that all of their suggestions will be accepted, but they do expect that they will be given serious consideration. We should create a climate of innovation. This will give associates the opportunity to criticize current practices and come up with their own original ideas. The old adage "If it isn't broken, don't fix it." must be replaced with "If it works now, it's probably obsolete."

Ten Tips on Coaching Associates

1. Meet with each associate on a regular basis to identify what that person can do to become more effective and what we can do to help.
2. Don't wait for a formal performance review to confront poor performance. Take action to correct it as soon as it is observed.
3. Keep a running record of each associate's progress. Include examples of successes and failures. Note areas where improvement is needed. Specify recommendations for that person's growth.

4. In training associates, keep in mind that people master tasks in small steps. Build the training by first giving the associate small tasks, then work up to more complex tasks.

5. Encourage slow learners by praising their efforts and reinforcing the training to help them catch up.

6. Rather than working to achieve several goals at once, help associates build their skills by working on one goal at a time. Once on the way to meeting it, add another goal.

7. We should be a role model to associates by our own pursuit of learning and our application of new approaches to the work.

8. Pass on tips, information, and ideas to team members. This may take the form of articles we read, Internet resources we e-mail to them or sharing new concepts orally.

9. Assign associates responsibility for all or part of a project and give them the leeway to do it without any interference.

10. If the coaching session doesn't result in improvement, ask these questions:

   - What was the purpose of the coaching session?
   - What did I do to achieve the purpose?
   - What action resulted from the session?

Have the team member answer the same questions, and compare the results.

Coaching the Team

Irrespective of work done in teams today, it is not enough to train each member of the team to perform exceptionally. Equally important is bringing together individuals into a coordinated working unit.

For a new team, it starts with a thorough orientation on the objectives of the team—what is expected from each associate, and from the team as a whole. This can be done in group sessions or, when a new member is added—one on one.

Let's look at Erica, leader of an information technology team. When the team is assigned a new project, Erica spends the first day or two of the assignment discussing it with team members—both individually and as a group. She draws on the experience that various team members have had with similar projects and together they plan the entire operation. As the project proceeds, she keeps tabs on each associate's progress and jumps in with assistance, added training, or whatever is needed to make them more effective on the job.

Give Pep Talks

Just as the coach of an athletic team gives pep talks to the team before the game and during breaks, team leaders find that pep talks stimulate production, and reinvigorate members when their enthusiasm wanes. A pep talk is more than yelling 'Go, team. Go!' The effective team leader provides the team with understanding of what they need to change to be more effective team members and works with them to make those changes.

Pep talks help push the team forward for a short term, and often that's enough to pull them out of a rut. For more lasting effect, we must keep the team alert to their progress. It is important to praise every accomplishment, celebrate the success of reaching interim goals, and give recognition to team members who do outstanding work.

Good leaders like good coaches, train people to give pep

talks to themselves. By showing associates that they have confidence in their abilities and in helping them build up self-confidence, managers are performing one of the most important functions of their job as manager/coach. Successful coaches work with people to keep up their spirits when they are depressed, to retrain them when they forget the fundamentals of the job, to revel with them about their triumphs, to understand their personalities, and model motivational programs to take advantage of these factors. Effective coaches do not give up easily when a few people do not meet their expectations. They work with their people and do their best to bring them at par with the high standards set for the team.

Managers can accomplish this by knowing their people and understanding their individual differences. As pointed out earlier, all people are not alike and one of the major errors in attempting to motivate people is to assume everybody wants the same from their jobs. It may be necessary to tailor a special motivational program for each employee. More commonly, supervisors find that each person is motivated by many different things. However, there are certain factors that can be built into most motivational systems.

Good leaders recognize superb performance as well as every improvement. When special achievements are accomplished, the leaders should praise the team and reiterate how the cooperative efforts of the team members contributed to the achievement. One manager makes a practice of having an impromptu pizza or ice-cream party when a significant part of a project is successfully finished; another manager hosts a barbecue at his home for all members and their significant others when a particularly complex project is completed.

Both Coach and Trainee Must Believe in the Vision

One of the most important concepts in coaching is having a vision or end goal in mind. Without that, people often lose sight of the importance of making the required changes. How we create this picture of what is possible is the central component of this step in the coaching process.

People with a clear vision of what the end result of coaching is, tend to move in that direction more quickly than those without. But it is critical the goal be owned by both the coach and the trainee. Without that sense of ownership, motivation may be lost. We focus on motivation and buy-in even more in the next step of the process, but this is where direction and motivation really begin.

Establish the Right Attitude

How well we really know our people may be determined by how quickly we know that we have the right people for the job and how they are motivated. This step is a critical part of the process of effective coaching. Without it we would spend a great deal of our time just overcoming resistance.

We often hear that people resist change. It isn't true, People resist being changed when they:

1) don't see the need,
2) don't want to do it, or
3) believe that the change is not possible for them.

Whenever people are asked to change without their buy-in, they create resistance. The effective coach creates an atmosphere where people are consistently motivated to attain high performance levels.

Provide Resources

The effective manager assures that all the resources needed for the training process are available. These include providing time, money, equipment, training aids, information, and upper level buy-in and support and most importantly, a personal commitment to success by everyone involved.

We must ensure that the appropriate resources are in place and available. Nothing is as frustrating as being promised something and then not getting it. It can make everyone feel like they have been set up to fail.

Identify Strengths and Opportunities for Improvement

Practice also allows the coach to identify strengths and opportunities for improvement. Some of the points to consider here are:

> How to encourage others to succeed
> How closely to monitor and when to let go
> How to hold others accountable for progress
> How to reinforce. Making progress is one thing, but without a way to reinforce and keep it in place people may quickly go back to the way they did things before. One of the biggest fallacies managers hold to is the assumption that if people know something, they will do it. People don't do what they know; they do what they have always done.

Some of the skills we must look into post reinforcement of coaching are:
> Empowering people to get results after they have learned new skills

- Giving the right kind of feedback
- Following up
- Handling non-performance issues
- Handling mistakes and people who get off track

Reward Achievement

One of the best ways to cement growth and progress is to reward it. What we reward gets repeated. What gets repeated becomes habit. Change is uncomfortable. That is why people often revert back to their former ways quickly if reinforcement and rewards are not there. Habit is stronger than knowledge. Suggestions on how to reward and praise has been discussed in Chapter 3.

Be a Mentor—Develop Others to be Mentors

One of the best approaches to develop our people is to encourage experienced associates mentor trainees. For example, a high-ranking manager takes a younger employee under his or her wing and becomes that person's mentor. This gives that person not only a head start for advancement, but will teach him or her know-how about the work, the subtleties and nuances incumbent to the company, and the "tricks of the trade."

It would be a major benefit to organizations if everybody had a mentor. As leaders, we should consider mentoring a job requirement not only for ourselves, but for all experienced team members. By structuring a mentoring program, and assigning the best people on our team the responsibility of mentoring a new associate, we take a giant step forward in making the newcomer productive and on the way to personal growth.

Organization leaders are busy people. Often they just don't have enough time to give to associates, particularly to newcomers in the team. One solution: appoint an experienced team member to mentor the newcomer. Don't always select the same member to be the mentor. Every associate should have the opportunity to undertake this role.

A structured mentoring program requires that people chosen to be mentors be willing to take on the job. Compelling someone to be a mentor is self-defeating. Everybody is not interested in or qualified to be a mentor. However, if in our judgment the person who declines the assignment is really qualified, but is shy or lacks the self-confidence, we should have a heart-to-heart talk about how by accepting the task, both the member and the team will benefit. New mentors should be trained by experienced people in the art of mentoring.

Both the mentor and the person who is being mentored benefits from the process of mentoring. Obviously, those who are mentored learn much more from the process, but equally important is what the mentors gain by sharpening their skills in order to pass them on. It heightens the mentor's sense of responsibility as they guide their mentees through the maze of company policies and politics. It also makes them more effective in their interpersonal relationships.

Ten Tips for New Mentors

When we are assigned to be a mentor, we should learn as much as we can about the art of mentoring. If we have had a personal successful experience with a mentor, use that as a model. If not, seek out another member who has been a successful mentor and learn from him or her.

Here are ten 10 things to keep in mind:

1. *Know the work:* Review the basics. Think back on the problems previously faced and how you dealt with them. Be prepared to answer questions about every aspect of the job.

2. *Know as much as we can about the company:* One of the main functions of a mentor is to help the trainee overcome the hurdles of unfamiliar company policies and practices. More importantly as a person who's been around the organization for some time, know the inner workings of the organization, the true power structure, the company politics.

3. *Get to know the mentee:* To be an effective mentor, you must take the time to learn as much as you can about the person you are mentoring. Learn about his or her education, previous work experience, current job, and more. Learn his or her goals, ambitions, and outside interests. Observe personality traits. Get accustomed to his or her preferred ways of communicating face-to-face, written memos, telephone, e-mail, Twitter, texting, etc.

4. *Learn to teach:* If you have minimal experience in teaching, pick up pointers on teaching methods from the best trainers you know. Read articles and books on training techniques.

5. *Learn to learn:* It is essential that we keep learning not only the latest techniques in our own field, but developments in our industry, in the business community, and in the overall field of management.

6. *Be patient:* Some people learn slower than others. This does not mean they're stupid. If the person you are

mentoring does not catch on right away, be patient. Slow learners often develop into productive team members.

7. *Be tactful:* You are not drill sergeants training a rookie in how to survive in combat. Be kind. Be courteous. Be gentle—but be firm and let the trainee know we expect the best.

8. *Don't be afraid to take risks:* Give the mentee assignments that will challenge his or her capabilities. Let the mentee know failures may occur, but that the best way to grow is to take on tough jobs. Failures should be looked upon as a learning experience.

9. *Celebrate successes:* Let the trainee know you are proud of the accomplishments and progress he or she made. When something especially significant is achieved, make a big fuss.

10. *Encourage our mentee to become a mentor:* The best reward we can get from being a mentor is that once the need for mentoring is done, [the mentee] carries on the process by becoming a mentor.

The successful man will profit from his mistakes and try again in a different way.

Dale Carnegie

Correcting Errors

Even the best people will make errors in their work from time to time. It is the manager's responsibility to correct these errors. To maintain morale and to get the best from our people, we must do this without causing resentment or making the associate feel inadequate or inferior. Although we may become frustrated, upset or even irate about the situation, this is not the time or place to lose our temper, rant and rave and bawl out the person who made the error. Address any situation as soon as it comes up. Unsure of our ability to communicate it well, we often wait until the situation reaches intolerable proportions, and then we explode in a rage. So act early, while the situation and our responses are manageable.

The Nine R's in Correcting Errors

Here are some suggestions on how to diplomatically correct errors, teach the associate how to correct them and avoid making future errors.

1. *Research*

Do the homework to make sure you have all the facts before discussing it with the associate. The aim is not to build a case as much as gather information. You must keep an open mind and look behind the facts to better understand motivations.

2. *Rapport*

When we meet the person who has made a mistake, it is best to begin by putting that person at ease and reducing the anxiety. One way to do this is to begin with honest appreciation that is supported by evidence. Instead of just giving a general compliment, choose a behavior that you have observed. Maintain a policy of keeping the business relationships warm so the other person is open to your input.

Conduct the discussion in private. Don't say or do anything that may cause the person to feel embarrassed or lose face in front of others. Adopt the attitude and actions we want the other person to exhibit. If we speak quietly and calmly, it is likely the other person will do so in return. If we view the fault as small and easy to correct, the other person may adopt the same attitude.

3. *Relate to the Situation*

Essential to success while correcting a problem is to focus on the problem and not the person. Eliminate personal pronouns and depersonalize the problem. It was the action that was wrong, not the person who did it. Give the other person a chance to explain what happened and then let that person know what you know about the problem. Listen to understand and to determine whether he or she is accepting responsibility or blaming and avoiding responsibility. The goal is to gather facts and information to be able to accurately identify the problem and determine why it happened. By reducing defensiveness and not jumping to conclusions, different perspectives will surface, and the root cause of the problem should be identified.

Instead of attaching a negative label or trait to the individual, phrase the comments in non-accusatory terms. Here are some examples:

Instead of saying: "There is not enough information about safety matters in the report," say: "This report is very comprehensive; it might be even more effective if the section on safety were more detailed. . ."

Instead of commenting: "Why were you so careless about these statistics?" If appropriate, supply an appropriate action step. "Joe Smith has the newest numbers you need. Can you get with him today?" or "Will you call Mary Ross at X-Tech to let her know the corrected shipping date?"

How the associate relates to the problem—their actions, attitude, and behavior in this decision—will determine the next moves.

4. *Restore Performance*

The purpose of this step is to remedy the problem, to reduce the chance of the mistake happening again, and to restore the person's performance. It also involves planning to devise a way to keep the problem from occurring again.

This step should be handled differently with the associate who accepts responsibility than with the one who blames and avoids taking responsibility. With the responsible employee, effective questioning, listening, and coaching can be used to encourage him or her to suggest ways to correct the situation. Involve the associate in the problem analysis and decision-making process.

For the "blaming" or "avoiding" employee, the manager may first need to reaffirm performance expectations and coach them to accept responsibility and to restore accountability.

5. *Reassure*

This step is focused on the person. Obviously a person who has made a mistake may feel, to some degree, like a failure and is likely to be less inclined to approach the next opportunity with confidence. Therefore, the manager needs to help the associate see the situation in a different context.

The associate needs to be reassured of his or her value and importance to the organization and of the manger's support and encouragement. The associate should leave the meeting motivated to achieve optimal performance because he or she perceives a solid relationship with the organization.

The "blaming" or "avoiding" person should leave with a sense of accountability and an understanding of what the company's expectations are. That person should also understand that we are interested in and committed to his or her success and growth.

6. *Retain*
If we handled the previous steps well, we have increased our chances of retaining the person, and enhanced his or her commitment. It also reinforces the morale of our whole team. This builds trust and increases the level of commitment and work ethic.

7. *Restate*
However, sometimes people resist the efforts to repair the situation, or refuse to relate to the issue. In such cases the next move is to restate the facts, the seriousness, the policy and the proper remedy to the issue. This gives the person one more chance to do the right thing.

8. *Reprimand*
When people refuse to accept responsibility, we may have to formally remind them in some way prior to further action. Most organizations have established policies and procedures that must be followed before disciplinary action can be taken. This is particularly important in companies with contracts either with individual employees or with a labor union. How to conduct such reprimands will be discussed in chapter 9.

9. *Remove*
Sometimes we find that the employee is not a good fit for a particular task, project, or in some cases a major part of the

department's activities. We may need to explore what his or her strengths, interests, and goals are and search for a better fit within the company. It is an injustice to employees and companies when we perpetuate a situation where individuals feel that they can never succeed.

The last resort after attempts to coach them for desired performance have been unsuccessful is to remove them from this area of responsibility—to replace, reassign or release them from the organization.

Remember to comply with all the organizations policies when making this decision.

Sum and Substance

> The leader's job is to ensure that all members of the group or team know the organization's goals and the latest methods and techniques that will enable them to reach those goals. They help them learn what they don't know and to perfect what they do know.

> Just as a coach of an athletic team is constantly on the alert to identify areas where improvement can be made for each team member, successful supervisors seek to work with each of their people to hone their skills so they can become even more effective in their jobs.

> To avoid resentment and assure cooperation when correcting an associate's mistakes, focus on the problem, not the person.

> In dealing with associates who have failed to meet performance standards, follow the 'Nine Rs' approach.

7

....

DELEGATING WITHOUT FEAR

Delegation is the process of assigning by the manager to one or more of his or her associates, the duties or responsibilities to be performed as well as giving the authority to commensurate with those responsibilities. By establishing and communicating performance standards, the manager creates accountability on the part of the delegatee. It is through the sharing of responsibilities by means of assigning combined with the assignment of authority and accountability that managers manage.

Reasons for Delegating

Managers may choose to delegate for many reasons. Some of these are:

▸ By shifting some of their workload, it frees them to work on other tasks that may be more complex, of higher priority, or require personal attention.

- Delegation is an opportunity to develop people via stretch assignments.
- It allows them to take advantage of the specialized skills or preferences of others on the staff.
- Delegation enables to distribute the workload, thus speeding up the process of getting things done.

Don't Be Afraid to Delegate

In order for most supervisors or managers to accomplish all their activities, it is essential that they delegate some of their work to their subordinates. Yet many managers are afraid to delegate. Let's look at some of these reasons:

- Fear of change and the unknown
- Inability or unwillingness to let go or known tendency to micromanage
- Believing that they are the only ones who can do the job properly
- Unwillingness to give up doing something they enjoy
- Lack of faith in subordinates' ability to perform and believing that "if we want something done right, we have to do it ourselves"
- Belief that it's quicker and easier to do a task personally than to train others to do it
- Ego-related fear that subordinates will outperform them or that they will become dispensable
- Lack of confidence in one's own ability to train, manage, and lead others
- Fear of imposing on or making demands others; not wanting to be "the bad guy"
- Fear of conflict

Building Self-Confidence

Most of the fears listed above are due to lack of self-confidence. One example is Paul, who fears that if a subordinate does too good a job, he or she will be a threat to him. "If the boss sees that one of my people can do what I can do, my job may be in jeopardy."

Although there have been situations where a manager has been replaced by a lower salaried subordinate, it usually has not been primarily due to this reason. As a matter of fact, the opposite is more usual. Most companies consider how effectively managers build up the capabilities of their people by evaluating their management skills.

By becoming as proficient as he can in his job, Paul will earn the respect of his supervisors and because he knows he is good at his work, it will build up his self-confidence. By making his people more effective in their work, he will be able to accomplish more in those aspects of the job that are of greater importance than those he has delegated to his subordinates.

Ellen's fear is more common: "If my subordinate messes up the assignment, I will be the one held responsible." All managers are held accountable for the work of their subordinates. In order to be assured that the work she has delegated to others is done correctly and on schedule, she should follow these steps in planning the delegation:

> Determine the capabilities of each of the people in the work that is to be performed. To delegate an assignment to one who is not able to do it properly dooms it to failure. If we do not have anybody who is capable, we have no choice but to

do it ourselves. If this is the case, the highest priority should be to train somebody to be able to handle this, so that the next time there is a need to delegate, a capable person will be available for the assignment.

➤ Determine how much training, guidance, and supervision the delegatee(s) might need in terms of time and attention, as well as what other resources might be necessary.

➤ Determine how delegating to this individual or these individuals will impact their current workload.

➤ If the delegatee does not report directly to us 100% of the time (e.g., with project teams), determine how to handle any potential conflict in priorities or issues with their other supervisors.

➤ In addition to keeping an eye on the task at hand, we should keep in mind the human aspect of managing and leading people. We should use interpersonal understanding techniques to see how delegates are feeling about how things are going. We should always be aware of their developmental progress, build their confidence, inspire them to perform and coach them to help maximize their potential. We must create a win-win situations whereby everyone will benefit from the fruits of their labor.

There is only one way. . . to get anybody to do anything. And that is by making the other person want to do it.

Dale Carnegie

Planning the Assignment

For any activity to succeed it must be planned. Too often supervisors do not take the time to prepare assignments.

They know what has to be done and assume by ordering an associate to do it, it will be done properly. Planning starts with having a clear concept of what must be accomplished. Even if one has done this type of work many times, it is important to think it through once again. We must put ourselves in the place of the associate. If we had never seen this project before, what would we want to know? List the objectives we wish to attain, the information needed to attain it, the materials, tools, support sources and whatever else is needed to do the work.

A very important part of the planning is to determine who will be given the assignment. In selecting this person bear in mind the importance of the assignment. If it is one in which it is essential that it be done rapidly and with little supervision, choose a person who has demonstrated ability in the past in this type of work. However, if it is an area where there is adequate time for you to provide guidance, it may be advantageous to assign it to a less skilled person and use this project as a means of training and developing that person's skills.

What is Delegated Should Be Communicated Effectively

Barbara was frustrated. She had given Carol a detailed description of what she wanted to be done and Carol had assured her she understood. Now, a week later, Carol turned in work that was all wrong. Her excuse: "I thought that's what you wanted."

Like many supervisors, when Carol said she understood, Barbara assumed that she really did understand. To be sure that a subordinate understands an assignment, don't ask "Do you understand?" That's a meaningless inquiry. Often the subordinate may think that he or she understands an assigned task, but really doesn't—and in good faith tells us that it is understood. Some people may be embarrassed to tell us that they do not understand and say that they do and then try to figure it out for themselves. Instead of asking "Do you understand?" ask: "what are you going to do?" If the answer indicates that it is not clearly understood, we can correct their perception of the assignment immediately.

Morton was upset. His boss had just given him a deadline that he felt was totally unrealistic. "He's out of line," Morton thought, "There's no way I can do this much work in such a short time. I'll do what I can, but I know I'm not going to make it."

With that attitude, it's unlikely that Morton will meet the deadline. In order to get full cooperation from a subordinate, it is important for that person to fully accept what it is we want. To gain acceptance, first let the subordinate know the importance of the assignment, then get him or her to participate in the planning process. "Mort, this assignment must be in the boss's hands by 10 tomorrow morning. When do you think you can have it?" Morton can now see the urgency of the work and together work out with us a realistic time table, which may include the need for additional help or authorization for overtime work.

Effective delegators design the communication strategy efficiently, thereby effectively presenting the assignment to their delegatees. This includes preparing to address any potential resistance, anticipating questions and concerns, etc.

Give the Delegatee the Tools to Get the Job Done

In Martha's company, computer time is always at a premium. When she delegated a project to one of her people, she neglected to arrange for computer time. As a result the entire project bogged down. Martha had the responsibility to assure that her subordinate had everything needed to do the job. By failing to do so, she doomed the project to failure.

Another type of "tool" the subordinate should be given is the authority needed to accomplish the mission. Martin was instructed to meet a tight deadline on the project. To do this it was necessary to work overtime, but Martin was not given the authority to order overtime work. This delayed completion of the project and resulted in missing the deadline.

Get a Plan of Action

On assignments that will take any significant amount of time, ask the associate to prepare a plan of action before starting the job. This should include just what is to be done, when it is scheduled to be done and what support may be needed.

Paul Cullen, founder of Cullen Electronics was retiring after 30 years on the job. His successor, Frank Ames, decided to have a gala celebration of his accomplishments and appointed his H.R. manager, Mark Lovett to arrange the affair.

Mark was to arrange travel plans for key employees, customers and vendors from all over the country to come to the celebration. Before starting the assignment, he wrote a plan of action to cover every aspect of the assignment including hiring a caterer, choosing the location, arranging for decorations, sending invitations and making airline and hotel reservations for out of town guests. The plan included time tables for starting and completing each phase and indication of what assistance would be needed for each phase. Mark reviewed this with Mr. Ames to assure all was in accord with his concepts. Mark wrote out the plan of action so that everyone involved in implementing the program were able to check at any time how the plan was proceeding and help to catch the problems early.

Set Control Points

Even if one delegates responsibility to the delegatee, managers are still held accountable. To assure that the assignments be performed correctly and on time, control points are set at places where one can check the progress of the assignments and if anything has gone wrong, it can be corrected before it goes too far. Control points are not surprise inspections. The associate knows when they will occur and what is expected at that point. For example, we give Ted an assignment on Monday that must be completed by Friday. We tell Ted: "We will meet tomorrow at 4 p.m. to discuss the project. By that time you should have completed Parts A and B." If at that time we uncover errors, they can be corrected before Ted continues. Another advantage of control points is that if Ted realizes at 11 a.m. that he will not be able to complete Part B by the 4 p.m. control point, he can ask for help early enough to keep the project from falling behind schedule.

Follow-Up

As managers are responsible for the actions of their subordinates, a system of follow-up is an essential management tool. To accomplish this without micromanaging can be a delicate matter.

When managers are constantly looking over the shoulders of their people, it engenders a feeling of distrust—and that can destroy the collaborative, cooperative atmosphere essential to true success.

Follow-up should be done in a particular manner. Instead of constantly overseeing the work or surprising subordinates with unexpected check-ups, the follow-ups should be built into the plan of action. Rather than superimpose a follow-up plan, the manager and the subordinates should develop the plan together. Control points should be incorporated throughout the project. When various phases of the project have been completed, the manager and the people performing the project will need to go over what has been done. The workers should be encouraged to critique the work and perhaps suggest new or additional matters that might be incorporated in the assignment. Of course, the manager would contribute appropriate comments and suggestions as well.

In this way the follow-up becomes part of the participative approach and acts as a stimulus for the subordinate to achieve even greater success in meeting the challenge of the assignment.

People rarely succeed unless they have fun in what they are doing.

Dale Carnegie

When We Delegate, We Do Not Abdicate

Managers should be available to help their people if need arises. When Duncan assigned a new project to Andrea, he told her: "I'm here to help you. If you have any problems, don't hesitate to bring them to me." Andrea took this literally and instead of trying to deal with her problems, she brought them to Duncan. This not only took an inordinate amount of Duncan's time, but did not help develop Andrea's skills.

The next time Duncan delegated a project to one of his people he again noted his availability to help them, but added: "Bring me your problems, but bring with them a suggested solution." This encouraged them to think about the situation and come to their own conclusions. Duncan would rather have them ask him: "Do you think this will work?" rather than "What should I do?"

Upon Completion of the Assignment

There is no one right way to do something. It's all about successfully achieving the desired result in the end. So even if something is not done exactly as we would have done it (most likely it won't be), that's perfectly okay.

Ask ourselves how we performed as the delegating manager. What things did we do right and wrong during this process? What, if anything, would we have done differently? What will we do differently in the future?

Analyze how the delegatee performed? Did he or she rise to the occasion? Was he or she stretched by the challenge or overwhelmed beyond his or her capabilities? Did we get personal feedback on how he or she thought things went? Did we take advantage of this developmental opportunity to provide the delegatee with praise or recognition, with rewards, if deserved, as well as providing fair, open, and honest constructive criticism?

Consider the ways in which your relationship with the delegatee may have changed from this experience and where things would go from here; how one might build on this progress or remedy any damage.

Finally, don't forget that you are ultimately responsible and accountable for the outcome when it comes time to report back to the superiors. As the manager and leader, your duty is to share the credit and celebrate the success with your delegatees. But the flip side of "wearing the crown" is that should things fail, the blame will lie solely on our head. In the end, that is what management and leadership is all about.

By following a systematic approach in delegating, you will accomplish more because other people would be doing those things which are more suited for subordinates freeing you for more significant work. You would also be accomplishing one of the most important roles of a manager—building up the capabilities of your staff. Delegation is one of the best means of giving people the experience important to their own development.

Delegating to Teams

When an organization is structured into teams, work should be delegated and assigned as a team activity. When people have some control over the assignments they get, they approach their work with enthusiasm and commitment.

When the boss gives a complex project, one should present it in its entirety to the team. Discuss with the team how to break the assignment into phases. Delegating each of the phases to individual team members will follow easily. Most members will choose to handle the areas in which they have the most expertise. If two members want the same area, let them iron it out with each other. But if it gets sticky, step in and resolve the problem diplomatically: "Gustav did the research on our last project, so let's give Liz a chance to handle it this time."

Certain phases of the assignment are bound to be tough or unpleasant. No one's really going to volunteer to do them. Have the team set up an equitable system for assigning this type of work.

As team leader, be sure that every member of the team is aware of everyone else's responsibilities as well as their own. In this way, everyone knows what everyone else is doing and what kind of support he or she can give or receive from others.

To keep everyone informed, create a chart listing each phase of the assignment, the person handling it, deadlines, and other pertinent information. Post the chart in the office for easy referral.

Sum and Substance

Some key points concerning delegation:

> Once the objectives have been established, the means of achieving them must be determined, after which the work to be performed and the associated responsibilities must be determined.

> It is because the necessary responsibilities are either too complex, diverse, or voluminous for one individual to handle that the need for delegation arises.

> While delegating work and the associated responsibilities to someone else, one must also delegate the appropriate degree of authority necessary to perform the delegated tasks. Delegation without empowerment will only lead to frustration and failure.

- Responsibility is the obligation of the delegatee to perform the required tasks. Accountability is the obligation of the delegatee to produce the desired results. Ultimate responsibility and accountability is the overarching obligation of the delegating manager to successfully achieve organizational objectives.

- Delegation takes time—planning, communicating, monitoring, etc.—but will save time in the long run. Delegation is not intended to be a quick fix (though it can be sometimes) but a long-term strategic approach to getting things done.

- Important: Remember that delegating responsibility, authority, is not delegating ultimate accountability! The delegating manager is still ultimately responsible and accountable for achieving the end result. Managers and leaders must take the good with the bad.

- Finally, remember the saying: "Delegation is not abdication." And, when successfully completed, it is important not to forget the recognition and the celebration!

8

ENCOURAGING INNOVATION AND
CREATIVITY

"More, better, faster with less" seems to be the mantra we hear so often today. How do we keep up with the changes and get in a proactive mode to deal with change?

It isn't just change that is so challenging. It is the speed of change. It comes faster each time. It is essential to the future of an organization.

The ability to create new products or systems innovation and develop existing products, services, or systems have been studied in many different ways over the years. Some researchers have sought to uncover and understand what makes a person creative. Others have examined the kind of environment that stimulates creative effort and enables it to thrive. Still others have focused on the development of creative products and services.

For centuries, people have been fascinated by the creative process—the series of ordered steps through which a person or group of people utilize the principles of creative thinking to analyze a problem or opportunity in a systematic, unbiased, and seemingly unconventional way. In recent times, modern research in the social and behavioral sciences demystifies the concept by showing how even modest powers of reasoning, analysis, and experimentation help us attain insights into the nature of innovation and its many faces and expressions.

This increased awareness and understanding captures the imagination of quality-conscious managers worldwide who recognize the enormous benefits of developing the creative powers and problem-solving abilities of their associates. In fact, surveys show that the ability to think creatively—to analyze problems and opportunities in new, innovative ways—is thought to be one of the most valuable skills we can develop within ourselves and within the organization.

Why? Because creative ideas result in new discoveries, better ways of doing things, reduced costs, and improved performances—issues vitally important to business people operating in modern competitive environments.

The Thinking Mechanism

The thinking mechanism of the human brain can be described as consisting of two elements: one part for uninhibited creative thinking and the other for analytical or judicial thinking.

The term "Green-Light Thinking" applies to the thought process most conducive to the generation of ideas. In this aspect, the quantity—not the quality—of ideas is emphasized.

The judicial part of the mind analyzes and evaluates ideas emanating from the creative, uninhibited part. Here, the focus is on the quality of ideas. The term "Red-Light Thinking" is often used to describe this process. "Green-Light" and "Red-Light Thinking" are two different processes and both are good and useful. They just cannot be applied at the same time. We often turn on the red-light when somebody presents an idea because we are thinking judicially before we have a clear concept of its ramifications.

This is not only true of our encouraging innovative ideas from others, but we internalize this and loath to open our own minds because most of our educational processes and systems have been devoted to developing the judicial thinking function (i.e., an ability to make decisions, compare and evaluate situations, distinguish between correct and incorrect, etc.), most people do not realize the extent of their own creative ability. In fact, our potential in this area is always present and can be developed to a much greater extent rather easily. We must never lose confidence in our own creative capabilities.

Keep your mind open to change all the time. Welcome it. Court it. It is only by examining and reexamining your opinions and ideas that you can progress.

Dale Carnegie

Everybody is Creative

Everybody is creative. Unfortunately, the creative juices which flow so easily when nurtured are cut off in most people—from childhood on—by the imposition of over-analysis and conformity by the authoritative figures in their lives. Too often creativity is blocked by red-light thinking:

"Stop this,"

"It's against company policy,"

"We never did it that way."

Instead of looking for reasons not to try new ideas, we should look at new ideas with open minds. Turn on the green light, Explore it further, Expand our thinking about it beyond the obvious.

Gary pondered about an idea that could increase productivity by a simple change in methods. Should he tell his boss? The last time he had made a suggestion, his supervisor rebuffed it. He said it wouldn't work. Never gave him a chance to explain it. Why bother now?

Just because we may believe our ideas may be rejected should not stop us from being creative. It is easy to give in to discouragement, but unless we keep coming up with ideas, we will stifle our own creative capabilities. Innovation must be honed by constant use. People tend to censor themselves by worrying about how others will receive their ideas. Self-censorship is far worse than criticism of others because it makes one feel inadequate. We will make mistakes; we will make suggestions that do not work; we may even be ridiculed by our bosses or our peers. Don't let this stop you. Einstein, Edison, Whitney and Watt were all ridiculed many times. Keep those creative ideas coming.

Blocking Creativity

Every idea is not necessarily going to work or is even worthwhile to pursue. However, by at least thinking about it and talking to others about it, we can explore its viability. If it is rejected, learn the reasons. Do not lose heart. Often the idea, as good as it appears, may not fit the specific application or be appropriate at that time. This does not mean it is not good. It also should not be interpreted as a personal affront. It was the idea that was rejected—not you.

Developing Creativity

Most people do not really believe that they are creative. All their lives they have been taught that creativity is some sort of special talent possessed only by artists, inventors and geniuses—not true. Psychologists have proven that creative thinking can be developed.

Here are some of the things we can do to make us more creative:

Observe

One doesn't have to dream up new ideas to be creative. By observing things around us and applying what we learn from other situations is just as creative as total innovation.

Stan, the manager of Hooper Steel in Las Vegas, noted that as more and more gas stations became "self-service" and no longer had facilities for oil change and lubrication of cars, rapid lubrication stations sprang up to meet this need. Stan used one of them for his car and was pleased with the speed and quality of the work.

For years Hooper Steel had sent its trucks to the service department of the dealer for their regular lubrications. This required sending two people to bring the truck to the dealer (one to drive the other back to the shop in his or her car), leave the truck at the dealer all day, and return later to pick up the truck—again using the time of two people.

"Why not use the rapid lube station for our trucks?"

thought Stan. The result: By sending one driver to the rapid lube station and having that person wait about 30 minutes while the truck was being serviced, Stan saved his company about $1600 a month in out-of-pocket service costs and lost time. In addition they had the use of the truck for most of the day.

Modify

Can we modify an existing product or concept to create something different? The founders of "Think Big" modified standard products by making enlarged versions of them. Their giant facsimiles of popular products ranging from pencils and telephone message pads to animals and furniture created a whole new market in advertising, decoration and novelties.

The growth of computer and electronic industry is based on modification by miniaturizing of electronic systems and components into microchips.

Substitute

Darlene, office manager of Mass Mailers, was having a difficult time retaining personnel in an extremely dull routine job: stuffing brochures and samples into envelopes. The nature of the job was such that it could not be done by the standard automated equipment. Not only was the cost of this turnover expensive, but she could never be sure that somebody would be there to do the job. She reasoned that if so-called "normal" people found this job so boring, perhaps mentally-challenged people might not. By filling the jobs with these "slow-learners," Darlene was able to hire workers who were not bored by the work and have become steady and valued employees.

Eliminate

Gil was irate. His company added still another form for salespeople to complete. How could he be out there selling when there was so much paper work that had to be done? When he complained to his sales manager, she shrugged her shoulders and said they needed the information "upstairs." Gil took all the forms he was required to complete, set them side by side and analyzed what information was required. It became apparent that there was a good deal of duplication of data. Instead of griping about it, Gil designed a new form that would provide the necessary facts to management and was easy to complete. This not only made the salesperson's job easier, but saved the company considerable time and money. An added benefit: it started the company on a systematic review and revision of all forms leading to elimination of many outdated and unnecessary reports.

These are only a few ways the creative juices can be stimulated. By stretching our imagination, by expanding our horizons, by breaking with conventional approaches to problems, we can become more inventive, solve difficult problems and initiate and implement exciting new concepts. This will not only be of benefit to the company, but will give us that great feeling of accomplishment when we see our ideas successfully implemented.

> *The person who goes farthest is generally the one who is willing to do and dare. The sure-thing boat never gets far from shore.*
>
> Dale Carnegie

Group Creativity

Most people visualize the creative person as one working along and generating ideas or inventions like Bill Gates or Steve Job. Actually many creative concepts come from groups of people working together. The interaction and cross-fertilization of ideas stimulates ideation.

The old adage, "two heads are better than one" and it's amplification that many heads are better than a few has been shown over and over again to be true. Group efforts in committees and conferences have helped solve many problems.

One approach that has been used effectively is *brainstorming*. Brainstorming is a technique for obtaining as many ideas on a subject as possible. The difference between the usual kind of meeting and brainstorming is that the objective is simply to generate ideas green-light thinking. To get the most out of a brainstorming session, red-light thinking is banned. Participants may not criticize, analyze, reject or accept any suggestion from any participant no matter how ridiculous or valueless or terrific it may appear to be.

The psychological principle behind brainstorming is called triggering. Any idea can trigger another idea in the minds of a listener. A dumb idea from one person can lead to a good idea from another. By allowing the participants to think freely and not concern themselves with how the idea will be received, brainstorming frees people to stretch their minds, and pave the way for an idea that may have value.

In a typical brainstorming session the group tackles a single subject, announced in advance of the meeting. Once the chair introduces the subject, he or she steps back and becomes just another member of the group. One person is appointed to list the ideas on a flipchart. Ideas are called out and recorded. No comments pro or con are made. Freewheeling is encouraged; the wilder the idea, the better. Success is measured by the number of ideas that are generated. Participants are encouraged to hitch-hike onto ideas that are presented. After the session a committee reviews the idea, investigates, and analyzes them. Only then red-light thinking begins.

Brainstorming is not appropriate for all types of problems, but can be very helpful in many situations. It works best in solving specific problems rather than determining long-term goals or general policies. Some examples of successful brainstorming are naming of a new product, opening new channels of distribution, making jobs less boring and developing non-traditional approaches to marketing a product or service.

Be Open to All Ideas

"Our company is different." How often have we heard this phrase? Many companies feel that they are unique and unless an idea, a process, or a program is created by them, it will not fit their needs. Of course, each company has its own culture and its own individuality, but we can learn a lot from other companies—even those whose business is considerably different from ours.

Get Out of the Rut

When people work together for a long time, they tend to think alike. Ideas presented by one may be accepted by all without critical analysis as all members of the group look at things in the same way. Alfred Sloan, one of the founders of

General Motors, recognized this. The company was about to undertake a major project. All members of the group involved, including Sloan felt it was a good idea. However, Sloan was uneasy about this. He told his group that they should give it more thought, check what problems other companies may have had with similar projects. He tabled the proposal for several months. When they met again about the same many problems that had been overlooked were discussed and what would have been instituted uncritically a few months earlier was *sent* back for serious reconsideration and refinement.

Benchmarking

One of the basic principles of the Total Quality Management concept is that successful companies are not afraid to seek out ideas from other organizations that may help them meet their goals. Indeed, one of the requirements in the Malcolm Baldrige awards—the U.S. government's highest recognition for high-quality businesses—is that participants share the methods and techniques used to achieve the award with all interested parties. This is called "benchmarking."

Direct Competitors

One may ask why a successful company would want to share what made them successful with their competitors. It is true that many organizations will not share trade secrets, but much of what leads to high quality is not so much a "secret" but a process that benefits all.

José operates a small appliance repair business in Gainesville, Florida. He is not doing as well as he feels he could do. José would like to ask Carlos, one of his successful competitors for advice, but knows he will probably be laughed at. Why should Carlos help a person who may take business away from him? But José is not limited to people who are his direct competitors. He learns from a trade publication that a small firm in Pell City, Alabama has overcome many of the problems he is facing. These people are not competitors and are much more likely to share some of their ideas with José. A telephone call or better, a visit to this firm would accomplish this.

Look to Other Industries

Our industry is not unique. Other businesses quite different from ours may have faced similar problems we have and solved them. They may be willing to help us.

One of the shuttle services that transported people from suburban New York to and fro the airports was plagued with complaints. Customers who telephoned for pick-ups had to wait through nine or ten rings before the phones were answered and then were put on hold for another few minutes. Finally, when they reached a clerk, they had to answer a variety of questions about their pick-up even if they had used the service over and over again.

The owner sought help from other transporters in various cities, but all had the same problem and had not solved them. As in most locations, they were the least expensive means of transportation, they felt that their low prices justified the delay.

One of the employees of this company told his boss: "I used to have the same problem when I ordered merchandise from L.L. Bean, a well-known outdoors clothing and equipment mail order firm. I would wait to be served, and then asked my address, credit card, sizes, etc. each time. Now when I call, they have all this on the computer. They answer the phone promptly and once I give them my name and phone number, all they need to know is what I want to order. I'm off the phone in a few minutes."

The owner made an appointment to speak with an L.L. Bean executive, who was happy to give him information about the computer program they were using. Within a few months they had installed a similar program which alleviated most of the problems they were facing.

A few years later he read about an improved system and upgraded his program so that when the caller-ID identified the caller, the computer automatically opened that customer's file displaying all the necessary information instantly.

Encourage Employees to Create Benchmarks

Learning from other companies is not limited to executives. Individuals should be encouraged to increase their skills by seeking out other people in their areas of expertize.

Melissa, a market research analyst, made a practice of attending meetings of the local chapter of the American Marketing Association. At one meeting she sat at the table with Angela, who was currently working on a marketing project that involved the use of some new techniques with which Melissa was not familiar. Angela invited her to visit her office to look over the system. Melissa suggested to her boss that she be allowed to spend some time at Angela's facility to study what they were doing. This resulted in Melissa's learning a new approach to her work which enabled her to do a more effective job for her company.

There is a certain special satisfaction in solving problems on one's own and this should not be discouraged. However, we are not the only ones in the world who have faced these problems. By researching what has been done by others and by seeking help from successful companies and people, much time and effort can be saved and solutions found that will keep us and our company on the cutting edge in our field.

Take a Chance

When Alex was a boy in Chicago, he and his friends were ardent Cubs fans. They were elated when their team won and unhappy when they lost. Alex felt the losses more than his friends. When the Cubs lost, he would be deeply grieved. After a particularly bad season, Alex thought, "It isn't worth it. I'm never going to get so involved with a team that I can feel this bad." From that time on he refused to commit himself to the Cubs or any team in any sport.

Alex carried this concept into all aspects of his life. His philosophy was: "If I don't become too involved, I can never be hurt." In his school and in his jobs, he always took the middle course. Indeed, Alex never did get hurt, but neither did he ever have any real joys. By not taking the chance that someone or something that he supports might not work out, he avoided the "agony of defeat," but never experienced "the thrill of victory."

Don't Fear Commitment

Teresa was all excited. After much thought, she came up with an idea that she felt would solve a major problem she faced on her job. When she presented it to her boss, he scoffed,

"It'll never work. Go back and rethink it." Some people may accept such a rejection, but Teresa was so sure it would work, she continued to refine the idea and in time convinced her boss that it was feasible.

Inventors and innovators have always faced ridicule. Jonas Salk was told over and over again that he was on the wrong track in his pursuit of a polio vaccine. Edison had tried and failed hundreds of times before succeeding in inventing the light bulb. Successful inventors must be willing and able to overcome the doubts and disappointments of defeat after defeat before reaching their goals.

Don't Be Reluctant to Disagree

Most people are uncomfortable when they are in the minority in opposing the way others in their group want to approach a problem. They feel that by disagreeing, the others might look down on them. The safe course is to go along and keep the disagreement to themselves. But if we are sure that the group may have overlooked an important aspect of the problem, it is crucial to risk being rejected and make an effort to present and prove what we believe.

Taking risks does not mean one must be a daredevil. Reasonable people take reasonable risks, but by definition, a risk may not succeed. Successful business executives take risks with every decision they make. However, they maximize their chances of success with careful research and analysis before making a decision. But when that decision finally has to be made, the manager must be willing to risk the possible loss of money, time, energy and emotion. Without risk, there is no possibility of gain.

Champions Take Risks

It is the end of the ninth inning. The Blue Jays lead the Yankees 2 to 1. The first two hitters strike out. Dave Winfield, the Yankee's ace hitter is at bat. The ball comes straight across the plate. Wham! a clean hit. Winfield races to first. He makes it easily. Should he try for a double? In microseconds, Dave must decide if he should play it safe or take the risk of trying for that extra base which would put him in a scoring position. If he fails, the game is over, but by taking a chance he increases the possibility of turning defeat into victory. Winfield is a risk taker and if there's a slightly better chance of success, he'll try for the double. Champions in life as well as in sports will take chances. That is what makes them champions.

What is the Worst that Can Happen?

In his book, *How to Stop Worrying and Start Living,* Dale Carnegie advises that when facing trouble: Ask yourself, "What is the worst that can possibly happen? then prepare to accept the worst; try to improve on the worst."

For example, Gil had not been able to obtain an appointment with Allen, the purchasing manager of a prospective customer. He had phoned, written letters and even "sat on his doorstep"— all to no avail. His colleagues advised him to forget Allen and to use his energies and time to develop other leads. But Gil was stubborn. There must be some way to get Allen's attention. He learned that Allen was to be a speaker at an industry workshop. "If I attend the workshop," thought Gil, "I can approach him after his talk, ask him some questions and then identify myself, so he'll at least know who I am."

His sales managers and co-workers discouraged this. "He'll be so mad he never will speak to anybody from this company again."

Gil responded by applying Carnegie's principles. "What is the worst that could happen? He won't do business with us. That's not so bad because he isn't doing business with us now, so we have nothing to lose."

By taking a chance, Gil reached an "unreachable" prospect and opened a very profitable account for his company.

> *Develop success from failure. Discouragement and failure are two of the surest steppingstones to success. Study them and make capital of them. Look backward. Can't you see where your failures have helped you?*
>
> *Dale Carnegie*

Being Creative Requires Us to Risk Failure

All of us have failed in various things we tried throughout our lives, but we learn from our mistakes and use what we learn to overcome them. The first time we try something new, it is likely we will not succeed.

When little Tricia tried to put together her first jigsaw puzzle, she cried in frustration. The parts simply wouldn't fit together. But with patience and some guidance from her mother, she began to identify patterns and in a short time her failures turned into successes.

Even when we have experience and know-how, we cannot always be successful. There will be times when we do fail, but we must not let the concept of failure overwhelm us. We should learn from our mistakes and apply what we have learned to overcome our failures.

We must all take risks if we want to make progress in our jobs and in our lives. By careful analysis we can minimize the chances of failure, but we can never eliminate them. Without pain there is no gain. By always playing it safe, we may avoid that pain, but we will never feel the great joy and satisfaction that results from overcoming obstacles and reaching our goals.

Sum and Substance

> ➤ The ability to think creatively—to analyze problems and opportunities in new, innovative ways—is thought to be one of the most valuable skills we can develop within ourselves and within the organization.

> ➤ In seeking solutions first use "green-light" thinking to develop new concepts, ideas or approaches. Then turn on the "red-light" to analyze and evaluate.

> ➤ Some of the things we can do to make us more creative are:
>   > ➤ Observe and apply what we learn from one situation to solve a different problem.
>   > ➤ Modify an existing product or concept to fit new situations.
>   > ➤ Substitute different method for less effective traditional approaches.
>   > ➤ Evaluate systems and procedures and eliminate duplications or redundancies.

> ➤ Use brainstorming to get a plethora of ideas, through group participation.

- By "benchmarking" we can learn how other organizations have dealt with similar problems as ours.
- Don't be afraid to take reasonable risks in tackling tough situations.

9

....

DEALING WITH LEADERSHIP
PROBLEMS

When we are promoted or assigned to a leadership position, we do not automatically acquire the skills and techniques that make us good leaders. We have to acquire them. It starts with earning the respect of our associates.

Be Good at What You Do

People respect professionalism. This does not mean that you have to be able to do the jobs that each of your people do better than them. Indeed, the higher one gets in management, the less likely that he or she can do many of the jobs that are done by their staff. The president of a company is unlikely to be able to operate every type of equipment or computers used in the organization. Even in the lower echelons of management, you would probably be required to supervise people who perform jobs quite different from your own. But, if you do whatever it is that you do in a professional manner, your people will respect you.

Treat People Fairly

Unless you deal with your people with an even hand, you will not only fail to gain respect, but will exacerbate resentment. This does not mean that everybody has to be managed in the same way. People differ one from the other and good leaders learn these differences and tailor the manner in which they deal with each of them and their individualities.

Stick Up For Your People

If your department is having a dispute with another department, you should stick up for your people even if it is not always politically expedient. Carey had tried her best to compete the work needed for a project her colleague, Stan, was working on. Due to technical problems with the new computer software, her people were not able to meet the deadline. Stan roared into her office. "What are your people trying to do? My staff can't start our phase of the project until you get them all the data. And don't give me that lame excuse that the computer is down."

Carey did not want to antagonize her colleague but she knew that her people had been doing their best to get the data and that they were really having those computer problems.

She responded: "Stan, we are just as anxious as you to get the data together, but the computer trouble is real, not just an excuse. I have had the tech people here to fix the problem and it should be on line today."

Give People Credit for What They've Done

Praise accomplishments. Let people know that their work is appreciated. On the other hand, one of the most devastating things a supervisor can do is to take credit for something one of his or her people has done and claim it as one's own.

Listen to Your Associates

Unless one listens, you cannot maintain an ongoing relationship with others. However, listening is more than just standing or sitting with our ears open. We must be active listeners. Active listeners ask questions about what has just been said. They paraphrase: 'So the way I see it is. . ..' When people realize that we really listen to them they know that we respect them and this will lead to more respect for us.

Support Your Staff

As discussed in chapter 6, give them the tools and teach them the techniques that will enable them to succeed in their jobs. Take time—even if it requires you to work extra hours or put off another project—to coach people when needed, to counsel them when they have problems, and to assure them that they are an integral part of your team.

Leadership Blunders to Avoid

Being a supervisor is never easy and it's particularly tough the first time one is promoted to a management position.

Let's look at a few of the common blunders supervisors often make.

Starting Out on The Wrong Foot

The first steps we take when starting our new assignments will set the climate of the department for months to come. If we have been promoted from the ranks, there is a good chance that other persons in the department had also vied for the job. For us to succeed, it's essential that we obtain their cooperation. To minimize their discontent, it is best that we not be the one to announce our promotion. It should be done by the person who made the decision, the boss. He or she should sit down with the unsuccessful candidates and say something like this:

> Tom, as you know you were one of the three people I was considering for the promotion. You were all highly qualified, but as there was only one opening I had to make a choice. It was a tough decision. I chose Susan for the job. This is not a negative reflection on your work, but as Susan has considerable knowledge of the new equipment, I felt that she could make the department more productive sooner. We are growing and additional opportunities will be coming up and you certainly will be considered for them. I would appreciate your giving Susan all the help you can to make this department as good as we know it can be.

When Susan starts, she should not call a meeting and say "I'm the new boss of this department and from now on we're going to do things my way." That is not the way to win friends and influence employees. Instead of calling a meeting, speak to each of the people in the department individually. Share some of your ideas. Elicit some of theirs. Ask for their cooperation. "I can't do this job alone. It is a team effort. I need your help."

As a new supervisor we may be desirous of making immediate and radical changes in the way things are done in the department. Don't! Change should be made by evolution, not revolution.

Dealing with employee-friends

How friendly should a supervisor be with their subordinates? Being too friendly can often interfere with the necessary control we should have, while being too aloof might cause resentment and lack of cooperation. Finding the middle ground is not easy.

Before Barbara was promoted to supervisor of the data entry section, she was particularly friendly with three of the ten women she now supervises. She is now their boss. Should she continue this relationship? She liked these women and didn't want to lose their friendship. However, the other workers in the department were jealous and although Barbara did her best to avoid any indications of favoritism, her actions were frequently interpreted negatively.

Upset about this, Barbara asked the advice of an experienced manager. "Probably some of the saddest things I had to do in my career," he said, "were to break the personal ties I had with former colleagues as I moved up the ladder, but it had to be done. Don't do it suddenly. Phase it out. Gradually cut out the after work socializing and the lunches. Start eating with other supervisors. In the beginning this may hurt your old friends, and you will not be happy, but unless you do this, you will not be able to run your department efficiently and your chances of getting ahead in this company will be reduced."

Lack of Recognition and Use of People's Talents

Claudia and Dave were very creative people. They had many good ideas that could have made the work in their department much easier for everybody. Yet their supervisor, Carla, insisted that everything be done "the way we always did it."

When Carla was chastised by her boss for the low level of production in her department, she fumed: "It's not my fault. My people just don't care about the work." Had she utilized the talents of Claudia, Dave and some of her other associates, not only would their contributions have improved production, but her people would "care about" the work, resulting in even better results.

Dealing with Negativism

In most organizations we will find negative thinkers. They always find some reason to oppose new ideas and argue with others on every point. Let's look at some of the problems negative people cause:

> *Resistance to change:* Even people with a positive attitude are reluctant to change. It's comfortable to keep doing things the way they've always been done. Positive people can be persuaded to change by presenting logical arguments. Negative people resist change just for the sake of resisting. No argument ever helps. They may even sabotage a situation so that they can say: "I told you so."

> *Impact on team morale:* Just as one rotten apple can spoil a whole barrel, one negative person can destroy the entire team's morale.

Control Emotions

It is easy to become impatient with negative people. However, it is not necessary—even if possible—not to show displeasure when somebody is constantly defying us. Instead of thinking "She's up to her old tricks. I'm not going to let her push me around," we must learn to think "She's manifesting her anti-authority feelings. It has nothing to do with the problem or with me." By not taking it as a personal affront, we can deal with it in a logical not an emotional manner.

Set Clearly Understood Guidelines

In dealing with negative people, instead of giving very specific instructions, where ever possible have the associates participate in how an assignment should be performed within deadlines of the work. Give them unambiguous performance standards that must be met, but let them determine what to do to meet them. This minimizes fighting over details and minor matters. Negative people will still find things to object to, but by giving them more control over their work, we eliminate the need to fight them on every point.

Listen to What They Don't Say

Negative people would not hesitate to tell us what is on their minds. However, the real issues may remain unsaid. A diatribe about some perceived mistreatment may be a subterfuge for hiding a fear that we do not like him or her. Often negativism is a cry for help. By filtering out from their complaints the areas that are not mentioned, we may uncover the real reason for the negative attitude.

In responding to such situations, determine what we can say or do at this moment to respond to the real situation as well as the perceived grievance. A non-opinionated, non-judgmental response will encourage the associate to reveal more layers of emotion until he or she feels understood. Once this happens, the person is more likely to cooperate.

If we sense that the employee is afraid that we do not like him or her, after we have approached the immediate problem, make a comment about some of the good things this person has done and reassure the employee of your appreciation and respect.

Work to Build a Positive Relationship

Negative people need constant reassurance. By making an overt effort to build a strong positive relationship with them, we may not change their personality, but we can make an impact on behavior.

Talk to them. Learn as much as you can about their interests, their goals, their real lives. Find out what they want out of this job that they are not getting now. If possible, offer training, support and coaching to help them overcome problems and reach their goals.

It isn't necessary to become their friend, but it is important that we are not their enemy. Take the time to explain your decisions. Ask for their ideas and input. Chat with them informally about non-business matters so they look upon you as a total human being, not just a boss or a representative.

By taking the time to learn about negative people and to change our thinking about them from that of a problematic employee to a human being with problems, we will find a smoother and more productive relationship developing.

Administer Discipline

One of the most unpleasant tasks of managers is staff discipline. When we hear the word "discipline," what is the first synonym that pops into our head? Most people say "punishment." We have always looked upon discipline as a means of punishing employees for violating company rules or not meeting production standards.

The traditional discipline system starts with a reprimand and if that doesn't work, more serious punishments ranging from formal written reports, probation, suspension and finally, termination. It is based on the concept that the employee must pay for his or her crime. This attitude is counter-productive. Punishment is viewed with resentment and hostility. A new approach, affirmative discipline, has been tried successfully by many organizations. This is accomplished through a series of reaffirmations of commitment rather than use of punishment.

Here's how it works:

➤ *Communication*: The employee is made fully aware of the company's rules and policies during the orientation process. He or she is asked to accept and commit to this policy.

➤ *Reinforcement*: After the first few months on the job, the employee meets with his or her supervisor and the rules and policies are explained again and the employee renews his or her commitment.

➤ *Violations*: If a violation of a rule occurs, the supervisor will initiate a conference with the employee and review that person's agreement to be committed to the company policies. The employee is asked to assure the supervisor that both the rule and the nature of that person's obligation is understood. This is confirmed in a memo signed by both employee and supervisor.

> *Second violation*: If the employee reneges on the commitment and repeats the violation, a second conference is held and the commitment is reinforced.

> *Final conference*: If the employee violates a minor rule for the third time within a specified period or a major rule for the first time, the supervisor asks the employee if he or she really wants to continue being employed with the company. If the employee states that he or she does want to continue, the employee signs a document stating that he or she is aware of the violation and that he or she will commit to abide by the commitment from now on.

> *Termination*: If the commitment is not kept, the employment will be terminated. Companies using this approach report that it is an effective way of maintaining high standards of conduct and employee morale.

Sum and Substance

Qualities of Outstanding Managers

Although individual strengths and abilities may vary, research indicates that outstanding managers view the world in similar ways. The following represent the most commonly observed qualities in outstanding managers and leaders:

> They hold strong values and high ethical standards.

> They lead by example, acting with integrity in both their professional and personal lives.

> They are knowledgeable about both corporate and departmental goals.

- They develop a vision of the future, and are proactive and self-motivated to achieve results.
- They are strong communicators and exceptional listeners.
- They earn trust, credibility, and respect.
- They are flexible under pressure and keep their emotions in check.
- They have a right versus wrong attitude. They invite constructive dissent and disagreement and are open to change and new ideas.
- They simplify ideas, concepts, and processes.
- They nurture the concept of team and respect diversity.
- They take the time to get to know what drives individual team members and enjoy motivating and helping them to succeed.
- They recognize and maximize strengths in others.
- They hold themselves and others accountable for results.
- They are efficient and manage their time effectively.
- They are creative and innovative.
- They exhibit excellent judgment while solving problems, making decisions, and resolving conflicts.
- They are committed to continuous learning and improvement.
- They look at discipline as learning rather than a punishing process.

Ten common mistakes managers make:

1. Relying on their title to gain respect.
2. Contradicting themselves or breaking their word.
3. Taking work-related issues personally.
4. Treating all employees the same versus understanding the diverse qualities and motivating factors of individuals.

5. Setting goals without fully understanding corporate objectives and strategies.
6. Neglecting to plan and prioritize goals of their departments.
7. Failing to clearly communicate objectives and to gain consensus.
8. Continue to do tasks that should be delegated.
9. Fail to act decisively when associates fail to meet standards.
10. Forget to show appreciation and recognition.

Appendix A

ABOUT DALE CARNEGIE

Dale Carnegie was a pioneer in what is now referred to as the human potential movement.

His teachings and writings have helped people all over the world become self-confident, personable, and influential individuals.

In 1912, Carnegie offered his first course in public speaking at a YMCA in New York City. As in most public speaking courses given at that time, Carnegie started the class with a theoretical lecture, but quickly noticed that the class members looked bored and restless. Something had to be done.

Dale stopped his lecture and calmly pointed to a man in the back row and asked him to get up and give an impromptu talk about his background. When the student finished, he asked another student to speak about himself, and so on until everybody in the class had given a brief talk. With the encouragement of their classmates and guidance from Carnegie, each of them overcame their fright and gave satisfactory talks. "Without knowing what I was doing," Carnegie later reported, "I stumbled on the best method of conquering fear."

His course became so popular that he was asked to give it in other cities. As the years went by, he kept improving the content of the course. He learned that the students were most interested in increasing their self-confidence, improving their interpersonal relations, becoming successful in their careers and overcoming fear and worry. This resulted in the emphasis of the course being shifted from public speaking to dealing with these matters. The talks became the means to an end rather than the end itself. In addition to what he learned from his students, Carnegie engaged in extensive research on the approach to life of successful men and women. He incorporated this into his classes. This led to the writing of his most famous book, *How To Win Friends and Influence People.*

This book became an instant bestseller and since its publication in 1936 (and its revised edition in 1981), over 20 million copies have been sold. It has been translated into 36 languages. In 2002, *How to Win Friends and Influence People* was named the #1 Business Book of the 20th Century. In 2008, *Fortune Magazine* listed it as one of the seven books every leader should have in his or her bookcase. His book, *How To Stop Worrying and Start Living,* written in 1948 sold millions of copies, has also been translated into 27 languages.

Dale Carnegie died on November 1, 1955. An obituary in a Washington newspaper summed up his contribution to society:

> *Dale Carnegie solved none of the profound mysteries of the universe. But, perhaps, more than anyone of his generation, he helped human beings learn how to get along together— which seems sometimes to be the greatest need of all.*

About Dale Carnegie & Associates, Inc.: Founded in 1912, Dale Carnegie Training has evolved from one man's belief in the power of self-improvement to a performance-based training company with offices worldwide. It focuses on giving people in business the opportunity to sharpen their skills and improve their performance in order to build positive, steady, and profitable results.

Dale Carnegie's original body of knowledge has been constantly updated, expanded and refined through nearly a century's worth of real-life business experiences. The 160 Dale Carnegie Franchisees around the world use their training and consulting services with companies of all sizes in all business segments to increase knowledge and performance. The result of this collective, global experience is an expanding reservoir of business acumen that our clients rely on to drive business results.

Headquartered in Hauppauge, New York, Dale Carnegie Training is represented in all 50 of the United States and over 75 countries. More than 2,700 instructors present Dale Carnegie Training programs in more than 25 languages. Dale Carnegie Training is dedicated to serving the business community worldwide. In fact, approximately 7 million people have completed Dale Carnegie Training.

Dale Carnegie Training emphasizes practical principles and processes by designing programs that offer people the knowledge, skills and practices they need to add value to the business. Connecting proven solutions with real-world challenges, Dale Carnegie Training is recognized internationally as the leader in bringing out the best in people.

Among the graduates of these programs are CEOs of major corporations, owners and managers of businesses of every size and every commercial and industrial activity, legislative and executive leaders of governments and countless individuals whose lives have been enriched by the experience.

In an ongoing global survey on customer satisfaction, 99 percent of Dale Carnegie Training graduates express satisfaction with the training they receive.

About the Editor

This book was compiled and edited by Dr. Arthur R. Pell, who was a consultant to Dale Carnegie & Associates for 22 years and was chosen by the company to edit and update Dale Carnegie's *How to Win Friends and Influence People*. He also authored *Enrich Your Life, the Dale Carnegie Way* and wrote and edited *The Human Side,* a monthly Dale Carnegie feature that was published in 150 trade and professional magazines.

He is the author of more than 50 books as well as hundreds of articles on management, human relations and self-improvement. In addition to his own writings, Dr. Pell has edited and updated such classics in the human potential field as Napoleon Hill's *Think and Grow Rich,* Joseph Murphy's *The Power of Your Subconscious Mind,* James Allen's *As A Man Thinketh,* Yoritomo Tashi's *Common Sense* and works of Orison Swett Marden, Julia Seton and Wallace D. Wattles.

Appendix B

....

DALE CARNEGIE'S PRINCIPLES

Become a Friendlier Person

1. Don't criticize, condemn or complain.
2. Give honest, sincere appreciation.
3. Arouse in the other person an eager want.
4. Become genuinely interested in other people.
5. Smile.
6. Remember that a person's name is to that person the sweetest sound in any language.
7. Be a good listener. Encourage others to talk about themselves.
8. Talk in terms of the other person's interests.
9. Make the other person feel important—and do it sincerely.
10. To get the best of an argument—avoid it.
11. Show respect for the other person's opinion. Never tell a person he or she is wrong.
12. If you are wrong, admit it quickly, emphatically.

13. Begin in a friendly way.
14. Get the other person to say "yes" immediately.
15. Let the other person do a great deal of the talking.
16. Let the other person feel the idea is his or hers.
17. Try honestly to see things from the other person's point of view.
18. Be sympathetic with the other person's ideas and desires.
19. Appeal to the nobler motives.
20. Dramatize your ideas.
21. Throw down a challenge.
22. Begin with praise and honest appreciation.
23. Call attention to people's mistakes indirectly.
24. Talk about your own mistakes before criticizing the other person.
25. Ask questions instead of giving direct orders.
26. Let the other person save face.
27. Praise the slightest improvement and praise every improvement. Be "hearty in your approbation and lavish in your praise."
28. Give the other person a fine reputation to live up to.
29. Use encouragement. Make the fault seem easy to correct.
30. Make the other person happy about doing the thing you suggest.

Fundamental Principles for Overcoming Worry

1. Live in "day—tight compartments."
2. How to face trouble:
   Ask yourself, "What is the worst that can possibly happen?"
3. Prepare to accept the worst.
4. Try to improve on the worst.

5. Remind yourself of the exorbitant price you can pay for worry in terms of your health.

Basic Techniques in Analyzing Worry

1. Get all the facts.
2. Weigh all the facts—then come to a decision.
3. Once a decision is reached, act!
4. Write out and answer the following questions:
   - What is the problem?
   - What are the causes of the problem?
   - What are the possible solutions?
   - What is the best possible solution?

Break the Worry Habit Before It Breaks You

1. Keep busy.
2. Don't fuss about trifles.
3. Use the law of averages to outlaw your worries.
4. Cooperate with the inevitable.
5. Decide just how much anxiety a thing may be worth and refuse to give it more.
6. Don't worry about the past.

Cultivate a Mental Attitude That Will Bring You Peace and Happiness

1. Fill your mind with thoughts of peace, courage, health.
2. Never try to get even with your enemies.
3. Expect ingratitude.
4. Count your blessings—not your troubles.
5. Do not imitate others.
6. Try to profit from your losses.
7. Create happiness for others.